THE FORSAKEN

From the Great Depression to the
Gulags: Hope and Betrayal
in Stalin's Russia

TIM TZOULIADIS

ABACUS

First published in Great Britain in 2008 by Little, Brown
This paperback edition published in 2009 by Abacus
Reprinted 2009

Copyright © Tim Tzouliadis 2008

The right of Tim Tzouliadis to be identified as author
of this work has been asserted by him in accordance with
the Copyright, Designs and Patents Act 1988

A CIP catalogue record for this book
is available from the British Library.

ISBN 978-0-349-11753-9

Typeset in Sabon by M Rules
Printed and bound in Great Britain by
Clays Ltd, St Ives plc

Papers used by Abacus are natural, renewable and
recyclable products sourced from well-managed forests and certified
in accordance with the rules of the Forest Stewardship Council.

Mixed Sources
Product group from well-managed
forests and other controlled sources
www.fsc.org   Cert no. SGS-COC-004081
© 1996 Forest Stewardship Council

Abacus
An imprint of
Little, Brown Book Group
100 Victoria Embankment
London EC4Y 0DY

An Hachette UK Company
www.hachette.co.uk

www.littlebrown.co.uk

For the innocent who lost their lives,
Of every nationality.

CONTENTS

1

THE JOADS OF RUSSIA

There is much to say about Soviet Russia. It is a new world to explore, Americans know almost nothing about it. But the story filters through, and it rouses heroism. As long as the Red Flag waves over the Kremlin, there is hope in the world. There is something in the air of Soviet Russia that throbbed in the air of Pericles' Athens; the England of Shakespeare; the France of Danton; the America of Walt Whitman . . . This is the first man learning in agony and joy how to think. Where else is there hope in the world?

New Masses, November 1926

Their story begins with a photograph of a baseball team. The year is 1934, the picture is in black and white. Two rows of young men pose for the camera: one standing, the other crouching down with their arms around each other's shoulders. They are all somewhere in their late teens or early twenties, in the peak of health. They appear to be the best of friends. We know many, if not all, of their names: Arnold Preedin, Arthur Abolin, Eugene Peterson, Leo Feinstein, Victor Herman, Leo Herman, Benny Grondon – the names themselves are unremarkable since none of the men are celebrities nor the sons or grandsons of the famous. They come from ordinary working families from across America: from Detroit, Boston, New York, San Francisco and the Midwest. Waiting in the sunshine, they look much like any other baseball team except, perhaps, for the Russian lettering on their uniforms.[1]

At first glance they might appear to be one team, but in actual fact there are two. On this occasion we can tell from their uniforms that the Foreign Workers' Club of Moscow are playing against the Auto Workers' Club from the nearby city of Gorky. But perhaps such details are unimportant since many of the American baseball players in the photograph will soon be dead. They will not die in an accident, in a train or a plane crash. They will be the witnesses to, and the victims of, the most sustained campaign of state terror in modern history.

The few baseball players who survive will be inordinately lucky. But they will come so close to death and endure such terrible circumstances that they too, at times, may wish they had lost their lives with the rest of their team. Only at that moment, as the camera shutter clicks in the warm summer air of Gorky Park, none of the American baseball players has any idea of their likely fate. Their smiles betray not the slightest inkling.

It was the least heralded migration in American history. Unsurprising perhaps, since in a nation of immigrants no one cares to remember the ones who left the dream behind – these forgotten exiles who stood with their families on the wooden decks of passenger liners, watching the Statue of Liberty fade into the distance as they left New York bound for Leningrad. A cross-section of America, they came from all walks of life: professors, engineers, factory workers, teachers, artists, doctors, even farmers, all mixed together on the passenger ships. They left to join the Five Year Plan of Soviet Russia, lured by the prospect of work at the height of the Great Depression. Qualified engineers on well-paid contracts jostled beside unemployed workers chasing jobs in Soviet factories and starry-eyed fellow travellers whose luggage was bursting with the heavy tomes of Marx, Engels and Lenin. Within their ranks were American communists, trade unionists and assorted radicals of the John Reed school, but most were ordinary citizens not overly concerned by politics. What united them was the hope that drives all emigrants: the search for a better life for their children and themselves. And in the eagerness of their departure, no wise eyes strained to foresee the chronicle of violence that lay in store in Russia, as the bronze-and-steel propellers laboured relentlessly across the grey-green ocean water towards Europe.

In the early 1930s, it must have felt as though America, caught in the clutches of the Great Depression, could not or would not keep her half of the social contract. There were more people out of work in the United States, both actually and proportionately, than in any other nation on earth. Thirteen million unemployed represented a quarter of the workforce in an age when, in most families, only the men held jobs. Now those millions stood in bread lines and queued up at soup kitchens waiting for their next meal. A ragged army of hoboes had taken to the highways and railroads of the continent in their search for work. Half the country was on the move, and not just the likes of Tom Joad driving to California in their Model As. To these people, the Great Depression's newly dispossessed, the abject failure of capitalism was not such a radical proposition so much as the straightforward evidence of their senses. They saw it, and smelt it, whichever way they turned.

The *New York Times* published a story on the new city that had risen next to Wall Street as a symbolic rival to the financial centre of the Western world: 'Campfires glowed last night in the Westside jungles. The jungle, bounded by Spring, West, Clarkson and Washington streets, looks, with its mounds of brick and its desolation like a shell-pocked village in France . . . Battered chimneys rise out of holes in the ground, where the unemployed have dug in for the winter. Shacks made of packing cases, old tin, dirty cement blocks, beams, tar paper, stand on some of the brick mounds, others are in the brick hollows.'[2] These brand-new Hoovervilles, built of corrugated iron and salvaged brick, had risen suddenly in every major American city and struck many as a warning of a civilisation dividing into alternate landscapes; as if competing visions of penury and plenty were being processed over one another, and the figures in the foreground were no longer sure to which their lives belonged or to which they now were heading. Almost overnight, pinstripes and spats had been replaced by worn-out denim and a sullen look, as the ranks of unemployed attempted to stay alive selling shoeshines or apples for a nickel apiece, competing with the countless others who had the same idea. On city sidewalks of America, the veterans of the Great War sold their decorations for valour won on the battlefields of France and Belgium. The going rate was one dollar and fifty cents.

In movie theatres, the newsreel pictures showed Franciscan friars doling out silver nickels to the homeless for a bed or a meal. Crowds of men stood smoking, their hats pulled down low over their eyes, waiting patiently to receive their solitary coin, tipping their hats as they walked past. It was an endless queue, and an anonymous haunted man who tries to cut in gets pushed back to the end of the line. The camera catches him in the act and preserves his despair for ever, like a Sisyphus of old New York. In Uniontown, Pennsylvania, the destitute were living inside coke ovens shut down by the crisis. Men with their entire families were living there inside. Kids with nothing looked curiously into the inquiring cameras, some with unnaturally stern faces, others with the shy grins of children for whom this is all still just fun and who had no idea quite how desperate their fathers had become. In Harrisburg a ragged army of unemployed stormed the state capitol demanding relief funds, while articles in the mainstream press carried portentous headlines warning of 'the Prospect of Violent Revolution in the United States'.[3]

Amid the enforced idleness, the bank failures, the sourness, and the blatant discontent, a bitter rage swept through American cities while the shock was still raw and the people angry enough to get out on to the streets. An international unemployment day was announced, and hundreds of thousands marched through the streets of New York, Detroit, Chicago, Milwaukee, Cleveland, Pittsburgh and the industrial heartlands. The general feeling of unease was impossible to resist; of disgust at the overwhelming power of money, which divided men from one another and added a layer of shame on to the hurt of what it already felt like to be absolutely poor. Reinforcing this nationwide shift towards radicalism – the sudden lurch of the entire political consensus to the left – was the growing awareness that all this unemployment and extreme hardship was ultimately unnecessary. The collective misery was simply the result of laissez-faire capitalism gone wild, the maniacal exuberance of Wall Street financiers who had stoked an express train until it careened off the tracks, leaving others to pick up the pieces of the wreck while the guilty fled the scene.[4]

Elected by a landslide, Franklin Roosevelt delivered his first inaugural address to a radio audience of sixty million listeners, roughly half the country eager to learn of a plan for a way out of the crisis:

> The rulers of the exchange of mankind's goods have failed, through their own stubbornness and their own incompetence, have admitted their failure, and abdicated. Practices of the unscrupulous moneychangers stand indicted in the court of public opinion, rejected by the hearts and minds of men . . . a host of unemployed citizens face the grim problem of existence, and an equally great number toil with little return. Only a foolish optimist can deny the dark realities of the moment . . . the moneychangers have fled from their high seats in the temple of

our civilization. We may now restore that temple to the ancient truths. The measure of the restoration lies in the extent to which we apply social values more noble than mere monetary profit.[5]

But many Americans no longer owned a radio to hear their President's calm words of reassurance. Such luxuries had long since been traded in for cash, along with the rest of their possessions. Thousands more had already left, choosing to chance their luck elsewhere and take a gamble on reports they read in newspapers of how Soviet Russia alone still had economic growth and jobs, and was planning a society that placed working men at its very centre, no longer merely the peripheral casualties of other men's greed. Searching for alternatives, for avenues of escape, they studied the glowing accounts of new factories being built in Russia surrounded by trees and flowers, with cafeterias and libraries for their workers, nurseries for the children – and even swimming pools, for crying out loud! At that moment, American curiosity to learn about the Soviet experiment was all-consuming. An English translation of *New Russia's Primer: The Story of the Five-Year Plan* had become the unlikely publishing phenomenon of 1931, an American bestseller for seven months and one of the highest selling non-fiction titles of the past decade.[6] Its simple explanations, written originally for Russian school-children, were read and reread by an American public searching for answers beyond the deadened reach of another decade of 'rugged individualism'. In the midst of Depression misery, who could not be attracted to the book's shared vision of future happiness and social progress?

All this will be written about us a few decades hence. He will work less and yet accomplish more. During seven hours in the factory he will do what now requires eleven and a half hours . . . Instead of dark, gloomy shops with dim, yellow lamps there will be light, clean halls with great windows and beautiful tile doors. Not the lungs of men, but powerful ventilators will suck in and swallow the dirt, dust, and shavings of the factories . . . Socialism is no longer a myth, a phantasy of mind . . . We ourselves are building it . . . And this better life will not come as a miracle: we ourselves must create it. But to create it we need knowledge: we need strong hands, yes, but we need strong minds too . . . Here it is – your Five-Year Plan.[7]

And who could blame those Americans, motivated as much by economic necessity as their own idealism, who gratefully accepted Joseph Stalin's open invitation to work in the Soviet Union? Skilled workers could even have their passage paid to the land where unemployment had been officially declared extinct. They saw themselves as the pioneers of a new frontier, moving slowly from west to east, lured not just by the idea of security in hard times but also the simple temptations of adequacy: of three square meals a day, a decent job, a roof over their heads, a doctor for the children and the knowledge that it could not all be taken away at the click of someone's fingers or the chatter of the stock-ticker.[8]

They left it to the social philosophers to speculate on the value of secure and decently paid employment to an individual's notion of identity or self-worth; let alone 'the pursuit of happiness', a phrase that provoked a certain mocking tone when spoken from beneath the corrugated roof of a brick shack. And if the President of the United States could talk to the nation of the flight of the money-changers from the temple without being called a 'Red', then presumably these American exiles could hold a similar view as they were drawn east to Russia like a beacon, a flickering flame in the white night of the Depression.

For the first time in her short history more people were leaving the United States than were arriving. And as the cutting edge of poverty sharpened their determination, the desire to join this forgotten exodus turned, as the saying goes, from a trickle to a flood. In the first eight months of 1931 alone, Amtorg – the Soviet trade agency based in New York – received more than *one hundred thousand* American applications for emigration to the USSR. Such was the overwhelming response to their newspaper advertisements publicising just six thousand jobs for skilled workers in Russia.[9] At the Amtorg offices in Manhattan, crowds of workers jammed the corridors with their wives, children and pets, pleading for a passage out to this 'promised land'. Ten thousand optimistic Americans were hired that year, part of the official 'organized emigration' who received their good news with a glee closer to that of lottery winners than economic migrants.

A business reporter was sent down to the unofficial Soviet embassy at 261 Fifth Avenue to look through one morning's applications. The occupations listed for those answering this 'Soviet call for Yankee skill' included 'barbers, plumbers, painters, cooks, clerical workers, service-station operators, electricians, carpenters, aviators, engineers, salesmen, printers, chemists, shoemakers, librarians, teachers, auto-mechanics, dentists, and one funeral director'. The would-be emigrants hailed from virtually every state of the union, and their principal reasons for leaving which they wrote on their job applications were: '1. Unemployment. 2. Disgust with conditions here. 3. Interest in Soviet experiment.'[10]

Following in the slipstream of this official organised exodus were unknown numbers of uncounted Americans, the waifs and strays of the economic times, who chose to dispense with bureaucracy and travel to Russia as tourists ready to pick up jobs just as soon as they arrived. The Soviet travel agency, Intourist, was happy to sell them one-way tickets with their tourist visas, while the sales agents of the shipping companies were telling all comers that Americans could find jobs in Russia whether they spoke the language or not. All they needed was enough money for their first week, which was as long as it took to find work.[11]

Already there were so many Americans writing to their government for information about work in Russia that as of May 1931 the Department of Commerce began replying to their letters with an official form response, entitled *Employment for Americans in Soviet Russia*. The Commerce Department's civil servants first told them what they already knew: 'At the present time a number of Soviet industrial organizations, operating through the Amtorg Trading Corporation in New York, are engaging American engineers and technicians in large numbers to work in Soviet Russia.' Then followed a catalogue of sensible advice concerning Soviet contracts and housing, along with some cautious insights into family life: 'It is not considered wise for wives and children to accompany the individual, if it is possible for them to be left. The strangeness of language, conditions and habits affects American women unfavourably, and the absence of educational facilities is a serious loss for children of school age.' Their government's advice was widely ignored – more often than not, the American emigrants took their wives and children with them. Where else were they going to leave them? The children, they reasoned, would find schools when they arrived.[12]

Other would-be emigrants addressed their letters directly to the State Department. Harry Dalhart, for example, wrote as the president of 'the Soviet emigration society' of Wichita, Kansas. In his letter Dalhart explained that his organisation had 342 members 'all under forty years of age. Ninety two are overseas world war veterans: all native born Americans.' The Kansan society sought advice concerning their emigration to Russia 'as a group'. Others intended to leave as enterprising individuals with an eye for the main chance. One resident of Denham, Indiana, wrote to the State Department offering his 'house, a lot, a truck, and a few household articles' he wished to trade with the government in exchange for his passage to Russia.[13]

On 4 February 1931, in the pages of the *New York Times*, 'the greatest wave of immigration in modern history' was being forecast by Walter Duranty, the celebrated Moscow-based reporter: 'The Soviet Union will witness in the next few years an immigration flood comparable to the influx into the United States in the decade before the World War ... it is only the beginning as yet of this movement, and the first swallows of the coming migration are scarce – but it has begun and will have to be reckoned with in the future.' Although the American exodus was as yet only in the thousands, Walter Duranty was confidently predicting that the Soviets would be welcoming two million a year in the not-too-distant future, with Cunard and the other shipping companies 'queuing up' for the passenger business. The American auto workers who had recently established themselves in Russia would soon be advising their friends to follow: 'When the day comes that foreign workers here may write home and say, "Things are pretty good here, why don't you come along? There are jobs for everybody and plenty to eat. Russia is not so bad a place in which to live and there are no lay-offs or short time and you get all that is coming to you" ... then immigration to the Soviet Union will begin to rival the flood that poured into America. At the present rate of progress that day is not far distant.'[14]

The article in the nation's most prestigious newspaper only hastened the deluge of American letters and visits to any Russian institution that might be willing to offer some assistance and advice. A San Franciscan mechanic wrote to a newspaper in Moscow asking if he ought to change his name 'before hand to a Russian name with that –ovitch or –itsky ending'. Others wondered if they needed relatives or friends in Russia to testify to their good character, supposing that the old rules of Ellis Island might somehow be reapplied by Russian immigration control. From Shenandoah, Virginia, a journalist reported that 'a group of miners is being formed to go to

Russia with their picks and drills and any other machinery that they have enough to buy'. And this news prompted a host of enquiries from depressed mining regions across the United States. One group asked if it was true that the Soviets were going to send a ship to 'rescue all the miners from their American misery, and would the metalworkers or the textile-workers be next?'[15]

At the docks of New York harbour, groups of jobless men shared the shipping page of the *New York Herald Tribune*, which published the dates of freighters leaving for Leningrad and Odessa. Word was passed around that those who could not afford the price of a ticket could work their passage, or stow away in one of the many crates of American machinery heading in the same direction. A dockside reporter described the zeal of a Milwaukee emigrant with the inspired idea that the 'mass transportation of "broke" Americans to Russia would be best solved by a winter walk from Alaska to Siberia over the ice of the Bering Straits – Just like Jules Verne described, just like Jules Verne!'[16]

Of course, the news of this sudden emigration from the world's wealthiest country was pounced upon by the Soviet press as evidence, not only of their own success, but that history was on their side. In an article titled 'Moscow the Magnet', the Russian journalist Boris Pilnyak recounted the story of a car journey through the Rocky Mountains in Arizona. One night some American miners had helped him repair his car and gathered around the campfire to listen to him talk of life in the USSR. Three years later in Moscow, the doorbell rang and 'a broad-shouldered man of about forty dressed in American working clothes entered. He smiled gaily and stretched his big hand over the threshold. "You don't recognize me?" he boomed. "Remember Arizona, that night by the gold mines? Your hand comrade ... I'm in Moscow!"'[17] No one knew how many American workers arrived on a wing and a prayer like this Arizonan gold-miner, having scraped enough money for a tourist visa, or slept third class or stowaway class. Unaccounted for in any records of state, they rated only a passing mention in a Soviet press article – a social phenomenon embodied by the nameless curiosity of a forty-year-old miner with a broad smile, a firm handshake and an overwhelming willingness to believe these grand accounts of Revolution.

If the Soviet emigration was not *the* most adventurous solution to the nation's Depression woes, it stretched the imagination to consider a bolder remedy. One group of American families sold their worldly goods to buy American machinery for a collective farm they were moving to outside Moscow. Another party of sixteen emigrants from San Francisco pooled their cash to buy tractors for the Portland Commune near Kiev. Between them they handed over their dollar savings, their tools and a Lincoln automobile. Others donated their entire life savings to the state, supposing that they would no longer need money in the new Russia.[18]

On 11 October 1931, George Bernard Shaw returned from Russia to broadcast a persuasive lecture on American national radio. Using the power of mass communication, the world's self-styled 'most successful playwright since Shakespeare' was only too delighted to share his thoughts on the Soviet experiment and demolish the myths that surrounded the world's first socialist state:

Naturally the contempt of the Russians for us is enormous. You fools, they are saying to us, why can you not do as we are doing? You cannot employ nor feed your people: well send them to us, and if they are worth their salt we will employ and feed them . . . They took command of the Soviets, and established the Union of Socialist Soviet Republics exactly as Washington and Jefferson and Hamilton and Franklin and Tom Paine had established the United States of America 141 years before . . . that Jefferson is Lenin, that Franklin is Litvinov, that Paine is Lunacharsky, that Hamilton is Stalin . . . Today there is a statue of Washington in Leningrad; and tomorrow there will no doubt be a statue of Lenin in New York. And now perhaps you would like to know what was my reaction to Russia when I visited it? . . . Well, my first impression was that Russia is full of Americans. My second was that every intelligent Russian has been in America and didn't like it because he had no freedom there. And now let me give you a few travelling tips in case you should join the American rush to visit Russia and see for yourself whether it is all real. If you are a skilled workman, especially in machine industry, and are of suitable age and good character . . . you will not have much difficulty; they will be only too glad to have you: proletarians of all lands are welcome if they can pull their weight in the Russian boat . . . there is hope everywhere in Russia because these evils are retreating there before the spread of Communism as steadily as they are advancing upon us before the last desperate struggle of our bankrupt Capitalism to stave off its inevitable doom. You will not go to Russia to smell out the evils you can see without leaving your own doorstep. Some of you will go because in the great financial storm that has burst on us your own ship is sinking and the Russian ship is the only big one that is not rolling heavily and tapping out SOS on its wireless.[19]

The sensational lecture was printed in full in the *New York Times* and, judging by the publicity it generated, George Bernard Shaw must have convinced many more Americans to emigrate or, at the very least, quelled the fears of those still making up their minds. It was plain from his assurances that Shaw, like so many intellectuals of the era, placed implicit faith in the motives of Joseph Stalin and gladly lent him his seal of approval. While the American emigrants themselves, believing they must find social justice somewhere on God's earth and persuaded by that hope, were willing to travel halfway around the world to join what was universally described as 'the greatest social experiment in the history of mankind'.

Few paused to distinguish whether they were being pulled by an ideology or pushed by their need. Nor were these Americans merely a confederacy of political fanatics, hopeless idealists, or naive adventurers. Theirs was a reaction to the actuality and future threat of poverty, and to understand them we must place ourselves momentarily in a similar position of unknowing: when the idea of the Soviet Revolution was still filled with hope and only the most perspicacious could discern the truth which lay beneath that promise. It was an era when the political system of communism had yet to be fully tested, just as once upon a time democracy, too, had presented an equally radical affront to conservative opinion.

And so, as perhaps the least significant, but most culturally enlightening consequence of this forgotten migration, there happened to be American baseball teams playing in Gorky Park in the very heart of Moscow; when its green acres were still known by its first Revolutionary name as the 'Central Park of Culture and Rest'. But maybe it was not so surprising after all. Immigrants have always brought their sports with them.

2

BASEBALL IN GORKY PARK

At one time America had been the remote star attracting all the unfortunate proletarians, serving as a lighthouse in their quest for liberty. The beacon, however, has become petrified. October lit a new star. The new fatherland of the proletariat has spread under this star over a sixth part of the globe, raising the scaffolding of its construction work from the Ruhr to Detroit, from red Wedding to Peking, the proletarians have risen and begin to march toward the star. This time they can be sure. The new star will not betray them.

Boris Agapor, *Za Industrializatsu*, 7 November 1931[1]

Every day between twenty and a hundred and fifty new American arrivals stepped down on to the platform of Moscow's Belorussky station. In early November 1931, the *Washington Post* reported the arrival of groups of miners from coal pits in Pennsylvania, Ohio, West Virginia and Illinois, and the metal shafts of Michigan, Utah and Montana. Steelworkers travelled from the shut-down mills in Pittsburgh and Gary to work alongside American carpenters, bricklayers, machinists and railroad men.[2] And no one could predict who might turn up next. There could be forty more miners with their wives and children from Pennsylvania, or eighteen Swedish-Americans from a Pacific coast lumber camp, or a couple of plumbers from Peru, Indiana, or a party of fourteen shoemakers from Los Angeles. As soon as the Americans left the train station they made their way down to the Intourist offices on Theatre Square to demand work – often to the astonishment of the Russian officials concerned. 'Barbers! We've got plenty!'

One party of three hundred American miners on their way to Leninsk in Siberia managed to have their passports 'misplaced' by a clerk, which created a storm of protest from their nervous wives. Half the group turned straight back home, the rest stayed. But for all the chaos of their arrival, two American reporters in Moscow, Ruth Kennell and Milly Bennett, understood their choices very well: 'Yet there are Americans who would rather have jobs in a land where poverty is general and hope is boundless – even standing in long lines to receive the food they pay for – than be idle in a land of plenty and despair.'[3]

By the winter of 1931, sufficient numbers had arrived for a weekly English-language newspaper to be established in Moscow, with the aim of reporting the 'truth about what the Soviet government is trying to do'. Staffed by young American journalists keen to salute the progress of the Five Year Plan, the *Moscow News* was the ramshackle brainchild of its editor Anna Louise Strong, a redoubtable progressive and personal friend of Eleanor Roosevelt. On her trips back to the United States, Strong was an occasional guest at the White House where the ever-curious President would pepper her with questions about Soviet Russia. How, Roosevelt asked, could Stalin afford to *buy* all those factories?[4]

In Moscow the new arrivals gave cheerful interviews to their newspaper along the lines of 'I'd rather be here than in the soup line in New York.' Some cracked wise about the social facilities they had heard were part of every factory worker's life – 'Where's the golf course?' – while others were more serious. 'It's hard to imagine conditions in the States if you haven't seen them,' wrote a Chicago woman. 'Public parks are crowded with sleeping unemployed lying on spread-out newspapers . . . a grocery store was broken into and robbed during the night.'[5] Letters arrived at the *Moscow News* offices on Strastnoi Boulevard from Americans searching for work. An ex-Follies dancer enclosed a photograph with her height and weight, asking if she could be of any use to the Five Year Plan? A Denver miner described how his wages in Colorado had been cut to thirty-five cents per ton which, after the company deductions for rent and groceries, left the miners with precisely nothing: 'Give us a chance to come to the Soviet Union. We are willing to work hard; to endure hardships, if need be. Here we have hardships, hunger too and no hope. Over there, you are building for tomorrow. Let us come and help. We will be satisfied with bread and carrots.'[6] Very soon, the sheer number of unemployed Americans turning up in Moscow was sufficient to create a headache for the Soviet authorities. In the *New York Times* of 14 March 1932, Walter Duranty described the number of new arrivals as still 'relatively small – say 1000 a week at the outside. But it is on the increase.'[7] The American reporters in Moscow were continually stumbling upon some poor lost soul worked down to his last dime, with nowhere to live, hoping to start life over in Russia, perhaps with a kid in tow, cap pulled down firmly over his eyes. Many had travelled completely of their own devices – they were neither qualified mechanics nor skilled workers on Amtorg contracts – and the Soviet government was completely unprepared for this sudden influx of tourists planning to stay and work, as in some latter-day Klondike rush to the land of zero unemployment. Soon an official edict was issued that in the future all tourists *must* carry a roundtrip ticket and would no longer be handed jobs because there was simply not enough space to house them all. Moscow and all the major Russian cities were already horrendously overcrowded. The Russians had to fight for a few square metres of living space, huddled together in single rooms shared by two or three families. The discomforts, they were told, were temporary. When the new socialist cities were built, there would be space enough for everyone. In the meantime they would have to make do.[8]

Meanwhile, the newspaper offices on Strastnoi Boulevard served as a social centre for the Americans. They organised Russian courses for the new arrivals, and English-language programmes on Soviet radio, as well as educational excursions, boat trips and, of course, a little music and dancing. On the evening of 21 October 1931 the *Moscow News* celebrated its first birthday with a party for three hundred guests crowded into the Foreign Workers' Club on Hertzen Street. Amid the usual speeches and high-flown rhetoric, the occasion was lent a touch of Bolshevik celebrity by a statement read out from Nikolai Bukharin. The diminutive revolutionary, who had once been one of Lenin's closest friends, welcomed the Americans to the USSR: 'To build up a new world is the highest joy for man. We greet everyone who is unafraid of difficulties and assists the Soviet Union!' And then, after midnight, a jazz band struck up and the guests danced away until the early hours. Did Bukharin stay for the American jazz? It was hard to resist the notion of Lenin's ideologue – the author of *The ABC of Communism* – skipping his dainty feet to the rhythm of saxophone and drums.[9]

Two weeks later, on 7 November 1931, one million Russians marched through Red Square for the fourteenth anniversary of the Revolution. Lost in this tide of humanity, the sixty staffers of the *Moscow News* joined a party of American auto workers who had recently found jobs at the assembly plant in Moscow. The children marched in front of their fathers, shouting 'Long live the American Pioneer Groups!' as they held up their banners in English, the Roman lettering strangely anomalous amid the long red streamers and bold Cyrillic propaganda slogans proclaiming the dawn of the Marxist–Leninist age.[10] Six months later, the Americans marched again for the May Day parade of 1932, those who did not yet understand Russian clustered around the ones who could translate and cheering their approval in English. 'Language did not matter. We were united by bonds closer than those of speech,' one of the marchers told a reporter. When the crowd passed into Red Square, the tall figure of the writer Maxim Gorky waved his hat and they cheered again. 'Where is Stalin? Isn't Stalin there?' asked a young American wearing a red tie in solidarity. 'Sure, there he is standing just on Gorky's right – see in the brown coat and brown cap, he's saluting now. And there's Molotov and Kaganovitch beside them.' And then the crowd swept on past the cathedral of St Basil, and out of Red Square until they merged with the million others on the embankment of the Moskva river.[11]

They played baseball almost as soon as they arrived. When the Moscow weather was fine enough, the young Americans formed their own teams and sprinted around the bases in Gorky Park on their free days and evenings through the short Russian summers – as though they craved to keep at least one strand of the familiar in their creation of this brave new world. There were at least two American teams playing in Moscow that year. The Foreign Workers' Club competed against a team from the Stalin Auto Plant, the auto workers taking a break from the assembly line to run the bases while curious Russians turned out to watch the sudden appearance of this strange new sport and their lively practice sessions in the park. In May 1932, the Foreign Workers' Club made an announcement in the pages of the *Moscow Daily News* (the newspaper was, by now, a daily title) that they were moving their whole summer programme to the park: 'Baseball players who have suits, gloves, and other baseball paraphernalia are requested to bring same to the club, as these things have never been made here.'

All summer long, the young Americans sauntered down to the park every other evening to play baseball. And as their shadows lengthened in the evening light, the numbers of Russian spectators grew ever larger, all striving to get a little closer to the action. The sight of the Americans sliding into bases and the dust flying over their bodies must only have added to the excitement. 'Niet out! Niet! Niet!' Some of the Russian spectators took to crowding around the bases, in spite of warnings that they might be hurt by bat or ball. Warnings which, we may assume, were met with friendly shrugs and smiles. 'Nichevo' – 'It doesn't matter' – and the game continued.

In the summer of 1932, the Soviet Supreme Council of Physical Culture announced its decision to introduce baseball to the Soviet Union as a 'national sport', part of a programme to foster athletic competitions in which the citizens of the first socialist state might effortlessly excel. The Supreme Council admitted they had studied the feasibility of adopting American football as well as baseball in Russia but, upon careful consideration, football had been rejected as 'too rough'. Baseball, on the other hand, had a much gentler appeal. The American Foreign Workers' Club soon began coaching a team of young Russians at Moscow's Tomsky Stadium. A sports reporter from the *Moscow Daily News* was dispatched to cover their first game, and wrote that the Russians could 'slam the ball all over the park' and throw just as well as the Americans, but 'catching the ball was their weakness'. The Russian players were also let down by not fully understanding the rules for stealing bases, evidently even a little indignant that such a plainly capitalistic aberration of 'Americanski beisbol' should ever be allowed in the USSR.[12]

Still the enthusiasm of the Russian youth was obvious to all, and the Soviet sports apparatchiks took quick notice of baseball's immediate popularity. Soon, they declared, the game would be played on a 'Union-wide scale', with the newly arrived Americans asked to volunteer as coaches. Orders would be placed to manufacture the necessary equipment, and the complicated rules would be translated into simple Russian for workers to learn. If there were still remote parts of the USSR where American workers had not yet emigrated then 'baseball will be taught by movies'. And as the Soviet press dutifully praised the 'grace and complexity' of America's national sport, the official admiration was inevitably reflected in the state propaganda. At the Stalin Auto Plant in Moscow, the headline of the factory newspaper exhorted the Russian workers to 'Play the New Game of Baseball!'[13]

The American emigrants brought with them enough children for an Anglo-American school to be set up in Moscow with 125 pupils on the register by November 1932, three-quarters of them born in the United States. Over the next three years, the numbers of pupils rose still further, and very soon the Anglo-American school was forced to move into larger premises at School Number 24 on Great Vuysovsky Street. Naturally the children were delighted by their new environment, enjoying a new woodwork shop, science labs, a music room, gymnasium and dining hall in space they never had before. The model pupils spoke approvingly of the progressive methods of their American teachers, who talked to them 'as friends' and 'not like bosses back home'.[14]

Inevitably the American students' lessons were very different from those they had been accustomed to back home, since the children were taught a Soviet curriculum which stressed the reasons *why* their parents had fled the capitalist crisis in the United States to join the forward march of Soviet Russia. It might, at first, seem startling that the classroom walls were decorated with brightly coloured pictures of Marx, Lenin and, of course, Comrade Stalin gazing down benevolently on the pupils as they chattered away in English and the Russian they had picked up with effortless speed. And the Russian textbooks used by the school made for some interesting reading at home: 'Is Henry Ford a capitalist? Yes Henry Ford is a capitalist. Was Lenin a great man? Yes Lenin was a great man . . . Is the Soviet Government a better form of Government than the American? The American form is better than other forms of Government but not better than the Soviet form.'[15]

Unsurprisingly many of the American engineers, in particular, complained that their children were turning out just a little too 'Red'. The indoctrination of their education was incessant, its effect magnified by the prevailing ideology of the Soviet state. An Associated Press reporter, Charlie Nutter, was somewhat disturbed when his young son Jimmy, who had consistently refused to say a single word, broke his silence one day by pointing a chubby finger at the picture on the front page of the newspaper. '*Eta Stalin!*' little Jimmy Nutter had gurgled in Russian with a smile, to the horror of his father, who immediately announced: 'We're going home ! I'm going to raise my kid to be an American!'[16]

For all the strangeness of their education, the pupils were still just normal American kids who happened to attend a school in Moscow. Their favourite books listed in the lending records of the school library were unexceptional: the three most popular were all by Jack London – *The Call of the Wild*, *The Son of the Wolf* and *White Fang*. In fourth place was *David Copperfield*, followed by more London and Dickens, before Mark Twain's *A Connecticut Yankee in King Arthur's Court*. Only far down the list in sixteenth place was there anything remotely ideological in Theodore Dreiser's *An American Tragedy*, just above John Reed's famous account of the Russian Revolution, *Ten Days that Shook The World* – at that time the bible of the American left.[17]

Nevertheless the Americans' school, just like their baseball teams, was a focus for intense Russian curiosity. A young cub reporter, Kamionski, visited the school to write a story for the *Moscow Pioneer*. In his article, Kamionski described both the children and their schoolteacher in suitably epic terms:

Every day new pupils come. They arrive with their fathers from the United States, from England, and from Canada. They cross the ocean, cross continents and enter the Great Vysovski Street . . . Here is Comrade Whiteman. He teaches physics, chemistry and mathematics. And the lads are very pleased. Thirty persons are in the class. The twenty-nine at the desks are white and the thirtieth on the platform is black. Comrade Whiteman is a Negro. Whiteman in English means a white man. The skin of Comrade Whiteman, however, is certainly not white. It is a greyish black color, a miserable negro skin. And the white family name was probably given in derision to an ancestor of Comrade Whiteman. Comrade Whiteman brought his mockery with him to the Soviet Union, where it is nobody's business what colour his skin is. He should have entirely forgotten about it, if not for the foreign journalists.

From young Kamionski we learn that the American children addressed their teachers as 'Comrade', that they studied collectively and wore the red ties of the Komsomol. More importantly, the cub reporter Kamionski also revealed how Soviet schoolchildren were taught to view the historical inevitability of their World Revolution: 'The man who goes up to the second floor not only crosses the Atlantic, he comes into a peculiar country, the America of the future.'[18] Eventually all American first-graders would patiently study their Marxism-Leninism. Until then there was School Number 24.

And in this startling vision of the 'America of the Future' we learn of the existence of a radical new method of discipline. On 6 January 1933, a group of delinquent American students, all aged between eleven and twelve, were brought for trial before a court of their peers, charged with 'petty thievery and attempts to disorganize the school'. After two and a half hours of careful cross-examination, the culprits were discovered to be suffering from 'poor home conditions' and one of them was motherless – all mitigating factors in their favour. Nevertheless the American child-prosecutors of the court noted the existence of 'a definite anti-social group' within their fold, and suspensions soon followed in this junior version of a show trial. It was a curious anticipation of what was come.[19]

The blonde president of the school's 'Anglo-American Pioneers' was a confident thirteen-year-old named Lucy Abolin, whose father had found work as a metalworker in Moscow. Lucy Abolin was a serious but pretty girl who wore a red handkerchief tied around her neck and helped to organise the school plays that year: a production of *Tom Sawyer* in English and Gogol's *Inspector General* for the children who could already speak Russian. Undoubtedly Lucy loved her new school and the responsibilities she was given. 'Even in America I was the leader of a dramatic circle,' she told a reporter from the *Moscow Daily News*. Some of the other American children found it hard to adjust but not Lucy, who had arrived two years earlier with her parents and brothers from Boston: 'Sometimes they are shy, sometimes just individualistic and find it hard to take part in group activities. We make friends with them, though, and they soon get over it. They see for themselves the difference between the Pioneers and the other children and they usually want to join.' And then this calm, self-possessed young girl, who already regarded 'individualism' as something of a character flaw, cheerfully explained how 'the Pioneers are so much more disciplined and more organized. If a boy or girl keeps on giving trouble, we take their red ties away from them and that means a lot.' Lucy Abolin was evidently happy and popular; and she no doubt basked in the limelight of her two elder brothers, Arthur and Carl Abolin, both regular starters on the Moscow Foreign Workers' baseball team.[20]

Over three seasons, baseball mania in the USSR had given rise to an emergent national league. In June 1934, the first inter-city game was played between the Moscow Foreign Workers' Club and the Gorky Auto Workers team, who arrived at the Moscow train station weighed down with the brand-new bats they had finished making in their factory just three days earlier. On this occasion Walter Preedin caught the eye playing in left field and hitting the ball all over the park, while his brother Arnold Preedin struck out the Gorky batters with metronome-like efficiency. On their home field, the Moscow Foreign Workers' Club won the game easily, sixteen runs to five, packing off their rivals back to the assembly lines of Gorky. While the American auto workers grouched about the trouble they had finding a place to stay in crowded Moscow and the fact that their game had not been properly advertised so the crowd was still only a couple of hundred. Their letters of complaint provoked a critical editorial in the *Moscow Daily News*: 'If baseball is to be rapidly popularised, as it deserves to be, such shortcomings must not be repeated, particularly as the Council of Physical Culture is considering the possibility of organizing this summer a six-city league and an All-Union tournament. Such a contest would be a tremendous encouragement to the American youth in the Soviet Union.'[21]

Four hundred kilometres north of Leningrad, the Americans of Petrozavodsk had already organised four baseball teams in their city. Hundreds of American teenagers had emigrated with their Finnish-American parents to this remote region beside the Russian-Finnish border. Amid the lakes of Karelia, baseball thrived despite the lack of a stadium or very much in the way of equipment. Here the baseball players had one bat between them in a very tired condition and had recently lost three precious balls into the river. The American baseball players had written home for new bats and balls, and one of their recruits, Alvar Valimaa, asked the *Moscow Daily News* if the newspaper could print the results of their local league each week with the batting averages of the best ten players. If baseball was all about statistics then in Soviet Russia it would surely thrive, as Hank Makawski hinted in a letter from Gorky: 'The fellows simply eat up baseball news from America, so you can be assured they are far more interested in baseball in the Soviet Union, where they themselves participate and are acquainted with the other teams.'[22]

In July 1934, one month after beating Gorky, the Moscow Foreign Workers' Club left on an eight-day tour of Karelia. In Petrozavodsk, their first game was broadcast live over Soviet radio, with play-by-play coverage in English and Russian. This time the match was heavily publicised by newspaper and poster advertisements all over the city, and attracted a crowd of two thousand fans who turned out to support their local team. The Karelian captain was Albert 'Red' Lonn, a young baseball fanatic from Detroit, who had emigrated to Russia with his most treasured possession: a baseball signed by his hero, Babe Ruth. In their two games, the Karelian Americans thrashed the Moscow Foreign Workers' Club, 12–7 and 12–2, with the big-city visitors excusing their poor performance with complaints of injuries, and the loss of their two best players to harvest time at the American collective farm.[23]

Their arguments were settled one month later in August, when Albert Lonn's team travelled down to Moscow for a return match at the Stalin Stadium, just across the street from Gorky Park. This time the American lumberjacks and ski-builders from Karelia scored six runs in the eighth inning to win 14–9, and the sports reporter from the *Moscow Daily News* wrote that the crowd had started shouting 'We want baseball' (meaning they wanted a national league) and noted that 'only hot dogs and pop were missing from a genuine American scene'. In a letter published in their newspaper, the captain of the Moscow team, Arnold Preedin publicly thanked these 'genuine fourteen carat rabid fans' for turning out in support, and graciously acknowledged that Albert Lonn's team deserved to be crowned 'the USSR champions of 1934'. Then the handsome Arnold Preedin – who in his photographs was usually pictured grinning beneath his mop of light-brown curly hair – promised them 'the sweetest trimming they ever got in their lives in 1935'. It would be the year hotdogs first went on sale in the streets of Moscow, another idea brought over by an enterprising American emigrant.[24]

Meanwhile, in an effort to popularise their sport, the American baseball teams had already played exhibition games for the Red Army, and during the half-time interval of the USSR–Turkey soccer match in front of a cheering crowd of 25,000 Russian spectators. In the summer of 1934, even the Dynamo Sports Club of the Soviet secret police showed an interest in learning the fashionable new sport. In June, the Foreign Workers' Club was invited to stage another exhibition game at Bolshevo, the model prison camp built for the rehabilitation of young criminal delinquents in parkland outside Moscow.[25]

Three years earlier, George Bernard Shaw had visited Bolshevo as part of his Soviet tour, and had been assured that this idyllic setting surrounded by trees and gardens was a typical example of a Soviet 'corrective labour camp'. The camp's buildings were finely constructed of wood and brick, and inside the dormitories were orderly lines of beds with clean white sheets, and sparkling washrooms.

Young delinquents, orphaned by the Revolution and Civil War, worked quietly at their chosen trades of metalwork or carpentry or engineering, and the boys never studied for more than six hours a day. Others simply concentrated on their schoolwork in bright classrooms with a gymnasium and auditorium attached. It was a prototype of the Soviet criminal justice system, a progressive showpiece for any Western intellectual, businessman or trade unionist who cared to visit this camp with no guards, whose gates were open and doors unlocked.[26]

The Americans' train left Moscow for Bolshevo at 10.15 a.m. Beforehand they had been informed that 'all ball players must turn out for this game', an instruction which sounded more like a warning than an invitation. No record survived of what took place that day on 18 June 1934 at Bolshevo, but their hosts must have been fairly impressed because the Dynamo Sports Club soon announced that they too would be preparing two baseball teams to play in the forthcoming Soviet league to compete against Arnold Preedin's Foreign Workers' Club and the other American teams.[27]

The Dynamo Sports Club had been founded a decade earlier by Felix Dzerzhinsky to provide rest and recreation to the Soviet secret police, known by its first Revolutionary acronym as 'the Cheka' – 'The Extraordinary Commission for the Combat of Counter-Revolution and Sabotage' – and later through the course of the next two decades by their ever-changing initials as the GPU, the OGPU and the NKVD. A neutral observer might have confidently predicted that any game between the OGPU and these brash young Americans would have been intensely competitive, with national pride at stake and tempers frayed over close calls, stolen bases and complex rules lost in translation on the baseball field. But the OGPU's interest in baseball would prove to be short-lived. Only their connection with the baseball players would last.

3

'LIFE HAS BECOME MORE JOYFUL!'

The abolition of the Ogpu, secret police organisation, and absorption of its functions into the newly created Commissariat for Internal Affairs [NKVD], was celebrated here today as a demonstration that the Soviet Union had turned the corner and at last could safely cast off methods by which the regime heretofore had stamped out enemies.

Harold Denny, 'End of OGPU Hailed as Defeat of Foes',
New York Times, 12 July 1934

As the two Foreign Workers' Club teams, the 'Hammer and Sickles' and the 'Red Stars', continued their practice sessions in Gorky Park or at the Stalin Stadium during the spring training of April 1935, the only problem they faced was the mischief of the Russian children who snuck into the ground to watch them play. In one tied game a foul ball was hit over the fence into left field where a gang of little faces was watching intently. Straightaway the kids grabbed the ball and ran away out of the stadium into their backyard to start a game of '*Americanski beisbol*' of their own. It was left to the captain, Arnold Preedin, to chase after them and persuade this Moscow Little League to return their precious ball, and let the Americans finish their game.[1]

By then the American baseball players had already gained their most celebrated team member. At the height of his fame, Paul Robeson arrived in Moscow to discuss acting roles with the Soviet film director Sergei Eisenstein, and to give concerts in Moscow factories where he was cheered by the American emigrants who worked there.[2] To the world's press, the thirty-five year old American actor and singer announced his passionate enthusiasm for all he had seen: 'In Russia I felt for the first time like a full human being – no color prejudice like in Mississippi, no color prejudice like in Washington.' Later Robeson revealed that his young son would start school in Moscow 'so that the boy need not contend with discrimination because of color'. Paul Robeson, Jr., was duly enrolled at the elite Moscow academy whose pupils included Stalin's daughter and Molotov's son.[3]

On New Year's Eve 1934, Paul Robeson had stepped into the party at the Foreign Workers' Club on Hertzen Street, perhaps out of curiosity or just because he was searching for somewhere to celebrate the New Year. In their club, the young Americans mobbed him as a hero of the progressive cause, and performed their initiation ceremony of throwing the six-foot-six-inch former All American football star three times into the air. At the invitation of the baseball players in the crowd, Robeson happily agreed to turn out for the Foreign Workers' Club when he returned to Russia in the New Year. 'I'll be a catcher,' he laughed and crouched down low to show them he still had the moves from his days on the Rutgers team that had beaten Princeton. And on a promise made around midnight, the Foreign Workers' Club baseball team gained an honorary new member, as Robeson and the young Americans raised their glasses and drank toasts, 'To the New Year, the third of our Five Year Plan.'[4]

'I was not prepared for the happiness I see on every face in Moscow,' Robeson told a reporter from the New York *Daily Worker*, 'I was aware that there was no starvation here, but I was not prepared for the bounding life; the feeling of safety and abundance and freedom that I find here, wherever I turn. I was not prepared for the endless friendliness, which surrounded me from the moment I crossed the border.' When asked for a comment on the recent executions of 'counter-revolutionary terrorists' announced in the Soviet press, Paul Robeson was frankly unconcerned: 'From what I have already seen of the workings of the Soviet Government, I can only say that anybody who lifts his hand against it ought to be shot! It is the government's duty to put down any opposition to this really free society with a firm hand . . . It is obvious that there is no terror here, that all the masses of every race are contented and support their government.'[5]

One of the new American baseball players to arrive in Moscow in the summer of 1935 was a nineteen-year-old from Buffalo, New York, with high cheekbones and brown eyes. Thomas Sgovio travelled with his mother and fifteen-year-old sister Grace, to join his father Joseph Sgovio, who had left America two years earlier. Sharing his father's gregarious nature, Thomas made friends easily within the American community in Moscow as he pursued his youthful ambition to become a fine artist. Perhaps one day he might see his work hanging in the Tretyakov Gallery across the river from the Kremlin, but in the meantime he waited patiently to be accepted into art school for the following year and took evening classes in charcoal drawing to help build up his portfolio.[6]

His father had found a job working as a pipe-fitter in a Moscow factory, and gave lectures to Soviet factory clubs on the evils of American unemployment his family had been lucky enough to leave behind.[7] Joseph Sgovio had been an active American Communist Party member in Buffalo, and was comfortable delivering radical speeches. In Russia the main difficulty these 'political emigrants' faced was overcoming the scepticism of their audiences. No matter how bleak a picture the American radicals painted of their hardships back home, the Russian workers would take one look at their fine clothes and boots, and not believe them. This political problem was addressed directly by Ben Thomas in a letter to the Soviet journal *Internatsionalny Mayak* in which he admitted that Russian workers still believed the Soviet newspapers 'exaggerate conditions of workers in America. They often judge of the conditions according to the clothes of the American workmen who come here. I tried to explain to the workmen that the persons arriving . . . have still retained their clothes doing their best to present an 'outward appearance' because in America a man with worn clothes is viewed with suspicion and turned out.'[8]

What set the American emigrants apart was always their clothing, which was closely examined by Russian workers, who touched their jackets and suits with expressions of approval and offered escalating sums of roubles to buy them, quite literally, off their backs. This Russian mania for American dress would last throughout the history of the Soviet Union, but it was particularly pressing in the thirties when both fashions and new materials were non-existent.[9] The best-dressed people on the streets of Russia's cities were always foreigners, while the mass of ordinary citizens looked on enviously. And the Americans, in turn, could not help but notice that the Russian faces, if not quite starving, were at the very least a little hollow.[10]

Joseph Sgovio's speeches provided his family with an extra food ration in the special stores, where they stood in line next to the German and Italian communists who had fled Fascism for the sanctuary of the USSR.[11] For some it came as a surprise that the system of Soviet food distribution was so heavily politicised. One American auto worker in Moscow reported six different types of stores selling items of varying quality to every class group.[12] While others, who had been in the Soviet Union much longer, were no longer shocked on seeing as many as seventeen different categories of wage and food rations. The mockery of the early American arrivals – 'Workers of the World Unite, and then divide yourself into seventeen categories!' – was entirely lost on the Bolsheviks.[13]

The most luxurious stores were exclusively reserved for the Bolshevik elites, and if a young American such as Thomas Sgovio did not know any better he might have suspected that a new privileged class had soon arisen from the ashes of the old. A sharp-eyed witness might occasionally catch a glimpse of a commissar or GPU officer stepping out of a store reserved for one of his own kind and turning the corner of a Moscow street clutching a precious food package wrapped in brown paper. But the Americans could hardly criticise when they themselves formed one rung on this escalating hierarchy of privilege. All those who arrived on official Amtorg contracts, as well as the political emigrants, gained access to the special food stores where scarce provisions could be bought in exchange for foreign currency. It was a gastronomic world above and beyond the subsistence tedium of black bread and soup reserved for ordinary Russian workers. Fortunately for the consciences of the Americans, Stalin himself had pronounced that strict equality – once the highest ideal of the Revolution – was now 'a piece of petty bourgeois stupidity, worthy of a primitive sect of ascetics, but not of socialists' society organized on Marxian lines.'[14]

Soon after his arrival in Moscow, Thomas Sgovio joined the Anglo-American Chorus, one of the cultural activities organised by the Foreign Workers' Club. The Chorus gave concerts with forty-five male and female voices singing a programme of 'Negro protest-songs and American cowboy tunes' conducted by Gertrude Rady, formerly of Broadway.[15] Very quickly these American singers were in great demand, invited to the Theatre of People's Art in Moscow, where they performed 'Dis Cotton Want a Picking' to great applause from a discerning Russian audience.[16] Their concert was filmed, and soon afterwards Thomas Sgovio joined his friends in a Moscow cinema to watch their performance projected up on to the silver screen at twenty-four frames per second. At that moment, they all must have felt as though they had really arrived.[17]

If only for a short while, the popularity of the Americans in Moscow was unrivalled. Everyone was keen to make friends with these optimistic, fun-loving and well-dressed new arrivals, including the sons and daughters of the Bolshevik elite. Thomas had recently made friends with Marvin Volat, a young American emigrant who hailed from his home town of Buffalo, New York, and was studying the violin at the Moscow Conservatory. It was Marvin who invited Thomas to meet his new Russian girlfriend, a nineteen-year-old language student named Sara Berman. Riding the tram over to Sara's apartment on Lubyanka Square, Marvin chattered excitedly: 'Just think! Her father is the chief of all the concentration camps in Russia! He knows Stalin real well.'[18]

As their crowded tram clanked slowly to their stop, Thomas Sgovio could hardly have considered the inadvertent warning that lay hidden in Marvin's words. What earthly significance could the *Glavnoye Upravleniye Lagerei* – 'the Labour Camps Directorate' whose initials formed the acronym 'Gulag' – have to a nineteen-year-old American art student? At the time, if either Matvei Berman or the Gulag meant anything at all, it was only as the faint reflection of the state propaganda which described the 'camps' as the unfortunate necessity of the post-Revolutionary era, required for the 'political re-education' of the remnants of the old Tsarist regime. Even Walter Duranty had agreed on the essentially benign nature of these 'concentration labor camps'. Their purpose, Duranty had written in an article published on the front page of the *New York Times*, was to 'remove subversive individuals from their familiar milieu to a remote spot where their potentially harmful activities will be nullified – the Bolsheviki add kindly – "where such misguided persons will be given a chance to regain by honest toil their lost citizenship in the Socialist Fatherland."' Duranty's best comparison was with the early American settlers of Virginia: 'Each concentration camp forms a sort of 'commune' where everyone lives comparatively free, not imprisoned, but compelled to work for the good of the community. They are fed and housed gratis and receive pay for their work . . . They are certainly not convicts in the American sense of the word.'[19]

Of course it was a strange coincidence that of all the millions of young women in Russia, his friend Marvin Volat had chosen to romance the daughter of Matvei Berman, the Gulag chief recently awarded the Order of Lenin for the 'glorious' construction of the White Sea–Baltic Canal.[20] But then it was equally surprising that two American teenagers should be riding a tram through 1930s Moscow towards the floodlit monolithic GPU headquarters on Lubyanka Square, whose blazing lights emitted a peculiar dark energy into the night. They had no idea, even then, that there were few Muscovites who would not make the necessary detour of a few city streets left or right to bypass Lubyanka Square.[21]

To make a little extra money on the side, Thomas was freelancing as a commercial artist at *Sovietland*, an English-language magazine published by the Soviet news agency, Tass, and intended as a cultural export for an English-speaking readership.[22] With no apparent sense of irony, the magazine's glossy pages were filled with articles such as 'Abundance!' which described how Moscow's department stores were overflowing with supplies of food, not to mention gramophones, vacuum cleaners, electric stoves and a cascade of other consumer goods. New cafés were opening in Moscow where 'payment was made by the honour system', although in a period of widespread shortages, exactly where such cafés were located no one was completely sure. But the magazine articles were pored over by readers in America who formed strong attachments from such slender means. The manufacture of certainty, it seemed, was the most successful export of the Five Year Plan.[23]

At the offices of *Sovietland*, Thomas Sgovio was introduced to Lucy Flaxman, who worked full-time on the magazine. Lucy was a pretty and rather light-hearted twenty-six-year-old from Boston, Massachusetts, who had arrived in Russia a decade earlier with her family. Naturally she knew a wider circle of people in Moscow, and could help Thomas with his faltering Russian. Thomas's first American girlfriend had returned home, so when Lucy Flaxman invited him to the prestigious House of Writers to dance the latest American crazes that were sweeping Moscow, he was only too happy to join her.[24]

Greater quantities of food were beginning to appear in the stores; if never in the quantities suggested by the *Sovietland* articles, then at least there was something to buy after years of acute hunger and terrible shortages. When people started talking of a new café which had opened up on Pushkin Square with music and dancing, it seemed as though the promised socialist 'good times' were finally on their way. The Communist Party had long declared itself to be 'dizzy with success', and the official slogan of 1935 was Stalin's own announcement that 'Life has become better, comrades; Life has become more joyful!'[25] It was seen everywhere across the USSR, the favourite catchphrase of a propaganda campaign announcing the arrival of socialism, the first step on the road to a fully communist society. 'Life has become more joyful!' was the front-page headline in the Soviet press on New Year's Eve, hung in banners over 'People's Parks' across the land, and celebrated in Red Army song. For a moment then, it seemed as though enjoyment itself, for its own sake, had received an official Kremlin blessing: carnival balls, new sports, new foods, dancing and jazz were all officially allowed, even encouraged.[26]

And so, as if obeying a stamped edict from on high, Thomas danced with Lucy Flaxman and their friends at the House of Writers, at the Metropol Hotel and the Foreign Workers' Club. The young Americans danced, played baseball, sang in choirs, acted in the Clifford Odets play *Waiting for Lefty*, fell in love with one another, and thanked their lucky stars that they had made the right decision to come to Soviet Russia. All of them were full of hope for the future, bursting with the can-do optimism of the young.[27]

4

'FORDIZATSIA'

Carbon is transformed into diamond
Russia into a New America
A new one, not the old America.

Alexander Blok, July 1919[1]

Far from congregating in Moscow, the American emigrants had scattered all over the Soviet Union. Wherever there was work to be done, there seemed to be a lean and eager American happy to make the journey, willing to travel across the length and breadth of the USSR, from remote eastern cities such as Nizhni Tagil tucked away in the Ural Mountains, all the way south to the oilfields of Azerbaijan. By the early 1930s, there were English-language schools established for the children of American workers in Moscow, Leningrad, Stalingrad, Kharkov and Nizhni Novgorod.[2]

Reports reached the *Moscow Daily News* of baseball teams organised in Yerevan, the capital of Armenia; and in the Ukraine, where the Americans working at the Kharkov tractor factory announced their desire to join the Soviet national league just as soon as their 'bush leaguers' got a little better. The Kharkov Americans had been getting along so far with one bat and two balls. The bat was all right but the balls were 'in bad condition after three seasons of mauling' and needed re-stitching after every game. They wrote that Russians were joining in their sport; and some Americans who had never had the chance to play baseball back home were learning for the very first time in the USSR.[3]

Did it strike them as strange that many of the Americans travelled to Russia only to find themselves working in brand-new Soviet factories built by the old capitalist titans of American industry? In the city of Nizhni Novgorod, 420 kilometres east of Moscow, the

Ford Motor Company had constructed a giant auto plant on the empty Russian steppe. Despite a ferocious record of strike-breaking in Detroit, Henry Ford had been only too delighted to sell the Soviets the necessary industrial blueprints and machinery, together with seventy-five thousand 'knocked-down' Ford Model As from the River Rouge plant. It was a deal sweetened by the guarantee of five years of tech nical assistance and the promise of American labour and know-how. The Soviet contract was worth a staggering forty million dollars and, lest we forget, these were 1930s millions, paid for in gold at the height of the Depression. No other firm in the United States, or even the world, conducted more business with Joseph Stalin than the Ford Motor Company between 1929 and 1936. For above all men, Henry Ford – 'the Sage of Dearborn' – understood very well that the power and allure of the automobile transcended ideology. The whole of mankind was in love with speed and, in that respect at least, the Bolsheviks were no different.[4]

In fact the cult of 'American mechanization' in Russia was as old as the Revolution. Lenin himself had been a passionate advocate of Ford's methods of mass production, and Ford's autobiography *My Life and Work* had long been a Soviet bestseller, going through four printings by 1925 alone. In remote Siberian villages, peasants who had not yet heard of Stalin knew all about Henry Ford; even his quip 'you can have any colour you like as long as it's black' hinted at a very mordant, Russian sense of humour. The Soviet press had long heralded the advent of 'Fordism' as the slogan for their industrialisation campaign.[5] But it was the motor car in particular, and Ford's role in its perfection, which set the standard for the modern age. The construction of a 'Soviet Detroit', therefore, was deemed essential to the Bolshevik cause. Henry Ford's unpalatable hatred of trade unions, not to mention his vast capitalistic fortune, would have to be politely ignored as the Soviet ideologues embraced Ford as a secular saint holding the keys to a mechanical heaven.[6]

In Detroit the River Rouge plant was universally recognised as 'the wonder of the industrial world'. The Rouge alone employed over one hundred thousand men, in factories constantly fed by snaking wagons of coal and iron ore bearing the Ford logo on their side. Henry Ford owned the railroad, the river barges, the coal and iron ore mines, the glass and tyre factories, even six million acres of Brazilian jungle bought for a rubber plantation named Fordlandia.

All of which converged at the Rouge, the industrial epicentre that employed five thousand workers just to keep the factories spotlessly clean, scrubbing floors, emptying trash every two hours, cleaning windows, endlessly repainting surfaces in the Ford colours of white and machine blue. There was no talking, no smoking, no more than fifteen minutes allowed for lunchbreaks, and instant firings for the slightest infraction of the rules.[7] Industry at the Rouge was all-powerful, unceasing and relentless: as one shift ended another began in the twenty-four hour production schedule; the Ford workers pouring out of the factories, most wearing flat caps and carrying lunch pails, a few grinning for the whirling cameras of the Ford Sociological Department, which were recording them for the Ford Motor Company archives. For among his many eccentricities, Henry Ford was most consumed by his company's much-vaunted history.

The Ford publicists boasted that the iron ore delivered at the River Rouge docks on Monday morning was transformed into a finished motor car to be sold in a Ford customer dealership by Thursday night.[8] The simplicity, speed and scale of the industrial operation was a miraculous achievement. It was also a uniquely American success, the pinnacle of mass production and the very starting point of modernity. Here in Dearborn, Michigan, was the distilled essence of the industrialised world, which every company around the world was so jealously striving to copy. By 1931 Henry Ford posed proudly for a photograph with his son Edsel in front of his very first and his twenty millionth car sold. No wonder Stalin gazed on so enviously, and sent his Russian emissaries to Detroit begging to learn how it was done.[9]

For his part, 'the Sage of Dearborn' could hardly suppress his delight at the prospect of being paid forty million dollars for the old Model A plant he had only been planning to scrap. From his point of view it was simply too great a business opportunity to refuse, although Henry Ford was perfectly aware of the grim reputation of the Soviet state. The Ford Motor Company had been trying to break into the Russian market since even before the Revolution. In the summer of 1926, Henry Ford had sent a party of five employees to investigate conditions in Soviet Russia and explore the idea of building a factory there. The group was led by the American engineer Bredo Berghoff, who quickly discovered that the existing Soviet industry languishing in a state of chaos. Their factories were burdened with endless workers' committees, reluctant management, widespread smoking, trash on the floors, crude oil in gas tanks, machine parts manufactured to random thickness – an endless litany of industrial despair. It was soon obvious that while a vast market in automobiles lay waiting in Russia, the construction of a privately owned factory at Ford's expense would be tantamount to economic suicide, liable at any moment to government seizure by the Bolsheviks.

Perhaps the most interesting section of Bredo Berghoff's report was the considerations of personal safety in Russia, which the engineer was very anxious to reveal to Henry Ford. The new Soviet leader was mentioned only in passing, in a cursory nod towards the well-known prejudices of his boss: 'The government of the USSR is today, just as it was before Lenin's death, controlled by one man, Comrade Stalin . . . an Asiatic whose iron control of Russia and the USSR befits his Name which means Steel. Stalin's real name is Joseph Vissarionovich Djugashvili, although he is said not to be of Jewish blood.' What Berghoff subsequently made plain was the range of repressive methods employed by the contemporary Soviet state. In particular he warned of the reputation of Felix Dzerzhinsky, the much-feared head of the Soviet secret police, who was 'considered responsible for the death of thousands upon thousands of people accused of not being in sympathy with Communist principles'. As Berghoff underscored the dangers, he added a request of his own that reflected this fear:

It is respectfully and urgently suggested that this copy of the Report on Soviet Russia and the USSR be kept at all times in a safe place and under lock when not under the holder's personal attention . . . The Soviet Government possesses an excellent system of espionage throughout the world . . . Any careless handling of the information contained herein might easily result in 1. No member of the present delegation being allowed to reenter Soviet Russia . . . 2. If allowed to enter the country prison terms and even violence might await any member who might thereafter be falsely accused of counter-revolutionary sympathies, as such has been practiced on other foreigners in the past.

In conclusion, Berghoff requested that the report be burnt immediately after it was read. Instead, it lay buried in the Ford Archives in Dearborn, an unheeded warning of the violence that might await any

American who ventured to Russia upon the business dealings of Henry Ford.[10]

Bredo Berghoff's presentiments of danger would prove to be well founded. But whereas Charles Sorensen – Ford's chief of production – was only too happy to drop the whole idea of the Russian venture completely, Henry Ford was never quite so easily deterred. With reports of Stalin extending courtship to the French auto giants Citroën and Peugeot, the prospect of losing the Russian market to an international business rival appeared more than Ford could bear.[11] The reluctant Sorensen was instructed by his boss to negotiate with Stalin's emissaries in Dearborn. If there could not be a wholly owned Ford factory in Soviet Russia, then perhaps a compromise might be reached? And so the hulking Danish-American industrialist Charlie Sorensen attempted to explain the strange vocabulary of capitalist ownership to the Bolsheviks, like a Roman senator pressing table manners on the hungry Goths.[12]

The startled American press pounced upon the leaked news of these negotiations. In an article titled 'Talk of Ford Favor Thrills Moscow', Walter Duranty attempted to explain the developments to the puzzled readers of the *New York Times*: 'Ford means America and all that America has accomplished to make her a model and an ideal for this vast and backward country . . . Cheap mass production is a Soviet goal, more precious from the practical standpoint than world revolution – Ford in Soviet eyes is the arch-mogul of that achievement. "Fordizatsia" – "Fordisation" – has become one of the "words of power" with which Soviet orators spellbind auditors.'[13] In Dearborn, real progress was made with the arrival of Valery Mezhlauk, a highly intelligent Soviet industrial commissar who struck up a warm and unlikely friendship with Charlie Sorensen. The agreement between the Ford Motor Company and the 'Soviet Supreme Council of National Economy' was signed on 31 May 1929, the forty-million-dollar deal completed in a mere seven pages of paperwork.[14] Henry Ford himself added his looping signature to the last page of the contract, and then happily posed to have his picture taken outside, standing between Valery Mezhlauk and Saul Bron, the Amtorg chief, as the photographers' bulbs flashed amid a general purr of mutual satisfaction.[15]

Two months after the agreement was signed, Charlie Sorensen was welcomed in the USSR as an industrial prince from the old New

World. For his visit, Sorensen was provided with his own private railroad car along with a personal chef, steward and valet to cater to his every whim on his journey across Russia. A private yacht was chartered to sail him down the Volga to view the site outside Nizhni Novgorod chosen to become 'the Soviet Detroit'.

At a truck factory in Moscow, Sorensen's arrival struck him as having made a 'good excuse for a holiday'. All semblance of work stopped, and to his surprise Sorensen heard shouts of 'Hello, Charlie!' and 'Charlie, how are you?' from former Ford employees greeting their old boss with an easy familiarity they would never have dared back home. Sorensen recognised some familiar faces from the Rouge, and noted that the Russians employed these Americans as 'experts' whereas back home they had been regular assembly-line Joes. At one point during his three days of negotiation in the Kremlin with Soviet industrial commissars, Sorensen was surprised to be greeted by another small, unnervingly familiar figure gliding past their table. ''Allo, Sharley', Joseph Stalin had murmured.[16]

Back in Detroit, bearing a parting gift of a silver jewellery box that had once belonged to Catherine the Great, Charlie Sorensen told Henry Ford that he would like to return to Russia to review the work they had set in motion. Ford's reaction, Sorensen later remembered, had been adamantly opposed: 'Charlie don't you do it! They need a man like you. If you went over there, you would never come out again. Don't take that chance!' If Ford's production chief could not be risked twice, no one seemed overly concerned for the safety of the company's present and former employees who would travel to Russia to assemble the Soviet Model As.[17]

The year the contract was signed, Ford's chauffeur pulled up outside the modest Detroit home of Sam Herman, an auto worker and naturalised American born in the Ukraine. Over afternoon tea, Ford easily convinced this spellbound employee that he should act as an interpreter for the Soviet deal. Sam Herman's youngest son, Victor, had sat in the room too overawed to interrupt their conversation. A teenage boy soon to become one of the American baseball players on the Gorky team, at the time Victor Herman was still just an athletic Detroit kid with pale blue eyes and a knack for getting into fights in their working-class neighbourhood. On Ironwood Street, the local toughs had thrown stones at the windows of the Herman family house because they were Jews, and Victor had learned to box to defend himself. When his father announced that the family would travel to Russia on a three-year contract to build cars, Victor had been only too delighted at the prospect of an adventure. He trailed along as his father helped persuade three hundred Detroit families to emigrate with them to the new 'American village' being built two miles outside the Ford factory in Nizhni Novgorod.[18]

Officially Victor Herman's father was now an employee of the Soviet trust Autostroi, although while he worked with the Russians at the River Rouge plant he was issued with a Ford Badge, No. H-9824, on 9 July, 1931, for which he had signed an official waiver for any claims for damage or loss to his person. The Ford badge allowed Sam Herman entrance onto the premises of the Ford Motor Company, and it stated in his contract that he would have to pay a five-dollar fine if the badge were lost.[19] Perhaps assured by this implicit moral covenant with Henry Ford, the Herman family emigrated on the passenger ship *Leviathan*, which sailed out of New York harbour on 26 September 1931.[20] Several hundred American auto workers and their families arrived in Nizhni Novgorod during the course of that year to join the crowds of that ancient Russian city with its blue onion-domed churches and muddy streets.

On a curve of the Volga river, at the junction of its tributary the Oka, where once there had been nothing but wheat fields and forests of dark fir trees, in fewer than two years a giant factory had risen from the Russian steppe.[21] An American construction company working under Ford supervision had begun the work in August 1930, and the factory was finished by November 1931. Given that half of the labour force was made up of Russian women equipped only with wheelbarrows and long-handled shovels, its completion was almost a miracle. Five thousand horse-drawn wagons had been used to move the building materials and heavy machinery since naturally there was a desperate shortage of trucks. Even the efficiency of these horses, the American construction engineers complained, was 'catastrophically reduced by the low supply norms of oats'.[22] During the winter in that part of central Russia the temperatures almost always fell below minus twenty degrees, and the ice on the Oka river froze at least four feet thick.[23]

In such conditions, despite all the obstacles, eventually a 'workers' city' was built beside the car factory, with rows of three-storey apartment houses specifically designed by their Bolshevik architects *without* individual kitchens since in the new Soviet era all cooking would be done in communal factory kitchens, signalling the 'death blow' to domestic bourgeois drudgery.[24] The architects had adorned their workers' city with all the conveniences of the model state: a cafeteria, a nursery, public baths, a 'palace of culture' and, of course, a crematorium.[25] It was, in every sense, a political showpiece of Joseph Stalin, to be heralded in Soviet propaganda as 'Detroit without Ford', whose 'masters are the working class, not capitalist kings'.[26]

The American workers simply christened their new home 'the Russian Fordville' – or 'Nizhni New York' – a faintly familiar copy of the River Rouge plant dropped down into the Russian wilderness.[27] And when the Americans arrived to work at their brand new auto factory, they could see from the distance the giant sign that read 'FORD'.[28]

5

'THE LINDBERGH OF RUSSIA'

We respect American efficiency in everything – in industry, in technique,
in literature, in life. We never forget the United States of America is a
capitalist country. But among the Americans are many sound persons
physically and mentally, sound in their approach to work, to action.
                            Joseph Stalin, interview, June 1932[1]

For a while, at least, Stalin loved to buy American. Considerations of
practicality were all but subsumed by the desire for symbolic achievement, with each new scheme designed to surpass the scale of the
American original, and rechristened 'the Soviet Detroit' or 'the Soviet
Gary' or 'the Soviet Muscle Shoals'. On Henry Ford's recommendation, the Detroit architect Albert Kahn designed the auto factory at
Nizhni Novgorod, and now opened an office in Moscow staffed with
twenty-five architects, all working non-stop to put up 521 new Soviet
factories in quick succession.[2] In the early thirties, Stalin's Russia was
being rapidly industrialised according to an American design. It was a
strange coalescence of expedience quickly consigned by both parties
into the dark interstices of history.

One thousand kilometres south of Nizhni Novgorod, along the
course of the Volga river, several hundred Americans had found jobs
working at the mammoth tractor factory built by Albert Kahn at
Stalingrad. If living conditions were initially somewhat primitive,
their deprivations were offset by feelings of solidarity, job security,
and higher pay. Robert Robinson was one of the lucky ones offered
a contract that almost doubled his existing wage. Working for Ford
in Detroit he had earned 140 dollars a month, whereas in the Soviet
Union he was offered 250 dollars a month, rent-free living quarters,
a maid, thirty days' paid vacation a year, a car, free passage to and

from Russia and the promise that 150 dollars of each month's paycheck would be deposited in an American bank. It was too good an opportunity to miss, especially since Robinson knew he might be laid off any day from his job at the Rouge.[3]

When Robinson arrived at the address advertised in the Detroit newspapers there was already a crowd of people hoping for the same chance.[4] Vast swathes of workers were being laid off in those Depression years; when wages at Ford's were almost halved from seven to four dollars a day, while the 'speed-up' was in full effect and becoming unendurable. By October 1932, the Ford workforce had been cut to just 15,000 men, and within months the entire River Rouge operation would be shut down completely.[5] The mass redundancies in Detroit were greeted with evident delight in front-page headlines in the Soviet press: 'Soviet Union Will Ask Fired Ford Men To Work Here'.[6] Robert Robinson was just twenty-three years old when he left Detroit, and he considered himself fortunate.

So it was bitterly ironic that as a black American who emigrated to work in Russia, the only racism Robinson encountered came from his white American co-workers. Arriving in Stalingrad, Robinson refused to take their casual threats seriously until, just two weeks into his contract, he was stopped by two Americans named Lewis and Brown, who first racially abused him and then threatened: 'You have twenty-four hours to leave this place or you'll be sorry.' On the banks of the Volga, a fight broke out in which Robert Robinson gave back as good as he got.[7]

Back home in the United States, such retaliatory violence might easily have led to Robinson being hunted down the next day. In Stalingrad, however, a Russian witness reported the ugly confrontation, and when Robinson turned up for work at the factory the next day, the Russian workers treated him as a hero. Four days later a well-organised demonstration took place outside the factory gates, with speeches condemning racism and calling for the punishment of Lewis and Brown. The Soviet newspaper *Trud* published the text of their resolutions: 'We will not allow the ways of bourgeois America in the U.S.S.R. The Negro worker is our brother like the American worker. We castigate any who dares to destroy in the Soviet land the equality we have established for all proletarians of all nations.'[8]

The Alabaman Herbert Lewis was locked up in a Stalingrad prison awaiting trial. His arrest – observed the visiting American reporter William Henry Chamberlin – seemed only to strengthen the 'racial chauvinism' of the three hundred other Americans working at the tractor factory. Chamberlin described a conversation he had with a 'middle-aged mechanic, of the type, who probably earned fifty or sixty dollars a week before the Depression, regularly voted the Republican ticket and belonged to the Methodist church'. This nameless mechanic had organised an American committee to free Lewis. 'You know, brother,' he said, 'it's been most humiliating for us, as Americans, to hear a lot of furriners get up and jabber about how our government was no good and how we couldn't make laws to suit ourselves. And what they're trying to do with this trial is to force on us something no white American will stand for: social equality with the colored race.'

The mechanic then showed Chamberlin a letter written on a sheet of paper, which Lewis had signed. The apology expressed his regret to 'the ladies of the American colony, to the workers of Russia, and to the workers of the whole world', part of the plea bargain struck to avoid a Soviet prison sentence. When Chamberlin asked about a line in the note that had been heavily crossed out, the Republican mechanic explained, 'That was a direct apology to the nigger. We crossed that out.'[9]

Taking into account the fact that the defendants had been 'inoculated with racial enmity by the capitalistic system of the exploitation of the lower races', the Stalingrad district court sentenced Lewis and Brown to expulsion from the Soviet Union as a substitute for 'the term of ten years for deprivation of liberty'.[10] The court case turned Robert Robinson into a minor celebrity in Russia and America also, where his story was quickly picked up by the press. For Lovett Fort-Whiteman, the teacher at the Anglo-American school in Moscow and co-founder of the American Negro Labor Congress, Robinson's case must have seemed the fulfilment of the great ideal of colour-blind justice. In the country Fort-Whiteman had left behind, black Americans were the last to be hired and the first to be fired, denied membership by the majority of white trade unions, thoroughly segregated and regularly the victims of racially motivated violence. In 1933, twenty-four black Americans were lynched in the United States, a practice that would continue with stubborn regularity for the next three decades.

Small wonder, then, that American emigrants such as Fort-Whiteman wanted so passionately to believe that a place in the world existed where man's essential brotherhood blinded him to differences of colour. In the USSR, he thought he had found it. How then could Lovett Fort-

Whiteman ever have foreseen that by being deported back to the United States for their assault Lewis and Brown would have their lives saved; while he, by staying on, would have his own condemned?

Herbert Lewis spent a month in jail, and nine days on trial, before returning to America. In an interview he gave to the *Chicago Tribune*, the Alabaman mechanic painted a grim picture of the living conditions for the 450 Americans (including eighty women and children) who he claimed were being 'held captive by Reds' in Stalingrad. Lewis stated that all of them were anxious to leave but were being refused exit visas and, meanwhile, were falling sick to 'typhoid, typhus, dysentery and scurvy'. Two Americans had already died and many others were seriously ill. Their communications with the outside world were heavily censored, and they had barely one hundred dollars between all of them. The American money, which was supposed to have been paid into their Detroit bank accounts, had never materialised, and they quickly discovered that their rouble salaries were virtually worthless. 'They were not there because they were Reds,' Lewis told the Tribune, 'they were there for the jobs, the salaries from $306 to $500 monthly.'[11]

Robert Robinson was never physically attacked again in Stalingrad. In the summer of 1933, he returned home to New York to visit his mother in Harlem. In the trough of the Depression, the poverty and misery on the streets of Harlem was unrelenting, and Robinson discovered also that as result of the publicity from his court case, he had been blacklisted by Ford's from all work in Detroit. Unable to find a job, Robinson returned to work at a ball-bearing factory in Moscow.[12] The following year, at a factory meeting on 10 December 1934, he was unexpectedly nominated to the Moscow Soviet. Once again the Soviet newspapers feted him as an example of how a black American, unwanted and persecuted back home, could be raised to the status of a big-city politician owing to the progressive nature of the Soviet state. Unanimously 'elected' with rising Communist Party apparatchiks such as Nikolai Bulganin and Nikita Khrushchev, Robinson's unlikely rise was featured in *Time* magazine's Christmas Eve edition of 1934. The magazine ran a photograph of the shy and studious-looking Robinson above the caption: 'The Coal Black Protégé of Joseph Stalin'. According to *Time*'s editorial: 'possession of a US passport is the sine qua non for Negroes whom the Soviet Government is training as Communist dynamite. Reason: they must be able to get home as bona fide US citizens to do any good when the hoped-for explosion of US Revolution comes.'[13]

In reality, Robert Robinson was a little panicked by his unexpected election. Fearing that he was already in well over his head, and not wishing to increase his indebtedness still further lest he might never be able to return home, Robinson refused Comrade Bulganin's offer of a central Moscow flat, a dacha, and a car in exchange for playing a more active role in the propaganda campaign. And, in the end, his American passport would prove no guarantee of his return.[14]

Meanwhile the city of Nizhni Novgorod had been renamed in honour of the Bolshevik writer Maxim Gorky, and its auto factory officially opened for full-scale production on 1 January 1932, with the usual fanfare of ceremonies and rhetoric: 'When we place the USSR at the wheel of an automobile, and a peasant on a tractor, let the venerable capitalists boasting of their "civilization" try to reach us!' The first Ford Model As began rolling off the assembly line beneath giant portraits of a disturbingly youthful-looking Joseph Stalin, his watchful gaze seemingly filled with satisfaction at the appropriation of one of the most famous brands of American industry. In the early days, the blue oval Ford badge was still stamped on the Soviet Model As, positioned next to the hammer-and-sickle and five-pointed red star on the front grille. The new cars were driven proudly out of the factory decorated with banners in Russian demanding: 'FULFIL THE FIVE YEAR PLAN! GIVE US SOVIET FORDS!'[15]

Within weeks the entire assembly line had been shut down amid reports of wildcat strikes due to food shortages, and the Red Army having to be called in to 'restore order'.[16] After production restarted in May, it became clear that for all the imported expertise of their 750 American workers the Soviet management had not yet grasped even the most basic principles of mass production. One American visitor watching the assembly line at Gorky noted a touring car, a closed car, a seven-passenger car and a truck emerging one after the other. Henry Ford would simply have fired everyone in sight.[17] Another Ford engineer just despaired: 'The Russians are a group of children playing with their first mechanical toys, they are smashing them, running them improperly, and generally making a mess of things.'[18]

Even the official Soviet production figure of just forty cars per day proved deeply suspect, since most of the cars emerged missing a fairly crucial element – spark plugs and steering wheels in particular. A thousand of these semi-cannibalised machines awaited delivery that first summer, before the Russian winter destroyed them. But at least the Five Year Plan was a little closer to being fulfilled. The Plan called for cars; it did not stipulate whether they arrived with their steering wheels attached.

Inside the factory, the native Detroiter Walter Reuther watched a Russian worker use his sleeve to wipe off a die because there was no cloth available. 'Nichevo' was the response as the acid burned through his coat. With the constant threat of sheared and falling machinery operated by inexpert hands, the Soviet Ford factory was an extremely dangerous place to work.[19] Young Russian women had to be persuaded to use tongs, not their hands, to remove material from the press. When an American worker tried to warn one woman, she only smiled and, with the air of a professional impatience to a timid novice, replied 'Nichevo.'[20] Fortunately a quick-thinking Ford engineer, Frank Bennett, was on hand when the wet paint on the Model As caught fire. If the paint drums stored next to the overheated ovens had caught light, the whole factory would have gone up in flames. But the drums were rolled out of the way just in time.

In Moscow, the 'Stalin' auto factory had been built to assemble the 75,000 knocked-down Fords shipped over from Detroit. The factory floors were still being laid when Frank Bennett arrived on an inspection tour. He noticed that the Russians did not use regular asphalt, which was immune to temperature fluctuations and was the accepted practice back in Detroit. Instead they preferred a 'low-grade concoction' reinforced with broken bricks from old buildings. Walking through the factory, the American engineer kicked a piece of brick and realised that it had come from a church.[21] As part of the atheist campaign, Moscow's Cathedral of Christ the Saviour had recently been dynamited to make way for Stalin's Palace of the Soviets. The demolition was filmed by Soviet newsreel as evidence of the final triumph of the Bolsheviks, with Stalin's functionary Lazar Kaganovich pictured standing on top of the ruins proclaiming: 'Mother Russia is cast down.'[22]

In retrospect the destruction of Christianity in Russia was a necessary precursor for all that followed. In the dictatorship of the proletariat, any civil institution that might provide a countervailing voice to the authority of Joseph Stalin was being systematically destroyed, or turned into an acquiescent imitation of self-parody. The rubble from the Russian churches was salvaged to be used for factory floors, and the church bells removed to a giant smelting works outside Moscow. Here – in a mountain of ancient gold and silver – lay the silence that had descended upon Russia like the first fall of winter snow.[23]

Shortly after his family's arrival in the USSR, Sam Herman was sent to Moscow from Nizhni Novgorod, as an official American representative of the Soviet Ninth Trade Union Congress. Scare stories of 'Nizhny Defeat' were unwarranted, Sam Herman told the Soviet press, 'mistakes have been made its true, but the plant has resumed operation'. With some justification he blamed setbacks on a shortage of essential tools 'such as Yankee screw drivers' and 'the inexperience of workers who never handled complex machinery before'. The Ninth Congress, Sam Herman pointed out, was 'the swellest Union convention ever witnessed, what impresses me about the Congress is the freedom with which workers criticize conditions in their plants. Could you imagine foreign workers scarcely employed a year at their trades elected to an AF of L. convention and actually stating opinions from the floor? In America this would be a pure fantasy. Yet here we are – a group of foreign delegates – three Americans and six Germans having the same rights as the rest.'[24]

On 26 April 1932, *Pravda* published the story of Joe Grondon under the headline 'The Man Who Abandoned Detroit'. Sam Herman's fellow union representative had been building Model As in Russia for the past four months, after fifteen years spent working at the Rouge. Joe Grondon made a passionate speech at the Ninth Congress describing how he had walked through a park in Dearborn before he left, and had seen an American policeman haul seven bodies of homeless workers out of the river:

I knew them – I had recently seen them alive. They had been working at our plant . . . I am a foremen of high qualification, and made good money at Ford's. But I asked myself: how about tomorrow? What will happen to me tomorrow? Shall I take walks in the park? Or will policemen carry my body out of the park? What guarantee have I that this will not occur? What security? There were 165,000 workmen in 1928 at the Ford plant where I was working. In 1931 there were only 35,000. Every one of these 35,000 spends all day in a state of feverish anxiety lest he be dismissed tomorrow.

In Detroit, Joe Grondon told his Russian audience, 'theft and murder were flourishing'. He had been mugged walking home from the plant, while unemployed auto workers were living in an abandoned Detroit fish factory in the dirt and soot, and fed once a day on soup. 'I decided to spend the rest of my days in the USSR,' said Grondon, who was fifty years old when he left the United States, 'I read in the bourgeois papers that the Bolsheviks are the enemies of culture and civilization. I came to the USSR and got employed as a foreman at the Nizhni Novgorod automobile plant . . . I see the enthusiasm of the workmen, I see their passionate desire to master new machinery . . . What an attitude they maintain towards me! How attentively they listen to every word I say!'[25]

It was always the political idealists like Joe Grondon and Sam Herman who had the hardest time adjusting to what they discovered in Russia, as they carried with them the seemingly irresistible hope that their situation would improve later that year, or the next, or the year after that, until it was all too late. Eighteen months after the union congress, Sam Herman's name appeared once again in the Soviet press with another update on news from Gorky:

The foreigner required real spunk to stick through the early stages – but we stuck. Things have definitely turned to a brighter side now. Life in the village is more comfortable; and the factory is working better each month . . . Shall I ever go back to the States again? . . . No I don't think so. I don't think any of us care to. Isn't there plenty to do right here? Our aim is to develop the Soviet automotive industry to the level of Detroit within the shortest time. Isn't that work enough for a specialist's lifetime?[26]

A convoy of the first thirty Ford cars and trucks built in the Gorky factory was ordered to be driven to Moscow for a propaganda display; a request that would have been easy enough to fulfil had there been sufficient workers who knew how to drive. But most of the Americans had been too broke to afford a car back home, and naturally very few Russians had learned to drive. So it fell to the Detroit teenager Victor Herman to get behind the wheel of a truck. On the journey to Moscow, Victor was amazed to see the Soviet militia turn out Russian villagers to tread down the snow in front of their convoy, making his route a little easier. In Moscow the atmosphere for the parade was strangely intense. There was hardly any cheering, the Russians appeared so genuinely moved by what they saw. Victor watched men and women openly weep at the sight of the brand-new Ford trucks and cars, 'made in the USSR'. On the street his observation was broken only by the voice of an educated Russian woman who tugged at his sleeve and whispered to him in English: 'Tell me why you do this. Why you help them, the Soviets?'[27] But it was only later, too late, that he understood the bewilderment resting in her question.

Afterwards, at their official reception in the Kremlin, Stalin himself made a rare appearance before the Gorky auto workers. He was much shorter than Victor Herman had expected, with a pockmarked face and yellow eyes quite unlike his idealised portrait. In a brief speech Stalin urged them all 'to try harder, produce more, give it all you've got', and was met by the familiar, thunderous ovation. An awestruck American engineer named McCarthy leant over and proudly told Victor that what they had just witnessed was 'an honour to them all'. Looking around the Kremlin banqueting hall, Victor Herman noticed that all the waiters had the clear outlines of revolvers bulging out of their jackets.[28]

After Stalin's speech Victor Herman met a Red Army officer in his mid-forties, with grey hair and an apparent sense of humour who introduced himself as 'Tukhachevsky'. By this stage Victor's Russian was fluent enough to ask the man if he was the son of the famous Civil War hero, to which the officer had only laughed and replied that he *was* Marshal Tukhachevsky. The Russian then questioned Victor on which aeroplanes he could fly, since he assumed that all Americans who could drive must be able to fly planes too. When Victor insisted that this was not actually the case, Tukhachevsky laughed again and asked if perhaps the young American might like to learn? Naturally, the excited Detroit teenager handed him his address at the American village in Gorky, and Marshal Tukhachevsky promised that all would be arranged. And, much to Victor's surprise, his new benefactor kept his word.[29]

It turned out that Victor Herman was not only a gifted athlete but a natural aviator, quickly graduating from flying planes to parachuting at an elite Moscow aviation academy. In September 1934, the nineteen-year-old Herman set the world freefall record, jumping from a plane at 24,000 feet and waiting 142 seconds before opening his parachute. From the ground, thirty thousand spectators watched him fall through the air holding the ripcord with his right hand and calmly eating an apple with his left. Victor later explained that he had been surprised to find the apple in his pocket – his pilot must have put it there for luck – and since apples were scarce at the time he thought he might as well eat it. His record, and the cool nerve he displayed in achieving it, turned him into another minor American celebrity of the Soviet emigration. The newspapers crowned Victor Herman 'the Lindbergh of Russia', while his story crossed the Atlantic into the pages of the *Detroit Evening Times* under the headline: 'Detroit Boy Wins Fame as "Lindy of Russia".'[30]

It was only later that the trouble started. The paperwork had to be filled out to gain credit for the jump from the world aviation authorities, and in the box marked 'nationality' Victor Herman had written 'USA'. Officials suddenly appeared from all sides, representing the Communist Party, the Red Army and the secret police. Questions were asked and arguments raged: 'How could an American be allowed to jump from a Soviet plane, flown by a Soviet pilot, on to Soviet soil?' Fortunately a quick-thinking official thought of a cheap solution to their problem. A new set of forms was filled out, and Victor Herman was politely asked to please write 'USSR' in the correct box. Full of a sense of his own invincibility, the naive blue-eyed Detroit teenager picked up the pen, paused for a moment, and then wrote 'USA'. And with those three letters young Victor Herman sealed his fate.[31]

6

'THE CAPTURED AMERICANS'

The slogan 'The Five Year Plan in Four Years' was advanced, and the magic symbols '5–in–4' and '2 + 2 = 5' were posted and shouted throughout the land. The formula '2 + 2 = 5' instantly riveted my attention. It seemed to me at once bold and preposterous – the daring and the paradox and the tragic absurdity of the Soviet scene . . . 2 + 2 = 5: in electric lights on Moscow housefronts, in foot-high letters on billboards, spelled planned error, hyperbole, perverse optimism, a slogan born in premature success tobogganing toward horror.

Eugene Lyons, American reporter in Moscow[1]

The Americans who found it hard to settle in Russia soon began to discover exactly how difficult it was to leave. In Moscow, one Californian machinist with two children was curtly told by the authorities that he was considered a Soviet citizen. His family was allowed an exit visa only after more than a year of protests and pressure from the American reporters who threatened to bypass Soviet censorship by mailing their dispatches to London and then have them cabled on to the States. Very quickly, the Californian's passport was returned and he was allowed to leave with his family. More usually, the Americans who arrived in Russia had their passports confiscated, and those whose initial fervour had quickly dimmed soon discovered they were on their own. In 1933, the United States still had no diplomatic presence in the Soviet Union, and after a while the American reporters simply shrugged their shoulders and offered not much more than sympathy. Privately they had already coined a name for these people; they became known as 'captured Americans'.[2]

The American press corps in Russia – Walter Duranty, William

Henry Chamberlin, Ralph Barnes, Linton Wells and Eugene Lyons, among others – were strangely reluctant to cover the story of the missing American passports, although it was a widely known practice at the time. In Gorky, the 'foreigners' bureau' at the auto factory was notorious for attempting to persuade American workers to take up Soviet citizenship, offering the lure of better food and housing, coupled with the threat of having to leave Russia at short notice. One group who had arrived in December 1931 were simply instructed to hand over their passports for registration which, they were told, would be returned to them when they left. The American auto workers were then given registration forms to fill out, and then abruptly informed that they had all become Soviet citizens. According to one witness there was an ardent American communist who worked in the bureau, named Sophie Talmy, who 'was responsible for causing many American citizens to apply unwittingly for and acquire Soviet citizenship'.[3]

After Herbert Lewis's expulsion from Stalingrad, both the *New York Times* and *Washington Post* carried a report from Peter Sutherland, a 44-year-old engineer from San Diego, on the 'enslavement' of Americans in the USSR by the confiscation of their passports, which Sutherland claimed were then used to slip communist agitators into the United States 'in the guise of returning American citizens'. Several men Sutherland had known personally in Russia had simply vanished. Meanwhile, an American military intelligence report sent from the Berlin Embassy to Washington DC, cited evidence 'confirmed by an authoritative source' that:

> American passports are stolen at every opportunity, as they can be sold to the Soviet government at a good price. Passports thus obtained by confiscation or theft are used for fraudulent entry of communists into the United States. The photograph is removed and a photograph of the communist user is substituted, who enters the United States under the name of the former owner. Counterfeit passports have also been used for the same purpose to some extent but the genuine passport, altered as described, is greatly preferred.[4]

Only a hopeless idealist – or the most blundering detective – could have failed to deduce that once an American passport was stolen and re-used, the true holder of that passport would become a rather inconvenient witness to an inelegant identity fraud. But the Berlin intelligence report was kept classified; and no one thought to warn the Joads still on their way to Russia.

Nor were the American reporters in Moscow ever likely to risk exposing the story, since their professional existence depended on the approval of the Soviet authorities, who censored their stories for the slightest transgression of the Bolshevik party line. The reporters understood very well that if they wrote anything remotely critical, they would be instantly harassed, have their visas revoked and shortly afterwards be declared 'hostile' to the Soviet Union and expelled. Over time, most of the foreign press in Moscow became browbeaten into repeating the themes their Soviet censors wished the American public to read. Consequently the news from Russia gradually acquired an Alice in Wonderland quality, as prescribed by the Soviet censor-in-chief Konstantin Oumansky, a young, multilingual, gold-toothed apparatchik.[5] And for their part, realising that it was pointless to write anything that would be censored anyway, the American reporters began to lose all measure of their critical faculties, lapsing into a stupefying form of self-censorship. If the story of the 'captured Americans' trapped in the USSR failed to register in the public consciousness back home, it was therefore hardly surprising. Especially when one considers how easily Konstantin Oumansky orchestrated the concealment of a far greater crime being committed at the time.

In March 1933, in response to the widespread rumours of a terrible famine in the Ukraine, Walter Duranty wrote an article for the *New York Times* entitled 'Russians Hungry But Not Starving'. Very carefully Duranty explained that reports of 'mass famine casualties' in the Ukraine 'were somewhat hasty'. Duranty himself was anxious to reveal the truth:

> I have made exhaustive inquiries about this alleged famine situation. I have inquired in Soviet commissariats and in foreign embassies with their network of consuls, and I have tabulated information from Britons working as specialists and from my personal connections, Russian and foreign. All of this seems to me to be more trustworthy information than I could get by a brief trip through any one area . . . And here are the facts: there is no actual starvation or deaths from starvation but there is widespread mortality from diseases due to malnutrition.[6]

Anyone who crossed paths with the travellers returning from Soviet famine areas understood very well the consequences of Stalin's collectivisation campaign. Jack Calder, the tall pipe-smoking American engineer who had built the tractor factory at Stalingrad, would sit at the bar of the Metropol Hotel in Moscow telling anyone who would listen the story of his recent trip through Soviet Central Asia. In Turkestan, Calder was chauffeured across the desert during a snowstorm. Through the car window, he noticed that the side of the road was lined with a continuous pile of logs, covered by the drifting snow. The logs had not been stacked correctly; often his chauffeur had to stop the car and move them over to the side of the road. When Calder asked where all the wood had come from in a desert region, the chauffeur had burst out laughing: 'Those aren't logs. This road leads out of the Soviet Union to countries where you can have food by merely going into a restaurant. Thousands of peasants . . . try to get out of Russia. Most of them are too weak to make it.'[7]

In Moscow, Jack Calder was celebrated as the American engineer 'Carter' in the Soviet play *Tempo* and, according to his contract in the Russian state archives, was earning a tax-free salary of ten thousand dollars per year, with all the perks of his position. But neither celebrity nor riches was sufficient compensation for the sights he had witnessed in Turkestan. Haunted by the dead, Calder packed his bags and returned home.[8]

Although other American engineers were bringing back similar eyewitness accounts of the terrible famine in the Ukraine – one stated flatly that Soviet border guards were opening fire on 'thousands' of Ukrainian peasants attempting to cross the frozen Dniester river at night – by their own admission the American reporters were more anxious to cover the forthcoming trial of a group of British engineers accused of espionage. Late one night in a Moscow hotel room, a Faustian pact was struck between Oumansky and the American press corps as to how they would cover the state-induced famine. Years later, Eugene Lyons, the United Press correspondent, confessed his own complicity in the deal: 'We admitted enough to soothe our consciences, but in roundabout phrases . . . The filthy business having been disposed of, someone ordered vodka and zakuski, Oumansky joined the celebration, and the party did not break up until the morning hours.'[9]

By September 1933, when the famine was over, the American press corps was finally granted permission to travel into southern Russia and the Ukraine. Walter Duranty was given a two-week head start, presumably as a form of payback for being the most vociferous champion of the non-existence of the starving millions. In a *New York Times* report entitled 'Abundance Found In North Caucasus', Duranty wrote: 'The use of the word "Famine" in connection with the North Caucasus is a sheer absurdity. There a bumper crop is being harvested as fast as tractors, horses, oxen, men, women and children can work . . . There are plump babies in the nurseries or gardens of the collectives . . . Village markets are flowing with eggs, fruit, poultry, vegetables, milk and butter at prices lower than in Moscow.'[10]

But Walter Duranty's private remarks were very different from his published story. To British diplomats, he admitted 'that Ukraine has been bled white . . . it was quite possible that as many as ten million people may have died directly or indirectly from lack of food in the Soviet Union during the past year.'[11] Perhaps as an Englishman he felt more at ease, and inclined to be honest, in the British Embassy overlooking the Moskva river.

The celebrated Walter Duranty was fêted by the American literary establishment. Awarded the 1932 Pulitzer Prize for his outstanding reporting from Soviet Russia, and rumoured to be one of the highest-paid foreign correspondents in the world, Duranty lived a life of unrivalled comfort in Moscow. With the success of his journalism his household expanded to include a fact-hunting American assistant, an elderly Russian cook, a young Russian housemaid, his chauffeur Grisha and his beautiful assistant Katya, who for a while 'ran the whole show' and bore him a son.[12] Together they lived in a luxurious apartment with four or five rooms – an unheard of living space in the desperately overcrowded city – with their own bathroom and a kitchen fitted with an electric refrigerator brought over from America, another luxury 'almost unique' in Moscow. His many guests noticed also, on very prominent display on the bookcase of his living room, a signed photograph of Joseph Stalin.[13]

At home, Walter Duranty would drink cocktails and make witty asides to his constant flow of visitors, while dictating effortless copy on the Five Year Plan for his American readership. And in the evening, the whole party moved on to the Metropol Hotel, where the fun really began.[14] All the rich Americans in Moscow would gravitate to the Metropol, with its long shining mahogany bar and jazz band blaring out syncopated rhythms, Soviet-style.[15] Couples danced, working their way around a circular fountain kept stocked with fish in the middle of the dance floor. Diners were encouraged to select their supper, at which point a net would be deftly flourished by the waiter, the fish caught and cooked and brought to their table. It was all part of the theatre, along with the Russian girls who walked through the dining room selling multicoloured balloons at five roubles apiece. Their customers would tie on a paper streamer, set it alight and watch the balloon float upwards. If it reached the ceiling intact there would be a burst of raucous applause. Who said you couldn't have fun in Moscow? The crowd at the Metropol was always 'a riot', amid the jazz and dancing and the waiters babbling away in the languages of the rich visitors passing through town. And then there was always the frisson of intrigue provided by the GPU and the Bolshevik apparatchiks, the only locals who could afford the prices. In public the Americans learned to follow the Russian example, and never mentioned the words 'GPU' or 'NKVD' out loud. Instead they joked about the 'Four-Letter Boys' or the 'YMCA' or 'Phi Beta Kappa' or 'the Society for Prevention of Cruelty to Bolshevism' or any other whip-smart euphemism that might confuse the listening waiters, secretaries and assorted informers of every stripe who surrounded them in the Metropol bar.[16]

The wealthy Americans – the industrial engineers, businessmen, reporters, and tourists – quickly discovered that tipping too, while officially abolished, was still very much in favour amongst the waiters themselves and ensured a stampede of service as soon as they sat down.[17] Their party at the Metropol became a weekly event to which everyone turned out, and the dancing would carry on until six in the morning, with the lonely Americans looking forward to the company of the sleek Russian girls who hung around the bar. All the Metropol hotel girls were 'swell dancers' and just happened to speak English, French and German.[18] They were always beautifully turned out with immaculate hair and make-up, and fashionable dresses impossible to come by at the time. Of course, it was widely known that these girls were handpicked by the GPU for their looks and ability to speak foreign languages. Almost without exception, they came from the former Russian aristocracy, the luckless generation of Anna Karenina's granddaughters made victims of the Revolution. As 'class enemies', the Metropol girls would disappear with heart-rending regularity only to be replaced by more of their kind. The rule among the Americans was 'not to get too attached', and to help things along they drank up the Metropol whisky, cognac and beer on sale at the better class of Chicago speakeasy prices. Vodka was, of course, cheaper and, for the more or less permanent resident, the drink of choice since the effect was quicker. The Russian vodka quickly drowned out the memory of the ever-changing faces of the Metropol beauties and allowed 'everyone to have a swell time anyway' as the photographer Jimmy Abbe put it.[19]

In the midst of the intrigue, Walter Duranty never missed the party. Duranty had lost half his leg in a train wreck and could not dance, but sat instead at his favourite table always 'romancing some dame'.[20] While the wits at the Metropol bar dreamt up plans for a population exchange between America and Russia. The Russians would bring to the United States their literature, art and music, and within a decade destroy American industry. The Americans would arrive in Russia and in that decade build up a fully functioning economy. Then both nationalities could go home again. It would take the Russians a further ten years to wreck their economy and the Americans the same amount of time to rebuild theirs, thus providing jobs and culture for all. Zara Witkin, a Californian engineer, even had the beginning of a show tune:

> *'USSR has some hope, but no soap*
> *USA has no hope, but some soap*
> *USA is losing its soap*
> *USSR is losing its hope.'*[21]

Occasionally a genuine American jazz band materialised in Moscow, and then according to one witness, 'the tide turned, and the boys put on some real American cloggin', the house broke out in a roar, and I heard a woman back of me saying "Marvellous, truly marvellous."'[22] For a moment then, with the blaring jazz and thunderous applause, the stamping feet and swinging arms, the pretty girls in expensive dresses and handsome men in black tie – if only for a moment – it must have felt as though the Depression had never really arrived and the Roaring Twenties roared on in one of Jay Gatsby's parties switched to snowy Moscow just for the thrill. And the rich American engineers and reporters who gathered at the Metropol to spend their dollars and savour the attention of Russian girls, so much more attractive than their company deserved, only had to put up with the occasional inconvenience, the occasional episode in the night to add to a vicious hangover and a very large bill. From the early 1930s, the rich Americans who shared their apartment buildings with the Soviet elite were already starting to be woken in the night by a pounding on their door from the GPU and a command barked in Russian, 'Open! Open!' They would answer bleary-eyed in a dressing gown at 5 a.m., only to discover that their wild-eyed night visitors had come to the wrong apartment: 'What do you mean coming around here at this hour waking people up? I am an American.'[23]

It was an experience that was becoming increasingly common with each passing month, and those American engineers who judged themselves to be immune from the threat were wrong. A few would be caught in the exit as they rushed for the doors. Their time was drawing ever closer, looming towards them with every passing week of the Metropol party, from out of the fog of the vodka, the girls, and the blaring jazz.

It was Walter Duranty, more than any other individual, who persuaded Franklin Roosevelt of the wisdom of granting diplomatic recognition to the Soviet government. Even before the inauguration, Duranty spent long hours briefing the President-elect on 'the Soviet experiment', elaborating on a theme he had first outlined in the *New York Times* of how 'the word "Bolshevik" has lost much of its former mystery and terror over here . . . such a concept of bolshevism as applied to the Union of Socialist Soviet Republics today is a trifle old-fashioned, to say the least.'[24] In the midst of a Soviet famine that was killing millions with calculated ruthlessness, the United States chose to make friendly overtures to Joseph Stalin. And President Roosevelt – while doubtless aware of the rumours of the famine – was either blind or inured to the scale of the horror; thanks in no small measure to Duranty.

In November 1933, as the Soviet Foreign Minister Maxim Litvinov crossed the Atlantic in the royal suite of the passenger liner *Berengaria* ready to negotiate the terms of the American recognition, a public relations campaign began. As the *Berengaria* steamed into New York harbour, Litvinov asked the captain to steer the ship closer to the Statue of Liberty. Standing beside him on the rail was Walter Duranty who wrote in the *New York Times* that the Soviet Foreign Minister admired the Statue of Liberty 'no less than the New York skyline'.[25] The *New York Times* reporter then assured the American public that the continued accounts of the Ukrainian famine were nothing but 'an eleventh-hour attempt to avert American recognition by picturing the Soviet Union as a land of ruin and despair'.[26] The tubby Soviet Foreign Minister, meanwhile, ensured himself a warm welcome at the White House by arriving with a complete collection of Soviet stamps issued since 1917, his personal gift for the philatelist President.[27]

After sixteen years as a pariah nation, the Soviet state once derided by the former Secretary of State Bainbridge Colby as 'illegal, irresponsible and without doubt impermanent' was now on the brink of legitimacy.[28] It was the American business community, in particular, who urged the President to help their firms export their way out of the Depression. For his part, Maxim Litvinov played the role of piper, forecasting more than one billion dollars of future trade orders, to mesmerise the two thousand American corporations already selling a shopping list of industrial equipment into the Soviet market. A cartoon published in national newspapers summed up their case: 'Starving in the Midst of Plenty' showed a very gaunt and hungry-looking Uncle Sam sitting next to the fat turkey of Russian trade.[29]

Stepping off the *Berengaria* – having travelled on the same crossing as Maxim Litvinov, albeit in steerage class – was William Gedritis, an American teenager from Chicago. Gedritis was followed shortly afterwards by his friend and co-worker in Russia, the fugitive American trade unionist Fred Beal, who was escaping the Soviet Union under a false identity. Sent by the Communist Party to work with the American emigrants at the Kharkov tractor plant, Beal had seen at first hand the foreigners of Kharkov under siege from Ukrainians desperate for food. The Americans, in particular, were known to be generous, and the locals knocked on their doors to beg for scraps or fought one another for the privilege of raking through their garbage. The foreigners' food stores were protected by armed guards, but the starving populace still attempted to break into them at night. In the autumn of 1932, seeking a break from the grinding desperation of city life, Fred Beal had taken an unsupervised trip out into the Ukrainian countryside. Walking through fields he stumbled upon fresh graves marked with crosses, and unburied bodies decomposing into the earth. As he continued walking he noticed the starving Ukrainian peasants running away from him, evidently mistaking him for the GPU.

Around six months later, in the spring of 1933, Fred Beal had made a second trip, this time to a Ukrainian collective farm, near the village of Chekhuyev, and walked several miles east. Here the atmosphere was thick with the cloying smell of death, hunger and despair. By the side of the road, the Massachusetts-born trade unionist came across a dead horse still harnessed to its wagon, and a dead man holding its reins in his hands. Walking into an empty village, Beal looked into a peasant hut and saw a dead man still sitting by a stove: 'His back was against the wall, he was rigid and staring straight at us with his faraway dead eyes.' On one village door someone had written: 'God bless those who enter here, may they never suffer as we have.' Inside the house, two men and a child lay dead beside the family icon. On his return to America, for all his radical contacts, Fred Beal could find only one newspaper willing to print his account of the famine that had claimed an estimated five million lives. The socialist *Jewish Daily Forward* of New York published his testimony in Yiddish.[30]

During the build-up to the US–Soviet recognition agreement, as the State Department officials busied themselves in Washington, they became aware of the pressing need to protect the Americans citizens who had already left to work in the USSR. Loy Henderson – soon to become First Secretary at the Moscow Embassy – later recalled how reports had been gathered as early as 1932, of the sudden and mysterious disappearance of American nationals in Russia. According to Henderson, some of the missing Americans had served sentences in Siberia and been allowed to leave, but others remained unaccounted for even as Litvinov was in discussions with Roosevelt at the White House.[31]

The day before their agreement was signed, Franklin Roosevelt exchanged a series of official letters with the Soviet Foreign Minister. With a cigarette burning in its ebony holder, tilted-up at a jaunty angle, and an ever-present smile flickering around the corners of his mouth, America's great optimist began:

> *My Dear Mr Litvinov,*
> *As I have told you in our recent conversations, it is my expectation that after the establishment of normal relations between our two countries many Americans will wish to reside temporarily or permanently within the territory of the Union of Soviet Socialist Republics, and I am deeply concerned that they should enjoy in all respects the same freedom of conscience and religious liberty which they enjoy at home. As you well know, the Government of the United States, since the foundation of the Republic, has always striven to protect its nationals, at home and abroad.*

The letter continued listing the presidential expectation of the rights of American citizens living in Russia:

> *We will expect that the nationals of the United States will have the right to collect from their co-religionists and to receive from abroad voluntary offerings for religious purposes; that they will be entitled without restriction to impart religious instruction to their children, either singly or in groups, or to have such instruction imparted by persons whom they may employ for such purpose; that they will be given and protected in the right to bury their dead according to their religious customs in suitable and convenient places established for that purpose ... Let me add that American diplomatic and consular officers in the Soviet Union will be zealous in guarding the rights of American nationals, particularly the right to a fair, public and speedy trial and the right to be represented by counsel of their choice. We shall expect that the nearest American diplomatic or consular officer shall be notified immediately of any arrest or detention of an American national.*

Perhaps Maxim Litvinov smiled when he read these words and, of course, he agreed wholeheartedly to every one of Roosevelt's demands, knowing as he did that the Soviet judicial process tended to conclude in only the swiftest extraction of confessions. The GPU, they said in Russia, 'could force the stones to talk'.[32]

At the official ceremony held at the White House on 17 November 1933, the United States recognised the existence of the Union of Soviet Socialist Republics. And in the subsequent press conference, President Roosevelt publicly reiterated to the two hundred gathered news reporters the guarantees he had gained for the protection of the American citizens living in the USSR. Even at the time, George Kennan, a young Russian speaker at the State Department who would soon arrive in Moscow, noted that the provisions of the agreement were inadequate. Among its many oversights, an American consul was not specifically entitled to visit with an American prisoner alone without the presence of the Soviet secret police. But in spite of his warnings urging more stringent safeguards, such flaws had been left unchanged in the final draft.[33] The President had sought to convey the impression of vigilance, when in reality the safeguards would prove unenforceable – and in the end were unenforced.

*

Afterwards at the celebratory banquet at the Waldorf Astoria, when Walter Duranty's name was announced, in the words of the *New Yorker* correspondent, 'the only really prolonged pandemonium was evoked . . . one got the impression that America, in a spasm of discernment, was recognizing both Russia and Walter Duranty.'[34] In this crowd there was only passionate agreement with Duranty's confidence in the new era of diplomatic friendship and cooperation between the United States and Soviet Russia. The American guests stood and cheered the 'King of Reporters', who told them that the methods of terror no longer existed in the modern USSR.[35]

Of course, every one of the American reporters in Moscow knew otherwise. Eugene Lyons had visited a Moscow theatre where the Russian comedian Vladimir Khenkin was performing his famous monologue. 'One night,' said Khenkin, 'I heard a vigorous knock at the door. So I took my little suitcase and went to open the door . . .' The Russian audience roared with laughter in a sudden release of nervous energy, and mutual recognition of their fear. They understood very well that the 'former' people were disappearing, and realized immediately that the little suitcase was the symbol of their departure. People had already begun packing these little suitcases in expectation, filling them with a change of clothes, something to stay warm, something to eat perhaps on the long journey to God-knows-where.[36] In retrospect the clues were all around them even then, if only they had the eyes to see and the sense to understand their significance. Adorning the walls of Soviet buildings in the early 1930s was one particularly uncanny propaganda poster. The image showed a large open eye watching over a work camp, above the slogan: 'GPU – THE UNBLINKING EYE OF THE PROLETARIAN DICTATORSHIP.'[37]

After several years in Russia, Eugene Lyons had become attuned to the low-frequency hum of the GPU; the soft burr of executions announced daily on Soviet radio and in the newspapers. His was a dawning comprehension of an approaching catastrophe. In the morning, Lyons would count out the death sentences handed down to the so-called 'enemies of Progress': the reactionary amalgam of wreckers, saboteurs, aristocrats, priests, businessmen, former White army officers – the list was endless.[38] At night, stumbling back from their parties more often than not the worse for wear, the American reporters had begun to notice strange new vehicles driving through the empty streets of Moscow that looked like moving vans from back home, except they had ventilation holes cut into their roofs. Late one night on his way home, Lyons had rung the bell of his courtyard gate and woken the concierge who was dozing. 'I thought it was the wagon again,' the sleepy-eyed man complained. 'Almost every night they come for somebody.'[39]

Meanwhile Eugene Lyons's colleague Walter Duranty returned from America with a shining new Buick. In December 1933, his young Russian chauffeur, Grisha, drove his master's limousine around Moscow at maniacal speed, and Duranty had a special GPU horn fitted which he took great delight in pressing as the terrified Muscovites leapt out of his way in panic. The horn on the Buick, Duranty later claimed, had been fitted through a 'fortuitous circumstance' but his fellow American reporters suspected otherwise. Linton Wells took a ride in the Buick late one night on a drunken spree, when his pal Duranty decided it would be a good idea to pay a call on some Russian friends. According to Wells, they pulled up outside an apartment building well past midnight, and the chauffeur began honking the Buick's horn to announce their arrival. Getting no response, Duranty and Wells stepped out of the car and rang the doorbell. Eventually a very frightened woman opened the door. 'We thought . . .' the woman whispered and then fell into silence. Inside the apartment Linton Wells could discern in the dim light: 'a dozen men, women and children huddled together, almost paralysed with fear. On every hand were indications that frantic efforts had been made to conceal everything and anything which might be regarded by the dread secret police as unworthy of being in a true proletarian's possession.'[40]

7

'THE ARRIVAL OF SPRING'

After 8 months of work I decided to go back to United States . . . They
told me they are not going to give my papers, because they need me as
a specialist in the factory . . . They scared me with threats to put me in
jail. They kept asking me why I wanted to go to the States, as there is
starvation. I told them that I would rather be in jail in America than an
employee in the Soviet Union. This made them angry . . . They told me
they would rather kill a person like me than let him out of the country
John Match to the State Department, handwritten letter,
6 May 1935[1]

Even before their Embassy had officially opened in Moscow, the first
American diplomats were set upon by their fellow countrymen desperate to return home. The First Secretary at the Embassy, Loy
Henderson, wrote that 'these unfortunate people were importuning
us in our hotel rooms'.[2] These American emigrants sought help to
gather the paperwork they needed to leave the USSR, help for their
friends who had been arrested and proof of their status as American
citizens to keep them safe from harm. And while 1934 was still very
much a honeymoon period for the American diplomats in Russia, a
time when they were able to move freely in Moscow as their governments warmed to each other, even in that first year of diplomatic
representation there were Americans disappearing.

As soon as he arrived in Moscow, the mild-mannered Loy
Henderson realised that the officials at the Soviet Foreign Ministry
were terrified of their own secret police and powerless to intervene.
A sixteen-year-old American girl called at the American Embassy to
plead for help to return herself, her mother, and two younger sisters
back home to the United States. According to Henderson, this

nameless girl was 'refused permission to visit the US embassy again' by the Soviet authorities. The young girl and her sisters remained on Loy Henderson's conscience as he wrote his memoirs several decades later. But she was not, by any means, an exceptional case.[3]

Working in the consular division of the Embassy, the thirty-one-year-old diplomat Elbridge Durbrow came into daily contact with Americans seeking new passports. Forty-seven years later he recalled their existence almost in passing, during an interview given in his retirement. According to Durbrow, their original American passports had simply vanished:

> A lot of them literally threw it in the Baltic Sea. Others claimed they didn't throw it away, it was taken when they got to Leningrad, when they printed in their visa or something, and never saw it again. Whether they were telling the truth, all of them, or not – but the stories jibed too well, at different periods of time, from people I don't think had met each other in the Soviet Union. They were dispersed all over. I had two assistants then, and we'd interrogate these guys for hours on end ... So we'd hear their story, check on where they'd lived in the United States, see if they knew something about Pittsburgh or Chicago or Washington, to check on their story. They'd all come over accompanied by their families. Some yes, some no, a lot of them were family and 'Daddy threw the passport away.'[4]

Elbridge Durbrow called them 'captive Americans' – too slight a variation on the reporters' expression 'captured Americans' to make a difference. Later Durbrow stated that he had helped five hundred to return home, in the days before their exit visas were stopped completely by the Soviets.[5]

It might seem strange that Durbrow was quite so tentative over what had happened, when the Soviet confiscation of American passports was so well-known at the time. On 5 April 1934, a satirical article entitled 'The Story of Two Passports Which Developed Into No Passport At All' was published in the German-language newspaper *Rigasche Rundschau*. After noting that two hundred Americans had arrived at the United States Embassy on the first day it opened, the German journalist proceeded to tell the story of an American engineer named William Smith – 'or any other name' – who had accepted a working contract in the USSR. Soon Smith is accused of espionage by the GPU and, to clear his name, was required to demonstrate his loyalty by taking up Soviet citizenship: He is told that he can be a Soviet citizen and remain an American. He will have two passports – a Soviet and an American passport.' William Smith's American passport is then confiscated and

> the Soviets inform his Embassy that he is now a Soviet citizen and point out that the Soviet passport is of a more recent date. The American ambassador says he is powerless to intervene. What is now to happen to poor Smith – that is the question that only the Gods can answer ... Each one of the two hundred Americans had passports, then they had two passports, and now, finally they have no passports at all. In respect to the simple workers and labourers the Soviets have quite simply stolen their passports. That was much easier, it made less work and it accomplished the same purpose ... Many tragedies in Russia have commenced with this matter of passports.

The American Embassy officials in Moscow not only read this startlingly accurate article, they had it translated and sent back to Washington.[6]

The difficulties of the ordinary American emigrants in Russia were worsened by the fact that so many were flat broke and unable to afford the price of a ticket home. Those not officially recruited by Amtorg were being paid the same rate as Russian workers, between eighty and 110 roubles per month, forty of which was spent on a place to sleep in a crowded room and the rest at the factory kitchen.[7] Shipping firms such as the Hamburg line, perhaps sensing the vulnerability of a captive market, were now charging 178 dollars for passage back to New York, a full 60 dollars more than the same journey in the opposite direction. For those Americans who had arrived on tourist visas and managed to find jobs working on an assembly line in Moscow or Gorky, it was an impossibly high price to pay.[8]

On 11 May 1934 the first US Ambassador to Russia, William Bullitt wrote to the State Department asking for a welfare committee to help destitute Americans return home: 'Most of the Americans in distressed circumstances still retain some sort of employment in the Soviet Union and despite the hardships they are encountering, are reluctant to return to the US for fear of being entirely destitute should they fail immediately to find employment . . . it is expected that many destitute Americans will appear in the future.' The State Department passed the financial responsibility on to the American Red Cross, who answered Bullitt's appeal with scant sympathy: 'the program of the Red Cross does not include relief for Americans abroad who find themselves in economic difficulties.'[9]

Meanwhile the State Department continued to receive numerous reports that Soviet authorities were issuing residence permits for shorter and shorter periods, forcing costly renewals unless the emigrants accepted Soviet citizenship, always given with the reassurance that their American citizenship would remain unaffected.[10] Although aware of the coercion involved, and the variety of methods used to part the American emigrants from their passports, the State Department did little to help them, even in those early honeymoon months when there was still an opportunity for negotiation. The American Embassy officials struggled to have their questions answered by the labyrinthine Soviet bureaucracy, and the 'captive Americans' remained in state-less limbo as the weeks and months ticked away. There were only a few thousand of them in Russia. Overwhelmingly they were just ordinary people with little influence or access to the high circles of state. The Soviet apparatchiks guessed, quite correctly, they would soon be forgotten.

Instead the American diplomats occupied themselves coping with the shock of their entrance into Soviet life. The chargé d'affaires John Wiley wrote to the State Department asking for Moscow to be placed on a list of 'unhealthful posts'. His seven-page letter listed the infectious diseases prevalent in Moscow that year: typhoid, malaria, smallpox, scarlet fever, diphtheria, dysentery and sixty-two reported cases of anthrax. 'A number of doctors,' Wiley added, 'including some who are believed to have accepted foreign currency for outside services, have disappeared within the past two months. The most competent dentist in Moscow disappeared two weeks ago when he was in the process of giving treatment to some members of the Embassy. Members of the Embassy who called on him in accordance with appointments found his doors secured with the seal of the OGPU.'[11]

Denied access to black market roubles by the high-minded prescription of Ambassador Bullitt, the young American diplomats and their wives busied themselves with the continual harassment of finding enough affordable food. At the foreigners' food stores the prices, starting at a dollar per egg and rising up to ten dollars for the whole chicken, were 'like eating gold'.[12] And when Irena Wiley discovered that their Embassy food supplies had been delayed at the border, she had to rush out and buy a very expensive and very thin Russian cow to be killed and butchered for a reception that day. At the dinner table, her husband quipped: 'You had better show our guests the horns, so that they'll know it isn't a horse.'[13]

Of course, none of these hardships made the slightest difference to the handsome, blue-eyed Ambassador William Christian Bullitt, whose private income derived from a trust fund of his wealthy Philadelphian family. Still only in his early forties, Bullitt arrived in Moscow very much in sympathy with the Bolshevik experiment. Like many others he regarded Stalin's economic planning as not so very different from the ideas Roosevelt was attempting in Washington, if just a few shades of red darker than the New Deal palette. As the American Ambassador settled into his official residence of Spaso House, the fine open rooms of the pre-Revolutionary mansion seemed to suit him and his little terrier, Pie-pie, very well. With great delight Bullitt wrote to his brother Orville that Pie-pie was 'lording it' over all Moscow since all the other pets in the city had disappeared after the chronic food shortages of the year or two before. Spaso House was described in the American press as one of the glories of the Tsarist era. The forty-room mansion, wrote one reporter, had once belonged to Russia's former sugar king, Tverkov, and 'had a tragic history. It was completed just before the war and the owner lived in it only a short time before the revolution broke out. In the civil war he was shot just at the steps where Ambassador Bullitt's car will draw up when he alights at his new home.'[14]

Unfazed by superstitious omens of bad luck, one of Ambassador Bullitt's very first actions was to place a bouquet of red roses on the grave of his friend John Reed at the Kremlin Wall. The Ambassador's marriage to John Reed's widow, Louise Bryant, had ended in bitter divorce just four years earlier, but this had not altered his affection for Reed. William Bullitt had attempted to buy a whole wreath for the grave of the American revolutionary, but this proved impossible in Moscow at the time. Even a dozen red roses tied together with wood-shavings (since there was no ribbon either) required the purchase of entire rose bushes, which at the artificially high exchange rate, ended up costing the Ambassador the princely sum of forty-eight dollars.[15]

But this political gesture did not pass unnoticed. Almost immediately, William Bullitt was invited to dinner at the mansion of the Soviet Defence Commissar, where he was introduced to Joseph Stalin. 'His eyes are curious,' Bullitt wrote in a letter to Roosevelt,

> giving the impression of a dark brown filmed with dark blue. They are small, intensely shrewd and continuously smiling. The impression of shrewd humor is increased by the fact that the 'crow's feet' which run out from them do not branch up and down in the usual manner, but all curve upward in long crescents. His hand is rather small with short fingers, wiry rather than strong. His moustache covers his mouth so that it is difficult to see just what it is like, but when he laughs his lips curl in a curiously canine manner . . . I felt I was talking to a wiry Gipsy with roots and emotions beyond my experience.

At Voroshilov's mansion Bullitt and Stalin became acquainted over the customarily lavish Soviet banquet, the food and wine of a quality that 'no one in America would dare serve nowadays'. After ten vodka toasts, Maxim Litvinov slyly noticed that Bullitt had started to only sip from his glass and quickly informed him that 'it was an insult not to drink to the bottom and that I must do so.' Another fifty toasts followed, which Bullitt survived thanking 'God for the possession of a head impervious to any quantity of alcohol'. He wrote that Joseph Stalin drank toasts to the 'American Army, the Navy, President and whole USA', while he himself reciprocated with 'the memory of Lenin and continued success of the Soviet Union'. Then an excited Stalin marched little Georgy Piatakov over to the piano and instructed him to play, standing behind the Deputy Commissar for Heavy Industry and squeezing his neck, as Piatakov 'launched into a number of wild Russian dances' with a manic furiosity at the keyboard, spurred on by Stalin's hands around his neck.

The music may have accounted for Stalin's evident good humour that night, as well as his open admiration for Roosevelt and his assurances to Bullitt that he could see him 'any time, day or night, you have only to let me know and I will see you at once'. As they left the mansion in the early hours, Stalin stopped the Ambassador to ask: 'Is there anything at all in the Soviet Union that you want? Anything?' The quick-thinking Philadelphian immediately requested seventeen acres of Lenin Hills overlooking the Moskva river as the site for the construction of the first American Embassy in the USSR in the style of Monticello. 'You shall have it,' Stalin answered and, brushing aside Bullitt's outstretched hand, took his head between his hands and kissed him. To the President, William Bullitt wrote: 'I swallowed my astonishment, and, when he turned up his face for a return kiss, I delivered it.'[16]

Ambassador Bullitt never lost his vision of a Monticello in Moscow which, he once quipped, would have a quotation from Thomas Jefferson over the entrance: 'God forbid that we should live for twenty years without a Revolution.'[17] He even obtained the necessary 1.2-million-dollar appropriation, a sum which caused a certain amount of controversy in Congress but was justified on the grounds of the expected 'Red trade offers'.[18] But Stalin never had any intention of giving up such valuable land in the centre of Moscow, so the money was never used, and Bullitt's kiss was returned in vain. Had he only thought of it, the American Ambassador might have asked instead for the release of the 'captive Americans' seeking exit visas from the USSR – a gift far easier to extract from the drunken Soviet dictator than seventeen acres of prime Moscow real estate. But he did not, and if there were a few more opportunities to make this request, they would all be squandered with the profligate expectation that such mistakes could later be corrected.

The new Ambassador did, however, gain permission to import the first privately owned aeroplane into Soviet Russia, along with carte blanche to fly 'wherever he wanted'. He also dispensed with the services of a chauffeur, and took to driving his own sports roadster around the streets of Moscow. According to his secretary, Charlie Thayer, the handsome Ambassador became very popular 'among the great mass because of his wonderful personality in crowds, his democratic leanings and his dashing ways ... Often on the streets the urchins who know the car shout at him as he goes by 'Your health Comrade Bullitt' which pleases him immensely.'[19] Even the news that Ambassador Bullitt had crashed his plane in a field outside Leningrad only added to his charisma. The plane had landed upside-down and was chased after by Soviet officials expecting to prise out the body of a dead Ambassador from the wreckage. Brushing himself down, William Bullitt climbed out of the airship completely unscathed 'and received them as if we were quite in the habit of landing upside down'.[20]

In the autumn, Ambassador Bullitt escorted his ten-year-old daughter Anne to the Moscow Children's Theatre. Visiting Moscow from her boarding school in Europe, Anne Bullitt was a pretty little girl with her mother Louise Bryant's dark hair and her father's calm gaze of self-possession. Together they met the Theatre's founder and director, Natalya Satz, and enjoyed a performance of *The Negress and the Monkey*: a moral fable of an African woman searching for her beloved pet monkey kidnapped by a party of capitalist big-game hunters. The play, Natalya Satz explained, promoted 'active sympathy for oppressed folks of far-off lands who, though their skins may be different, are human beings, experiencing the joys and sorrows of human beings'. Anne Bullitt then happily posed for a publicity photograph for Miss Satz and her new theatre; while her father expressed his approval to the press: 'Every time I visit the Children's Theater I am more impressed by the profound understanding that Miss Satz possesses not only of the art of the theatre but also of the nature of children.'[21]

In a letter, President Roosevelt had suggested to Bullitt that 'it seems to me highly desirable that an effort should be made to provide the Embassy and Consular staffs with a certain amount of American recreation'.[22] Pursuing the President's idea, the Ambassador wrote to A.G. Spalding and Bros of New York requesting the delivery of sports equipment to Moscow: a dozen baseballs, six bats, one catcher's mask, two catcher's mitts, sixteen gloves, one body protector, one set of bases, home plates, and shoes and uniforms for four teams.[23] The handsome Bullitt easily charmed Betty Glan, the director of Gorky Park, into providing the American Embassy with its very own baseball diamond in the park's green acres.[24] And so, with the President's blessing, baseball in the Soviet Union took a further fragile hold, as the diplomats, just like the Americans emigrants before them, attempted to play their national sport and feel a little less sick for the home they had left behind.

The newness was scuffed off the Spalding baseball gear at the first Embassy ballgame held on the Fourth of July 1934. Unsurprisingly the team of diplomats soundly thrashed the newspaper reporters, whose taste for late nights seen through empty vodka glasses was reflected in their athletic performance. The reporters lost twenty-one runs to three, with Bullitt himself driving home the first run. 'The Ambassador,' reported Harold Denny in the *New York Times*, 'had a perfect batting average with five hits in five times at bat, and he actually made a double play unassisted. It was that kind of a game.'

That night at Spaso House, the Ambassador hosted a Fourth of July party for a few hundred American guests, with a Soviet jazz orchestra hired to belt out a welcoming rendition of 'The Star-Spangled Banner'. Unfortunately the Russian musicians had borrowed their score from a phonograph disk on which several variations of the American national anthem were recorded. Bewildered by this unfamiliar degree of choice, they had naturally preferred the jazz version as the most authentically American. With hundreds of guests standing to attention, the Soviet orchestra blared out the Star Spangled Banner with 'saxophones crooning and an occasional bewildering 'Hey nonny nonny and hotcha cha.'[25]

The diplomatic baseball played in the Moscow summer evenings was captured on film by the visiting American documentary film-maker Julian Bryan. Miraculously his rushes from Gorky Park survived, and the black-and-white images brought to life a game watched by crowds of small boys as the athletic figure of William Bullitt jogs up to the pitcher's mound smiling and wearing a big white hat and grey flannel trousers. The Ambassador pitches fairly fast, winding up and firing the ball down to a catcher standing with the proper protection behind home plate, while languid American women sip champagne and look on from deckchairs at the side of the field. This was the Embassy crowd at play: quite literally a different league from the hard-edged competition of the American emigrants. Later on, the Ambassador steps up to bat and strikes out as the spluttering film jump-cuts into another sequence in which Bullitt attempts to teach some Russian boys and girls to hit and catch. They swipe and miss, learning that it is very easy to miss but so satisfying when the bat connects and the ball flies away into the air. It is a warm summer day; people are sipping their cocktails as the baseball equipment is stacked up for a photograph, the bats in a pyramid, the protector and the facemask at the front. Young men and women grin at the camera as a baseball is presented to a girl with smiles and handshakes.[26]

Since all forms of photography in the Soviet Union were subject to draconian censorship and interminable delay, Julian Bryan's film left the country in the diplomatic bag to be edited and screened in American cinemas as part of the *March of Time* newsreel. On

29 August 1934, President Roosevelt wrote a congratulatory letter to Bullitt: 'It is grand about . . . the baseball. By the way, as an expert I want to compliment you again on your excellent Russian in that picture. All you need to do now is to swallow some lubricant just before starting to speak. It will give you the necessary speed-up!'[27]

Of course, there were a few mocking articles in the American press. John Lardner, in his column 'From the Press Box' wrote,

> our Ambassador is a first baseman. Nobody knows how good a first baseman he is. But he doesn't have to be good to fool the Russians. If the Hon. William C. Bullitt scores a few putouts . . . the Russian ball writers will be calling him another Hal Chase and comrades all over the Soviet Union will bring their children up to be first basemen . . . In no time at all the natives would be falling over themselves in their eagerness to form a club of their own, the Kremlin Wildcats, or the Moscow Maroons, or possibly, when the game takes hold in all sections of the country, the Nevsky Prospect Red Sox . . .[28]

What the mockers never knew was that the clubs already existed, although the American emigrants' fledgling baseball league and the diplomatic games belonged to two separate worlds. The Moscow Foreign Workers' Club was formed from American electricians, steamfitters, linotype operators, machinists and truck drivers who played baseball to a level comparable with the average industrial league in the States; with a few of their players even described as having 'semi-professional and professional experience'.[29] It was possible that an occasional young American such as Arnold Preedin, or Thomas Sgovio might have dropped in to play a game with the diplomatic corps. But it was equally true that the sons of radical metal-workers and machinists were unlikely to mix easily with their State Department peers, who were predominantly wealthy and Ivy League-educated. Other than their nationality they had little else in common. It was simply a case of money and class and the separation both bring: twin social forces which applied just as equally in Moscow as any city back home.

As if to highlight this very difference, the following year William Bullitt hosted an Embassy ball themed on 'the Arrival of Spring', its size and sheer extravagance so typical of his character. For one night in April 1935, the ballroom of Spaso House was decorated in a colour scheme of green, white and gold – with green trees, white tulips, white goats with gilded horns, and white roosters in gold and glass cages. Since Moscow was still blanketed in snow, Charlie Thayer had telegraphed south to Odessa for birch trees to be flown up and placed under sunlamps ready to burst into leaf. Lambs were ordered from a collective farm, but the Americans received sheep instead which had to be shampooed to rid them of their overpowering smell, only to be replaced by kid goats anyway. The director of Moscow Zoo agreed to loan the crazed Americans a bear cub, and took to calling up his co-conspirator Irena Wiley whenever a new animal was born: 'Do you need a giraffe, a wolf, a baby llama?' Nothing was beyond the imagination of these Americans, if the zoo director took his cue from Mrs Wiley's idea to have the ballroom floor glassed over and the space filled with water and brightly coloured tropical fish. It would make a sensational aquarium on which the Ambassador's guests could dance their hot American jazz.

Either practicality, or an understandable uncertainty over Soviet glass manufacture, spared the tropical fish, but not the rest of the zoo's menagerie. As Ambassador Bullitt greeted his guests from the top of the stairs of Spaso House, the gilded bear cubs, kid goats and cockerels encircled the floodlit ballroom. Around them a consignment of blooming white tulips, flown in from abroad, was made to sway in the breeze by means of a concealed electric fan. While imported champagne and delicacies were laid on to satisfy the tastes of the invited guests, whose social hierarchy ranked from Max Litvinov, the tubby Soviet Foreign Minister bursting out of his white tie and tails, all the way down to Mikhail Bulgakov, the penurious writer whose wife had nervously worried about what they might wear to the grand American ball. In the event, the guests' costumes were hardly noticed amid the slides of flowers projected on to the ballroom walls and the vast nets glinting with gold powder that had been stretched across the ceiling from four marble pillars, creating a vast aviary for hundreds of chattering greenfinches on loan from Moscow Zoo.

Naturally the animals caused a sensation. The Soviet general Aleksandr Yegorov picked up a bear-cub in his arms, only to have the bear redecorate his uniform. Yegorov left, cursing, but returned an hour later, newly resplendent, and stayed until dawn. Amid the laughter, another Red Army General, Semyon Budenny, folded his arms across his chest and started to dance Cossack style, his long waxed moustache glinting under the lights, while Ivy Litvinov, the wife of the Foreign Minister, clutched one of the kid goats to her chest, and Karl Radek, the editor of *Izvestiya*, attempted to pour champagne into the bear cub's milk bottle. Amid the lights and general commotion, no one noticed that in the aviary above them the greenfinches were dying. When the jazz orchestra burst into 'The Star Spangled Banner', the birds had flown into a 'heart-breaking' panic, crashing into the golden nets and getting tangled in their mesh. The fortunate few who managed to escape were trapped in the house for days.[30]

Quietly observing this celebration of American bravura, Mikhail Bulgakov would borrow a host of details for his novel *The Master and Margarita*, whose scene from 'Satan's Ball' was bewitchingly similar to the real-life American affair down to the 'green tailed parrots and white tulips' and an 'unbearably loud jazz band'. Even one of Bullitt's guests, Baron Boris Steiger, the unofficial liaison officer between the diplomatic community and the NKVD, became recast by Bulgakov as 'Baron Meigel, employee of the Spectacles Commission in charge of acquainting foreigners with places of interest in the capital'. Mikhail Bulgakov would write his masterpiece during the height of the Terror over the next three years. But the novel's principal theme of the devil's reappearance in modern-day Moscow meant that it could never be published in Russia while Stalin was still alive. The analogy was far too blatant.[31]

Like its fictional counterpart, the American ball continued through the night and was interrupted only at daybreak, when the gold-painted cockerels began to crow inside Spaso House. The animal noises were drowned out by the jazz band that kept on playing, since none of the gathered guests showed the slightest desire to leave, dancing as if half-conscious they would never had this chance again. It was nine o'clock in the morning before the last party-lovers were shepherded away into their waiting limousines.

Rumours of Bullitt's extravaganza quickly travelled around the world. One of the gossip columns in the American press called it 'the swellest party Moscow has seen since the Revolution'.[32] The piece was spotted by the eagle-eyed Roosevelt who had it clipped and sent in the diplomatic mail to his ambassador.

*

Less than a year after he hosted the ball the Terror had begun. Ambassador Bullitt wrote to his friend R. Walton Moore, the Assistant Secretary of State:

> The stories which are reaching us from Leningrad sound unbelievable ... The British Vice Consul there reports that 150,000 persons have been exiled from the city and 500,000 from the Leningrad Oblast. In Moscow the OGPU is now carrying out arrests every night. I know, personally, of three recent cases. In each case, at 2AM, the secret police appeared, entered the apartment, took all papers, sealed whatever room contained books, and removed the head of a family. Since the disappearances, wives and children have been unable to get any information as to whether fathers or husbands are alive or dead.[33]

During his brief tenure in Moscow, Bullitt's Russian friends had already begun to disappear. Natalya Satz, the director of the Moscow Children's Theatre, had been arrested; as had Betty Glan, the director of Gorky Park. Natalya Satz was imprisoned as a 'wife of a traitor to the motherland'. In her 'corrective labour' camp, the Children's Theatre director fell ill with typhus and became so exhausted that, according to a fellow prisoner, she 'resembled a puny little girl, though her head was gray'.[34] Their disappearances rid William Bullitt of all trace of his romantic preconceptions of the Revolution. In his final dispatch to the State Department, dated 20 April 1936, the Ambassador issued a frank warning: 'The problem of relations with the Government of the Soviet Union is ... a subordinate part of the problem presented by communism as a militant faith determined to produce world revolution and the "liquidation" (that is to say murder) of all non-believers. There is no doubt whatsoever that all orthodox communist parties in all countries, including the United States, believe in mass murder ... The final argument of the believing communist is invariably that all battle, murder, and sudden death, all the spies, exiles and firing squads are justified.'[35]

At the State Department offices in Washington, Bullitt's sudden hostility might well have seemed exaggerated. Unless witnessed personally, the scale of what was taking place in Russia was difficult to comprehend. In June 1936, on his way to the American diplomats' rented dacha outside Moscow, Elbridge Durbrow watched a train of fifty cars 'loaded down with prisoners, men, women and children together, coming out of Moscow'.[36] No one knew who these people were or their destination, but the prison trains had been seen in operation for several years now by American witnesses from all over Russia. Some, such as the young American writer Ellery Walter, sensed their significance straightaway and took the trouble to report them: 'I counted 13 trains, each with 2000 men and women and children bound for Siberia.'[37] Others, such as American engineer Bredo Berghoff, had chanced upon a prison train while searching for his trunk along a railroad yard. Through the narrow steel-barred windows Berghoff could see young men whose eyes stared back at him from the darkness.[38]

Packed with several thousand human beings, each train was destined to travel hundreds, and often thousands, of stifling kilometres to its hidden end-point. The system of repression was kept secret, but it had grown so vast there were continual gaps in the fabric of its concealment. The American witnesses had seen the suffering of those trapped within the carriages, and in an exchange of looks, their fearful eyes carried their own message.

William Bullitt was far from alone in realising the truth of what was taking place around him. One of the American reporters, William Henry Chamberlin, left at the same time in the early summer of 1936. 'I went to Russia,' Chamberlin later wrote, 'believing that the Soviet system might represent the most hopeful answer to the problems raised by the World War and the subsequent economic crisis. I left convinced that the absolutist Soviet state . . . is a power of darkness and of evil with few parallels in history . . . Murder is a habit, even more with states than with individuals.'[39] Perhaps it was not accurate to say that the Terror had begun then. In truth, it had been in existence for many years. But Bullitt's departure did coincide with a vast expansion and *acceleration* of the process, as if what once had been mere habit had now been transformed into an overwhelming compulsion and inexorable desire.

Several months after Bullitt's departure from Moscow, in October 1936, a small party of young American diplomats sat listening to a radio broadcast of the World Series. Late into the night, they gathered in the study of their absent Ambassador to eat hot dogs and follow the sixth game of an all-New York contest between the Yankees and the Giants played at the Polo Grounds on West 155th Street. The radio commentary over the airwaves to Moscow was uncannily clear that night: the diplomats could hear the ball as it was struck, the roar of the crowd from the bleachers, and the fizzing words of the announcer as he called out the names of Lou Gehrig and Joe DiMaggio, the Yankee clipper, from six thousand miles away in New York. Every now and then, through the crackle and the pop, came a moment of crystal clarity – a New Yorker shouting 'Robber, Robber! Kill the umpire! Fan him out!' or a salesman crying, 'Peanuts, popcorn, chewing gum and candy.'[40]

It was unlikely that any of the 'captive Americans' living in Russia had a radio capable of picking up the World Series. In any event, by October 1936, listening to a foreign-language radio station in Moscow would have given cause for suspicion among their neighbours in the communal apartments in which they lived. All trace of baseball's fragile existence in the USSR was disappearing from the stage. A few practice games had been played earlier that summer, but there was an edginess about it all, as if the American players began to sense the danger of sticking their heads above the parapet of ideological conformity. 'Where are the old baseball enthusiasts and why have they not been coming around to practice sessions?' a *Moscow Daily News* reporter asked in an article written that year. 'Nothing has been heard in Moscow from cities such as Petrozavodsk, Gorky and Leningrad this season.'

The first baseball game of the Moscow season was played in July 1936, when the Red Stars beat the Hammer and Sickle team by four runs to three in a game at the Lokomotiv stadium. The Moscow team captain, Arnold Preedin, hit the only home run in the sixth inning, and Thomas Sgovio hit a triple in the seventh to lend strength to the batting line-up of the Foreign Workers' teams.[41] But just one month later, in August, the first of the great show trials opened in Moscow. At the trial of the Trotskyite–Zinovyevite Terrorist Centre, the prosecutor Andrey Vyshinsky jumped to his feet in a furious rage at the defendants, angrily demanding that 'these rabid dogs must be shot to the last one'.[42] And suddenly baseball in Soviet Russia seemed so evidently strange, so anomalous, so utterly divorced from the terrible events taking place all around them that it became a danger to its participants.

Even Gorky Park, for all its popularity, and millions of visitors, had fallen uncannily silent. The atmosphere had puzzled the visiting American critic Edmund Wilson, who walked among these silent crowds. When Wilson mentioned the silence, there was a long pause before his female Russian companion whispered an explanation in French: '*C'est que tout le monde a très peur.*'[43]

Amid this general ever-increasing fear, baseball stopped being discussed or reported in the press, and very soon was no longer played. The Soviet Union's newest national sport simply vanished from the stage, the taint of its association with capitalism judged too overpowering. And the American baseball players also began to disappear one by one, their photographs fading into sepia as if they had never been real human beings at all, just phantoms of a passing age. Baseball in Gorky Park had lasted just a few brief summers, which had come and gone so quickly. And very soon all trace of its existence was removed from life in Soviet Russia, and all that would remain were a few still photographs in black and white and some long-forgotten newsreel buried in a dusty archive of the Library of Congress.

There were still a few English-language programmes broadcast on Soviet radio for the American emigrants, but their propaganda was growing ever more hectoring: 'It must be remembered also that the radio hour is not only an opportunity for enjoyment and recreation, but can also be a powerful weapon in the greatest of all battles, the struggle for a classless socialist society'.[44] At the radio centre in Moscow, a few American contributors gamely discussed: 'How shall we spend our holidays this summer? Shall we go to a Rest Home or Sanatorium? Or travel on our own? Shall we go to the North to the Arctic or to the South, the Caucasus or the Black Sea?'[45] But their stilted conversations had developed an element of staged unreality, like the vast Stars and Stripes hauled up in front of the American Embassy on Mokhovaya Street facing the Kremlin, with its implicit promise of guardianship over the lives of the American emigrants.[46]

The previous year, the American Embassy had requested, through the pages of the *Moscow Daily News*, that all Americans in the USSR should come into the building to register their passports. A list, they said, was being compiled so that the diplomats might know their whereabouts and 'in order that protection might be extended in the event that such an occasion should arise.'[47]

In retrospect, it seemed that the American diplomats, at least, were well aware of what was about to happen. By the summer of 1936, sufficient numbers of their friends and acquaintances had already disappeared. Loy Henderson, for one, observed the growing uneasiness among the Russian members of the staff within the building.

In August, he found one of the female employees 'hunched over her typewriter sobbing'.[48] It had been not even three years since the US–Soviet recognition agreement had been signed, when *Time* magazine wrote that 'President Roosevelt cast the cloak of his popularity over Dictator Stalin'.[49] In exchange for a long list of unfulfilled promises and the lure of a trade bonanza that never arrived, a moral legitimacy had been granted to Joseph Stalin which he would continue to flaunt through the very worst of the Terror. And through it all the Stars and Stripes would float in the breeze opposite the Kremlin, although Ambassador Bullitt had long since departed in disgust, and the diplomatic staff he left behind in Moscow had been 'pared to the bone'.[50]

The Bolsheviks had once described the American radicals as '*poputshiki*' – 'fellow-travellers' – whose path coincided with theirs for a certain distance until the time came when they would have to part.[51] And although, in theory, there was still an institution to protect the welfare of the American emigrants, in practice the Stars and Stripes on Mokhovaya Street, rather than being a source of their salvation, became instead the cause of their death.

8

THE TERROR, THE TERROR

Little apple, little apple, where are you rolling to?
Are you rolling to the Cheka?
Then you will never come back . . .

Anonymous[1]

On 1 December 1934, in an empty corridor of a Leningrad office building, a waiting assassin stepped out and shot the party boss Sergei Kirov at point-blank range. Although Kirov had been Stalin's personal friend, subsequent evidence pointed towards the premeditated assassination of a political rival. The day after the assassination, Stalin boarded a train to Leningrad, and 'retaliatory' violence quickly followed in his wake. Kirov's principal bodyguard was summoned to appear before Stalin, but arrived dead at an NKVD hospital, having been thrown from a moving truck. Stalin himself, meanwhile, interrogated the assassin Leonid Nikolaev, asking why he had killed Kirov. According to one witness: 'Nikolaev answered that he killed Comrade Kirov on the instruction of a person employed by the Cheka, and at this pointed to the men from the Cheka sitting in the room . . . "They forced me to do it." The NKVD agent then knocked Nikolaev to the floor with a blow to the head, and he was removed.'[2] The assassin Nikolaev was tried and executed, and the NKVD officers in Leningrad were arrested and sent to the camps, where they would later be shot. In a subsequent show trial, the NKVD chief Henrikh Yagoda was charged with organising Kirov's murder as part of a 'Trotskyite conspiracy'.[3] But in truth, the Kirov assassination was only ever a pretext for what was to come.

The night of Kirov's murder, a reception was held at the American Embassy attended by the usual gathering of the Soviet elite. Irena Wiley was talking to Karl Radek, the editor of *Izvestiya*, when a Russian interrupted their conversation to whisper in Radek's ear. On hearing the news, she watched the colour drain from Radek's face as he leant against the wall in shock. Immediately Radek made his excuses and left, and within minutes every Russian at the party had disappeared without a word of goodbye. That night John and Irena Wiley were visited by their friend, the diplomatic liaison officer Baron Boris Steiger. 'Take it very seriously,' said Steiger, explaining the reason for the mass departure. Afterwards Steiger revealed that every day 'seven thousand' people were being arrested and 'exiled' to the Arctic Circle or Central Asia.[4]

Two days later, on the afternoon of December third, Elbridge Durbrow invited the Soviet vice-president of Intourist, George Andreytchine, into his apartment above the Embassy to talk with Loy Henderson and John Wiley. Andreytchine appeared extremely distressed as he attempted to explain that the death of Kirov was an act of terror, which 'could trigger acts of repression on the part of the Soviet regime that would make even the collectivization campaign of 1930 look mild'. As an insider, George Andreytchine had the clearest understanding of the mechanics of Stalin's power.[5] His prediction proved correct, and he himself was one of those about to be arrested. From this point onwards, the disappearances within Soviet society became ever more noticeable and, by their very abruptness, so much harder to conceal. At an American Embassy bridge party, Irena Wiley's partner, the Soviet diplomatic chief of protocol Florinski, was called to the telephone. He returned to their table smiling with the news that he would have to leave for just a few minutes but would return shortly, and would they please wait for him?[6] Florinski never returned to finish his hand.

The only elliptical explanation for the disappearances was in a film playing in Moscow cinemas during the winter of 1936. The Hollywood feature *The Invisible Man*, based on the novel by H. G. Wells, had been dubbed into Russian and was advertised in the Soviet press: 'One stormy night an unknown, uncanny man, his eyes completely hidden by enormous black glasses, enters a rural English inn. The stranger removes his hat, then his glasses – and his head disappears completely then his hands and feet, until nothing but terrifying emptiness remains where he has been standing . . .'[7]

The Soviet Union no longer teetered on the brink. The Revolutionary state had already fallen into the abyss, pushed by the ministrations of the force whose name could not be mentioned. Above all else, the NKVD commanded fear since their power over every citizen was beyond all justification. The time to leave Russia had long passed. Now the only hope for protection lay in obscurity, to hide far from people and abandon any position of responsibility or town of any size. The most astute unaccountably walked away from careers as industrial managers to become bricklayers, or abandoned their surgical duties to tend horses on a collective farm. Those who had read the signs in time slipped away to reappear, if they were lucky, among the community of Russian exiles in Paris or Nice. It was a time – in the words of the poet Alexander Blok – to be 'quieter than water, lower than grass.' But by 1937 the Soviet borders were sealed tight. All opportunities for flight were exhausted, and what was once impending had now arrived.

Who in Soviet Russia dared speak out? Hardly a soul when the consequence was not a dissident's imprisonment but immediate execution. Besides which, no medium for protest existed outside the state's control. Among Russia's intellectuals the clear-sighted had long recognised the murderous capacity of the Revolution. The father of modern psychology, Ivan Pavlov, was eighty-five years old on 21 December 1934. His experiments in behaviourism had earned him the Nobel Prize, and his international scientific reputation made him virtually untouchable. Following the mass arrests in Leningrad, Pavlov had written an angry letter to the USSR Council of People's Commissars: 'You believe in vain in the all-world revolution . . . You disperse not revolution, but fascism with great success throughout the world . . . Fascism did not exist before your revolution . . . You are terror and violence . . . We are living now in the atmosphere of terror and violence . . . Am I alone in thinking and feeling this way? Have pity on the Motherland and us.' When Ivan Pavlov died two years later, the NKVD had collected five volumes of informers' denunciations against the figurehead of Soviet science.[8]

Russia's only other living Nobel winner, Ivan Bunin, had collected the 1933 prize for literature in Stockholm as a stateless exile. Like Pavlov, Bunin had been aware of the violence of the Revolution from the very beginning. In March 1918, he asked a telephone operator to put him through to a literary magazine and instead was accidentally connected to a conversation within the Kremlin: 'I have fifteen officers and Lieutenant Kaledin. What should I do with them?' The voice on the end of the line did not hesitate: 'Shoot them right away.'[9] Later Bunin received an order requiring the registration of 'all bourgeois', which prompted the question in his diary: 'How is one to understand this?' His suspicions that their registration was the prelude to execution proved entirely correct. Fortunately Bunin managed to flee Russia into exile and saved his life. In his private diary he wrote: 'the "Great Russian Revolution" is a thousand times more bestial, filthy and stupid than the vile original which it claims to copy because it exceeds – step by step, item for item, and in a horribly shameless and explicit way – the bloody melodrama that had played itself out in France.'[10] The events of 1937 would turn his words into understatement.

In March 1937, Joseph Stalin made a speech to the Central Committee that was published across the Soviet Union, and signalled a further escalation of the Terror:

> The sabotage and diversionist work has reached to a greater or lesser extent, all or practically all our organizations . . . Soviet power has conquered only one sixth of the world and five sixths of the world are in the hands of capitalist states . . . As long as our capitalist encirclement remains, we will always have saboteurs, diversionists, and spies . . . the real saboteur must from time to time show evidence of success in his work, for that is the only way in which he can keep his job as a saboteur . . . We shall have to extirpate those persons, grind them down without stopping, without flagging, for they are the enemies of the working class, they are traitors to our homeland![11]

It was as if an angel of death had descended upon Russia, and the sound of its beating wings grew louder and louder as the months wore on. Only their nocturnal visitor wore the uniform of the NKVD and, far from being one single entity, arrived as an army of one third of a million. There was a saying in Moscow at the time: 'Thieves, prostitutes and the NKVD work mainly at night'. The Russians had learned that the peak calling hours for Stalin's secret police were between one and five in the morning, when the 'ravens', the prison vans, began scouring the streets for 'enemies of the people', taking with them their families, their friends and even simple acquaintances seized for 'prophylactic purposes'. Each arrest sparked a new series of detentions in a chain reaction which rapidly developed a momentum of its own. So many people were being arrested that the black vans were painted with signs advertising 'Bread' or 'Meat' or even 'Drink Soviet champagne!' in a shallow effort not to alarm the frightened public.[12]

As the Terror picked up speed, it was enough to crack a joke, to show ironic hesitancy over state propaganda, or even to collect foreign stamps, to be judged an 'enemy'. Mass indoctrination was broadcast from blaring loudspeakers put up on street corners. A simple mistake of a factory manager, the miscalculation of an engineer, a broadcaster's choice of light-hearted music on the anniversary of Lenin's death – all became evidence of an organised conspiracy of saboteurs operating in their midst. The Soviet public was encouraged to search for hidden fascist symbols and coded messages, and quickly found them disguised in seemingly innocent book illustrations or newspaper photographs. Denunciation boxes appeared in factories and on street corners, and were soon crammed to bursting with claims made against fellow citizens; the denouncers vainly believing that by accusing others they might somehow save themselves. In such a society pure malice was given free rein. The secretary of Stalin's henchman Lazar Kaganovich, for example, while typing out an arrest list quietly added the name of her neighbour. When her neighbour was arrested, she moved into the apartment she had coveted.[13]

'Conciliators' – those citizens who advocated leniency towards the 'enemies of the people' – were themselves arrested. 'Failure to denounce' had become a crime, and there were provocateurs who made false statements just to report those who failed in their duty to the state. A fourteen-year-old boy who had informed on his peasant father for hoarding grain – and was then murdered by outraged neighbours – was turned into a Soviet national hero. 'Pavlik Morozov' statues were commissioned for parks and squares across the Soviet Union, so many, in fact, that the statue's sculptor was killed in an accident caused by the state's production demands. No one stopped to appreciate the irony, and who could believe the rumours that the fourteen-year-old informer had, in fact, been murdered by the NKVD, who executed thirty-seven of his village neighbours, including Morozov's grandfather, grandmother, uncle and cousin?[14]

Not only were Soviet schoolchildren expected to denounce the 'enemies of the people', they were also specifically instructed to inform on their parents, their teachers and their friends. Young

Pioneers who accepted the new morality took part in 'socialist competitions' with awards given for those who could inform upon the greatest number of 'enemies'. One homeless child of the 1930s, a waif named Voinov, remembered his teacher walking into their classroom one morning with a smile across her face. 'Vasiliev is the pride of our school,' the teacher began. 'He sets an example that should be followed. He's only a boy, but he has proved that he is a responsible citizen of our country . . . With vigilance worthy of a real Bolshevik, Vasiliev has revealed and unmasked an enemy of the people. Of course, this is the duty of every Soviet citizen – you're right. But Vasiliev did more. He has acted like a hero. He conquered family prejudices and denounced his own father!' Vasiliev sat in the classroom wearing a new suit, his reward for having reported seeing his father reading the banned works of Trotsky.[15]

Wise parents stopped talking when their children came home from school. When both parents were arrested, their children were sent to NKVD orphanages where they learned the consequences of being the sons and daughters of 'enemies of the people'. A future Soviet dissident, Yelena Bonner, remembered how her nine-year-old brother innocently accepted the guilt of their father, arrested in 1937. 'Look what those enemies of the people are like,' he told his sister. 'Some of them even pretend to be fathers.' Yelena Bonner's father was shot, and her mother sent to the camps.[16]

Desperate to avoid the same fate, millions of Soviet citizens voted for death sentences in public demonstrations across the Soviet Union. The first generation of Bolsheviks responsible for the Revolution was almost entirely annihilated by Stalin. Vladimir Antonov-Ovseenko, who had led the storming of the Winter Palace in 1917, was one of those given 'the supreme measure of punishment'. Their executions removed the eyewitnesses of the origins of the Revolution, leaving a blank canvas upon which Stalin and his historians could paint any interpretation they desired. The recent past was erased and replaced with an alternative vision in which the primacy of Stalin emerged unchecked, shoulder to shoulder with Lenin throughout, directing the events of 1917. Any other interpretation – or even memory of the Revolution – became a secular heresy to be stamped out with ruthless and unyielding brutality. Thus, of the 1,966 People's Deputies of the Seventeenth Party Congress of 1934, 1,108 were arrested on charges of 'anti-Revolutionary crimes'. The so-called Congress of Victors had greeted Comrade Kirov's speech with a little too much enthusiasm, thereby hastening both Kirov's death and their own. And the execution of the Bolshevik cadres was merely the public face of a vast hidden realm of terror.[17]

During the summer of 1937, Stalin's chief henchmen – Kaganovich, Molotov, and Khrushchev, among others – were sent out to the provinces to oversee 'the purge of the party and state apparatus'. Old slogans in the factories were replaced by stark warnings: 'We shall destroy the enemies of the people, Comrades!' and, as the Soviet press and radio broadcast incessant reports of conspiracies against Stalin's life, the NKVD adopted efficiency targets to speed their plan for arrests, confessions and executions.[18]

In their eagerness to over-fulfil their plan, the internal NKVD sections bickered with one another for promotion and reward. One department complained that another had preselected married men with children for interrogation who, as every agent knew, were the quickest to confess. The NKVD was expanding ever outwards, recruiting and controlling an ever larger network of informers. While the secret departments watched from within, and like a Russian doll, those departments had special sections to watch the watchers. These were the 'special tasks' operatives entrusted with hunting down the Russian agents and diplomats who had refused to come home from abroad. Assassination squads travelled across Europe and America to silence the defectors.[19]

In Moscow a dwarf-like apparatchik named Nikolai Yezhov had been promoted from the provinces and had risen rapidly to succeed the fallen Commissar Henrikh Yagoda. Standing barely five feet tall even wearing the peaked cap of the NKVD, Yezhov scarcely came up to Stalin's shoulder, and Stalin was himself a small man. Besides his stature, it was Yezhov's eyes that caught people's attention, 'grey-green, fastening themselves upon his collocutor like gimlets, clever as the eyes of a cobra'.[20] Every day, the gimlet-eyed Yezhov would visit Stalin at his Kremlin office or 'Dacha Number One' outside Moscow. In Stalin's official register of visitors, it was recorded that Yezhov spent several hours each day conferring with the Great Leader.[21]

Together they worked on the lists of those about to be destroyed. In the Lubyanka, Yezhov would create the lists of names, which Stalin would read and sign, and afterwards watch a movie for relax-ation. At one Central Committee meeting, Stalin presented lists for

Molotov, Kaganovich and Malenkov to co-sign which sentenced 230,000 people to their executions. During 1937 and 1938, Yezhov faithfully brought Stalin 383 lists for his examination.[22] Unlike Hitler, the Soviet dictator never had any qualms about adding his personal signature to genocide, scanning thousands of names into the night, occasionally marking off a famous writer such as Boris Pasternak as 'not to be touched'. Such dispensations were, of course, extremely rare. On one of the lists Yezhov claimed to be checking, Stalin wrote: 'No need to check. Arrest them.'[23]

Telegrams were sent by Yezhov from Moscow to regional districts across the USSR. The messages conveyed succinct instructions: 'You are charged with the task of exterminating ten thousand enemies of the people. Report results by signal.' And the replies from the local NKVD chiefs would be swiftly telegraphed back to the Centre: 'The following enemies have been shot . . .'[24] In their haste, the NKVD provincial chiefs often attempted to outperform one another, and as they struggled to over-fulfil their execution norms, the wave of judicially sanctioned murders escalated still further. Unprecedented in its scale, the same measures were simultaneously applied in every city, town and village of the Soviet Union. There was no recourse to an appeal.

One NKVD deputy commander, Iakubovich, attempted to increase the number of arrest warrants he could sign in one minute, timing himself as he furiously initialled sheaves of papers with a red pencil.[25] When the Western Siberian NKVD were informed they had achieved second place in the killing spree, the mood, according to one operative, Tepliakov, 'reached ecstasy'.[26] On 23 July 1938, an NKVD chief named Gorbach wired Moscow from the city of Omsk asking for an increased quota of thousands more executions since his men had already fulfilled their plan. The request was approved by Stalin personally, who promoted Gorbach to a larger district, where he over-fulfilled the quota once again. Meanwhile, Yezhov sent out threatening telegrams of encouragement to the others: 'Beat destroy without sorting out . . . A certain number of innocent people will be annihilated too . . . act more boldly, I have already told you repeatedly.'[27]

On 4 August 1937, Popashenko, the NKVD chief of the Kuibyshev region, issued a detailed set of instructions to one of his underlings, a Captain Korobitsin, on how to proceed with the executions:

1. Adapt immediately an area in a building of the NKVD, prefer-
ably in the cellar, suitable as a special cell for carrying out death
sentences . . . 3. The death sentences are to be carried out at
night. Before the sentences are executed the exact identity of the
prisoner is to be established by checking carefully his question-
naire with the troika verdict. 4. After the executions the bodies
are to be laid in a pit dug beforehand, then carefully buried and
the pit is to be camouflaged. 5. Documents on the execution of
the death sentences consist of a written form which is to be completed and signed for each prisoner in one copy only and sent in
a separate package to the UNKVD [local administration of the
secret police] for the attention of the 8th UGB Department
[Registrations] UNKVD. 6. It is your personal responsibility to
ensure that there is complete secrecy concerning time, place and
method of execution. 7. Immediately on receipt of this order you
are to present a list of NKVD staff permitted to participate in
executions. Red Army soldiers or militsionery are not to be
employed. All persons involved in the work of transporting the
bodies and excavating or filling in the pits have to sign a document certifying they are sworn to secrecy.[28]

Similar instructions were ordered in other districts, supporting
the conclusion that this was the universal method. In Novosibirsk,
in July 1937, the NKVD chief Mironov charged his local opera-
tional chiefs with the task of: 'Finding a place where the sentences
will be executed and a place where you can bury the corpses. If
this is in a wood, the turf should be cut off beforehand so that for
full secrecy's sake the place can be covered with this turf after-
ward.'[29] And with exacting premedation, the turf was cut and
the graves were dug, ready to conceal their victims. By the autumn
of 1937, the pressure to achieve arrests was so great the NKVD
interrogators began picking out the names from the telephone
directory.[30]

Their victims were killed with a shot to the back of the head. From
a mass grave at Vinnytsia in the Ukraine, 9,432 bodies were taken
for examination, of whom two-thirds had required a second shot to
end their lives. Seventy-eight people were shot three times and two
victims were shot four times.[31] Others had their skulls staved in by
the force of a blunt object. The victims were buried in a pear

orchard, which the NKVD surrounded with a high fence for secrecy. Nevertheless, curious locals had peered through holes in the fence, or climbed trees to look into the orchard where they had seen the bodies stacked up awaiting burial. Most of the victims were male, but the bodies of a number of women were found in the graves also, some of whom were buried naked.[32]

In the mass graves of Kuropaty, near Minsk in Byelorussia, it was reported that sand thrown over each layer of victims was seen to be moving some time afterwards.[33] Here the graves extended across acres of woodland, the victims executed on the edge of the pits. At Kuropaty the executions continued for four and a half years, as pit after pit was dug and filled with bodies. Just as in the Ukraine, around the execution grounds the NVKD had built a fence ten feet high. This time the local villagers heard the pleas of the victims echoing across the night air. Even in the final stages of the Terror, when the Nazis were bombing Minsk in July 1941, the executions continued, and by the outbreak of World War II a quarter of a million people lay buried in one of eight killing fields located around Minsk.[34]

The victims' families were not informed of the executions. Instead they were told their relatives had been given ten-year sentences in the camps 'without the right of correspondence'. Outside prisons across the Soviet Union long queues formed of women and children seeking word of their disappeared loved ones. Under the Soviet criminal code, political prisoners not yet convicted were allowed to receive fifty roubles while in prison. Waiting in line for news of her husband, the German communist Margarete Buber noticed a little girl about ten years old join the queue behind them. In her hand the girl was clutching several rouble notes. 'Who are you paying in for, dear?' a voice from the queue asked gently. 'Mummy and Daddy,' the ten-year-old girl replied.[35]

As an organisation, the NKVD was expanding so rapidly the agents making the arrests were often little more than teenagers themselves. When confronted by any unforeseen obstacle, they had to telephone back to base for instructions. Edmund Stevens, an American reporter living in a Moscow building which had already been visited several times, remembered one night when the NKVD arrived just after two o'clock. Their teenage agents wore the caps of cornflower blue with red piping marked with the badge of the hammer and sickle, the faces of their victims reflecting back at them from the shining visors. Years later, Stevens could still not rid himself of the screams of hysteria as a young mother was torn away from her two-month-old baby, and she and her husband were dragged down into the van waiting for them on the street below.[36]

In Moscow at the height of the Terror, it was if the whole city was waiting to be arrested. Another American reporter, Louis Fischer, watched a Soviet official sitting on a balcony with his little suitcase packed ready, killing time before the night when the visitors would arrive. Fischer watched the official for three weeks that summer before the NVKD finally took him. More than half of the 160 apartments of his eight-storey building had already been subjected to the nocturnal arrests. The rest of his neighbours were waiting and the apprehension itself became part of the repression. At night, feigning sleep, the Soviet citizens listened out for the sound of the brakes on the wheels of the van, and the crunch of boots as the NKVD agents leaped down onto the pavement and began pounding up the stairs.[37]

In Leningrad another sleepless witness, Lyobov Shaporina, the fifty-eight-year-old wife of a composer, noticed how people would repeat the news of the disappearance of an acquaintance as calmly as saying 'he went to the theatre'. Shaporina wrote in her diary that the atmosphere was 'like walking through a cemetery pitted with freshly dug graves. Who will fall in next, will it be you?' At three o'clock in the morning of 22 October 1937 she had woken suddenly. Outside the night air was still and there were no trams or cars to break the silence when she heard a burst of gunfire. The noise was repeated ten minutes later, and then at intervals through the night until five o'clock in the morning, when the city of Leningrad gradually awoke to its normal routine. Walking to her window, Shaporina concluded the shooting had come from the fortress of Saint Peter and Paul, used as a jail by the NKVD. And then calmly she realized that she had spent the night listening to executions.[38]

During the 'Yezhov days' people shrank away from one another in fear, unsure if a casual acquaintance was an informer or, worse yet, an 'enemy' who might implicate them by association. With denunciations reaching saturation point, friends stopped recognising one another on the street, fearing the consequence of unnecessary social contact. And thus, ironically, Soviet Russia became transformed into a nation of fearful individualists, their eyes flicking across to each other and then swiftly away, as each citizen reminded himself not to speak unless it was strictly necessary, to remain silent at all times, except when silence itself gave cause for suspicion. Then they would applaud with all the energy a threatened life could muster, until their hands shook white and still they dared not stop. At a party rally or a factory meeting, if an ovation lasted twenty minutes – no thirty minutes – for a speech made by Comrade Stalin, then so what? Everyone sensed they could not be the first to stop when 'the angels' were watching. The first to break the applause would be arrested. So the crowds kept pounding their hands together, shouting out their praise for Comrade Stalin, sensing rightly that their lives depended on it. And so it continued, day after day and night after night.[39]

In the autumn of 1937, writers and journalists were disappearing so quickly their names were no longer painted on the doors of publishing companies, or newspapers such as *Izvestiya*. The response of the frightened writers was to shout their chorus of approval still louder, putting forward sincere proposals to rename the Volga river after Stalin, or the city of Moscow, or even the moon. Of the seven hundred writers who had attended the First Congress of Soviet Writers three years earlier, only fifty survived the Terror. Their past work was there for all to scrutinise, their fate a lesson to others: 'If you think don't speak! If you speak don't write! If you write don't publish! If you publish recant immediately!'[40]

In such an atmosphere, famous cultural figures were shot without fanfare. The writer Isaac Babel was arrested at his dacha. His subsequent trial lasted twenty minutes, and he was shot the next morning. The internationally renowned theatre director Vsevolod Meyerhold was arrested and executed in similar circumstances. Weeks after his arrest, his wife Zinaida was discovered in her apartment murdered. The poet Osip Mandelstam suffered an ignominious death in a transit camp in Far East Russia. Once he had joked: 'Russia is the only place where poetry is really important. They'll kill people for it here.' After Stalin closed his opera *Lady Macbeth of Mtsenk*, Dmitry Shostakovich took to sleeping in the corridor outside his apartment so that his arrest would not disturb his family. Shostakovich was ordered to appear before his NKVD inquisitor Zanchevsky in the spring of 1937, accused of involvement in a plot to assassinate Stalin. The shocked composer denied the charges but was given the weekend to think it over: 'I can give you until Monday. By that day you will without fail remember everything. You must recall every detail of the discussion regarding the plot.' Returning to the Lubyanka on Monday morning, Shostakovich was told, 'Zanchevsky is not coming in today.' On this occasion it was the inquisitor, not his victim, who was taken.[41]

Since 'enemies of the people' were being discovered everywhere else, then why not within the NKVD itself? There was an old saying from the 1920s: 'A Chekist who has shot fifty prisoners, he deserves to be shot as the fifty-first.' And thus the Terror began to consume both its 'enemies' and the minds of those who had imagined them, fuelled by Stalin's ever-present desire to rid himself of the witnesses of his crimes. Several NKVD officers committed suicide in anticipation. It was reported that a knock on the door of an NKVD residential building in central Moscow triggered a multitude of gunshots within adjacent apartments. Others threw themselves from the top-floor windows in a rash of suicides, their bodies hurtling to the ground in full view of passers-by. Rumours of the news spread rapidly over Moscow, panicking the population still further.[42]

In a totalitarian and paranoid state, nothing was beyond the reach of politics. Professor Kalmonson of Moscow Zoo was arrested for 'wrecking' activities, after the zoo's monkeys died of tuberculosis. In jail, the Professor was thankful to have only been arrested as a 'wrecker' and not a 'spy', which carried a greater certainty of death. In December 1937, fifty-three members of a deaf mutes' association were arrested in Leningrad, and thirty-three were sentenced to death for conducting 'conspiracies' in their private language. Philatelists and Esperantists were arrested for their past dealings with foreigners. Anyone who had been outside the borders of the USSR in any capacity became an immediate suspect. With the prisons filled beyond capacity, two- or three-man NKVD committees – the dread 'dvoiki' or 'troiki' – began handing out death sentences after ten-minute trials. Willingly the NKVD pursued their nightly task as a bleakly efficient killing machine, immune to reason or restraint; which in the morning left behind only the red seals on the apartment doors of their victims, as evidence of their presence, like the aftermath of a plague.[43]

Fearful in the midst of the mass arrests, waiting anxiously for salvation, were the foreigners of the Soviet Union. Most bewildered of all were the Americans, coming as they did from a nation with no history of state terror. No longer the welcomed guests of the Revolution who arrived to help 'build socialism', the foreigners were now regarded as potential spies plotting its destruction. Officially, from Stalin himself they had received the mark of Cain:

> It has been proved as definitely as twice two are four, that the bourgeois states send to each other spies, wreckers, diversion-ists and sometimes also assassins ... The question arises why should bourgeois states be milder and more neighbourly towards the Soviet Socialist state ... Would it not be more true, from the point of view of Marxism, to assume that to the rear of the Soviet Union the bourgeois states should send twice and three times as many wreckers, spies, diversionists and murderers?[44]

After such well-publicised pronouncements, all foreigners became a special target, with Moscow's embassies recast as hostile outposts to be watched over with all the suspicion that a notoriously paranoid organisation could devote. Orders were given that these 'potential intelligence bases' of 'enemy states' were to be placed under contin-uous observation. Every foreigner entering and leaving the embassy buildings who did not possess cast-iron diplomatic or journalistic credentials became subject to investigation.[45]

Aping their bosses in Moscow, the regional NKVD were, if any-thing, even fiercer in their witch hunts against the foreigners. The Krasnoyarsk NKVD chief, Sobolev, proclaimed enthusiastically: 'All these Poles, Koreans, Latvians, Germans etc should be beaten, these are all mercenary nations, subject to termination ... All nations should be caught, forced to their knees, and exterminated like mad dogs.' The term 'mad dog' had become an essential part of the Soviet lexicography, the choice of language reflecting a dehumanising process that facilitated the destruction of their victims. Amongst the Polish community residing in the Soviet Union, 144,000 people were arrested, and of these 111,000 were executed. It beggared belief, but such was the power of the NKVD.[46]

All communication with foreigners became dangerous, and ordi-nary Russian citizens shrank away from them in fear. Propaganda posters depicted a Nazi spy choosing which mask to wear, the choice of labels communicating the hierarchy of suspicion: 'Foreign spe-cialist', 'Tourist', 'Writer' and 'Victim of Fascism'. Viewing such posters, the American emigrants must have realised they were suddenly very vulnerable as they waited, transfixed by the events taking place around them. For most, the Terror was impossible to understand; it was easier to believe in the guilt of the arrested than to contemplate the notion that the Soviet state was now intent upon their destruction. Some Americans found solace in the recently published *Stalin Constitution*, which guaranteed: 'the citizens of the USSR are ensured inviolability of the person. No one may be subject to arrest except by decision of a court or with the sanction of a state prosecutor.' But fate made a mockery of their hope, as the authors of Stalin's so-called 'Bill of Rights' were themselves arrested.[47]

The direst warning had stared them directly in the face. The year before, Nikolai Yezhov's appointment as the People's Commissar for the NKVD had been announced with a banner headline in the *Moscow Daily News*. On the front page, his photograph had gazed out at the American readers. Picking up the newspaper that day, did they really believe Yezhov's 'grey-green gimlet eyes' would miss them?

9

'SPETZRABOTA'

Or be that fairy tale you've dreamed up,
So sickeningly familiar to everyone –
In which I glimpse the top of a pale blue cap
And the house attendant white with fear.

Anna Akhmatova, 'To Death'[1]

With every passing week, Stalin's portrait had multiplied. His gaze was there whichever way the Americans turned, a constant reminder of their powerlessness. Uncannily in an atheistic state, Stalin's image had acquired a sacramental quality, demanding the very greatest reverence from his subjects. Nothing could be placed over it, the slightest fun could not be made of it, nor could it be even accidentally tarnished – not that any sane person would ever dream of committing such an offence. Most disturbing of all were the portraits of Stalin held aloft in crowds, emerging in successive waves of marching acolytes, watched over by the same face looking down in approval from surrounding buildings. At the Tushino air fête, a crowd of half a million spectators gathered under a slow procession of hot-air balloons, carrying monumental fifty-by-thirty feet photographs of Stalin and the Politburo, moving gently across the summer sky. '*Long Live the Brain, the Heart, the Strength of the Party and the Soviet peoples, our Beloved Leader and Teacher, Comrade Stalin!*'[2]

It was Stalin who personally instructed the NKVD to torture their prisoners to extract confessions, writing 'beat, beat!' next to his victims' names. When Khrushchev visited Yezhov in his Central Committee office during the Terror, he noticed bloodstains on the front and cuffs of Yezhov's shirt. Catching his gaze, Yezhov replied that, 'One might be proud of such spots, for it was the blood of the enemies of the Revolution.'

By now, Stalin had nicknamed his favourite Commissar *Ezhevichka* ('the little bramble') and entrusted him with the order No. 00447 to 'put an end, once and for all' to anti-Soviet elements within society.[3]

At the height of the Terror, Stalin promised: 'We shall annihilate every one of these enemies, even if he is an Old Bolshevik. We shall annihilate him and his relatives, his family. Anyone who in deed or in thought, yes, in thought, attacks the unity of the socialist state will be mercilessly crushed by us. We shall exterminate all enemies to the very last man, and also their families and relatives!'[4] Naturally there were those who privately speculated on the mental health of Stalin, this small man, rather thin and quite frail, whose jacket hung off him and whose face was pockmarked by smallpox scars and had grown deathly pale from his nocturnal schedule. They questioned whether Stalin had not descended into a psychopathic paranoia, concealed by a functioning intelligence. A childhood friend, Ioseb Iremashvili, later wrote that 'undeserved terrible beatings made the boy as hard and heartless as his father himself. Since all men who had authority over others either through power or age reminded him of his father there had arisen a feeling of revenge against all men who stood above him. From his youth the realization of his thoughts of revenge became the goal toward which everything was aimed.'[5]

There were many who believed Stalin was insane, such was the scale and senselessness of his wrath. The Dearborn negotiator Valery Mezhlauk wrote to his brother, who was organising a Soviet exhibition in Paris, that Stalin was ill from 'acute' paranoia. What other explanation could there be? To infer that Stalin was deliberately scything through every class of Soviet society to maintain an absolute and critical hold on power seemed either fantastical or diabolical in its cruelty. Such a conclusion went beyond the deductive logic of even a highly intelligent Bolshevik Party member such as Mezhlauk. To have reached this political conclusion would also have required the realisation of his own impending death, and his brother's also.[6]

Even by speculating on Stalin's mental health, Mezhlauk was guilty of 'thought crime', a very real transgression in a state that demanded only the appearance and actuality of capitulation. The Polish writer Czeslaw Miloscz later described the rationale of their guardians: 'The enemy, in a potential form, will always be there; the only friend will be the man who accepts the doctrine 100 per cent. If he accepts only 99 per cent, he will necessarily have to be considered a foe, for from that remaining 1 per cent a new church can rise.'[7] In the mind of Stalin, the killings had become a necessity for the entrenchment of power. And the 'captured' Americans – although only a negligible fraction of a percentage of the population of the USSR – were as subject to the mechanics of Soviet power as any of those around them; perhaps even more so, since every American emigrant carried with them the threat of revelation to the outside world.

Arthur Talent arrived in Moscow in the 1920s as a seven-year-old with his family from Boston. The shy boy was a gifted violinist who won a place at the prestigious Moscow Conservatory to study music. As a young man, Arthur Talent offered a room in his family's apartment to John Goode, the brother-in-law of Paul Robeson, and received as a gift a brand-new suit from America. In the political atmosphere of the day, even such a simple exchange could condemn both parties. On 28 January 1938, Arthur Talent was arrested by the NKVD, and the young violinist vanished.

In the late 1990s transcripts of his interrogation were released by the Russian security services. The yellowed sheets of paper in Arthur Talent's NKVD file recorded his steadfast denial of the accusations thrown at him in the Lubyanka. His interrogation ended abruptly, only to be resumed thirty-eight days later, when Talent began a full 'confession' to an NKVD agent named Salov. The methods used to change Talent's mind were commonplace; the transcript failing to convey the mechanical cadences of an exhausted victim who prefers death over that which he has just endured: 'You are arrested and accused of espionage activities in the USSR in favour of a foreign state. Do you plead guilty?' 'Yes! I plead guilty of being involved in espionage in favour of Latvia. After thirty-eight days of denial, I have decided to tell the inquest the whole truth.'

Arthur Talent confessed that Paul Robeson's wife, Eslanda, had brought him the American suit during a previous visit to Moscow, at the request of her brother, John Goode, who was staying at his apartment, which had become a 'centre for foreign espionage'. He confirmed that John Goode was an 'agent of a foreign state', and the suit was proof of payment for his espionage. Pressed for more information and the names of his accomplices, Arthur Talent proceeded to denounce his friends involved in his 'crimes', including Jim Abolin and his two sons who played on the Moscow Foreign Workers' baseball team. A slip of paper inserted at the end of the file revealed that Arthur Talent was then taken from his prison cell and driven to the countryside outside Moscow. At the execution grounds at Butovo on 7 June 1938, he was shot. He was twenty-one years old.[8]

On 10 May 1936 Paul Robeson had given an interview to Ben Davis, Jr., of the *Sunday Worker* describing a visit he had made to the apartment of his brother-in-law John Goode: 'While in the Soviet Union I made it a point to visit some of the workers' homes . . . and I saw for myself. They all live in healthful surroundings, apartments, with nurseries containing the most modern equipment for their children. Besides they were still building. I certainly wish the workers in this country – and especially the Negroes in Harlem and the South – had such places to stay in. I visited the home of my brother-in-law, his apartment had plenty of light, fresh air and space. Believe me he is very happy.' John Goode was a mechanic and bus driver living in Moscow whose existence Robeson was careful to publicise.[9]

What the American singer never mentioned in any interview was the news that he had helped to engineer Goode's escape from Russia at the end of his concert tour. His brother-in-law fled with just one suitcase to add credence to their story that he was taking just a short vacation outside the USSR. And by means of this subterfuge John Goode's life was saved from the NKVD decree of 19 February 1938 ordering his arrest.[10] But if any of the young American baseball players of Moscow were hoping for similar intercession by Robeson on their behalf, they were to wait in vain. There is no record of any statement made by the honorary catcher of the Moscow Foreign Workers' baseball team in support of his young American friends. Nor did Robeson make any attempt to denounce the Terror, which he knew was taking place within the Soviet Union. The most famous bass voice in world music had fallen unaccountably silent.

In February 1937, as the Stalin Constitution was being ratified, Paul Robeson returned to Russia for a concert tour with the Moscow State Philharmonic. At a performance at the Bolshoi Theatre in Moscow, the audience suddenly stood and began to cheer furiously. Joseph Stalin was standing in a box on the right, smiling and applauding. Later Robeson described his feelings: 'I remember the tears began to quietly flow and I too smiled and waved. Here was clearly a man who seemed to embrace all. So kindly – I can never forget that warm feeling of kindliness and also a feeling of sureness. Here was one who was wise and good – the world and especially the socialist world was fortunate indeed to have his daily guidance. I lifted high my son Pauli to wave to this world leader, and his leader.'[11]

That summer, Eslanda Robeson visited the American Communist Party leader Eugene Dennis at the Hotel Lux in Moscow. When she asked Dennis if they should keep Paul Robeson, Jr., at school in Moscow, his advice was straightforward: 'If you do so, I urge that you make it publicly well-known, and be sure the practical arrangements are such that you can take him home whenever you wish.' Eugene Dennis was speaking from experience; he had been forced to leave his son behind in Moscow when he first left the USSR. Tim Dennis was eight years old and could not speak English at all – although both his parents were American – and when the couple left Moscow again, he was raised in a Soviet state orphanage.[12] Heeding Dennis's advice, the Robesons took their son with them on a summer vacation with the family of Oliver Golden, a black American cotton specialist who had arrived in the Soviet Union in 1931 with his wife Bertha, and settled in Tashkent. Oliver Golden spoke Russian with a Mississippi accent, and joked about returning home 'when elephants roost in the trees'.

During their vacation at the elite rest home on the Black Sea, the ten-year-old Paul Robeson, Jr., explained to his father how the parents of his Moscow school friends were being arrested. The children of the Bolshevik elite had learned to walk outside into the playground if they wanted to talk about their parents, for fear of their conversations being recorded. Paul Robeson, Jr., then recounted how he had stood with his friend Misha watching the return of the Soviet hero-explorers from their North Pole expedition. As they stood watching the propaganda parade, Misha explained that the light ash falling from the sky 'came from the crematoria in the cellars of prisoners where the firing squads were working overtime'.[13]

In the face of such revelations, it was unsurprising that the Robesons' Black Sea holiday was marred by arguments. Oliver Golden's daughter remembered how her father and Paul Robeson had been locked in 'heated political discussions'.[14] Given that both were dedicated Communists, it was uncertain who was defending the status quo, but it transpired also that Robeson had been unable to find any of the Russian friends he had made on his earlier visits. Returning to Moscow in August 1937, Robeson asked to meet Ignaty Kazakov, a doctor and Shakespeare scholar who had made friends with his young son. Although warned that Kazakov had already disappeared, Robeson insisted and quite unexpectedly the Russian doctor telephoned to invite him to lunch at the Metropol

Hotel. Arriving with two 'translators' as his escort, Kazakov sat down for a two-hour lunch as if nothing was wrong. Only at the end of the meal, when the doctor announced that he must return to his medical institute, did he manage to whisper 'Thank you' into Robeson's ear.

Six months later, Ignaty Kazakov's name appeared as one of the defendants of a Moscow show trial, accused of having used his medical clinic for political assassinations. His guilty verdict and swift execution prompted an argument between Paul Robeson and his young son, who had since been moved to the Soviet diplomatic school in London. With a child's instinct for justice, Paul Robeson, Jr., understood very well that the charges were fabricated, and he accused his father of inaction: 'We all knew he was innocent, and you never said a word.' In his memoirs, Paul Robeson, Jr., wrote that a few days later his father had explained how *sometimes great injustices may be inflicted on the minority when the majority is in the pursuit of a great and just cause*.[15]

After their vacation, Oliver Golden returned to the 'House of the Foreign Specialists' in Tashkent, only to discover his neighbour's apartment door was sealed with red wax. Concerned friends told Golden that while he was away the NKVD had arrived in the night to arrest him. As a dutiful communist, the American cotton specialist immediately took himself down to the NKVD headquarters. 'You came for me,' he said boldly. 'Arrest me if you think I'm an enemy of the people.' Then something remarkable happened. The NKVD officer in charge advised him to calm down: 'Comrade Golden, don't get so upset. We've already fulfilled the plans of arrests for your area. Go home and work in peace.' And by this stroke of good fortune, Oliver Golden lived another three years. According to his granddaughter, he died of heart and kidney failure in the land of his dreams.[16]

Lovett Fort-Whiteman disappeared soon after applying for permission to return home to the United States. His exit visa was refused, and the former teacher at the Anglo-American school, born in Dallas and educated at the Tuskegee Institute, was denounced as a 'counter-revolutionary' by a lawyer from the Communist Party of the United States. Three weeks later Fort-Whiteman was arrested and sent to a 'corrective labour camp' in Kazakhstan. In Moscow, Robert Robinson heard more news from a Russian friend who had returned from the same camp. According to this witness, Fort-Whiteman had been severely beaten because he had failed to meet his work quota. In the camp, he had died of starvation, a broken man whose teeth had been knocked out.[17] It was difficult to comprehend how such a robust figure, so physically strong and an avid boxer, could have died so quickly. But the truth of the sighting was confirmed when Lovett Fort-Whiteman's NKVD file was discovered in the late 1990s. The NKVD recorded the date of his death as 13 January 1939, at the age of forty-four. The fingerprints taken from his corpse were still attached to the back of his file.[18]

Sympathy for the Soviet cause was no guarantee of safety; instead it attracted suspicion. The Reverend Julius Hecker, for example, was a Methodist academic from Columbia University who published several books defending communism before moving to Russia with his American wife and three young daughters to teach philosophy at Moscow University. According to the American Embassy, in earlier summers, when Moscow was crowded with tourists, Julius Hecker had made 'speeches almost daily to the visitors on the subject of religious tolerance in the Soviet Union.'[19] His daughter Marcella Hecker remembered the day the NKVD came to take her father away. 'He was asleep in a little room which I occupy now,' she said. 'Although my mother opened the door very, very quietly, Father must have had some terrible dream, because he woke up at once with a jerk, and immediately understood everything. They bore him away and we never saw him again.' Julius Hecker's wife remained convinced that her husband's arrest was just a terrible mistake and waited long years for his return.[20] She never learned that just two and half months after his arrest, on 28 April 1938, Professor Julius Hecker confessed to being an American spy who had written his books merely to draw attention away from his espionage. Two hours after making this false confession, he was shot.[21]

There were those – the majority – who waited in the night like Julius Hecker. Only a very few sought sanctuary with friends, hidden away in attics like Soviet Anne Franks. But in the communal apartments of overcrowded cities, it was almost impossible to hide without being noticed. Some fugitives moved cities and kept on running, hoping to buy false papers and new identities, and keep one step ahead of the overburdened NKVD. There were always more than enough 'enemies' to arrest who remained in their apartments, paralysed by fear. But it was difficult to flee if you were a foreigner, let alone an American, whose particular Russian accent automatically attracted attention, and thus suspicion. Those who left the cities to live in remote villages, or arrived at a new construction site in search of work, only came under the scrutiny of fresh pairs of NKVD eyes, eagerly scanning residence lists in search of names.[22]

In 1937, Victor Herman, 'the Lindbergh of Russia', was expelled from his elite parachute academy outside Moscow, stung by the taunts of the school's Political Commissar: 'You are an enemy, Herman! Your kind does not belong here! All enemies are being weeded out!'[23] Now in his early twenties, when Victor took the train back to the Ford auto factory in Gorky, he discovered the once lively American village had become deserted. Recognising two Americans in the cafeteria, Victor was shocked to realise they were too fearful to say hello. When he questioned his father, Sam Herman instinctively looked over his shoulder before whispering: 'Leave here with your sister . . . Take Miriam and return to Moscow. You are to go straight to the American consulate there. You will tell them you wish to go home immediately. I want you to promise me, Vickie, you will not leave that building until they send you and your sister home.' Later his father told him that of the hundreds of Americans who had come to work at the auto factory in Gorky, only twenty were left.[24]

The American workers had been disappearing from the auto factory for some time. Joe Grondon, the former Ford employee and trade unionist briefly made famous by *Pravda* as 'The Man Who Abandoned Detroit', had been arrested at home in the American village some two years earlier. From the State Department records we know that his son Benjamin Grondon reported his father's disappearance to the American Embassy on 6 May 1935.[25] What happened to Benjamin Grondon, who had played as an outfielder on the Gorky baseball team, we do not know. But during the intervening period, virtually every Russian engineer who had any connection with Detroit was arrested. An anonymous American engineer who visited the Gorky car plant during the Terror discovered to his amazement that the production cost of each Soviet automobile was around 'twenty thousand dollars'. The latest engineers were all 'high school graduates' with virtually no one aged over thirty left working in the factory.[26]

On 7 October 1937, *Pravda* ran an article accusing the Gorky Automobile Plant of 'shameful' work. The machinery installed by 'wreckers' had become worn out due to 'carelessness and insufficient care'; while expensive technology bought from abroad had not been used at all for 'fear that if improperly installed the machinery might not function'. If it was obvious that the Soviet Detroit was nowhere near as productive as Henry Ford's, then clearly 'wreckers' must be to blame. Valery Mezhlauk and Saul Bron – the two Russians photographed on either side of Henry Ford after signing the Amtorg contract in Dearborn – were both arrested and summarily executed. Sergey Dyakanov, the director of the Gorky plant, whose photograph Henry Ford had once generously signed 'from the American Ford to the Soviet Ford' was arrested and shot in the Lubyanka on the day of his trial. In Dyakanov's NKVD file, his interrogator Lieutenant Shevilyov noted that he had carried out the sentence personally.[27]

In such circumstances, any promise Victor Herman made to his father in the American village was impossible to keep. Those who tried to escape Gorky could not get far. The NKVD were everywhere, constantly checking identity papers, and someone like Victor never really stood a chance. He was arrested on 20 July 1938, bundled into the back of a Ford Model A. Like the others, the bewildered Victor Herman attempted to protest his innocence: 'I am an American! You will pay for this! This is kidnapping! You cannot do this to an American!' But the NKVD lieutenant remained impassive, watching his victim with detached amusement before nodding towards some pedestrians staring at them from the street: 'Look, Lindbergh of Russia, the people are applauding.'[28] In Russia, the Americans were carried away in the very cars they had left Detroit to build. For Henry Ford's contract signed in Dearborn had supplied the NKVD with their entire fleet, missing only the uniformed drivers and the blue stars on the windscreens.[29]

Through the course of 1937 and 1938, Americans such as Victor Herman began to disappear, one after another. Many of the arrested were shot not long afterwards, often with their fathers who had brought them to the USSR. After their denunciation, the baseball players from Boston, Arthur Abolin and his younger brother Carl, were both arrested and executed with their father James Abolin in 1938. Their mother died later in a concentration camp. Only their younger sister Lucy Abolin – the precocious drama student of the Anglo-American school – was left untouched.[30] Other records emerged which revealed how certain victims were forced to testify against their family members in so-called 'confrontation interrogations'. In March 1938, a twenty-five-year-old New Yorker named Victor Tyskewicz-Voskov confessed that his mother had been recruited into 'espionage in favour of Germany'. Under extreme duress, Tyskewicz-Voskov denounced his mother to his interrogator as a 'Trotskyist, inclined antagonistically against the Soviet power'. The NKVD officers then placed his forty-three-year-old mother in the same interrogation room while her son repeated his denunciation in front of her. His mother bravely confessed her own guilt while steadfastly refusing to implicate her son. They were both executed on 7 June 1938.[31]

In the killing fields of Butovo, twenty-seven kilometres south of Moscow, the depressions in the ground later revealed themselves in aerial photography. The mass graves ran for up to half a kilometre at a time. Nor was there anything particularly unique about Butovo. Within the Soviet Union such 'zones' were differentiated only by their location. Orders sent from Moscow were applied uniformly throughout the USSR, from the Polish border across one sixth of the surface of the earth to the Pacific ocean. If the NKVD were instructed that 250,000 people should fill one of the eight mass graves in Byelorussia, then a similar ratio was applied to every other Soviet republic, and every regional district of Russia too, including the Moscow region itself. At Butovo, exactly the same procedure was followed by the NKVD brigades as elsewhere.[32]

In the 1990s, a Russian society for the rehabilitation of Stalin's victims, located within the files of KGB pensioners a 'Comrade S.', the first *komendant* of an NKVD execution squad, who was willing to be interviewed for the historical record. Comrade S. happily discussed his *spetzrabota* – the so-called 'special work' – which he had performed with his team of a dozen executioners during the *Yezhovchina*, 'the days of Yezhov'. Comrade S. remembered how his unit had waited in a stone house on the edge of the killing fields while their prisoners' files were checked. How they led their victims to the edge of the pit and held the standard-issue Nagan pistol to the backs of their heads. How they pulled the trigger and watched each body crumple and fall into the hole in the earth. And then how they repeated the process over and again until, like every other Soviet worker, they had met their quota for the night's work. At the end of their shift, Comrade S. and the dozen members of his squad would retire to their stone headquarters exhausted, to drink the litres of vodka specially allocated for the job in hand. Obviously their masters understood the traumatic effect the *spetzrabota* had on the minds of the executioners. The vodka salved their consciences as the dawn rose over Moscow, and a new day began for the city's fear-filled inhabitants.[33]

In the mornings at Butovo, the executioners heard the sound of the bulldozers covering over the mass graves, and the fresh graves being hollowed ready for the next night's work. In their stone house they washed their hands and faces, removing the inevitable back-spray of blood, and doused themselves in cheap eau de cologne, once again provided by their masters, who seemed to have thought of everything and understood that the smell of death clings to those who administer it. Although they were given leather aprons, gloves and hats to protect their uniforms from the spattered gore of blood and skull and brain, the men found that it was impossible to stay pristinely clean.[34]

Judging from the undisturbed recollections of Comrade S., the NKVD guards remained convinced they were not murderers but righteous executioners sanctioned by their state. With prolonged ideological training, their moral sense became disguised and distorted by euphemism. The brigade was enforcing the 'supreme penalty for social defence', or administering the 'nine-gram ration'. Words such as 'liquidation' or 'repression' inadequately concealed the simple act of murder. While, numbed by the repetitiveness of their 'special work', the executioners became as passionless as slaughtermen, too busy for introspection. Their *spetzrabota* did not end for many years; it kept arriving until it was hardly special any longer, just monotonous in its routine.[35] There was, however, one unexpected consequence to their lives. Their work made them wealthy. Each NKVD executioner was paid special rouble bonuses for killing people in 'the zones', so much in fact that their increased salaries excited the envy of their NKVD colleagues not selected for this work. And the rouble bonuses mounted up as night after night the pits were filled and new ones were dug again the next morning.[36]

In the fields of Butovo, apple trees were planted over the dead. In Depository No.7 at the Lubyanka, the NKVD entered their names in four hundred bound volumes. Each name was marked with a red pencil and the note 'sentence carried out'. From these books, researchers later calculated that eighty-five per cent of the dead were non-Communists, ordinary people who mostly came from the Russian peasantry. Given the scale of the genocide, the fate of the Americans was scarcely a matter of significance. The statistical evidence had no regard for the captain of the Moscow Foreign Workers' baseball team, Arnold Preedin, or his brother Walter Preedin, from Boston, Massachusetts, who lay buried in an apple orchard, twenty-seven kilometres south of Moscow.[37]

Virtually every day in Moscow, Thomas Sgovio heard the news of the arrest of friends such as Arnold Preedin and his family. At the Foreign Workers' Club on Hertzen Street, the Americans shrank away from one another in fear before deserting the building completely. Soon the premises were shut down, along with virtually every other institution associated with the world beyond the borders of the USSR, including the Anglo-American school, whose teachers were now accused of running a 'spy centre'. After his father Joseph was arrested, Thomas Sgovio quite naturally panicked. Not knowing where else to turn, he approached the only place he thought might possibly help a twenty-one-year-old from Buffalo, New York, thousands of miles from home. Like many others before him, Thomas Sgovio walked into the sanctuary of the American Embassy on Mokhovaya Street.[38]

At the time virtually every embassy in Moscow was besieged by desperate men and women attempting to flee the USSR. As well as Americans there were thousands of other foreigners – Italians, French, Spanish, Greeks, Austrians, Germans – all in a similar position of realising too late what a terrible mistake they had made in emigrating to Soviet Russia. And while it was obvious that the Russian public had no protection whatsoever from the ferocity of the NKVD, collectively the foreigners still clung to the hope that their governments might save them.

The staff at the American Embassy were inundated with requests for help, but this still did not explain their slow, and strangely ambivalent, response. In fear for their lives, American emigrants were turned away by their diplomats, often on the flimsiest of grounds. Those who had lost their passports to the coercive schemes of the NKVD were informed that they would have to be subject to lengthy periods of investigation, when there was no time to lose. Those whose passports had lapsed were refused new ones on the grounds that they lacked the necessary photographs, or the two-dollar fee at a time when possession of foreign currency was a criminal offence in the Soviet Union. Meanwhile, lurking outside the Embassy gates, the NKVD agents were waiting for the emigrants to emerge. Many American citizens were arrested in this way, on the pavement just yards from the Embassy. Alexander Gelver, a twenty-four-year-old from Oshkosh, Wisconsin, was one of those picked up outside. He was executed on New Year's Day 1938.[39]

Thomas Sgovio's friend Marvin Volat was also arrested leaving the American Embassy on 11 March 1938. The violonist and musician was accused of 'counter-revolutionary activity' and espionage for foreign powers. His interrogation lasted two long months, but eventually Marvin confessed to having taken clandestine photographs at Moscow's military airport. He was convicted and sentenced to hard labour in the camps. On the final page of his NKVD file, an official hastily recorded that Volat died in February 1939. None of his former Soviet friends could help him. His girlfriend, Sara Berman, was herself arrested as a 'CH-S', a family member of 'an enemy of the people'. Her father Matvei Berman, the former Gulag chief, had already been executed on Stalin's orders.[40]

Ten days after his friend Marvin's arrest, on 21 March 1938, Thomas Sgovio walked into the American Embassy. The midday emptiness of the waiting room surprised him. On his first visit the room had been crowded with people waiting patiently to be seen. This time Thomas was told once again that the officials were reviewing his case and that he should return in a week or so. No one warned him that his appeals and repeated visits were only placing his life in greater danger. Instead, ever hopeful and respectful of their advice, Thomas Sgovio left the American Embassy at 1.15 p.m., and was immediately arrested by the NKVD on Sverdlov Square. That afternoon it was his turn to be pushed into the back of a black Soviet Ford Model A and begin the short journey that ended in the Lubyanka. He was twenty-one years old, and had been in the Soviet Union just two and a half years.[41]

Inside the Embassy offices, the American diplomats had known about these disappearances at least as early as 4 April 1934, when Henry Maiwin had visited to register his American passport and subsequently vanished. In a memo dispatched to Washington DC, a diplomat wrote that 'persons living in Mr. Maiwin's apartment house advised an inquirer that Mr. Maiwin had been arrested by the OGPU and shot'.[42] A year later, on 16 February 1935, the chargé d'affaires, John Wiley, had reported the Soviet surveillance of United States passport and registration applicants, before stating drily: 'If American citizens can disappear in the Soviet Union without leaving a trace, the ability of the Embassy to extend protection to such citizens becomes distinctly impaired.'[43]

It is not certain what lay behind the diplomats' reaction. Perhaps they viewed these American exiles with disdain, as men and women who had turned their backs on their country and were now suffering the consequences. Perhaps the State Department was unwilling to countenance the return to the United States of those they saw as economic misfits and political radicals of varying leftist stripe whom they could scarcely have regretted to see leave. While serving in the American Consulate in Berlin in February 1931, George Kennan had written a memo on 'the status of American communists' living in the USSR: 'The question naturally arises as to whether they should be allowed to retain their American passports and citizenship . . . it is evident that American citizens become to a certain extent naturalized as soon as they step on Soviet soil.' Kennan had then advocated the use of delay as the best procedure to follow: 'If anyone is to take the initiative in getting this matter cleared up, it would apparently have to be Consular officers in the field, who could either submit reports on expatriation or hold up the renewal of passports in cases of this sort . . . Outside of new legislation, at any rate, this is the only possible means I can see of bringing about the legal expatriation of those whose moral expatriation has long since been a fact.'[44]

Whether or not his advice was put into practice at the American Embassy in Moscow at the height of the Terror we do not know. But it was certainly true that the American diplomatic staff found themselves having to explain to the visitors who had lost their American passports and their citizenship that the process was irreversible. The Soviets had simply claimed them as their own, and there was very little countervailing desire to question their judgement.[45] In Moscow, the American diplomats understood very well that low-level negotiation with the Soviet Foreign Ministry was entirely useless, given the fact that the entire Commissariat was petrified of the NKVD and were themselves the frequent victims of the Terror. Clearly more forceful intervention was required at the very highest levels of government. Had the diplomats been willing, action might still have been taken, and the lives of the American emigrants might well have been saved.

But what was abundantly clear was that if this was about to happen, the 'captured' Americans needed a heroically protective figure to intervene on their behalf – someone with the courage of Oskar Schindler or Raoul Wallenberg – someone willing to lend sanctuary, to hand out passports, to speak to the President, and to kick up a very loud and very public fuss in a time of peril. Someone, in short, who might hold a protective hand over them when their lives were so evidently endangered.

What they got, instead, was Ambassador Joseph Davies.

10

'A DISPASSIONATE OBSERVER'

To grief, even at night, the road is bright.

Innokenty Annensky[1]

Joseph Davies was a liberal lawyer who had married an heiress and thereby ascended into the rarefied world of America's multi-millionaires. As legal counsel to the General Foods empire, Davies had been invited to a dinner party of mainly anti-Roosevelt business-men hosted by the company's owner, Marjorie Merriweather Post. Their romance began when Joseph Davies launched into a passionate attack on the 'Liberty League' guests present at the table, whose conversation was spent running down Roosevelt as a man who had betrayed his class. The New Deal, retorted an indignant Davies, had not only rescued millions of unemployed American families from hunger but saved the nation from the threat of imminent revolution: 'Where would your millions be then?' The speech overwhelmed his glamorous hostess who swiftly got up from her chair and, paying no attention whatsoever to her startled guests, walked over to Davies and kissed him: 'That's what I've been wanting to say to this crowd!'[2]

Marjorie Merriweather Post was well known to the American press as 'the Lady Bountiful of Hell's Kitchen' for gifting 700 free meals every day to the destitute women and children of New York. Her press critics sniped that this was merely good public relations for a fortune that had survived the Crash unscathed, her generosity being well within her means, especially given the food business was notoriously Depression-proof. Each time one of 130 million Americans consumed an array of General Foods products – Instant Postum, Post Toasties, Sanka Coffee, Grape-Nuts, Log Cabin syrup, Swans Down cake mix, Jell-O, Minute Tapioca, Calumet baking powder, Baker's chocolate, Maxwell House coffee or any of the Birdseye frozen foods – Marjorie became a few cents richer.[3]

The profits of her brand-laden business financed one of the most lavish lifestyles in America. Luxury mansions on manicured estates scattered from Palm Beach to the Adirondacks were periodically filled with vast parties featuring 'elephants from Ringling Brothers– Barnum and Bailey Circus, and cooch dancers'. The twenties had been a sparkling decade to be very rich, and it took a while for the hosts and their guests to realise that the gilded era of conspicuous consumption was gone. From the German shipyards of Kiel, a 357-foot yacht, *Sea Cloud*, was commissioned and launched in 1931 as one of the final unwitting tributes to a decade of excess.[4] As the Depression's woes became fully apparent, Marjorie and her second husband spent long expanses of the year aboard the world's largest privately owned yacht, with its immaculately uniformed crew of seventy in attendance. It was, all conceded, so much easier to enjoy life on the high seas than back home, where the backwash of poverty left a guilty aftertaste, no matter how many mothers and their children were being fed in Hell's Kitchen.[5]

A year after their fateful dinner party, Joseph Davies married Marjorie Merriweather Post, both bride and groom having divorced their respective spouses – in Davies' case his wife of thirty-three years. Details of their wedding – Marjorie's third – were supposed to be secret but, of course, were leaked to a press eager for tales of high living in those Depression years. The wedding was reported to have cost one hundred thousand dollars, nearly five thousand of which was spent on chrysanthemums, dyed blush-pink to match the bride's dress, and an enormous three-hundred-pound wedding cake which, one reporter calculated, worked out at seven dollars per slice. If the cost was scandalous, the indignation of the press soon trailed off in the wake of the *Sea Cloud* as the couple honeymooned on a cruise through the Bahamas; and Joseph Davies contemplated his elevation to a lifestyle immune from the misfortunes of the Depression. For a man rumoured to have lost much of his own personal fortune in the Crash, it must have come as some relief.[6]

While the gossip columnists who wondered what exactly the groom had brought to their union, aside from his evident love and persuasive oratory, had underestimated the consolations of the world of politics. For Joseph Davies had remained a personal friend of

Franklin Roosevelt's from their days working together in the Wilson administration. When Davies' own political career had stalled in a failed Wisconsin Senate campaign, he clung to the coat-tails of an altogether more successful politician. And since both Davies and his new wife were very generous contributors to Roosevelt's 1936 re-election campaign, there was an outstanding favour to be returned. So when the President was casting around for a sympathetic progressive to appoint as the second American Ambassador to the Soviet Union, naturally he turned to his good friend Joe. It was a very suitable wedding gift, said the press, for the woman who had everything. And the title Ambassadress lent official recognition of an elevated status far above the mere ordinariness of uncommon wealth.

It did not seem to matter that Joseph Davies had no previous diplomatic experience, nor that he spoke not one word of Russian. All Roosevelt required was a friend whom he could trust 'to be his eyes and ears on the ground'. Leaving for Moscow, the new Ambassador was by no means overawed. He told the press that his mission was to 'counter prejudice and misinformation' and that his mind was ready for 'dispassionate observation'. In retrospect, it was difficult to imagine a worse choice to send to Soviet Russia at any time, least of all at the very height of the Terror.

In January 1937, the Davies' entourage arrived in Moscow on a special train waited on by a small army of footmen, secretaries, chauffeurs, a chef, a hairdresser and a masseuse – making up sixteen servants in all, with an attendant mountain of luggage. Stepping off the train dressed for the Russian winter in a thick fur hat, immaculately tailored coat and gold-topped cane, Joseph Davies glanced around for the first secretary of the Embassy, Loy Henderson, who recognised the Ambassador's 'flashing, probing eyes' and noted his fine clothes. Marjorie Davies, the secretary observed, was almost fifty years old but looked 'exceptionally young' and 'not travel worn in the least'.[7]

The scene at the railway station was chaotic. The Moscow police had cordoned off the entire square, and the station was crowded with Soviet apparatchiks, American diplomatic staff and a kaleidoscope of dignitaries from foreign embassies who had turned out to greet the new American Ambassador. Fighting for space in the crowd were the photographers from the Soviet and American press popping flashbulbs, while their newsreel colleagues worked under lights, with the whole circus shepherded by the NKVD. The Russian cameramen paid special attention to the gold-braided American flag attached to the left-side fender of the Ambassador's waiting limousine.

From behind the wheel of the enormous twelve-cylinder Packard shipped over from America, the Ambassador's chauffeur, Charlie Ciliberti, watched them photographing the Stars and Stripes from every angle. He also noticed how the couple's designated Soviet fixer, Philip Bender, barked orders in Russian to the station porters, who leapt to his every command with puzzling speed. In New York, Ciliberti concluded, someone like Bender 'would probably have had his ears slapped down' for taking such a tone. But in Moscow, the home of the working man, the situation appeared very different.[8] Here Philip Bender fairly exuded authority and parted crowds by showing a card in his hand to the Moscow militia, who sprang into action. Loy Henderson often felt that it was Bender rather than the American Ambassador whom the Moscow police were attempting to help.[9]

Emerging from the press frenzy, Ambassador Davies and his wife were driven slowly away from the station. The Ambassador had brought with him a home movie camera, which one of the passengers used to film through the window of the Packard as it cruised along the snow-laden streets of Moscow. Caught on film were the ordinary citizens of Moscow wrapped up in black overcoats as they ran out in front of the limousine, chasing after trams hooked up to electric cables running overhead.[10] For a crowded metropolis Moscow was unusually quiet. The streets were teeming with people but strangely empty of cars, and the majority of traffic consisted of overcrowded trams, or horses and carts, with just the occasional truck or car, whose engine noise was muffled by the snow packed down on the roads. The atmosphere was like living in a silent movie, of mute monochromatic figures silhouetted against the snow.[11]

Their chauffeur drove the American couple the short distance to their new home at Spaso House. The grand mansion with its black railings and garden covered in snow had an outwardly unwelcoming appearance, but inside, the ambassadorial residence had been extensively remodelled with furnishings and furniture imported from the United States. An interior decorator, Harry Benson, had been dispatched several months earlier to raise the mansion to the level accustomed by Marjorie Davies, and in a frantic burst of activity the tired building was transformed with all the urgent taste a multi-million-dollar fortune can command. A crystal chandelier, said to have been insured for ten thousand dollars – which took two men several days to shine – was suspended within the central dome of the ballroom forty feet high.[12] On a tour of the finished project, Elizabeth Hampel, the wife of a military attaché from St Louis, marvelled at 'oil paintings in bathrooms and gold rimmed glasses and cut crystal bottles and too much of everything that was too expensive'.[13]

In the basement, a Belgian electrical engineer had installed the twenty-five deep freezers required for two train-cars of American frozen food shipped ahead to Russia. Steaks, fowl, wild game and exotic fruit and vegetables were all now on the daily menu, with four hundred quarts of frozen cream specially imported to soothe the Ambassador's troublesome stomach. News of the couple's 'desert-island' food supply was soon leaked to the press, irritating the Soviet censors with its presumption that there was no decent food to be had in Moscow, and adding to the rolling Davies news story. The publicity only worsened when, within days of their arrival, the freezers shorted out the Spaso House generator, causing a catastrophic melt. The idea of American appetites overwhelming Soviet electricity supply became an irresistible target for mockery.[14]

On the couple's first afternoon in Moscow, Charlie Ciliberti had driven the Packard to Red Square, and the Ambassador and Mrs Davies got out to stretch their legs around the Kremlin. From the railway station they were followed, and when the Ambassador stepped out of the car, two men walked behind him at a distance. From that moment onwards, if the Ambassador ever came close to anyone who looked as though he might engage him in conversation, the lurking NKVD escort cut in very quickly. They would remain at his heels for the rest of his stay in Russia. Officially assigned for the Ambassador's personal protection, the Soviet secret police would equally ensure that no one else came near. It would not, however, prevent them from trying.[15]

Just two days after his arrival, Joseph Davies attended the second of the great Moscow show trials, the major international news story of the day. Whereas the majority of Stalin's victims were stealthily eradicated, the most famous Bolsheviks were periodically tried in a Soviet court of law. Pleased by his timely arrival, the new Ambassador assiduously attended the six-day trial, with George Kennan whispering a simultaneous translation beside him in court. They sat together at the very front of the Hall of Columns, once a ballroom of the Tsarist aristocracy, whose high ceilings and faded blue walls lent an atmosphere of decaying splendour to the proceedings. The court-room was filled with four hundred spectators, with the defendants placed in an adjacent box guarded by four soldiers standing to atten-tion, their rifles resting on the floor. Recording the scene were the microphones of the radio broadcasters and the lights and cameras of the photographers of the world's press.[16]

The American Ambassador's highly visible attendance in court was heavily publicised in the Soviet media, his presence lending to the proceedings a veneer of legitimacy, which Stalin so clearly craved.[17] The German diplomatic corps had notably stayed away en masse; and according to his secretary, the German Ambassador Schulenburg was full of 'indignation and bewilderment' at Joseph Davies' promi-nent place in the courtroom. It was, he said, as if Davies viewed the show trials 'as innocently as the dances held in the nobleman's ball-room in the Tsarist era'.[18] Quite unaware that he had managed to concede the moral high ground to the diplomatic representatives of Nazi Germany, at lunch Ambassador Davies asked George Kennan to run off for some sandwiches while he turned to chat with the boys from the American press. The publicity-hungry Ambassador courted the newspapers at all times, and perhaps realised that he could stand to use a little help with some background material.[19]

The show trials had a long and very chequered history in the Soviet Union. A decade earlier, when the trials were still in the process of being properly managed, there were obvious kinks in the mechanism, missteps in the elaborate choreography between prosecutor and defendant. These were the cases when the victim, expected only to confess, remained silent before shouting: 'Comrades how could I not sign?' and then tore off his shirt to reveal a tortured back 'streaked with deep, purple bruises and swollen welts'.[20] In past trials brother had testified against brother, and a teenage son against his father, all anxious to profess their greater loyalty to the Soviet state: 'I denounce my father as a whole-hearted traitor and an enemy of the working class. I demand for him the severest penalty. I reject him and the name he bears. Hereafter, I shall no longer call myself Kolodoob.'[21] The teenager's confession was published in the morning edition of *Pravda*, and wise readers understood very well its beckon-ing subtext of implicit violence.

In previous prosecutorial fiascos, defendants had supposedly met with people already dead, in places – such as the Hotel Bristol in Copenhagen – that turned out to have been demolished some twenty years earlier. The French President Raymond Poincaré, one of the accused Russian spies' alleged controllers, had very derisively responded that 'there must be rather gullible people in Moscow, if some actually believe or believed those fairy tales'. And the obvious question was 'Why have a prosecutor at all?' The ashen-faced defendants were always so free with their confessions, talking their lives away in fantastical conspiracies led by Raymond Poincaré or Winston Churchill or Lawrence of Arabia, or whichever other unlikely foreigner was cast as the mastermind of the Revolution's evident ills.[22]

Even in the current trial, mistakes had crept into the most carefully planned testimony. The newcomer Joseph Davies looked on as the piano-playing former Soviet Industrial Commissar Georgy Piatakov was accused of having met Leon Trotsky at an airfield in Oslo. The trembling Piatakov resembled, according to one witness, 'not Piatakov but his shadow, a skeleton with his teeth knocked out'.[23] Such was the fate of the Bolshevik once described by Lenin as 'unquestionably a man of outstanding will and outstanding ability'. Piatakov had been tortured for thirty-three days before he was broken and ready to appear before the show trial. According to Yezhov's report to Stalin, during his interrogation Piatakov volunteered to act as a prosecutor, asking that 'they allow him personally to shoot all those sentenced to be shot in the upcoming trial, including his former wife'. But Stalin had refused the request, commenting only that it would turn the trial into 'a comedy'.[24]

For the next six days, Ambassador Davies listened to the confessions of the defendants. During one intermission, he turned to a British journalist, Alfred Cholerton of the Daily Telegraph, to ask his opinion of the trial. Cholerton answered that the Soviet Union seemed to move only through convulsions, and that this, being the latest, was the most violent of all. When Davies insisted, 'No, no I am quite serious, I would like your opinion of this trial,' the incredulous Cholerton replied, 'Mr. Ambassador, I believe everything but the facts.'[25] Another reporter, from the Austrian newspaper Neue Freie Presse, wrote a more straightforward summary of the atmosphere in court: 'No analogy from modern European history is aroused in western brains when hearing of this deathly tragedy of marionettes. It is necessary to go far back, to the Middle Ages, if one wants to find a similar fervent longing for execution, a similar tired "only quickly, only quickly the end".'[26]

But still it seemed Joseph Davies could not grasp the essential idea that the entire legal proceedings were staged, an elaborate deceit played out after torture. This obvious notion seemed too fantastic, despite the prompt retort from the Norwegian government stating that the airfield cited in the supposed Trotsky–Piatakov meeting had been closed at the time to all civilian traffic. 'To have assumed that this proceeding was invented and staged as a project of dramatic political fiction,' wrote Davies back to Washington, 'would be to presuppose the creative genius of a Shakespeare and the genius of a Belasco in stage production.' The clever Cholerton might have done better to quote *Macbeth* to the Ambassador, so ever appropriate for Stalin's Russia: 'By the clock 'tis day, And yet dark night strangles the travelling lamp'.[27]

In the early hours of a January morning, 200,000 factory workers from Moscow's night shift gathered in Red Square in a 'spontaneous demonstration' to demand death sentences for the accused. The crowd was addressed by the forty-year-old Nikita Khrushchev: 'The enemy of mankind, the mad dog, the murderer Trotsky is a faithful ally of the fascists – the instigators of a World War ... The Trotskyites reptiles have been crushed. But this must not lull our vigilance ... Long live the leader of the world proletariat, the perpetrator of the cause of Lenin – Comrade Stalin!' In minus twenty-seven degrees centigrade, the crowd roared back their approval, each individual careful to display a frenzied enthusiasm to their neighbour.[28] The death sentences demanded by the prosecutor Vyshinsky were handed down to all but four of the defendants. The *Izvestiya* editor Karl Radek was given a notional ten-year sentence only to be murdered in jail. Perhaps it was vengeance for Radek's veiled irony during the trial: 'for nothing at all, just for the sake of Trotsky's beautiful eyes – the country was to return to capitalism.'[29]

Joseph Davies, meanwhile, had cabled President Roosevelt with his observation that 'the confessions bore the hallmarks of credibility'. In his diplomatic report Davies described how Stalin had uprooted 'a clear conspiracy against the government'. And as if to underline his point, the Ambassador bought up English translations of the trial – quickly published by Tass in Moscow – to send to his friends back home. Almost without exception his staff in Moscow were sceptical. George Kennan wrote to the State Department that there was 'in actuality . . . no real evidence – nothing, in fact, except vague and general contentions to show that these men ever constituted anything resembling an organization'.[30]

Shocked at the apparent naiveté of their new boss, the American diplomats met secretly in Loy Henderson's rooms to consider a mass resignation in protest.[31] Had they actually done so perhaps subsequent events might have taken a different course, but at the critical moment the officials lost their nerve and stayed silent, reasoning that Joseph Davies would be in Moscow only for another year or possibly two, and they would wait it out. Then the steady Loy Henderson warned the younger officers that while serving under Joseph Davies 'they should not indicate by word, gesture, or even facial expression a lack of respect of him'.[32]

In the meantime, life was very stressful for the American diplomats, with the demands of Joseph Davies' arrival and the stream of desperate Americans begging at the Embassy for passports or harassing them on the streets for their help. At least the ban on black market currency dealings had been abandoned. Now even the lowest-ranking diplomats could buy roubles at fifty to the dollar on the black *bourse* in Paris, which financed a handsome lifestyle in Moscow. A group of the younger American staff officers rented a dacha in the countryside outside Moscow, staffed with Russian servants, and treated themselves to 'great spoonfuls' of caviar for breakfast. There were weekend retreats of blissful calm in the midst of the Terror, in which they relaxed from the stresses of Moscow city life. In the winter of 1937, Elbridge Durbrow and Charlie Thayer brought some American records over to a public skating rink, which they managed to have played over the loudspeakers, and everyone danced along to the beat. Later they took their expensive American skis out for a run across the countryside, chased after by excited Russian children yelling 'Capitalists! Capitalists! Capitalists!'[33]

Oblivious to the mutinous intrigues of his staff, Joseph Davies cultivated the friendship of Kremlin insiders. On 17 February 1937, he entertained at lunch Boris Steiger, the Soviet diplomatic liaison officer. After a long talk over foreign affairs, Davies drew Steiger aside and asked him confidentially how he was 'faring personally' in the midst of the purges. The Russian merely shrugged his shoulders and pointed with his index finger to the back of his neck. Was this witty élan or the calm resignation of someone who knew the end was nigh? The ever-charming Steiger endeavoured to become a Davies family favourite, accompanying them to the royal box for the opera. After one performance, Steiger invited Davies' daughter Ekay and her friends to dinner and dancing at the Metropol Hotel. Shortly after midnight, while seated at their table, he was tapped on the shoulder by two men in civilian dress. Steiger excused himself and left, saying he would be back shortly. He was never seen again.[34]

A more superstitious man might have steered well clear of the American Ambassador that year. A month after Steiger's disappearance, Davies invited a party of sixty Red Army high commanders to dinner at the American Embassy, laying on the very best meal his French chefs could offer, with 'all the capitalistic trimmings' and old-fashioned American cocktails that seemed to go down very well with the Soviet military elite. Marshal Tukhachevsky was placed next to Ekay Davies, who had learned some Russian while studying law at Moscow University. The Red Army Marshal and the Ambassador's daughter had a long discussion about communism and women's rights in the USSR. Toasts followed, with Ambassador Davies proposing the health of the Red Army.[35]

Within nine weeks of the dinner, most of Davies' guests, including Marshal Tukhachevsky, had been shot. Their arrest, closed trial and execution made headline news all over the world, with political repercussions in Washington, London, Berlin and Tokyo. Naturally the Ambassador's opinion was called for, and once again Davies attempted to substantiate the charges made against his former guests: 'The best judgement seems to believe that in all probability there was a definite conspiracy in the making looking to a coup d'état by the army.' One month later, Davies continued his theme in a letter to the Secretary of State: 'It is scarcely credible that their brother officers . . . should have acquiesced in their execution unless they were convinced that these men had been guilty.'[36]

The Red Army officers who signed Tukhachevsky's death sentence were themselves executed, one by one, over the course of the year. The rationale for their deaths was that the survivors might become resentful, a state of mind that Stalin referred to as an 'unhealthy mood'. General Pavel Dybenko, one of the commanders who conscientiously signed the death warrants, was himself accused of being an American spy. Pavel Dybenko had once been described by John Reed in Ten Days That Shook the World as 'a great bearded sailor, with the clear eyes of youth, (who) prowled restless about, absently toying with an enormous blue-steel revolver which never left his hand ... giving rapid orders right and left'. Now the former Revolutionary hero was reduced to writing desperate pleas to Stalin from captivity: 'I don't know the American Language, Comrade Stalin. I beg you to look into it thoroughly.' His pleas fell on deaf ears, and Dybenko was shot along with the others. Nor were their families spared. Tukhachevsky's wife and brother were executed, while his daughter and four sisters were sent to the camps.[37]

Barely three months after his arrival in Moscow, Joseph Davies sailed back to the United States to brief Roosevelt on the Soviet criminal procedure he had watched so carefully during the Moscow show trial. What the new Ambassador never discussed, or even mentioned at the time, was the plight of the American exiles or their evident desperation to leave the USSR. This was not through ignorance, since Davies was well aware of both their existence and continued requests for help. But the Ambassador and his new wife always appeared to have more pressing business to attend.

Throughout their stay in Moscow, the American couple were consumed by an acquisitive desire for Russian art, jewellery, and pre-Revolutionary treasures on sale at the Soviet commission shops. Joseph Davies clearly understood the provenance of these items, as he revealed in a letter to his daughter Eleanor: 'These resemble our antique shops and are run by the state and sell all manner of things brought in by the owners, from pictures to bedroom sets, and from jewels to china.' Even on his industrial tours of the USSR, Joseph Davies found time to buy paintings from these commission stores, closely watched over by an NKVD officer who, if an item was oversold or misrepresented, demanded a quick refund on behalf of the grateful Ambassador. During the summer of 1937, Joseph Davies admitted his compulsion in a letter to his daughter, Ekay: 'Marjorie was much pleased with your selections at the Commission shops. As usual, we cannot resist them and have been having somewhat of an orgy again in picking up these interesting souvenirs. I definitely made up my mind not make any more purchases of pictures, but apparently I can withstand anything but temptation and I fell for four or five more very lovely ones.'[38]

Other diplomats behaved with more restraint, their consciences overcoming the bargain-hunting instinct. On one visit, Irena Wiley had encountered a distinguished-looking elderly Russian dressed in threadbare clothes. His feet were wrapped in newspaper as he offered a silver cup for sale, evidently a family heirloom. At the counter, the old man was offered such a low price that despite his obvious poverty, he declined. Outside, Irena Wiley offered to buy the cup from him at a price she thought was fair, and he accepted. When she took her purchase home and polished it up, she discovered it was an eighteenth-century silver goblet with a Moscow hallmark, worth a hundred times what she had paid for it. Then she realised that every item in the Soviet commission stores was bought on the suffering inflicted upon the Russian people. The thrill of the bargain hunt was immediately replaced by guilt; and she, for one, never went back.[39]

But Joseph and Marjorie Davies' desire for such treasures never wavered. Their keenest interest was usually in the possessions of the former Russian aristocracy, sold at discount by their executioners: 'Marjorie dearest: Here is the letter from Paris descriptive of the Orlov Tea Service and the items which we procured, for your files . . . I have talked over with Bender all of the matters you had in mind. I think I shall send him to Leningrad personally within the next few days and he will look into the matter of the Vladimir plates, the Greuse head, the tea set, and the other items.'[40] In gratitude for his ability to facilitate their acquisitions, Philip Bender soon acquired the trappings of the Davies family retinue. His fine American clothes only added to his authority.[41]

There were no exact figures, but it was clear that a significant portion of Marjorie Davies' fortune was leveraged to fund the couple's spending spree. At the time the German diplomat Hans Von Herwarth wondered if the Americans were buying 'not individual objects but whole museums' and later he would be proved correct. In the meantime, the most immediate effect was that the American couple managed to drive up the black market rouble rate in Moscow. Too busy augmenting their collections to question their behaviour, the couple kept a catalogue of their purchases that told its own story. Second on the list of Joseph Davies' Russian icons was 'an interesting example of sixteenth or seventeenth century art' taken from the Chudov Monastery during the destruction of the atheist campaign. The icon was simply titled 'Descent into Hell'.[42]

Throughout March 1937, Charlie Ciliberti was approached almost every day on the street by desperate Americans, either too scared or too well-informed to venture into the Embassy but still attempting intervention at a higher level of authority than the nay-saying official-dom of George Kennan. The chauffeur passed on the information he learned to the Ambassador during their car journeys around Moscow, but it seemed that Joseph Davies was strangely unmoved by the plight of his fellow citizens even though his public profile – and hence his ability to intervene – could scarcely have been any higher. In mid-March 1937, Joseph and Marjorie Davies were photographed holding hands and laughing for the front cover of *Time* magazine, over a quote hinting at the magnificence of their lifestyles: 'The exaggerations give both Mrs Davies and me a big laugh!'[43]

At the very moment when his presence was most urgently required in Moscow, the laughing Ambassador arrived back in New York City on 6 April 1937, pursued by a press forever hungry for news from the closed world of Soviet Russia. With the Terror entering its bloodiest phase, Joseph Davies briefed the American media on his recent observations: 'A wonderful and stimulating experiment is taking place in the Soviet Union. It is an enormous laboratory in which one of the greatest experiments in the realm of state administration is being accomplished. The Soviet Union is doing wonderful things. The leaders of the Government are an extremely capable, serious, hardworking and powerful group of men and women.' His comments were widely reported in the Soviet news-papers and left even their most vigilant censors with nothing to add.[44]

In New York, Davies made no mention of the reports of the dis-appearances of Americans in Russia, or the trainloads of prisoners seen by his Embassy officers pulling out of Moscow, or even the frantic telephone calls received after their friends had been arrested.[45] Most tellingly, he kept absolutely silent regarding the sounds that had kept his wife awake in their bedroom in Spaso House. Only years later, after their divorce, did Marjorie Merriweather Post reveal how she had listened to the NKVD vans pulling up outside the apart-ment houses that surrounded the Spaso House gardens. In the middle of the night, she had lain awake listening to the screams of families and children as the victims were taken away. These had con-tinued night after night.

Like many other historical witnesses of the Terror, Marjorie Davies was also regularly awoken by the intermittent sound of gun-fire. Once, when the noise of the guns interrupted her sleep, she turned to Joseph Davies to tell him: 'I know perfectly well they are executing a lot of those people.' To which the American Ambassador replied soothingly: 'Oh no, I think it's blasting in the new part of the subway.'[46]

None of this was mentioned at the press conference in New York. Instead, Joseph Davies travelled on to Washington DC to brief the President on the show trials and his tour of the Soviet industrial showpieces. From Ambassador Davies, Roosevelt discovered that the Soviets were introducing capitalist foundations into their economy: returning to a system of personal incentives, piece rates and new technology. At the White House, Davies exhibited the wonderful collection of Russian art he had accumulated during his short stay in Moscow. Wheeled around the pictures hanging in the East Room, President Roosevelt remarked that he 'particularly liked the vividness and beauty of the snow scenes'.[47]

11

'SEND VIEWS OF NEW YORK'

Apostle Peter, if I go away
forsaken, what will I do in hell?
My love will melt the ice of hell,
and my tears will flood hell's fire.

Nikolay Gumilyov[1]

Joseph Davies returned to Moscow via London, where the Ambassador and his wife had been invited to the coronation of George VI. At the Coronation Ball, the Ambassador noted that Marjorie 'created a sensation' with her jewels and white satin gown outshining even the maharajas and European royalty gathered at Buckingham Palace. Outside, the crowd had started to cheer Marjorie when she waved to a child, accidentally mistaking her for the princess of a monarchy as yet undeclared.[2] In London, Davies' thoughts on the Moscow show trials gave the sceptical Winston Churchill a 'completely new concept of the situation'. This English understatement was taken at face value by the delighted Ambassador, who embarked on a leisurely tour of European capitals before eventually returning to his post in Moscow on 24 June 1937.[3]

His diplomatic staff had spent the intervening weeks investigating Soviet attempts to bug the Embassy and the Ambassador's residence. Below stairs in Spaso House, the Russian servants ate at separate tables from the Americans, officially because the two groups could not understand each other.[4] But there was also a certain strangeness among the Russians, who often spoke better English than they let on and seemed to live in fear of an employee named Sam Lieberman. Strange wiring had recently been discovered in Spaso House, artfully concealed yet comically betrayed by a pile of fresh cigarette butts found next to a hiding place in the attic. A trap was set to catch the chain-smoking spy with trip-threads running across the attic attached to an alarm. But each morning the young American diplomats discovered the threads cut and the power to the alarm switched off, until eventually their cat-and-mouse game ended when they stayed up all night to catch Sam Lieberman red-handed, emerging from the attic. Lieberman admitted everything quite brazenly but received only a reprimand.[5] The day after his return to Moscow, Ambassador Davies declared their efforts a complete waste of time. There was 'nothing to hide' from the Kremlin.[6]

Instead, Davies treated the prevalence of microphones, hidden all over the Embassy and Spaso House, as a source of his own amusement. At the British Embassy, the Ambassador had met a Welsh military attaché, and for fun they conspired privately to speak the language of Davies' grandparents over the telephone. Not long after their conversation began all the phone circuits were cut, and a short while later rumours began circulating the diplomatic community that America and Great Britain were engaging in war plans. Conversations had been heard in an 'American-Indian language' that no one in Moscow could translate.[7]

While driving the Ambassador around Moscow, wherever his chauffeur Charlie Ciliberti parked the shining Packard, a crowd of Russians would immediately stop and gather around. Ciliberti understood people's natural curiosity but winced at the fingerprints smeared over the car's immaculate body and windows. Children especially felt compelled to touch the beautiful American machine, whose wing mirrors were constantly being twisted by mischief-makers trying to catch sight of their own reflection. Tired of having to shine the expanse of bodywork at almost every stop, when one of the mirrors and a door handle went missing Ciliberti sought the counsel of his Russian chauffeur friends. They advised him to adopt the practice of the Soviet elite, whose luxury cars were protected by an electric current which gave curious hands a nasty shock. Using a battery, coil and plumb, Ciliberti engineered a similar system for the Packard, and very soon when he was parked on Moscow's city streets no one dared come too close.[8]

Only the American emigrants were drawn almost irresistibly to the beautiful electrified limousine – just as they had been drawn into the Embassy on Mokhovya Street. The gold-braided Stars and Stripes flown from the fender of the Packard, and the car's familiar

New York licence plate, carried a similar promise of salvation.[9] In June 1937, a harassed Ciliberti was parked on Stoleshnikov Pereulok, waiting for the Ambassador to emerge from his latest shopping trip. Their NKVD escort was somewhere in the vicinity but not especially close that day, and Ciliberti happened to meet another American on the street and stood idly chatting as the Moscow crowds milled around them. Quite unexpectedly, in the midst of their conversation, Ciliberti noticed a blonde girl standing close by, watching them intently and smiling as if she understood every word they were saying. Glancing round, Ciliberti asked the girl in Russian if she spoke English. 'I was born in Cleveland,' she replied deadpan.

Unaware of the extent of the emigration, and having no sense of the number of young Americans, just like this blonde eavesdropper, who were trapped in the Soviet Union, Charlie Ciliberti and his friend stood on the street quite amazed. When they asked, the girl told them that she had been brought to Russia by her parents six years earlier, when she was fifteen. But just as she started her story, Ambassador Davies reappeared quite suddenly, and Ciliberti had to jump back into the Packard to drive him on to his next destination.

The American chauffeur was thirty-one years old when he arrived in Moscow by way of New Jersey. A handsome man personally chosen by Marjorie Davies – whose appreciation for beauty appeared to extend to her employees – Ciliberti's intelligence was revealed when he voluntarily chose to study Russian during his evenings off and quickly acquired a conversational ability that neither the Ambassador nor his wife ever came close to matching. Perhaps in a 1930s novel, the bright working-class chauffeur from Jersey City might have defied authority and leapt to the rescue of this young girl from Cleveland, driving her back into the safety of the American Embassy. And Ciliberti did meet the girl again, either by accident or because the Packard was so easy to spot, on the same street a week later. But this was reality, not fiction.

At their second meeting Ciliberti learned only that she was a twenty-one-year-old American citizen; and did nothing more than advise her to present herself at the Chancery. Recalling the episode in a memoir published nine years later, Ciliberti revealed an unapologetic indifference towards the fate of the girl whose name he did not recall:

Whether or not she tried to get out I do not know. If she did she probably was picked up, since the Chancery was watched as closely as the Embassy and anyone who visited there was suspect. If she really was an American, the American authorities would do all they could for her. She had told me she could get the money for her passage. If she did get picked up, it was either because she went into the Chancery, or because she talked to me when the GPU was with me. I know one of the GPU heard her speaking English to me and I didn't like the look in his eye. He was a new boy. We had lost two of our old GPU guard.[10]

Later Ciliberti wrote that he did not want to go 'out on a limb' in case the girl was a 'phony'. Not wishing to risk his job, he chose to do nothing at all for the Cleveland girl, who must have known the risk she was taking by meeting him twice on the street but would have calculated that it was less dangerous than walking into the Embassy.[11] Given his status and close relationship with the Ambassador and his wife, Ciliberti had sufficient authority to protect her life if he chose. But he was either unwilling or persuaded by his uncertainty. Charlie Ciliberti elected to remain safe and warm in the fur-lined American coat bought for him by Marjorie Davies. He never saw the girl again.

Rather than risk the antagonism of the NKVD escort, Ciliberti chose instead to win their friendship. At first he tried bribing them with cartons of Camel cigarettes, or by slowing down when their tailing car stalled to allow them time to catch up with the Packard. Later he worked out a system of warning blasts on the horn to give the NKVD enough time to warm up their unreliable Soviet Ford engine before departure. In return, Ciliberti received a nightly ride back to his hotel from the NKVD, after he had dropped off the Ambassador at Spaso House.[12] Soon Ciliberti was supplying the NKVD agents with gifts from America – they asked for contraceptives in particular – and as a consequence of this favour swapping he remained untouched when virtually every other Davies family servant was arrested on the streets of Moscow during the course of the year.[13] Agar Lindstrom, Marjorie's hulking Swedish masseur, was picked up in broad daylight soon after leaving the Italian Embassy where he had gone to give a massage to the Italian Ambassador's wife. The brawny Swede refused to go quietly, and a mighty struggle ensued until the NKVD agents were persuaded to drive Lindstrom back into the American embassy.[14] Perhaps it was because Ciliberti was never arrested that he had so little sympathy for the 'captured' Americans. 'They made their bed, let them sleep on it,' was his attitude, which ultimately was much the same as that of Ambassador Davies, who shrugged his shoulders and politely sighed that there was nothing to be done.[15]

Shortly after their return to Moscow, Joseph Davies and his wife embarked on a summer cruise around the Baltic. Before he ordered the *Sea Cloud* to be sailed to Leningrad, Davies had first consulted with Maxim Litvinov to check whether such a defiant expression of American capitalism might offend the Soviets. His question had only made the jovial Foreign Minister laugh. 'Why of course not, Davies. We respect and trust you even though you differ from us in political ideology.' The Ambassador's next question revealed the full extent of his naiveté of the first principles of this totalitarian state: 'Now then, Litvinov, I want to ask you a still more delicate question. Do you think that it might possibly be blown up in the harbor by one of your Bolsheviks?' Once again, Maxim Litvinov struggled to hide his amusement: 'Davies, it will be safer in the harbor of Leningrad than in the harbor of New York . . . Our police force are more efficient.'[16]

In his journal Joseph Davies wrote that he had smiled at Litvinov, who smiled back, 'for he knew that I had seen their visits in the night to take heads of family into custody never to be seen again'. But in public, Davies gave not even the slightest hint of his knowledge or disapproval at the time. That summer the *Sea Cloud* motored out of Leningrad harbour on a Baltic cruise, escorted through the minefield by a naval vessel of the secret police. The Ambassador then very politely invited his NKVD guardians aboard to watch Hollywood movies in the ship's cinema. After a long discussion and 'much amazement', the men in the pale blue caps accepted his invitation.[17]

Charlie Ciliberti, meanwhile, was left behind in Leningrad with Philip Bender. Picking up a telegram at the Hotel Europa, Ciliberti accidentally walked through the wrong door into a room where twenty men and women were studiously bent over desks writing screeds on pads of paper. Among them he recognised the Russian woman who had been their guide in Leningrad. When Cilberti asked Bender what it was he had just seen, Bender only smiled. 'What do you think?' he said. 'She is probably writing up everything we said today,' Ciliberti answered. And Philip Bender, who had spent his youth working as an organiser for the Industrial Workers of the World in San Francisco, and had long exhausted his life's given supply of irony, merely replied, 'Charlie, you catch on quickly.'[18]

It was the normal course of events in Soviet Russia. The longer an American stayed, the more likely this painted world was to reveal itself. Although there were obvious exceptions to the rule – most notably the Ambassador, now happily watching movies aboard the *Sea Cloud* with his friends from the NKVD. The summer weather was so blissful and the sea air so bracing that Joseph Davies declared the *Sea Cloud* would become 'his floating Embassy' in Russia. Presumably by doing so, he would avoid any more unwelcome confrontations on the street.[19]

While Davies cruised the Baltic on his yacht, letters continued to 'pour in' at the American Embassy in Moscow, and the State Department in Washington, from anxious relatives across the United States searching for their missing loved ones in Russia. These letters would carry on arriving throughout the course of 1937 and 1938, and intermittently thereafter for the next two decades.[20] Some were sent by Americans who had been freed from the camps in the early thirties and managed to return home. Emma Popper, for example, wrote on behalf of Timothy Belakoff, whom she described as an American passport holder who had arrived to work in Russia as an engineer on an Amtorg contract in 1931, only to be arrested shortly afterwards. She had met Belakoff in a prison hospital suffering from malnutrition and in a 'worsening' state of health. In her letter sent from New York, Emma Popper enclosed a small piece of black bread, which she said she had brought back with her from her Gulag camp as evidence of how little they were given to eat. A State Department official read her letter, filed it and then placed the morsel of Russian bread in an envelope, where it remained, dried and preserved in the archives for the next seventy years, a strange relic of the lost American emigration to Stalin's Russia.[21]

Some of the correspondents had lost their entire families. Mrs Edythe Habacon of the Bronx, New York, wrote asking for news of her parents, brother and sister, all missing in Russia. Her brother and sister, named Carl and Sirkka Hakanen, she wrote, were born in Boston and had simply disappeared. Another letter came from Lillian Burton, of Detroit, seeking help on behalf of her father, Paul Burton: 'I am writing concerning the disappearance of my father from his home in Russia . . . I am sure my dad would not willingly stop writing to us . . . therefore I am trying to locate him as I feel something is wrong. Can you help me find my father?' Sarah

Dansky's brother was searching for his sister, who had volunteered to work in Russian hospitals as a doctor before vanishing: 'On account of late purges in that country, we feel that she may have met with foul play.' Bennett Cooper of Wilmington, Delaware, wrote on behalf of his brother John Cooper, an American engineer whose regular correspondence had ended abruptly: 'it is unlike him to forget or neglect'. Bennett Cooper's reply from the State Department was typical of the official reaction to such letters: 'Since Mr Cooper no longer has the status of an American citizen, this Department is unable to take any steps which may assist in the obtaining of information with respect to him.'[22]

A letter from Mrs Hilma Oja of 1999 Madison Avenue, New York, dated 24 October 1938, provided evidence of hundreds of Americans in the same position:

> Dear Secretary Hull, We the parents of Mrs Bertha Kylma, (nee Bertha Kortes – born in Painestale, Michigan, December 26, 1915) want to report that she, a citizen of the United States, is being held against her will in Carelia, Russia, USSR! Please reply at once what can be done to enable her to return to the United States. We have definite proof, from her – by letter, that she is being held prisoner for no reason at all and that she is being forced to suffer untold misery. She says several hundred other women of American citizenship are also being imprisoned on several islands which are in Lake Ladoga.[23]

An insurance salesman, B. Jaffe, wrote to the State Department on 2 May 1938 asking for assistance for his brother Harry Jaffe, who had lived in Russia since 1933, working for the *Moscow News* before becoming an English teacher. Harry Jaffe had written home every two weeks until February 1938, when his correspondence abruptly stopped.[24] This was surely the same Harry Jaffe who had sung the tenor solos beside Thomas Sgovio in the Anglo-American Chorus. The father of another one of Thomas's friends, Abraham Volat of 458 East Ferry Street, Buffalo, New York, addressed a handwritten letter to the American Secretary of State:

> In 1932, my son Marvin Volat, age 20, applied for a passport to go to Europe to study music. The passport was granted to him and he left the state. He was in London and Paris but could not

stay there on account of the world depression. Then he decided to go to the Soviet Union . . . A year ago last March we received a letter from a lady friend of his telling us that Marvin was in an accident. She did not specify the nature of the accident. That was the last we heard of him . . . Mister Secretary as a citizen of this country and Marvin born in Buffalo, I appeal to you to take a hold of this matter through our Embassy in Moscow to find out whatever became of him . . . I sincerely hope my wish will be fulfilled under your supervision,

Yours truly,

Abraham Volat.

Eleven days later, Abraham Volat received a terse reply from the State Department: 'Since your son no longer has the status of an American citizen, this Department is unable to take any steps to which may assist in the obtaining of information with respect to him.'[25]

Another father, Yakim Dubin of 233 Tenth Street, Pottsville, Pennsylvania wrote asking for help for his son Ivan, who had called at the American Embassy on 1 March 1938 to apply for a passport and had been told that he was missing the required photographs and to come back when he had them. His father had called in at his Congressman's office excited because he had discovered the address of Ivan's concentration camp in Russia. Now, apparently, the State Department could do something.[26]

But no concerted action was ever taken on their behalf, at the State Department in Washington or the American Embassy in Moscow, or from the Presidential office at the White House. Instead there was just an uncomfortable silence, and these missing men and women and their children were simply left to their fate. In 1937, at the height of the Terror, Ambassador Joseph Davies contrived to remain outside Soviet Russia for precisely 199 days of the year, either at home in the United States, touring Europe or cruising the Baltic on his yacht. Anywhere save the very place his presence was so urgently required.[27]

Only rarely did the news of the arrest of an American in Russia ever make it into the newspapers back home. Joseph Davies was away in December 1937 when an American reporter told Embassy officials of the sudden disappearance of his neighbour, Donald Robinson, from the National Hotel, the building adjacent to the American Embassy. When Angus Ward and Loy Henderson knocked on the door of Room 333, Donald Robinson's wife told them that her husband had fallen sick and been taken to a hospital, where he was being kept in an 'iron lung'. The American diplomats returned to the hotel room the following day, only to discover that Ruth Robinson had also disappeared.

On this occasion, news of the couple's mysterious disappearance bypassed Soviet censors to become a sensational crime story in the American national press. The mystery deepened when a State Department investigation revealed that the American passports issued to Donald and Ruth Robinson had been obtained in the United States by fraud. The Soviet newspapers, meanwhile, denounced the couple as 'American Trotskyite spies', the news of which prompted Max Schactman, a friend of Trotsky's, to reply acidly: 'There is nobody in Russia, except the Government, who can cause people to disappear like that. The Soviet Union has no private gangsters who kidnap people and hold them for ransom ... If the couple are alive today, they are in some dungeon in Lubyanka Prison.'[28]

In her passport photograph, Ruth Robinson gave the impression of a very attractive woman in her late twenties, with hazel eyes and light brown hair styled in a fashionable bob. Loy Henderson, who had met her briefly in her hotel room, wrote to the Secretary of State that her 'speech and gestures were those of an American woman who has lived for the most part in native American environments and who has had at least a secondary education. She did not appear to be Jewish.' Quite why Henderson chose to speculate upon her religion was less surprising – given the anti-Semitism of many within the State Department at the time – than the subsequent FBI discovery that Donald Robinson was, in fact, a Latvian Communist whose real name was Adolph Rubens. It was confirmed, however, that his wife was indeed an American citizen, and Ruth Rubens's only mistake appeared to have been marrying a man who had used her for his own ends. On 28 December 1937, Constance Boerger was interviewed by the FBI, and positively identified her younger sister, Ruth, born in Germantown, Pennsylvania. She told the investigators that her sister had left behind a daughter in America. On 30 December 1937, the *New York Daily News* printed a photograph of Ruth Delight Rubens, aged seven, with her dog Brownie, taken at her grandparents' home in Miami, Florida.

In Moscow, because of the publicity their disappearances had received in the United States, the American Embassy officials were finally spurred into action, and pressed to be allowed to visit Ruth Rubens, whom everyone knew was being held in custody by the NKVD. After a lengthy delay, the Soviets bowed to pressure and gave unprecedented access to Ruth Rubens, held captive in Moscow's notorious Butyrskaya prison.

At four o'clock on the afternoon of 10 February 1938, Loy Henderson was driven into the prison. A huge sliding iron door, operated by heavy machinery, opened slowly to allow his car into the courtyard. The First Secretary was then escorted down a maze of corridors into an interrogation room where he was introduced to Major Yamnitsky of the NKVD. A bell was rung and Ruth Rubens suddenly appeared, led under guard into the room dressed in a 'simple woollen American house-dress with low neck and long sleeves'. The twenty-nine-year-old American prisoner, wrote Henderson in his report, was 'under complete domination of Major Yamnitsky . . . who insisted that English questions and answers be translated into Russian.' Loy Henderson then described how Ruth Rubens had

changed greatly in appearance since Mr Ward and I had seen her in the National Hotel on night of December 8th. Her face was puffy and swollen. She had a sallow complexion and seemed completely broken in spirit. Although she appeared to be listless, and talked in a monotonous tone of voice, I could ascertain from the clenching of her hands and other involuntary movements that she was under severe nervous strain . . . she kept her eyes fastened on Major Y, until he told her that she could sit in a chair at the side of his desk between him and us.

When Loy Henderson asked if he might offer her a cigarette, the NKVD Major snapped, 'there was no reason why Mrs Rubens should be given a cigarette'.

Their interview lasted forty-five minutes, at least half of which was spent translating the questions and answers into Russian for the benefit of Major Yamnitsky. Ruth Rubens confirmed that she was born in Philadelphia on 27 May 1908 and explained that her husband had given her the passport in the name of Robinson: 'I know my husband has committed a serious crime against the Soviet Union and I feel that the Soviet authorities are justified in their actions against me. I quite understand their reasons for holding me. I am grateful for your offer of assistance, but I request you not to try to help me. I intend to stick to my husband.' At this point Loy Henderson asked if she had any children, and showed her the picture of Ruth Delight cut from the New York *Daily News*. The little girl's mother looked at the picture, and tears welled in her eyes as she confirmed that this was indeed her daughter. Their interview continued rather abjectly – 'Do you have an attorney?' 'Not yet.' 'Do you desire the services of an attorney?' 'No.' – until Major Yamnitsky decided he had heard enough and rang the bell again, which brought the armed guard back into the room. At this point Henderson wrote, 'Mrs Rubens stood up, and at signal from Major Y turned a right-about-face and marched out with the guard without a word of farewell and without even a backward glance.'[29]

During his debriefing in America, the Soviet defector General Walter Krivitsky revealed to the FBI that when Stalin was first told of the procedure for American naturalisation and citizenship, his reaction had been one of delight: 'Wonderful – send a thousand men to America at once and let them sit there.' Krivitsky also confirmed that Adolph Rubens had been

> sent to the US to get genuine American passports which could be used with no alteration preferably, or with merely a change of photograph if alteration were required. He said that prior to the adoption of the new style passport by this Department it had been possible to manufacture in Moscow the passports needed, taking apart genuine passports, washing the pages, and making up new ones to suit their needs. They found it impossible to remove the covers and take apart the present style passport without the operation leaving noticeable marks.

As well as explaining the mystery of the couple's disappearance in Moscow, Krivitsky provided further corroborative testimony as to why the NKVD had been so keen to confiscate the passports of the American emigrants to the Soviet Union.[30]

But it seemed that few people were willing to take Krivitsky's statements seriously, or his frequent complaints that Soviet agents were tracking him for the past two years in New York. In December 1939,

Krivitsky telephoned Loy Henderson 'very alarmed for fear that attempts upon his life might be made immediately'. Henderson's response was to advise him to call the New York Police Department. On 10 December 1941, the body of Walter Krivitsky was discovered lying in pool of blood in a room at the Bellevue Hotel in Washington DC. A bullet from a thirty-eight-calibre revolver had passed into his right temple. An alleged suicide note was found at the scene, but one month before his death, Krivitsky had told a friend: 'Don't you ever believe that I will be a suicide. They have shot everybody else and they are going to shoot me.'[31]

According to Loy Henderson's memoirs, 'the Soviets never once informed American diplomatic or consular officers of the arrest of an American citizen within time limits. Usually we learned of the arrest through letters received from US, through persons in the Soviet Union acquainted with the person under arrest, or from a person who had met the arrested man in prison.'[32] Occasionally a press article was brought to the attention of an American diplomat, and the relevant cutting would be attached to an existing or newly created file. By this means the State Department learned of the imprisonment of George Sviridoff, 'a sixteen- or seventeen-year-old fair-haired boy' who had been discovered as a stowaway on the steamer *Kim*, leaving the USSR bound for the United States. For the 'crime' of attempting to exit the Soviet Union illegally the American teenager was sentenced to ten years' 'corrective labour'.

Remarkably, and almost uniquely in the case of George Sviridoff, two handwritten letters sent from his concentration camp reached his father in America, most likely via an intermediary living in Russia. His father had then passed these letters on to the State Department in an effort to impress upon them the severity of his son's ordeal. The first letter was dated 10 July 1936:

Dear Papa,

I am now in the far North in Vorkuta, not far from the island of Varchaga. I am working at present as a driller and in general work in a mine as a miner. The material conditions are all right but you know, Papa, in one word, a camp gets you in the end, no matter how good it may be, but you are subject to the regulations of arrested persons and cannot live in peace . . . Send food suitable for the North, photographs, views of

New York, one sweater with a fastener, Papa, answer immediately.
The post here does not operate accurately. Time is precious . . .
    Your Loving Son,
        George.

A year later a second letter arrived from Vorkuta, the Gulag centre
in northern Siberia, located above the Arctic Circle. The second letter
was dated 17 July 1937:

Greetings dear Papa
    . . . I have had one letter from you during three years and
two months. All hope has collapsed . . . Dear Papa, I did not
want to upset you up to now, but it would be even sadder were
you not to know my actual situation and whereabouts . . .
Now Papa my fate is sealed. I have left you, lost my country,
lost my freedom, lost all the delights of life . . . there remains
only to lose in addition my head, which may happen not being
able to live through it all. Today is a day which brought me
much unpleasantness. I refused to work in the mine.
    Your loving son,
        George Sviridoff.[33]

His case, in particular, sparked a moment of compassion from the
State Department officials. On 1 June 1938, George Kennan wrote a
lengthy note, attached to Sviridoff's case file:

The Soviet Government has the administrative power to arrest
and hold incommunicado indefinitely any American citizen in the
Soviet Union . . . Should this person have at the time of his arrest
only American nationality the Soviet authorities apparently have
only to notify us that he has been admitted to Soviet citizenship
in order to create a situation in which under our usual practice
we would not press further representations in his behalf . . . The
upshot is that in reality no American citizen resident in the Soviet
Union has any assurance that we will be able to help him in case
the Soviet authorities should take repressive action against him.
The situation is such that these people are virtually at the mercy
of the Soviet authorities . . . Logically we should refuse to recognize the naturalization of Americans in the Soviet Union as
voluntary and valid in the absence of confirmation of the

voluntary character of the act on the part of the person concerned ... An alternative would be to give publicity to the real
situation, with a view to relieving the Department and the
Embassy at Moscow of further responsibility for the protection
of our citizens resident in the Soviet Union.[34]

George Kennan's belated recognition of the coercion used to strip
Americans of their citizenship and his idea of publicising their existence was, in retrospect, their only hope of salvation. But no such
publicity was ever attempted, and Kennan was unwilling to act
alone. Just like the others, he remained silent.

12

'SUBMISSION TO MOSCOW'

To save one life is as if you have saved the world.

The Talmud

As the Terror worsened, Joseph Davies wrote steadily more bizarre cables to the State Department: 'The secret police is the personal agency of Stalin and the party. It is in the saddle and riding hard! The new head of the organization, Ezhov, is comparatively a young man. He is constantly seen with Stalin and is regarded as one of the strongest men in the government. His effectiveness and ability are greatly respected . . .' At the celebrations for the twentieth anniversary of the Revolution, Davies had watched Yezhov – 'a man of very short stature almost a dwarf but with a very fine head and face' – standing constantly close to Stalin, 'whispering and joking with him.'[1]

By the spring of 1938, the Ambassador's diplomatic staff in Moscow were reporting the daily arrests and disappearances of friends and their relatives. One member of Davies' staff witnessed 'a struggling unfortunate being arrested and torn from his eleven-year-old child on the street in front of the adjoining apartment house at 3.30 a.m.'[2] In March, as Charlie Ciliberti waited for Ambassador Davies, the chauffeur watched the NKVD struggling to pull a fourteen-year-old boy into their car. The boy refused to go quietly and a silently sympathetic crowd of Muscovites gathered to watch the scene. When the American Ambassador unexpectedly appeared, as if by a miraculous force the NKVD released the boy immediately. It was proof that the Ambassador had the power to save lives, if only by his presence. But Joseph Davies deigned to use this power only by accident, and never by design.[3]

Instead, that same month, Davies attended the last of the Moscow

The Moscow Foreign Workers' Club vs the Gorky Auto Workers Club baseball game, Moscow, June 1934 (Sgovio Collection)

George Bernard Shaw tours Russia in the summer of 1931, gathering material for a radio lecture to an American audience (Russian State Archive of Film and Photographic Documents)

Henry Ford after the Amtorg deal is signed in Dearborn, 31 March 1929 – Ford stands between the Soviet commissar Valery Mezhlauk and Amtorg chairman Saul Bron, both of whom will be executed during the Terror (Collection of the Benson Ford Archives)

Stalin's love for the automobile, undated 1930s (David King Collection)

The atheist campaign in Nizhni Novgorod – rubble from the demolished churches was used for the construction of the new auto factories (Dmitriev photo archive/Nizhni Novgorod City Museum)

The first American Ambassador William C. Bullitt arrives at the Hotel National in Moscow, circa December 1933. The permanent American Embassy is still under construction next door on the site of a demolished Russian church (William C. Bullitt Papers, Yale University)

The American reporters vs diplomats baseball match in Gorky Park, 4 July 1934 (William C. Bullitt Papers, Yale University)

Laughter during the Terror: Ambassador Joseph Davies and Marjorie Davies on the front cover of *Time* magazine, March 1937
(Time & Life Pictures/Getty Images)

SPASO HOUSE

Enclosure No. 5 to SECTION II
(CONTINUED), 3, QUARTERS, of the
report on the Moscow Embassy,
dated March 15, 1937.

MOKHOVAYA BUILDING

Top: Spaso House in winter – at night from her bedroom Marjorie Davies listened to
the screams of her neighbours being arrested

Bottom: The American Embassy on Mokhovaya Street – the American emigrants
were arrested on the pavement outside (National Archives II, College Park, Maryland)

Ambassador Joseph Davies and Marjorie Davies dressed for a Moscow winter (Marjorie Merriweather Post Collection, Hillwood Museum and Archives, Washington DC)

The Ambassador's Packard draws a crowd – the twelve-cylinder Packard attracted the attention of curious Muscovites wherever it was parked, including the American emigrants drawn to its NY licence plate and the Stars and Stripes on the fender (Charles Ciliberti, *Backstairs Mission to Moscow*)

The American chauffeur as a witness – Charlie Ciliberti poses in front of the Packard with his NKVD escort watching in the car parked behind (Charles Ciliberti, *Backstairs Mission to Moscow*)

'The Floating American Embassy' – Marjorie Davies's yacht *Sea Cloud* in full sail, 1939 (Mystic Seaport, Rosenfeld Collection)

Stalin beside Commissar Yezhov at the Moscow-Volga Canal. After his subsequent execution, the image of Yezhov disappears from the picture (David King Collection)

An NKVD execution squad, 1936 (David King Collection)

show trials. Sitting once again at the very front of the court, on this occasion the Ambassador knew personally many of the famous names sitting in the defendants' box just ten feet away. Among them was Doctor Pletnev, the Kremlin cardiologist who had treated him several times in Moscow. In his diary Joseph Davies wrote that he found it difficult to look at Pletnev: 'for fear our eyes would meet. They faced death and were in a desperate and hopeless plight.'[4]

Beside Pletnev in the defendant's box sat Arkady Rosengoltz, the former Commissar for Foreign Trade, who had entertained Davies and his family in his mansion as the two men spent long days negotiating the Soviet debt. During the trial, Rosengoltz was mocked by the prosecutor, Vyshinsky, because his wife was discovered to have sewn into his jacket a copy of the Ninety-First Psalm.[5] During the Great War, Russian soldiers had carried excerpts of the psalm either in an amulet or sewn into a piece of their clothing to offer protection from the bullets and shells. Twenty years later, Stalin's prisoners were repeating the old traditions of Mother Russia:

> *Thou shalt not be afraid for the terror by night;*
> *Nor for the arrow that flieth by day;*
> *Nor for the pestilence that walketh in darkness;*
> *Nor for the destruction that wasteth at noonday.*
> *A thousand shall fall at thy side, and ten thousand at thy*
> *right hand; but it shall not come nigh thee.*

In the courtroom for a special report, Walter Duranty noticed, high above the judge's table, a space resembling a window, which was screened so that nothing could be seen through it bar the occasional lighting of a match, or the glow of a cigarette. In this small room overlooking the courtroom, Duranty wrote that Stalin sat watching the enactment of the confessions his NKVD interrogators had so carefully scripted.[6]

This third show trial was even more fantastic than its predecessors. First up on to the witness stand was Nikolai Bukharin. Once described by Lenin as 'the most able man in the Party', he was now accused of plotting the murders of both Lenin and Stalin, of conspiracy to return capitalism to the USSR, and of having worked for British and German imperialists since 1921.[7] Preserved in the Russian state archives is a letter – dated 13 March 1938 – which Bukharin wrote to Stalin from his prison cell, pleading for his life:

The former Bukharin has already died, he no longer lives on this earth. If physical life were to be granted me, it would go for the benefit of the socialist motherland, under whatever conditions I would have to work: in a solitary prison cell, in a concentration camp, at the North Pole . . . let a new, second Bukharin grow . . . great historical frontiers will be crossed under Stalin's leadership, and you will not lament the act of charity and mercy that I ask of you: I shall strive to prove to you, with every fibre of my being, that this gesture of proletarian generosity was justified.[8]

The Party's former ideologue ought to have known the futility of asking for 'proletarian generosity' from Stalin, the man so dedicated to 'proletarian ruthlessness'. Bukharin had devoted his entire life to the ends of the Bolsheviks. He once told William Bullitt that on the ninety-first day of the Revolution, Lenin had wrapped his arms around him, saying: 'Isn't it wonderful? We have lasted 91 days, one day longer than the French Commune!' Now Bukharin poured out his confession to the court and waited for his sentence to be announced, like a carpenter who has laboured furiously day and night only to step back and discover he has constructed his own gallows.[9]

Beside him in court sat Henrikh Yagoda, the once-feared GPU chief who had persecuted the Soviet regime's enemies mercilessly throughout a long and very bloody career. Now Yagoda confessed to a conspiracy with Trotsky and of having masterminded espionage for Germany all along. Yagoda also claimed responsibility for the assassination of Kirov, the murder of the writer Maxim Gorky, and a plot to kill his successor Yezhov by redecorating his office with poisonous paint. Awaiting trial in his prison cell, Yagoda joked of his sudden belief in the existence of God. 'It's very simple,' he told his guard. 'I deserved nothing but gratitude from Stalin for my loyal service. I had earned the severest punishment from God, however, since I broke his commandments a thousand times. Now look where I am – and decide for yourself whether God exists.'[10]

Only one of the old Bolsheviks, Nikolai Krestinsky, was willing to disrupt the smooth flow of their confessions. As Deputy Commissar for Foreign Affairs, Krestinsky had accepted the diplomatic credentials of Joseph Davies on his arrival in Russia. Now Krestinsky astounded the court by announcing he was 'not guilty' of all charges. The consternation forced the presiding Judge, Vassily Ulrich, to call for an immediate adjournment. The following day, normality returned as Krestinsky requested to change his plea to guilty: 'Yesterday, under the influence of a momentary strong feeling of false shame caused by the atmosphere of the prisoners' dock and the painful impression created by the reading of the indictment, aggravated by my poor state of health, I could not bring myself to speak the truth, could not bring myself to say that I was guilty. And, instead of saying – yes, I am guilty. I replied almost mechanically – no, I am not guilty.'[11] A friend who had known him before the Revolution commented at the time: 'You know they must have done something awful to Krestinsky because I simply didn't recognize him on the second day. Even his voice was somehow different.'[12] Later it was discovered that Krestinsky had been severely tortured and admitted to Butyrskaya prison hospital for treatment to his back, which was described as being 'like a single wound'.[13]

Privately the defendants were reminded of the methods to be used against them if the 'correct' testimony was not received in court. Their fate, therefore, depended not only on what they said but *how* they said it. Thus when Judge Ulrich gave Bukharin the veiled hint that he was defending himself, Bukharin responded frantically: 'This is not my defence. It is my self-accusation! I have not said a single word in my defence!'[14] His subsequent confession was abject: 'I am responsible as one of the leaders and not merely as a cog . . . I do not want to minimise my guilt, I want to aggravate it.'[15] As the old Bolsheviks reeled off their crimes in self-abasement, the sweat poured from their faces in front of the blinding Klieg lights dazzling the courtroom for the newsreel cameras of the world's press.

At 4 a.m. on 13 March 1938, Judge General Ulrich once again read out the defendants' names, followed by a monotonous drone of death sentences: 'To be shot, to be shot, to be shot, to be shot.' In the majority of cases their family members were also arrested and sent to the camps, the promises of leniency revealed as yet another cruel deceit. Thus Bukharin's young wife, Anna, was torn from her one-year-old child and sentenced to twenty years' imprisonment. To entertain his boss Stalin's bodyguard, Karl Pauker re-enacted the moment when Bukharin was led away to his death, kicking and screaming and clinging to the shoulders of his guards shouting: 'Please, somebody call Joseph Vissarionovich!' Watching Pauker's impersonation, Stalin laughed uncontrollably, tears streaming down his face, until he had to wave to his bodyguard to stop. Later Pauker too, was shot.[16]

From Mexico, the last survivor of the Revolution, a scornful Leon Trotsky, likened the proceedings in Moscow to the 'witch-trials of the medieval inquisition'. Stalin's most famous living enemy had already noted that 'Krupskaya once said in 1927 that if Lenin were alive he would probably be in a Stalinist prison.'[17] Now Trotsky set to work destroying the credibility of the trial: 'the whole Communist Political Bureau and almost the whole Communist Committee of the heroic period of the Revolution, except for Stalin, are proclaimed agents of the restoration of capitalism. Who will believe this?' Within three years Trotsky, too, would be murdered by the 'special tasks' agents of the NKVD, but not before his rhetorical question was answered. The one man willing to believe every word was sitting at the very front of the court.[18]

From Moscow, Ambassador Joseph Davies wrote to Secretary of State Cordell Hull: 'After daily observation of the witnesses, their manner of testifying, the unconscious corroborations which developed ... it is my opinion so far as the political defendants are concerned sufficient crimes under Soviet law ... were established by the proof and beyond a reasonable doubt to justify the verdict of guilty of treason.'[19] No other American diplomat working under Davies shared his view. His diplomatic aide, Charlie Thayer, summed up their consensus in his diary entry for 2 March 1938: 'I have this moment heard the indictment on the Bukharin trial read over the radio. A more incredible document I could hardly have imagined. *Gulliver's Travels* sounds in comparison like a scientific exposition of Euclid ... The Russian may be naïf, but this is too much for a dog to believe.'[20]

Considering the Ambassador's reaction to the trial, it was unsurprising that Davies did so little to help the American emigrants being arrested in Russia. While run-of-the-mill emigrants lacked sufficient influence to bypass the ranks of Embassy officials, the Ambassador did occasionally receive one of the more highly placed of the exiles. Shortly after the end of the Bukharin trial, he sat down for a meeting with Tamara Aisenstein, a naturalised American artist whose husband had signed on as an engineer for the Soviet Oil Trust before he was arrested. As an enthusiastic art collector, Joseph Davies might have sympathised with the fate of Tamara Aisenstein, whose paintings of Californian landscapes had recently been exhibited at the Moscow Union of Soviet Artists. Her West Coast impressionism had only attracted the hostility of Soviet art critics, the hyper-vigilant guardians of Stalin's socialist realism: 'We are faced with a naive, slightly lady-like art with a clear and even deliberate bent towards infantilism . . . they lack life, they are not pervaded with a sense of reality, nor warmed with the breath of living man.'[21] Sitting in his office, Ambassador Davies patiently explained to Mrs Aisenstein that since both she and her husband had received Soviet citizenship, they were no longer entitled to his protection. And, like many others before her, she was forced to leave the Embassy empty-handed.[22] She, too, was arrested shortly afterwards and little more was said on the matter. Only Monroe Deutsch, the provost of the University of California at Berkeley, wrote a letter, in vain, to Secretary of State Hull asking for intervention on behalf of his former student, who was 'well known to many engineers in the region and his artist wife Tamara, who had left behind many good friends in California.'[23]

If Davies' conscience troubled him, there is no evidence to suggest so. Above all else, the Ambassador sought to avoid even the slightest appearance of conflict with the Soviet authorities. He left complete responsibility for the protection of American citizens to his staff. If pressed by the State Department, according to Loy Henderson, he would talk to the Foreign Minister Litvinov 'in an apologetic manner as though he were asking a personal favour'.[24] According to Maxim Litvinov's official diary, preserved in the Russian state archives, at one particular lunch party Joseph Davies *did* politely ask about an arrested American citizen whom he requested to be released and expelled '*if possible*'. But Litvinov had simply sidestepped the issue, explaining that he was leaving Moscow soon, and requesting that Davies address the matter to the 'Third Western Division of the Soviet Foreign Affairs' – the usual bureaucratic dead end for American diplomatic enquiries. In an internal memorandum drafted to his Soviet colleagues, Litvinov added, 'I see no need for explanations with the NKVD. The Ambassador named the prisoners, but I cannot recall them.'[25]

Clearly Maxim Litvinov had not the slightest desire to entangle himself in the affairs of the NKVD, especially when he was in fear for his own life. From 1937 onwards, the Soviet Foreign Minister slept with a revolver next to his bed, 'so that if the bell rang in the night, he would not have to live through the consequences'. But unlike Litvinov, Ambassador Joseph Davies could never claim his life was in danger. Only at the very end of his Moscow posting did the puzzled First Secretary, Loy Henderson, understand the real reason for the American Ambassador's curiously supine behaviour. But by then it was already all too late.[26]

At the beginning of one of the hottest Russian summers in living memory, on 5 June 1938, Ambassador Davies was summoned to the Kremlin to exchange diplomatic farewells with Maxim Litvinov on the eve of his departure from the USSR. When Joseph Stalin unexpectedly walked into the room, a meeting took place that Davies later described as causing 'nothing short of a sensation in the Diplomatic Corps'. For the past several years, Stalin had consistently refused to meet the ambassadors of even the great powers.[27] Through the course of the Terror, the Soviet Leader had grown ever more reclusive, appearing in public only rarely, on May Day or at the anniversary of the Revolution, when he would stand and wave from Lenin's Mausoleum, above the roar of the crowd below.

Catching sight of the almost mythic figure of Stalin walking towards him, Joseph Davies leapt to his feet and began an off-the-cuff speech describing how he had 'heard it said that history would record Stalin as a greater builder than Peter the Great or Catherine'. Davies then explained how honoured he was to meet 'the man who had built for the practical benefit of common men'. Well used to such sycophancy, Stalin showed no surprise at the unctuous flattery pouring from the mouth of the American Ambassador. Instead he preferred to talk business, asking what was holding up Soviet arms purchases from the United States; and why, when he was offering a hundred million dollars in cash, were the Americans so reluctant to sell them their latest battleships? Soviet representatives were locked in their thirteenth month of negotiations with Navy officials in Washington, although Roosevelt himself had already approved the deal. Ambassador Davies duly promised to expedite matters, and the two men continued a two-hour discussion ranging from the political situation in Europe to the personality of Franklin Roosevelt.[28]

Returning to his office at Spaso House, Joseph Davies was unable to contain his joy, telling Henderson: 'I have seen him; I have finally had a talk with him; he is really a fine, upstanding, great man!' Loy Henderson later described how the Ambassador confided that 'this was one of the great days of his life, that the President had instructed him that his main mission in Moscow was to win the confidence of Stalin, to be able to talk over Soviet–American relations frankly and personally with Stalin, that he had been striving ever since his arrival in Moscow to carry out this mission, and that just on the eve of his departure he had finally succeeded'.[29] After the meeting, in a letter to his daughter Davies wrote that Stalin 'gives the impression of a strong mind which is composed and wise. His brown eyes are exceedingly kind and gentle. A child would like to sit in his lap and a dog would sidle up to him.'[30]

On their departure from Russia, once again the diplomatic corps turned out to see the American couple off from Moscow's Belorussky station. A delighted Marjorie Davies was presented with the parting gift of a pair of vases from the Sheremetev Palace and, just before the train departed, the Soviet chief of protocol, Vladimir Barkov, rushed up to the Ambassador and handed him a silver frame with four red stars embossed in its corners, holding an autographed photograph of Joseph Stalin.[31] The gift gave Davies an opportunity to write Stalin a gushing letter of thanks:

I shall always value it. It will occupy a prominent place in my photographic gallery of the Great of the Earth. May I say, also, that I was deeply gratified at the opportunity of meeting you personally before I left Moscow. It has been my privilege to meet the most (and to know quite well some) of the great men of my time. I was, therefore, very glad to meet, and measurably to feel that I now know, the leader of the Great Russian people; and to find in him a greatness of spirit that is absorbed in the cause that he is serving, and one who has the courage to dare and to do what he considers to be for the benefit of the common man.[32]

True to his word, Joseph Davies kept the signed photograph of Joseph Stalin in its silver frame on prominent display in his library for years to come. It was an inadvertent reminder of the lives he had not saved, and of the man who had killed them.[33]

Faced with similar circumstances, other diplomats behaved very differently. Dr Heinrich Pacher-Theinburg served as the Austrian Ambassador to Moscow through the worst period of the Terror. During the summer and autumn of 1937, small groups of Austrian emigrants had sought refuge at their embassy as they attempted to escape the predations of the NKVD. The conservative and aristocratic Pacher-Theinburg was faced with a difficult choice in respect of these

Austrian asylum seekers, whose left-wing politics he plainly did not share. Like his American contemporaries, Pacher-Theinburg clearly understood that all foreigners were being methodically arrested in Stalin's Russia, often immediately after they left their embassy buildings. Like the Americans, too, he was fully aware of the consequences of NKVD arrest: the reports circulating Moscow of torture, executions and concentration camps were impossible to avoid. Unlike his American counterparts, however, Ambassador Pacher-Theinberg felt sufficiently compelled to save the lives of his fellow Austrians by offering them shelter in the basement of the Austrian Embassy.

Just feeding these refugees during their months of confinement stretched the resources of Pacher-Theinburg to their very limit. Quite predictably, the Soviet authorities did their utmost to obstruct this small ark of salvation from the Terror. But fearful of an international scandal, eventually the regime allowed the lucky group of refugees a negotiated exit from the Soviet Union under Pacher-Theinburg's protection. According to Loy Henderson, the Austrian Ambassador saved the lives of between twenty and thirty young men in this way. He had little opportunity to do more. By March 1938, Hitler's *Anschluss* had deprived Pacher-Theinburg of a country to represent. The Austrian diplomat returned with his family to Vienna and severe financial hardship. For rare individuals, the choices they made in response to the crimes of totalitarianism were relatively simple. There was no other acceptable moral alternative.[34]

For their part, the American Embassy staff did attempt to keep a list of Americans in the USSR. But given the disinclination of the NKVD to inform the Embassy whenever they arrested another American emigrant, unless the diplomats learned of the disappearance from a relative in the United States or through a personal friend of the victim contacting the Embassy, they remained none the wiser. Even the starting point for their list was wrong since there were no records for the majority of Americans who had arrived at the beginning of the Depression, during the three years before the Embassy opened. Instead, the diplomats resorted to advertising in the pages of the *Moscow Daily News* to gain a clearer picture of the numbers. Although they gathered sheets and sheets of American names, many of which they subsequently marked with a cross or an asterisk to signify their arrest, the project remained fraught with error.[35] Neither Thomas Sgovio nor any member of the Sgovio family, for example, ever appeared on the American Embassy list, although Thomas had visited the Embassy at least twice before his arrest. The American Embassy list – unlike Oskar Schindler's four years later – became a source of self-deception rather than salvation.

In April 1937, during one of Joseph Davies' lengthy absences, Ambassador J. K. Huddle visited the Moscow Embassy in his role as the State Department's Inspector of Posts. In his official report Huddle wrote that he discovered the Moscow Embassy in a state of considerable disarray: 'When I arrived I must regretfully state that morale was almost at the breaking point ... The embassy in Moscow is afflicted with a tenseness, a nervousness, an apprehension of the unseen – a victim as is everything and everyone else in Moscow of the OGPU. Members of the staff and their families have been arrested and held temporarily on numbers of occasions, American members, even officers.'[36]

Among his recommendations, Huddle criticised even the creation of this fragmentary list of Americans on the grounds of sheer wastefulness:

In January and February of each year almost the full time of one stenographer seems to be required for ten days for the work of typing a descriptive list of American citizens residing in the Soviet Union ... Of the 872 listed ... only 100 were persons whose presence in the Soviet Union has any political and economic significance to the Government of the United States. The other seven eighths of these persons now living in the Soviet Union represent merely flotsam and jetsam on the sea of life. They are born, live and die, and their existence has probably no individual effect on any governing or supervising authority.

As well as substantially underestimating the number of American emigrants in Russia, Ambassador Huddle regarded this 'flotsam and jetsam' as valuable only in terms of a footnote for the State Department files. With bureaucratic detachment, Huddle acknowledged there might be cases of 'intense human interest and such a case report might be of later historic value'. As an example, he quoted the letter of 'lad born in Ohio in 1918' who had written to the Embassy for assistance on 15 January 1937. The unnamed nineteen-year-old boy was obviously desperate:

I beg you once more to do something for me as soon as possible because I can't stand it here any longer. I am learning now and it is very hard for me to live. I have no place to live and only get

eighty rubles a month, and you know yourself that on eighty
rubles a month you can't live. I have a grandfather, grandmother,
aunts and uncles in the United States and I know I won't have to
suffer there like I do in the Soviet Union. 'A free country'. That's
what the Russians say, but for me it is not a free country.

What happened to this nineteen-year-old Ohioan, Huddle never
recorded, nor was the government inspector moved to action. As one of
the 'flotsam and jetsam' in Russia, it appeared this American teenager's
life held no significance to the government of the United States.[37]

Alexander Kirk was the senior diplomat left in Moscow after
Joseph Davies' departure. In the summer of 1938, Kirk wrote to
Secretary of State Hull, informing him of the disappearance of further 'former Americans' after they had visited the Moscow Embassy.
Elmer John Nousiainen, an American passport holder from
Daisytown, Pennsylvania, had arrived at the Embassy on 18 July
1938 with news of mass arrests of the American emigrants in
Petrozavodsk. Directly from this eyewitness the diplomats learned
how 'hundreds of families have been broken up and the morale of
the inhabitants completely broken'. In the preceding fortnight, two
hundred Americans had been arrested when the NKVD launched an
'industrialization drive'. The majority were young men taken in the
night. Elmer John Nouisiainen gave chilling details in his statement
to the diplomats: 'No cause is given. The sons are not even allowed
to say good-bye to their mothers; the apartments are always
searched; all things foreign are taken by the authorities ... The
young people are afraid to go home. Several girls have been arrested.
One in the last stages of pregnancy was left behind with the warning
that her case would be settled later.' The city's ski factory, which had
once employed 160 Americans, was shut down and all its workers
rounded up after local Communists accused 'all foreign-born persons of being spies, wreckers, saboteurs'.[38]

Elmer John Nousiainen was twenty-two years old at the time,
his biography that of a typical American emigrant to the USSR. In
Pennsylvania during the Depression, his father was a miner put out
on the dole. His mother and father had sold their home and packed
up their belongings in search of work in Russia.[39] After delivering
his report on the Terror among the Americans in Karelia, Elmer was
allowed to leave the Embassy building in Moscow. No attempt
was made to warn him, to hide him or even to delay his departure.

Outside on Mokhovaya street, the twenty-two-year-old Pennsylvanian was arrested by the NKVD.[40]

In a memo copied into Nousiainen's file and sent on to Washington DC, Loy Henderson expressed a certain weariness and attempted to excuse the Embassy's inaction:

> It appears that persons who are considered by the Soviet government to be Soviet citizens are from time to time arrested if it is ascertained that their call at the Chancery is for the purpose of endeavouring to establish American citizenship or if they insist that they are also American citizens . . . I fear there is little which the American Government can do in this matter. No protest or action, in my opinion, can change these Soviet practices . . . Our citizens fare no worse than other foreigners in Soviet Union. In fact, the citizens of a number of other countries have encountered treatment which in so far as I know has not been meted out in our generation by one country to the citizens of another with which it has formally friendly relations. You will recall the recent despatch from our Embassy, for instance, containing the statement that more than 20,000 Greek citizens have been arrested.[41]

The snatched arrests of American nationals outside the Embassy had been taking place for the past four years, and yet each new case was treated as if it were the first. Later two more American exiles, Henry Webb and Bruno Wuori, were stopped outside the Embassy building – but, for unknown reasons, were released. They then returned inside the building to 'point out their interrogators to members of the Embassy staff as being the two plain clothes individuals whose custom it was to loiter or stand in front of a shop window between the Hotel National and the Embassy building within approximately forty paces of the entrance to the Consular Section'. By December 1938 an unnamed American embassy official, presumably a recent arrival, had typed another note to Washington: 'Formerly there was a steady and considerable volume of correspondence between the Embassy and Americans of dual nationality, most of whom are young, in connection with their efforts to renounce Soviet citizenship, but during last year there has been a noticeable decline in this class of correspondence, which the Embassy is at a loss to explain.'[42]

*

On his return to the White House, Joseph Davies gave a full briefing to President Roosevelt on his lengthy conversation with Stalin. At the Soviet Embassy in Washington, Davies explained to Konstantin Oumansky – the former censor turned diplomat – how Roosevelt had questioned him closely and he had described Stalin as 'a sage, simple man, who can look ahead and combine dignity with affability'. For his part, Oumansky wrote back to Moscow that Joseph Davies had told him that he 'took all measures to stop the campaign on the Rubens case organized by officials from the American Embassy in Moscow in his absence without any pressure from Washington'.[43] It seemed the American Ambassador was apologising for the attempted intervention on behalf of Ruth Rubens in Butyrskaya prison.

Despite an intense lobbying campaign, Franklin Roosevelt passed Joseph Davies over for the promised Berlin ambassadorial post, with the tactful excuse that to appoint someone of his 'high profile' might send the Nazis the wrong message. The world travels of the 'freshman ambassador' had already prompted a sceptical reaction in the American press, and the President was acutely sensitive to bad public relations and obviously wary of a repeat performance in Berlin. As a consolation, Joseph Davies was appointed ambassador to Belgium, where the potential for damage was obviously more limited. After brief service in Brussels, Davies turned his attention to writing *Mission to Moscow*, a memoir of his diplomatic service in Russia, full of praise for Stalin's tough-minded ability to protect himself from internal threat.

Quickly re-titled *Submission to Moscow* by the diplomats who had served under him, Davies' book was published in 1941, just as America entered into a wartime alliance with Stalin. For an American public still reeling from the shock of Pearl Harbor the book provided welcome reassurance that their democracy was in alliance with a fair-minded and trustworthy Soviet leader, as characterised by Davies, rather than the ruthless and genocidal dictator already responsible for the death of millions. *Mission to Moscow* became a runaway international success, selling 700,000 copies in the United States alone, and topping the bestseller lists in the thirteen languages into which it was translated. On the flyleaf of the personal copy he kept at his bedside, President Roosevelt wrote the words 'this book will last'. Buoyed by the success of the President's favourite memoir, Joseph Davies returned to his wife's Florida estate at Mar-A-Lago to recuperate. For the Americans he had left behind in Russia, life was to follow a very different course.

13

'KOLYMA ZNACZIT SMERT'

> Whoever was tortured, stays tortured. Torture is ineradicably burned into him.
>
> Jean Améry, *At the Mind's Limits*[1]

After his arrest outside the American Embassy, Thomas Sgovio was escorted to a Moscow militia precinct before being placed in a Soviet Ford and driven the short distance to the Lubyanka. Almost immediately an NKVD officer began the interrogation: 'Tell us of your espionage activities. We know you are a spy. You have to tell us.' Usually the arrested prisoners were met with a cascade of blows, but Thomas was not beaten, perhaps because early on in the interrogation he admitted to being homesick. His words were written into his NKVD file as a confession: 'When I came to the USSR everything was so strange and I felt hostile to the Soviet system so I decided to return to America which is my real homeland.'[2]

Later Thomas was taken to Taganka prison for processing. Here the prisoners were fingerprinted, photographed and strip-searched. Barbers cropped their heads with clippers and shaved their bodies; buttons were cut off, belts and shoelaces confiscated, pockets turned inside out, and those with gold teeth were taken to the prison dentist. Then the arrested prisoners were pressed into the already desperately overcrowded cells. There were 165 men in Thomas's cell in Taganka prison – so many they could barely shuffle their feet.[3] In the midst of this ordeal, when Thomas heard the piercing screams of the men and women inside the jail, he still did not fully understand what was taking place around him. A fellow prisoner had to explain that the unearthly noise was simply some poor soul being beaten. Even then, Thomas's reaction was one of naive amazement. He was not yet willing to believe that a person could be tortured within the Soviet prison system.[4]

The prisoners were beaten by teams of NKVD interrogators working in shifts, who kept their victims awake for nights on end until they signed the confessions placed before them. Usually the more fantastic the charges, the greater the ferocity required in a system known by prisoners and guards alike as 'the conveyor'. In the memoirs of the survivors, there were many examples of those driven mad under the strain of their ordeal. A tortured Red Army officer, Colonel Vikhorev, asked his interrogator, 'Tell me, this counter-revolutionary organization of which I am a member – does it really exist?[5] A member of the Communist Party of Palestine, Ephraim Leszinsky, was beaten so savagely to force him to confess the names of his 'accomplices' that he broke down in tears in his cell, banging his head against the wall and shouting, 'What's that other name I've forgotten? What's that other name I've forgotten?'[6] Often the final outcome of the 'conveyor' was mental breakdown. Lucien Blit, a Jewish Bundist, recorded the outburst of a powerfully built peasant from Kolno, who awoke the entire cell to tell them he was Jesus Christ and that it was time they took him down from the cross. His screaming lasted for five days.[7]

In Taganka, Thomas Sgovio's cellmates included Harry Jaffe, the tenor from the Anglo-American Chorus, and Michael Aisenstein, the naturalised American engineer from California whose artist wife had attempted intervention with Ambassador Davies. The oil engineer explained that he had been arrested after an informer had denounced his unwise comment that 'in America the unemployed were better off than Soviet engineers'.[8]

In the city of Gorky – 420 kilometres east of Moscow – between 'fifty and seventy bodies' were removed each day from the NKVD headquarters on Vorobievka Street. According to one survivor, a prisoner was nominated to whitewash the cell walls to remove the names left behind by the dead. The desire to leave some trace of their existence appeared to have been a common impulse among those who sensed the end was fast approaching.[9] At night in Gorky, screams were heard emerging from the NKVD prison courtyard – 'No. Don't shoot, Comrades! Don't shoot me, I have done nothing wrong!' – followed by the crack of a gunshot, a brief silence, and then another shot to make sure.[10]

Inside this building, another surviving American was taken from his prison cell for interrogation. Victor Herman was confronted by the figure of a swaying, slightly drunk NKVD guard who introduced himself as 'Citizen Belov' and then demanded: 'You will tell me about your counter-revolutionary activities. I will hear every one!' When Victor failed to respond, the heavy-set interrogator ordered him to turn around and face the wall. Then Belov began to punch the twenty-three-year-old Detroiter with steady blows to his kidneys.[11]

Torture was a legally sanctioned method of inquisition in the USSR. Stalin had issued an explicit instruction for a long-standing practice on 20 January 1938: 'physical pressure in NKVD practice is permissible . . . physical pressure should still be used obligatorily, as an exception applicable to known and obstinate enemies of the people, as a method both justifiable and appropriate.' Many NKVD interrogators framed these words on their desk to act as a continuing threat when they grew physically tired of beating the prisoners.[12] Nor was there ever a shortage of men such as Belov, happy to don a new uniform and, in exchange for increased living space and food allowances, to torture these 'enemies of the people'. A newly hired NKVD staff member earned between 1200 and 1500 roubles per month, roughly twice the income of a Soviet official with ten years' experience, and that was excluding the potential bonuses for their 'special work'.[13]

The moral boundaries had been redrawn some two decades earlier. The arrested were no longer to be regarded as fully human, worthy of compassion. Instead, they were re-categorised as something 'other', outside the fold of 'progressive' humanity, whose excision could only benefit the construction of a classless, socialist society. Within this totalitarian underworld, an enthusiasm to inflict physical violence upon such 'enemies' was regarded as a cherished character trait by an organisation that elevated the psychotic to the heroic and feted their most successful. This was the NKVD's heralded 'revolutionary instinct' with teeth barred, which turned a brutal interrogator such as Belov into a local celebrity – the generator of corpses collected every day from the building on Vorobievka Street.

Each night Belov would punch Victor Herman's back three times on his right side, and then again on the left. He would pause, pacing himself by stopping to drink a beer or whisky, before starting up again with steady deliberation. Shortly after midnight, Belov would begin and he would continue until dawn. On the first night Victor Herman managed to stay on his feet, but on the second night he fell, and every night thereafter. On the eleventh night, Belov pressed his fingertips across the length of Victor's back, in a macabre imperson-ation of a medical doctor asking his victim where it hurt. Victor remained silent, but when he flinched, Belov sensed he had found his mark. After the fifteenth night, Victor began bleeding from his penis, his rectum, his nose and his eyes. He was returned to his cell each morning at dawn. Eventually the cell 'elder' pleaded with him to talk – 'Save your life, American' – but Victor Herman stubbornly refused to confess to a crime he had not committed.[14]

On the fifty-third night of his torture, he was told he would be released if he only signed a list of names. When Victor again refused, he was taken to a basement cell and beaten by a gang of men with clubs. The next morning he was coughing up clots of blood, and the following night he was beaten again and told he was going to be killed. Losing consciousness, Victor was woken by the sensation and smell of his leg being burned to bring him back round. On the fifty-fifth night, believing that he was about to die and knowing that he might never get the chance again, Victor Herman spat in Belov's face. He woke up in the prison hospital.[15]

Lying beside him in the hospital ward was a prisoner named Romanoff, who had also emigrated from Detroit to work in the Soviet Ford factory. Romanoff was in a terrible state but seemed oddly cheerful; he said he would soon be released and then find a way to return home to Detroit. When Victor asked how this was possible, Romanoff told him that he had signed a confession denouncing McCarthy, an engineer at the auto factory, as an American spy. The following night, Romanoff died in the hospital of internal injuries. At this point, convinced that he too would be beaten to death, Victor Herman signed the confession placed before him. He was immediately returned to his crowded holding cell, where he recognised another American from the auto factory, a man named Janssen, lying prostrate on the concrete floor with blood bub-bling from his mouth. A few hours later Janssen's body was removed from the cell.[16]

A Polish prisoner, Z. Stypulkowski, detailed the psychological effect of torture by the NKVD: 'After fifty or sixty interrogations with cold and hunger and almost no sleep, a man becomes like an automaton –

his eyes are bright, his legs swollen, his hands trembling. In this state he is often convinced he is guilty.'[17] With sufficient beatings, a prisoner lost even the sense of his own self, which had been broken and replaced by an overwhelming fear. New prisoners quickly learned the value of confessing their 'crimes' and spitting out names. Their compliance often saved their lives.[18] Some chose to incriminate everyone they knew, hoping vainly to overload the system of terror. Others attempted to name only the dead. But given time, even the toughest minds dissolved under the brutality of the conveyor. Under extreme duress, it was easier to consider oneself a Trotskyite spy working for Germany or Japan than to keep hold of your past. In such circumstances the mind gently protects the body from that which it can no longer endure.

Between interrogation and sentencing, Victor Herman was transferred without warning into a very different cell, which held just nineteen prisoners in far less crowded conditions. As he entered the doorway he saw a perfectly clean white towel laid out in front of him. As soon as he stepped around this towel, two heavily tattooed prisoners jumped down from their bunks to attack him. What they did not expect was that Victor Herman was a trained boxer who, even in his weakened condition, could fight off two untrained men. When a third prisoner came towards him with a prison-made knife, Victor worked him like a heavy bag in the gym, holding the man's body up over his shoulder and continuing his frenzied attack until the man slumped to the floor. At this point, the atmosphere in the prison cell changed dramatically.[19]

Thrown in with a group of Russian criminals, or *urkas*, Victor Herman discovered that his savage fighting skills had won their immediate respect. A heavy man with a scarred face and dark eyes beckoned him over: 'I am the Atoman, the chief here, and you, fighter, what are you? A wolfblood, yes? One of us, yes?' Far from being angry, the Atoman appeared pleased: 'Hey fighter! . . . Next time you wipe your feet on the towel, yes?' And thus began Victor Herman's first lesson on how to pass among the criminals, a casual introduction into the subculture of murderers and thieves used by the Soviet authorities to terrorise the 'enemies of the people'. From the Atoman, Victor learned why he had been transferred to that particular cell: 'They put one in here, and we do the rest, you know?' And when the NKVD guards returned to find the wrong body lying on the floor, the Atoman explained that there had been an accident. 'It was a bad fall,' he shrugged.[20]

Perhaps because they were both young and physically fit, Victor Herman and Thomas Sgovio survived their months in prison. In time each was convicted of 'crimes' against the Soviet state, and each was handed a piece of paper with their name and a number written on the back and circled in red.[21] Victor Herman received a 'ten', whereas Thomas Sgovio's paper showed only a 'five', but their sentences carried a purely arbitrary quality since their prosecutors did not expect them to survive. And for their part, all the prisoners sent out into the 'zone' of the 'corrective labour camps' would look back upon their time spent in jail with the curious nostalgia reserved for the easiest part of their sentences. Within the Gulag, both Victor Herman and Thomas Sgovio would suffer ordeals far worse than that which they had already known. For suffering comes not only from the pain one receives, but also from the pain one inflicts on others in trying to survive.

On the night of 24 June 1938, Thomas Sgovio left Moscow sealed into the carriage of a prison train with roughly seventy other prisoners. They formed one unit of a transportation of prisoners, packed tight onto the train for their long journey east. These NKVD prison trains had been specially modified with steel spikes under the carriages to prevent escape and machine gun emplacements on the roofs. The number of cars on each train ranged from between 60 and 120, allowing several thousand prisoners to be moved at a time to destinations across the Soviet Union's vast Gulag system. The prison trains moved slowly, in part because of the number of cars on the line but also because the drivers feared the consequence of an accidental derailment. And the slow progress was regularly interrupted by guards, who hammered on the walls, ceilings and floors of the train with wooden mallets to check that the prisoners were not attempting an escape.[22]

None of the prisoners knew their final destination, although there was an expectation that the further they travelled the worse it would be – and to a certain extent this was true. But the measure was only relative, not absolute. While Victor Herman's journey ended in the forest wilderness of central Russia, Thomas Sgovio was transported across the entire length of the USSR, to the very end of the line. His ten-thousand-kilometre journey locked in the carriage lasted twenty-eight days, and every stop along the way was marked by the burial of prisoners who had died on board the train. This too, was completely normal.[23]

A month after his train's departure, Thomas arrived starved and traumatised at a vast transit camp near Vladivostok, on Russia's Pacific coast. His transportation was still not over. Here the prisoners waited within a barbed wire enclosure, inside a vast city of eighty thousand souls, ready for the next stage of their descent.[24] It was the place from which the poet Osip Mandelstam managed to send his last letter in December 1938, the month of his death: 'My health is very poor. I am emaciated in the extreme, I've become very thin, almost unrecognisable, but send clothes, food and money – though I don't know if there's any point. Try nevertheless, I get terribly cold without any [warm] things . . . This is a transit camp. They didn't take me to Kolyma. I may have to winter here.'[25]

All prisoners would experience the same shock of the vertiginous fall into the abyss, and at every moment when they believed they had reached the final depths, they would fall again, lower and lower, until they scarcely recognised themselves as human beings. Only then – when they had lost all self-awareness and respect – when they existed only in the most savage primal sense as men stripped bare of all humanity; only then would they have arrived at the very heart of the Gulag. And in this state of starving desperation they would hardly recognise their loss. They would be dismissive of even the notion of freedom – like Kant's dove, which feels the weight of the air on its wings and thinks that it can fly better in the void.

The Vladivostok holding camp was a vast field where, according to one survivor, 'as far as the eye could see there were columns of male and female prisoners marching in one direction or another, like armies on a battlefield. A huge detachment of security officers, soldiers and signal corpsmen with field telephones and motorcycles, kept in touch with headquarters, arranging the smooth flow of these human rivers.'[26] At intervals the guards would shout warnings – 'Those who are bored with life should take one step out of the column' – while unlocking the bolts of their rifles. Their prisoners had little idea what awaited them, nor were there any explanations. In the holding camp, they died by the score in epidemics of typhus and dysentery, or they were murdered by the criminals in their midst. Attempting to survive, the English-speaking prisoners of Thomas Sgovio's transport grouped together. With Michael Aisenstein, Thomas came across an American bootlegger who had escaped jail in California only to be arrested in the Soviet Union. The American had sold off all his clothes and was left in a pitiful, ragged condition, swearing, 'I'd kiss a skunk's ass to be in a prison in California again, even if it was for life.'[27]

After weeks of waiting, the prisoners were eventually marched down towards a fleet of ships waiting at anchor in the Vladivostok dockyard. The NKVD ships were old tramp steamers, which once had names like *Commercial Quaker*, *Ripon* and *Dallas*, and had been bought up in America and Europe for rock-bottom prices after the Crash. The smokestacks of the Gulag fleet were painted in the blue of the NKVD, but the ships themselves were always at the very margins of seaworthiness. Already old and decrepit when they were bought, the fleet had since been corroded by the fierce weather, the sea salt, and the ice floes.[28] Now Thomas Sgovio found himself being pushed down a steep and slippery wooden stairway into the filthy depths of the ship. It took a while for the prisoners' eyes to adjust to the dim light of the lower decks, but looming out of the darkness was a scene that one survivor compared to a nightmarish vision by Francisco Goya.'[29] In the cavernous depths of each ship were crammed five or more levels of wooden bunks containing thousands of battered men and women who had been arrested from all over the Soviet Union. Thomas Sgovio was pressed into the human cargo of the steamer *Indigirka*, which ferried between three and five thousand other prisoners north across the Sea of Okhotsk, into another world. He remembered the date of his transportation exactly. It was 2 August 1938, three years to the day since he had left New York harbour on the deck of a passenger liner, waving goodbye to the Statue of Liberty bound for Soviet Russia.[30]

The *Indigirka* steamed north out of Vladivostok towards the Arctic Circle, passing through the narrow Straits of La Perouse and across the Sea of Okhotsk. The voyage of the prisoners could last up to two weeks depending on the sea conditions, and during that time no guard ever ventured down into the hold. They feared the savagery of the criminals who reigned in the darkness below, robbing the political prisoners of their food and clothing. Their attacks were impossible to withstand; if any political prisoner dared resist, a pack of criminals simply murdered them. One fallen Red Army general, Aleksandr Gorbatov, who had survived five sessions of torture by the NKVD in Lefortovo prison, described having his boots stolen by a gang of thieves in the hold of the *Dzhurma*. His decision not to fight back very likely saved his life.[31]

Terrible events regularly occurred on these sea transports. The criminals would often break through the thin partition walls of the hold to attack the female prisoners who travelled with them. These mass rapes were reported in many survivor accounts and appeared to have become a ritualised part of the Sea of Okhotsk crossing. One female witness remembered watching the horror of the violence inflicted upon her fellow prisoners in close proximity. Over the screams of their victims, the criminals most violently abused the women who resisted. In one instance, two female prisoners were left dead in the bottom of the hold.[32]

Although the escorting guards were heavily armed, their usual response to such events was to do nothing. Only if the riots below decks became too unruly would any action be taken. Then the hold would be drenched with freezing ocean water from the fire pumps. One ship, the *Kim*, set out from Vladivostok carrying three thousand prisoners. When the prisoners mutinied, starting a fire below deck, the guards simply flooded the hold and the prisoners arrived in Magadan frozen from hypothermia.[33] Similarly, if one of the Gulag ships was caught in a storm or ran aground, its human cargo would be abandoned to their fate as the guards attempted to save their own lives, firing shots at the prisoners to prevent their escape.

Fifteen months after Thomas's transportation, on 13 December 1939, the *Indigirka* ran aground on a reef in shallow waters just a mile off the coast of Japan. At the time the ship's hold contained 1,200 highly skilled engineers and scientists specially selected from the Gulag population to return to the 'mainland' as part of the Soviet preparations for war. Three days after the wreck, the Japanese authorities learned from the *Indigirka*'s captain that he had abandoned the ship with the prisoners still alive inside, trapped under the upturned steel hull in only a few feet of water. A Japanese rescue team was dispatched to the wreck with cutting torches but they found only corpses trapped in the cold dark space. The prisoners had clambered on top of each other in their desperation to survive. Just twenty-eight prisoners were discovered alive at the top of this pyramid.

It was the end of the ship built in 1920 in Manitowoc, Wisconsin, and originally named the *Ripon* in honour of the town where a group of American Republicans first announced there could be no political compromise with slavery.[34]

Thomas Sgovio spent six days and nights trapped inside the darkness of the *Indigirka*. As the atmosphere grew overpowering, the

Americans compared their fate to that of African slaves transported to the United States. Then one of their group reminded them that while a slave might have been sold for several hundred dollars, their lives were no longer worth 'two kopecks'.[35] From a Russian prisoner they learned that the ship was bound for Kolyma, in the far north-eastern corner of the USSR. It was an area so remote it could only be reached by sea, and so cold it was called 'another planet' by its prisoners:

> Kolyma, Kolyma wonderful planet,
> Twelve months winter – the rest, summer.

In Kolyma, the coldest temperatures on earth had been recorded at below minus sixty degrees centigrade.[36] Officially a rule existed in the camps that the prisoners' work was cancelled if the temperature fell to minus fifty degrees. But the rule was never enforced, and the prisoners never saw a thermometer. Instead, they judged the temperature by other means: at minus forty, the human body made a clinking sound as it exhaled; at minus fifty-five degrees, the man in front disappeared as the air froze into an impenetrable fog; below minus sixty degrees spit froze in mid-air.[37] In Kolyma, nature was said to be 'in league with the executioner', the extreme cold accelerating the destruction of its victims. Alexander Solzhenitysn would later describe the region as the 'pole of cold and cruelty' of the Gulag Archipelago. And, like the train timetables of Auschwitz, the logbooks of Andrei Sakharov's 'death ships of the Okhotsk Sea' would reveal the scale of the tragedy that took place in this one unknown corner of the Soviet Union.[38] In complete secrecy, the NKVD fleet had been silently ferrying its human cargo since 1932, and the ships would continue their operations for the next two decades. During this period, millions of prisoners would be disembarked onto its rocky shore, the majority never to return.

On his arrival at the port of Nagaevo, Thomas Sgovio was ordered down the gangplank to join the column of prisoners for roll call. The prisoners were routinely referred to as 'slaves' by their guards. Even the word used for their death was one not normally applicable to human beings: in Russian, they would use 'paddochnicht', meaning to 'croak'.[39] From the shore of Nagaevo Bay, the prisoners were force-marched up the cliffs to the city of Magadan, the wind howling all around them, drowning out the commands of the guards and the barking of the Alsatians which, when let loose, could knock a starved prisoner down with ease.[40] Thomas Sgovio was marched up these cliffs at night, the guards holding lanterns amid the barking of the dogs. To distract himself from his fear, and the sudden coldness of the air, he started humming the 'St Louis Blues'.[41]

As elsewhere, Stalin's portrait dominated Magadan, a declaration of both his authority and responsibility for the crimes taking place within its hinterland. Hung across the buildings and streets were red banners with slogans: 'Glory to Stalin, the greatest genius of mankind' and 'Kolyma Welcomes You!'[42] As if the prisoners could feel welcomed after their arrival in the hold of a ship. Most had already heard the rumours describing Kolyma as 'the land of white death' or 'the white crematorium'. Or there was the most straightforward warning of all: 'Kolyma znaczit smert' – 'Kolyma means death.'[43]

Columns of prisoners were marched though the city streets of Magadan, named after the ever-changing chiefs of the NKVD. Above them, guards aimed machine guns from watchtowers, and searchlights reflected back their shadows across the snow and ice. The whole of this closed city was effectively one large concentration camp policed by rifle butts and baying dogs, one of 'the slave capitals' of the Soviet Union. Marched out of Magadan, the first prisoners had been harried along the only road north into the Arctic wilderness, towards their designated camps and the primitive mines hollowed out of the earth with pickaxes.

To the outside world Kolyma was a void, not even a mystery, just another closed zone of the Soviet Union where no cameras or foreign visitors were permitted to travel. As for the millions of people who vanished into it, the Western world had no idea they even existed. In 1942, the *New York Times* reporter Walter Duranty wrote of between 'thirty or forty thousand' killed during the Terror. If a Pulitzer Prize winner could publish an error of such magnitude without immediate public derision, what hope did anyone else have of discovering the truth? After all, how could an empty space be detected in a hermetic, totalitarian state unless the witness himself happened to be a prisoner?[44]

Unwittingly the Soviet Union's own statisticians provided an oblique form of an answer in the results of the 1937 census, which revealed a dramatic shortfall in the Soviet population. According to a report from *Mech* – a Russian-language weekly published in Poland – the census declared a population total of 159 million, instead of the projected 176 million, amounting to 17 million people who had disappeared.[45] The Soviet defector Walter Krivitsky, who had access to the NKVD files, quoted the same statistical shortfall as 26 million.[46] Whichever number was closer to the truth, the results of the 1937 census were suppressed and Stalin reacted to the news by having the hapless statisticians shot. A new census was ordered whose experts learned from their predecessors' mistakes and wisely presented the 'correct' set of results. Years later a secret report ordered by Nikita Khrushchev revealed that between 1935 and 1941 the NKVD arrested more than nineteen million citizens. Seven million of the arrested were shot straightaway. An unknown proportion of the rest perished later, by the many means there were to die in the concentration camps of the Gulag.[47]

Down this pathway of arrest, imprisonment, execution or the Gulag were driven the American emigrants to the Soviet Union. There was a selection process and those who survived, like Thomas Sgovio or Victor Herman, were delivered to work their sentences in the camps. Strangely it was only the consequence of their labour, never the circumstance of their disappearance, that caused alarm in the capital cities of the West.

14

THE SOVIET GOLD RUSH

When we are victorious on a world-wide scale, we will make public
toilets out of gold on the streets of the world's largest cities.
                                                    Vladimir Lenin, 1921[1]

From the early 1930s, the American Secretary of the Treasury's first
appointment was an early morning meeting in the President's bedroom at the White House. According to Henry Morgenthau's diary,
Franklin Roosevelt 'would lie comfortably on his old-fashioned,
three-quarter mahogany bed. A table stood on either side; on his left
would be a batch of government reports, a detective novel or two,
and a couple of telephones. On his right would be pads, pencils, cigarettes, his watch, and a plate of fruit.' Refreshed after a night's
sleep, Roosevelt would eat soft-boiled eggs while Morgenthau
reported on the behaviour of the gold and commodity prices.
Together their strategy was to keep the gold price moving upwards
by intervening in the markets and, by boosting the price of every
other commodity in its wake, to claw the American economy out of
the Great Depression.

However, to prevent speculators from predicting future price
increases, they deliberately varied the amount they wished to raise it
by each day. On 25 October 1933, for example, the President took
one look at Morgenthau, who was feeling 'more than usually worried about the state of the world', and suggested a price rise of
twenty-one cents. 'It's a lucky number,' said Roosevelt with a smile,
'because it's three times seven.' In his diary, Morgenthau noted
gloomily that 'if anybody ever knew how we really set the gold price
through a combination of lucky numbers, etc, I think they would be
frightened.'[2]

'Henry the Morgue', as the President liked to call his rather dour Treasury Secretary, owed his position to his predecessor's sudden ill health. One reporter described him as the 'most obscure Secretary of the Treasury this country has ever had' – not long earlier he had been a New York apple farmer in Dutchess County, next to the Roosevelt family estate.[3] Unexpectedly elevated early in the first New Deal administration, Morgenthau was naturally nervous. If the American economy was the sickest of patients, he was the least experienced of physicians.

Four years later, in April 1937, a substantial increase in the world's gold supply was creating an inevitable downward pressure on price, and Morgenthau was forced into buying ever-increasing quantities to maintain the US government's fixed price. There was no secret where this surplus gold was coming from since the Soviet Union had been openly selling shipments of bullion on the metals exchanges of London, Paris and New York. Here, then, was the explanation behind the sudden cash wealth in Moscow that had allowed Stalin to buy up American factories like so much confetti, and wave one-hundred-million-dollar naval contracts beneath the nose of Joseph Davies, salted with ironic promises to help 'alleviate American unemployment'.

Furious that his first term's work might soon be undone, Henry Morgenthau summoned Konstantin Oumansky to his office in Washington. Very bluntly the Treasury Secretary asked what the Soviets thought they were playing at: 'the Russians were children about international finance, I used to call them American Indians. They dumped commodities like quicksilver and killed their markets.' But in response to Morgenthau's irate line of questioning, Oumansky steadfastly refused to reveal either how much gold was being produced or the amount still held in reserve. Stone-faced, Oumansky volunteered nothing, and so resolutely feigned either real or pretend ignorance that the frustrated Morgenthau found himself having to teach him how the central banking system worked.[4]

Unbeknown to the Soviet diplomats, the Treasury Secretary had been conducting a private investigation of his own. Shortly after his arrival in Moscow, a carefully briefed Joseph Davies had written a report back to Morgenthau: 'I have been making every effort to try to get a line on the gold reserve here. It is practically impossible to get anything definite. It is more or less a military secret which is guarded with care ... The other day I was privileged to see the collection of treasure and jewels at the State Bank. What surprised me was the size of the gold nuggets. They had two nuggets of solid gold ranging between forty and fifty pounds each. From their appearance I should judge that they were practically pure gold.'[5] Six months later Davies wrote again describing a meeting with Foreign Minister Maxim Litvinov in which he had asked straightforward questions about Soviet gold production and reserves. The wily Litvinov volunteered that 'he could state confidentially that current estimates were rather exaggerated'. In his letter, Davies suggested that the Soviet government was 'jealously guarding the facts with reference to the gold supply . . . constantly exaggerating its size for propaganda purposes and its possible effect on their enemies'.[6]

As so often before, Ambassador Davies' deductions were completely misplaced. Ironically, the one expert who could answer Morgenthau's questions was lurking right beneath the Ambassador's nose. Stranger still, this expert was an American mining engineer and frequent guest of the American Embassy in Moscow. In almost a decade's service to the Soviet government, Jack Littlepage had played a crucial role in their gold industry.

When Littlepage first arrived in Russia, it seemed self-evident that the fledgling Bolshevik state was teetering on the brink of bankruptcy and ruin. After the role of the market was abandoned, prices in the USSR were no longer used as a mechanism for the allocation of resources. With inflation running out of control, most Western economists were confidently predicting the imminent collapse of a regime they perceived as an economic absurdity. Within the Soviet Union itself, everyone understood that the rouble was virtually worthless. Whenever the government required extra money, the State Bank simply printed more and more notes, often with identical serial numbers and on paper so thin it literally fell apart in your hands.[7] And although the Wall Street Crash was greeted by Soviet ideologues as obvious proof of the Marxist conception of history, their evident satisfaction was tempered by the increasing awareness of the damage inflicted upon the Five Year Plan. All the factories and specialists arriving from Detroit or Cologne had to be paid for in precious, and fast-diminishing, foreign currency. After the Crash, the Soviet commodity exports were suddenly worth only a fraction of their former value.[8]

Thus the Kremlin's schemes to gather hard currency were driven by a mounting sense of desperation. In one project, the NKVD began counterfeiting hundred-dollar bills for distribution across Europe and China, forcing the American Federal Reserve to issue widespread warnings against the excellent forgeries.[9] At the same time Stalin authorised the Soviet Art Export Trust to sell off art treasures accumulated over generations by the Tsars. Very quietly a selection of Old Masters from the Hermitage Museum was delivered to the auction rooms of the West. In one deal, worth over seven million dollars, some twenty-one masterpieces, including Raphael's 'Alba Madonna', Titian's 'Venus With A Mirror' and Velazquez's 'Innocent X', were all sold. The paintings were simply taken down from the walls of the Hermitage, while the curators rearranged the remainder to cover the gaps, their absence to be later explained by the 1931 fire or the Nazi siege.[10]

Fortunately the principal buyer in the latest Soviet art sale happened to be an American citizen equally anxious to maintain the secrecy of the deal. And for good reason, since the gentleman in question happened to be none other than Henry Morgenthau's predecessor in office. At the time, Andrew Mellon was an elderly, frail man with high cheekbones, sharp blue eyes and a slight stammer. Ultra-reserved, he ranked alongside Henry Ford and John D. Rockefeller as one of the world's wealthiest men – the Mellon family fortune dominating the American banking, oil, steel and shipbuilding industries. As America's Secretary of the Treasury through the Roaring Twenties, three Republican Presidents – Harding, Coolidge and Hoover – were all said to have 'served under him'. And while publicly Andrew Mellon ran the nation's finances as he saw fit, privately the scant responsibilities of laissez-faire appeared insufficiently fulfilling for the Republican statesman. Privately, Andrew Mellon was consumed by an altogether more demanding passion: the desire for fine art, regardless of its provenance.

Even while his art dealers were negotiating with their Kremlin intermediaries, Andrew Mellon was responsible for the American government's economic policy with the USSR – including the vexed question of the first exports of Gulag labour into the American market. It was, of course, a direct conflict of interests. However, in a more discreet age, secrecy remained assured on both sides; and the flow of pictures by Hals, Rembrandt, Rubens, Van Eyck, Van Dyck, Raphael, Velazquez, Botticelli, Veronese, Chardin and Perugino continued to disappear from Leningrad's Hermitage Collection to reappear, as if by magic, on the walls of Andrew Mellon's private apartment at 1785 Massachusetts Avenue, Washington DC.[11]

The truth became public only in the spring of 1935, under the bright lights of a tax evasion case. In court, Andrew Mellon was forced to reveal both the value and origin of the art collection he intended as a gift to the nation. His lawyer David E. Finley spoke on his behalf: 'Mr Mellon wanted to keep the thing a surprise until the right moment. It probably would not have been very good politics for the Secretary of the Treasury to spend millions for rare paintings at a time when the government was swamped with unemployment, bank failures and general distress.' Mellon would die before the completion of his National Gallery in Washington DC, but when asked why he had collected the paintings his answer had been characteristically concise: 'Every man wants to connect his life with something that is eternal.'[12] It was a strange echo, albeit from the opposite end of the economic spectrum, of the cause that had drawn so many American emigrants to Russia.

And while it was suitably ironic that the finances of the USSR were being saved, at least partially, by millions of dollars from the very men the Revolution had sought to destroy, it was also apparent that Stalin's state coffers required a more constant source of replenishment. Through the early 1930s, a campaign was launched across the USSR obliging all citizens to hand in their gold to the state. Cash rewards were offered for the denunciation of neighbours' hoards as investigators from the GPU hunted for gold, foreign currency, and jewellery, tearing through apartments in their quest. In the midst of universal shortages, 'gold stores' were opened, fully stocked with every conceivable item to be priced and paid for in metal, the scales on their counters weighing wedding rings and christening spoons. Naturally the state robbed its citizens blinder than a Chicago loan shark – the American reporter Eugene Lyons calculated that a pair of shoes was charged at twice its weight in silver. There was also another hidden danger to the transaction, since the stores were carefully watched by the GPU who checked the identities of the customers, ready to arrest them if they considered it worthwhile.[13]

When private pockets were exhausted, more radical solutions had to be found. In the Kremlin, Stalin ordered the translation into Russian of books on the Californian gold rush and summoned the pre-Revolutionary Bolshevik Alexander Serebrovsky to a meeting.[14]

In the Caucasus, Serebrovsky had earned a reputation as 'the Soviet Rockefeller' for returning the oilfields to production after the Civil War. Now Stalin instructed him to repeat his success in the Soviet gold industry. Their plan was to duplicate American mining techniques, and exactly one week later, Alexander Serebrovsky was dispatched to Alaska.[15]

Described by Littlepage as 'a medium-sized, inconspicuous man, smooth-shaven, with American clothes and an American air', Serebrovsky posed as a humble 'Professor of Mines' as he toured the Alaskan gold mines. He met Jack Littlepage in one of the first mines he visited, and was impressed by this tall, lean American engineer who worked alongside his miners and knew how to get the job done quickly. In Alaska, Serebrovsky was surprised by the lack of class distinction between the engineer and the miners. 'Isn't it the same way in Russia?' asked Littlepage. 'It's not that way yet,' Serebrovsky replied with some honesty.[16]

But when Serebrovsky asked if he would like to work in Russia, Jack Littlepage had refused point-blank, stating bluntly that he 'did not like Bolsheviks'. 'You don't like Bolsheviks? Well what's wrong with them?' wondered the astonished Serebrovsky, who had joined the Party in 1903. 'They seem to have a habit of shooting people, especially engineers,' replied Littlepage, who even then had read the reports of show trials. But Serebrovsky was unfazed by the 'misperceptions' of the bourgeois press, and quietly allayed Littlepage's fears: 'Well, I am a Bolshevik, and have been one for many, many years. Do I look so dangerous?'[17]

In a Soviet propaganda pamphlet, Serebrovsky described the American engineer as 'drawn to the Soviet Union by the grand scale of our construction work, the ideas of great Stalin, the chance to unfold his talents freely'. If the financial allure was left unstated, it was also clear that Serebrovsky was a sound judge of character. Jack Littlepage arrived in the Soviet Union on 1 May 1928, with his wife, Georgia, and their two young daughters. Quickly renamed 'Ivan Eduardovich', he soon learned to speak Russian and, with an indefatigable energy, 'set about verifying calculations, designs, estimates, plans of work'. In the next six years, the USSR outstripped America in gold production figures and was ready to overtake the world's number one producer, the British Empire, which controlled the vast gold wealth of South Africa.[18] Jack Littlepage's career as the Deputy Commissar of the Soviet Gold Trust was so successful that he was decorated with the Order of the Red Banner of Labour and rewarded with a Soviet Ford Model A, among the most prestigious gifts of the era. Publicly praised in an article in *Izvestiya*, he was sent back to the United States several times to recruit more engineers, 'the beginning of the great American invasion' hired to oversee work in the Soviet gold mines. In those Depression years, there was never any shortage of willing recruits.[19]

On his way to Moscow via Berlin, one of the Soviet apparatchiks had taken a shine to Jack Littlepage and offered him some advice that he later remembered: 'He said I needn't get worried if Russians working with me suddenly disappeared under what would seem to me to be mysterious circumstances. There wasn't any other way to manage things at present, he told me, and I would find the police active in the mines and the mills. He told me I should take it that the police were helping rather than hindering my work, and not be bothered by them.'[20] Although Jack Littlepage was never forced to take up Soviet citizenship or stripped of his American passport, he was required to turn a blind eye to the scenes he witnessed of Russian peasants driven from their homes and forced to work in the gold mines. Later he claimed to believe the confessions of the Bolsheviks in the show trials, and their wild accusations that 'wreckers' and 'saboteurs' were responsible for the lamentable performance of Soviet industry. In the midst of the repressions, Jack Littlepage continued to fulfil his role as a Deputy Commissar, advising Serebrovsky on the use of Alaskan-style prospecting parties working in twos and threes to scour the vast unexplored lands of the USSR in search of gold.[21]

In 1932, a geological prospecting team made its way to the remote corner of north-eastern Russia. It was, they said, a wasteland of such cold and darkness that it had never been permanently settled by man. In the valley of the Kolyma river, the prospectors discovered vast placer deposits of gold, often lying in nuggets close to the surface of the earth. But who would volunteer to work in this god-forsaken wasteland whose winter temperatures were colder and more extreme even than those at the North Pole? The answer, of course, was simple since, as Jack Littlepage himself had recognised elsewhere in the USSR, 'the secret police have an advantage over other Soviet organizations as they can always count on a steady supply of labour, no matter what kind of living conditions exist, where the given task has to be done'. While Tsar Nicholas II had once made the decision that the conditions in Kolyma were too atrocious for human beings to live or work, Stalin never had such qualms.[22]

In exchange for the soft yellow metal, Stalin offered up the lives of legions of prisoners, safe in the knowledge that he possessed an almost inexhaustible supply. If, after all, Matvei Berman had consumed up to a quarter of a million lives in the construction of the White Sea–Baltic Canal, how many more would the Kolyma gold be worth? A vast new Soviet enterprise was called into being, given the euphemistic title of the 'Far North East Construction Trust' and known by its Russian acronym as Dalstroi. The trust would control an area three million square kilometres in size, larger than western Europe, and the ships of the NKVD fleet were purchased at auction ready to deliver their labour force.[23]

The first waves of prisoners were marched under guard across the snowfields. In Kolyma they were forced to build their own camps beside the newly prospected gold mines, and those who faltered or lagged behind were shot. These early camps were primitive affairs regularly cut off from the new city of Magadan by the ferocity of the winters. Supplies often failed and when communications were restored – days, sometimes weeks, later – there were, at times, no survivors left to continue. From the early years, it was said that only one in every hundred survived, and these 'last of the Mohicans' reported watching Eduard Berzin, the first Dalstroi chief, travel along the main highway to inspect the mines in a Rolls-Royce that had once belonged to Lenin, the reward from Stalin for his success.[24]

From Dalstroi's inception, Stalin kept close control over its operations, demanding regular updates, which required its top officials to report back personally to Moscow.[25] The Politburo resolutions for Dalstroi were obscured by layers of official secrecy. Selected items from key reports were placed in special folders for 'eyes only' secrecy, and relevant Party officials were allowed to read just one or two points from the whole report. Only Stalin and the highest levels of the NKVD hierarchy had knowledge of and responsibility for the whole enterprise – both in its creation and continued expansion in the annual prisoner transfers across the first 'open water'.[26]

In his first two years, Eduard Berzin delivered the news that Dalstroi's harvest of gold had leapt tenfold. In response, Stalin poured more and more prisoners into the wilderness, and the production rose still higher.[27] But however much gold Berzin sent back to Moscow, it was still never enough. Above all, the gold plan must not just be fulfilled, it must be over-fulfilled; and during the Terror, Stalin came to the conclusion that Berzin had been 'coddling' his prisoners. The powerful Dalstroi chief was lured to a meeting with a visiting NKVD delegation in Magadan, who promised further medals and arrested him on the airfield. Flown in handcuffs to Moscow, Eduard Berzin was executed in a basement of the Lubyanka. The 'Berzin affair' resulted in the execution of several thousand of the Dalstroi apparat. Collectively they were accused of a conspiracy to turn Kolyma into 'the 49th state of the USA'.[28]

The effect on his successors was predictably savage. In time, Berzin was replaced by a functionary named Pavlov and his deputy Garanin, a thirty-nine-year-old NKVD colonel whose response to Moscow's demands for gold made him notorious in the camps. Colonel Garanin personally oversaw the prisoners' line-ups, when those who had not fulfilled their work quotas were ordered to step forward. The NKVD colonel then walked down the line personally executing the 'enemies of the people', closely followed by two guards who took turns reloading his revolver.[29] The prisoners' corpses were then stacked up at the gates as a reminder to the rest. While executions continued throughout the Gulag, under Garanin a camp named Serpantinnaya was specifically constructed in the wilderness, several hundred kilometres west of Magadan. This camp became widely known as an extermination centre. The weakest prisoners were transported there in trucks to be executed en masse. They were described by surviving prisoners as being 'sent to the moon'.[30]

Less than a year into his reign, Garanin was himself arrested and shot as a Japanese spy. All his subordinates, from executioners to gravediggers, followed in the Kremlin's methodical effort to conceal what had already taken place. New Dalstroi functionaries arrived in 1938 and, like their predecessors, did not last long, since the exigencies of the Terror applied just as equally within Kolyma as every other region of the Soviet Union.[31]

Eventually an NKVD general, Ivan Nikishov, was appointed as the new Dalstroi chief, and a degree of stability was re-established. Still in his forties, Nikishov had been promoted from his ruthless administration of the Terror in the Soviet Republic of Azerbaijan.[32] A powerful man, he was selected for his pragmatic cruelty which allowed him steadily to over-fulfil the plan for gold. Quickly made a

Soviet 'hero of labour', Nikishov pursued his given task with the grim fixation of a man who knew his life depended on it. In his ascendancy, he divorced his wife and remarried a pretty twenty-nine-year-old named Aleksandra Gridassova, well known to the female prisoners as the commandant of a Magadan women's camp. Thanks to Nikishov's patronage, Gridassova had risen through the Gulag hierarchy until she was responsible for the lives of thousands of female prisoners, who christened her 'Catherine the Fourth' for the peremptory way she decided human destinies and the lavish lifestyle she created for herself and her husband in Kolyma.[33]

Together the couple occupied a country house to the north-west of Magadan, surrounded by luxury, with the usual retinue of chauffeurs, cooks, maids and personal doctors provided for the Soviet elite. The couple organised their own 'cultural brigade': a slave theatre of singers, actors and ballerinas whose lives were saved from the mines in return for their performances. Gulag society, in the form of the camp commandants and their wives, attended Magadan's Gorky Theatre to watch their gala performances, as the gaunt former stars struggled to reproduce past glories in costumes flown in from Moscow.[34]

Two decades after the Revolution, Lenin's promise that the leaders of the Revolutionary state would 'receive the same salary as an average worker' had long been forgotten. It was all as hopelessly naive as another Leninist prediction, that under communism, gold would become 'valueless', used only for the building of public conveniences. Instead, millions of prisoners' lives became subject to the regime of Dalstroi, forced into hard labour to maintain the steady supply of gold flown back to Moscow in NKVD planes, and ready to be sold in the markets of the West. By the end of the 1930s, Dalstroi was producing annually more than eighty thousand kilograms of chemically pure gold, worth over a hundred million dollars at the price kept fixed by President Roosevelt and Henry Morgenthau. It was precisely this gold that resuscitated the ailing Soviet economy and ultimately kept Stalin in power. And Stalin understood this economic imperative only too well.[35]

Dalstroi's successful operation meant that Alexander Serebrovsky's services were no longer quite so essential to the Soviet state. Calling Milchakov, his Russian deputy into the Kremlin, Stalin explained that Serebrovsky had been 'unmasked' by the NKVD as a 'vicious enemy of the people' responsible for the delivery of fifty million gold ingots to Trotsky. Milchakov was then ordered to shadow Serebrovsky until the moment arrived for him to be publicly denounced. The 'Soviet Rockefeller' was soon executed, while Milchakov lasted only two months before he, too, was arrested.[36]

Politically tainted by his close friendship with Serebrovsky, Jack Littlepage found himself unable to work. Terrified Russian employees refused even to come near him, carrying as he did the double stain of his status as a foreigner and his friendship with a prominent 'enemy of the people'. Fortunately, either because Littlepage had carefully guarded his American passport or because he had acquired a valuable reputation for keeping his mouth shut, the American engineer was allowed to leave Soviet Russia unhindered.[37] On 22 September 1937, Jack Littlepage called at the American Embassy before his final departure. He told the diplomats that he had been asked to investigate alleged 'wrecking activities' by Soviet industrial commissar Georgy Piatakov in various gold mines, and reported his conviction that 'there had been deliberate wrecking in these mines and he was of the opinion that this wrecking had been ordered by Piatakov'. An American official described Littlepage's rationale as being 'somewhat vague', but it appeared that his real motive had been overlooked. Jack Littlepage was simply paying for his ticket home, and the safety of his life in America.[38]

On the train out of Russia, Littlepage wore his Order of the Red Banner of Labour prominently displayed on his jacket, evidently anticipating last-minute difficulties. But the only reaction came from a Polish customs official on the other side of the border, who saw the medal and snapped, 'Take that thing off.'[39] In a series of articles for the *Saturday Evening Post*, Littlepage described how 'the Far Eastern gold rush continues. An army of intrepid men and women push ever farther into the unexplored wastes of Eastern Siberia, Yakutia, and Kazakstan. Prospectors work in blinding blizzards and tropical heat, and penetrate into districts which man may never have seen before.'[40] Only later, in secrecy, would Littlepage answer questions from the American War Department. Marking a map of the Soviet Union, he wrote the number one in a circle over Kolyma and informed the intelligence officer that here was 'the richest gold field in the world from which the gold can be produced by placer mining without refining process . . . twice as much can be obtained from this one field alone as we are now getting from all of Alaska'.[41]

In neither case did he mention the existence of legions of prisoners marched out into the frozen wasteland to extract the gold.

Dumped from the hulls of the slave ships, the prisoners' lives would soon be exhausted. When their bodies became useless for the mines, the last iota of strength was squeezed from them in road-building tasks before the end claimed them falling down by the side of the road or from the bullet of a gun. Into this infernal world had fallen Thomas Sgovio, just one of the millions of prisoners whose life would be governed by the unremitting demands of Dalstroi.[42]

Meanwhile, in his offices at the Treasury Department in Washington DC, Henry Morgenthau had long been aware that the Soviet gold was mined by 'forced labour'. If Jack Littlepage stayed largely silent about the horrors he encountered, other American mining engineers had been more forthcoming in their reports. As early as 1932, Raymond Vandervoort had briefed a State Department officer in Berlin:

A good deal of the labor employed in the gold mines is forced labor and that the casualties among these people are exceedingly heavy and he estimates that 50 to 60 thousand a year die from exposure, hardship, and cold throughout Siberia . . . They are the most persecuted people on the earth . . . The attitude openly expressed by officials with regard to the casualties among the workers is one of unparalleled hard-heartedness. They take no notice of the deaths and insist that through these casualties they have less persons to feed . . . The Russians butcher and butcher and butcher. There has been no let-up in the number of executions.[43]

By the late 1930s, Raymond Vandervoort's estimate of the annual mortality rate had become a distant memory long surpassed. And through all those years – as the Gulag casualties mounted by orders of magnitude – Soviet gold bonds were offered for sale as a guaranteed investment to the American public, freely advertised in the financial pages of the *New York Times*: 'Facts and Figures prove the economic growth of the Soviet Union . . . a series of accomplishments unparalleled in the history of modern nations . . . the second largest producer of gold in the world.'[44]

Nor did Henry Morgenthau have any intention of antagonising Stalin when upbraiding the Soviet diplomats on their gold sales. It was simply a question of commerce, not morality, as the Treasury

Secretary made clear when he assured Oumansky that 'the methods they used were of no interest to the American government'.

All the pragmatic Morgenthau wished for was the markets to function smoothly. In pursuit of this end, he suggested the formation of a direct liaison committee between the Soviet State Bank and the American Federal Reserve to facilitate the sale and transit of Soviet gold to the United States.[45] In 1937, Konstantin Oumansky was invited to Morgenthau's Washington home and complimented on 'the finesse of the refining of the Russian bars' which Morgenthau recognised as 'second only to American' in purity and weight accuracy. The Soviets had sent sixty million dollars' worth of gold to America just in the past month, to be sold at the guaranteed price of thirty-five dollars an ounce. The glimmering bars of chemically pure yellow metal arrived stamped with the emblem of the hammer and sickle.[46]

Had Henry Morgenthau considered his actions more carefully he might have concluded that he was actively facilitating the deaths of countless innocent men and women and, as we shall later discover, children too, by allowing the gold mined by Soviet prisoners in Arctic temperatures to be transferred to the Federal deposit in the blue hills of Kentucky. We can be fairly certain, however, that the Treasury Secretary did not see that far along his particular chain of moral responsibility, and rested peacefully at night, ready for his early morning meetings with the President.[47]

15

'OUR SELFLESS LABOUR WILL RESTORE US TO THE FAMILY OF WORKERS'

So few my roads, so many my mistakes.

Sergei Esenin[1]

In Kolyma, Thomas Sgovio awoke each day in a realm of suffering at the cruellest margin of human existence. Death was all around: for saying the work was too harsh, for not responding to the orders of a guard, for remaining silent when a crowd of prisoners shouted, 'Long Live Stalin'. Silence was a crime, refusal to work was a crime, to consider oneself innocent was a crime – 'The Five Year Plan is the law! Not to carry out the Plan is a crime!'[2] Next to gold, human life was an ill-valued commodity that Dalstroi only suffered to support. Orders came down to carry out executions at the slightest slow-down, with individual camp commandants given a free hand to take whatever measures they considered necessary to maintain the supply.[3] One NKVD 'camp doctor' explained the situation to the prisoners in the starkest terms: 'You are not brought here to live, but to suffer and die. If you live it means that you are guilty of two things: either you worked less than was assigned, or you ate more than your proper due.'[4]

As the operations of Dalstroi consumed the prisoners' lives, it created the continual need for their replacement. This, too, was a predetermined and carefully calculated policy, since the Plan for gold included a measure for the consumption of life. With remorseless logic, the labour force was to be replenished in proportion to the projected mortality rate, which was one target that never fell below the norm. Lev Inzhir had once been the chief accountant of the Gulag before he was himself arrested. To a fellow prisoner, Inzhir revealed how he had monitored the flow of life through the camps from his offices at the Lubyanka in Moscow. The daily accountancy was dominated by two headings: 'Arrivals' and 'Deaths'; and it seemed to Inzhir that the whole of the Soviet Union was about to be absorbed into these two columns. With his colleagues in the upper echelons of the NKVD the accountant discussed how they might steady the ever-rising death rate, and instructions were sent from the Centre to the individual camp commandants. Although it was impossible to investigate thousands of deaths per day, a maximum permitted rate was agreed, and as long as the mortality did not exceed this norm then it was deemed to be acceptable. Instructions arrived from the NKVD headquarters specifying that the Dalstroi prisoners were to be delivered to Magadan 'completely healthy', not as physical wrecks, worn half dead by the corrosive regime of prison, train, holding camp, and ship.[5]

Within the bureaucracy of the Gulag, a human being became a mere abstraction, a biological machine stripped of all essential worth beyond his or her utility to the state. The logical consequence of such thinking was that the numbers of casualties within this grand 'social experiment' ceased to bear any meaning to the camp administrators. Each incremental zero in a column of statistics required only the necessary dispassionate Bolshevik logic to proceed on to the next. And all regulatory agreements between the Moscow administrators and the camp officials were always to ensure the efficiency of the mechanism, which, in their eyes, was ultimately the most important value. Once the mortality was set at the agreed rate, the hands of this mechanism were left to turn, and millions of lives were eventually consumed without conscience or respite, over the next two decades. Thus the deaths of the Gulag's victims became the *cause* as well as the effect of Stalin's mass repressions. Viewed from the methodology of power, the mechanism had become self-perpetuating.

Of course, Lev Inzhir's privileged insights did nothing to help in the camps. Desperate to save his life and conceal his status from those who hunted down his kind, Inzhir became a camp informer and eventually fell victim to the system he had worked so hard to perpetuate. Then the Gulag's former chief accountant was transformed into another statistic in a mortality column sent back to Moscow.[6]

*

From the Magadan transit camp Thomas Sgovio was transported by truck four hundred kilometres north, and force-marched another seven kilometres to the goldfield Razvedchik.[7] On arrival at their camp, the new prisoners were immediately sent out to work between fourteen and eighteen hours per day, the first twelve hours at the goldfields and the remainder spent digging infrastructure projects.[8] They arrived in the midst of the 'Garanin days' during the winter of 1938, when lists of names were read out after roll call throughout the Kolyma camps, and thousands were sentenced to be shot. Colonel Garanin himself visited Razvedchik only once. Entering the camp barracks, he discovered two criminal prisoners refusing to work and shot them both on the spot.[9]

For many the shock of arrival was too great. Such men suffered an immediate psychological collapse, which led quickly to their death. After the first day in Camp Razvedchik, one of the Americans slashed his wrists with a razor blade. The victim was Harry Jaffe, the tenor who had once stood next to Thomas Sgovio singing solos in the Anglo-American Chorus in Moscow. For the others, Jaffe's suicide strengthened their awareness that they had been abandoned to their fate, since his brother was rumoured to be a committee member of the American Communist Party. If any of the Americans had a chance of being rescued, it was him.[10] A short while after Jaffe's death, on 28 January 1939, the *New York Times* carried an article: 'American in Russia believed arrested'. The report stated only that Harry Jaffe of New Jersey, a former employee of the *Moscow News*, 'is believed by persons who knew him to have been arrested a year or more ago'. Later Senator James Slattery wrote to the American chargé d'affaires in Moscow in response to a letter from the seventy-eight-year-old Rachel Jaffe of Chicago seeking news of her son 'who had volunteered for service in the US Navy during the World War'. From Moscow, Angus Ward answered that Harry Jaffe had expatriated himself, and advised his relatives to 'address themselves to the Soviet Embassy in Washington'.[11]

The prisoners who wanted to live were forced to mine the Kolyma gold, pushing vast wheelbarrows filled with earth up runners into the sluices to be washed. Officially they were allocated three days' rest per month, but such measures were universally disregarded by the authorities. All prisoners were worked every day of the year – if they lasted a year – knowing that to refuse would be the end of their ordeal.[12] Intellectuals who expressed doubt over their capacity for hard labour were mocked by the criminals: 'Don't worry, here they'll give you a twenty kilogram "pencil" (a crowbar) and you can "write" in the quarry.'[13]

From the old-timers, the new arrivals learned that it was impossible to survive on the meagre food they were given. Each prisoner received a ration based upon the work completed. But the calories used up in fulfilling, or over-fulfilling, the 'norm' were always greater than those in the food itself. Similarly, falling below the 'sixty per cent norm' resulted in a penalty ration, which accelerated the process of starvation. Thus the prisoners learned the course of action that would preserve their strength for as long as possible, or kill them the most slowly. Even achieving this sixty per cent 'norm', their labour stripped first the fat from their bodies and then burned up their muscles too, until nothing was left but their skin and bones. It was a physiological certainty that hard labour combined with starvation in sub-zero temperatures would end only in their death.[14]

From breaking the ground with picks and pushing the endless wheelbarrows filled with frozen earth the prisoners' hands became grotesquely misshapen into blackened claws which ached through the night as they tried to sleep. At dawn, Thomas Sgovio would wake up, unable to open his fingers, and try to summon the strength of will to survive another day. His youth and good health were important factors in his favour, but such qualities alone were insufficient defence – both disappeared very quickly with each march out of the wooden stockade of the camp into the goldfields, under the sign over the gates that read 'LABOUR IN THE USSR IS A MATTER OF HONOUR, COURAGE AND HEROISM.'[15]

Although he had not been brought up in a religious family, Thomas Sgovio began to pray. In the midst of despair and with no hope of human intervention, he prayed with all the faith of someone who, until then, had none.[16] With nothing left to lose, he prayed for his life as he swung his pick into the frozen earth. And through prayer, Thomas discovered a stubborn streak within himself which presupposed that the worse his world became, the stronger would be his resolve to live – so that if, by some miracle, he ever returned to America, he could at least tell his father's friends what life was really like in 'the workers' paradise'.[18]

There were many innocent prisoners in Kolyma who prayed as faithfully as Thomas Sgovio but lost their lives. Why one man is saved and another is lost is a mystery, just as faith itself remains a mystery. Rationally, of course, some would survive, and perhaps it was all just pure luck. Perhaps the real mystery was why the innocent were being killed with such unrelenting cruelty.

Every ten days the prisoners were forced to endure a visit to the bathhouse, where they noticed the bones poking through their disappearing flesh. With a thousand others, Thomas was forced to stand in the cold waiting his turn. They were then ordered to undress, their prison clothes thrown into a giant heap while they were given a cup of cold water and a cup of hot water to wash: 'And how could you wash? And my hands were just like monkey's hands, black, all chapped with blood.' Sexual violence occurred regularly within the bathhouse walls, as the criminals abused the weakest and most vulnerable of the prisoners. Their visits were followed by a fight to retrieve their clothes. The strongest and most brutal grabbed first choice – and their bodies, protected from the cold, became a little stronger. While the weakest were left with the most worn and fragile remainders from the pile, which only steepened the trajectory of their descent. In the extreme cold of Kolyma, the prisoners' clothing was as vital as food: 'We killed each other. We tore each other's eyes out for these clothes.'[18]

Those left without gloves had to fashion their own, and if a prisoner woke in the morning, and the man in the next bunk had died, he considered himself fortunate to take the dead man's clothes and perhaps find a hidden portion of bread. The camp barracks were constructed with sleeping platforms on two levels, with a stove in the middle to provide some warmth. But there was no insulation, and often the roofs were so poorly built the prisoners could see the stars above them. In winter, the temperatures inside could fall below minus forty degrees, with no blankets to cover them. Each night Thomas bowed his head and whispered the Lord's Prayer; using his rag boots as a pillow and his outer jacket as a blanket, he would attempt to sleep knowing that he would have to get up during the night to warm himself by the stove.[19] And then a new work day would begin with the morning roll call, when Thomas would stand waiting to shout out his name, year of birth, and sentence under the Soviet criminal code.[20]

By necessity Thomas's Russian quickly improved, since very soon there was no one left who could speak English. Of the twelve

Americans, or Russian-Americans, who had arrived with him on the transport, ten had died within the first year. Overall, three-quarters of the prisoners did not survive their first winter. One survivor testified that the 'average lifespan of a convict at Kolyma is usually taken as four months. People with a weaker constitution are, as a rule, finished by the end of the second or third week. For reasons that I do not know, their leg and arm joints soon begin to swell; later on the swelling spreads to the face and in a few weeks they die.' According to the Polish prisoner Kazimierz Zamorski, 'the number of so-called "three year men" that is, prisoners who have survived three Kolyma winters, was very small indeed. They could be easily recognized by their dark-coloured cheeks, a stigma of numerous frostbites. They were highly respected by their fellow-prisoners as heroes of the incessant and hard struggle for existence. Every one of them had had at least one toe amputated . . . Generally not more than fifteen per cent of the prisoners survived the first winter.'[21]

The larger men died first, since they needed the most food. Prisoners from the Baltic States, for example, died more quickly than Russians because they tended to be physically larger and needed more calories to sustain their work.[22] The most susceptible to the cold and disease were the Central Asian prisoners. Transported from their subtropical homelands into Arctic temperatures, according to one prisoner, 'they died like flies. All their vital forces were numbed as soon as they went out into the terrible cold . . . They stood motionless, their arms crossed, their bowed heads hunched between their shoulders, waiting for the end.'[23] Only the prisoners who had once been peasants or labourers could withstand the shock of heavy manual labour. Worst off were the intellectuals or former office workers, who were persecuted at every turn by the NKVD guards and doomed by their education to the hardest labour. Their mortality was amongst the highest.[24]

Such men and women quickly degenerated into '*dokhodyagas*', the walking skeletons whose ironic name derived from the Russian verb *dokhodit*, meaning 'to arrive'. Within the camps the *dokhodyagas* were those who had 'arrived' as the finished citizens of their model socialist society.[25] They could hardly be missed: their faces were taut and sharpened by starvation, their unfocused eyes lost deep in their sockets, their cheekbones protruding, and their gait uncertain as if their every next step would be their last.[26] Such men would collapse and die quite suddenly, often while working. They would swing a pick, stumble, and fall face down to the ground. Their physical deterioration created a feeling of helplessness and passivity. In this condition, on the threshold of death, it became difficult to distinguish one from another, or even men from women.[27]

The conditions of camp life were such that even healthy-looking men could be transformed into *dokhodyagas* with startling speed. Michael Aisenstein was one of the first from Thomas's group to deteriorate. The engineer had been assigned to a different work brigade, and had his American camel hair coat stolen on the first day. Thomas saw him lurking around the camp kitchen, gathering empty plates from the mess tables, his listless eyes scanning them for scraps of food. When Thomas approached, Aisenstein looked right through him as though he did not recognise his friend. That winter, when Aisenstein disappeared, Thomas presumed he had died.[28]

In the context of the Gulag, grief became a superfluous emotion to those preoccupied with their own survival. Within the camps, the death of their fellow prisoners was normal and to be expected, most commonly dismissed with a shrug and a laconic eulogy learned from the others: 'You die today, I die tomorrow.'[29] As the temperatures fell steadily that winter, Thomas felt the stinging sensation on the tip of his frozen nose, and was taught to take his hand from his mitten to cover his nose and warm it a little, careful not to rub it, or the skin and tissue would fall off. Gradually the survivors' faces became covered in scabs, which they were warned not to touch: 'Let them heal by themselves – otherwise you'll find yourself without a nose in the spring.'[30]

Worse torments came from the criminals who preyed upon the political prisoners in the camps just as they had in the prisons and along their transport. Within the hierarchy of the Gulag, the criminals were favoured by the guards with an ideological status higher than the 'enemies of the people'. The criminals were thus encouraged to act as an internal killing machine. One Kolyma camp survivor, Anatoly Zhigulin, recalled that 'their moral impact on camp life was boundless, they beat to death dozens of thousands. They corrupted hundreds of thousands. And those they corrupted equally ceased to be human.' Within the camps, these criminals were not just physically stronger; they hunted in packs and possessed few, if any, moral prohibitions to limit their violence.[31]

They did, however, possess a peculiarly human weakness, reported time and again in the accounts of the survivors. Starved of entertainment, the criminals loved to listen to stories, not only anecdotes or jokes, but whole works of literature told, if possible, in an educated manner. In the camps there were prisoners who created a niche for themselves as storytellers, recounting the novels of Dumas, Conan Doyle or H. G. Wells from memory in exchange for an extra ration of bread.[32] In this way, too, Thomas Sgovio's life was saved, as the criminals asked him curious questions about America and he told colourful stories of famous gangsters such as Al Capone and John Dillinger or of the St Valentine's Day massacre. When Thomas used up all his gangster tales, he would switch to the stories of O. Henry, which carried a satisfying twist in the tail for his discerning audience.[33]

Later they taught him how to make tattoos with home-made needles and ink from a chunk of burnt rubber mixed with a little sugar and water. On their bodies, Thomas Sgovio inked the markings of their subculture, from simple scrolls – 'I love my mother' – to elaborate tableaux of a bottle of vodka, the ace of spades and a naked girl – 'Our Ruin'.[34] The criminals' tattoos carried an ever-present symbolism created to inspire fear in others. Skulls on fingers counted the number of murders committed, the spires of cathedrals or monasteries the number of years spent within the prison system. On their shoulders the criminal leaders had tattooed the epaulettes of the White Army, and by this self-identification a strict hierarchy was enforced.[35] In Thomas's camp, a criminal leader named Goncharov had taken a shine to the young American and offered him some advice: 'We give you extra food. Just don't let your spirits fall. If you live through this first winter, the chances are about fifty-fifty that you'll survive the next. You're still young.' With this help, Thomas Sgovio survived his first winter in Kolyma, while the others were dying all around.[36]

To survive long term was much harder. Each prisoner had to find a way to remove themselves from the physical labour in the goldfields. There was a common piece of advice in the Soviet concentration camps – 'You can only survive on a function' – which emphasised the necessity of finding a precious job as a cook, a camp clerk or a medical orderly, or any other role away from the mines which killed without fail.[37] 'All the fools croaked,' the criminals would grin. 'Only the smart ones made it.'[38] Thomas's function came when the camp authorities chose to make use of his expertise as a signwriter for their propaganda displays. Transferred to a new camp, he gained temporary respite painting the slogans chosen to boost the morale of the prisoners sent out to work. 'OUR SELFLESS LABOUR WILL RESTORE US TO THE FAMILY OF WORKERS' was a typical example of a propaganda slogan inscribed over the gates of the Kolyma camps. It was the Soviet precursor to '*Arbeit Macht Frei*'.[39]

Now Thomas was fearful lest he ruin his good fortune by making inadvertent grammatical mistakes in his rudimentary Russian. The rest of the Americans from his transport were dead, so he was surprised one afternoon when he heard a voice call out 'Hello' to him in English. He turned to see the smiling face of Alex Shopik, one of the Pittsburgh miners who had been sent to Kolyma on the same transport as Thomas's friend, Marvin Volat. Although Marvin had died in the camps, Alex Shopik had survived thus far working in the camp engineer's office, where he was given the task of translating the instruction manuals for two American excavating machines, newly imported to boost Dalstroi's gold production. Thomas Sgovio and Alex Shopik's friendship would, however, prove to be only fleeting. When Shopik's translation duties ended, he was reassigned to general work and quickly became a *dokhodyaga*. In the ever-worsening conditions, and despite Thomas's efforts to send him extra food, he soon died.[40]

In 1931, Alex Shopik had been one of a party of seventy-five American miners emigrating to the USSR from Pittsburgh, Pennsylvania. At the beginning of the decade, their stirring speeches had been reported in the newspaper *Sovietskaya Sibir*: 'We the members of the fifth group of miners which have been exploited by the bosses of Amerika, and thrown out of work for our services into the thirteen million army of unemployed have decided to leave that capitalist country and help the Soviet Union . . . We, ourselves, have come to Soviet Russia not to sleep but to work and work with all our power to help and complete the Five Year Plan.'[41] No one counted how many of the seventy-five American miners ever returned home, or how many of their lives ended in solitary deaths, scattered in the camps across the Gulag archipelago. In their eagerness, they had all been as innocent as children.

In a camp hospital in Kolyma, Elinor Lipper, a young Dutch socialist arrested in Moscow, had gained temporary reprieve as a nurse. With almost no resources she attempted to help the prisoners regain their strength, but her best efforts were mostly in vain. Their cause of death was invariably starvation or the consequences thereof, which left the body utterly vulnerable to disease or the slightest infection which would quickly kill.[42] Elinor Lipper noticed that the female prisoners seemed to survive in greater numbers than the male, perhaps because they had a greater determination to live, or possibly because they were marginally better treated. But her observation was only relative. The female prisoners also succumbed to the starvation and disease, and were subject to executions just like the men.

Of the many women coerced into prostitution to save their lives in the camps, some became pregnant, but they were kept at work until their final month of pregnancy. The mothers were allowed to nurse their babies until they were nine months old, at which point the children's heads would be shaved before they were transferred to the camp orphanage. Growing up in camp conditions, the children ran wild, unable to speak because they were hardly spoken to, communicating in grunts and howls. There were so many young babies in one orphanage that it took a prisoner-nurse an hour and a half to change all their nappies. Uncared for and deprived of a mother's attention, the youngest ones died in droves.[43] Only very occasionally could it be clandestinely arranged for a mother to see her child. Thus a three-year-old girl whose entire life had been lived within 'the zone' was led to see the face of a prisoner through a snow-covered window. And then a very frightened woman spoke to her for the first time: 'Daughter, I'm your mother.'[44]

The older surviving children were taught songs: 'I'm a little girl, I sing and I play. I haven't seen Stalin but I love him each day.'[45] On every orphanage wall was hung the same picture that could be seen all over the Soviet Union. It showed Stalin, 'the Greatest Friend of Soviet Families', holding a pretty little girl in his arms above the inscription: 'THANK YOU, COMRADE STALIN, FOR A HAPPY CHILDHOOD.' The photograph became a ubiquitous image of Stalinism. Later it was discovered that the six-year-old girl's father and mother had both been killed in the Terror.[46]

In Elinor Lipper's hospital a group of prisoner-doctors attempted to keep a record of the crimes they had witnessed, so that future generations might at least be informed of what had taken place within the camps. But as so often happened – since every aspect of Soviet life was riddled with informers – their plan to create a historical archive was betrayed. The doctors judged to be ringleaders were shot, and the rest given lengthy additions to their sentences. As one of the few survivors, Elinor Lipper resolved to commit to memory all she had seen, for the sake of those who lost their lives.[47]

Several thousand kilometres further west, in central Russia, another surviving American, Victor Herman, was suffering equal hardships in a concentration camp named Burelopom or 'Stormbeaten'. Within the Gulag there was a policy of naming many camps after themes from nature – Mineral, Mountain, Oak, Steppe, Seashore, River, Lake and Watershed – which belied their ferocity.[48] Like all the others, Victor Herman's camp was encircled by a wooden stockade and guarded by watchtowers standing at diagonal corners. Its commander was known as a sadistic killer who gave Burelopom the justified reputation of a death camp.

Starvation here, too, was routine. The prisoners attempted to trap rats with sticks or pull up weeds to chew on their roots and supplement their meagre ration. Every day they were marched out into the forest to cut down the surrounding birch, maple and pine trees. During the winter, as the snow fell ever thicker, more and more prisoners fell short of their norms and, on punishment rations, died of starvation. The few who attempted to escape were either shot immediately or hunted down by dogs and returned to the camp. They were then placed in an isolator dug into the frozen ground into which the guards would throw water until their victims froze in the winter temperatures.[49]

Just as in Kolyma, Victor Herman witnessed scenes of extreme violence committed by the criminals, and condoned or encouraged by the guards. Often the violence was inflicted only out of boredom, almost casually, for 'fun'. Across the Gulag, the criminals played a card game called 'loser cuts', in which a knife would be taken to the nose, ear, or head of a randomly selected victim. In the barracks, Victor Herman once overheard them discussing the rules: 'See that one there – the bald one? His nose. The one with the scar over his eye and the limp? Him. His life.' On another occasion, he witnessed the NKVD guards lead a gang of criminals out into a clearing of the forest to rape a transport of female prisoners newly arrived by train and still dressed in their summer clothes. A criminal leader who attacked a heavily pregnant woman was hacked to death in front of them all.[50]

It was then, as he struggled to survive in their midst, that Victor

Herman became aware of the degenerative effect such violence was having upon his psyche. Worse yet, he was conscious of a vague feeling of 'excitement' or 'zest', provoked by his exposure to this violence. In the camps, he felt an increasing sense of shame and wondered if something 'evil' had not begun to grow inside him that caused him to stay silent, and the other political prisoners to keep away.[51]

After torture in prison, anger was always very close to the surface. Victor Herman had fought to gain a place on the upper bunk of the train during his transportation, which protected him from being crushed with the other prisoners, some of whom had died even before the train had even left the station. Transferred on to a new camp from Burelopom, Victor fought again for a place nearest the stove, when the prisoners were forced to live in tents covered in Iceland moss.[52] Soon they were shipped further north, to a place named Fosfortinaya, where he was ordered to cut down pine trees and punished for infractions by being sent to work into the phosphorus mine next to the camp. After only two or three days' work in the mine, the weakest prisoners began to cough up blood and quickly died. Victor was sent to the phosphorus mine seven times, but on each occasion he survived his punishment and was returned to general labour cutting down trees.[53]

Transferred back to Burelopom, at hard labour camp number 231/1, he met other American emigrants from Detroit and elsewhere. Among them he befriended Albert 'Red' Lonn, the former captain of the American baseball team of Petrozavodsk, the champions of 1934. All that was lost after Lonn's arrest as a 'Very Dangerous Person' and his three-year sentence in the camps. With him in Burelopom were others whose names Victor remembered as Benny Murrto, 'Blackie' Pessonen and Jim Domyano. Together they reminisced about the lives they had left behind in Detroit and tried to encourage one another to survive. Albert Lonn's warmth and good humour, in particular, helped to restore a feeling of humanity to Victor, which he knew he had lost in the violence of his ordeal. Albert also told him that the guards in Burelopom did not want the prisoners to survive. The Americans never walked through the camp alone. They travelled in groups, armed with clubs, to ward off the criminals' attacks.[54]

Victor Herman was briefly transferred to prison in Gorky, his presence required there by the unexplained machinations of the

NKVD. On his return to Burelopom, he discovered that Benny Murrto had died. He was then transferred once again to build another sub-camp for the ever-expanding numbers of prisoners. After a punishment in the camp isolator, his toes became frostbitten. The camp doctor removed the dead flesh with a pair of scissors and Victor Herman was again sent out to work.[55]

None of the Americans surviving in the Soviet camps had any idea of the wider world around them. Transported to the remote outposts of a totalitarian state, they were cut off from the outside world, with no knowledge of the rapidly unfolding pace of world events. While public opinion in the West showed little concern for the existence of the millions in the Gulag camps, whose lives were reduced to a daily struggle to survive the greater purpose organised to kill them.

By the end of the decade, very few Americans could even remember the emigrants who had travelled to Russia at the Depression's height. At the New York World's Fair in 1939, few protested against the grand opening of the Soviet pavilion, or the party for a thousand VIP guests at which an orchestra alternately played 'The Star Spangled Banner' and the 'Internationale' for the latest NBC television cameras. Drawn by the fanfare and publicity, millions of American visitors flocked to see this lavishly expensive pavilion which advertised the bold achievements of the Soviet Union to the world. Ordinary New Yorkers jostled into its entrance marked by twin columns of marble, each carved with the giant faces of Lenin and Stalin. Beneath Stalin's profile was the inscription: 'FOR THE USSR, SOCIALISM IS SOMETHING ALREADY ACHIEVED AND WON.' Then they marvelled at the life-size replica of Mayakovsky Square metro station, and believed these words to be true.[56]

At the opening ceremony, Stalin's regime received the enthusiastic endorsement of the popular Mayor of New York, Fiorello LaGuardia, who delivered a warm welcoming speech in front of the microphones:

The Soviet architects deserve the highest praise for the beautiful concept and design of this building. I believe that in your exhibition here the opportunity will present itself to show to the American people what has been accomplished by a young government in an old country. After all our own country, our own concept of government was the result of a bloody revolution. We did not obtain freedom by requesting it on a postcard and receiving it on an engraved certificate. We fought for it. And you know, Mr Ambassador, our young republic was not so very popular with the dynasties of Europe at the time ... All beginnings are difficult. But I believe that there are contributions that have been made by your government which should be recognized by all.[57]

Outside the Soviet pavilion, a 250-foot-tall stainless steel statue of a heroic 'Soviet Worker' had been constructed to serve as a landmark and tourist attraction. The statue was quickly christened 'Big Joe' by New Yorkers, and held in its outstretched hand a five-pointed red star measuring ten feet in diameter. At night the star was lit with the powerful brightness of a 5000-watt lamp. The Second World War had just recently begun, and across the Lagoon of Nations other pavilions representing the independent democracies of Poland and the Baltic States were consumed in the aftermath of the Hitler–Stalin pact. But in the cool night air of fall, 'Big Joe' held the red Soviet star aloft high over the World's Fair, shining out beyond the fields of Flushing Meadows, and across the whole of old New York.[58]

16

22 JUNE 1941

> Imagine that you are creating a fabric of human destiny with the object of making men happy in the end, giving them peace and rest at last, but that it was essential and inevitable to torture to death only one tiny creature – that baby beating its breast with its fist, for instance – and to found that edifice on its unavenged tears, would you consent to be the architect on those conditions?'
>
> Fyodor Dostoyevsky, *The Brothers Karamazov*[1]

The build-up to World War II changed Kolyma. By 1939, the system of repression in the Soviet Union was bursting at the seams. The NKVD was operating beyond capacity, gathering information faster than it could be used – one tenth of the population might possibly be arrested, but never half. And so, quite abruptly, the Terror was scaled back. Overnight, the orders of the NKVD were no longer approved by 'the Commissar of State Security, Nikolai Yezhov'. Instead a story appeared on the back page of *Pravda*, just a few lines to say that Yezhov had resigned, and immediately afterwards his photograph disappeared from the public sphere.

At the closed military tribunal, the fallen Commissar pleaded vainly for his life: 'I was always by nature unable to stand violence against my person. For that reason I wrote all sorts of rubbish . . . I was subjected to the severest beating.'[2] Yezhov even attempted to defend himself: 'If they now accuse me of violating legality let them first of all ask that bitch Vyshinsky . . . he was the Union Procurator, not me. He had to take care of legality. By the way, comrade Stalin knew all about it.'[3] Yezhov was shot as a 'British spy' since, during the period of Stalin's alliance with Hitler, the spies of the Soviet Union had, with preternatural cunning, switched their allegiances from Nazi Germany to the 'British imperialists'.

When the German Foreign Minister, Joachim von Ribbentrop, flew in to Moscow to sign their pact, the Soviet chiefs of protocol realised late that there were no Nazi flags available to greet him, and in a panic they had to use stage props from an anti-Nazi propaganda film. As a Soviet military band played the unfamiliar 'Horst Wessel' song to welcome their guests, Gebhardt von Walther, an attendant German diplomat, whispered to his colleague, 'Look how the Gestapo officers are shaking hands with their counterparts of the NKVD and how they are all smiling at each other. They're obviously delighted finally to be able to collaborate.'[4]

At 2 a.m. on 24 August 1939, the pact was signed by Ribbentrop and Vyacheslav Molotov, who had recently replaced Maxim Litvinov as the new – and necessarily non-Jewish – Soviet Foreign Minister. In the Kremlin ceremony, a delighted Stalin raised his glass in a toast: 'I know how much the German nation loves its Führer,' said Stalin, ' I should therefore like to drink to his health.'[5] The official German photographer, Helmut Laux, snatched a picture of the Soviet dictator at that moment with his glass raised, which caused Stalin to suggest that it might not be wise to publish that particular photo. When Helmut Laux started to remove the film from his camera, Stalin waved him to stop: 'I trust the word of a German,' he said. And thus, over champagne toasts in the early hours of the Kremlin morning, the Second World War had effectively begun.[6]

One week after their pact was signed, Hitler's armies invaded Poland from the west. Two weeks later, on 14 September 1939, the Red Army occupied their predetermined portion of eastern Poland almost unnoticed. The cynical choreography of the division prompted Benito Mussolini's observation: 'Bolshevism is dead. In its place is a kind of Slavonic fascism.'[7] In Moscow, a programme of cultural exchange was organised to strengthen ties between the two totalitarian regimes, with Wagner's *Ring Cycle* arranged for the Bolshoi Theatre, and German businessmen once again crowding the tables at the Metropol Hotel.[8] Over Soviet radio, Foreign Minister Molotov broadcast lectures on the 'progressive' nature of the Nazi regime, which had successfully eliminated unemployment with its autobahn construction projects. Fascism was now simply 'a matter of taste'.[9]

In December 1939, an exchange of telegrams between Hitler and

Stalin was published in the Soviet press: 'Mr Joseph Stalin, Moscow. Please accept my most sincere congratulations on your sixtieth birthday. I take this occasion to tender my best wishes. I wish you personally good health and a happy future of the people of the friendly Soviet Union. Adolf Hitler.' To which Stalin politely answered: 'Herr Adolf Hitler, Head of the German State, Berlin. Please accept my appreciation of the congratulations and thanks for your good wishes with respect to the peoples of the Soviet Union. J. Stalin.'[10] Such courtesies would, of course, soon be excised from Soviet history, along with every other trace of the Hitler–Stalin pact. During the war, even to mention its existence became punishable with a ten-year sentence under Article 58 of the Soviet criminal code. In such circumstances, people quickly lost their ability to recall.[11]

As France and Norway fell before the Nazi blitzkrieg, and with London bombed relentlessly through the Blitz, Stalin lifted not one finger in support of the Western democracies. Even the notion of Soviet assistance was absurd, as the Red Army invaded Finland in the so-called 'Winter War' of December 1939. On 18 June 1940, after the collapse of France, Vyacheslav Molotov sent Adolf Hitler a message of praise via the German Ambassador Schulenburg, to express 'the warmest congratulations of the Soviet Government on the splendid success of the German Armed Forces'.[12] Fulfilling his role as Hitler's ally, Stalin authorised the export of the necessary raw materials required by the Nazi blitzkrieg. Through the course of 1940 Joseph Stalin delivered over 700,000 tons of Russian oil to the victorious Nazi armies. Travelling west across the Soviet– German frontier, alongside cargoes of iron ore and wheat, was a hidden trade in human beings. Since, as one of the conditions of their pact, Adolf Hitler had demanded that which Franklin Roosevelt scarcely knew existed: the return of his nationals from the USSR.[13]

Those Germans and Austrian nationals still alive in Soviet prisons or camps were ordered to be sent back to the Reich. Thus the Austrian Communist Franz Koritschoner, who had been arrested in Kiev in 1936 and tortured into an abject confession by the NKVD – 'I stand as a criminal before Soviet power . . . I request nothing more than to be shot as soon as possible as a criminal. My many years of service to the Communist cause are not grounds for mercy' – was delivered into the arms of the Gestapo.[14] Margarete Buber, the wife of a German communist, was removed from the brutal Karaganda

Gulag and returned to Moscow for questioning: 'Has your health suffered in any way during your stay in the reformatory camp?' 'Good heavens, no. What a question!' The NKVD kept her until her hair grew out and she had put on sufficient weight for her return to Germany, since in the words of another survivor: 'They don't want to hand over a band of skeletons; it would look bad.'[15]

At Brest-Litovsk, Margarete Buber watched as the SS and the NKVD exchanged salutes and pleasantries while the latest consignment of fifty prisoners was exchanged over the bridge. Photographs were taken of the Soviet and Nazi secret police socialising in their respective uniforms over a triumphal archway decorated with both a swastika and the hammer and sickle, next to the ubiquitous portrait of Stalin.[16] Along with the German prisoners, the NKVD handed the SS their official documentation, presumably as some form of professional courtesy. Virtually all the German prisoners were avowed anti-Nazis destined to be transported directly into Hitler's concentration camps. Franz Koritschoner was murdered at Auschwitz in June 1941. Margarete Buber was consigned to the women's camp at Ravensbrueck, where she found herself shunned by those German communists who had never been to Russia. They accused her of spreading lies about Stalin and the Soviet Union.[17]

In occupied Poland, Red Army soldiers experienced a similar conflict between ideology and the outward expression of reality. 'Comrade Colonel,' one soldier was reported to have asked, 'didn't we come to Poland to liberate our brothers, oppressed by landowners and capitalists? . . . A peasant has three or four horses, five or six cows, there is a bicycle in front of every house. Workers wear suits, hats – the same as a big Soviet director. There is something here that I don't understand.'[18] The Red Army soldiers of the Polish campaign brought back news of shops piled high with goods, a world without queues or ration cards where the ordinary workers' flats had running water and two taps: 'You turn one tap and you get hot water; you turn another – it's cold.' Poland was almost miraculous, as if communism had finally arrived in the very place it had never been attempted.[19]

Inevitably, the NKVD followed in the Red Army's wake to clear the population of all 'enemies of the people'. In this process, approximately 1.7 million Poles were arrested and transported east into the Soviet camps.[20] The Polish families were separated, the men from the

women and children, although the NKVD did not inform them at
the outset in order to avoid needless hysteria and consequent delay.
Rather they were told to pack their toiletries separately since they
would be led to separate places for a sanitary inspection.[21] The Poles
were then pressed and shut into crowded cattle cars, to be tormented
by thirst and cold during the long journey to the terminal points of
the Gulag. At Kotlas, in the northern Russian province of Archangel,
the trains travelled slowly for ten days across a landscape of barbed
wire and watchtowers. A Polish survivor recounted how twelve railroad tracks conjoined at the end of the line, each one occupied by a
prison train disgorging thousands upon thousands of frail human
beings, their faces blue with cold, shivering in temperatures well
below freezing. This mass of humanity was then divided by the tall
figures of the NKVD officers wearing long coats, black leather boots
and guns.[22]

With the world's attention focused on the fall of France, the Red
Army occupied the formerly independent Baltic States almost unnoticed. Just as in Poland, the NKVD arrested the 'enemies of the
people' en masse. Approximately 1.2 million Latvians, Lithuanians
and Estonians were deported by train, and disappeared into the inexhaustible Gulag.[23]

What serious hope did President Roosevelt have when he asked
his acting Secretary of State, Sumner Welles, to negotiate with Soviet
Ambassador Konstantin Oumansky in Washington? The President's
intention was to persuade Stalin to withdraw from his alliance with
Hitler, which Roosevelt light-heartedly described as 'Stalin's
Mugwump policy'.[24] As Sumner Welles sat down to barter with
Oumansky, the lives of the Americans in Russia depended on the
negotiating skills of this childhood friend of Roosevelt's, like him a
product of Groton and Harvard. When Oumansky asked for
American engineers to be sent to Russia to provide technical assistance for the manufacture of high-octane aviation fuel, Sumner
Welles refused the request: 'So long as American citizens were not
given freedom of movement and were not allowed at will to appear
at the American Embassy at Moscow, this Government did not feel
that it could afford to facilitate the visits of American citizens to the
Soviet Union by the issuance to them of passports.'

His statement showed that, at the very least, the Acting Secretary
of State was aware of the American emigrants' continued existence
in Russia. For his part Oumansky cynically wondered if these

citizens 'really were Americans at all' and answered that he would have to report back to Moscow.[25] But whereas Adolf Hitler had successfully managed to retrieve his nationals from Russia only to have them killed out of 'motiveless malignity', neither Sumner Welles nor Franklin Roosevelt was willing, or even attempted to force the diplomatic issue any further.

Although he was warned by American and British intelligence for several months beforehand, the Nazi invasion of 22 June 1941 appeared to take Stalin completely by surprise. It was left to Molotov to break the news to the public over the radio:

> Citizens of the Soviet Union: the Soviet government and its head, Comrade Stalin have authorized me to make the following statement. Today at 4 o'clock in the morning, without any claim having been presented to the Soviet Union, without a declaration of war, German troops attacked our borders at many points . . . The attack on our country was perpetrated despite the fact that a treaty on non-aggression had been signed between the USSR and Germany, and that the Soviet Government has most faithfully abided by all the provisions of this treaty . . .[26]

For the Red Army officers who had survived the Terror, the outbreak of war represented their best hope of salvation. Eighty per cent of the Red Army command, from majors up, had already been killed by the NKVD. Marshal Rodion Malinovsky, the Soviet Defence Minister after Stalin's death, later quoted a figure of 82,000 executions. It was, said Malinovsky, as if a crystal vase containing their most experienced commanders had been wantonly smashed, and 'on the eve of the war, we found ourselves decapitated'.[27] For the Russian officers who survived the Terror, the Second World War would prove to be a safer experience. Fewer would die on the Eastern Front, the greatest theatre of conflict in modern history, than had been already killed by the NKVD. Thus Konstantin Rokossovsky, a future marshal of the Soviet Union and defence minister of Poland, was flown back from Kolyma ready to resume his military career with his teeth kicked out. In the Kremlin, Stalin questioned him, 'Konstantin Konstantinovich did they beat you up there?' 'They did, Comrade Stalin,' replied Rokossovsky.[28]

For ordinary citizens the outbreak of war was a breathing space in

Russia, a time of relative freedom after the overwhelming fear that had dominated their lives before. Foreigners discovered Muscovites to have become peculiarly more cheerful on hearing the news of war. The visiting American writer Erskine Caldwell wrote that: 'On face after face smiles broke out, plainly indicating genuine happiness that at last they would give full vent to their long-pent-up emotions.'[29] Meanwhile Joseph Stalin had disappeared from sight altogether, refusing to meet any of his staff between 24 June and 2 July 1941, a week that Khrushchev later claimed had been lost to a drinking binge.[30] Stunned by the rapid German advances, and fully aware that his personal safety was at risk, Stalin retreated to his dacha outside Moscow. When Politburo members arrived to visit, Stalin shrank away from them in fear, his voice becoming tense as if he expected to be arrested. 'What have you come for?' Stalin asked. The loyal functionaries replied that they wished to create a State Committee for Defence with Stalin at its head.[31]

It took until 3 July 1941 for Stalin to finally address the nation for the first time in three years. His radio speech was made at 6 a.m. without any forewarning, just a statement that loudspeakers should be left on at that time. The reason for the strange scheduling, the visiting American journalist Alice-Leone Moats learned, was because Stalin spoke Russian with a thick Georgian accent, 'like an Italian waiter in an American movie speaks English'. When the Great Leader sipped his water, the clink of the glass was heard from Moscow to Vladivostok: 'Comrades, citizens, brothers and sisters, fighters of our Red Army and Navy! I am speaking to you, my friends!'[32]

In the Ukraine, villagers greeted the invading Nazi armies with the traditional Slavic gifts of bread and salt. The older peasants touched the black crosses on the German tanks in awe, naively believing them to be emissaries of Christ.[33] Statues of Stalin were pulled down and beaten furiously with pickaxes, and when Soviet planes were shot down the villagers laughed and clapped their hands announcing that Stalin's regime would soon fall.[34] The Ukrainian famine had taken place just eight years earlier, followed by a vengeful and very bloody Terror. Millions of Ukrainian lives had been already lost to Stalin. Perhaps if a father watches his children starve to death in his arms, he might welcome the devil himself.

In Moscow the chimneys of the offices of the Soviet government billowed with smoke, as the records of the NKVD, the Foreign

Ministry and the Prosecutor's Office were burned, destroying the evidence of their crimes. In October 1941, the first snows settling in Moscow were 'sooty with burnt paper'. As the German armies advanced to the very outskirts of the city, witnesses saw Communist Party members committing the ultimate sacrilege of tearing up their Party cards and flushing away the pieces into the sewers. Others just tossed their cards into the street, with their names and pictures safely scratched off. They littered the Moscow pavements. The action was both a measure of the people's fear and an assessment of the likelihood of Moscow's fall, amid well-founded rumours that brigades of the SS were executing Communist Party officials. Moscow's Jewish population was particularly conscious of the horror that awaited them if they were caught in the city.[35] The Luftwaffe had recently dropped leaflets over Moscow with the words 'Death to all Jews' written in heavy Teutonic typeface. Underneath was the information that the leaflet should be kept as a guarantee of safe conduct to the German side.[36]

That summer Moscow was lit up with anti-aircraft fire shooting red, green and orange tracers into the night sky. The defence of the city against the Luftwaffe was deafening as shrapnel rained down over rooftops and city streets.[37] The Soviet commissariats were evacuated, and the most famous buildings and bridges in Moscow were all mined with explosives. During the night, the embalmed body of Lenin – the most sacred relic of the atheist state – was removed from its marble mausoleum in Red Square. Vladimir Ilyich was evacuated on the same train to Kuibyshev as the American diplomatic corps and reporters.[38] Earlier that day, on 15 October 1941, the Americans had gathered in the courtyard of Spaso House amid the noise of approaching gunfire. A thousand-pound German bomb had recently blown out the Spaso House windows, and now a Russian chauffeur was taking bets on whether Nazi tanks had already entered Moscow.[39]

It was during the diplomatic evacuation that many of the confidential files of the American Embassy in Moscow were destroyed, and much of the history of the American emigration to the USSR was lost.[40] Appropriately enough, the evacuation train carrying Lenin's body and the American diplomats had cars attached filled with prisoners, since even in moments of the gravest crisis the needs of the Gulag were met and the system of repression remained firmly intact. When the American diplomats reached the safety of Kuibyshev, their NKVD minders stood out even more conspicuously in this closed city on the banks of the Volga. Eight hundred kilometres south-east of Moscow, the same faces patrolled the relocated buildings of the foreign embassies, in case anyone should have the foolish idea that the normal rules no longer applied.[41]

In Kuibyshev, just as in Moscow, the diplomats were harried by a few surviving American exiles, often female family members who had escaped the NKVD thus far. Anna and Anastasia Wardamsky, for example, called at the new American Embassy building in February 1942, hysterical after their father had disappeared, and their third sister Helena had fallen 'sick with nerves'. The Wardamsky sisters described how their American passports had been confiscated by the Soviet authorities, and Anna frantically complained that 'the Embassy was not protecting them'. As their family waited for the hundreds of dollars they needed to pay their passage home, the sisters received the written assurance from American diplomats that 'should the Soviet authorities attempt to prevail upon you to accept Soviet passports, or should efforts be made to force you to accept Soviet passports, you may inform them that any attempt on their part to force any American citizen to bear a Soviet passport involuntarily is a matter of the gravest concern to the Embassy and will be brought to the urgent attention of the Government of the United States of America.'

Inevitably their case became mired in bureaucracy, not helped by the telegrammed refusal of Sumner Welles to issue an emergency repatriation loan. As their case dragged on, the Wardamsky sisters were ordered by the NKVD to leave the closed city of Kuibyshev. In May 1942, Helena telephoned the American Embassy to let them know that her sister Anna had been arrested. After the arrest, Helena continued to write frantic appeals to the diplomats asking for intervention on behalf of her missing sister. She was still waiting for the State Department to act when she received the official news that Anna Wardamsky had died in an NKVD prison, supposedly of 'heart-failure'.[42]

As might be expected, the death certificates of Americans in Soviet custody were regularly falsified to disguise the true cause. On 8 December 1942 and 9 January 1943, Embassy officials were allowed to visit the imprisoned Isaiah Oggins, a 45-year-old from Willimantic, Connecticut, after a sustained letter-writing campaign by his wife Norma in the United States. In her letters, Norma Oggins had stressed the need of their eleven-year-old son Robin to see his father. The boy, she wrote, was 'as promising a young American as ever lived'. Although the American diplomats were allowed to visit Isaiah Oggins, nothing more was done to obtain the release of the former American Communist Party member, imprisoned since February 1939.[43]

For their part, the Soviet security services had no intention of ever allowing Isaiah Oggins to return home. A letter was sent from Victor Abakumov – a protégé of the new secret police chief, Lavrenty Beria – to Stalin in connection with the case:

> The appearance of Oggins in the USA might be used by persons hostile to the Soviet Union for active propaganda against the USSR. Based on this, the MGB of the USSR considers it necessary to execute Oggins, and then to report to the Americans that after the meeting of Oggins with the representatives of the American Embassy in June of 1943, he was returned to the place of confinement in Norilsk and died there in 1946 in hospital as a result of tuberculosis of the spine. In the Norilsk camp archives we will reflect the course of Oggins' illness and medical and other aid rendered to him. Oggins' death will be recorded officially in his medical records along with an autopsy and burial certificate . . . I request your instructions. Abakumov.[44]

Soon afterwards, Isaiah Oggins was executed in Moscow by poison administered by an NKVD doctor named Grigory Mairanovsky. The official Soviet documentation recorded death due to 'paralysis of the heart owing to acute sclerosis of the coronary artery with associated angiospams and papillary carcinoma of the urinary bladder'. In the chaos of war, hardly a soul knew or cared about the solitary deaths of such victims.[45]

Nor was it easy to imagine there were still a few naive Americans attempting to emigrate to the USSR. Edward Speier was a thirty-six-year-old metalworker from Detroit who had taken the latest proclamations of Soviet–American friendship perhaps a little too seriously. With the United States not yet in the war, Speier chose to help the Soviet cause by stowing away in a boxed locomotive loaded on to a Soviet steamer in Richmond, California. Before organising his departure he had told his mother, Henrietta Speier, that he believed 'the Russians would welcome the services of a skilled mechanic'. He was arrested on his arrival in Vladivostok in September 1941.

Unusually, American diplomatic officials were allowed to visit Edward Speier twice during the relatively brief period of his detention, a possible sign of Stalin's new concern for American friendship. The first visit took place only weeks after Speier's arrest, on 20 December 1941. In his interview, the rugged-looking metalworker – whose black hair and hazel eyes stared out defiantly from his photograph – described himself as one of 'Uncle Sam's disinherited sons, kicked around and not given a chance to work . . . in every country there are good and bad people, but whereas in the United States the bad people are running the Government in the Soviet Union the bad people are all in jail.' Edward Speier claimed that he had been persecuted many times in the United States for 'stealing food and eating in restaurants without paying'. The American vice-consul, Donald Nichols, was left unimpressed by the visit, describing Speier in his dispatch back to Washington as 'a very uncouth person who seasons his conversation liberally with profanity and obscenities'.

Six months' incarceration in an NKVD prison changed Edward Speier's attitude completely. By his second visit, on 25 March 1942, Speier was denying that he had ever felt badly about the United States and begging the American consul to help him return home. Twice the Soviet authorities asked the American officials if they wanted him back, otherwise 'normal Soviet law would be applied'. But nothing was done to save Speier, and his subsequent fate was all too predictable. According to the Soviet death certificate issued to the American diplomats, Edward Speier died on 3 January 1943 at 7 a.m. The chief of the prisoners' convoy testified that he died of pneumonia on a prison train, 'No. 74', en route to a 'reformation-labour camp' at Karaganda. His corpse, they said, was forwarded for burial at the camp. With exacting thoroughness the Soviets listed his personal effects: '1. Warm jacket old. 2. Brown fur hat, old. 3. Knitted black hat, old. 4. Sweater woollen, old. 5. Woollen trousers, green, torn. 6. Pillow, filled with feathers. 7. Leather shoes, torn. 8. Leather shoes, torn. 9. Leather slippers, torn.'[46]

On hearing the news of her son's premature death, Henrietta Speier of San Bernardino, California, wrote a series of three letters addressed to the American diplomatic staff in Kuibyshev which she requested to be forwarded to the Soviet authorities. In her handwritten letters Mrs Speier's spelling was often less than perfect:

*In the very heart of your beloved land of Russia is buried my
dear son Edward Henry Speier exact location being 300
meters west of the hospital of the 4th district in Karaganda
Reformatory Labor Camp . . . I his mother knows that if
there's any way of one knowing what happens after death to
ones body I know that my son would be well pleased to be
buried where he is deep in the heart of Russia. The country he
learned to love and admire through books and liditure he's
read . . . the only thing that might sadden my son's heart
would be the thought of having to lay in a prison and paupers
grave after all his efforts to help our beloved allies. He
perhaps offered his services but not being trusted had to be
detained. I his mother worry about his burrial. Did he have a
coffen? And a rough box? you know its my very own flesh
and blood no one knew and understood what a real noble
heart he had. Can any one tell me how long my son was ill
before he died? Did the people in who's costidy like my son?
Did my son suffer hard or long before he died? Did he leave
any message? To anyone. Did he work or serve Russia? . . .
did my son have cloths on when buried? Was he buried
dishonarably? Hope not. Can we visit his grave after the war?
. . . Can the Dr at the dispensary or Drs on train no 74 who
treated my son in his illness tell me anything how my son
contacted pneumonia.*

   Sincierally Yours,

     Mrs Albert C. Speier.

PS Can you answer me?'

Lacking an answer to her questions, Henrietta Speier found her
grief could only worsen. In her second letter, she continued:

*All I hoped was that my son had left a last letter or made a
spoken last request to me his mother as most folks do when
they become very ill. I hope my son wasn't put to death by
Russian government by my son entering their country in
wartime. Truly he only wanted to offer his services to our
allies . . . as there been so much talk in Russian lititure stating
that there was a great need for skilled help. Seeing I cant or
havnt had a better explanation about cause of his death I feel
so sad and fear foul play theres such a haunting unrest in my*

heart. My son's spirit haunts me kindly forward this to Russian officials who had charge of my son during his illness and death and buerial. Tell them I expect to come to Russia after war and if possiable have my sons remains removed to a private buerial grounds. I had a dream of a man leaving a train woke up frightened then several mo's later I got word my son passed away on train always feared my son tried to escape and was shot we're honest folks and neither our government or Russian need fear he ment to harm either government.

　Sincierally Yours
　　Mrs Henrietta Speier.
Kindly forward.

Henrietta Speier's third and final letter reflected a mother's gradual understanding of the truth behind her son's death:

I'm worried to distract when I read all his cloths and shoes had holes in them. No wonder my son took down with phnuemoni . . . We can thank God we live in a land of plenty among people who believe in treating prisoners of war and I'll bet even stowaways like my son was would at least be given warm enough cloths to keep them from getting ill. Like my son did. Are my letters sent direct to the Russian government? Everthing seems so hushed not enough in detail conserning my sons illness I fear he met with a terriable fate perhaps put to death . . . Sincierally Yours, Mrs Henrietta Speier, I wonder how cold it was on Jan 3, the year my son died at Karaganda Kasah? Is it very cold at Karaganda Kasah in Jan ??? . . . My God I prayed every day to God for my sons welfare surly God must of heard me. And I trusted God that he wouldn't let any harm befall my son.[47]

There was no record of any answer to Henrietta Speier's letters.

By the end of 1942, the conditions within the Soviet concentration camps were already well known to the American authorities. In the early stages of the war, Stalin allowed an army to be gathered from the survivors of the 1.7 million Poles consigned to the Gulag in 1939. The American journalist Alice-Leone Moats happened to be present in Kuibyshev in 1941 when a trainload of two thousand

Poles arrived back from one of the camps. She found their condition heart-rending:

> There were sixteen corpses in the cars – men and women who had died of hunger on the way ... By a strange coincidence I encountered a man in his thirties whom I had known well in Vienna ten years before as a rather fat and very gay young blade. It was not until he told me his name that I recognized him. Although six feet tall, he weighed only one hundred and twenty pounds; his face was gaunt and gray, most of his teeth were gone, and the short stubble of hair just growing in from the prison haircut was white. Just three days before the signing of the Russo–Polish agreement he had been condemned to death and was still dazed by his miraculous escape. A doctor who had been allowed to treat his compatriots in one camp told me that all had dysentery from hunger, one in three had scurvy, and fifty per cent of those under twenty had tuberculosis.

The so-called 'Anders army' had been granted permission to leave the USSR to fight alongside the British. One Polish survivor of the camps remembered: 'The Russians had a hard time seeing us leave. The elderly ones said it is a miracle, a true miracle. This never happened before. The younger ones envied us.'[48]

As the Poles gathered in Iran, Lieutenant-Colonel Henry Szymanski, an American military liaison officer, wrote a detailed report dated 23 November 1943, describing the facts he had learned concerning the earlier deportations of Polish men, women and children into the Soviet Gulag:

> The plan was very carefully worked out, and its purpose was the extermination of the so-called intelligentsia of Eastern Poland ... Families were broken up and in many cases the husband shot. Very little time was given for preparation. One or two suitcases were all that was permitted to be taken ... the destinations were forced labor camps, concentration camps, and prisons ... because of the lack of vitamins, scurvy, beriberi and many other diseases were prevalent. Night-blindness and loss of memory resulted from the same causes ... Pictures taken by men in Pahlevi indicate the privations that those people had to undergo in the land of the Soviets. The children had no chance. It is

estimated that 50% have already died from malnutrition. The other 50% will die unless evacuated to a land where American help can reach them. A visit to any of the hospitals in Teheran will testify to this statement. They are filled with children and adults who would be better off not to have survived the ordeal.'

In his report sent back to Washington DC, Lieutenant-Colonel Szymanski emphasised that 'overwork and undernourishment . . . have done the job of bullets'. Among the witness statements, he quoted a letter from Stanislaus Haracz to his brother in Brooklyn, New York, describing his journey to Siberia. Of the seventy people packed into their train car, 'not a single child arrived at destination, my three children died; their bodies were placed on the snow beside the car and the train moved on; that was their funeral'. Near the end of this startling document, which read as a shocked American soldier's first encounter with genocide, Lieutenant-Colonel Szymanski added: 'One of Mr Willkie's secretarys stated to me in Tehran, that Russia and the United States will dictate the peace of Europe. When I repeated this (without mentioning the source) to a very prominent Pole in Tehran, he at first begged me not to jest, and then very sadly said to me that "In that case Poland has lost the war and the Allies have lost the war." The choice in Europe is not merely: Democracy vs Hitler, as so many Americans seem to think it is.'

Almost as an afterthought, tucked in a folder at the very end of the report, Szymanski enclosed a series of black and white photographs taken of the starved Polish children in the hospitals of Teheran. It was the pictures of these children, even more than the written accounts of their suffering, which conveyed the immediate truth of what was then taking place within the Gulag camps. Here was possibly the first photographic evidence of the consequences of Stalinism on the human body. The Polish children gazed back at the camera lens unaware of their unexpected reprieve. Their tiny bodies were only skin and bone, and their bulging eyes stared out in lifeless accusation.[49] Of the 1.7 million Poles deported into Soviet Russia, only 400,000 returned and were saved. What happened to the rest – the remaining 1.3 million who simply disappeared – was revealed in the eyes of the child who was spared.

A Polish survivor of the Soviet camps, Antoni Ekart, wrote in a memoir that the 'deliberate NKVD policy of undernourishment makes it difficult to regard the majority of the camps, especially those in the North and the so-called Penal Settlements, as being in any way different from the German concentration camps with their crematoria and gas chambers. The death rate is the same.'[50] One significant difference was the lack of photographic evidence ever to emerge from the Gulag. Nor was this accidental, since photography within the wider Soviet Union, let alone the camps, was always one of the most heavily proscribed activities, guaranteed to lead to swift arrest unless overseen by the NKVD. And without the photographic evidence of their victims, the essential inhumanity of the Soviet camps never fully entered into the Western public's consciousness, where such issues were open to judgement. Later the written evidence from the survivors might be understood intellectually, and their drawings and sketches from memory acknowledged. But, as was undoubtedly true in Nuremberg, it was only the photographic evidence which elicited true comprehension from all parties irrespective of their politics. We trust, it seems, only with our eyes.[51]

It might, therefore, appear criminally unjust that such rare evidence gathered in the early stages of the war was judged too politically sensitive ever to see the light of day. Lieutenant-Colonel Szymanski's report, and its photographs, were classified as 'secret' and buried away in an archive in Washington DC – 'This document contains information affecting the national defense of the United States within the meaning of the Espionage Laws, Title 18, U.S.C., Sections 793 and 794. The transmission or the revelation of its contents in any manner to an unauthorized person is prohibited by law.' And thus its revelations were safely hidden from the public gaze by the moral exigencies of the American–Soviet alliance.

With much of European Russia occupied, and Leningrad and Stalingrad under siege, it was perhaps difficult to rationalise how Stalin was prepared to use valuable men and scarce resources to keep millions more imprisoned. But this would be to overlook the fact that in Soviet Russia, just as in Nazi Germany, the consequences of totalitarianism accelerated in the shadow of the Second World War. In Kolyma, General Nikishov's principal difficulty was managing the shortage of materials he required to keep his vast operation running. Remarkably, his predicament was solved by the intervention of the United States government.

17

THE AMERICAN BRANDS OF A SOVIET GENOCIDE

> So that prisons should vanish forever, we built new prisons ... So
> that work should become a rest and a pleasure, we introduced forced
> labor. So that not one drop of blood be shed any more, we killed and
> killed and killed.
>
> Andrei Sinyavsky, *On Socialist Realism*[1]

One month after the invasion of Russia, in July 1941, Roosevelt's
most trusted adviser, Harry Hopkins, flew into Moscow. A key policy-
maker of the New Deal, the hollow-faced Hopkins was described
by one Democratic party rival as having 'a mind like a razor, a tongue
like a skinning knife, a temper like a Tartar and a sufficient vocabulary of parlor profanity ... to make a muleskinner jealous'.[2] In the
Kremlin he was welcomed with open arms by Joseph Stalin.

The Soviet leader now declared President Roosevelt the 'best
friend of the world's down-trodden', and was asking for American
troops to be sent to Russia to fight alongside the Red Army under
their own chain of command. It was a project involving up to thirty
Allied divisions, which Winston Churchill described as 'a delusion'
not least because in the summer of 1941 most military intelligence
experts were predicting an imminent and total Soviet collapse. Even
Roosevelt's cabinet members were making private bets on whether
the cities of Leningrad, Moscow, Kiev and Odessa would all fall before
1 September 1941.[3]

For Hopkins' visit, Stalin ordered the portraits of Marx and
Engels to be taken down and replaced by two large paintings of
Mikhail Kutuzov and Alexander Suvorov, the traditional Russian

military heroes of the pre-Revolutionary age.[4] The gambit appeared to work very well: 'It is ridiculous to think of Stalin as a Communist,' Hopkins reported back home, 'he's a Russian nationalist.' In an American magazine article Hopkins went still further in his praise:

> He talked as he knew his troops were shooting – straight and hard ... an austere, rugged, determined figure in boots that shone like mirrors, stout baggy trousers, and snug-fitting blouse. He wore no ornament, military or civilian. He's built close to the ground, like a football coach's dream of a tackle. He's about five feet six, about a hundred and ninety pounds. His hands are huge, as hard as his mind. His voice is harsh but ever under control.'[5]

Harry Hopkins returned with a list of Soviet military requirements and a glowing impression of the Soviet dictator who had spoken so sincerely of 'the necessity of there being a minimum moral standard between nations'.[6]

In response, Henry Morgenthau noted in his diary, President Roosevelt 'went to town in a way I have never heard him go to town before. He was terrific. He said he didn't want to hear what was on order, he said he wanted to hear only what was on the water.' Attempting to gain swift Congressional approval for 'Lend-Lease' aid to Russia, Roosevelt set out to persuade the American public that Stalin's regime was at the forefront of 'peace and democracy in the world'. At a White House press conference, the American President even ventured to claim there was freedom of religion in the Soviet Union: 'As I think I suggested a week or two ago, some of you might find it useful to read Article 124 of the Constitution of Russia,' Roosevelt patiently explained to the White House press corps. When a reporter interrupted to ask him what it said, the President amiably continued: 'Well I haven't learned it by heart sufficiently to quote – I might be off a little bit, but anyway: freedom of conscience ... freedom of religion. Freedom equally to use propaganda against religion, which is essentially what the rule is in this country; only, we don't put it quite the same way.'

In the aftermath of the controversial press conference, Secretary of State Cordell Hull was immediately instructed to wire Moscow with the request that the President wanted from the 'highest authorities of

Soviet government some statement which can be sent to the press in this country' to confirm the truth of what he had just said. Stalin, of course, was only too happy to oblige.[7]

In Moscow, the celebrated American photographer Margaret Bourke-White was given permission to take pictures of overflowing congregations in Russian churches. The images were rushed into publication for a book entitled *Russia at War*, with her husband Erskine Caldwell responsible for the unconvincing copy: 'The Protestant Churches had gained much with the coming of the Soviet regime and they were quick to recognize it ... The coming of Bolshevism meant for them a chance to worship in peace, unaided by the Government, but unpersecuted by it.'

Inside the Kremlin, Margaret Bourke-White was given rare permission to photograph Stalin himself. Unnerved by her proximity to absolute power, the sympathetic Bourke-White appeared to have fallen headlong into the Leni Riefenstahl school of totalitarian devotion, dressing up especially for the occasion in a pair of red shoes with a red bow in her hair. Later she described their meeting: 'I thought he had the strongest face I had ever seen. When I dropped to my knees to get a low camera angle he began to laugh. And when he pressed his interpreter into work, changing flash bulbs and holding reflectors for me, he chuckled.' Afterwards, as Bourke-White packed away her photographic equipment, she noticed Stalin's expression had changed: 'When the smile ended, it was as though a veil had been drawn over his features. Again he looked as if he had been turned into granite, and I went away thinking that this was the strongest, most determined face I had ever seen.'[8] In the Kremlin, Stalin smoked his favourite brands of American cigarettes – the Camels, Chesterfields and Lucky Strikes delivered as a courtesy by the American Embassy along with his regular consignment of Hollywood movies. During their small talk, Margaret Bourke-White never mentioned the names of her Russian friends in government who had helped her on her previous visits to photograph the Five Year Plan. They had all since vanished, and the American visitors understood that it was impolite to mention the missing. From 1938, their diplomats had coached them on the correct etiquette of silence.[9]

Had there been the slightest desire, the State Department need only have consulted their own files to correct the President's claim, and confirm the truth that Russian priests of every denomination had been among the first to be arrested and killed in the 'atheist campaigns'. Some of the victims were personally known to the American diplomats in Moscow. In November 1936, the Reverend Strekh, a Lutheran evangelist pastor who risked his life to minister to the American Embassy, was arrested on the day he was supposed to perform a marriage ceremony for the American vice-consul in Moscow.[10] The following year, Loy Henderson reported that Monsigneur Frison, the Apostolic Administrator of the Crimea, 'the last Catholic bishop remaining in the USSR' had been shot on 27 June 1937.[11]

For years the State Department had been sent correspondence from Americans asking for intervention on behalf of the persecuted Russian clergy. A recent example was a letter sent on 29 July 1941, from Pastor Alfred Anderson of the Salem Lutheran Church of Brooklyn, New York:

> *Dear Mr President . . .*
> *Kindly have Mr Hopkins inquire of 'Comrade Stalin' where the*
> *40 theological students of a few years ago in the Lutheran*
> *Seminary in Moscow are today . . . Also where the 318*
> *Lutheran pastors of that date are. We know some were shot,*
> *some sent into the woods as slaves, but where are the rest?*
> *Their blood cries up to heaven.[12]*

Other letters had asked for protection for missing American clergymen in Russia, for example from M. A. Matthew of the First Presbyterian Church of Seattle, Washington:

> *My Dear Brother*
> *I am writing you in behalf of Rev. John S. Voronaeff and*
> *his wife, Katherine Voronaeff, American citizens who have*
> *been imprisoned in Russia. Rev. Voronaeff preached here for*
> *years, had a church in this city . . . That infernal, hell bound*
> *country of Russia has no right to imprison American citizens.*
> *Will you see that these two good people are released at*
> *once . . .?[13]*

Even the question of freedom of religion, and what had happened to Russia's missing clergy, had been answered candidly by Joseph Stalin himself in an audience given to a visiting American delegation just a few years earlier: 'The Party cannot remain neutral regarding the propagators of religious prejudices, with regard to reactionary clergy poisoning the minds of labouring masses. Have we annihilated the clergy? Yes we have annihilated it. The trouble is that it is not yet completely liquidated.'[14] When Stalin made statements using verbs such as 'annihilate' or 'liquidate', the result was always organised violence on a mass scale. After the fall of the Soviet Union, the former Politburo member Alexander Yakovlev led a human rights commission, which concluded that 200,000 Russian clergy had been executed during the Stalinist period.[15]

While Winston Churchill all but bankrupted the Bank of England to pay for American arms, Soviet Lend-Lease was funded on generous credit terms destined never to be repaid. 'I think it is a mistake at this time to bother Stalin with any financial arrangements and take his mind off the war,' Henry Morgenthau told Hopkins in October 1941. 'It would make him think we are nothing but a bunch of Yankee traitors trying to squeeze the last drop out of him. Do you feel or does the President feel that because the English paid down so much cash that we have to get so much gold from the Russians?'[16] During the course of the war the United States shipped fifteen million tons of materials to the Soviet Union, valued at eleven billion dollars, less than half of which were munitions. An endless supply of American equipment began arriving at the wharves of Magadan, and at any other Soviet port with open water. Inevitably, the American cargo was unloaded by Gulag labour.[17]

The master of the SS *City of Omaha*, Captain J. S. Schulz, spent ten months trapped in the new port of Molotovsk, thirty-five kilometres west of Archangel, penned in by ice and German bombing. The port, named after the Soviet Foreign Minister, had three concentration camps attached, and the Gulag prisoners who unloaded the American ships were starved to the point where they risked eating the raw flour spilled on to the decks, although they knew the penalty for such behaviour was death. In his report, Captain Schulz wrote that the Soviet authorities 'were very careless about life over there. It means nothing. If a convict steps out of line – any small thing at all – they kill him.' When the scrapings of the ship's garbage was taken away in trucks to be fed to pigs, Captain Schultz watched one prisoner 'rummaging in a garbage-filled truck and, upon refusing to leave when warned by a soldier, was bayoneted and shot.' Another Gulag prisoner was killed on the *City of Omaha*'s deck, and was left lying there until the American crew objected and the body was taken away. In his report, Captain Schultz noted that the Soviet prisoners were worked fourteen or fifteen hours a day, and included young women just seventeen years old.[18]

Approximately half the American Lend-Lease cargo was shipped to the Soviet Far East ports where the conditions in the camps were, if anything, worse than Molotovsk. In Magadan, much of the cargo intended for use in the war against Germany was channelled by General Nikishov into the service of Dalstroi. Brand-new American icebreakers were used by the Soviets to keep sea lanes open around Magadan, further extending the transportation season for the Dalstroi fleet. Having delivered their cargos, the American Liberty ships were then converted to transport prisoners into Kolyma; while the ageing Dalstroi fleet was sailed across the Pacific to shipyards on the West Coast for expensive overhaul and repair. In the United States, the NKVD steamers were reconditioned at the expense of the American taxpayer before their quick return to service as 'the death ships of the Sea of Okhotsk'.

On 31 January 1942, for example, the *Dzhurma* arrived at a Seattle shipyard for an overhaul costing over half a million dollars. Before the war the *Dzhurma* had caught fire in a riot below decks and limped into Magadan with the prisoners still locked in the hold. Three years later, when the American fitters opened up the hold, they were met by the appalling stench of death.[19] Nothing was said or done as one Dalstroi ship after another arrived in America for refitting and, having been made seaworthy again, returned to Vladivostok to pick up more prisoners, often on their very next voyage. Without the NKVD fleet, the operations within Kolyma would have become impossible to sustain. The ships were an essential link in the mechanism required to replace the prisoners who had died, and to expand still further the network of concentration camps. It was as if the Reichministry had arranged to have their railway engines repaired in Philadelphia and then shipped back across the Atlantic to recommence their journeys to Auschwitz.

At the time, it was the surviving American prisoners, such as Thomas Sgovio or Victor Herman, who felt the keenest sense of outrage at the most famous brand names of American industry being used in the service of the death camps. In Kolyma, Thomas Sgovio witnessed the arrival of enormous black, fifty-ton American Diamond trucks with trailers and iron sides, and the five-ton Studebakers that could easily manage the unforgiving terrain. These American trucks were used to transport prisoners across the vast distances of Russian wilderness into the camps.

Within the Kolyma camps and mines, suddenly everything was American: the machinery, the tools, the shovels, even the detonators and blasting equipment, were all 'Made in the USA'. In one camp, the prisoner Varlam Shalamov, a former law student from Leningrad, described watching the NKVD guards eating 'magical jars of American sausage'.[20] Meanwhile Thomas Sgovio was fed a new kind of soup, one that tasted very different from any other he had been given and, astonishingly, contained meat and bones. For two weeks the prisoners ate what they were given, reassuring themselves that the meat must be reindeer from the Yakut breeding farms. Eventually they heard that the cooks in the camp kitchens had stolen the American canned pork and replaced it with the bodies of the dead. The prisoners hardly flinched when they heard this news. They were all too starved to care.[21]

In her women's camp, the Dutch nurse Elinor Lipper blessed the Americans for delivering their flour in such splendid white bags. The bags could be turned into extra clothing to protect the prisoners from the extreme cold, a practice which spread rapidly through the camps of Kolyma. And thus the starving Gulag legions became clad in American flour bags, whose brand names ran across their emaciated bodies in irregular patterns, like a Cubist rendering of suffering.[22] The prisoners' desperation for food was revealed when the American bulldozers were first delivered, each with its own barrel of machine grease. Varlam Shalamov watched one barrel attacked by a crowd of starving prisoners who convinced themselves that the grease was 'Lend-Lease butter'. By the time a guard arrived to protect the 'food for machines', only half the barrel was left.[23]

Nor did the arrival of the bulldozers ease the burden of the prisoners' labour. Shalamov witnessed how the first American bulldozer was driven out of the camp *away* from the mines, to the place where a series of stone pits had begun to slide down the mountain. The pits contained the bodies of the male and female prisoners who had been shot, beaten or starved to death at that particular camp. Newly exposed to the elements after months or years underground, their bare skeletal bodies had been perfectly preserved by the extreme cold. Standing on the side of the mountain watching the bulldozer rebury the bodies, Varlam Shalamov described how even the expressions on the faces of the dead could still be recognised: 'They were just bare skeletons over which stretched dirty, scratched skin bitten all over by lice ... eyes burning with a hungry gleam.' He also realised that what he had witnessed was only a pitifully small part of a vast world of hundreds of camps, and that so many more 'could be hidden in the folds of a mountain'.[24]

At the end of the war, Allied investigators found it difficult to comprehend how one million people could have been killed in the few acres of the Nazi extermination camp at Treblinka. Only after the downfall of the regime, and the arrival of the victorious Allied armies, could the enormity of the crime be revealed and later, at Nuremberg, a measure of justice brought to bear. In the Soviet Union there was never a victorious army to expose the consequences of Stalin's rule, nor would there ever be a Nuremberg. Instead, the victims of Kolyma, and every other terminal point of the Gulag, remained concealed even as the killings continued unabated. In Kolyma, the rhetorical question Joseph Goebbels had asked in his diary actually came true: 'For when we win who will question us on our methods?'[25]

Vast territorial losses in western Russia only accelerated the destructiveness of the NKVD. Foreigners from within the Gulag population, in particular, were targeted for execution. In Kolgma they were placed into convoys of trucks driving towards the extermination centre at Serpantinnaya. Thomas Sgovio was selected for the Serpantinnaya list three times. On each occasion his life was saved by the intervention of an NKVD officer who had taken a personal interest in the young American prisoner. To circumvent the order, Lieutenant Terentyev would telegraph headquarters stating that he required Sgovio's sign-painting skills. Spared by the miracle of a compassionate NKVD officer, Thomas continued his 'function' as a signwriter in the war – 'A GRAM OF GOLD IS A CANNON SHOT IN THE HEART OF THE ENEMY! THE FATHERLAND DEMANDS MORE GOLD!' But his good fortune could not last forever.[26]

All prisoners were regularly transferred within the system of camps to prevent over-familiarisation, and soon Thomas Sgovio was returned to gold mining. His situation worsened further with his transfer into the so-called Valley of Death, located some 600 kilometres north of Magadan.[27] In his new camp, Thomas watched twenty-strong brigades of prisoners, who themselves had no more than a month or two to live, making two trips daily up a slope just over two kilometres from the compound. On their shoulders they carried the frozen corpses of prisoners to a burial site. When three or four hundred bodies were stacked like logs on the slope, a burial brigade bored holes into the frozen earth and blasted out pits with explosives. The pits were then filled with the dead.[28]

There was no electricity at Camp Seven since it was too far north. At night the darkness concealed a level of violence so high that the guards did not attempt to step inside.[29] Driven to fury by hunger, all human qualities became submerged beneath the animal desire to survive the work and the killings within the zone. And even as the prisoners died, a steady stream of new arrivals filled their ranks, delivered in the holds of the Gulag fleet. Reduced by overwork to a ninety-pound skeleton, Thomas Sgovio gradually realised that he too had become a *dokhodyaga*. Anticipating his death, Thomas tattooed his name on his hip so that if, years later, his body was ever discovered frozen in the ground, someone might at least know of his existence.[30]

Instead, another intervention occurred. His brigadier, a Russian engineer named Dmitry Prokhorov, took pity on him and sent him for a medical examination. When Thomas undressed for the first time that winter in the local camp hospital, every bone was projecting from his body. The doctor who examined him told him, 'You are as emaciated as any living skeleton I have seen, but it's amazing you have the heart of a horse. I can't put you in the hospital at all.' Thomas was then returned to work in Camp Seven. Days from death, he received a second respite: 'It was always like this, every time I was about to die, something happened. God saved me, I think.'[31]

His brigadier Prokhorov had spoken to the camp bread-cutter, who commissioned Thomas to draw a series of nudes in a notebook in exchange for a consignment of bread. While Thomas was completing the artwork, he would be excused work and gain time to regain his strength. Prokhorov persuaded the other prisoners in the brigade to agree to the deal: 'Look he's American, he's young, aided by some miracle – he'll go back to America and tell the world about Kolyma.' Perhaps the rest of the brigade realised that Thomas was scarcely fit for any work at all, but it was also true that all prisoners dearly craved a witness for their suffering. Realising that their own deaths were likely and impending, above all else they wanted the outside world to learn of their fate.

After their bargain was struck, Thomas attempted to straighten his gnarled hands and make his blackened fingers supple enough to draw. At first he could barely hold the pencil he was given, but eventually his work improved. 'I said what does he want, does he prefer blondes or brunettes? He said anything I don't care, as long as they have big breasts.' In Camp Number Seven of the Valley of Death, Thomas's teenage ambition to become an artist in the Soviet Union was finally fulfilled, drawing pictures of naked women to save his life.[32]

Hunger had always been a necessity of the Gulag, a calculated policy since it was understood that a starved man became more pliable, more passive and more easily stunned into submission. Starvation turned the prisoners into automata, quite incapable of acts of conspiracy or resistance. Across the Gulag, food became so scarce that each prisoner ate his thin ration of soup while running from the others. Out of calculated desperation, increasing numbers of prisoners chose self-mutilation in an attempt to be moved to lighter duties. At first, they hacked off their fingers and toes, then they paid others to remove a whole leg or an arm using either an axe or a detonator charge. The self-mutilators reasoned, and not without a certain terrible logic, that it was better to lose a limb than one's life. Within the camps of Burelopom, Victor Herman heard how prisoners had disappeared in the woods, falling down only to be attacked by the criminals for whom the fallen man was 'nothing but food'. What remained afterwards was buried beneath the snow.[33]

Victor Herman, too, was singled out for extermination. Shortly after his arrival in Burelopom, he was marched with eighteen other foreigners from Sub-camp Number Five. A guard then ordered that 'the filth from the capitalist nations' must each load a sixty-ton railroad car with lumber before he would be allowed to eat. With the treeline more than a mile away, it was a deliberately impossible task. But Victor had noticed a cache of logs that formed a ramp next to the railway track on to which timber was rolled up into the train. Using this wood, over the course of the next three days without food, he loaded his railway car, spacing out the stacks to cover the gaps so that the wagon appeared to be full. By this subterfuge he survived the task while the other seventeen foreigners died of exhaustion and exposure. When his cheating was eventually discovered, he was put into a punishment cell, beaten regularly and kept on a starvation diet of thin soup.[34]

After a year in solitary confinement, Victor was returned into the general population of the camp. At this point, he was too close to death to be able to work at all. He had started to go blind, and when his emaciated body was dumped face down in the frozen mud of the camp, he found he was too weak even to lift himself up. There he might have died, his fate ignored by the other prisoners – since within the camps a dead body attracted no attention – but the next morning he was recognised by his friend Albert Lonn, who picked him up and carried him back to his barracks: 'Son of a bitch, look what they did to old Vic. Hey, old Vic, look what they did to you, lad. Why I bet you don't weigh twenty-three pounds.' For days afterwards, Albert Lonn shared his precious ration of bread and nursed Victor Herman back towards life.[35]

In the midst of the war, Albert Lonn's gift of food carried a far greater significance than the small number of calories it contained. Fragments of the best of human nature endured even in the darkest hours of a concentration camp in Burelopom. Albert's compassionate action provided hope for the spirit, and with hope came a renewed willingness to seek and find a means of survival. While he lay hidden under Albert's berth, Victor had the idea of trapping the rats he had seen in the camp outhouse where the prisoners' corpses were stored. Using a trap built for him by Albert, he caught and ate those rats until he was strong enough to return to work.[36]

It was while cutting lumber in the snow that Victor Herman first saw the NKVD guards opening cans of Campbell's Pork and Beans, Franco-American Spaghetti, and Dinty Moore's Beef Stew. When he recognised the labels on the cans from his childhood in Detroit, Victor became so enraged that the guards waved a machine gun at him and threatened to kill him. Then he sat back down in the snow and wept.[37]

In Kolyma, Thomas Sgovio's original five-year sentence had long expired, but he clung to the faint hope that if he could survive another day or another week, he might perhaps be unexpectedly transferred or reprieved. Every prisoner's life depended on such fragile glimmers of hope, on rumours of change, or of people arriving from far-off places who might bring intervention or respite.

In the spring of 1944, another rumour swept the camps of Far East Russia. The Soviet Union, it was whispered, was preparing to cede Kolyma to the Americans in return for the Lend-Lease aid. The sale of vast swathes of frozen wasteland was, after all, an old Russian tradition: had not Tsar Alexander II traded Alaska to the United States in the nineteenth century? The Tsar had also freed the Russian serfs, two years before President Lincoln freed the American slaves. Perhaps this, too, was an omen of freedom? And the Kolyma prisoners noticed other strange changes taking place in their midst. Another rumour began to circulate, as the wooden watchtowers lining the access roads to Magadan were dismantled, and thousands of starving prisoners marched out of the city – the Vice-President of the United States of America was arriving on a visit to Kolyma. And this time, as fantastic as it seemed, the rumour was true. The American Vice-President was on his way.[38]

18

AN AMERICAN VICE-PRESIDENT IN THE HEART OF DARKNESS

Show us not the aim without the way. For ends and means on earth
are so entangled, that changing one, you change the other too; each
different path brings other ends in view.

Ferdinand Lassalle, *Franz von Sickingen*[1]

As a politician, Henry Wallace was never quite of this world. In the early
days of the New Deal, the former Secretary of Agriculture had devised
a scheme to raise farm prices by ordering farmers' crops to be ploughed
under and their livestock slaughtered. To his critics, the wastefulness of
the cure only magnified the Depression misery of American farmers. In
cabinet, Secretary Wallace read long-winded statements on agricultural
economics whose every sentence seemed to end in a question. Even the
President found it hard not to mock him: 'That is very nice Henry. Now
suppose you write the answer to all your own questions.'[2]

After two New Deal presidencies, the native Iowan's manner was
still viewed with some unease by his colleagues. But Roosevelt gifted
Henry Wallace the vice-presidential nomination in 1940 as a reward
for his loyalty and hard work. 'Henry's a good man to have around
if something happened to the President' was Roosevelt's public justification, which provoked the fury of southern Democrats, for
whom Wallace's union ties and early denunciation of racial segrega-
tion branded him a high-risk deputy for the third term. 'They'll go
for Wallace or I won't run' had been Roosevelt's laconic riposte.[3]

After Roosevelt's third election triumph, Henry Wallace inherited
the vice-presidency from 'Cactus' Jack Garner, the Texan Democrat
who had first deemed the office 'not worth a pitcher of warm piss'.[4]

Whatever influence Wallace was supposed to wield behind the scenes in the Senate was lost after he ordered the removal of Cactus Jack's bourbon bar and urinal from the vice-presidential office. As a teetotaller and fitness fanatic Wallace attempted to cajole the Senators into taking up paddleball, boxing and rowing. Unfortunately few shared his advanced views on the value of exercise, preferring hot baths and rub-downs in the Senate gym. Very soon they stopped dropping by the office at all.[5]

In the circumstances it hardly mattered. Henry Wallace was destined to hold the vice-presidency during the most critical period of modern history. After the outbreak of the Second World War, his oratory made him internationally famous as he delivered speech after speech on his favoured theme of the 'Century of the Common Man'. Even before Pearl Harbor, Wallace had been unafraid to issue unpopular warnings that 'civilization was burning' and that America would soon have to defend herself against Nazi aggression. The tall Iowan, with his high forehead and the strained eyes of a prophet, took upon himself the role of passionate interventionist in a war in which, the opinion polls revealed, a substantial majority of Americans were happy not to be involved.[6]

Throughout the course of the Hitler–Stalin Pact, as Luftwaffe bombs rained down on London in the Blitz, left-wing protesters kept up peace vigils advocating America's non-intervention in this 'imperialist war'. Outside the White House, advocates such as Woody Guthrie and Pete Seeger sang protest songs declaring that their government meant to have American boys 'plowed under' just as Wallace had done with the farmers' hogs:

> Remember when the AAA
> Killed a million hogs a day
> Instead of hogs it's men today
> Plow the fourth one under . . .
> (Don't you . . .) Plow under
> (Don't you . . .) Plow under
> Every fourth American boy[7]

The day after the invasion of the Soviet Union, this chorus ended as abruptly as a needle lifted from a record. The same voices were now united in favour of immediate intervention. But Roosevelt's attempts to mobilise support for a Soviet Lend-Lease programme were still faced with continued conservative opposition. An obscure Democratic senator from Missouri, Harry Truman, pithily endorsed the majority, isolationist position: 'If we see that Germany is winning the war we ought to help Russia; if Russia is winning we ought to help Germany and that way let them kill as many of each other as possible.'[8]

The national hero, Charles Lindbergh had become the leader of the 'America First' campaign. On 11 September 1941, Lindbergh gave a speech in Des Moines, Iowa, in which he identified a coalition of 'warmongers' hastening America into the conflict – the Roosevelt administration, the British and the Jews. 'Instead of agitating for war,' Lindbergh warned ominously, 'the Jewish groups in this country should be opposing it in every possible way for they will be among the first to feel its consequences.' His audience responded with a standing ovation. Only the former President Herbert Hoover advised Lindbergh that the speech was a mistake, in particular his statement that the Jews were responsible for the war. When Lindbergh insisted that what he said had been 'moderate and true', Hoover answered, 'When you had been in politics long enough you learn not to say things just because they are true.'[9]

Steering a course through the isolationism and prejudices of the left and right, Henry Wallace championed America's intervention in the war, and lent his considerable support to the Soviet cause. Addressing a 'Russian Aid' rally at Madison Square Garden, the American Vice-President announced his belief that the American and Russian Revolutions were both part of 'the march of freedom of the past 150 years. It is no accident that Americans and Russians like each other when they get acquainted. Both peoples know their future is greater than their past. Both hate sham.' Nor was Wallace content to leave his support merely at the level of progressive rhetoric. Evidently something more substantial was required.[10]

In May 1942, the Soviet Foreign Minister Vyacheslav Molotov arrived on a clandestine mission to the United States. At the White House, a moment of comedy ensued when the American valets unpacking Molotov's suitcase discovered a large hunk of black bread, some Russian sausage and a revolver. Eleanor Roosevelt wondered quizzically if 'Mr Molotov evidently thought he might have to defend himself, and also that he might be hungry'.[11] While the White House press reporters were informed that Molotov was travelling under the pseudonym 'Mr Brown' and were asked to observe a news blackout for the duration of the visit. Apart from an obviously face-tious question asked by one of the reporters – 'Why not Mr Red?' – no one was at all disturbed that Stalin's henchman-in-chief who had signed the death lists through the course of the Terror as well as the pact with Hitler, was now an official guest at the White House. He was placed in the bedroom next to Harry Hopkins.[12]

Over dinner, Roosevelt attempted to loosen Molotov's tongue by plying him with brandy and champagne cocktails. Obviously this was a strategy doomed to failure, since a Soviet apparatchik forced to binge-drink litres of vodka by Stalin would obviously find the President's 'Haitian libations' as pleasant as a summer's walk around Gorky Park. When Roosevelt informed him that Lend-Lease ship-ments might have to fall to cover the Allied Second Front, Molotov had looked at the President with disapproval: 'the Second Front will be stronger if the First Front stood fast'. But such minor differences caused no lasting damage, and did nothing to prevent Roosevelt from raising his glass in a toast to the health of Joseph Stalin.[13]

For his part Henry Wallace met with Molotov in Washington to discuss his idea for a grand project in the spirit of the New Deal. Ever the visionary, Wallace spoke passionately of an international public works programme that would symbolise the bond between their two great nations, and bring them still closer together. What Wallace had in mind was a great 'highway and airway' stretching west from Chicago, over and across Alaska to Siberia, and onwards to Moscow. The hard-boiled Molotov – who had arrived in America to obtain increased Lend-Lease shipments and an immediate second front in Europe, not to listen to wild schemes of highways in the sky – nevertheless quickly agreed, and extended an invitation to the American Vice-President to visit his embattled country. In prepara-tion for which a delighted Wallace began taking Russian lessons.[14]

On 21 April 1944, Henry Wallace issued a press release describing his hopes for his trip to the 'Wild East' of Russia, where 'the common men of the world will fill up the vacant spots as they try to attain a fuller and deeper life by harnessing nature. This is the kind of job with which our fathers and grandfathers were fully familiar.' In Siberia he 'expected to feel that grandeur that comes when men wisely work with nature'.[15] The journey had been carefully planned at the White House, with President Roosevelt's enthusiastic approval – 'Oh you must go, I think you ought to see a lot of Siberia.' In the midst of the Second

World War, the American Vice-President was resolved to travel to the place he envisaged as the Russian starting-point for his great highway. Unbeknown to Wallace, the land already had its own, darkly tragic, purpose. Unable to sustain human life, it was being used by Stalin to end it. It was Kolyma.[16]

What happened next is well documented. On 23 May 1944, Henry Wallace climbed the steps of a silver Skymaster plane waiting at a military airport in Alaska, and set out on the short flight over the Bering Strait. Travelling with him on the plane, and documenting their journey, was Professor Owen Lattimore from the Office of War Information, one of America's most gifted Orientalists who maintained a keen interest in Soviet affairs. Professor Lattimore's published views on the Moscow show trials made interesting reading. In Lattimore's opinion the trials had given 'the ordinary citizen more courage to protest, loudly, whenever he finds himself being victimized by "someone in the Party" or "someone in the Government." That sounds to me like democracy.'[17]

Coincidentally the pilot of the plane, Colonel Richard Kight, had also flown Wendell Willkie on the Russian leg of his world tour just the year before. In an article for *Reader's Digest* magazine, the defeated Republican presidential candidate had hinted darkly at the presence of concentration camps in the Soviet Union, to which his party had been refused access. It was one of many warnings that Henry Wallace might have heeded before he left. Over dinner at the British Embassy, Sir Oliver Lyttelton had warned him that Stalin held an estimated 'sixteen million' Russians imprisoned in such camps. In his diary, Wallace's reaction to this news was openly sceptical, noting that 'the figure seemed to be quite fantastic and Lyttelton's motives seemed to be so obvious that I did not question his statement'.[18]

Henry Wallace landed at the airport in Magadan as the highest-ranking American politician ever to visit the USSR. He was greeted with an official banquet of welcome hosted by General Sergei Goglidze – formerly the People's Commissar for Internal Affairs in Georgia during the Terror – now the NKVD 'plenipotentiary' for the whole of Far East Russia.[19] The American Vice-President appeared completely uninformed of his host's grim reputation, and was impressed only by the fact that Goglidze was known to be an 'intimate friend' of Stalin. Nor was Wallace overly concerned that the Americans were surrounded at all times by officials of the

NKVD. In his diary Wallace described his guardians as 'old soldiers with blue tops on their caps. Everybody treated them with great respect'.[20]

Sergei Goglidze introduced Wallace to plain 'Mister' Ivan Nikishov, the Dalstroi 'director' having mysteriously lost the rank of an NKVD general and donned a grey civilian suit. 'Magadan was founded by volunteers from all over the Soviet Union,' Nikishov explained, and helpfully characterised Dalstroi as 'a combination of the TVA and Hudson's Bay Company'. Without batting an eyelid, Nikishov boasted that they 'employed' some three hundred thousand men in more than one thousand mining operations across Kolyma. The walls of his office were lined with the minerals these 'employees' spent their lives extracting: samples of lead, tin, uranium, and, of course, gold.[21]

Standing in front of this display, Nikishov and Goglidze presented a uniquely convincing NKVD double act. Between them the two high-ranking NKVD administrators were personally responsible for the death of hundreds of thousands – if not millions – of Stalin's victims, in Georgia, Azerbaijan and now Kolyma. But their capacity for mass murder was hidden by an affable demeanour, as Nikishov was filled with loquacious enthusiasm for his American audience, and Goglidze teased his colleague's officiousness: 'He runs everything around here. With Dalstroi's resources he's a millionaire!'[22]

Together they led their American guests down to Magadan harbour, which Henry Wallace admired, noting how unusual it was for such a remote location to be able to berth three ships simultaneously. The *North Wind*, an American-built icebreaker, could be seen offshore. 'We use it to keep the sea open for shipping,' Nikishov explained as they walked past lines of Studebaker trucks stored in Dalstroi warehouses. Henry Wallace discovered that his Soviet hosts were very appreciative of the American materials. The latest US industrial machinery was clearly identifiable in the factories of Magadan; and Professor Lattimore, in particular, had no doubt about the warmth of Russian feeling for American aid. As they walked through one factory, they were greeted by ripples of 'spontaneous' applause.[23]

The minutely calibrated deceptions would continue through the length of the visit as the American Vice-President was walked through a charade designed to conceal the true nature of what was taking place around him. Like a moving stage set, everything in Kolyma had been carefully managed for Wallace's willing eyes. No beguiling detail was left untouched in the Soviet effort to convince Wallace that what lay before him was a vision of Pioneers at work, not the reality of a network of death camps. The NKVD guards with their baying dogs had vanished, along with the skeletal prisoners. The watchtowers and searchlights had disappeared. Wondrous selections of food now filled the shops of Magadan. There were even greenhouses on show, built to provide 'much-needed fruit and vegetables for the vitamin-starved miners of the Arctic'.[24]

Meanwhile any schemes that a surviving American prisoner, such as Thomas Sgovio, might have hatched for contacting their Vice-President were dashed by the unprecedented security. Barring the NKVD interpreters, no English speaker was allowed near Wallace's party, and Sergei Goglidze seldom left his side. Judging by a character sketch in his diary, Henry Wallace had grown quite fond of his company: 'Goglidze is a very fine man, very efficient, gentle, and understanding with people.' Professor Lattimore's notes went even further in their praise: 'Quiet but humorous. Gentle, cultivated, yet obviously a man of great organizing and executive ability.' Ivan Nikishov, the American professor compared to 'a top flight industrial or business management man. As somebody said, put him in Wall Street and in ten years he'd own half of General Electric.'[25]

With their NKVD escorts leading the way, the American visitors were launched on a twenty-five-day tour of Kolyma and Far East Russia. As they inspected a series of mines, collective farms and factories, Henry Wallace was always ready to practise his rudimentary language skills on any terrified Russian who crossed his path. On one occasion Wallace's restless energy led him ahead of the game. Breaking clear of his guardians, he hiked up a hillside in Magadan alone, only to be chased after by an irate NKVD major who barked at him to 'come down at once'. His host's nervousness was justified. In Kolyma, no one could be sure what sights lay in store over the next ridge, or opened up from the side of a mountain as the earth shifted in the briefest of summers. About to take offence, the Vice-President was calmed by an interpreter's assurance that what the major had actually said was 'Dinner is ready.'[26]

Two days into the trip, Goglidze and Nikishov had sufficient confidence to lead Henry Wallace into a gold mine in the Kolyma valley. Here the Americans were shown Lend-Lease shovels and the huge Bucyrus Erie machines with forty-foot cranes which had been intended for earth moving on the Eastern front, not mining gold. The American Vice-President was introduced to a group of miners – 'big husky young men who came out to the Far East from European Russia' – who told him how they had written to Comrade Stalin asking to be sent to the front, but Stalin had replied they were needed right there. Mr Adagin, their 'union leader', stepped forward and asked Henry Wallace to send 'his best regards to American unionists'. Noting that the Russian miners had good clothing and plenty of roubles to spend, Wallace wrote in his diary that he 'could not help but wonder how much better off these people were than they had been under the Tsars'.[27]

For his part, Professor Lattimore seemed very pleased that these Russian gold miners were so obviously 'very healthy, well-fed and strong; intelligent'. In his journal, the Professor recorded with some satisfaction that the State Department lawyer in their company, John Hazard, 'had been led to expect from the literature on the subject, that they would all be kulaks and other forced labour'. As the gold miners shook hands with the American Vice President, Lattimore busily took photographs to illustrate the article he was writing for *National Geographic* magazine.[28]

Judging by their physical condition these strong, healthy 'miners' could only have been NKVD guards playing the part for the American visitors. Their smiles for Lattimore's camera carried all the sincerity of successful conmen, their eyes gleaming with cunning in the pale summer sunlight. While the persecutors took on the roles of the persecuted for a few hours, the real miners waited hidden in the shadows, worked close to death and clothed in American flour bags. Their faces would never grace the pages of *National Geographic*.

Later, still unsuspecting, Henry Wallace walked through the taiga with Ivan Nikishov. In his diary, Wallace wrote that Nikishov 'gamboled out like a calf enjoying the wonderful air, the larches putting out their new leaves and the valley looked marvellous against the snow covered mountains, thirty miles away in every direction'.[29] Kolyma's physical beauty was often remembered in the memoirs of those prisoners who survived. The white nights of summer were adorned by the Northern Lights, flickering in violet and blue across the horizon. For the prisoners, the natural beauty of this wilderness served only as a reminder of the contrasting brutality of the camps all around; man's contribution to the landscape being nothing more than the means of their suffering. Here in the camps of Far East

Russia was 'the common man' of the twentieth century, in extreme representation as a concentration camp prisoner and guard. All that was missing from the triptych was the third party, the bystander, in this case a naive American visitor from Adair County, Iowa. Always at the end of the road lay the camp unseen – the hidden endpoint of this grand experiment in human evolution, the futile attempt at the perfectibility of mankind.[30]

Henry Wallace's tour continued amid the elaborately choreographed deceptions. At a collective farm, the Vice-President had no idea of the confusion he caused with some harmless questions about pigs. According to Elinor Lipper, the girls tending the animals were actually NKVD clerical staff, hand-picked to play the role normally filled by female prisoners. Never having been near pigs in their lives, the secretaries had no idea how to answer the former Secretary of Agriculture. Once again, an NKVD interpreter volunteered a vaguely plausible response, which left Wallace none the wiser.[31] On another occasion, the Americans stopped to dig one of the many 'victory' gardens in Magadan. Both Ivan Nikishov and Sergei Goglidze happily joined in the manual labour: 'What a story the gardener will have to tell tomorrow,' Ivan Nikishov had joked.[32]

At night the Americans were entertained by a group of Russian singers and musicians whose depth of talent Henry Wallace found quite remarkable for such a remote place. In fact, they were almost too good. When the Russian speaker John Hazard questioned Nikishov about the extraordinary professionalism of their theatre, the Dalstroi Chief became quite defensive: 'We ought to have some very good people, for these are the exiles from Leningrad.'[33] Earlier Nikishov had explained the need for entertainment in their town, since in the winter 'the men do not work outside when the weather is below forty degrees below zero.' Professor Lattimore heard someone remark how 'high-grade entertainment just naturally seems to go with gold'.[34] Of course, the truth was the artists all belonged to Nikishov's 'Cultural Brigade' – the former professional singers and musicians saved from the gold mines by their talent. When the applause ended, they were herded into trucks and returned to their imprisonment.[35]

Although Thomas Sgovio never witnessed their performance, later he met a former opera singer from Leningrad who explained how the Cultural Brigade had sung, 'Okay – America–Soviet Union' as a welcoming overture. The NKVD had tried to teach them more English, but there had not been enough time. Naturally all the singers in the Cultural Brigade who could actually speak English were not allowed to participate. The rest were forced to sign an oath promising to behave as 'loyal Soviet patriots' in the presence of their American audience. One word, or sign of their status as prisoners 'would be considered an act of treason' which, in case they needed reminding, carried 'the supreme penalty'.[36]

Another evening's entertainment was provided by a film screening at the Magadan theatre. General Goglidze started the night with a documentary on the siege of Stalingrad, accompanied by serious-minded applause. Henry Wallace reciprocated with the Soviet premiere of the movie *North Star* in a print with Russian subtitles, which he had brought with him. On screen was the Hollywood version of life on a Soviet collective farm, complete with Ukrainian peasants dancing around a perfect set with pressed white shirts and flowers in their hair, playing balalaikas and accordions. The film was made by Sam Goldwyn as a favour to the President – with his son Eliot Roosevelt in charge of production. To say that it lightened the mood was an understatement. How could the NKVD Generals not stifle their laughter? 'It's marvellous that Americans would produce such a picture about us,' proclaimed Mrs Nikishov, as the Vice-President modestly insisted that what they had just seen was only 'an artificial reality built for a film-set' whereas the Soviet achievements here in Kolyma were both real and substantial. 'Hollywood built an entire village only to demolish it. Magadan's not such a synthetic town. It has solid underpinnings,' said Henry Wallace.[37]

Filled with the evangelical fervour of someone who is sure because he has seen with his own eyes, Henry Wallace embarked on a series of speeches across Siberia using the Russian language skills he had struggled so hard to master. In his booming Midwestern accent, he addressed his assembled Russian audiences: 'Siberia used to mean to Americans frightful suffering and sorrow, convict-chains and exiles. For long generations Siberia remained thus without appreciable change. Then in this generation during the past fifteen years, all has been changed as though by magic. Siberia today is one of the world's largest lands still open to pioneer settlers.'

His words were accepted as a propaganda coup by his grateful hosts, who heavily featured them in the Soviet press as an endorsement of their way of life. TASS reported more praise from Wallace in a speech made in Irkutsk:

> There are no more similar countries in the world than the Soviet Union and the United States of America. The vast expanse of your country, its virgin forests, its broad rivers and great lakes, all types of climate from tropical to polar, its inexhaustible natural riches remind me of my own homeland. The history of Siberia and its heroic population remind me of the history of the Far West of the United States. The pioneers of our countries in the titanic struggle with nature and with hard conditions of life went forward fearlessly, building new towns and villages, new industry and a new life for the welfare of their homeland and of all humanity . . . Free people, born on free expanses, can never live in slavery.[38]

At their parting in Magadan, the indebted Nikishov presented Wallace with two framed pictures of embroidered landscapes, a much-coveted item collected by the wives of the Kolyma elite. But even this simple gift carried the threat of revelation. When the American Vice-President innocently asked who had made them, Nikishov replied that he could not possibly know all the sewing women in the city. Later Wallace was told they were the work of Nikishov's wife, Gridassova. The truth, according to Elinor Lipper, was that the embroideries were another by-product of the camp labour system. Female prisoners, often former nuns, received an additional ration in return for their needlework which, because of their pitiful working conditions, ruined their eyesight. The America Vice-President left Soviet Russia with the landscapes in his luggage, having written an open letter to Comrade J. V. Stalin to express his 'deep gratitude for the splendid cordial hospitality shown to me'.[39]

In an American national radio broadcast, Henry Wallace had nothing but praise for his Russian hosts, eulogising their 'development' of Siberia and the patriotic spirit of the masses of 'volunteers'. Millions of Americans read more about the Vice-President's expedition in the December edition of *National Geographic* magazine. In his article, Professor Lattimore praised Nikishov and his wife's 'trained and sensitive interest in art and music' and their 'deep sense of civic responsibility'. Pictured also were the 'Far North's Husky Miners' grinning at the camera, over the caption which read that 'these men had volunteered for war, only to be ordered to stay at work because of Russia's need for gold'.[40]

A short while afterwards a documentary film was released by the Office of War Information using footage shot by Soviet cameramen. 'Soviet and Central Asia, America's New Gateway to Asia' was written and edited by the industrious Professor Lattimore, its script narrated in the excited baritone of 1940s newsreel: 'Never before had so important an American representative visited these little known territories, the Soviet authorities threw everything open to him. Soviet cameramen made a continuous record of the journey. And OWI now presents to you this film made by our Soviet allies, about a journey through lands and among people destined to be better known to Americans in the years after the war.'

In the film, American cinema audiences watched their Vice-President picking and eating a crisp cucumber grown in the special greenhouses of the North, 'as characteristic of Siberia as the hot-dog is of America'. Henry Wallace smiles and grins at the camera, as happy as an Iowan farmer at harvest time. Later the American visitors are shown attending the village soviet of the 'Red Dawn' collective farm, as Professor Lattimore tiptoes through the nuances of Stalinist democracy: 'A village Soviet in Siberia is a forum for open discussion like a town meeting in New England.' And thus with dismal conviction, the American professor transformed the scene of mass murder into possibly the saddest piece of American wartime propaganda. Its final reel ends with Colonel Kight, the pilot of the good plane *Polar Bear*, waving at the camera, and to the soundtrack of blaring trumpets 'the mighty C54 heads for the snow-capped mountains and distant capital of our ally China'.[41]

Amid rumours circulating Washington that he was about to be dumped from the ticket for Roosevelt's fourth term, an anxious Henry Wallace arrived at the White House on 10 July 1944 bearing presidential gifts of an Uzbek robe and a set of Outer Mongolian stamps. At their meeting Roosevelt cheerfully explained that, while Wallace was his personal choice for the nomination, many of his visitors disagreed, and many looked upon Wallace as a 'Communist or worse'. However, the President understood that there was 'no one more American, no one more of the American soil'. A few days later Roosevelt explained that he was going to write a letter to Senator Sam

Jackson of the Democratic National Committee explaining that if he were a delegate at the Convention he would vote for Wallace. And then Franklin Roosevelt turned on his full charm: 'While I cannot put it just that way in public, I hope it will be the same old team.'[42]

The night of the vice-presidential nomination at the Democratic National Convention in Chicago, Wallace's liberal supporters raised the roof for their man. There were tremendous ovations for Wallace, with placards waved proclaiming, 'THE PEOPLE WANT WALLACE', 'ROO-SEVELT AND WALLACE' and 'WE WANT WALLACE!' It was clear, however, that the Democratic Party bosses were following other instructions. Bob Hannegan and Mayor Ed Kelly approached Senator Jackson: 'You've got to adjourn the convention,' Hannegan demanded. 'The crowd's too hot,' Jackson replied, 'I can't.' 'You're taking orders from me,' answered Hannegan, a hulking Irishman from St Louis. 'And I'm taking orders from the President.' Calls for adjournment were greeted by choruses of 'No', to which Senator Jackson promptly purred, 'The ayes have it!' The following day the Wallace supporters were kept out of the convention. They found themselves with the wrong kind of tickets, the top galleries were cleared, and speakers for Wallace had their microphones unexpectedly switched off.[43]

In a Gallup poll for the vice-presidential nomination taken four days earlier, Senator Harry Truman registered scarcely two points to Henry Wallace's runaway sixty-five-point lead.[44] No one seemed to know too much about Harry Truman, save for the fact that he had risen up through 'Boss Tom' Pendergast's corrupt Kansas City machine. At the Chicago convention, the former sins of the 'Senator from Pendergast' were charitably forgotten and when the votes were counted, it was Harry Truman who won. Meanwhile the Democratic Party bosses of the self-styled 'conspiracy of the pure in heart' were delighted at their timely work. Years later, 'Boss' Bob Hannegan told friends that his epitaph should read: 'Here lies the man who kept Henry Wallace from becoming President of the United States.'

For the rest of his life, Henry Wallace would attempt to recover from the shock of what was done to him in Chicago. Though he had lost the presidency by a whisker, Wallace's political nemesis had hardly begun. And as in an Aeschylean tragedy it would be ghosts – the ghosts of Kolyma – which would return to deal the former vice-president his final blows.[45]

19

'TO SEE CRUELTY AND BURN NOT'

You know I am a juggler, and I never let my right hand know what my left hand does . . . I may be entirely inconsistent, and furthermore I am perfectly willing to mislead and tell untruths if it will help win the war.

Franklin Roosevelt, May 1942[1]

Days after Henry Wallace flew out of Russia, the prisoners in Kolyma were marched back to work as the watchtowers and searchlights rose above them once again. Later, Thomas Sgovio was asked by a Soviet supply officer to meet him at a warehouse. The building stood apart from the rest of the camp, its floor littered with American newspapers used to pack the Lend-Lease equipment. Shutting the door behind him, the NKVD officer handed Thomas a picture from a newspaper. 'Don't tell anyone I let you see these. I'm supposed to burn them, before I do, tell me what's written here?' he asked, pointing to a picture of a fashion model in tights. Thomas replied it was an advertisement. 'And this?' the Russian asked holding out another picture. 'The same,' Thomas replied. 'What the hell, your newspapers are full of advertisements!' As a reward for his translation, Thomas was allowed to read from a stack of American newspapers, at which point he discovered that the United States and Great Britain were fighting in an alliance with the USSR in the Second World War.[2]

For weeks after Wallace's visit, Thomas became the butt of camp jokes, his presence greeted by taunts of 'You Americans are really stupid.' There was hardly a single prisoner in Kolyma who had not heard of the Vice-President's visit. And if the jokes themselves were insufficient reminder of Wallace's folly, the camp commanders and their wives deepened the ridicule by dressing up in expensive American clothes. Attached to each item delivered to Kolyma was a handwritten tag with a message in English, and the name and address of a donor from the Californian branch of the 'USA–USSR Friendship Society'. Thomas watched the Gulag officials' wives fighting over the clothes in the warehouse to which they were delivered. It was concentration camp chic, the Rodeo Drive of the damned.[3]

The starvation of the Gulag prisoners never diminished throughout the war, despite the ships loaded with American food supplied to the USSR. One prisoner, who had the task of processing the dead, took Thomas Sgovio to a mortuary where the dead prisoners' frozen hands were amputated before their meagre bodies were taken away to be buried. The hands were kept on hooks until they thawed so that fingerprints could be taken for the camp files. In the mortuary the prisoner, named Vassya, explained how all the dead had to be properly accounted for – with their palm and finger prints made on three sets of forms attached to their NKVD files. Thomas sensed that the man only wanted a witness for the duties he was forced to perform.[4]

It was at this time that Thomas Sgovio briefly met John Pass, another young American surviving in the Kolyma camps. Born in the Midwest, Pass had emigrated to the USSR as a child in the early 1930s with his family. He had been arrested in 1940 for possession of a copy of John Reed's *Ten Days That Shook The World*. The book had been banned in the Soviet Union because 'it did not show the leading role of Stalin during the October Revolution'.[5] In Reed's account, it was Trotsky who appeared most often by Lenin's side directing the events of 1917, and Stalin was hardly mentioned. Had the author still been alive in Soviet Russia, he would most certainly have been shot for such heresy – his body dumped face down in a mass grave, not buried as a Revolutionary hero at the Kremlin Wall. Instead, it was his readers who were punished vicariously, some twenty years later. In Camp Seven, John Pass had survived thus far on a 'function' as the English teacher to the commandant's wife. But his friendship with Thomas Sgovio was brief. As was Kolyma's transitory nature, Thomas would be transferred on again to a new camp, and he never learned if Pass managed to survive.[6]

Towards the end of the war, Thomas was moved to a camp further north, as Dalstroi expanded to make room for the new waves of prisoners arriving in the holds of the Gulag fleet. When he had first arrived the so-called 'road of bones' leading out of Magadan was already 400 kilometres long. Seven years later, it stretched 1000 kilometres into the wilderness, and every extra metre was built on the lives of the weakest prisoners. From this main highway, countless tributaries ran off into the landscape, each leading to a network of mines and camps.[7] As Kolyma expanded, the newspaper *Izvestiya* described how 'the total number of new names marked on the map of the region during the Dalstroi era exceeds ten thousand and includes all kinds of mining centres, gold fields, fishing villages, government farms, and so forth.' In the Soviet press, the existence of the prisoners, of course, was never mentioned.[8]

Within this expanding world, with his original five-year sentence long since expired, Thomas Sgovio was kept as 'an over-timer', one of the prisoners 'retained in the Corrective Labour Camps until Special Orders'. His latest camp was a twenty-kilometre forced march from the highway's northern end. In Camp Victory Thomas survived once again as a sign painter, lettering the production signs of the work brigades, along with their percentage targets and propaganda slogans: 'THE FATHERLAND DEMANDS METAL!' While every day the rest of the prisoners were marched out into the goldfields.[9]

Meanwhile in Moscow, a fresh crop of patriotic American war reporters flew in to write stories on the burgeoning American–Soviet alliance, or how Stalin's 'democracy' was – with a few minor indiscretions – so much like their own. Inevitably the reporters learned the awkward truth of the former existence of the American emigrants in Russia. But they mentioned them only in passing, almost as a historical curiosity, before moving on to the more pressing issues of the war.

Often the reporters hired the daughters of the American emigrants to work as bilingual assistants, since they themselves spoke little, if any, Russian. This was how the Associated Press chief, Eddy Gilmore, first encountered Lydia Kleingal, a young girl born in St Louis whose family had left Missouri in search of work in Russia. Lydia's father had already been shot, and soon she too was arrested in the midst of the wartime alliance. Not yet realising the consequences of his actions, Eddy Gilmore then hired Alyce Alex, the daughter of a River Rouge auto worker who had left Detroit to build Soviet Fords in September 1931. Alyce was born in Brooklyn and had managed to keep hold of her American passport throughout her stay in Russia.[10]

In quick succession she too disappeared, but unlike her predecessor, Alyce managed to send Gilmore a note from her camp, pleading for his help. The message arrived a year later in an envelope pushed under his door, with his name and address written in Russian. Eddy Gilmore recognised Alyce's handwriting straightaway: 'Dear Mr Gilmore, I'm at a camp near Kirov. Won't you please ask the American Embassy to help me? Forever grateful, Alyce.'

The Associated Press reporter took the letter down to the American Embassy on Mokhovaya Street, and handed it to the same disinterested Third Secretary to whom he had first reported Alyce's arrest. 'You've been here long enough to know we can't do anything,' the anonymous diplomat replied. And upon that judgement and with an indifferent shrug, the young girl from Brooklyn, New York, was left to fend for herself in the concentration camp of her country's wartime ally.[11]

All the reporters heard one version or other of the American emigration during the early years of the Depression. In the account William White was told, the Americans had freely given up their passports and voluntarily acquired Soviet citizenship. In a wartime memoir, White wrote, 'under any interpretation of international law they were indistinguishable from any other Soviet citizen, bound to their assigned jobs and with no hope of leaving'. White discovered how the emigrants had once clamoured at the doors of the American Embassy begging for help. As the Soviet Union's foreigners were transported into the Gulag, 'all trace of them was lost and no longer could they plead with their embassies in Moscow'. Not having been in Soviet Russia long enough to understand their true narrative of deception, coercion, and arrest, White regarded the emigrants as the authors of their own misfortune, no longer in any true sense 'American' or deserving of real sympathy.[12]

And yet some of the scattered families of the Americans still survived. During a Moscow air raid, the reporter Wallace Carroll woke up in a metro station next to a young girl who asked him, 'What time is it?' in perfect American-accented English. Carroll described the girl as a 'thin woman with deep lines under her eyes and a grey shawl over her head'. She was from Minnesota, one of the Finnish-Americans who had arrived in 1934. 'Yes there were lots of us,' she whispered, 'but I am alone here now. They don't trust us Finns. They send us to Siberia. That's where they'll send me too.' Wallace Carroll christened them 'Exiles in Utopia'.[13]

But rather than worry over their fate, the American reporters and diplomats whiled away their free evenings playing in a jazz band. The Kremlin Krows were named after the birds that flew around the Spasski Tower in the Kremlin and featured George Kennan on guitar, Eddy Gilmore on drums, with assorted American clerks and military attachés filling in the other spots in the line-up. At night in wartime Moscow, the Kremlin Krows thumped out 1940s jazz favourites for the endless round of Embassy parties, while their compatriots clung to their lives in the camps.[14]

All the old faces were returning, including Ambassador Joseph Davies who had arrived in Moscow in May 1943, on a mission to arrange the first meeting between Roosevelt and Stalin. The Ambassador brought with him the perfect ideological olive branch in the form of a special print of the movie *Mission to Moscow* complete with Russian subtitles. At the White House, the President had passed Davies's bestseller across the table to his guest, Jack Warner. 'Jack, I see you're in the army,' said Roosevelt, acknowledging Warner's uniform. 'As one officer to another, I suggest you do a film based on this book ... Our people know almost nothing about the Soviet Union and the Russian people. What they do know is largely prejudiced and inaccurate. If we're going to fight the war together, we need a more sympathetic understanding.' The Hollywood mogul had agreed to make the film there and then, without opening the book.[15]

On the evening of 23 May 1943, Stalin welcomed Joseph Davies with a Kremlin banquet in his honour. The Soviet banquets had continued throughout the war, with no concession made to the million Russians who were starving to death in the still-besieged city of Leningrad. The menu for Davies' reception began with a choice of cold appetisers of 'soft and pressed caviar, white salmon, pink salmon, herring with garnish, smoked shamaia, jellied sturgeon, cold suckling pig with horseradish, English roast beef with garnish, cold ham with lanspig, wild game and shefru in aspic, braised duck galantine, "Olivier" and "Spring" salads, fresh cucumbers, garden radishes, assorted cheeses, butter and toast.' The hot appetisers were listed as 'champignon au gratin, and medallion of wild game poivrade', followed by a main course of 'soupe de poularde à la reine, pirogi pies, consommé, borsht, white salmon in white wine, roast veal with potatoes, roast turkey and chicken with lettuce, cauliflower, asparagus'. Then, finally, a dessert menu offered 'strawberry parfait, ice cream, coffee, assorted cheeses, fruits, petit-fours, almonds, and liqueurs'.[16]

At the end of their dinner, Stalin abruptly got up from the table to announce that they would all now watch *Mission to Moscow* in the Kremlin cinema.[17] According to Joseph Davies' account the film 'caused a great deal of joking' not least because of its dramatisation of the lives of those watching in the elite audience. The inner circle of Stalin's court were all present, including Beria, Voroshilov, Mikoyan, Litvinov, Vyshinsky and Vyacheslav Molotov, who personally congratulated Davies on this high-budget Hollywood adaptation of his service in 1930s Moscow. Ambassador Davies had been allowed to introduce the film with a monologue delivered directly to camera, a picture of Marjorie hanging on the wall behind him: 'There was so much prejudice and misunderstanding of the Soviet Union, in which I partly shared, that I felt it was my duty to tell the truth . . . while I was in Russia I came to have a very high respect for the honesty of the Soviet leaders.'

The same Soviet leaders now watched a Stalinist version of the history of the Terror projected on to the silver screen. Naturally the Show Trials were presented as a truthful account of real events: from explosions in Soviet factories to scenes of Nikolai Bukharin nefariously conspiring with the Japanese ambassador. On screen, the actor Walter Huston, playing the part of Ambassador Davies, declared his undisputed opinion that 'based on twenty years of trial practice, I'd be inclined to believe these confessions'. There was even a dramatic recreation of Bukharin's confession: 'One has only to weigh the wise leadership of the Soviet government against the sordid personal ambitions of those who would wish to betray it, to realize the monstrousness of our crimes.'

Joseph Stalin watched his own likeness quite unperturbed. As the credits rolled, he told Davies that he 'liked Walter Huston particularly'. And with Stalin's approval, *Mission to Moscow* was scheduled for distribution across the USSR. The simple fact that the totalitarian regime saw no apparent need for censorship tells us all we need know of the film's historical accuracy and worth; its failings no more surprising than the fawning dedication Joseph Davies wrote in a copy of his book he presented to Stalin:

To one of the very great men of this era of history – Joseph V. Stalin Premier of the Government of his People, Marshal of their

Great Red Army, Whose Vision, Power, and Greatness enabled his people to save themselves and their land from enslavement by the Hun. And but for whose Valiant and Immortal Defense of the Ramparts of Liberty and Freedom, that Civilization which Free Men must have to live, would have been utterly destroyed, With the great respect and sincere admiration of His Friend.[18]

Hidden away in the film, like an unconscious clue of self-incrimination, was the most fleeting allusion to the American emigrants, in whose fate both Stalin and Ambassador Davies had been so instrumental and so complicit. Almost in passing, as the briefest introduction to a scene set during the Terror, an Embassy secretary walks into Davies's office at Spaso House holding a sheaf of documents. 'More applications for American passports, sir,' the secretary declares. 'The pile's getting bigger every day,' Walter Huston replies, 'It reminds me of animals scurrying for shelter from the storm.'

As specific thanks for the film, Stalin awarded Joseph Davies the Order of Lenin. The medal was later presented by the show trial prosecutor Andrei Vyshinsky, who assured him that 'the Soviets had no higher honour'.[19]

The subject of the Americans executed in the Terror, and those still imprisoned in the Gulag, became one of the unspoken taboos of the wartime alliance. Although both the disappearance of the Americans and the deaths inflicted within the Gulag were known of at the time in the highest levels of the American government. But of this sensitive issue never a word was spoken publicly. Soon after the war, the Acting Secretary of State, Sumner Welles, had sent cables to the American Embassy in Moscow authorising appeals to Stalin for the arrested Americans 'solely on the grounds of international courtesy and for humanitarian reasons'. But no further action was taken, nor was the issue ever pressed.[20]

In Spaso House, Averell Harriman, the latest in a succession of wealthy American ambassadors, was not about to involve himself in a wartime confrontation over the fate of a few thousand of his not quite forgotten countrymen who, if they were alive at all, were cast to the four corners of the USSR. Ambassador Harriman could scarcely save the few Americans who worked for him directly at the Embassy. On 24 March 1944, he was informed of the Soviet request to discharge the Embassy employees Theodore Okkonen, his wife Freda and their American-born son, Olav. The Okkonen family were Finnish-American emigrants who had arrived in the USSR in the early 1930s and found jobs at the American Embassy. They were now accused of espionage 'on behalf of Germany and Finland'.

Ambassador Harriman wrote to Washington that the Okkonen family had worked for the Embassy as domestic staff for a number of years. Theodore and Freda 'both were of simple type and mentality and it was difficult to believe that either would have the ability to engage in espionage.' Their son Olav was a

> dual national, born in the United States, who came to the Soviet Union as a minor and who has a longstanding application to renounce Soviet citizenship and return to the United States. He has rendered exemplary services for a number of years . . . Since he is an American citizen under American law and is officially employed by an agency of the United States government, I desired, before taking any action, to report this matter to the Department with a view to receiving appropriate instructions . . . It is my intention to continue to endeavour to persuade the Soviet authorities to withhold insisting on the request that these servants be discharged. However, I feel that I will eventually have to accede to their demands if pressed. There is no doubt that their discharge will lead to arrest and severe punishment.[21]

In response to Harriman's request for 'comments or suggestions', the State Department replied that 'experience . . . has demonstrated that in cases of this character the Soviet authorities directly concerned are inclined to be arbitrary and adamant in maintaining the validity of the charges and consequently the Foreign Office is usually powerless.' All three members of the Okkonen family were then given up with scarcely a murmur of complaint.[22]

According to the memoirs of Harriman's secretary, Robert Meikeljohn, the phone in Spaso House practically never rang, and the Ambassador stayed in bed most mornings, rarely getting dressed before midday unless he happened to be visited by one of the American military contingent passing through Moscow. In the afternoons, Harriman would sit in his comfortable armchair by a roaring fire, dictating memos so slowly that Meikeljohn could 'usually steal a nap between words without him noticing'. Harriman would then go over these sentences, 'changing words, phrases and paragraphs time after time till nobody but him has the slightest idea of what the end product is'. His staff detected that the Ambassador took his lack of access to Stalin rather personally. There was a period in the first winter when Harriman 'took to his bed with a sinus infection and didn't get out for six weeks. He was obviously suffering some kind of psychosomatic trauma'.[23]

In the afternoons, a recuperated Harriman played badminton or skied with his twenty-six-year-old daughter Kathleen on slopes outside Moscow, nervously followed by one of his escort of four NKVD guardians. In the evenings, there was the usual round of diplomatic receptions to be attended either as a guest or host. On 30 January 1944, for example, the American Ambassador threw a party in honour of President Roosevelt's sixty-second birthday whose long guest list included the highest-ranking officers from the NKVD, including Lieutenant-General P. V. Fitin, Major-General Ossipov and, of course, Lavrenty Beria himself – if they could only drag themselves away from the burning lights of the Lubyanka to enjoy the American hospitality. As these parties continued, Robert Meikeljohn expressed in his diary his increasing sense of unease: 'It is a strange country where an American Ambassador takes pride in having the head of the secret police, probably as big a murderer as Himmler, dine with him.'[24]

But then the incomprehension worked both ways. On one social outing, General John Deane, the head of the American military mission, was invited to Aragvis – a Moscow restaurant so exclusive and expensive that he had never been able to afford its prices. Over dinner, the NKVD Major-General Ossipov gravely broke the news that a group of American oil engineers had been overheard discussing the forthcoming 1944 presidential election at an oil refinery in Azerbaijan. One of them, Ossipov confided darkly, had called Roosevelt 'a son of a bitch who should be taken out and shot'. It seemed the NKVD general had delivered this intelligence with the evident expectation of a request for 'special work' to be carried to protect the President from the conspiracy. It was left to General Deane to explain how 'colorful language' was often used during the American electoral process.[25]

As the official hostess of Spaso House, the glamorous Kathleen Harriman noticed how the Red Army officers were very careful to keep their distance from the NKVD guests invited to the American receptions. Once she noticed an NKVD general standing apart from the rest of their group and politely invited him to join their table, where he was scrupulously ignored by two Russian Air Force generals. At the time, Kathleen Harriman reasoned that their silence was caused by 'jealousy' of the NKVD's power, never sensing their natural abhorrence for the executioner in their midst. It was precisely this naiveté that the NKVD chose to exploit when the exposure of a scene of a mass murder threatened briefly to disturb the night-water of the American–Soviet alliance.[26]

In January 1944, Kathleen Harriman was invited to visit a clearing in the Katyn Forest of Byelorussia where the mass graves of several thousand Polish officers missing since 1940 had been discovered. At Katyn, half the Polish officer corps lay buried in pits alongside several hundred Polish doctors, university professors, and priests.[27] The massacre had first been uncovered during the Nazi occupation, when Joseph Goebbels took full advantage of this propaganda coup to accuse Stalin of having ordered the killings. As the Second World War progressed, the Red Army had since recaptured the lost ground and, one year later, the Soviet propaganda machine now sought to convince the world that the Katyn massacre was, in fact, a Nazi atrocity all along.

An international press corps was gathered to attend an official 'Soviet Commission of Enquiry' at the site, and the Ambassador's daughter was selected as a prized witness, invited as a representative of the Office of War Information. Kathleen Harriman was driven into the Byelorussian forest in a Lend-Lease jeep. At the site of the murders, she gazed down into the pits and watched Red Army soldiers prising out the decomposing bodies, stacked in layers face down and twelve deep. Standing next to the Associated Press journalist Homer Smith, Kathleen Harriman had 'moaned and choked' at the stench of death.[28]

The Polish officers had all been shot in the back of the head. A few had broken jaws and bayonet wounds, evidence of a struggle at the end. At the forest site, the Soviet forensic scientists proceeded with their demonstration whose purpose was to explain how all this was the work of the SS. Their lecture was a long and unconvincing affair, not least because the bodies had been removed from the graves dressed in heavy winter clothes. When a reporter asked why this was the case, given that they said the Germans had allegedly killed the

Polish officers in August, there was a moment of confusion. After a short consultation, the Soviet investigators replied that the weather in Byelorussia was extremely variable in August: people there often wore heavy winter clothing even in the height of summer.

However shallow, such explanations were enough to convince Kathleen Harriman. From Moscow, by confidential telegram, her father cabled President Roosevelt the news that his daughter could confirm that in 'all probability the massacre was perpetrated by the Germans'.[29]

If the American government wished to continue to portray Stalin's regime as worthy of the public's wholehearted support, then the suppression of the NKVD's culpability for the Katyn massacre became an essential part of the Allied war effort. All evidence to the contrary would have to be buried – just as the reports of the missing Americans had been buried – under a mountain of classified material, left to gather dust in the archives in secrecy until no one could remember why any more and all the protagonists had long since left the stage.

In fact, President Roosevelt had already been fully briefed on the events that had taken place at Katyn Forest. On 13 August 1943, Roosevelt received a classified British intelligence report accompanied by a personal letter from Winston Churchill, which made it transparently clear that the Soviets were responsible for the mass murder. The details provided in the report were precise and unremitting. In its pages, Roosevelt learned how the Polish officers had scratched on the train wagons 'don't believe that we are going home'; how their letters to their relatives had abruptly stopped in March 1940; how Katyn Forest had been a well-known killing ground of the NKVD 'used by the Bolsheviks in 1919 as a convenient place for the killing of many Tsarist officers'; how 'if a man struggled, the executioner threw his coat over his head, tying it around his neck and leading him hooded to the pit's edge – in many cases a body was found to be thus hooded and the coat to have been pierced by a bullet where it covered the base of the skull'; how the bullets penetrated the skulls from close range or with the muzzle pressed against the base of the neck; how the wounds were regular, as if fired by experienced hands; how the bodies were stabbed with four-edged bayonets of a Soviet issue.

The report read as a letter of protest from its author Owen

O'Malley, the British Ambassador to the Polish government-in-exile:

> We have been constrained by the urgent need for cordial rela-
> tions with the Soviet Government to appear to appraise the
> evidence with more hesitation and lenience than we should do in
> forming a common-sense judgment on events occurring in
> normal times or in the ordinary course of our private lives; we
> have been obliged to appear to distort the normal and healthy
> operation of our intellectual and moral judgments; we have been
> obliged to give undue prominence to the tactlessness or impul-
> siveness of Poles ... We have in fact perforce used the good
> name of England like the murderers used the little conifers to
> cover up a massacre ... we now stand in danger of bemusing not
> only others but ourselves: of falling ... under St. Paul's curse on
> those who can see cruelty and burn not.[30]

The truth of O'Malley's observations was later found in the Soviet
archives. On 5 March 1940, a 'top secret' NKVD memo had been
sent from Beria to Stalin:

> A large number of former Polish army officers ... and others are
> at the present moment being kept in the camps of the NKVD
> USSR for prisoners-of-war and in the prisons of the western dis-
> tricts of Ukraine and Byelorussia. All of them are bitter enemies
> of the soviet power, filled with enmity for the soviet system ...
> The NKVD USSR considers as essential: 1. Recommend the
> NKVD USSR to the matter of the 14,700 persons ... apply
> towards them the punishment of the highest order – shooting. 2.
> The matter is to be looked at without summoning the arrested
> and without the presentation of evidence.

Across the first page of the memorandum was scrawled Stalin's signature, followed by those of his Politburo functionaries – Voroshilov,
Molotov, Mikoyan, and the votes of Kalinin and Kaganovich added
by the recorder in the margin: 'For'.[31]

In terms of the history of the Soviet secret police, Katyn was a standard operation that just happened to have been discovered. But the
threat of exposure never materialised from the White House. Instead,
Owen O'Malley's report was locked away in Roosevelt's 'safe files',
never to see the light of day until decades later. And its pages revealed

two further pieces of incriminating information. The first was that the American President encouraged Henry Wallace to visit Kolyma, even after the region had been clearly identified as another place of execution of Poles in Russia. The second was that President Roosevelt was fully aware of Stalin's capability for mass murder, even as he was making preparations to meet him. But no one, it seemed, believed in the curse of St Paul at the dawn of the atomic age.

At the White House, when William Bullitt tried to warn Roosevelt about Stalin's true intent, the President lost patience with him. 'Bill, I don't dispute your facts, they are accurate,' Roosevelt replied, 'I don't dispute the logic of your reasoning. I just have a hunch that Stalin is not that kind of man. Harry says he's not and that he doesn't want anything but security for his country, and I think that if I give him everything I possibly can and ask for nothing from him in return, noblesse oblige, he won't try to annex anything and will work with me for a world of democracy and peace.' Bullitt purposefully reminded the President that 'when he talked of noblesse oblige he was not speaking of the Duke of Norfolk but of a Caucasian bandit whose only thought when he got something for nothing was that the other fellow was an ass'. But Roosevelt had heard enough: 'It's my responsibility and not yours, and I'm going to play my hunch.'[32] (Like most leaders, Roosevelt preferred the company of those whose views he shared, notwithstanding his affection, at the time, for Bullitt. In the last week of November 1941, Roosevelt had warned his first Ambassador to Soviet Russia against travelling across the Pacific: 'I am expecting the Japs to attack any time now, probably within the next three or four days.'[33])

At Teheran on 28 November 1943, Franklin Roosevelt met Joseph Stalin for the first time with only interpreters present. 'I am glad to see you,' said Roosevelt, 'I have tried for a long time to bring this about.' For security reasons, the American President was housed in the compound of the Soviet Embassy, pushed into and out of buildings by his valet on a system of ramps, and lifted in and out of cars while Secret Service agents kept him surrounded.[34] In their long conversations Roosevelt happily discussed issues ranging from the future of India – 'The best solution,' said Roosevelt, 'would be reform from the bottom, somewhat on the Soviet Line' – to the future liberty of Poland, a political question that Roosevelt reminded Stalin had domestic considerations upon 'six to seven million Americans of

Polish extraction, and as a practical man he would not wish to lose their vote'. Stressing the need for free elections in the once independent Baltic states, Roosevelt agreed that he 'personally was confident that the people would vote to join the Soviet Union'.[35]

For his part, Stalin's contempt for the perceived weakness he saw in Roosevelt was revealed at the end of a morning session in Teheran. Roosevelt genially announced to the conference table, 'now we can adjourn and let's go have some lunch'. After everyone got to their feet, the Soviet interpreter Valentin Berezhkov heard Stalin mockingly remark: 'Some will walk and some will ride.' When Berezhkov asked if this comment should be translated, Stalin answered, 'Niet'.[36]

With the other interpreters, Berezhkov worked around the clock translating Roosevelt's private conversations, since his living quarters were, of course, bugged by the NKVD. These conversations were not hostile in the slightest, so much so that Berezhkov wondered if perhaps Roosevelt was speaking not only to his American aides but also to the microphones.[37] Later, at Yalta, a perplexed Stalin would ask: 'What do you think? Do they know that we are listening to them? . . . It's bizarre. They say everything in the fullest detail.'[38]

At Teheran, the most revealing conversation was made quite openly, over dinner on 29 November 1943. Stalin twice proposed that after the war in Germany 'at least 50,000 and perhaps 100,000 of the German Commanding Staff must be physically liquidated'. Franklin Roosevelt, evidently believing that the Soviet leader was joking, suggested that only 'forty-nine thousand' should be killed. Winston Churchill got up from the table and left the room in disgust. 'I was deeply angered,' Churchill later wrote, 'I would rather, I said, be taken out into the garden here and now and be shot myself than sully my own and my country's honour by such infamy.' Both Churchill and Roosevelt had read Owen O'Malley's report of the Katyn massacre just three months earlier.[39]

After his return from Teheran, the President broadcast a fireside chat to the nation: 'To use an American and somewhat ungrammatical colloquialism, I may say that "I got along fine" with Marshal Stalin. He is a man who combines a tremendous, relentless determination with a stalwart good humor. I believe he is truly representative of the heart and soul of Russia; and I believe that we are going to get along very well with him and the Russian people – very well indeed.'[40] Nor was this simply a public facade, designed to reassure the American public. In her memoirs, Eleanor Roosevelt confided that her husband had been 'impressed by the strength of Stalin's personality. On his return he was always careful in describing him to mention that he was short and thick-set and powerful . . . He also said that his control over the people of his country was unquestionably due to their trust in him and their confidence that he had their good at heart.'[41]

Just over a year later, the ailing American President was once again lifted 'into automobile, to ship, to shore and to aircraft' to travel around the world for a second meeting with Stalin this time at the Soviet leader's summer retreat on the Black Sea. In the newsreel pictures taken at the Yalta Conference of February 1945, Roosevelt appeared pale and very drawn, struggling to summon his customary bright smile for the cameras. At their photocall, the three most powerful men in the world sat on a simple bench with their aides gathered behind them. In the newsreel, on a whim Stalin gets up to shake Churchill's hand, and for a moment Franklin Roosevelt is left sitting on the bench alone, wearing a black cloak fastened at his throat with a chain, looking around him forlorn and somewhat confused.[42]

Inside the Livadia Palace, Joseph Stalin raised a glass to his Allies: 'I am talking, as an old man; that is why I am talking so much . . . In an alliance the allies should not deceive each other. Perhaps this is naïve? Experienced diplomatists may say, "Why should I not deceive my ally?" But I as a naïve man think it best not to deceive my ally even if he is a fool. Possibly our alliance is so firm just because we do not deceive each other, or is it because it is not so easy to deceive each other? I propose a toast to the firmness of our Three Power Alliance.'[43]

Leaving us to wonder if such elegant rhetoric – such deceiving words on the nature of deception – was even necessary given Roosevelt's deteriorating health and his belief in 'noblesse oblige'. At their very first session in Yalta, Roosevelt announced that 'the United States would take all reasonable steps to preserve peace, but not at the expense of keeping a large army in Europe, three thousand miles away from home. The American occupation would therefore be limited to two years.' Churchill described the statement as 'momentous'.[44] What hope had Eastern Europe, or even Poland whose liberty had been the very starting point of the war? When Roosevelt asked Stalin how soon it would be possible to hold elections in Poland, Stalin crisply replied 'within a month', and the American President appeared to believe him. 'The elections,' Roosevelt emphasised to Stalin, 'must be above criticism, like Caesar's wife. I want some kind of assurance to give to the world, and I don't want anybody to be able to question their purity.'[45]

In private telegrams to Churchill, Roosevelt often referred to Stalin as 'UJ' or 'Uncle Joe', with an avuncular affection he clearly wanted others to share. It was a fantasy Roosevelt continued to believe almost to the very end. On his return from Yalta, the President described Stalin's character to his assembled Cabinet as having 'something in his being apart from this revolutionist Bolshevik thing'. Warming to his theme, Roosevelt suggested that Stalin's early training as a priest meant that 'something entered into his nature, of the way in which a Christian gentleman should behave'. Perhaps Roosevelt wished to cling to the notion of their wartime alliance as morally unambiguous: a straightforward triumph of good over evil as scripted by the Office of War Information. Perhaps Roosevelt wanted to conceal from himself and others the bitter similarities between the two totalitarian dictatorships. Perhaps Roosevelt genuinely believed the views of his closest advisers, the publicly expressed enthusiasms of Joseph Davies, Sumner Welles, Henry Wallace and Harry Hopkins. We do not know, since the American President always reserved the ability to hide the truth, if need be, even from himself.

Winston Churchill, at least, recognised the reality behind the facade. At the Livadia Palace in Yalta, when the British Ambassador Archibald Clark Kerr raised his glass in a toast to Lavrenty Beria, 'the protector of our bodies', it was Churchill who growled back at him, 'No, no, Archie. None of that.' The perspicacity of Churchill shone through the smoke and subterfuge of stateroom diplomacy. Unlike Roosevelt, Churchill never harboured any illusions over Soviet intentions, and he understood very well that Stalin made good on his threats.

Two years earlier, in August 1942, Churchill had visited Stalin in Moscow to discuss the delay of the second front. During their late-night conversation, Churchill asked if the strains of the Second World War were any worse than during the collectivisation period a decade earlier. 'Oh no,' Stalin replied. 'The collective farm policy was a terrible struggle.' Churchill then mentioned that Stalin had dealt with not just 'a few score thousands of aristocrats or big landowners, but with millions of small men'. At which point Stalin corrected him:

'Ten millions.' When Churchill asked what had happened to this *kulak* class, Stalin explained, 'Many of them agreed to come in with us. Some of them were given land of their own to cultivate in the province of Tomsk . . . or further north, but the great bulk were very unpopular and were wiped out by their labourers.' There was then a 'considerable pause' while the British Prime Minister understood the significance of the destruction of approximately one eighth of the Russian population judged to be part of this *kulak* class.[46]

At Yalta, both Roosevelt and Churchill agreed to repatriate 'without exception and by force if necessary' all former Soviet prisoners of war, fugitive Soviet nationals and fleeing citizens of satellite nations. It did not require too much political acumen to predict what fate awaited these men once they were returned to the USSR. Stalin himself had publicly warned that 'in Hitler's camps there are no Russian prisoners-of-war, only Russian traitors and we shall do away with them when the war is over'. But Churchill's signature remained on the document that settled the fate of approximately two million Russian prisoners of war at the conference on the Black Sea. Churchill christened the retreat 'the Riviera of Hades'.[47]

At Yalta, when Churchill asked for some lemon for his gin and tonics, he awoke the next morning to discover a lemon tree growing outside his palace window. Even this humble lemon tree concealed a private tragedy which linked the forgotten Americans to this historic setting. Albert Troyer had been a citrus specialist, a graduate of the University of Nebraska, who arrived in the Soviet Union from his native Alabama in 1932, ready to take on the responsibility for revitalising the moribund Soviet citrus industry. In the sunny climate by the Black Sea, Albert Troyer had diligently crossed and grafted lemons for four years until his arrest in 1936 and subsequent sentence to ten years in the Gulag. Eventually his wife's parcels to him were returned and Eva Troyer was informed that her husband had been 'transferred to an undisclosed destination'. She had reported his arrest to the American Embassy: 'My husband is an old man – 71 years old. He has been a horticulturist practically all his life, with no definite political interests. He is essentially an idealist and an altruist. For fifteen years he taught agriculture in the Calhoun Colored School of Calhoun, Alabama . . . He believed his difficulties arose chiefly because of his inability to understand the Russian language.' But no help was ever forthcoming for this humble lemon farmer from Alabama.[48]

*

Returning from Yalta, the USS *Quincy* stopped in Algiers to allow Harry Hopkins to be taken off on a stretcher and flown to the Mayo Clinic for treatment of the cancer that would take his life within the year. Another one of the President's closest aides, General Edwin 'Pa' Watson, was confined in an oxygen tent after collapsing from a heart attack, and would die en route. Roosevelt himself, according to an eyewitness, looked worn out. His college friend Alexander Kirk commented: 'This is really a ship of death and everyone responsible for encouraging that man to go to Yalta has done a disservice to the United States and ought to be shot.'[49]

Two months later, Henry Morgenthau visited the President at the Little White House at Warm Springs, Georgia. The ever-faithful Treasury Secretary discovered Roosevelt 'sitting in a chair with his feet up on a very large footstool with a card table drawn up over his legs. He was mixing cocktails.' When he saw Roosevelt's face, Morgenthau was shocked, describing in his diary how the President 'had aged terrifically and looked very haggard. His hands shook so that he started to knock the glasses over, and I had to hold each glass as he poured out the cocktail . . . I noticed that he took two cocktails and then seemed to feel a little bit better. I found his memory bad, and he was constantly confusing names. He hasn't weighed himself so he didn't know whether he had gained weight or not. I have never seen him have so much difficulty transferring himself from his wheelchair to a regular chair, and I was in agony watching him.'[50]

The next day before lunch, Roosevelt was having his portrait painted by Elizabeth Shoumatoff, a White Russian artist whose family had fled the Revolution. As Shoumatoff mixed her watercolours, she glanced up at the President, who was working on some government papers. The grey, drained look on his face had disappeared, and he seemed in good colour, remarking, 'We have fifteen minutes more to work.' As the cerebral haemorrhage struck, Franklin Roosevelt's right hand passed over his forehead several times, his head bent forward in his chair, and he lost consciousness. Two hours after his collapse, at 3.35 p.m. on 12 April 1945, Franklin Roosevelt died.[51]

At 6.45 p.m. on the same day, Chief Justice Harlan Stone administered the oath of office to Vice-President Truman. Harry Truman's shock and surprise at the news was such that he forgot to raise his right hand when he repeated the oath of office with his left hand on the Bible. Chief Justice Stone had to quietly remind him of this obligation.[52]

Three months later at their meeting at Potsdam in the ruins of Berlin, Stalin charitably advised Truman that 'a man must conserve his strength. President Roosevelt had a great sense of duty, but he did not save his strength. If he had, he would probably be alive today.'[53] Given that it was Stalin himself who had twice in rapid succession summoned the ailing, wheelchair-bound President around the world to his very doorstep, it appeared that the Soviet dictator was having a private joke with himself.

But that seemed to be Stalin's way. When Averell Harriman left Moscow, Stalin presented him with a gift of two horses that the American Ambassador had admired in the newsreel of the Red Square victory parade. One of the horses was given with special thanks to the Ambassador's daughter, Kathleen Harriman. At Soviet state expense, the thoroughbreds were transported across the Atlantic – with an escort of a Russian vet, a jockey and two grooms – to the Harriman family estate in New York. Upon their arrival, Kathleen Harriman was photographed standing beside a magnificent sixteen-hand bay stallion named 'Fact'. The horse's Russian documentation, bound in red leather and presented with the gift, revealed that Fact had been bred at the military farm of the First Cavalry Army. The stallion was the offspring of a sire named 'Pharaoh' and a dam named 'Liquidation'.[54]

20

'RELEASE BY THE GREEN PROCURATOR'

> The General Assembly signed the agreement on genocide . . . . We signed the convention. Of course, 1937 was not genocide. It was the destruction of the enemies of the people. There was no reason not to sign the convention.
>
> Varlam Shalamov, *Graphite*[1]

Stalin declared Victory Day in the USSR to be 9 May 1945, exactly one day after the Allies. On the morning of 10 May, a crowd of joyful Russians gathered outside the American Embassy cheering the Stars and Stripes and refusing to move on. From the balcony, George Kennan made a short speech – 'Congratulations on the day of Victory. All honor to the Soviet allies' – and then the crowd remained on the street waving and cheering until evening. No spontaneous mass demonstration had taken place in Moscow since the Revolution. As George Kennan recalled: 'Not even a sparrow had fallen . . . for twenty-seven years and now suddenly this!' It seemed that the suffering of the Russian people during the war, and their courage in withstanding the invasion, had also given rise to a certain boldness in its aftermath.[2]

In July 1945, a scene was reported by an American witness one night outside a restaurant in the centre of Moscow. A Russian man and a woman were confronted by several policemen including one plain-clothes man who appeared to have a pistol in his hand. Astonishingly the Russian civilian refused to be arrested and instead shouted in the street: 'I served the whole war on the front. And where did you serve, eh? Where did you serve?' In his choice of language, the former Red Army soldier used the familiar form of the Russian 'you', signifying his contempt for the secret police. He then strode off down the street and was allowed to walk away.

Within the Soviet Union it was evident that the defeat of Nazi Germany contained the possibility for new liberties at home. If, therefore, the post-war period was rapidly transformed into a new pre-war prelude, then this was never merely an accident of historical circumstance.[3]

Within the Gulag, the end of the Second World War made little difference, save for its continued expansion. New waves of prisoners began filling the camps in the summer of 1945, including the so-called *spetz* men, the Soviet prisoners of war whose fate had been sealed months earlier at Yalta. In the Allied-controlled prisoner-of-war camps of France and Germany, NKVD agents identified the men they wanted back. They handed out propaganda leaflets and posters showing a beautiful Russian woman stretching out her arms, 'Come home, dearest son, your motherland calls you'. After the propaganda was distributed, the NKVD agents read promises from the Soviet government that no prisoner of war would be prosecuted in his native land. Of course, they were universally disbelieved.[4]

During the post-war deportations, an estimated forty thousand Russians were hunted down in free France, with the assistance of the French police.[5] In one example, French witnesses looked on as a Russian former prisoner of war, Nikolai Lapchinski, was beaten and dragged across the street into a waiting car by the agents of the NKVD. The inside of his safe-house apartment showed the aftermath of a desperate struggle. The walls were covered in blood, the furniture smashed, and a broken kitchen knife lay on the floor. The measure of violence revealing how well their victim understood what was at stake.[6]

The captured Russians joined thousands of others in transit camps in the Soviet zone of eastern Germany. At Sachsenhausen, Buchenwald and elsewhere, prisoners were once again clothed in the familiar striped pyjamas the world knew so well.[7] Among them was John Noble, a twenty-one-year-old American interned by the Germans and arrested by the Soviet police. As a prisoner-clerk at the Soviet jail at Munchenerplatz, John Noble learned of the guards' 'humane' method of execution. On execution days a prisoner was undressed and walked down a corridor. As he turned a corner, he was shot in the back of the head. At the end of the day the bodies were piled up, ready to be doused in gasoline and set alight.[8] Five years after the end of the war, while still a prisoner in Buchenwald, John Noble learned there were prisoners who had suffered in this camp under the Nazi and the Soviet regimes. The bodies of approximately seven thousand prisoners who had been starved to death were taken out to the forest and buried in mass graves. In Sachsenhausen in the early 1990s, forensic investigators found 12,500 bodies buried in 50 mass graves around the camp, dating from its period as a Stalinist transit camp from 1945 to 1950.[9]

The surviving prisoners began the long journey east, transported into the Gulag on prison trains until they arrived in the dense and endless forest of barbed wire, watchtowers, searchlights, dogs and guards that was the camp complex of Vorkuta. John Noble was given a black uniform with the number '1–E–241' sewn into the cloth and sent to work in the mines. When he arrived in October, the summer was over and the ground was already covered in snow. After work, Noble watched the prisoners gather the snow into blocks and build them up around the barracks in preparation for winter, when the temperatures in this Gulag centre above the Arctic Circle fell to between forty-five and sixty-five degrees below zero. On a daily diet of approximately 1400 calories, and performing heavy labour of pushing a two-ton car of slate through the mines, John Noble's weight dropped to 95 pounds. Bones protruding, face gaunt, he joined the army of skeletal cadavers who universally weighed between seventy-five and 115 pounds. Almost all the prisoners had half their teeth missing through scurvy, they fell out while they were eating. John Noble was not due for release until the mid-1960s.[10]

Many other Americans were caught up in the mass deportations into the Gulag after the war. Mieczyslaw Rusinek was an American citizen born in Detroit and brought to Poland as an infant by his parents. Although Rusinek was issued with an American passport in 1940, he was arrested by the NKVD during their operations in Poland. On 8 February 1945, he was placed in a transport of 3800 Polish men and women pressed into sealed wagons for the six-week journey. 'About half the people died during the journey,' Rusinek later wrote. In the camp 'we received to eat only nettle and some ivy and 400 grams of bread daily ... only 25% of our transport survived the camp.'[11]

A German woman, Marga Sochart, wrote to the American

Consulate in Bremen describing how she had been placed in a stock car containing ninety prisoners, where she had met a nineteen-year-old American citizen named Anneliese Thamm, captured by the NKVD with her mother in Elbing, West Prussia, where she had been 'beaten and raped by Russian troops'. The mother and daughter were then transported to a camp in Turkmenistan, where they 'performed hard labour, though inadequately fed ... Of the 3500 inmates of the camp about 3000 died.' Mrs Thamm suffered continually from heart attacks and died in July 1945. Her daughter Anneliese died later the same month. Marga Sochart wrote that: 'Their bodies were stripped of their clothes and were buried in a common grave with 10 to 20 others in the cemetery.'[12]

The Gulag collected prisoners from all over the world, including the United States. According to British and American military intelligence estimates, approximately one in ten soldiers fighting in the German army during the D-Day invasion of France was a former Soviet citizen, more than a million of whom had been enlisted.[13] In encouraging these Russian troops to surrender in Normandy, the US Army psychological warfare operatives had given these soldiers their assurance, in leaflets, that 'they would be sent to America for the duration and subsequently would not be required to return to Russia'.[14]

At Fort Dix, New Jersey, a riot broke out when Russian prisoners of war discovered they were about to be repatriated. Tear gas and rifle-fire were required before the prisoners were finally clubbed into submission. Three men were found hanged in their barracks, and several others were hospitalised with self-inflicted injuries.[15] From Camp Rupert, Idaho, eleven hundred Russians were dispatched on to ships leaving from the West Coast. Once again, three men attempted to commit suicide, and two bodies were later found floating in the water.[16]

The British authorities resorted to deceptions of their own. One captured Cossack battle group was given Allied uniforms and promised that ninety thousand men would be allowed to serve in the British army. The Cossacks were asked to turn in their weapons before being given a standard-issue supply. Once disarmed, they were handed over to the NKVD. Knowing their likely fate, the Russian prisoners of war physically resisted their embarkation on to the trains. Since the NKVD lacked the necessary manpower and could not yet shoot the prisoners on the spot, it was left to the American and British military police, using tear gas and baton charges, to club them on board. In one, not untypical group of three hundred Russians, nine men hanged themselves, one stabbed himself to death and twenty others preferred hospitalisation with self-inflicted injuries rather than risk being sent back to the Soviet Union.[17]

A British witness watched a disembarkation of former Russian prisoners of war in the northern port of Murmansk that lasted four and a half hours. The sick prisoners, those with broken legs, the amputees, the dying, and the failed suicides were 'marched or dragged into a warehouse fifty yards from the ship and after a lapse of fifteen minutes, automatic fire was heard coming from the warehouse; twenty minutes later a covered lorry drove out of the warehouse and headed towards the town. Later I had a chance to glance into the warehouse when no one was around and found the cobbled floor stained dark in several places around the sides and the walls badly chipped for about five feet up.' The executioners were Russian youths with automatic rifles, between fourteen and sixteen years old.[18]

In the Soviet Union, many of the Russian prisoners of war who had enlisted in General Andrei Vlassov's 'Russian Liberation Movement' were executed as traitors. The rest of the *spetz* men – mainly ordinary Russian prisoners of war guilty of nothing other than having been captured in battle – were handed twenty-five-year sentences and transported to the harshest, and most remote, camps. But whereas the mass of Gulag prisoners before the Second World War had been mainly civilian victims unused to violence and preyed upon by the criminals, the *spetz* men were different. They arrived marked by the habits of war, and placed their trust in the gun, not Soviet propaganda. This made them especially dangerous.

Varlam Shalamov would later describe the fate of Lieutenant Yanovsky, a Red Army officer and former prisoner of war in Germany who refused the Vlassov emissaries' invitation to fight against the Soviet Union. Instead Yanovsky had managed to escape a Nazi camp and make his way back across enemy lines to his own side. He was immediately arrested by the NKVD and handed a twenty-five-year sentence. Eventually Yanovsky was transported to Kolyma, where one glance at his fellow prisoners convinced him they had been delivered to their deaths. Resolving to save himself once again, he spent the winter of 1945 planning one of the few armed conspiracies in the history of the Kolyma Gulag.

His conspirators learned the information required to make their operation successful: the guard duty, the location of the munitions stores, the geography beyond the wire. According to Shalamov's account, Lieutenant Yanovsky spoke to many men who refused to join the escape, but no one betrayed him and twelve agreed to risk their lives for the chance of freedom. Their plan was to overpower the guards, steal a truck and head off into the taiga towards the nearest military airport, where they would hijack a plane to Alaska. Nor was this scheme quite so far-fetched as it might at first have appeared. Its very audacity worked in its favour. Only the year before, three Russian pilots had escaped from a Nazi prison camp, seizing Luftwaffe planes and flying out of Germany to what they had believed was the safety of Byelorussia.[19] Far from being welcomed as heroes, the Russian pilots were arrested and sent to Kolyma. But in Alaska, Yanovsky reasoned, the Americans would not treat them like the NKVD.

In the spring of 1946, the Yanovsky conspirators killed two guards, changed into their uniforms and overpowered the whole guard block. Taking food, weapons and ammunition, they drove a truck out of the camp. There were several military airports in the vicinity, and the men headed for the nearest. When their truck ran out of fuel, they got out and ran across the taiga. Every available NKVD troop in the heavily garrisoned area was sent after them. Adopting guerrilla tactics, the escapees split into two groups: a main group of eight, and a reconnaissance patrol of four led by Yanovsky. The advance party soon encountered a unit of soldiers whose dogs had picked up their scent. Three of the men were cut down by rifle fire, and only Yanovsky himself escaped. The main group of eight were caught in a flanking movement by the NKVD. Pinned down by crossfire, the soldiers formed a circle and fought at each other's side until their ammunition was exhausted and they were shot down. Only one of their group was captured, wounded but alive. He was taken to a camp hospital, where he was treated until he recovered and then executed.

Perhaps, before he was killed, the wounded escapee had gained some grim satisfaction from the camp doctors' assumption that the World War Three had begun, so numerous were the NKVD casualties. And it might have comforted the lone Russian to learn that, despite every effort, Lieutenant Yanovsky's body was not recovered. The Russian lieutenant had promised his men liberty, and had delivered, if only for a few precious hours spent running across the taiga.

The conspirators had expected nothing more, and no one in their camp questioned their choice.[20]

Thomas Sgovio personally witnessed what happened to the *spetz* men in the Kolyma camps. Kept shackled with no names only numbers on their backs, they were subjected to the very worst conditions of food and labour. Very few survived their sentence – for most, the maximum life expectancy was two years.[21]

Desperation at their lengthened sentences led many prisoners to make individual escape attempts from Kolyma in the spring of 1946. 'Release by the green procurator' almost invariably ended in failure, since there was nowhere to run to in that vast wilderness. The nearest human settlements were hundreds of kilometres away, and the local nomadic tribesmen were promised flour and vodka for every escapee they returned. The bounty was only rarely collected. Most escape attempts were quickly ended by experienced teams of 'head hunters' who tracked the runners with dogs and planes, shooting their victims on sight. They dumped the bodies in the wasteland and amputated their hands for identification.[22] Early on in his sentence, Thomas Sgovio had heard that two criminals named Prosolov and Novikov were planning an escape and were looking for a third person to join their party. All the experienced prisoners wisely refused, but eventually a new arrival was persuaded to join them. The young man could hardly have realised that the criminals were merely planning to use him as a food source. Somewhere along the way they killed their victim. Both men were then hunted down and shot by the guards.[23]

And yet, for all the overwhelming odds against them, there were still a few individuals who managed to escape the Gulag. In the chaos at the end of the war, a few 'captive' Americans turned up in Moscow in ones or twos, always furtive and clearly desperate. At the Associated Press offices in the Metropol Hotel, the American reporter Homer Smith answered a call from a man asking for Eddy Gilmore. Since the bureau chief was away, and knowing that the Metropol was closely watched, Homer Smith suggested a meeting at the Moscow Post Office. There he met a 'heavy set, sallow-complexioned man' whose hands were 'calloused as a stevedore's'. Together they took a metro train to Sokolniki Park in north-east Moscow, and, sitting on a park bench, 'K.' told Smith his story.

The American was a former union activist from California who had arrived in Soviet Russia as 'political immigrant' in 1930. Soon afterwards his criticism of Stalin's regime had led to his arrest and deportation to Kolyma. Having survived fourteen years in the Gulag, K. explained that he had escaped from a prison train on a transfer in the Urals, and six weeks later arrived in Moscow. In the city he had acquired false identity papers, and was hidden in the basement of a Russian widow who had lost her husband during the Terror. Then in Sokolniki Park, K. attempted to describe to Smith the conditions he had witnessed in Kolyma – 'the inhumanity, brutality and horrors of life'.

Two days later K. met Smith again, this time in Gorky Park. He asked Smith if he would be willing to drive him into the American Embassy. Homer Smith refused but gave him the name of a friend who might be able to help. Later Smith heard that the Californian unionist had stayed in the American Embassy basement for a week, where he was interviewed and given new clothes. K. was not, however, granted asylum and his escape from the USSR remained his own initiative. Two attempts to cross into Romania and Finland both ended in failure. Weeks later, K. met Smith for the last time in Moscow, with a plan to cross the Polish border. Once again Homer Smith chose not to become involved, claiming that he was unsure if the Californian was the 'real thing' or an NKVD agent. In the circumstances Smith's caution was understandable. Before he was hired by Gilmore at the Associated Press, Homer Smith had been just another American emigrant like K., who had arrived in the early 1930s to work at the Moscow Post Office. His press accreditation offered him a measure of protection, but he must have known of the disappearances of Lydia Kleingal and Alyce Alex.[24]

Often American fugitives such as K. encountered the same diplomats who had failed to protect them several years earlier. After his return to Moscow to maintain his Russian language skills, Elbridge Durbrow was presented with the case of Nathan Coalman, 'a man claiming to be American citizen', who called at the American Embassy on 26 October 1945. In a telegram to the State Department, Elbridge Durbrow wrote that Nathan Coalman 'was at his rope's end . . . He stated that if we could not assist him or give him asylum in Embassy we should turn him over to police in order that we would know that the police had him and furthermore that the police would be cognisant of the fact that we knew of his case.

He was persuaded to leave the premises but in all probability will return within a day or two for a final answer . . . if he calls again and demands asylum he will be refused unless Department feels otherwise.'

Three days later, just as predicted, Nathan Coalman returned to the American Embassy and was once again persuaded to leave. 'If possible,' Durbrow wrote, 'urgently request reply to his citizenship status since if impossible to try to protect him as American citizen I see no alternative but to turn him over to the authorities if he shows up here again.'[25] Durbrow's telegram was the last official trace of the existence of Nathan Coalman. In the USSR, it was only a question of time before a problem like Coalman would disappear. And while Joseph Stalin urgently coveted the return of every national back into the Soviet orbit 'without exception', the same could not be said for the new administration of Harry S. Truman.

Like Durbrow, George Kennan had been posted back to the American Embassy in Moscow. On 14 November 1945, as Minister-Counselor he wrote to the new Secretary of State James Byrnes 'transmitting a report on Soviet Treatment of American citizens'. In his letter Kennan described the fate of hundreds of Americans caught 'between the Soviet and American worlds' whose treatment could be 'little different if our country were in a state of war with the Soviet Union'. Kennan's letter showed a level of concern largely absent in the decade before the war:

> The individuals affected are mostly little people. The officials involved are minor officials. Soviet cynicism with respect to capitalist society readily suggests that neither the individuals nor the officials will normally be able to make their voices heard in the councils of the United States Government, and that even if they do, the issues will be too petty and too confused to enlist any dangerous degree of official indignation. Banking on this, they feel that they can safely continue to follow a policy of unconcealed arrogance and hostility in this obscure field of inter-governmental relations, so important to them and – as they imagine – so unimportant to us.

Once again, Kennan suggested that the whole hidden issue of the American emigrants should be presented openly: 'if we were to find means to state frankly to the American public what the situation is with which we are faced in this respect . . . I would recommend that this particular compartment of Russian–American relations, which has long remained so dark and so replete with uncertainty and unpleasantness, be given its airing and illumination.'[26]

Attached to Kennan's letter was a report from Roger Tyler Jr., the Second Secretary at the Moscow Embassy and head of the consular section. Tyler's report contained the first official admission of the diplomats' earlier hostility towards the American emigrants: 'It cannot be denied that during the years where there were no diplomatic relations between the United States and Soviet Russia, a general feeling existed that any one who came to the Soviet Union was a damned Bolshevik and deserved what he got.' Tyler then continued:

> An examination of the citizen files in the Embassy reveals with stark clarity the force, deception and threats employed by the Soviet authorities in preventing many American citizens from maintaining their citizenship status . . . The files are full of pleas from desperate people who want to come to Moscow to explain their cases . . . few of those who were persuaded by propaganda to leave America in times of Depression or on contracts signed with Amtorg . . . had any idea that they would be under great and sometimes irresistible pressure to part with their American citizenship and never be allowed to return to the United States.

To underscore his point Roger Tyler highlighted the precarious existence of three young Americans – Dora Gershonowitz, Alexander Dolgun and Isaac Elkowitz – who had all found temporary sanctuary working in clerical jobs at the American Embassy. His report also cited the case of Lillian Boft, an American citizen brought to the Soviet Union as a child. Her sister Edith Boft had recently written to the Embassy: 'Lillian used to keep a diary, and wrote in it that she would kill herself if she could not get back to the United States. We didn't believe her.' Tyler then added: 'the record shows that while on vacation in Odessa, she hanged herself'.[27]

George Kennan sent his letter with Tyler's report to Washington but the publicity he asked for failed to materialise. Instead, the material was classified as 'Top Secret' and filed once again in the archives. Nor were the American diplomats in Moscow willing to break the silence without official sanction. Three months later, Kennan wrote another, much longer telegram advocating the policy of 'containment' in America's relationship with the Soviet Union. The eight-thousand-word telegram was quickly passed around US government circles and the resulting publicity made Kennan internationally famous as a Cold War strategist. His earlier plea on behalf of the Americans trapped in the Soviet Union received no such publicity, and was soon forgotten, even by its author.[28]

21

THE SECOND GENERATION

Under the spreading chestnut tree
I sold you and you sold me.

George Orwell, *Nineteen Eighty-Four*

Within the camps, the American survivors clung on, preoccupied with survival and waiting for a new turn of events. In theory, at least, all prisoners remained subject to the laws of the Soviet judicial system, which retained an arbitrary quality described by one survivor as 'like playing chess with an orang-utan'.[1] In September 1946, eight and a half years into his five-year sentence, Thomas Sgovio was unexpectedly fingerprinted and asked to sign a warrant. As an 'over-timer' he was informed that although he was not allowed to leave the Kolyma region, he could seek work among the free settlers shipped in to colonise the empty spaces of the north.

Now aged thirty, Thomas found a job drawing maps for a geological prospecting group. In the evenings he taught the geologists English, although his lessons grew less and less popular as the superpower relationship deteriorated. All over the Soviet Union, from this tiny ice-bound settlement in Kolyma to the busy streets of Moscow, the public loudspeakers were barking a daily diatribe against America 'the warmonger and imperialist oppressor'. With bewildering speed, the United States was transformed from World War ally into Cold War foe.[2]

Nine months later, 'the hand of the orang-utan' reached out to make another move. The petitions sent by his mother and sister in Moscow had finally reached the desk of a Soviet official willing to grant Thomas Sgovio permission to leave Kolyma. Once again without explanation, he was issued an internal passport authorising leave for the 'mainland'. Gathering his scant belongings in a knapsack, he hitched a ride south towards Magadan. On his arrival, he found the city filled with bewildered Japanese prisoners of war, who could make little sense of what was taking place around them.[3] One of the Japanese asked a former prisoner in pidgin Russian, 'Japanese soldiers walk down road, Russian soldiers guard. We understand – war! Russian ladies walk down road, Russian soldiers guard. We do not understand.' And who could begin to explain the nature of Stalinism that had led the Russian women to this end?[4]

In Magadan, Thomas bought his first apple in nine years and began the interminable bureaucratic battle to gather the necessary travel and identity papers required by an ex-prisoner to leave this closed zone. As the months wore on and his funds ran low, Thomas started to despair but was helped by a Russian translator friend, who told him that there was another American living in Magadan and working as a free-citizen engineer. His name was Aisenstein, 'perhaps he might be able to help?' Clutching the address on a slip of paper, Thomas Sgovio hurried down to the port ready for a reunion with his friend who had been saved from starvation in the camp by his qualifications as an engineer. But Michael Aisenstein greeted him at the door stony-faced, and after a few cold questions and answers, Thomas left empty-handed. Many of the former prisoners were too fearful to risk even a conversation.[5]

Instead, Thomas's salvation came in the unexpected form of an alcoholic NKVD guard whom he ran into on the streets of Magadan. Lieutenant Vassilyev's only words of English were 'Hey Thomas! Intelligence service!' First the NKVD lieutenant roared out his greeting, and then advised him to hurry down to the post office and send a telegram to Moscow. Thomas's sister, Grace Sgovio, was by now an employee at the British Embassy, and thanks to her intervention and the generosity of a British diplomat, she managed to wire her brother the necessary funds. Using this cash, Thomas bribed his way on board a flight leaving Magadan for Khabarovsk, the city six hundred kilometres north of Vladivostok. On the long train journey back to Moscow, his ragged clothes and knapsack made him instantly identifiable as a survivor from 'over there'. But no one shunned him; instead the Russian travellers treated him like a long-lost brother. Almost everyone, it seemed, had lost a family member or friend to the Terror.[6]

Exhausted by his journey, Thomas arrived to a joyous reception at his mother's flat in Moscow. In the family's shared room, his sister Grace played American records on their gramophone while they talked, since she assumed 'the walls were listening'. When Thomas asked for news of their father the mood turned more sombre. Very calmly, Grace explained that after Joseph Sgovio's arrest in 1937, no one had heard any news of his fate for the next ten years. Then, in January 1947, just three months earlier, she had answered the door to a decrepit old man dressed in rags. Thinking he was just another one of Moscow's beggars made homeless by the war, she had turned towards the kitchen to give him some food. Only when the figure whispered, 'Grace, Grace is that you?' did she realise that this old man, too frightened to follow her into the hallway, was her father.[7]

On the verge of collapse, Joseph Sgovio had summoned the strength to return to his family after ten years in the camps. Estranged from his wife, and without permission to remain in Moscow, Joseph had left just ahead of a visit from the secret police. On a collective farm in Tashkent he was hospitalised, but he managed to return once again to his family in Moscow. On his second visit, Grace Sgovio sent for a private doctor, who examined her father's skeletal body and diagnosed a combination of the typical illnesses of a Gulag prisoner: dysentery, pellagra, malaria and pneumonia. It was also very likely that he was suffering from tuberculosis, since he was coughing up blood. There was little that could be done, and a short while afterwards Joseph Sgovio died with his family by his bedside, having begged their forgiveness for ever bringing them to the Soviet Union. At the very end, he held their hands: 'Forgive me . . . goodbye.'[8]

It was a condition not uncommon among the survivors of the camps. Some men could wilfully cling on to life with stubborn tenacity. No matter how hard the circumstances they defiantly survived, exhausting their bodies' final reserves in an effort to see their families again. Once this end was achieved, they died very quickly. As Grace Sgovio recounted her father's death the gramophone played a hit record from 1929 – one that her brother had brought with him from America – 'I'm Only Painting the Clouds with Sunshine'.[9]

Happier times were to come. In the months after his return, Thomas was reunited with Lucy Flaxman, his former sweetheart, who was still living in Moscow – her family having survived the purges unharmed. In spite of the years that had passed since Thomas's arrest, their romance was rekindled in long walks through the pine woods outside Moscow. But when Thomas asked Lucy if she thought she might ever return to America, she always had trouble answering. And she always asked him not to discuss the camps: 'I'm really very weak. If ever they arrest me and interrogate me about you – I'd honestly be able to answer I know nothing.'[10]

Later, to lighten the mood, Lucy Flaxman told a joke that was going round Moscow at the time: 'When you find yourself in the company of three be careful what you say! One of you is certainly a secret agent, if not two, perhaps all three!' Thomas warned her to be careful, since jokes such as these could have disastrous consequences. But Lucy had only laughed, just as she always did, and claimed he was exaggerating. 'I've told them before. How come I was never arrested?' In reply, Thomas could only mumble an expression he had picked up in the camps: 'When it happens to you, you'll know that it was true.'[11]

As a former prisoner, Thomas was not allowed to live in Moscow or any major city of the USSR. So he found work as a sign painter in the industrial town of Alexandrov, 120 kilometres north-east of Moscow. Months later, his romance with Lucy was moving closer to marriage. At the same time, the political atmosphere in the USSR was deteriorating steadily, with a new ideological campaign launched against the crime of 'cosmopolitanism' and all foreign influences 'infecting' Soviet society.

If the latest anti-foreigner campaign had been confined to Soviet plays ridiculing President Truman, the abandoned Americans might only have suffered another period of nervous apprehension. But Stalinist propaganda was seldom unaccompanied by repressive action. In 1948 and 1949, new articles were added to the Soviet criminal code banning 'Praise of American Technology' and 'Praise of American Democracy' as offences carrying a sentence of twenty-five years.[12] Prisoners were no longer being released from the Gulag, and those who had been freed were being re-arrested in alphabetical order. The survivors understood what was approaching. In truth they had never really been free at all: their release was simply the interval between two arrests. Survivors like Thomas Sgovio were always destined to become future detainees, marking time until Stalin 'felt hungry again'.

As the Berlin Airlift threatened to escalate into a Third World War, Stalin tightened his grip still further and a new wave of Terror broke across the Soviet Union. Within the American community, along with the survivors disappearing in the latest arrests, a second generation of American sons and daughters suddenly became vulnerable. They had survived the pre-war Terror because they were children at the time. But by 1949, this was no longer the case, and that year would become known as 'the twin brother' of 1937.[13]

The three Americans mentioned by name in Roger Tyler's report were still working as clerks or translators at the Embassy in Moscow. Dora Gershonowitz had arrived in Russia as an eleven-year-old child, and had been trying to return to her birthplace, in Paterson, New Jersey, since the age of fourteen. On 18 December 1945, she wrote a letter addressed to Secretary of State James F. Byrnes, describing how: 'I was deemed expatriated as a result of my failure to return to the United States ... I have done everything humanly possible to obtain a Soviet exit visa – have been refused several times. I have never discontinued my efforts to obtain a visa and as a result have been waiting one and a half years for an answer from the Presidium of the Supreme Soviet of the USSR, in order to be able to return to my native country ... I am requesting your intervention on my behalf ... I would not have turned for assistance to you if I were not desperate.'[14]

Letters such as Dora's prompted Byrnes to telegram the Moscow Embassy on 23 May 1946:

> Long accumulation of unsolved cases has resulted in embarrassment to Dept in its communication with persons in US interested in American nationals in Soviet Union. Dept desires that discussions with Foreign Minister be on a plane of utmost frankness ... Soviet authorities have since resumption of diplomatic relations molested and in numerous instances arrested American nationals who have called at the Embassy, some of whom have disappeared and Embassy has been unable to ascertain their whereabouts or fate ... Dept is considering the disclosure of facts of this situation to American public.[15]

While the machinery of the State Department considered how to act, Dora Gershonowitz was arrested. Although she was both an

American citizen and an employee of the American Embassy, little was done to protect her from her ordeal.

Eight years after her disappearance, in March 1956, a released German prisoner named Vera Kemnitz reported having seen her alive in Camp Nineteen at Potma, approximately 350 kilometres south of Nizhni Novgorod. Vera Kemnitz described Dora Gershonowitz as being of 'slight build, approximately one hundred pounds in weight, dark brown hair, brown eyes and she is suffering badly from the effects of tuberculosis'. As proof of her identity, Dora had asked Kemnitz to remember the names of two diplomats she had worked with at the American Embassy: 'Robert Tyler Jr, and Louis Hirschfeld, both US citizens.'[16]

Like Dora, Alexander Dolgun was employed as a clerk at the American Embassy. His father had brought him to Moscow as a seven-year-old boy, having signed up on a dollar contract assembling Fords at the Stalin auto factory in 1933. Now aged twenty-two, Alexander Dolgun was stopped on a Moscow street by a secret police officer and bundled into the back of a car to be driven the short distance to the Lubyanka. His reaction was almost identical to his American predecessors ten years earlier: 'What is all this about! Don't you know you are dealing with a citizen of the United States of America!'[17]

After the official Embassy requests to visit Dolgun in prison were refused, there seems to have been a collective bureaucratic shrug. From New York, Alexander's sister wrote frantic appeals to her senator, and received a reply from an Assistant Secretary of State that 'every feasible means will be employed to ascertain Mr Dolgun's status'. But a short while afterwards, a minor official from the Embassy wrote back suggesting that it would 'be useful' if they were authorised to dispose of some of her brother's belongings 'by giving them to needy persons'. On an internal note, another diplomat had handwritten, 'Do you remember him?'[18]

In the Lubyanka, Alexander Dolgun's MGB interrogator took evident pleasure in ridiculing an American letter of protest written on his behalf: 'Fuck your embassy. That's all you are going to hear from them. That's the end of it. That's all they are good for. You are going to be here for the rest of your life, do you understand that?'[19]

Transferred to the notorious Lefortovo prison, Dolgun was put on the 'conveyor' and placed in an isolation cell painted black. Severe physical abuse continued for nine months, as his interrogators attempted to force his confession to an alleged espionage plot while screaming at him, 'the State fucks you, you stupid son of a bitch'. As the starvation and torture continued, Dolgun's hair fell out and his weight dropped to less than ninety pounds. By early 1950, when his condition had degenerated to the point where he could hardly walk, he was sentenced to twenty-five years at the Gulag camp of Dzhezkazgan in the deserts of Kazakhstan.[20]

On his arrival at the camp, the American Embassy clerk was distracted by the sound of an orchestra, drifting out from inside. The gates opened and an army of skeletal prisoners marched out in lines of five, wearing black jackets with white numbers, looking straight ahead and keeping time to the march. The camp's ragged orchestra consisted of a tuba, a trumpet, a drum, an accordion and a violin, and Alexander Dolgun noticed how 'the eyes of the brass players looked profoundly hollow over their puffed cheeks.' The new prisoners were then forced to undergo a selection: those who still had flesh on their buttocks were sent directly to the mines. Given his already starved condition, Dolgun was chosen for outdoor construction work breaking stones, and was thus denied an early death. Later a Latvian prisoner-doctor chose to train him as medical orderly in exchange for English lessons. And by the shelter of this 'function' Alexander Dolgun's life was saved from the mechanism of a camp that killed one third of its population every year.[21]

Who, then, could blame a very frightened Isaac Elkowitz when he refused even to leave the safety of the American Embassy at all? Like the others, the twenty-year-old Ike had been vainly attempting to gain an exit visa back to New York, his former home and place of birth. His family had tried to leave the Soviet Union in the summer of 1941, but his parents had been killed during the war, and Ike found himself in an orphanage with his sister. During this period he lost his sister too, and having nowhere else to turn, he travelled to the American Embassy in Moscow, where he found temporary sanctuary in his job as a telephone operator.

Denied permanent asylum in the Embassy building, Ike Elkowitz was called up for Soviet military service. Weeks later he was arrested and held in Lefortovo prison, still wearing a Red Army uniform but with its insignia torn off. Ike was then accused of 'having betrayed his homeland', an offence which carried a twenty-five year sentence or 'the supreme measure of social justice'. He briefly recounted his story to another prisoner who survived Lefortovo and later remembered his existence. But no one knew what happened to Ike Elkowitz after his imprisonment.[22]

The three Americans mentioned *by name* in Roger Tyler's report ought to have been among the safest of the American emigrants' children, not just because all three worked at the American Embassy. Official records were kept of their identities, and their disappearances were immediately noticed and reported. If the safest could not be saved, then what hope had the rest of the American survivors? In Moscow, the American diplomatic officials no longer wrote individual replies to the requests sent by their relatives from back home. Instead, they sent out form responses to those asking for help for their loved-ones who had disappeared: 'The embassy regrets, that due to the great number of welfare and whereabouts enquiries received and the inability of the Consular Section to increase the staff to handle them because of the housing and office space shortage, a form letter must be used in reply to your letter.'

Privately, in a secret memorandum dated 12 January 1949, an American diplomatic official admitted their failure to protect: 'With the exception of the period preceding the War of 1812, perhaps never have so many American citizens been subjected to comparable discriminations, threats, police interrogations, and administrative punishments, all for no greater offence than that of attempting to assert their American citizenship and depart from a country whose regime they abhor more strenuously than many of their more fortunate fellow citizens residing in the United States.'[23] The latest US Ambassador, Walter Bedell Smith, did put forward a proposal to exchange the 'estimated two thousand Americans being held in the Soviet Union' for the remaining Russian former prisoners of war in the American zone of West Germany. But as they always did the Soviets blocked the scheme, and this faint hope soon came to nothing.[24]

Thomas Sgovio knew personally many of the Americans who disappeared at this time. His friend Sam Freedman was arrested and executed. Before her arrest, Dora Gershonowitz had visited Thomas with her mother, and he had told her the little he knew of the fate of Dora's father, Abe Gershonowitz – a mechanic from New Jersey – who had shared a cell with Thomas in 1938 and later died in the camps.[25]

Lucy Abolin, the former young pioneer at the Anglo-American

school, was another one of the post-war American victims. She had already lost most of her family in the Terror of 1937 and 1938: her two brothers from the American baseball team and her father. During the Second World War, the American Embassy had attempted to hire Lucy as a telephone operator. Ambassador Standley had telegrammed Washington describing how Lucy Abolin had told him 'her position has been made very difficult and that she has been ordered to stop seeing her American friends and forbidden to come to the Embassy. Her application to renounce her Soviet citizenship has never been approved. Please instruct what action, if any, Department desires taken on her behalf.' A five-word reply had come back from Secretary Cordell Hull: 'Subject: Lucy Abolin. No intervention.' By 1949, Lucy Abolin was old enough to be arrested by the secret police. That year, Thomas Sgovio learned that she had been sent to the camps.[26]

Like the others, Thomas understood that his own rearrest was fast approaching. But whenever he voiced his increasing concern to Lucy Flaxman, she would always reassure him that he had nothing to worry about – everything would be fine. Although this was obviously untrue, Lucy projected such optimism that eventually Thomas became angry. One evening in his room in Alexandrov, Thomas persisted with his questions, sensing that she knew something more, until Lucy broke down in tears: 'All right, I'll tell you, promise you'll never tell . . . they'll give me twenty-five years'. And then she confessed that she was an informer for the secret police.[27]

It had happened, she explained, after she had first applied for an exit visa to return to the United States some two years earlier. Within days of her refusal, Lucy Flaxman was arrested and taken to the Lubyanka. There, the MGB agents had sworn at her and demanded to know if she was really 'a loyal Soviet citizen'. When Lucy replied that she was, her interrogator responded that she would have to prove it by 'cooperating' with them. At first she refused, but they threatened her with deportation and degradation in the camps. Thoroughly frightened, Lucy Flaxman agreed to do as they asked, and was instructed to begin work straightaway. Assigned the code name 'Nora', she was ordered to inform on other Americans in Moscow, and to report to the secret police once a week at the Moscow Hotel and private apartments located around the city. Tearfully, Lucy explained to Thomas that they had never asked if he was loyal, and that she had always praised him anyhow. They knew all about their relationship. She was sure he would be safe.[28]

What Lucy Flaxman experienced was common among those Americans left 'untouched' by the attentions of the Cheka and allowed to live outside 'the zone'. Margaret Wettlin had once been a teacher at the Anglo-American school in Nizhni-Novgorod, before facing a similar recruitment at the Lubyanka in Moscow. Her fate and that of others was to join an alternate existence offered to a smaller number of the American emigrants who escaped execution or imprisonment.[29] In Margaret Wettlin's case, the new career of the young schoolteacher from Rhode Island was accompanied by a rapid rise in her fortunes, as she moved from teaching to broadcasting the news in English on Radio Moscow.

Of course, the most valuable benefit was also the simplest: by informing on others, they saved themselves. Only later, as the years wore on, did Margaret Wettlin realise she had became part of 'an enormous, impersonal, diabolical machine'. Once she had informed on a 'Mrs Davis', an American Communist who foolishly mentioned that she hated Stalin. After Mrs Davis disappeared, Margaret Wettlin abruptly understood 'the evil of it, and that I was supporting evil'. There were others who perceived the stark moral choice straight-away and refused the coercions of the secret police – preferring instead to suffer the consequences. But they were always very few, and seldom, if ever, lived to tell their stories.[30]

Three days after Lucy Flaxman's sudden confession, Thomas Sgovio was once again arrested.

From his prison cell, Thomas heard the miraculous sound of a famil-iar bass voice singing in English, broadcast over a loudspeaker. In 1949, Paul Robeson was giving a concert in Moscow, preserving the myth of freedom of expression in a nation whose lips had been 'sewn shut' with fear.[31] While every other American artist was being exco-riated in the 'anti-cosmopolitan' campaign, Robeson alone remained untouchable – that year the Soviets had named the highest mountain peak in the republic of Kirghizia in his honour. And with such exalted status came other privileges not normally paid to an ordinary visitor. On his arrival in Moscow, Paul Robeson asked to meet two Russian friends he had made in America during his wartime support for 'the Jewish Anti-Fascist League'.

In the summer of 1943, at New York City Hall, the poet Yitzhak Pfeffer and actor Solomon Mikhoels had been honoured by Fiorello LaGuardia, the New York City Mayor, who brushed interpreters aside and spoke to the Soviet cultural ambassadors in Yiddish. On 8 July 1943, at a mass rally at the Polo Grounds, 47,000 New Yorkers had gathered to welcome them – 'Sholom Aleichem, Brothers!' – in a show of solidarity between American and Soviet Jewry with entertainment provided by Eddie Cantor, Larry Adler and Paul Robeson.[32]

Six years later in Moscow, Robeson was told that his Russian friends were both away on holiday. When the American singer insisted, the poet Pfeffer was eventually found and arrived to meet him in his hotel room. The meeting was uncannily similar to the one Robeson had with Ignaty Kazakov a decade earlier, before Kazakov's show trial and execution. But on this occasion, Yitzhak Pfeffer arrived at the Hotel Moskva alone and dressed in a suit, although obviously in great distress. Knowing their hotel room was bugged, Pfeffer resorted to sign language and handwritten notes in an attempt to answer Robeson's questions. The actor Solomon Mikhoels, Pfeffer explained, had been 'murdered on Stalin's order', and Pfeffer was himself imprisoned in the Lubyanka. When Robeson asked what would happen to him, the Jewish poet was unequivocal: 'They're going to kill us. When you return to America, you must speak out and save us.'[33]

In an interview, Paul Robeson, Jr., explained that afterwards his father had written a letter to Stalin on Pfeffer's behalf and sang a song in Yiddish at a Moscow concert, in a coded protest against the ongoing persecution of Soviet Jewry.[34] But Robeson refused Pfeffer's request to speak out publicly upon his return to the United States. Instead the American singer rejected as anti-Soviet propaganda the rumours of mass arrests, and refused to denounce Stalin's methods although he had met the victims personally. To a reporter from *Soviet Russia Today* Robeson denied the reports of a purge against the Jews in Soviet Russia, stating that he had 'met Jewish people all over the place. I heard no word about it.'[35]

At the beginning of the 'anti-cosmopolitan campaign', the Politburo member Andrei Zhdanov had publicly promised: 'Since it is quite natural to punish failure in industrial production, how much more serious is ideological failure in cultural production. Consequently the punishment of literary and artistic offenders has to be most severe.'[36] Three years later, in August 1952, Yitzhak Pfeffer was executed along with four other Jewish writers and poets and ten leading Jewish cultural and scientific figures, all falsely convicted of espionage during their wartime membership of 'the Jewish Anti-Fascist

Committee'. One after another, they were taken down to a basement cell of the Lubyanka prison and shot.[37]

Nor did Paul Robeson attempt intervention on behalf of the Americans in Russia. When Robert Robinson first tried to enlist Robeson's help, he was met with suspicion from one of Robeson's entourage: 'What do you think you are doing, Robinson, running away from here? You must stay right where you are. You belong here for the good of the cause. Or maybe you're trying to tarnish Paul's reputation, by getting him involved in your attempt to leave. That is all I have to say to you. You may go now!'[38] Two years later, perhaps disbelieving that his message ever got through, Robinson appealed directly to Eslanda Robeson for help with an exit visa for Ethiopia. Robeson's wife listened and then explained the situation firmly on her husband's behalf: 'We have thought about your request, and he has decided that he cannot help you. You see, we do not really know you well enough, to know what is in your mind. Suppose he were to help you leave, and then when you arrived in Ethiopia, you decided to turn anti-Soviet. We would find ourselves in trouble with the authorities here.'[39]

By a curious coincidence another sympathetic American celebrity, the writer John Steinbeck, had chosen to visit the Soviet Union just two years before Paul Robeson. For his many readers, Steinbeck wrote an account of his Russian tour of 1947, surveying the aftermath of the Second World War in the company of the Magnum photographer Robert Capa. A Russian Journal was, for the most part, simple reportage made in the company of his Intourist guides. John Steinbeck's published journal was only indirectly political, when he highlighted the overwhelming nature of Stalin's personality cult: 'His portrait hangs not only in every museum, but in every room of every museum. His statue marches in front of all public buildings. His bust is in front of all airports, railroad stations, bus stations. His bust is also in all schoolrooms, and his portrait is often directly behind his bust. In parks he sits on a plaster bench, discussing problems with Lenin . . . At public celebrations the pictures of Stalin outgrow every bound of reason. They may be eight stories high and fifty feet wide. Every public building carries monster portraits of him.'[40]

Even Intourist could not conceal the fearful atmosphere that permeated Stalin's Russia at the time. Privately Steinbeck renounced any political sympathies he might once have shared with the Bolsheviks. *The Grapes of Wrath* had been published eight years earlier in 1939, its pages filled with the high notes of 1930s radicalism: 'Here is the node, you who hate change and fear revolution . . . If you could separate causes from results, if you could know that Paine, Marx, Jefferson, Lenin, were results, not causes, you might survive. But that you cannot know.'[41] One long lean decade after the Crash, the American public recognised the hard choices of the Depression years, and bought Steinbeck's novel by the million. To Steinbeck's readers, Tom Joad was always a kind of hero, a tarnished hero maybe, but a hero nevertheless. 'A red is any son-of-a-bitch that wants thirty cents an hour when we're paying twenty-five!' . . . 'Well, Jesus, Mr Hines. I ain't a son-of-a-bitch, but if that's what a red is – why, I want thirty cents an hour. Ever'body does. Hell, Mr Hines, we're all reds.'[42] Eight years later, John Steinbeck's factual description of the 'monster portraits' of Joseph Stalin made him persona non grata in the USSR.

By the time of Paul Robeson's concert tour, Steinbeck revealed in a letter to a friend how far his political views had changed:

I have been horrified at the creeping paralysis that is coming out of the Kremlin, the death of art and thought, the death of individuals and the only creative thing in the world is the individual. When I was in Russia a couple of years ago I could see no creative thing. The intellectuals parroted articles they had read in safe magazines. It makes me more than sorry, it makes me nauseated. And of all the books required and sent to Russians who asked for them, not one arrived, and even the warm sweater and mittens for a girl, and a doll for a little girl – not even these were permitted to arrive. I can't think that wars can solve things but something must stop this thing or the world is done and gone into a black chaos that makes the dark ages shine. If that is what we are headed for, I hope I do not live to see it and I won't because I will fight it . . . I do not think any system which uses such force can survive for long but while it does – it can ruin and maim for such a long time to come.[43]

Thus the creator of the Joads was converted to an unflinching anti-communism he would hold for the rest of his life. It was a common enough journey among those who had seen the truth at first hand in the USSR, and lived to report their experience. Only the American emigrants in Soviet Russia were seldom so lucky. Their Damascene conversion arrived too late, and without the protecting cloak of international celebrity. It came at midnight in the back of a prison van, or after their first beating in a basement cell of Lefortovo Prison, or pressed down in the hold of a slave ship on the Sea of Okhotsk, or standing at the edge of an execution pit in Butovo. And there was no one to write their collective story, or even to wonder what had happened to these real-life emigrants whose destination had been Russia not California.

Theirs was a Depression migration altogether more epic in its scope and more transgressive in its revelations of human nature than fiction ever could allow. In Soviet Russia, a free spirit like Tom Joad would have been dragged into a cell and beaten unconscious for weeks on end, until all the defiance had been knocked out of him and he mumbled a false confession through broken teeth. Then his father, grandfather, uncle and brothers would have been taken away to be shot, and his mother and sisters would have disappeared into the camps of the Far North. But there never was a Steinbeck to write the story of the Preedens or the Abolins or the Gershonowitzs or the Hermans or the Sgovios or the many others like them.

The surviving Americans in Russia never learned that back home the Depression poverty had been eclipsed by the full employment generated in the build-up to the Second World War, and the golden economic boom that followed over the course of the next three decades. In Moscow, the American reporter William White had noticed that few people living inside this carefully controlled world had any real notion of what life was like outside the USSR. They were told over and over again that capitalism was on the brink of collapse, and the state's propaganda was carefully edited to reflect that view. Only very occasionally did the clunking machinery of monolithic censorship make an inadvertent error. During the war, White happened to watch a Soviet newsreel when a feature appeared on the Detroit race riots. On the Moscow cinema screen was projected a close-up of a black American getting beaten by the Detroit city police. The effect on the Russian audience was, according to our American witness, immediate and 'electric'. In the darkness of the cinema, the Russians jumped up to their feet. 'Look,' someone cried, 'at that wonderful pair of shoes the Negro is wearing!'[44]

Convicted of 'intention to betray the Fatherland', Thomas Sgovio was again marched from his cell on to another prison train to be transported to a lumber camp in central Russia. In a camp at Boguchanni, the rearrested were told that although they were 'not considered prisoners . . . any attempt to escape would result in a twenty-five-year sentence'. Thomas was then sent out to work chopping down trees in the neverending forest, his isolation broken only by occasional reminders of the outside world. In Boguchanni the prisoners were allowed to watch old black-and-white American movies confiscated by the Red Army from the ruins of Berlin. At night in the darkness of the Russian forest, Thomas Sgovio watched James Cagney dubbed into German with Russian subtitles, and Henry Fonda playing the part of Tom Joad in *The Grapes of Wrath*.[45] As the cult of Stalin loomed ever larger, no one could possibly have imagined that this lost tribe of Americans had ever existed, let alone had once played baseball in Gorky Park.

Similar circumstances faced another American survivor, the Detroit-born Victor Herman, who had served out his ten-year sentence in the camps of Burelopom to be freed in October 1948.[46] From his camp, Victor was exiled by railroad car to Krasnoyarsk, the city in central Siberia north of the Mongolian border. There he found a job coaching athletics and teaching the Siberians to box. In the brief space between arrests, he fell in love for the first time and married a Russian gymnast. Together the couple started a family of their own, and for three brief years Victor Herman lived the semblance of a normal life.

His fleeting happiness was ended by his arrest in the summer of 1951. Nine months later, Victor was arrested again, doubly suspect as an American and a Jew at the height of Stalin's anti-Semitic campaign. After his second arrest, he was sentenced to exile hundreds of kilometres further north in the wilderness, where he was ordered to live a prescribed distance away from the nearest village settlement and forced to cut a house for himself out of the permafrost. There he lived alone until he was eventually joined by his wife and one-year-old daughter, who walked through a snowstorm to reach him. The Herman family survived by selling wood to passing villagers.[47]

To pass the time Victor Herman would tell Russian fairy tales to his daughter, and also tales from his life in old Detroit. These stories would always begin the same way: 'Once upon a time there was a place called America . . .' Until eventually his little girl – perhaps sensing her father's homesickness and the change in the tone of his voice when he spoke of home – no longer asked to hear the fairy tales. Instead she would chirp, 'Tell America, Papa, tell America.'[48]

22

AWAKENING

In a totally fictitious world, failures need not be recorded, admitted or remembered. Factuality itself depends for its continued existence upon the existence of the nontotalitarian world.

Hannah Arendt, *The Origins of Totalitarianism*, 1951[1]

Of the millions incarcerated in the Soviet camps very few had managed to escape and publish their stories in the West. After the war it seemed their potential audience had already grown weary of narratives of violence and human suffering. The existing horrors were more than enough – the clear confirmation that the Allied nations had been fighting a justified war against a manifest evil as represented by the vérité of the black-and-white newsreel from the Nazi camps. The most terrible crime of modern civilisation was more than sufficient. To add a concurrent notion of a Soviet genocide, and one from within the wartime Alliance, was perhaps too much to bear. And so, although reports had begun to emerge, to begin with at least they were disregarded. If public opinion in the West found the accounts difficult to accept, then this too was understandable in many ways. There seems to be a natural human instinct to turn one's face from suffering. Few had believed the scale of the reports from Poland or, in the early stages of the Holocaust, had dismissed them as 'atrocity tales'. How much more incomprehensible, then, that a society predicated on the equality and fraternity of mankind could commit a crime even remotely equivalent?

From Stalin's realm emerged no newsreel or photography, just the fragments of witness statements illustrated by drawings from memory by those who had escaped. Swathes of public opinion suspected the vehemence of these survivors; their claims against Stalin and the

USSR could all too easily be characterised as 'hysterical anti-communism', prone to exaggeration, bursting with fanatical damnation, susceptible to a host of suspicious criteria which rendered their statements inaccurate if not completely false. After the onset of the Cold War, Western intellectuals began to wonder if such voices were not merely serving a darker purpose, concocting useful anti-Soviet propaganda to justify the pregnant wishes of Langley or the Pentagon, and reinforce the spending requirements of America's rapidly escalating defence budgets. Sceptical of the truth that was emerging from the Soviet Union, there were many who fell into the trap of denial.

In France, a court case that centred on just such evidence was attracting international publicity. Victor Kravchenko had been a Soviet Lend-Lease official who had defected in 1944 while stationed in New York. At the time the Soviet Embassy had tried hard to force Kravchenko's extradition as a wartime 'deserter', and had engaged the willing intervention of Ambassador Joseph Davies to their cause. What followed was the farce of the FBI having to call up Kravchenko anonymously to tip him off that 'the heat was on' from the State Department and warn him that he should 'carefully hide himself'. But Kravchenko's English was not yet up to such head-spinning machinations, and the FBI agent had to repeat the whole conversation to a friend, who took the appropriate evasive action on his behalf.[2] Joseph Davies, meanwhile, appealed directly to the President and Secretary of State to have Kravchenko sent back to Russia. The moral issue of his inevitable execution was elegantly side-stepped by Harry Hopkins, who argued that if Kravchenko was returned, no one would *know* what happened to him.[3] Only President Roosevelt had sensed a fast-approaching political calamity: 'Will you tell Joe that I cannot do this?' he instructed his secretary, and the defector's life was spared.[4]

Why the Soviet diplomatic machine went to such lengths to have him extradited was revealed when Kravchenko published his autobiography *I Chose Freedom*, after the war. The book was a factual account of the crimes of Stalin, seen through the eyes of a mid-level Soviet industrial manager. Its pages contained detailed eyewitness descriptions of the Ukrainian famine – 'little children with skeleton limbs dangling from balloon-like abdomens. Starvation had wiped every trace of youth from their faces' – the mass arrests and disappearances of the Terror, the Gulag labour delivered to the factories that Kravchenko had once managed: 'Their unsmiling silence was more terrible than their raggedness, filth and physical degradation. They went about their work like people doomed, too pathetic to examine their surroundings or to commune with the free workers near them.' One prisoner in particular haunted Kravchenko. His face 'was of pasty gray hue and looked like a death mask. A raw gash, purple with congealed blood, zigzagged from one temple almost to his chin.'5 From his privileged position within the Soviet industrial elite, Kravchenko reported that there were fifteen million such prisoners kept in Gulag camps by Stalin, and more recently, closer to twenty million.6

Quite predictably, the publication of Kravchenko's book in the West was greeted by furious attacks from Soviet critics. The former prosecutor Andrei Vyshinsky – whose career had risen from the show trials to presenting evidence at Nuremberg – now led the campaign to characterise life in the 're-education camps' as an entirely 'happy' experience.7 In a bid to smear Kravchenko's reputation, the French Communist magazine *Les Lettres Françaises* accused him of never having written the book at all. His authorship was an impossibility, their editorship alleged, since Kravchenko was, in fact, an illiterate. *Les Lettres Françaises* reassured the French public, and in particular the quarter of the electorate who had recently voted for the French Communist Party, that *I Chose Freedom* was, in fact, written by an American intelligence agent.8

In February 1949, Victor Kravchenko arrived at the Palais de Justice in Paris to fight a libel trial. Smoking a cigarette and flanked by lawyers, he strode to the top of the steps to make a statement to the press: 'I assure my friends and all my readers that I will do my best, with their moral help in order to show the truth during the trial and show to the world public opinion the horrors of Soviet reality.'9 At the so-called 'Trial of the Century', a succession of Kravchenko's former colleagues were flown in from Moscow to testify against him. But this tactic backfired, since the world of Stalin transplanted to Paris scarcely made any sense at all. Without an all-embracing fear, it was impossible not to suppress a smile at the absurdity of the evidence. Victor Romanov, who had worked alongside Kravchenko in New York, now accused him of the cardinal sin of 'forming impressions of America in a personal manner', which brought wry amusement to the courtroom. Kravchenko's ex-wife took the stand only for it to emerge that the NKVD had executed her father in 1937. One exchange in particular cut to the quick:

Kravchenko: It is one thing to repeat resounding formulas in
   honour of the 'beloved chief Stalin' . . .
Kolybalov (angrily): You will please not mention in this place
   the name of my beloved leader Stalin! . . .
(Jeers, catcalls, and roars of laughter from the spectators.)
Kravchenko: And it is another to manufacture pipes. I can
   speak of your leader because I am in free France. I spit on
   your beloved leader! I have been waiting for this moment all
   my life.'
(Tumult in the court.)[10]

After two months of argument the French high court handed a
hollow victory to Kravchenko, with one-franc damages. The verdict
was immediately headlined across the front pages around the world.
But in spite of the overwhelming evidence, there remained a reluc-
tance to believe or – to express this reaction more pointedly – an
apparent *willingness to deny* the truth of what was still ongoing
within the Soviet Union. Jean-Paul Sartre was one of the more
brilliant intellectuals who dismissed Kravchenko, supported the
Communists in North Korea – 'Any anti-Communist is a dog!' – and
justified the use of terror as the 'midwife of humanism'.[11] Thus Sartre
lent intellectual credence to voices such as Pierre Daix, the editor of *Les
Lettres Françaises*, who wrote that 'the camps of re-education of the
Soviet Union are the achievement of the complete suppression of
the exploitation of men by men'.[12] Or the French Communist Party
leader Maurice Thorez, who made a public speech in February 1949
declaring that if the Soviet army 'defending the cause of freedom
and of socialism, should be brought to pursue the aggressors onto
our soil, could the workers and people of France have any other attitude toward the Soviet army than have been that of the peoples of
Poland, Rumania and Yugoslavia?'[13]

Turned by such men, the wheels of justification ground black into
white and, if need be, back to black again, depending upon the
ideological vagaries of Moscow. And always hidden from view was
the sight of a starved and bloodied prisoner, cowed, his teeth knocked
out, his eyes swollen with fear, frantically confessing his guilt. Thus the
celebrated words of Jean-Paul Sartre lent existential apology to the fists
of torturers such as Belov and provided moral comfort to listening
ideologues and embryonic tyrants such as the Cambodian student
named Saloth Sar, who joined the French Communist Party in Paris in

the early 1950s and would become better known to the world as 'Brother Number One' or Pol Pot.[14]

Nor could Sartre possibly claim ignorance. He had only to step into any library and take down from the shelves André Gide's account of his visit to Soviet Russia in 1936 whose publication had caused a sensation in France: 'The smallest protest, the least criticism is liable to the severest penalties, and in fact is immediately stifled. And I doubt whether in any other country in the world, even Hitler's Germany, thought be less free, more bowed down, more fearful (terrorized), more vassalized.'[15] Gide had been a Communist when he arrived in Russia, and was predictably eviscerated upon his return to France. But his response to the Stalinist critics was unequivocal:

> When I told you the apple was worm-eaten, you accused me of blindness . . . It is high time that the Communist Party of France should consent to open its eyes, high time that their lying should cease . . . The USSR is prolific enough to allow murderous drives to be made among its human live-stock without its being apparent . . . Those who disappear, who are made to disappear, are the most valuable . . . I see those victims, I hear them, I feel them all around me. Last night it was their gagged cries that woke me; today it is their silence that dictates these lines.[16]

To Gide the truth was always more important than the consolations of ideology. He had seen through the deceptions of the French colonial authorities in the Congo and simply reapplied the same instincts to the USSR.

But the most damning evidence came long after the fury of Kravchenko's court case was over, when few people could remember the ferocious arguments his name had once caused in France. As with so many other Russian defectors before him, no one had taken seriously Victor Kravchenko's repeated claims that Soviet agents were trying to kill him. In 1966, his body was discovered in his Manhattan apartment. The gunshot wound, the authorities stated at the time, was self-inflicted.[17]

The truth, although it may be initially disbelieved, will always surface. During the post-war period, two more witnesses escaped to the West, both survivors of the Soviet camps. The first was Vladimir Petrov, formerly a Leningrad law student, whose 1935 arrest had consigned him to the Kolyma gold mines. Much like Thomas Sgovio and Victor Herman, Petrov had survived his sentence by courage and repeated good fortune – the most essential prerequisite of all. At one point he had been transferred to the eighth unit of the Shturmovoy mines, where the life expectancy was 'less than a month', and was saved by the intervention of a friend in the camp bureaucracy, who transferred him in time. Later on, Petrov attempted to escape Kolyma with two others on home-made skis. After three days he turned back, realising that only death rose up to meet him in that frozen wasteland.[18]

Vladimir Petrov's case was unusual because he was released from Kolyma early on in the war, before the official order to keep all the 'overtimers' had been introduced. Using the chaos of war to his advantage, Petrov returned to his mother's village in the Ukraine and then retreated west with the German armies, always conscious of the need to stay ahead of the NKVD. His refugee odyssey ended in America in 1947, where he settled and wrote several magazine articles describing the atrocities he had witnessed in Kolyma, later expanded into a book. The future Georgetown University professor's literary efforts were coolly received by many within the intellectual establishment, who viewed his descriptions as little more than the Cold War ravings of a Nazi sympathiser.[19] There was, however, one famous American Progressive who was profoundly disturbed by the articles he read – so much so, in fact, that he sought an interview with their author. His name was Henry Wallace.

At this point, Wallace had already descended far down the glassy slide from political powerbroker to nonentity to pariah. Firing him from his Roosevelt appointment as Secretary of Commerce, President Truman scathingly described Wallace as 'a pacifist, a dreamer who wants to disband our armed forces, give Russia our atomic secrets, and trust a bunch of adventurers in the Kremlin Politburo'.[20] In the 1948 presidential election, Wallace ran against Truman as the leader of the Progressive party. There was courage, at least, in his campaign in the Deep South, where Wallace refused to stay in segregated hotels and slept instead in the homes of his black supporters. 'Go back to Russia, you nigger-lover,' was regularly shouted at him with all the raw hatred that prefigured physical violence.[21] But ultimately Wallace's campaign self-destructed into failure amid bitter accusations of Communist Party infiltration. Now a chastened man, he met with Vladimir Petrov in the fall of 1949 to talk to the Russian about his experiences in Kolyma. Strangely, the two men became friends, and Wallace publicly apologised for having allowed himself to be fooled by the Soviets.[22]

His belated apology was never enough to save him from his many enemies, as the once shining liberal icon became firmly caught in the McCarthyite snare. Always under the surveillance of J. Edgar Hoover – whom Wallace had once derided as 'our American Himmler' – the former vice-president was now suspected of being a Soviet agent and of passing atomic secrets to the Russians. In closed testimony before the House Un-American Activities Committee, Lieutenant-General Leslie Groves, formerly the director of the Manhattan Project, accused Wallace of advocating the transfer of uranium to the Soviet Union during the war. The FBI, on behalf of the Senate Judiciary Committee, began investigating claims that Wallace had met 'a subversive agent during the war with data on the atomic bomb'.[23] In response, Wallace hired a lawyer and wrote to Albert Einstein, asking for a 'powerful statement enlightening the public with regard to the utter insignificance of five hundred pounds of uranium oxide and five hundred pounds of uranium nitrate even for experimental purposes'.[24] Wallace's FBI file contained more than two thousand pages of accumulated surveillance, including details of the meetings he held with Molotov and Andrei Gromyko while planning his fateful journey to Kolyma. No evidence was ever brought against him in court, nor was Henry Wallace ever charged with any crime. But just as he was getting back up on his feet, another Kolyma survivor was about to kick him back down.

After concerted diplomatic pressure, the Swiss government had obtained an exit visa for Elinor Lipper, whose life had been saved by her job as a nurse in a Kolyma prison hospital. After sixteen years in the camps, and through the miracle of a Swiss citizenship by marriage, Elinor Lipper was placed in the hold of a Dalstroi ship with another woman prisoner and delivered from Magadan back to 'the mainland'. During the return voyage, a group of criminals gang-raped her companion, and Elinor Lipper was forced to witness the violence unfolding in front of her. She was eight months' pregnant at the time, and gave birth to a baby daughter in a transit camp on the mainland. Only a year later, with the continued intervention of the Swiss Red Cross, was she finally allowed to exit the Soviet Union.[25]

True to her promise to the executed camp doctors, Elinor Lipper published an account of the Kolyma camps to a disbelieving world in 1950. The following year, when Henry Wallace appeared before a Senate Internal Security Committee to answer questions about his vice-presidential visit to Kolyma, it was Elinor Lipper's testimony that inflicted the very worst damage upon his reputation. In front of a row of hostile Senators, Wallace was forced to listen to his behaviour compared to that of an American visiting Auschwitz only to compliment the SS on their work. His public defence was simply that in 1944 'there was no way in which I could learn the full truth'. But this reply was not quite accurate. The evidence had been there, but Henry Wallace had chosen not to believe it.[26]

At his farm in South Salem, New York, Wallace began to receive hate mail. 'Shame on you Henry Wallace, for letting Stalin make a sucker out of you. Mr Wallace you owe those tortured millions something, you helped Stalin. Do something. Get going! Faster! Faster!' Opinion polls rated him 'the second least approved man in America', just a few percentage points ahead of Lucky Luciano.[27] In the panic of the time, a New York school board banned the book *Twenty Famous Americans* for its offending chapter on the country's former Vice-President.[28]

As Henry Wallace's reputation disintegrated, his colleague on the Kolyma trip, Professor Owen Lattimore, was accused by Joseph McCarthy of being Soviet Russia's 'top secret agent in the United States'. At the senatorial investigation, Professor Lattimore proved to be a ferociously determined opponent: 'I am not and never have been a member of the Communist Party, I have never been affiliated with or associated with the Communist Party, I have never believed in the principles of Communism, nor subscribed nor advocated the Communist form of government either within the United States, in China, in the Far-East or anywhere in the world ... I hope the Senator will in fact lay his machine-gun down. He is too reckless, careless and irresponsible to have a licence to use it.' Joseph McCarthy sat, with his thin black hair and bull figure, grimacing in response. The witness Louis Budenz testified that Owen Lattimore had belonged to a Communist Party cell, based on the information he had received from Moscow while working as the editor of the *Daily Worker* newspaper. There were many who discounted Budenz's testimony as just another McCarthyite smear from a turncoat twisting to absolve himself of blame. Lattimore himself launched a waspish counter-attack: 'Now gentlemen, I of course do not enjoy being vilified by anybody: even by the motley crew of crackpots, professional informers, hysterics and ex-Communists who McCarthy would have you believe represent sound Americanism.'[29] Five years on, the final charges of perjury against him were dismissed, and Lattimore left America to take up an academic post in England. Unlike the remorseful Wallace, Owen Lattimore never apologised for his portrayal of their visit to Kolyma. Instead he attacked the veracity of Elinor Lipper's account, accusing her of being a McCarthyite pawn.[30]

In 1995, it was publicly disclosed that the FBI had secretly collected coded telegrams sent from the Soviet Consulate in New York during the Second World War. The so-called 'Venona Project' only began decoding these cables in 1946, when resources became available. The messages revealed not only the extent of the Soviet spies' penetration of the Manhattan project, but also the recruitment of American espionage agents from the very highest reaches of government. Less than half of the Soviet code names were ever discovered as named individuals but among them, 349 American agents were revealed to be working for Stalin. Given that only a small percentage of the Soviet cables were ever decoded, the actual number of agents was, of course, likely to be higher. But because of the need to maintain the confidentiality of this source the existence of the Venona Project was kept secret, and its evidence was never used in a courtroom prosecution. Had the decryptions been admissible, much of the legal and journalistic wrangling over the guilt or supposed innocence of controversial figures such as Alger Hiss or Julius Rosenberg would have been cut like the Gordian knot.[31]

The Venona decryptions served as confirmation for what was already known at the time. As early as 2 September 1939, Whittaker Chambers, a former American Communist Party member and Soviet military intelligence agent, gave a long interview to Adolf Berle, the Assistant Secretary of State, revealing the names of several Soviet agents working inside the State Department and other branches of the US government, including Alger Hiss and his brother Donald. According to Chambers' account, Adolf Berle immediately passed this information on to Roosevelt's secretary, but Berle had been unable to take seriously the notion that the 'Hiss boys' were planning to 'take over the United States' government'.[32] And no one had prevented Alger Hiss from travelling to Yalta as the State Department's leading strategist to President Roosevelt. Sitting five feet from Stalin, Hiss had passed handwritten notes to the ailing and increasingly forgetful American President. He was one of, at least, six confirmed Soviet sources working within the State Department.[33]

Also named by Chambers in 1939 was Henry Morgenthau's assistant secretary of the Treasury, Harry Dexter White, whose career in government would continue for another decade. White's influence over American foreign policy was considerable, including his recommendation of a ten-billion dollar loan to Stalin, and his authorship of the 'Morgenthau Plan' advocating the partition and de-industrialisation of Germany after the war. Eventually White was promoted to become the director of the International Monetary Fund. In August 1948, days after denying espionage in front of the House Un-American Activities Committee, Harry Dexter White suffered a heart attack and died.[34]

Four months later, White's colleague at the State Department, Lawrence Duggan, having been questioned by the FBI on charges of espionage, fell sixteen floors from a Manhattan skyscraper. The former Acting Secretary of State Sumner Welles had always maintained Duggan's integrity as his protégé.[35] While Welles praised Duggan in public, privately he wrote that 'there was not the slightest motive for suicide in his case . . . He is certainly the last man on earth whom one could think to have wished to take his life.' Three days after attending Duggan's funeral, Sumner Welles was himself discovered unconscious and frostbitten beside a stream on his private estate in Maryland. The author of the Atlantic Charter had lain there all night and was found the next day close to death. The American public had no knowledge of why Sumner Welles had been forced to resign in 1943 – Roosevelt had attempted to keep secret the affidavits of the Pullman porters of the Presidential train to whom Welles had drunkenly offered escalating sums of money for sex. But the scandal of Welles's erratic behaviour became widely known in Washington, and the Truman Committee reported rumours of 'various demands being made by Russia and that Russia had Welles sewed up . . . Russia knew about Welles having been caught in these acts.'[36]

After he was pulled from the stream unconscious, Sumner Welles spent several months in hospital recovering from tissue and nerve damage. Later he claimed not to remember the circumstances of the accident, but there were many who remained unconvinced. The American reporter Jay Franklin wrote in his column of 4 January 1949: 'the death of Larry Duggan was followed shortly after by the discovery of his friend and sponsor, Sumner Welles, lying half-frozen in a Maryland field . . . it requires a heroic degree of self-control not to speculate as to whether – just as with Larry Duggan – there is not more to the tragic accident than the outward appearances.' It seemed unlikely that Soviet intelligence would miss such a straightforward opportunity for blackmail. Alcohol addiction, suicide attempts and depression would haunt Sumner Welles for the remainder of his life. Such was the fate of the former Acting Secretary of State, whose face had once graced the cover of *Time* magazine. On Welles's shoulders had rested the slender hopes of all the American emigrants in the USSR.[37]

During the Congressional hearings of December 1949, Major Robert Jordan testified that in 1943 he had inspected a Soviet Lend-Lease plane at Great Falls airport in Montana, that had been filled with black patent-leather suitcases sealed with white cord and red wax and marked 'diplomatic'. Working at night with a flashlight in the hold of the aircraft, Major Jordan pulled detailed scientific information from the suitcases. From one case opened at random, Major Jordan's eye had been caught by a piece of stationery marked 'THE WHITE HOUSE, WASHINGTON'. At the top of the second page of a letter addressed to Anastas Mikoyan, the Soviet Commissar of Foreign Trade, he copied the words '. . . . . had a hell of a time getting these away from Groves'. The letter was signed by Harry Hopkins and attached to a thick map, which Jordan unfolded into a technical drawing larger than his extended arms in size. The drawing was stamped with the notice 'OAK RIDGE, MANHATTAN ENGINEERING DISTRICT' and included documentation marked with the name 'HARRY HOPKINS'. The top secret scientific language of the report was unfamiliar to Major Jordan, but he carefully noted the words 'cyclotron . . . proton . . . deutron' and another unusual phrase, 'uranium 92'.[38] The Soviet plane was one of a regular series of flights carrying similar cargoes of diplomatic suitcases out of Great Falls airport. The following month, according to Jordan's testimony, Harry Hopkins had telephoned to authorise a shipment of uranium to the USSR 'off the records' but sent through the channels of the Lend-Lease programme.[39]

During the Second World War, neither Harry Hopkins's loyalty nor his authority could be questioned. Who could doubt the integrity of the right hand of the President, who had an office and a bedroom at the White House, whom Roosevelt sent on his most confidential missions to the Soviet Union? Throughout the wartime alliance Hopkins had never shied away from expressing his wholehearted sympathy for the Soviet government. In a public speech at Madison Square Garden, he proclaimed: 'We are determined that nothing shall stop us from sharing with you all that we have . . . Generations unborn will owe a great measure of their freedom to the unconquerable power of the Soviet people.' And privately he advised the Vice-President, Henry Wallace: 'Henry, don't let anybody tell you that the Russians are against their regime.'[40]

In the face of Major Jordan's evidence, Hopkins's friends defended him, claiming he had not 'the faintest understanding of the Manhattan Project, and didn't know the difference between a uranium and a geranium'.[41] Only after the fall of the Soviet Union did the KGB defector Oleg Gordievsky reveal how he had attended a lecture at the Lubyanka given by Iskhak Akhmerov, the controller of Soviet intelligence in America during the war. To his KGB colleagues, Akhmerov identified the 'most important of all Soviet war-time agents in the United States' as Harry Hopkins.[42]

At Potsdam, when President Truman revealed to Stalin the secret of the atomic bomb – the most devastating weapon in the history of mankind – the Soviet dictator took what was surely intended as a surprise with the calm shrug of old news. Both Churchill and Truman suspected that Stalin had failed to understand the true significance of what he had just been told, since he expressed no curiosity and asked no further questions. It did not occur to either of them that the reason for this unnatural lack of inquisitiveness was simply that Stalin had no questions left to ask. The NKVD had successfully delivered the secrets of the Manhattan Project, with 'atomic spies' from a number of sources passing a steady flow of scientific data from the United States back to Moscow.[43]

Even with the most detailed American technical plans and the resources of the entire Soviet state, it would take Stalin another four years to duplicate the atomic bomb. In the meantime, in anticipation of an imminent war with the 'imperialist powers', it soon became apparent that Stalin had taken some counter-measures of his own. And thus a third generation of Americans was transferred into the Gulag camps.

23

'CITIZEN OF THE UNITED STATES OF AMERICA, ALLIED OFFICER DALE'

You are waiting for your friends, the Americans and the British, to come and rescue you from our hands, aren't you? Well, they will never reach these shores! And even if they do we shall blow up the mine entrances and you will die like rats, two thousand yards below without seeing a single American or British uniform!

MVD officer to Michael Solomon, Kolyma prisoner, 1950[1]

The year 1949 was like any other in Magadan, with summary executions continuing in the camps. In one scene, German prisoners of war looked on as the Russian prisoners were lined up and thirteen were ordered to step forward. A German survivor described what happened next: 'Most of these Russians were immediately clubbed to death with crowbars, the rest finally shot with pistols. This took place in front of all men.' In December 1949, during an indoctrination session, a Soviet MVD officer told these German prisoners that many of them would be released: 'to make room for American prisoners-of-war who soon would fill the camps'.[2]

In the late 1990s, the United States government published a report that drew upon the evidence of a former Gulag prisoner initially identified as 'Witness A'. Later the prisoner's name was revealed to be Benjamin Dodon. In the summer of 1948, Dodon wrote that he had seen a group of American prisoners arrive at the Magadan transfer point in the Bay of Nagaev. Fourteen men were disembarked in the usual helpless condition of Dalstroi transportees: exhausted by the long sea crossing, hungry, cold and disorientated. He could not remember any one face in particular since they all appeared to be 'uniformly lifeless'. There was little opportunity to communicate with them since one night they were 'taken off to the depths of Kolyma, into the abyss of its vastness'.[3] Elsewhere in the Gulag, another contemporary Russian witness reported having seen a similar column of prisoners, half-frozen in threadbare clothes, driven forward like cattle by their NKVD guards. Unable to speak Russian, these men could only repeat 'American, American' and 'eat, eat'.[4]

Three years later, in January 1951, Benjamin Dodon was flown out towards the island of Dikson in Siberia, approximately eight hundred kilometres north of the Arctic Circle in the Kara Sea, just two hours' flight from the North Pole. An emergency had occurred at the mine next to the Gulag camp Rybak, and as a qualified engineer Dodon was enlisted to repair the damage. In response to his request for an experienced 'pyrotechnic and demolition specialist', Dodon was brought a prisoner whom he described as 'tall, exhausted by hunger and the Arctic, with a very characteristic, slightly elongated artistic face with an unnatural protrusion of gray eyes in sockets sunken from emaciation'. In a Russian accent 'clearly that of an English-speaker' the prisoner identified himself as 'a citizen of the United States of America, Allied Officer Dale'.

Working in the mine under the surveillance of the guards, Dodon had been unable to talk freely with Officer Dale. Before entering this closed zone, he had been strictly forbidden to communicate with any prisoners he met there. Six days later, Dodon was flown back to Dikson and informed that he had been working in a uranium mine in an area used for the testing of nuclear weapons. On his return to Krasnoyarsk in Siberia the engineer was required to sign a secrecy agreement covering all he had seen or heard at Rybak. Confidentially a fellow camp survivor told him that many of the Americans 'who had fallen into our hands in 1945 from the liberated Fascist camps' were being held there.[5]

Nor did the sightings of American prisoners end there. After Dodon was transferred to work in a gold-prospecting brigade in the Krasnoyarsk region, he met a new radio-operator who had worked on a fishing trawler of the Far East fleet. The radio operator told him they had recently received a message ordering all ships in the area to search for a shot-down American plane. No survivors were found, and the following week it was announced that the plane's crew had perished. Two months later, however, the trawler's captain told the radio-operator privately that the American crew had been picked up alive and were being held in pre-trial solitary confinement in the city of Svobodnyi, near the Chinese border. When asked what would happen to them, the captain replied they would be squeezed for 'what is required' and then 'finished off'. Straight from the trains, the captain said, men had been killed in Svobodnyi 'like nothing at all'.

After his release from his sentence Benjamin Dodon gathered one final piece of news on the fate of the missing American aircrew. The information came from a former Dalstroi official who told him that although ten Americans had been captured alive, 'the guys from within worked them over so badly only eight were taken to Svobodnyi. Do you know what sort of arrogance they had? They were Americans! You understand!' Later, from another former official, Dodon learned the names of two Americans from the plane's crew: 'Bush and Moore', who would 'remain forever in the soil of the Khabarovsk Region'.[6]

Shocked at the fate of Russia's former allies, Benjamin Dodon began writing his memoirs. Like many survivors of the camps, he wrote with little expectation of ever being published, the manuscript destined only for the desk drawer. Although he did not realise it at the time, Dodon's would prove to be only one of a large number of eyewitness accounts documenting the existence of American servicemen held captive in the Gulag from the end of the Second World War and through the course of the Cold War. Within the camps, the sightings of this 'third generation' of American prisoners became relatively frequent and unambiguous. And as the Cold War threatened to escalate into all-out confrontation, it appeared that Stalin's policy of hostage taking was being quietly stepped up. The unacknowledged presence of these Americans would remain an official secret – guarded by both governments – until the fall of the Soviet Union.

Weeks before he died, Franklin Roosevelt made repeated personal requests to Stalin to allow the US Army Air Forces permission to evacuate sick and wounded American prisoners of war from Poland. On 17 March 1945, Roosevelt telegrammed once again: 'I have information that I consider positive and reliable that there are a very considerable number of sick and injured Americans in hospitals in Poland ... This government has done everything to meet each of your requests. I now request you to meet mine in this particular matter.' Roosevelt's appeals for the evacuation were consistently refused by Stalin; the Soviet dictator claiming, with cynical disingenuity, that he lacked sufficient authority: 'I must say that if that request concerned me personally I would readily agree even to the prejudice of my interests. But in this case the matter concerns the interest of the Soviet armies at the front and Soviet commanders who do not want to have extra officers with them.'[7]

In the closing phases of the Second World War, Stalin's well-documented suspicion was already starting to build. Five days before Roosevelt's death, Stalin telegrammed the American President to complain of how the Germans on the Eastern Front 'continue to fight savagely with the Russians for some unknown junction Zemlianitsa – 'Little Strawberry' – in Czechoslovakia which they need as much as a dead man needs poultices, but surrender without any resistance such important towns in Central Germany as Osnabrük, Mannheim, Kassel. Don't you agree that such behaviour of the Germans is more than strange and incomprehensible . . .'[8]

In his memoirs, Major-General John Deane, the head of the American military mission in Moscow, wrote that American prisoners 'are spoils of war, won by the Soviets. They may be robbed, starved and abused – and no one has the right to question such treatment.'[9] From the vantage point of the American Embassy in Moscow, Elbridge Durbrow understood very well the dangers of the situation. In a letter, he expressed his misgivings following the failure of the American mission to Poland, and its subsequent return to Moscow: 'This quite naturally caused us to be deeply worried about the fate of the many thousands of American prisoners of war being liberated at that time. Because of the past record of the Soviets, we became particularly concerned that they might not allow our liberated prisoners of war to be repatriated immediately, might have tried to propagandize many of them before they were released, cause other completely unjustified delays, or even retain some without our knowledge.'[10] Elbridge Durbrow did not mention the past experience upon which his fears were based. The diplomatic class of 1937 had all seen first-hand the methods of the NKVD. They realised also that the history of the Soviet Union was one of endless and very tragic repetition.

Using persistent negotiation and the lure of economic aid, the West German government had managed, by the mid-1950s, to secure the release of thousands of German prisoners of war who remained in captivity in the Soviet Union. Almost a decade after the end of the Second World War, the survival rate of these veterans of the Eastern Front was very low, but those who did survive surely owed their lives to the fact that their existence had been officially acknowledged. The Soviets were obliged to present at least some notion of account to a democratic government actively demanding the prisoners' release. At one point, the German Chancellor Konrad Adenauer issued a forthright statement that the Soviet armies had captured three and a half million *Wehrmacht* soldiers at the cessation of hostilities. According to Tass the Soviets had repatriated, or accounted for, almost two million. What, asked Adenauer, had happened to the remaining one and a half million?[11] Of course, the question was only rhetorical. Of the 93,000 German soldiers marched through Moscow in a propaganda display after the surrender of the Sixth Army at Stalingrad in February 1943, only 6,000 returned home.[12] What had happened to the remaining German prisoners of war was clear. They had been subjected to the accelerated mortality of the 'corrective labour camps'.

In a study made by the US Army Headquarters, out of a sample of 2,658 Germans released from Soviet captivity in 1955, almost two-thirds had no known affiliation with the Nazi Party.[13] Not that the mechanism of the Gulag was ever mindful of ideology or nationality. Among the millions in the camps were representatives of virtually every nation on earth: Germans, Austrians, Italians, French, Yugoslavs, Greeks, Rumanians, British, Poles, Norwegians – the list was endless. Spanish soldiers from Franco's Fascist Blue Division were transported into the same camp system that imprisoned hundreds of Spanish Communists who had fled to Russia in the wake of their Civil War. The children of these Spanish refugees were also consigned to the same fate.[14] In 1948, the Italian defence minister Luigi Gasparotto reported that '94 percent of Italian prisoners in Russian concentration camps have perished'. It was the remainder – the fortunate ones – who brought back news of the Americans.[15]

Between 1947 and 1956, the US Air Force interviewed approximately 300,000 former German and Japanese prisoners of war who had returned from the Soviet camps. During this period, the US Air Force sought to gather intelligence material for bombing targets in the USSR, in the event of the outbreak of World War III. But their interviewees, quite unexpectedly, volunteered first-hand accounts of American servicemen detained with them in the camps. For nine years, these so-called 'Wringer' reports were meticulously logged, marked 'secret' and classified away in the military archives. From their pages emerged accounts of 'silence' camps in which the prisoners were forbidden to receive any contact with the outside world. Three-quarters of the prisoners held in such camps had been sentenced to life terms, and the rest to twenty-five years. It was the legacy of a war that never came, and the last trace of the Americans who never returned.[16]

Viewed at random, the Wringer files spoke of men such as Gerhard Klueck, a tall blond-haired American with blue eyes and broad shoulders, who had been seen wearing an American major's uniform in the camps at Vorkuta, approximately one hundred kilometres north of the Arctic Circle, after his kidnap from Berlin in April 1945.[17] From a camp near Petropavlovsk on the Kamchatka Peninsula, another survivor described an unnamed 'brown-eyed, dark-haired' American from Fredericksburg, Virginia, who wore a pilot's suit and had received a twenty-five-year sentence. The pilot spoke broken German with an American accent, and his gold teeth had been removed by the camp dentist. The interviewee then drew a sketch of the face of this Virginian held with him in the camp.[18]

A thirty-eight-year-old German serviceman named Guenther Kloose returned from war and subsequent incarceration with his right eye missing, his left eye partially blind, and nearly every tooth lost from his upper jaw. From April 1943 until December 1947, Kloose was interned in a 'silence camp' among prisoners of all nationalities, who were forced to work the mercury mines in the South Ural mountains. Because of his poor physical condition, Kloose was assigned an office job where he worked with the camp files listing the prisoners by nationality. In this particular camp Kloose recalled there were 2,800 Germans, 460 Italian soldiers, 210 French, twenty-four British and six Americans, the last two groups listed in the records as 'intelligence officers'. The Americans had all arrived in the camp between the end of 1945 and the beginning of 1946. 'None of the prisoners are supposed to be discharged and they are not authorized any connection with the outside world,' said Kloose. 'Mortality is very high.'[19]

The information given by those interviewed was often scarcely more than a location and brief description of the American prisoner. But occasionally more details could be supplied. Thus Doctor Anton Petzold, a German civilian returnee – who was 'intelligent and cooperative' according to his debriefer – brought news of a 'Major Thompson' captured by the Soviets after a forced landing in 1944. This American major had been incarcerated in Budenskaya prison until 1948, and was then sent to Tayshet camp on a twenty-five-year sentence for espionage. Major Thompson had told Doctor Petzold that he was from San Antonio, Texas. Doctor Petzold added the details that Thompson was thirty-eight years old, 1.85 metres tall, with fair hair and blue eyes. He was one of five Americans imprisoned in the USSR, mentioned in that day's report.[20]

Another German witness, Doctor Geismann, described six Americans arrested by Soviet forces in Germany, two of whom were still being held in the Vorkuta camps in 1953. Doctor Geismann remembered that one of the men was called Nielsen, a naturalised American born in Denmark who had won a gold medal for boxing in the 1936 Berlin Olympics. Although there is no record of a medallist at the Berlin Olympics of that name, a 'Hans Jacob Nielsen' was listed as having won a boxing gold in the 1924 Paris Olympics.[21] Other survivors brought similar fragments of information to be entered into the files. They spoke of an American consular secretary from a Balkan country named Peters who had been kidnapped from a steamer after the war. An American civilian employee of the Moscow Embassy named Brown who liked to talk about classical music and the operas he had seen in New York City. An American sergeant named Henry P, who spoke 'broken German' and had 'three nearly destroyed chevrons' still recognisable on his uniform.'[22] Or a US Army Air Forces bombardier named Joe Miller from Chicago, shot down over Berlin in 1945, whom a former German prisoner explained was a 'staunch believer in democracy' who had been 'severely beaten and starved by the Soviets' before being sent to the Karaganda Gulag where he was 'very weak physically and was suffering from malnutrition.'[23]

After the first Soviet atomic bomb was successfully tested on 29 August 1949, a succession of events quickly unfolded that led the world to the brink of nuclear war. According to Gavril Korotkov, a former Soviet military intelligence officer, Kim Il-Sung secretly visited Moscow in February 1950 to inform Stalin that North Korea was not yet ready to launch an invasion of the South. Stalin's response to the North Korean dictator was straightforward: 'they were ready to start the fighting and couldn't wait'. Kim Il-Sung was then sent out of Stalin's Kremlin office to 'think it over'. Four months later, on 25 June 1950, the North Korean armies, supplied with Soviet arms and air support, launched their invasion.[24]

Over the course of the next three years, the Korean War took the lives of approximately two and a half million soldiers and civilians, including more than thirty-three thousand American servicemen and women with approximately eight thousand listed as missing in action or unaccounted for.[25] During the conflict Americans fought Russians directly in combat for the first time since the Russian Civil War of 1919. Although neither side could admit this fact openly, the American pilots recognised the faces of Russian pilots wearing Chinese uniforms flying the MiG fighter planes in the skies over Korea. In the heat of combat, the political instruction to issue commands only in Chinese was quickly forgotten, as Russian swearing could be clearly heard over the airwaves.[26]

On 15 November 1951, Colonel James M. Hanley, the Judge Advocate General of the Eighth Army in Korea, jointly accused the Chinese and Korean communists of the murder of American prisoners of war. Colonel Hanley provided the names of 2500 captured American soldiers. Nine months earlier, General Matthew Ridgway, the commander of American forces in Korea, sent a film back to Washington that showed the recovered bodies of American prisoners of war shot in the back of the head and buried in mass graves with their hands still tied behind their backs. One decade after the Katyn massacre, the method of their execution was identical.[27]

In the United States, all the precursors to a Third World War were being carefully noted by intelligence agencies. The children of Soviet representatives in America had all been evacuated. The Soviet consulates in Los Angeles, San Francisco and New York were closed, and the Amtorg offices in New York were finally shut down. All Soviet bullion funds on deposit in the United States were withdrawn from the Federal Reserve and cash balances run down. At the same time, a Soviet defector disclosed that there were four million Gulag prisoners in Far East Russia building the military infrastructure necessary for hostilities. On the Chukovsky peninsula, the Soviet Fourteenth Landing Army had gathered with the strategic mission of landing in Alaska to launch a southerly offensive along the Pacific coast in the event of an all-out nuclear war.[28]

On 7 May 1951, President Truman publicly addressed this

prospect in a speech at the Civil Defense Conference in Washington DC. The President had already raised the spectre of a Third World War to the American nation on national television, his round glasses reflecting back the camera lights aimed at his taut, lined face:

> The threat of atomic warfare is one which we must face, no matter how much we dislike it. We can never afford to forget that the terrible destruction of our cities is a real possibility . . . Our losses in an atomic war, if we should have one, would be terrible. Whole cities would be casualties. Cleveland or Chicago, Seattle or New York, or any of our other great cities might be destroyed . . . Even with our losses, I think this country would survive and would win an atomic war. But even if we win, an atomic war would be a disaster. Communist aggression in Korea is a part of the world-wide strategy of the Kremlin to destroy freedom. The defence of Korea is part of the world-wide effort of all the free nations to maintain freedom. It has shown free men that if they stand together, and pool their strength, Communist aggression cannot succeed.[29]

Very quietly, in the midst of this epic confrontation, a press release was issued by the State Department. Given an unassuming title – 'Soviet Refusal to Grant Exit Permits to American Citizens in the USSR' – and dated 20 March 1950, the government memo carried the straightforward admission of 'considerable evidence that repressive measures have been taken by Soviet authorities against American citizens attempting to arrange departure from the Soviet Union'. The State Department officials then explained that 'two thousand citizens' were estimated to be trapped in the USSR. It was the first public acknowledgement of the lost American families of the Depression emigration.

Finally in the midst of conflict, the existence of the forsaken had been publicised. But when the American diplomats in Moscow were planning the destruction of the Embassy records by the use of thermite bombs – which, they observed, would have the disadvantage of destroying the Mokhovaya building in which they would be imprisoned 'to try and dissuade US Air Forces from attacking Moscow with atomic weapons' – the fate of a couple of thousand American civilians hardly seemed a priority. Of the American servicemen who had so recently joined their ranks, nothing at all was admitted, although their sightings within the Gulag continued, and the Korean War only increased their numbers.[30]

At the end of 1951, and in the spring of 1952, a Greek refugee from the Soviet Union was interviewed by the American Air Liaison office in Hong Kong. The Greek witness stated that he had seen 'several hundred American prisoners-of-war being transferred from Chinese to Russian trains at Manchouli near the border of Manchuria and Siberia' and heard three prisoners of war under guard 'conversing in English'. Their uniforms had American sleeve insignia, and among them were a 'great number of Negroes', a race the witness had not seen before. The American prisoners were carrying no belongings except canteens, and the Chinese guards transferred them through a gate bisecting the platform directly into the custody of their Soviet counterparts, who escorted them on to a waiting prison train. The first time he saw the prisoners transferred, there had been sufficient numbers to fill a seven-car train; however 'these shipments were reported often and occurred when United Nations forces in Korea were on the offensive'. In his report, the American air attaché noted that 'the source is very careful not to exaggerate information and is positive of identification of American POWs'.[31]

This information was corroborated when Yuri Rastvorov, a Russian diplomat and lieutenant-colonel of the MVD, defected from the Soviet mission in Tokyo. In a debriefing document dated 31 January 1955, Rastvorov stated that 'US and other UN POWS were being held in Siberia'. The Soviet defector had received this intelligence information from 'recent arrivals – 1950–1953 – from the Soviet Union to the USSR's Tokyo Mission'.[32] Philip Corso, a retired American Army intelligence officer, later described how Rastvorov had told him that 'several hundred' American prisoners of war had been sent to Siberia. According to Corso, President Eisenhower had received this intelligence but had not wished to force the issue for fear of escalation into nuclear war: 'the general feeling in policy-making bodies was that direct confrontation with the Soviets could be disastrous'.[33]

Yuri Rastvorov's report remain classified for the next four decades, along with other evidence such as a CIA report, dated 30 April 1952 that detailed the transfer of 'approximately 300 prisoners-of-war' by rail from China to Molotov (the Russian city now known as Perm):

The prisoners were clad in Soviet-type cotton padded tunics with no distinctive marks. They were first transported from the railway station to the MVD prison and then sent by rail, in a train consisting of 9 wagons to Molotov on or about 5 April 1952. The train was heavily guarded by the MVD ... According to information gathered between April 1 and 20 a certain number of American POW officers, among them was a group referred to as the 'American General Staff', were kept at that time in the Command of the Military District of Molotov ... They have been completely isolated from the outside world.[34]

Sightings of the American prisoners in Soviet camps continued to be reported throughout the 1950s. Often former Gulag prisoners simply walked into American embassies in Western Europe to offer up their information voluntarily. Thus an Austrian former prisoner, Adalbert Skala, told American officials in Vienna of his meeting with a 'Lieutenant Racek' in Prison Number Two in the city of Irkutsk, and later in the Lubyanka in Moscow. The Austrian witness remembered Racek as a 'lieutenant of armoured troops' captured in Korea. Lieutenant Racek gave him the address of his father in New York City to let him know he was still alive. Skala warned his interviewer that the American lieutenant's health was not good, 'having had a number of front teeth knocked out, having lost his hair, and generally having suffered the effects of mistreatment'.[35]

Occasionally an American diplomat received a direct appeal from an American prisoner, smuggled out of the camps by a freed German or Polish prisoner, although the messengers' prison clothes were always thoroughly checked for just such contraband. On 22 August 1956, a letter was delivered via the German Embassy in Moscow from a camp at Potma in the Komi Republic, west of Archangel: 'I am in camp 7 eleven years without any help whatsoever. I have tried to get in contact with my friends and relatives in the States and so far have had not luck. I wonder if you will be so kind as to help me and send me something here.'[36] Two years earlier, in March 1954, the employees of a German import-export firm discovered a tag wrapped in a bundle of hides exported from the Soviet Union. The tag was a wooden rectangle about five centimetres long by three centimetres wide, with a round hole drilled into an end – similar to those used by Gulag authorities to identify the bodies of the dead prisoners. The wooden tag was taken as evidence to the local police station, who reported it to the US Army headquarters in Heidelberg. In tiny letters on both sides of the tag, a desperate plea had been written in English: 'I AM IN JAIL IN RUSSIA. GO TO THE NEAREST POLICE STATION AND REPORT IT. MATTER OF DEAD OR LIVE. SAVE ME PLEASE AND ALL THE OTHERS. KRISTIAN HJALTSON.'

Rather than forming a banner headline in newspapers across the free world, the discovered message was sent directly to the State Department, where an anonymous official placed the tag in an envelope marked 'confidential', and this small artefact of Cold War history disappeared into the archives. There it lay, waiting to be rediscovered, decades after Kristian Hjaltson's life had ended.[37]

And still the sightings continued. In July 1956, a German journalist named Werner von Borcke visited the American Embassy in Vienna to explain how, before his return from a twelve-year sentence in the camps, he had sewn the names and addresses of two American prisoners into his clothes. The Russians had replaced his uniform and the names were lost, but Werner von Borcke remembered the first American had been a woman arrested in Berlin who had sustained a grave injury to her leg while felling trees in the forest. She had looked ten years older than she was, her brown hair was streaked with grey and her health was poor. The second had been a 'typical American' man, 'tall, slender with dark hair and good build, about thirty-five years old, but with the fourth finger of the left hand missing'. He was a lieutenant in the US Air Force who had fought in Germany during the war, and who spoke of New York and Milwaukee. The other prisoners assumed that he had been captured in Korea. The American was a silent person, and 'after his interrogation by Soviet officers became yet more silent and depressed'.[38]

On 5 September 1960, a Polish prisoner, Richard Romanowski, walked into the American Embassy in Brussels, having survived a seven-and-a-half-year sentence in the Soviet camp No. 307, near Bulon, in Eastern Siberia. After his sentence, Romanowski had been returned to his native Poland, but had successfully crossed the Iron Curtain into West Germany before claiming political asylum in Belgium. Two American prisoners, both captured in Korea in 1951, Lieutenant Ted Watson from Buffalo and Sergeant Fred Rosbiki from Chicago, had asked Romanowski to report their presence to the American authorities. Both men, said Romanowski, were in poor health, having been forced to work in a phosphorus mine. At the Brussels Embassy, the Polish survivor then carefully explained how the phosphorus attacked the head and liver, bending down to show his own scaling scalp. The American diplomat in Brussels noted in his report that although Romanowski was 'almost destitute' and living off only a dollar a day, at no point in their interview had he asked for any money for this information, which he had given voluntarily. The Polish survivor had accepted two dollars only 'very reluctantly' to help him return the one hundred kilometres back to his home in Liège.[39]

That same year Heinz Meier, a printer, had escaped East Germany. On 27 July 1960, Meier called at the American Embassy in Bonn to report a tour he had made with an East German delegation of the Soviet printing industry. Their group had visited a camp 7.5 kilometres from Novosibirisk where between '12,000 and 13,000 men' were being used as Gulag labour. In the camp, Meier 'was approached by two persons who identified themselves as US nationals who had been taken prisoner in Korea, taken to Red China for a year, and then transferred to the USSR'. Heinz Meier described a 'C. Colman, about 42–44 years of age, who had light blond hair' and was from Philadelphia. The other American, standing nearby, told Meier he was a second lieutenant from New York City. 'Colman said there were originally 28 Americans in the group, but that it had been broken up, and there now "6 or 7" still together.'[40]

Few stronger bonds exist than those forged by soldiers during and in the aftermath of conflict. This phenomenon appears to transcend the differences of race and religion. In December 1956, a former prisoner of war from Niigata, Japan, sent a report to the American Embassy in Tokyo. Keihachi Sakurai was very anxious to describe the fate of his friend, an American prisoner:

I was taken prisoner by the Soviet forces at the end of August 1945 and led a miserable life of slavery for twelve years at concentration camps in the Taishet region, north of Lake Baikal in Siberia . . . During my detention at the said concentration camps I happened to become acquainted with an American of German descent. He and I helped and encouraged each other all the time to get through the various difficulties of our captive life . . . I fear his release may be difficult because he had such a strong spirit of hostility that he always made anti-Soviet acts and remarks even while working at the concentration camps. From his condition at that time, I am anxious that he may not escape dying of sickness if some steps are not taken to save him. I stayed with him in Concentration Camp no 19 of the Taishet region from 1950 through 1951. He was about five inches and five feet high, slender, long-faced, smart in style and very cheerful.[41]

There was no logic within this hidden underworld in which American soldiers were held captive with German and Japanese prisoners – their wartime enemies – in camps run by their former Soviet allies. Both German and Japanese survivors kept promises they had made to the Americans to let their relatives know they were still alive. But only very rarely did a report of the sighting of an American prisoner in the USSR ever reach the international news media. In a press conference given on 3 November 1953, Secretary of State John Foster Dulles referred to new information gathered on 'Americans reported to be in Russian prison camps. We have asked Ambassador Bohlen to take their cases up with the Soviet Government.' Days earlier, seven Norwegians, who had been released after eight years' imprisonment, had informed their national press that the Soviets were holding 'scores of other Western prisoners including an American major'. The item only ever made a minor story in the newspapers, and was soon forgotten.[42]

Two years later, on 11 July 1955, officials at the State Department recommended that President Eisenhower 'seek an opportunity at the next summit meeting to take up with Soviet Premier Bulganin the general question of American citizens held in custody in the Soviet Union, basing his approach on the eye-witness informants who have reported having been in everyday contact with these imprisoned Americans.' In the State Department report prepared for Geneva, it was decided to concentrate their efforts on behalf of the pilots of a US Navy plane shot down over the Baltic on 8 April 1950 and eight other American citizens. An internal policy document stated that: 'It is recommended that no publicity be given to the Department's representations in these cases. The Department particularly desires no publicity regarding Major Wirt Elizabeth Thompson since without confirmation it hesitates to raise the hopes of this man's parents. They know nothing of his reported presence in the USSR.' This document then touched on the fate of the original American emigrants to the USSR: 'two thousand claimants to American citizenship . . . have not been able to communicate with the American Embassy in order to have their citizenship established. Of this number approximately 704 have been verified as American citizens . . . It is believed that no mention should be made at the "Summit" meeting of this group of claimants, our representations in their behalf being confined to approaches from the American embassy to the Soviet Ministry of Foreign Affairs.'[43]

Nothing was ever achieved at Geneva, if the issue was ever raised at all. Nor did President Eisenhower ever present the matter to the American public. As superpower summits came and went, the faint trace of the existence of those left behind in Russia was all but washed away. Outside national security circles, the Americans imprisoned in the Gulag hardly existed at all, nor were they likely to be officially recognised by the Soviet authorities, since their incarceration was without doubt a contravention of international law. Beyond the corridors of the State Department or Langley or the Pentagon, very few officials knew of their existence, or even suspected they might be there. In the United States, the families were told that their loved ones were dead or missing in action, presumed killed. As the Cold War settled into the quiet tension of mutually assured destruction – punctuated by violent proxy conflicts around the world – gradually the American officials responsible retired and died. And then, inevitably, the issue became lost with them.

Why quite so little was done to help these men and women is uncertain. The evidence of their existence may well have been deemed too sketchy or inconclusive, or perhaps a calculated decision was made that pursuing their fate would only have edged the superpowers still closer to nuclear confrontation, risking the lives of millions. All mid-level State Department enquiries were either denied or delayed by the Soviets, and there seemed to have existed an unspoken willingness on both sides never to press or publicise the issue. That Western diplomats had a disturbing habit of turning away their gaze had already been proven in the case of Raoul Wallenberg, the Swedish diplomat who saved the lives of thousands of Hungarian Jews at the end of the Second World War before his capture by the Soviet secret police. With Wallenberg imprisoned in the Lubyanka, the Swedish government immediately requested American diplomatic assistance to free him. From Moscow on 25 September 1945, George Kennan sent a telegram addressed to the Secretary of State: 'Soviet authorities pay little attention to our enquiries re welfare whereabouts American citizens in Soviet Union ... they are particularly reticent in cases of person in hands of NKVD and if Wallenberg is alive it must be presumed that he is in custody of that organization which rarely pays even perfunctory heed to the normal demands of diplomatic practice. We consequently feel that any action here on our part on behalf of Wallenberg, a Swedish national, would serve no useful purpose.' Later, Dag Hammarskjold, the UN Secretary-General, expressed a similar weariness more succinctly: 'I do not want to begin World War Three because of one missing person.'[44]

According to the memoirs of Pavel Sudoplatov, a retired Soviet NKVD agent, Raoul Wallenberg was held for two years in Lefortovo Prison and at the Lubyanka: 'My best estimate is that Wallenberg was killed by Maironovsky, who was ordered to inject him with poison under the guise of medical treatment . . . One of the reasons I believe Wallenberg was poisoned is that his body was cremated without an autopsy, under the direct order of Minister of Security Abakumov . . . The regulations were that those executed under special government decisions were cremated without autopsy at the Donskoi cemetery crematorium and their ashes buried in a common grave.'[45]

Whether motivated by tempered disbelief, or the cynicism of realpolitik, a third generation of Americans were abandoned to their fate in the camps. How many could only be estimated, but their existence was incontrovertible. The Gulag lasted longer than any other system of concentration camps in modern history, and the Americans remained at the behest of one man. The NKVD reports returned to Stalin always began with the words: 'In accordance with your instructions . . .'[46]

In September 1952, Joseph Stalin and the Politburo held a meeting with Chou En-lai, and a party of Chinese communists, to discuss the ongoing war in Korea. According to the minutes of the meeting, preserved in the Russian state archives, Stalin had lectured Chou En-lai on the subject of prisoners of war, putting forward a 'proposal' that 'both sides temporarily withhold twenty per cent of the prisoners-of-war.' Stalin's explanation for this gambit was simple: 'Americans do not want to hand over all the prisoners-of-war. The Americans will keep some of them, intending to recruit them. It was like this with our prisoners-of-war: every day now we catch several [former] prisoners-of-war whom the Americans send to our country. They detain prisoners-of-war not because, as the Americans often claim, the prisoners say that they do not want to return, but in order to use the prisoners for espionage.'

When Chou En-lai asked for a letter he might take back to Mao, Stalin explained that 'it is better to manage without a letter, that he sees that Chou En-lai is taking notes and that he trusts him fully'. Later, when Chou En-lai asked for 'instruction', Stalin replied 'instruction or advice?' The Chinese Foreign Minister's answer was both deft and psychologically revealing: 'From the point of view of Comrade Stalin, this is perhaps advice, but in its presentation it is instruction.' In the early 1950s – well before the Sino–Soviet quarrels – if Stalin's 'advice' had called for the retention of twenty per cent of UN prisoners of war during the Korean War, then to the Chinese such a 'proposal' carried the sanctity of a commandment from the 'Great Leader' of the Communist cause. It was Joseph Stalin, after all, who had armed the sixty Chinese divisions poured into the conflict in Korea.[47]

24

'SMERT STALINA
SPASET ROSSIIU'

And we will cut heads off mercilessly. We will crush sedition, eradicate the treason . . . A kingdom cannot be ruled without an iron hand . . . I stand alone. I can trust no one.

Sergei Eisenstein, *Ivan The Terrible*, Part One, 1944[1]

That Stalin could hold untold numbers of Allied servicemen hostage was unsurprising given his state of mind. By the early 1950s, the 'Cult of Personality' had taken on a fervour and fanaticism seen only in the early stages of mass religious movements. Stalin, the former seminarian, had built a socialist religion with himself at its centre: a god who demanded belief without rationale, obedience without a moment's hesitation. That hundreds of millions of people – the entire populations of the Soviet Union, China and the newly satellite nations of Eastern Europe – could have their lives controlled by one man, who had usurped the entire power of a World Revolution, was too much for ordinary citizens to contemplate. Far easier and far safer, then, to believe. But their collective adulation only magnified and reinfected Stalin's megalomania.[2]

How else could one describe the actions of a leader who personally signed a Politburo order on 2 July 1951, authorising thirty-three tons of copper to be used for the construction of a gigantic statue of himself, built beside the Volga-Don Canal, a project which had killed thousands of its prisoner-labourers?[3] The colossal statue was built with an electric current running through its head to prevent migratory birds from defacing the idol. The birds would land and be electrocuted, their feathered bodies falling to the ground in silent tribute to this Soviet Ozymandias, the shoemaker's son from Gori, Georgia.[4]

Viewed through the methodology of power, the personality cult had a calculated purpose. The psychological effect of Soviet 'giganticism' was always intended to create a feeling of awe, which rendered the individual meaningless beneath the towering ubiquity of the Great Leader. The blind adulation of the cult leader erased the notion of the self as a free-thinking individual and in its place created an acolyte. Twice a year, Stalin's tiny arm would wave from Lenin's Mausoleum, and a million marchers roared back their approval in regimented unison into the Moscow air.

Most disturbingly, the essence of Stalinism was never based on fear alone. There were millions who supported Stalin with genuine fervour – who had adapted themselves to the demands of the Soviet state. These were his willing volunteers, the Stalinists who chose to subjugate their judgement to the will of the Leader and the Party. If they must pay a peculiar sacrifice – in the strange denominations of a father, mother, brother or sister – then so be it. They remained convinced that their cause would provide the ultimate justification for the Party's excesses. To such steadfast disciples, Stalin represented the essence of a society that would never change, the security of an individual whose every choice has been taken away.

There were those who convinced themselves that Stalin's actions were for the benefit of all. These apologists could not separate the suffering of the Russian people during the Second World War – and the courage and sacrifice of the Russian soldiers in defeating the Nazi invasion – from the actions of the tyrant who ruled their state. This was always a strange paradox: for the love of Russia, to grant approval to the very man who had killed so many millions of their countrymen. Since of the myriad nationalities of the Soviet Union, it was the Russians themselves who suffered the most casualties to the regime. But then nationalism, like a distorting mirror at a fairground, bends the critical capacity of the beholder; and those who distinguish their personal identity by an accident of geography will always, in a sense, remain vulnerable.

In the Kremlin, the late night banquets had descended into drunken farce, with Stalin forcing his henchmen into vodka-drinking contests, declaring, 'Everyone must guess how many degrees below zero it is, and everyone will be punished by drinking as many glasses of vodka as the number of degrees he has guessed wrong!' The visiting Yugoslav Communist Milovan Djilas reported how Lavrenty Beria had erred by three degrees and then claimed afterwards to have done so deliberately in order to drink more vodka. At one point Stalin left their table to put some music on a huge record player. He tried to dance, but quickly became exhausted. 'Age has crept on me and I am already an old man,' said Stalin, looking around him to watch their reaction. 'No, no, nonsense you look fine. You're bearing up wonderfully. Yes, indeed, for your age ... ' The surviving Politburo members had grown wise to their master's wiles. When Stalin put on his favourite record of an opera soprano accompanied by the howling and barking of dogs, the most powerful man in the world would listen and laugh, and the chorus of faces made pale by their nocturnal Kremlin hours would laugh along with him.[5]

During a state visit Mikhail Kalinin, the ageing figurehead President of the USSR, had asked Comrade Tito for a Yugoslav cigarette. 'Don't take any – those are capitalist cigarettes,' snapped Stalin, who watched Kalinin drop the offending cigarette through trembling fingers, and then began to laugh. 'The expression on his face was like a satyr's,' wrote Djilas. Kalinin's wife had been arrested and was a prisoner in a Gulag camp, given the task of picking the nits out of the prisoners' clothes at the camp bathhouse.[6]

In 1949, Joseph Stalin again suggested at a Kremlin meeting that he was getting too tired for the job; perhaps it was time for someone else to step into replace him? Immediately the protestations began: 'No, no, in Georgia people lived to be 160!' Stalin wondered if the leaders of the Leningrad siege should replace him as premier and General Secretary? The rest of the Politburo chorused 'No, no, Comrade Stalin!' But when Aleksei Kuznetsov and Nikolai Voznesensky hesitated, Stalin had them arrested. At the end of the show trial known as 'the Leningrad Affair', the former Soviet war heroes were draped in white shrouds and led out of the courtroom to be shot one hour later.[7]

Once again the Soviet Union was enveloped in a tyrant's fury. In a rare moment of candour, Stalin told Khrushchev, 'I'm finished. I trust no one. Not even myself.'[8] On New Year's Eve 1951, the former Foreign Minister Maxim Litvinov was killed in a car accident. According to the Politburo member Anastas Mikoyan, a truck had been deliberately driven into Litvinov's car as it rounded a bend in the road leading from his dacha. Stalin had met with the MVD department responsible for political assassinations and 'instructed them personally'.[9]

In June 1946, Maxim Litvinov had briefed Richard Hottelet, a correspondent for CBS, 'to warn the western world that the Kremlin cannot be trusted and cannot be appeased'. Litvinov explained that each concession of Stalin's demands would lead to 'the West being faced, after a more or less short time, with the next set of demands'. Litvinov then went on to discuss the political consequences of Stalin's death, thus ensuring he would never live to witness the event.[10]

The assassination of Litvinov marked an intensification of Stalin's anti-Semitic campaign. In November 1952, Stalin ordered the arrest of the mainly Jewish Kremlin doctors, including his own physician Vladimir Vinogradov, who had treated him for years. Stalin wrote his instructions on the interrogation report of one of the doctors: 'Put them in handcuffs and beat them until they confess.'[11] The order was accompanied with a threat to Semyen Ignatiev, the Minister of State Security, 'if you don't get the doctors' confessions, you'll find yourself shorter by a head'. When the confessions duly arrived, Stalin passed them around the Politburo. 'You are like blind kittens,' he said. 'What will happen without me? The country will perish because you don't recognize enemies.'[12]

In January 1953, an article was published in *Pravda* entitled 'Assassins in white coats'. The prose was a straightforward attack on the Jewish doctors and, by extension, all Soviet Jews. It was written in Stalin's own style, recognisable because every grammatical or spelling mistake had been left uncorrected by the fearful editors. (According to his interpreter, Valentin Berezhkov, for each one of Stalin's errors an impression was formed that 'perhaps now we should write this word in this way'.[13]) The latest propaganda onslaught was filled with diatribes against the 'disease of contamination' of the healthy Soviet body politic by these Jewish doctors. Those who had taken Russian names were identified in the press with their former Jewish surnames in brackets, lest there be any doubt.[14] Cartoonists depicted them in anti-Semitic caricatures, the general hysteria reflected in the language of the charges: 'It has been established that all these killer-doctors, monsters in human form, tramping the holy banner of science and desecrating the honour of the man of science, were hired agents of foreign intelligence services . . . established by American intelligence services for the alleged purpose of providing material aid to Jews in other countries.'[15] In *Pravda*, it was announced that the trial of the Kremlin doctors would take place at the Hall of Columns on 5 March 1953.[16]

By February 1953, Stalin was an elderly man who often failed to recognise his henchmen as he sat in Dacha Number One, protected by rotating shifts of twelve hundred armed secret police.[17] Towards the end he filled his time planning show trials to mark the beginning of the latest clampdown. Lists of questions were drawn up for the Politburo members, together with the confessions they would provide. The fear of neglected victims haunted Stalin, flashing in the corners of his paranoid, yellow-filmed eyes. At this point, even Vyacheslav Molotov's life was in danger: he was replaced as Foreign Minister three years earlier, when Stalin ordered the return of the original documents of the Molotov-Ribbentrop pact to be used as evidence against him.[18] Years later, in retirement, the former Soviet premier admitted, 'I think that if he had lived another year or so, I might not have survived.' Molotov had been forced to attend a Politburo meeting to authorise the arrest of his Jewish wife, Polina. At the meeting, he had abstained from the vote, but later regretted this veiled display of opposition and wrote to Stalin: 'I hereby declare that after thinking the matter over I now vote in favour of the Central Committee's decision ... Furthermore I acknowledge that I was gravely at fault in not restraining in time a person near to me from taking false steps.'[19]

At this time Stalin's daughter visited her father at his dacha. In her memoirs, Svetlana Alliluyeva described how surprised she had been to see pictures pinned up on the walls of the dacha. Her father had surrounded himself with enlarged magazine photographs, mostly pictures of young children: a little girl drinking goat's milk from a horn, a boy on skis or children having a picnic under a cherry tree.[20] This was the private life of the most powerful man on earth, a recluse who held the destiny of the world in his well-guarded, incommunicative reverie. According to Svetlana, 'he saw enemies everywhere. It had reached the point of being pathological, of persecution mania.' Once, Stalin even turned on his daughter, shouting angrily, 'You yourself make anti-Soviet statements.' Svetlana was, of course, watched over at all times 'for her protection', but she was still aware of the truth of the society in which she lived. Her imprisoned aunt had told her how she had signed her own confession: 'You sign anything there, just to be left alone and not tortured! At night no one could sleep for the shrieks of agony in the cells. Victims screamed in an unearthly way, begging to be killed, better to be killed.'[21]

But all men are mortal, even Stalin. The knowledge kept the Gulag prisoners alive, including Thomas Sgovio who was still cutting down trees in Boguchanni during the winter of 1953. For a prisoner with the same routine, time starts to bend: each day seems interminable, and yet the minute hand of the Gulag swept years into decades. Early on in his sentence, Lucy Flaxman had visited him in Boguchanni, but the couple quarrelled after she told him that she had informed on an English journalist in Moscow. They agreed to go their separate ways, and as Thomas's isolation continued, time fell away until 5 March 1953.[22]

In the early 1930s there had once been a joke that 'SSSR' – the Russian initials for the Soviet state – stood for '*Smert Stalina Spaset Rossiiu*' ('Stalin's death will save Russia').[23] The Russian people had waited long and grief-stricken decades to find out. In the camps, the prisoners scrutinised photographs of 'the Moustache' or 'the Old One', as Stalin was called, by those who knew better than to speak his name out loud. One prisoner was heard to mutter, 'He doesn't look well to me. See his eyes – how old and tired they are.' And when the news reached them that Stalin had been taken ill, many prisoners openly prayed, 'May the devil take his soul today!' One old man fell to his knees in the water of a mine: 'Thank God someone still looks out for the wretched.'[24]

On 5 March 1953, Thomas Sgovio spent the day felling trees as normal. Only when he returned from the forest did he hear the rumours that Stalin was dying. The local store was suddenly filled with customers buying vodka to carry home in silence, ready for their secret celebrations. Across the camps of the Soviet Union, millions of prisoners marching under guard passed the news along in excited whispers: 'He's croaked! He's croaked!'[25] The 'Greatest Friend of Soviet Families' had suffered a stroke in his dacha outside Moscow, lying untreated on his bedroom floor for several hours, his bodyguards too fearful to disturb him. Surrounded by terrified doctors, Stalin's final hours were slow and agonising. His face altered shape and grew dark; his lips blackened and his features became grotesque, his lungs struggled for breath, his body gasping as if he was being slowly strangled, choking to death in front of his henchmen. At the final moment, according to Svetlana, her father suddenly opened his eyes and cast a glance over everyone in the room:

> It was a terrible glance, insane, or perhaps angry and full of fear of death and the unfamiliar faces of the doctors bent over him. The glance swept over everyone in a second. Then something incomprehensible and awesome happened . . . He suddenly lifted his left hand as though he were pointing to something up above and bringing down a curse on us all. The gesture was incomprehensible and full of menace, and no one could say to whom or what it might be directed. The next moment, after a final effort, the spirit wrenched itself free of the flesh.[26]

In the early hours of 6 March 1953, Radio Moscow broadcast the news of an important announcement in fifteen minutes. The time passed in silence only for the message to be repeated. Finally at almost 4 a.m., the news was confirmed that Stalin had died at 9.50 p.m. the night before.

That morning Moscow was covered in red flags with black borders, and the newspapers carried the markings of national grief.[27] As preparations began for the state funeral, the whole of the Soviet Union fell into solemnity, everyone consciously watching their neighbour's reaction to the news. For some, it was a moment of suppressed joy. Others shed tears, if not for the man then for the years they had lost and the loved ones who had disappeared. And there were those who could not distinguish between public grief and private feeling. They had pretended for so long now that their self-deception had become real. As Radio Moscow broadcast requiems into the March air, green funeral wreaths were placed as tokens of mourning on trams and taxis.[28] Overcome with hysteria, grown men and women sobbed. They held Stalin's portrait aloft like an icon: the man who had promised them heaven on earth, and delivered an unremitting hell.

Millions converged from across the Soviet Union towards the Hall of Columns, where the body of Joseph Stalin was lying in state. Did they esteem him so much, or did they want to make sure he was really dead? It was easy to believe in the immortality of evil, to forget that every dictator must eventually die. Although even from beyond the grave, Stalin would demand a final sacrifice. Rows of trucks had been placed around the building as a security barrier, and as the crowds surged, people began to be crushed against them. Eyewitnesses reported that hundreds were killed, screaming 'Save me! Save me!' as they were pressed and trampled underfoot.[29] The Moscow morgues were filled to overflowing, although there was never any public record of this disaster published in the Soviet media. When Robert Robinson went to view Stalin's body the following day, the crowds were still overwhelming. Caught in a surge, for fifteen seconds he felt his feet leave the ground and he was treading on thin air.[30]

At the front of the funeral cortège, holding Stalin's coffin, Lavrenty Beria marched with his black coat falling past his knees, a stern expression on his bespectacled face. Beside and behind him were the rest of the inner circle: Malenkov, Molotov, Bulganin, Kaganovich and Khrushchev, each looking suitably austere. The pall-bearers carried Stalin's coffin decorated with a solitary marshal's cap, the plexiglass dome covering his face and lending the proceedings a strangely futuristic air. As the apparatchiks strained under Stalin's weight, they passed slowly out of the Hall of Columns. The coffin was then placed on a gun carriage and ceremoniously marched to Red Square, passing in front of the American Embassy on Mokhovaya Street, where the Stars and Stripes was flown at half-mast as a mark of respect.

After the funeral eulogies, the embalmed body was carried down into Lenin's Mausoleum in Red Square, on which Stalin's name was already carved into the red marble. The American chargé d'affaires Jacob Beam – as instructed by Washington – tendered 'the official condolences' of the United States government.[31]

At the United Nations Plaza in New York, the flags of sixty nations were taken down as a mark of respect for one of history's greatest mass murderers. Only the United Nations flag was flown at half-mast. In America, the recipient of the Stalin Peace Prize for 1952, Paul Robeson, led the eulogies at a memorial meeting: 'Slava – slava – slava – Stalin, Glory to Stalin. Forever will his name be honored and beloved in all lands . . . Yes, through his deep humanity, by his wise understanding, he leaves us a rich and monumental heritage . . . He leaves tens of millions all over the earth bowed in heart-aching grief. But, as he well knew, the struggle continues. So, inspired by his noble example, let us lift our heads slowly but proudly high and march forward in the fight for peace . . .

To you Beloved Comrade, we make this solemn vow
The fight will go on – the fight will still go on.
Sleep well, Beloved Comrade, our work will just begin.
The fight will go on – till we win – until we win.'[32]

After the funeral in the Soviet Union, there was an immediate less-
ening of the psychological pressure – as if the strong hands on the
windpipe had lost their grip and the body was finally able to draw
breath. The poet Yevgeny Yevtushenko wrote of fear 'slinking away
from Russia', as people sensed instinctively that Stalin's death must
change things. The Kremlin doctors awaiting trial in the Lubyanka
were immediately released, their coerced confessions disregarded. For
the Gulag prisoners, Stalin's death was not yet sufficient cause to
grant them freedom. Another man would have to die to allow them
that hope, and thousands more casualties would follow as events
proceeded apace.

In the power vacuum after Stalin's death, Lavrenty Beria held
the entire machinery of repression in his hands. Several divisions
of Ministry of Interior troops, brought to Moscow to supervise the
funeral, were left in the city to maintain order, ready, so it appeared,
for a coup. But Beria was impatient and lacked his master's political cunning. Knowing what lay in store for them should Beria
claim power, Nikita Khrushchev and the rest of the Politburo acted
decisively.[33]

At a Central Committee meeting in July 1953, Khrushchev delivered a speech in front of a shocked Beria accusing him of crimes
against the state. In a carefully planned manoeuvre, a buzzer was
pressed under the table and ten armed men burst into the room seizing the most feared man in the Soviet Union. Apparently
spontaneously, a Politburo bodyguard then stepped forward to
inform them that Beria had raped his twelve-year-old stepdaughter.
It was a common accusation made against the secret police chief,
who was known to cruise the streets of Moscow in his armoured
limousine looking for young girls to abduct. Four decades later, the
workmen at the site of Beria's former mansion at number 28
Kacholovna Street – now the Tunisian Embassy – discovered a dozen
skeletons buried in the grounds.[34]

At his closed military trial Beria appeared calm and insolent. Only
after the death sentence was pronounced did his confidence evapo-
rate. When he realised that his execution was to be carried out

immediately, he 'lost control completely'. According to General Ivan Konev, who presided over the trial, Beria 'flung himself about the courtroom weeping and begging for mercy'. He was led away to a cell, where his hands were tied behind his back and attached to a hook driven into a wooden board on the wall. He tried one last time to talk his way out: 'Permit me to say . . . ' but the Procurator General ordered the guard to gag his mouth with a towel. An officer then stepped forward and fired a bullet through the middle of Beria's forehead. Simultaneously across the Soviet Union every school, library and research archive was shut to allow staff time to tear Beria's photograph from their collections.[35]

Following his arrest, Army detachments stormed the Lubyanka, and Beria's key supporters in the secret police were all detained. Those who resisted were shot in their offices. After organising the security at Stalin's funeral, Sergei Goglidze had been flown out to East Berlin with orders to crush the nascent democratic uprising. A Polish railroad employee working at the border reported, 'The Russians have shipped about forty thousand East German men, women and children to the USSR on this line after June 17th 1953.' In Berlin, Sergei Goglidze, too, was arrested and transported back to Moscow to be executed on 23 December 1953.[36]

Within the camps, Stalin and Beria's deaths, in such quick succession, changed the atmosphere immediately. The prisoners began a series of mass uprisings in protest against their sentences, seizing control from their guards and killing the informers in their midst. At the Vorkuta camps, the American prisoner John Noble learned of the attempted rebellion in East Germany from hundreds of young Berliners, aged between sixteen and twenty-two, who had been added to the camps' population. In Mines Seventeen and Eighteen, on the side of the coal cars someone dared to write in chalk: 'To hell with your coal. We want freedom'.[37] Quickly a strike spread across the one hundred thousand prisoners of Vorkuta, their demands voiced by Gureyvich, a former Soviet diplomat, who called for a reduction in sentences and freedom for the men who had already served ten years. A former Russian professor of history from Leningrad gave a speech: 'Never in the story of man has working slavery been so extensive or cruelly exploited as here in the Soviet Union – the liberator of the working class!'[38]

At first the MVD's response was cautious. But by early August

1953, the Deputy Minister of the Interior Ivan Maslennikov, was sent to end negotiations and reassert control by the traditional methods. Striking prisoners who refused to return to work were fired on with automatic weapons. In one volley more than a hundred prisoners were killed, and five hundred badly wounded. In the week after the general return to work at Vorkuta, three hundred of the strike's leaders were executed.[39]

Working as an orderly in the camp hospital of Dzhehkazgan, in Central Asia, the former American Embassy clerk Alexander Dolgun gave comfort to the prisoners who were dying. In Dzhehkazgan, Dolgun heard of the rebellion at the Kengir camp, just twenty-seven kilometres away.[40] On 16 May 1954, eight thousand male and female prisoners had taken over the camp. In *The Gulag Archipelago*, Alexander Solzhenitsyn chronicled the uprising, describing the scenes of Ukrainian girls meeting their husbands whom they had secretly married with the blessing of imprisoned priests. Services for all religions were conducted in the mess hall according to a fixed timetable. The Jehovah's Witnesses were free to observe their own rules and, refusing to stand guard, volunteered to wash dishes instead. For forty days the prisoners of Kengir were free once more, albeit barricaded within the camp. From the point of view of the authorities, their existence was now a threat to the state.

At first the Soviet police units punched holes in the camp walls, thinking that all but the ringleaders would flee. When this ploy failed, in the early dawn of 25 June 1954, parachute flares lit up the sky and cannon fire was heard overhead as tanks rolled into the Kengir camp. The assault was filmed by the cameras of the secret police: ranks of Ukrainian women dressed in the embroidered dresses which at home they wore to church, linked arms and, holding their heads up, marched forward believing they might stop the assault. But the tanks only accelerated, driving over their bodies. Then the MVD troops started shooting in a massacre which began at three o'clock in the morning and continued for the next five hours. When the fighting was over, a secret police officer who had been seen shooting more than two dozen prisoners with his revolver, placed knives in the hands of the dead, ready for a photographer to record the pictures of these 'gangsters'.[41]

In 1953 and 1954, similar events were recorded across the Gulag Archipelago, proof that the pitiless functionality of the Soviet state had continued after Stalin's death. In Kolyma, an underground opposition group had been formed calling itself 'the Democratic Party of Russia'. Little is known of the Russians who led the uprisings here – the documentary evidence of their existence is limited and there appear to have been few survivors.[42] But although their collective rebellions were all crushed, the political message was not lost on Stalin's successors. It was evident that ever-increasing levels of violence would be required to keep the Gulag legions in timid acquiescence. Over the next two years, between 1954 and 1956, Nikita Khrushchev ordered the release of millions of prisoners from the camps. And among the millions freed from their sentences were two surviving members of the ill-fated American baseball teams of the 1930s: Thomas Sgovio and Victor Herman.

Their lives were saved in different ways. Thomas Sgovio survived thanks, in part, to the gift of his artistic talent, and Victor Herman through his ability to fight. Born within months of each other, they were both young men when first arrested and they were both relatively short, wiry and extremely tough. Such physiological characteristics were important factors in their survival. But the most essential quality of all was luck. Their stories were extraordinary because the camps of Kolyma and Burelopom were not places from which prisoners normally returned. The Gulag itself was a system where men died; and that these two Americans survived should not deflect us from this essential truth. Both Thomas and Victor escaped death on several occasions and only by the narrowest of margins, and each believed himself to have lived a charmed existence. Most importantly we know of their existence only *because* they survived. There were many others just like them, the overwhelming majority in fact, of whom we know almost nothing at all – save for a passing reference in a chauffeur's memoir, a reporter's fleeting encounter in a subway shelter or a forgotten face smiling in a baseball team's photograph.

In his analysis of the Holocaust, Bruno Bettelheim wrote that concentrating on the few who survived, must not draw our 'attention from the millions who were murdered'. The same lesson is surely true for the victims of Stalinism, the other great tragedy of the twentieth century.[43]

There was, however, a sense in which survival had an abiding moral quality, even when the life saved was simply one's own. Survival was also an act of resistance, hope and triumph, in as much as it allowed an individual to bear witness on behalf of those who had lost their lives.[44] Both Thomas Sgovio and Victor Herman would fulfil this duty for the remainder of their lives. Eighteen years after they were first sentenced, each received an amnesty from the Soviet authorities for their respective 'crimes'. From his exile in the remote wilderness, Victor Herman returned with his family to the city of Krasnoyarsk to resume his career as a boxing coach.[45] While Thomas Sgovio took the train, for a second time, back to his mother and sister in Moscow. On 24 March 1954, his sister Grace had written her latest appeal to the Soviet President Malenkov requesting Thomas's release: 'Please remember that of the nineteen years my brother has lived in the Soviet Union, sixteen of them have been in prison.'[46]

In the backlash against the old regime, after his return to Moscow Thomas discovered that Lucy Flaxman had been arrested as a 'spy' and sentenced to a twenty-five-year jail term.[47] The MVD had come for her on 5 March 1953, the day of Stalin's death. Her son Evgeny remembered clearly how the police had arrived at six o'clock in the morning. Suddenly the lights were switched on and a voice told him, 'Don't get up.' Then the uniformed men ordered his mother to 'Get dressed.' Lucy Flaxman had looked back at them in surprise and incomprehension, 'In front of you?'

After they took her away, the search of their apartment continued until four o'clock in the afternoon. One of the Chekists had told Evgeny: 'You are going to write a letter? Well don't address it to Beria.' And for years afterwards Lucy Flaxman's son would wonder how this man knew that Beria would soon be arrested. All his mother's possessions were confiscated, including her clothes and the family's precious television set. Evgeny was expelled from university the next day and drafted into the army. After his mother's sentencing, he was allowed to visit her before her birthday on 25 September 1953. At the Moscow prison they were separated by two sets of bars and a guard. In six months Lucy Flaxman had lost some weight but 'she did not look awful'. She told her son that since the 'Leader of Nations' had died, she hoped she would be freed soon: 'I have signed everything they gave me,' she said. 'I can't bear it when they beat me.'[48]

Lucy Flaxman's fate was that of so many women, both those who had been coerced into working for the regime and those who had refused. Later Boris Pasternak remembered their lives in the fate of

Lara, the beloved heroine of *Doctor Zhivago*. Pasternak's novel was banned in the USSR, since the author was savagely critical of the Soviet regime. But ordinary Russians paid vast sums of roubles for the samizdat version on the black market. And in its pages they read a description of what had happened to their missing loved ones: 'One day Lara went out and did not come back. She must have been arrested in the street, as so often happened in those days, and she died or vanished somewhere, forgotten as a nameless number on a list which later was mislaid, in one of the innumerable mixed or women's concentration camps in the north.'[49]

Thomas Sgovio never saw Lucy Flaxman again. Instead, in Moscow, he came across other Americans, far guiltier than Lucy, who had survived. These were men like Bernie Cooper, Eddie Ruderman and Joe Adamov, whom he remembered as 'the Hatchet Man of the American community'. Seeing Thomas approach, they crossed the street to avoid him.[50]

25

FREEDOM AND DECEIT

I wouldn't want to go back to my family. They wouldn't understand me, they couldn't . . . No man should see or know the things I have seen or known.

Varlam Shalamov, *Graphite*[1]

In Moscow, Thomas Sgovio realised that everyone seemed to know something about Kolyma. The name had become a household word signifying the very worst of the camps. From the mid-1950s, the millions who returned brought back explicit accounts of suffering which, until then, had been concealed from the Soviet public. The survivors reappeared with little else besides the lost years, their lives, and a continuing trauma. 'All I have left is the bones in my body and the skin stretched over them,' was one description, repeated in endless variations by those who attempted to adjust to life outside 'the zone'.[2]

Some managed to create new lives and remarried. Others refused to have children, citing the simple reason, 'I don't want to be the father of slaves.'[3] Their return was often the point at which the prisoners realised it had not been enough to survive. Their essential task was yet harder: to survive and keep one's soul intact. There were men and women who walked around the streets of Moscow 'with horrifyingly empty eyes'.[4] It was an easy condition to recognise, even after the weight had returned and the rags were replaced by clean clothes. They walked and yet they hesitated, unsure of what to do without instruction. For many who had spent long years confined within the regimen of prison cells and concentration camps, the idea of even limited freedom was terrifying. Crossing the street seemed a feat of extraordinary magnitude.[5] Even their journeys *away* from the camps had been difficult to bear. The prisoners returned in passenger trains whose mirrored bathrooms were often the cause of distress. One female prisoner described washing her face and catching the sight of a haggard old woman staring back at her. Frightened, she ran into the corridor and returned with a guard. Of course, there was no one there.[6]

As a survivor, the former law-student Varlam Shalamov described the process by which human emotions returned to a prisoner saved from the prospect of imminent death. Out of nothingness first a degree of indifference was felt, then fear, then envy. Love resurfaced last, if at all.[7] As the literary chronicler of Kolyma, Shalamov's own life would end tragically. Forty-five years after his first arrest, he was confined in a Soviet psychiatric institution for his final incarceration. Only his prose remained to lend meaning to his tragic life, and provide a degree of understanding to his future readers: a testimony to the events that had taken place in that far north-eastern corner of Russia.[8]

Like Shalamov, many survivors who had witnessed the execution of their fellow prisoners attempted to document their stories, anxious lest they should die and then, according to Ivan Okunev, 'they won't know where those who were killed were buried'. Okunev was a survivor sent to Kolyma as a twenty-year-old in the terrible year of 1938:

> Instead of shoes they gave us two sleeves from worn-out work coats and one pair of mittens and that was all for two years. We worked at the face in the goldmines and the sleeves quickly tore on the chippings at the face and the padding came out and our bare toes would become frozen . . . Not far from our camp there was a hill and a tractor stood on it. They brought [prisoners] in from the other mines in trucks covered with canvas they cried farewell as they drove past our camp. There they stood people by the readymade trenches started up the tractor and shot them with a machinegun . . . There were thousands . . . Excuse the handwriting I have been paralysed twice and as I write now my shoulder is trembling. I am crying I remember what I've lived through. I would call it the Road to Calvary.'[9]

Although they reawakened the events the former prisoners had endured, such memoirs were also a form of catharsis, an unburdening that provided a degree of comfort to the survivor. In any case, it was impossible for the human mind to remain unscathed. Those who had denied themselves all feeling in order to survive discovered themselves to be something less than human when they left 'the zone'. At night the survivors lay sleepless, wide-eyed with fear lest they be arrested and sent back 'there'. Some were quite literally unable to close their eyes from this all-consuming anxiety. The Greeks had invented a term for this condition of extreme shock, *lagophthalmia*, fusing together the words for 'hare' and 'eye', since the hare was believed never to close its eyes. The survivors wondered when the knock on the door in the night might come, and in the morning they attempted to live.

Such were the consequences of severe trauma. There were those who remembered too much and went mad under the strain. Others remembered too little and became amnesiacs trying to piece together their fragmented minds. For many, their condition within the camps had been so unbearable, so traumatising, that they lost all knowledge of both their families and themselves. One scientist named Nikolai Timofeev recalled: 'I remembered only that the name of my wife was Lyol'ka, but I forgot her full name. I forgot the names of my sons. I forgot everything. I forgot my last name. I remembered only that Nikolai was my first name.' The same amnesiac response to severe trauma was recorded among the survivors of the Holocaust.[10]

Some prisoners suffered the cruelty of losing the ability to make choices, and had to request that the choice be made for them; anxious to only get what they were given, since they were unable to cope with the expression of individual identity or desire. Their sense of self no longer existed. Some did not want to leave the camps at all. If they could, they would have chosen to remain within the zone. Such psychological conditions fell within a whole range of experience. But there was one, very revealing, phenomenon reported among the survivors of the Kolyma camps in particular. They hated the sight of gold.[11]

For some of those whose actions had consigned these people to the camps, the return of the 'ghosts' was too much to bear. Alexander Fadeyev had once been a famous writer whose novel *The Young Guard* sold over three million copies in the USSR. As the secretary of the Writers' Union, Fadeyev had also signed the arrest lists of his fellow authors. A long-term alcoholic, at first he had tried drunkenly to befriend his former victims who survived. Then, quite suddenly, Alexander Fadeyev stopped drinking and wrote a letter addressed to the Central Committee of the Communist Party. The suicide note was retained by the KGB, but its contents were clear from Fadeyev's bitter complaints: 'I thought I was guarding a temple, and it turned out to be a latrine.' And then he shot himself.[12]

Like Fadeyev, Ivan Nikishov, the former Dalstroi chief and deceiver of an American vice-president, had lapsed into alcoholism. After the war, anonymous reports had been sent to Moscow informing on the 'unworthy behaviour of the head of Dalstroi, Comrade Nikishov'. An MVD investigation in Magadan revealed the widespread abuse of state funds, and lavish drinking and debauchery on the part of Nikishov and his wife: 'Nikishov and Gridassova organize binges on board the ships that arrive from America; afterwards, absolutely drunken Nikishov is being carried into his car in sight of all the personnel of the harbour.' The secret police report described the 'hand-kissing and sexual degeneracy' of Gridassova and likened the atmosphere to that of a royal court: 'Presents from America were not distributed among those who needed them; instead, they were given to Gridassova.'[13] In 1956, the disgraced Nikishov died in a bath, apparently another suicide. He, too, left a note of self-justification: 'Yezhov and Beria demanded to fulfil the plan of gold production by any cost: "Do not be sorry for prisoners. You will receive workers always when steamers can bring them" ... I do not feel guilty ... I was only an executor. Here are the copies of Yezhov's and Beria's orders. I kept them because I knew that I might be asked.'[14]

That year, Alexander Dolgun, the former clerk of the American Embassy, was finally released from the camps, eight years after his arrest on a Moscow street. His freedom was, of course, only relative, since he was warned that if he ever attempted to leave the USSR, his punishment would be a life sentence in a closed prison. He discovered that his mother had also been arrested after she had asked for news of her son. Meeting her again in Moscow, Alexander Dolgun was shocked that she looked twenty years older than her actual age; her fingernails were 'twisted and torn, and her temples and forehead were scarred'. Like many prisoners, Mrs Dolgun had suffered a severe mental breakdown in response to her torture, and was subsequently placed in a Soviet psychiatric institution. Twice a week, Alexander Dolgun visited his mother in hospital, where she would reminisce about her life in New York and her sister living in New Jersey. Once, Dolgun was approached by a hospital psychiatrist who explained that his mother was suffering from severe paranoia combined with the most intricate delusions: 'She has told me the most vivid stories about living in New York City. Can you believe that? She describes the streets and the buildings with such clarity that I find myself believing her. I have seldom seen such an advanced case. I am sorry to have to tell you that she is very, very far gone into a world of her own making.'[15]

At the American Embassy, Alexander Dolgun was invited to collect some money that he was owed. Accompanied by a KGB escort, he was offered a thousand dollars in back pay and asked how he would like to receive the money. When Dolgun requested to be paid in roubles, his only counsel came from his KGB minder, who advised him that he should not have changed the currency since 'you could buy a lot with a thousand dollars in Moscow'. An Embassy official told Dolgun that his belongings were stored in a warehouse but they would take some time to find. His reaction to this news was muted: 'But all the time I was running the consular file section, the records were in excellent shape.'[16]

In 1956, there were still Americans imprisoned in camps who were forced to write to friends abroad in code. One letter was sent from 'Vincent W.', who substituted the word 'uncle' for the American Embassy in Moscow, and 'aunt' for the Soviet secret police: 'I can tell you that I received from my uncle a letter from Moscow; he writes very nicely, he did not give me up, I am considered their son.' After Vincent W.'s release from the camp, he wrote again: 'I was not permitted to see the uncle, the aunt herself talked to me for four hours . . . Please speak with my uncle who lives with you.'[17] In September 1956, Alyce Alex was still appealing to the American Ambassador from her prison camp, by means of a letter delivered by hand: 'I am in camp seven years without any help what so ever. I have tried to get in contact with my friends and relatives in the States and so far have had no luck. I wonder if you will be so kind as to help me . . . Please help me.'[18]

On 10 August 1956, State Department officials met with the American Red Cross to ask them to 'bring up the question of the release of American citizens imprisoned in the Soviet Union'. Mr Ellsworth Bunker, the President of the American Red Cross, replied that 'the Red Cross delegation had given careful consideration to this problem and had decided that it would be best to avoid raising the question which would be considered by the Soviets as a political issue'.[19] The attitude of the American Red Cross had remained unchanged since the Terror. Ten years earlier a British enquiry for intervention on behalf of a missing legal adviser had received the following reply from Ralph Hubbell, the Red Cross director: 'We have made it a practice, if not a policy, however, not to make inquiries about those whom we know are political prisoners; those arrested by the Soviet police; those we know are domiciled in NKVD camps . . . in our opinion, inquiries about persons in this category would tend to be a source of annoyance, if not embarrassment.'[20]

After midnight on 25 February 1956, at the final day of the Twentieth Party Congress, Nikita Khrushchev unexpectedly announced that proceedings would continue in a closed session. A summons was issued to the Communist Party delegates staying in nearby hotels, and within half an hour the Congress hall was full. Then Khrushchev stepped up to the podium and, without warning, launched into a four-hour speech listing Stalin's crimes against 'socialist legality' and the Communist Party. The delegates listened in silence, their shock interrupted only by the occasional expression of astonishment and indignation.[21]

In his so-called 'Secret Speech' Khrushchev acknowledged for the first time the catalogue of 'mass arrests and deportations', 'cruel and inhuman tortures' and the lists that Stalin signed condemning 'thousands of honest and innocent Communists'. The new Soviet leader mentioned several innocent parties by name, and attributed personal responsibility to Stalin for their deaths. At a stroke, the principal charges made against Stalin, so ferociously denied for so long, were suddenly accepted as truths by his successor. As Khrushchev candidly admitted to his audience: 'Stalin was a very distrustful man, sickly suspicious. We know this from our work with him. He could look at a man and say: "Why are your eyes so shifty today?" or "Why are you turning so much today and avoiding looking at me directly in the eyes?"'[22] An American writer described quite perfectly the shock of Stalin's former followers as they listened to Khrushchev's speech: 'In the eyes of a Communist, it was as if St Paul, suddenly and without warning, had bitterly charged Christ with depravity and deceit.'[23]

Of course, Khrushchev's candour only went so far. The issue that could never be addressed by the new General Secretary was that the Communist Party of the Soviet Union was not only the victim, but also the institution that had allowed a judicially-sanctioned genocide to occur. In terms of responsibility, the Communist Party had actively encouraged, and continually excused, the actions of its leader. Untold fanatical believers had pursued Stalin's will through conviction, not just fear, and one of those had been Khrushchev himself. So if the 'Secret Speech' stunned its audience, it left a great deal else unsaid. The camps themselves were never mentioned, and while Khrushchev alluded to the 'illegal' execution of 'thousands' of Communists, he could never fully acknowledge the death of millions of innocent victims of the Terror.

After the speech, Khrushchev cautiously remarked that 'we must not carry out a St Bartholomew's Massacre', and explained how bringing to account all those who had participated in Stalin's crimes would have incarcerated more people than had just been released. His own passionate speeches in defence of the Terror were erased from the record, just as he made certain to conceal his personal role in the mass arrests in Moscow and the Ukraine during 1937 and 1938. According to Semyon Vilensky, a Gulag survivor and the head of a support group for its victims, thousands of documents were burned during the Khrushchev regime as 'people wanted to eliminate the traces of their crimes'.[24]

To admit openly the enormity of the crimes against humanity, let alone the lies concealing it, would surely have sounded the death knell of the Soviet Union, and privately Nikita Khrushchev himself worried lest the 'thaw' turn into a flood that might wash the regime away.[25] Instead of openness, Stalin's inheritors – the willing Stalinists of the past – chose first partial revelation, and then to continue what Boris Pasternak described as 'the inhuman power of the lie'.[26]

In the following months, new death certificates were delivered to the families of the victims. The causes of death were entirely fictional and yet medically plausible: dysentery, typhus, tuberculosis, pneumonia, heart attacks – the list was endless. Oscar Corgan had once been a leading organiser of the Finnish-American emigration to Karelia, before his arrest and disappearance during the Terror. After Corgan's posthumous rehabilitation under Khrushchev, his family were issued a death certificate which stated that Corgan had died of stomach cancer on 18 July 1940, the place of death unknown.

Decades later the family received a second certificate, somewhat closer to the truth: Oscar Corgan had been shot on 9 January 1938, the place of his execution still unknown. The 'inhuman power of the lie' was a function of the regime regardless of its leadership.[27]

After his release Thomas Sgovio bought a ticket to a Moscow cinema where a documentary on Kolyma was about to be screened. Ten minutes into the film, Thomas began to feel unwell, unable to cope with the images he saw on screen. The film showed pictures of beautiful pine-covered hills, of Yakut villagers herding reindeer as the narrator praised 'the heroic deeds of the Komsomol' in opening up these new Soviet lands. The emaciated prisoners, the frozen corpses, the guard dogs and the watchtowers had all been quietly erased from the official record of Soviet history.

Watching the documentary pushed Thomas towards the realisation that applying for an American passport to leave the USSR was too much to hope for, even in the heady days of the Khrushchev 'thaw'. Instead, he used his father's ancestry to obtain an Italian passport and an exit visa. Eventually in 1960, Thomas Sgovio was permitted to leave Moscow on an Aeroflot plane bound for Italy, and from there he travelled on to New York. After years of exile, most of which had been spent as a prisoner, he had finally returned home. When Thomas Sgovio left the United States, President Franklin D. Roosevelt was battling the Great Depression. On his return, John F. Kennedy was promising 'the New Frontier'. A quarter of a century had passed.[28]

By strange coincidence, Nikita Khrushchev arrived in America before Thomas Sgovio's return. It was the first visit of a Soviet leader to the United States, and Khrushchev had remained in ebullient humour throughout, confidently declaring 'your grandchildren will live under communism'. In New York, Khrushchev explained how the 'conical shape of A-bomb waves made tall buildings situated even at great distances from ground zero more vulnerable to destruction'. When he confided that the Soviets were building not more than 'four or five' storeys high, an American aide remarked that perhaps soon they would 'all live underground'.

Unfazed by the shadow of Armageddon, Khrushchev appeared to enjoy the United States very much, and took the evident economic prosperity in his stride, ready with a quick-fire answer for every eventuality. The American automobiles, he reluctantly admitted, were 'impressive', but in the Soviet Union they were setting up large rent-a-car garages for the people to use collectively rather than creating all this wasteful individual ownership. And Khrushchev reminded American businessmen that in earlier days trade between their countries had been 'rather extensive and that Ford, for example, had found it profitable to deal with the USSR'.[29]

In San Francisco, Khrushchev was greeted by cheering crowds and his warmest reception yet. A lone dissenting voice came from the leadership of the United Auto Workers' Union. Walter and Victor Reuther were among a party of American trade unionists invited to a reception at the Mark Hopkins Hotel. When Victor Reuther greeted the Soviet leader in Russian, quite naturally questions were asked, with Reuther explaining that he had spent the years of 1934 and 1935 with his brother working at the Gorky Automotive Works 'named in honour of Molotov. Is it still called that?' '*Niet*,' snapped Khrushchev. The Reuther brothers had managed to leave Russia in 1935, but there had been disappearances even then, and they never believed the official explanation that the Americans had left voluntarily. For his part, Khrushchev reacted to their criticism with predicable ill temper. Later, at a summit meeting in Vienna he told President Kennedy, 'We hanged the likes of Reuther in Russia in 1917.'[30]

In Los Angeles, Twentieth-Century Fox organised a reception in Khrushchev's honour – a glittering occasion attended by Hollywood's leading producers, directors and movie stars. The rotund Khrushchev happily posed for cameras surrounded by scantily clad showgirls from the set of *Can-Can*, with Shirley MacLaine and Frank Sinatra lending a touch of glamour to what was essentially a public relations campaign. One week later, just hours before his plane left for Moscow, Khrushchev broadcast a live speech on American television: 'Everybody in the Soviet Union wants our two countries to live in peace, everyone wants peaceful co-existence . . . What do we have in mind? To abolish all armed forces completely . . . Everyone in the Soviet Union enjoys real freedom . . . Good-bye, good luck, friends!'[31]

Three years earlier – with Khrushchev's approval and to lend 'fraternal proletarian solidarity' – Soviet tanks had crushed the democratic uprising in Budapest. Three years later, the Soviet premier would precipitate the Cuban Missile Crisis, which brought the world to the brink of destruction. Those who saw Khrushchev only as a rotund smiling red-faced peasant perhaps had second thoughts. Next to Stalin, of course, he appeared to be a saint.[32]

On 13 July 1956, five months after Khrushchev's revelations and a month after the 'Secret Speech' was published in the *New York Times*, Paul Robeson appeared before the House Un-American Activities Committee. No hint of apology was forthcoming from Robeson, who claimed forgetfulness for his long years of obeisance to Stalin, before launching into a counter-attack of his own:

Congressman Arens: While you were in Moscow did you make a speech lauding Stalin?

Robeson: I do not know.

Arens: Did you say in effect that Stalin was a great man and Stalin had done much for the Russian people, for all of the nations of the world, for all working people of the earth? Did you say something to that effect about Stalin when you were in Moscow?

Robeson: I cannot remember.

Arens: Do you have a recollection of praising Stalin?

Robeson: I can certainly know that I said a lot about Soviet people, fighting for the peoples of the earth.

Arens: Did you praise Stalin?

Robeson: I do not remember.

Arens: Have you recently changed your mind about Stalin ?

Robeson: Whatever has happened to Stalin, gentlemen, is a question for the Soviet Union and I would not argue with a representative of the people who, in building America wasted sixty to one hundred million lives of my people, black people drawn from Africa on the plantations. You are responsible and your forebears for sixty million to one hundred million black people dying in the slave ships and on the plantations, and don't you ask me about anybody, please.

Arens: I am glad you called our attention to that slave problem. While you were in Soviet Russia, did you ask them there to show you the slave labour camps?

The Chairman Representative Francis Walter: You have been so greatly interested in slaves, I should think that you would want to see that.

Robeson: The slaves I see are still as a kind of semi-serfdom, and I am interested in the place I am and in the country that can do something about it. As far as I know about the slave camps, they were Fascist prisoners who had murdered millions of the Jewish people and who would have wiped out millions of the Negro people could they have gotten hold of them. That is all I know about that . . . You are the non-patriots, and you are the un-Americans and you ought to be ashamed of yourselves . . . You want to shut up every colored person who wants to fight for the rights of his people.[33]

In answer to direct questions on his membership of the Communist Party, Robeson pled the Fifth Amendment over thirty times, until the hearing was adjourned. Paul Robeson's steadfast campaign for civil rights in America made his acquiescence to Stalinism all the more tragic. There were many American Communists who recanted once they understood the nature of the crimes committed in the USSR. There remained, however, a psychological conflict among those who understood, yet whose pride or ideology could not allow them to admit their error. Robeson's actions and speeches had justified, and therefore contributed to, the crimes of Stalinism, and for that at least he was morally culpable.

In 1961, after his passport was restored by a Supreme Court ruling, Paul Robeson was free to travel once more to the Soviet Union, for his first visit since the death of Stalin. In a Moscow hotel room, the American singer attempted to end his life by slashing his wrists with a razor blade. His son, Paul Robeson, Jr., would later assert that his father's mental breakdown was fashioned by a CIA agent who drugged his drink at a cocktail party earlier that night. An alternative, and perhaps more likely, explanation was that Robeson had succumbed to the same spiritual despair as Alexander Fadeyev.

After an extended convalescence in London, Robeson returned to America on 23 December 1963. According to press reports, at the airport he looked 'at least fifty pounds underweight, his face gaunt and his hair gray . . . the basso profundo that thrilled the world was silent.' When his wife Eslanda died of cancer in 1965, Robeson retreated still further into isolation. The rest of his life would be scarred by a series of nervous breakdowns, bouts of depression and a complete withdrawal from society. His last decade was lived as a recluse in his sister's house in Philadelphia, until his death on

Stalin shakes the hand of Joachim von Ribbentrop, the Nazi foreign minister. In the Kremlin during the signing of the Nazi–Soviet pact, August 1939 (David King Collection)

Harry Hopkins meeting Joseph Stalin in the Kremlin, July 1941 (Time & Life Pictures/Margaret Bourke-White/Getty Images)

'I thought he had the strongest face I'd ever seen' – the American photographer Margaret Bourke-White's portrait of Stalin (Time & Life Pictures/Margaret Bourke-White/Getty Images)

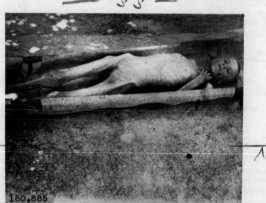

180,885

Ten year old girl — Polish evacuee from Russia — Aug. 1942.
Photo by Lt. Col. Szymanski. *U.S. Army.*

180,886

Three sisters, Ages 7, 8, and 9 — Polish evacuees from Russia — Aug. 19
Photo by Lt. Col. Szymanski.

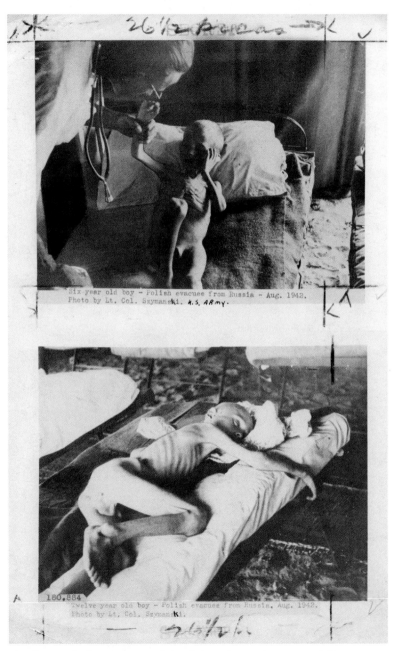

Six year old boy - Polish evacuee from Russia - Aug. 1942.
Photo by Lt. Col. Szymanski. U.S. ARMY.

180.884

Twelve year old boy - Polish evacuee from Russia, Aug. 1942.
Photo by Lt. Col. Szymanski.

The photographs from Lieutenant-Colonel Henry Szymanski's report, 1942

Above: An NKVD mass grave at Katyn

Below: The identification papers of the Polish officers taken from the site (National Archives II, College Park, Maryland)

The American Vice-President, Henry Wallace, meets the Dalstroi chief, Ivan Nikishov, in Kolyma, 1944 (Henry A. Wallace, *Soviet Asia Mission*)

Henry Wallace shakes hands with Kolyma's 'gold miners' (Henry A. Wallace, *Soviet Asia Mission*)

The sincerity of successful conmen – 'The Far North's Husky Placer Miners', Kolyma (Owen Lattimore)

Roosevelt and Stalin at the Yalta conference – sitting at the President's left is Alger Hiss
(UPI/Bettmann/Getty Images)

Stalin's personal gift to Kathleen
Harriman – 'Fact' the horse from
'Pharaoh' and 'Liquidation' –
delivered to the USA
(National Archives II, College Park, Maryland)

Russians celebrate the end of the Second World War, outside the US Embassy, Moscow – the first spontaneous mass demonstration since 1917 (National Archives II, College Park, Maryland)

The Soviet Ozymandias – Stalin's personality cult at its height (Time & Life Pictures/Margaret Bourke-White/Getty Images)

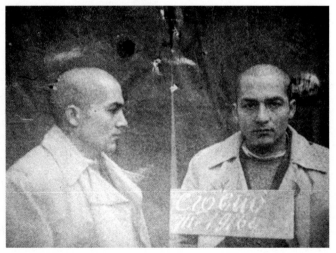

Thomas Sgovio's second arrest photograph, 1948 (AP/Press Association)

Paul Robeson at a party to celebrate the thirty-third anniversary of the Revolution at the Soviet Embassy, Washington DC, 1950 (Bettmann/Corbis)

An abandoned monument to Stalinism – a rusted locomotive on a disused prisoner-built railway line of the Far North (Central Moscow Archive for Documents on Special Media, and the Russian State Archive of Film and Photographic Documents)

23 January 1976. It was, according to a former friend, 'a great whis-per and a greater silence in black America'. The honorary catcher of the American baseball team of Gorky Park was gone.[34]

Of course, those without ideology, only cynical expedience, suffered no particular trauma at all. In the early 1950s, Joseph Davies was briefly caught up in the McCarthy era, forced to defend the movie *Mission to Moscow* from the Un-American Activities Committee attacks, while his marriage was plagued by rumours that Marjorie Davies had interests elsewhere. Ever the chameleon, Davies emerged mauled but relatively unscathed, having learned to brandish his cre-dentials as a corporate lawyer and businessman: 'I was one of the birds who in the 1920's put great business combinations together . . . all strictly within the law . . . and I made a fortune doing it.' But his access to presidential power was cut off, and without this rejuve-nating oxygen Joseph Davies grew old and sick very quickly. It was as if he had nothing else to live for.[35]

In 1952, Marjorie Davies sued for divorce citing 'mental cruelty and incompatability', her husband's 'whiplash temper' and 'the lack of basic straight thinking that was awfully hard to live with'. Three years later she married the nephew of Davies' first law partner. After her fourth marriage, Marjorie moved into another Washington man-sion, which she filled with her vast collection of Russian art brought back from Moscow during the Terror. In the garden, just outside the back door of the house, she had a shelter dug to withstand a Soviet nuclear attack. At the Hillwood mansion, she lived quietly until her death in 1973. In her will, Marjorie Merriweather Post instructed that the mansion be converted into a museum and opened to the public. The collection included the vast Socialist Realist painting, 'Peasant Holiday in the Ukraine', which Joseph Davies had given her as a fiftieth birthday present in 1937. The painting depicted a colour-ful, bucolic Ukrainian peasant scene, which the museum's curator carelessly chose to hang in the public dining room. Occasionally this cultural negation of a famine that killed five million attracts the com-plaint of an elderly Ukrainian-American visitor, but there it remains, waiting for someone with sufficient grace to take it down.

In the years after his divorce, Ambassador Joseph Davies was left alone in Tregaron, the Washington mansion bought by Marjorie, who generously placed his name on the title deed. There was enough Russian art to fill this house, too, and the portrait of Stalin in its silver frame to remind the Ambassador of his former proximity to power, if not the lives he had not saved. His children from his first marriage attempted to contrive a reunion with his first wife, but by this stage Davies was already a sick man. After months of invalid care, he died on 9 May 1958, of a cerebral haemorrhage. His offer to gift Tregaron to the nation as a vice-presidential mansion was declined.[36]

Walter Duranty died just six months earlier, at the age of seventy-three, in retirement in Orlando, Florida. The former 'King of Reporters' had stopped writing years earlier, and was living in genteel poverty before the onset of a sunset romance with a rich Floridian widow, which ended in a marriage at his hospital deathbed. Walter Duranty's son and former mistress had been left behind in Russia, and were long forgotten. Many years later, Victor Hammer – the brother of the notorious American businessman, Armand Hammer – told an investigative reporter that Duranty had reported regularly to the OGPU throughout his period working for the *New York Times* in Moscow. According to Victor Hammer, Duranty had had a weakness for young girls, and his brother, Armand, had kept him supplied. But by his death in October 1957, the name Walter Duranty meant very little to the American public.[37]

During the McCarthyite period, while dining with a friend one night, Henry Wallace confessed that he did not want to live in America any more. The treatment he was being subjected to, he said, was hardly what any citizen, much less a former vice-president, should expect. By the outbreak of the Korean War, Wallace had taken to making lengthy public apologies for his former support for the Soviet Union. He now understood that the 'Soviets wanted the Cold War to go on indefinitely, even if it led to a hot one'. His nemesis, J. Edgar Hoover, remained unimpressed: 'Old bubble head has seen the light at last, but all too late.' Henry Wallace retreated to the isolation of his farm in upstate New York to cultivate strawberries and gladioli. He died in the mid-sixties of Lou Gehrig's disease; after a long illness and unable to speak, he was forced to communicate with his final visitors on a slate.[38]

Before his illness, Henry Wallace had given a long interview to Columbia University. As an old man, he spoke of his earliest memories, of getting lost in a cornfield in Iowa, aged three or four. The young Wallace recalled how he had wandered deep into the field where the sand burrs got into his socks and started to hurt his feet.

And then he began to cry 'Where is Mama's baby? Where is Mama's baby?' until his family heard his shouts and found him. Later Wallace told his interviewer how he had genuinely loved Franklin Roosevelt for his 'capacity to radiate joy and confidence to other people', and how he often dreamed that the President could rise up from his wheelchair and walk. In the last days of his illness, perhaps Henry Wallace found comfort in his recurring dreams of walking beside Roosevelt, the man with the 'golden heart'.[39]

Henry Ford's famous good health deteriorated soon after he suffered a stroke in his River Rouge cinema while watching the black-and-white newsreel taken from Majdanek concentration camp at the closing stages of the war. In the theatre, it appeared that Ford, the former publisher of *The International Jew*, had a sudden awareness of the consequences of his actions. The silver-haired billionaire had once given away his violent pamphlets against the Jews personally, saying proudly, 'This came out of our factory.' The Nazi propaganda machine had turned his hateful book into a bestseller in Germany, reprinting it throughout the Holocaust, by which time it had been translated into a dozen languages and distributed through the occupied capitals of Europe, with a swastika on its title page. The world-famous figure of Henry Ford had lent his name and reputation to the anti-Semitic cause, paving the road to the Holocaust like a highway for one of his cars; which led its victims on the short journey to the crematoria. For Ford's words, once written, could never be taken back.[40]

Two years after suffering his stroke, Henry Ford died on 7 April 1947 at his home at Fair Lane on the banks of the river Rouge. On the day of his funeral, the bells of Detroit City Hall and every church in the city tolled, and the whole state of Michigan stopped to observe a minute's silence for America's greatest industrialist. In all the eulogies what was never mentioned was that Ford had been one of the few American businessmen to have maintained ties with both totalitarian regimes simultaneously.

Three years before his death, Henry Ford had sent a message to Joseph Stalin, brought to the Kremlin by Eric Johnston, the young head of the American Chamber of Commerce. From the record of the meeting, preserved in the Russian state archives, we know that on the evening of 26 June 1944, Eric Johnston told Stalin that he had talked with Henry Ford in Detroit before his departure and that

Ford had requested him to pass along his personal greetings to the Soviet leader. Stalin replied that he had not expected to receive greetings from Henry Ford: 'We owe Henry Ford a lot, he helped us to construct automobile plants.' At this point, Johnston conveyed Henry Ford's willingness to help the Soviet Union again in the future, to which Stalin answered that 'the Soviet Union would repay Ford for his help', just as they had done in the past. The Soviet stenographers then recorded that Johnston complimented Stalin: 'In his opinion J.V. Stalin is in fact a real businessman.' To which Stalin replied that, 'if he was born in America and lived there he would probably have really become a businessman'.[41]

The Ford Archives, almost a mile of boxed records of the Ford Motor Company's history, were stored at Ford's mansion in Fair Lane, Dearborn. According to the memoirs of Charles Sorensen, Henry Ford liked to roam among them in his old age. The octogenarian industrialist would step quietly past the records of those people he had dispatched around the world to do his bidding. Hidden in these archives lay the single slip of paper that had issued a Ford badge to Sam Herman, the defining gesture which began the Herman family's emigration to the USSR. And there, too, were the names of the other former Ford auto workers who had followed him on their doomed journey to Nizhni Novgorod.[42]

In the last decades of the Cold War, very little was heard from the surviving Americans in the Soviet Union. Among the millions of Stalin's victims, the American emigrants scarcely registered as just one small tile in a vast mosaic of suffering. And of the thousands who had left in the early thirties, only a handful ever returned home in the footsteps of Thomas Sgovio. One of the few was Victor Herman, who managed to send a letter to a law firm in New Orleans addressed to a cousin he had never met. After long years of bureaucratic struggle and harassment, Victor Herman finally received an American passport and was allowed to leave the USSR in 1976. Forty-five years after he had departed New York as a teenager on a passenger liner bound for Leningrad, he returned home to Detroit. He was sixty years old, and his story was featured in the pages of the New York Times.[43]

In America, Victor Herman wrote a memoir of his experiences entitled Coming Out of the Ice: An Unexpected Life, which received a measure of critical attention, almost as an anomaly of the Cold War, a historical curiosity. Although his family was eventually allowed to join him in Detroit, the trauma of the camps of Burelopom remained with him and left him no peace. In the early hours of the morning, Victor Herman would awake with a start from his dreams, convinced that he was still starving and desperate for a scrap of food. The following year, he launched a ten-million-dollar lawsuit against the Ford Motor Company charging that it had abandoned his family to their fate in the Soviet Union. The Ford Company lawyers responded that Sam Herman had never actually worked for their company, and the case was dismissed by the Federal District Court of Detroit. Seven years later, on 25 March 1985, Victor Herman died of a heart attack in his home town, at the age of sixty-nine.[44]

After the advent of glasnost, a few more Americans returned to the United States in the late 1980s, like Rip Van Winkles whose lives had flashed by from youth into old age. As individuals they were not welcomed with any fanfare, just shrugs; scarcely a footnote of history, a few wide-eyed old men and women shuffling into airports, ready to be interviewed by the FBI checking they were the same people who had left in the 1930s, not Soviet agents who had already been caught using the American emigrés' identities. The collective existence of the American emigrants was hardly acknowledged in the short history of the young Republic. And yet their lives held a moral significance far greater than their numbers.

Abe Stolar's father had worked for the *Moscow Daily News* before his arrest and execution in 1937. Abe Stolar was wounded serving in the Red Army during the war, and his sister was sent to the camps in 1951. After years of waiting, Stolar was finally allowed to return to America in 1989: 'I cannot find words. It has been a long time. I tried very hard to get here.' In Chicago, he walked the streets of his youth, asking for places that had not existed for decades, his accent and speech still anchored in the 1930s. In fifty years virtually everything had changed in Chicago; all the old landmarks were long gone. Only Wrigley Field remained standing, and the Chicago Cubs were still playing in the old baseball park. One more time, after almost sixty years, Abe Stolar was able to watch his beloved Cubs take to the field. Only baseball had remained unchanged, as though awaiting his return:

> *Take me out to the ball game,*
> *Take me out with the crowd;*

Buy me some peanuts and cracker jack,
I don't care if I never get back . . .[45]

Other Americans stayed on in Russia. Albert 'Red' Lonn also survived his sentence in Burelopom, although Victor Herman had
believed he had died in the camps. On his release, Lonn returned to
his wife in Karelia, after fourteen years of imprisonment. In the small
town of Suojarvi, Albert Lonn worked quietly as an electrician, and
started teaching a new generation of children the rules of baseball.
He could not show them the baseball signed by Babe Ruth he had
brought with him from America; but he always remained the captain
of the 'championship' winning team of 1934. And, despite his every
hardship, Albert Lonn stayed a baseball fanatic until the very end.

Lucy Flaxman was held as a prisoner in the camps for three years
before her rehabilitation and release in 1956, under the general
amnesty. On her return to Moscow, she received four hundred roubles
compensation for her confiscated belongings, and her son gave her
enough money to buy some material to have a suit made. She then
worked as a literary translator at the Soviet news agency Novosti.
Until her death, Lucy Flaxman never allowed anyone to say a bad
word about Nikita Khrushchev. 'He gave freedom to thousands of
people,' she would say. Her son remembered his mother as 'always
young in her soul' who never had much interest in politics. She
worked hard, and liked to take her granddaughter for a walk to the
shops, and celebrate the holidays. 'She was a very easy-going person,
and did not reflect much, which was certainly for the best in the
USSR.' In 1965 she met Aleksandr Fisson, a retired prosecutor from
the Far East fleet, and the couple lived happily together in Moscow. In
1979, Lucy Flaxman died of cancer, which had progressed very
quickly.[46]

Of the American servicemen held captive in the Soviet Union after
World War II, nothing more was known. The American intelligence
files remained closed, left buried in the vaults to accumulate dust and
gradually be forgotten by succeeding generations of operatives. It
seemed the conscience of the world lay dormant through the Cold
War, locked in the embrace of superpower antagonism. And while
the Gulag camps lost the vast majority of their prisoners after 1956,
the system was never completely shut down.

The state repressions continued until the very end of the Soviet regime. Through the 1960s and 1970s, political dissidents in the USSR were routinely diagnosed as suffering from 'mental illness' by Soviet psychiatrists and placed in institutions to be force-fed drugs, or subjected to electroshock 'therapy' until cured of their stubborn desire for freedom of speech. In the mid-sixties, the dissident Vladimir Bukovsky met someone in a special clinic who had been there almost a decade for demanding an enquiry into Stalin's crimes.[47] Another dissident, Andrei Sinyavsky, was arrested and put on trial in February 1966 for the 'crime' of having his books published abroad. At Sinyavsky's trial, the judge's questions echoed the absurdity of a regime that had cut itself off from the world – 'Do you think reactionary publishers would have printed your books so beautifully if there had been nothing anti-Soviet in them? Just look at this paper, just look at this book jacket.' – before he sentenced Sinyavsky to seven years in 'strict-regime' labour camps.[48]

Within the Soviet Union, the United States had always to be portrayed as in a state of semi-permanent crisis, if Friedrich Engels was to be considered justified in calling Karl Marx 'the Darwin of History'. Upon this historical necessity – an idea as fragile and finely-crafted as a Fabergé jewel – was hung the whole justification for the Soviet regime's existence and the endless sacrifices borne by its people.[49]

After Nikita Khrushchev was overthrown in the coup of Communist Party hardliners of October 1964, the business of running the Soviet state was quickly returned to normal. Gone was the vain pretence of recognising Stalin's 'mistakes'. It was far simpler instead to restore Stalin's name to uneasy eminence in the Soviet pantheon. After the coup, Nikita Khrushchev was turned into a 'non-person', kept under house arrest by the KGB in a dacha twenty miles west of Moscow until his death in September 1971.[50] During the stagnation and repression of the Brezhnev years, an endgame was taking place, although few were aware of it at the time. As a young Central Committee secretary, Mikhail Gorbachev remembered overhearing an ageing Leonid Brezhnev turn to ask Yuri Andropov, 'How's my speech?', to which the KGB chief answered, 'Good, good, Leonid Ilyich.' Later, when Gorbachev enquired which Marxist-Leninist message Leonid Brezhnev was referring to, Andropov explained he had misunderstood: 'Leonid Ilyich was having increasing trouble speaking.'

As the Soviet Union slipped away into a gerontocracy, one ageing

Leninist hero with a chestful of medals succeeded another in a patient shuffle to the front of the queue, their collective belief in the socialist society lost to the evidence all around them. At the end, the entire country was still queuing for food. And in 1987, two years *after* Gorbachev had come to power, the Russian writer Leonid Borodin was still serving a prison sentence for advocating religious freedom in the USSR.[51]

And there perhaps our story might have ended, except where Russia is concerned little is straightforward and all endings seem false. In the summer of 1989, a Hungarian prime minister whose name few people can now remember, made the fateful decision to open the border and allow East Germans permission to cross freely into Austria, thereby setting off the chain of events that led to the fall of the Berlin Wall. Perhaps Miklós Németh was delivering a 'fraternal thank-you' for the 'socialist assistance' of 1956.

In the Kremlin, the final Soviet leader, the one man with sufficient power to halt the peaceful revolutions of Eastern Europe, chose not to maintain the status quo through violence. Mikhail Gorbachev's grandfathers had both been arrested during the Terror, and his wife Raisa's grandfather was executed in 1937. This family history might help to explain why Gorbachev was not prepared to follow the actions of the Chinese Communist Party leadership, who ruthlessly ordered in tanks to kill the Chinese students protesting for democracy in Tiananmen Square that summer. After the failure of the hardliners' coup against him in August 1991, Mikhail Gorbachev announced his resignation as General Secretary of the Communist Party of the Soviet Union.

The 'greatest social experiment in the history of mankind' ended on Christmas Day 1991 as the red flag was lowered from the Kremlin and the new Russian President, Boris Yeltsin, declared that the Soviet Union had ceased to exist. And only then could the final act of a tragedy begin to unfold.

26

THE TRUTH AT LAST

The Trojan War
Is over now; I don't recall who won it.
The Greeks, no doubt, for only they would leave
So many dead so far from their own homeland.
                    Joseph Brodsky, *Odysseus to Telemachus*[1]

Visiting the United States in 1992, President Boris Yeltsin made an unexpected announcement to the news media. In the early 1950s, he said, Soviet forces had shot down an American plane and taken its dozen-member crew hostage. Although the Russian officials accompanying their erratic new President made efforts to backtrack on the details of his statement, the end result was a 'Joint Commission of Investigation' called into existence by the American and Russian governments. The commission was authorised to discover 'whether American servicemen are being held against their will on the territory of the former Soviet Union and, if so, to secure their immediate release and repatriation; to locate and return to the United States the remains of any deceased American servicemen interred in the former Soviet Union, and to ascertain the facts regarding American servicemen who were not repatriated and whose fate remains unresolved.'

At a press conference in the White House Rose Garden on 16 June 1992, President George H.W. Bush pledged, 'I want to assure all Americans, and particularly those families of the American POWs and MIAs that we will spare no effort in working with our Russian colleagues to investigate all information in the Russian archives concerning our servicemen.' President Boris Yeltsin reciprocated in the spirit of the new Russian–American entente: 'I can promise that the joint commission which will be established . . . will report to the

American public all the information that will be found in the archives that we are going to open for it . . . the archives in the KGB, in the Central Committee of the Communist Party, regarding the fate of the American POWs and MIAs.'[2]

In a television interview, Yeltsin gave clues as to what may have happened to the missing Americans: 'Some of them were transferred to the former Soviet Union and were kept in labour camps. We don't have complete data and can only surmise that some of them may still be alive. That is why our investigations are continuing. Some of them may have ended up in psychiatric asylums.'[3] The following day in the White House East Room, Yeltsin was asked by a reporter 'if Gorbachev or any of his predecessors, even going back to Stalin, Khrushchev, Brezhnev, knew about the possibility that Americans were being held?' His reply was frank: 'Well that's just the point. They did know. That's the very point, that they kept it a secret. The point is that that era, when we kept the truth from each other, has come to an end and we will now tell the truth to each other person to person.'[4]

Decades after the first American prisoners of war had been reported missing, 'Task Force Russia' began its investigation from offices at the American Embassy in Moscow. To begin with, at least, optimism ran high, although the eight American investigators always maintained that much would depend on the good will of their hosts. In the first flush of the anti-communist Yeltsin government, a degree of progress was made. The leader of the Russian side, the historian General Dmitri Volkogonov, unearthed a KGB document revealing the existence of a plan 'to deliver knowledgeable Americans to the USSR for intelligence purposes'. It was the first official recognition that the imprisonment of American servicemen had been an approved, not merely accidental, policy of the Soviet government.

There were other notable early discoveries. In one find, Volkogonov reported that 119 American prisoners of war were held back by Stalin after the end of the Second World War, because their names had 'Russian, Ukrainian or Jewish' origins. But even a Russian general found it difficult to discover the extent of the disappearances. The former Soviet archives were vast, their guardians were recalcitrant, and incriminating documents had often been sequestered or destroyed. As Volkogonov attempted to explain to the

American side, 'My own father was shot in 1937 and, to date, I can't establish where he is buried.'[5]

Three years into the investigation Dmitri Volkogonov, already suffering from cancer, died of a heart attack. His Russian successors, meanwhile, denied all knowledge of the so-called 'Volkogonov plan' or even the document outlining its existence, and the investigation's progress inevitably became mired in bureaucratic intransigence. As the decade wore on, Task Force Russia turned into a weathervane for the changing fortunes of the Russian–American relationship, veering from guarded cooperation to complete breakdown, depending on the political circumstances of the day. When American F-16s bombed the former Yugoslavia in 1997, for example, Task Force Russia was shut down completely and its investigators expelled, in a rerun of an old-fashioned Cold War spy drama.[6]

It soon became apparent that the wheels of bureaucracy turned as slowly in the new Russia as they had ever done in the past. Nor was the culture of secrecy vastly different, since the former Soviet officialdom below the highest ranks had survived completely intact. The KGB changed its name to the 'new Russian' FSB, but this was a not uncommon gambit for the organisation, and the faces within the offices at the Lubyanka remained unchanged, the officials overwhelmingly reluctant to offer American investigators full, or even partial, access to their archives. Privately, many on the American side conceded, there was a growing preference for the investigation to wither and die for lack of access to documentary materials.

Such views were candidly expressed in declassified American policy documents:

What started out as a dictatorship can also end up as a dictatorship ... The Russians with whom we must deal sense instinctively that, sooner or later, the boot may come down on any neck that has been extended, dirtied their hands with the POW issue ... [The Russian security forces] have not diverged from their planned course and, when confronted by potentially damaging evidence by the US side, they react swiftly and aggressively, quickly moving to put the US representatives on the defensive. They appear willing to lie openly and repeatedly. Some Americans may have difficulty grasping this fundamental fact of Russian diplomacy ... security services have lost much of their earlier fear of the President and may be as willing to lie to him or to stonewall him on the POW issue as they are apt to do to the US side . . . The possibility also exists that President Yeltsin has undergone a change of heart as regards his full support for the resolution of this issue. He may have been informed of some details that he, too, finds too sensitive to release.[7]

Such analysis appeared uncannily accurate when President Yeltsin ordered Stalin's personal archives to remain closed for forty years.[8] It quickly became apparent that old views lived on in the new Russia. In the wake of national publicity over the search for missing American pilots, a letter from Lieutenant Colonel Anatolij Dokuchaev was published in the newspaper *Red Star* in February 1993:

> They say that angels from abroad were simply flying when they were shot down by vampires. Peaceful, bubbling with life Roberts and Johns perished. They were shot down by dour, Russian Ivans . . . There is sympathy not for our lads defending the Fatherland, but for the boys from abroad bringing us 'happiness' from bomber hatches . . . Did they forget something at our borders? . . . Dostoeyevsky in his masterwork *The Brothers Karamazov*, depicted Smerdlyakov as a synonym of sadness, of obsequiousness before all foreigners and westerners. But the modern day Smerdlyakovs have gone even further – from obsequiousness to spitting on everything that is ours, everything Russian.[9]

In the former Soviet days, carefully phrased letters from members of the public were often used as a signal for changes in the party line. The subtext could be construed as a repetition of the Soviet reflex, which carried with it the undercurrent of threat, which had begun to re-emerge even then. Yuri Smirnov, a Russian parliament member and head of a subcommittee on POW/MIA affairs stated that he had been warned: 'You're working too hard on the subject and should back off.' Mail sent by Gulag survivors to the Joint Commission offices disappeared or was intercepted. Other witnesses who came forward were warned off by anonymous visitors and, quite naturally, became reluctant to go public.[10]

And yet, for all the limitations of the process, documents were discovered in the Russian state archives that – the American investigators stated in their joint meetings – referred to 'American POWS in Soviet camps during 1946 and 1947 in a seemingly matter of fact way'.[11] From the State Archives of the Russian Federation, one document referred to '2,836 Americans' held in the Komi Republic, in the far north of European Russia. These Americans belonged to a larger group of foreigners kept as prisoners during the early 1950s. The response of the Russian side to such information was always sceptical. At their joint meetings, a view was proposed that perhaps these prisoners had been deemed Americans as part of a 'criminal fabrication' and then a familiar question was raised: 'Are any of these 2,836 Americans mentioned in this document American citizens in the traditional sense of the term? ... Such a possibility cannot be excluded.'[12]

Searching for corroborative evidence, the American investigators re-examined their own archives. From thousands of boxes of information, the Wringer reports of the early 1950s were unearthed, and the evidence of the sightings of Americans by German and Polish survivors was presented to the Russian side. One report retrieved from a German lieutenant described the Gulag camp of Atkars, five hundred miles south-east of Moscow, where between 'three and five hundred' Americans were being held in June 1945. All had citizenship papers and had been interned first by the Germans during the war, before being captured by the Russians. Half of the group had been forced to hand over their identity papers, but the German witness had seen camp files with one column headed 'citizenship' filled with at least ten to twenty 'USA's written by the camp inmates.[13]

Another German prisoner of war, interviewed in 1947, reported '130 US Navy personnel' held in the Gulag camp at Kashgar. The German witness stated that these men were the survivors of two American submarines sunk in the Pacific, who had been picked up by a Russian tanker. The Americans had arrived in Kashgar in July and August 1944 and had then been isolated, with the German prisoners becoming aware of their presence only after the Americans had thrown notes to them over the fence. When the Germans left in July 1946, around 'thirty' of these Americans were already dead. Five decades later, the search for the existence of these men led nowhere, and the American investigators' requests for access to the Soviet secret police archives was consistently stonewalled. Amid claims, counter-claims and denials, the work of the Russian-American commission continued through the 1990s.[14]

Meanwhile, other national organisations searching for their missing citizens in Russia appeared to be achieving better results. The Association Edouard Kalifat – named after a missing French prisoner of war and dedicated to tracing the hundreds of French nationals who vanished in the Soviet Union during and after the Second World War – found a fresh source of information in the St Petersburg Medical and Military Archive. Buried in the sixty million files held on patients treated in combat the French investigators discovered evidence that, far from dying in battle as they had been told, many French servicemen had been imprisoned in Gulag camps. With the KGB archives still sealed, the St Petersburg Medical Archive held the promise of a uniquely useful resource. But when the Americans knocked on their door, they were politely told that the archive was undergoing 'restoration', and turned away. On another occasion, while investigating reports of 'six or seven' American prisoners of war held in a camp in Tambov, the American investigators interviewed a Russian archivist, Yuri Dulensky, who confided that many records had been destroyed 'for unknown reasons'. The camp archives had been 'cleaned up' over the years by their administrators fearing retribution.[15]

Over the course of the 1990s, the relatives of missing American servicemen had grown weary of the interminable delays. A coalition of families based in Roanoke, Virginia, issued a press release: 'Promises can evolve into action taken, or they can deteriorate into lip service. We are waiting with growing impatience to see some leadership.' Some families expressed their view that the Joint Commission was, in their words, 'nothing but a front office, bent on managing a potentially explosive issue to the least harm for America's political relationship with Russia'. Harried by such criticism, the American investigators continued their search across the former Soviet Union, travelling to the remote locations of former prisons and camps where prisoner lists were sampled for known names under variations of Russian spelling. Appeals for information were broadcast on Russian radio and television, and limited access was negotiated with the archives of the Russian Ministry of Defence, the Navy and the Coastguard.[16]

Public appeals made in the newly independent Baltic States brought forward several former Gulag prisoners who remembered Americans imprisoned with them in their camps. One Latvian survivor spoke of a pilot named 'Jimmy Braiton or Baker . . . 180 cm tall with dark eyes, and a limp which required him to walk with a cane.' Another witness reported the existence of an American pilot imprisoned in Norilsk in 1949 'called Tim or Tom, although that was not his real name. The pilot was 175–180cm tall; handsome with dark hair . . . After being implicated in a plot to steal a plane in the spring of 1949, Tim/Tom disappeared.' In Tallinn City Museum, a notebook was discovered filled with prisoners' portraits. One picture carried a dedication in English 'for Good memories', dated 2 October 1952. Over the man's face the artist had written the word '*Yankee*' in Estonian.[17]

A portrait or an artefact always carried a tangible feeling of presence. In April 1995, another Gulag survivor handed in a ring that he said had belonged to an American pilot, Captain Oliver Rom, who was born in 1923, a native of Minnesota, and had been shot down over Germany and subsequently imprisoned in a Gulag camp in Karelia. It was reported that Captain Rom had been shot by a guard in December 1958, some five years after Stalin's death.[18]

In response to a newspaper advertisement, a Russian citizen named Yury Khorshunov wrote a letter from Nizhneudinsk, in the Irkutsk region of Siberia, addressed to the American Embassy in Moscow, 'fulfilling the will of my late mother'. The author explained that his mother had worked as a conductor on the railways after the war. In March 1946, Mrs Khorshunov was employed servicing the trains delivering prisoners to the camps of Far East Russia. Eight prisoners had died on that particular section of the journey, and their bodies were unloaded from the prison train and placed on a sledge for burial. As Mrs Khorshunov was returning home from her shift, the driver of the burial sledge stopped to ask her 'what he was supposed to do, since one of the dead prisoners seemed to breathe, and putting a live person into a grave did not correspond to Christian traditions'. Faced with a choice, Mrs Khorshunov decided to bring this prisoner back home with her.

Over the next three days this man began to speak a language Mrs Khorshunov could not understand. All she could grasp was that the prisoner pointed a finger to himself and said, 'American.' Then he asked for a paper and pencil, and with difficulty drew a picture of a 'falling aircraft, three human figures, and then poles with barbed wire'. In another picture, the American prisoner drew several storeyed buildings and repeated the word 'Kanifol'. He also told Mrs Khorshunov his name. His Christian name was 'Fred', and his surname, she remembered, sounded like 'Collins'.

Perhaps because she had lost two brothers in 1937, Mrs Khorshunov felt both a heightened sense of compassion for her patient and an awareness that there was nowhere she could turn to for help. One week later, 'Fred Collins' died, and the Khorshunov family dug a grave and buried him, along with his few possessions: a small book and a badge or medal hidden in the sole of his boot. For many years Mrs Khorshunov tended this unmarked grave, and her son, too, followed her there sometimes. Decades later, fulfilling his duty to the American prisoner, Yuri Khorshunov sat down to write his letter to the investigation: 'There may be nonsense in my writing to you, since one human life is really nothing for such a great country like yours, though the relatives of that man may still be waiting for some information about him. If you have any questions, I will be glad to answer them.'[19]

Other Russian witnesses emerged with evidence gained from within the Soviet state. Vladimir Trotsenko, for example, had once been a Soviet army sergeant assigned to the aviation transport regiment of the 99th Soviet Airborne Division. In November 1951, Trotsenko broke his leg in a parachute training accident and was sent to an Air Force hospital in the small town of Staraya Sysoyovka, north-east of Vladivostok. Due to a bed scarcity, Trotsenko was taken to a separate facility on the second floor. There he was placed in a room next to four prisoners, whose door was latticed with metal bars. A guard was posted outside, but whenever this private needed a break he asked Trotsenko 'to keep an eye on the Americans'.

According to his testimony, although Trotsenko could not speak English, he managed to communicate with the four Americans using sign language. The prisoners were convalescing in bandages and plaster casts, and their treatment was periodically interrupted by the interrogation of a visiting Soviet captain who, on one occasion, pulled out the round medallion hanging around each man's neck to confirm his identity. Trotsenko remembered that one of the American pilots had his right arm in a new cast. This man would slowly repeat 'America – San Francisco, Cleveland, Los Angeles, Chicago', indicating the home city of each of his fellow patients. He also pointed to a crewman in a body cast and 'would make cradling motions with his arms indicating that the man had left two small children back home'. The American had blue eyes and light-coloured hair, was around six feet tall and was from Cleveland. A fifth American had died and was buried in the hospital cemetery.

Forty-four years after this meeting in the hospital, Vladimir Trotsenko saw an advertisement in a Khabarovsk city newspaper, and came forward with his evidence. The American investigators interviewed Trotsenko twice and were convinced of his authenticity. But when they put their findings to the Russian side of the Joint Commission, the information was received with overt scepticism and the accuracy of Trotsenko's account was called into question. According to a Russian Colonel Vinogradov, 'there are many inventive people in Russia who can conjure up good fairy tales'. Three visits were made to the hospital, and it was discovered that Trotsenko's memory for key details of the building and its grounds were correct. A US Navy historian also confirmed that between 1940 and 1956 the dog tags issued had been round and not rectangular. The grave of the fifth American was searched for in the hospital cemetery, and although remains were exhumed they were not matched by DNA testing for ethnicity. Of the four surviving Americans, no further evidence was discovered, barring the self-evident fact that they had been seen alive in a Russian military hospital as prisoners, and had never returned home.[20]

Another witness, a former Soviet MVD colonel, Vladimir Malinin in response to an advertisement claimed to have seen a group of foreign prisoners in a Leningrad KGB prison in 1953 or 1954, who had waved at him from a separate room and shouted, 'American, American, American.' Later, on duty in Kolyma, Malinin was told, 'there was a nuclear power generating plant far north of Magadan and that a number of uranium mines were located within eighty kilometres of the plant. Foreign prisoners were used exclusively in this work area . . . prisoners who were sent there were not expected to return.'[21]

General Georgi Lobov, the former commander of the Soviet 64th Fighter Aviation Corps, was interviewed by a Russian journalist for a newspaper article: 'I know that in summer [of] 1952 at least 30–40 American POWs were placed in a separate and closely guarded carriage, attached to a goods train, and sent to the USSR . . . They must have been a treasure-trove. I imagine that it was specifically from these people that the GRU's remarkable knowledge of our adversary came. Incidentally I know that it was accurate information of this sort, gathered from these Americans held on Soviet terrritory, which in 1951 helped us seize a Sikorsky helicopter from the Americans . . . That is what I know for certain. As regards the subsequent fate of those 30-40 Americans, I, like yourself, can only guess.'[22] Colonel Pavel Derzskii, the former adviser to the Soviet Ambassador in North Korea, told the American commission that there had been a standing order to send captured American pilots back to the Soviet Union. Another witness, Colonel Gavril Korotkov, stated that he had personally interrogated two American prisoners of war in Khabarovsk during the Korean War.[23] In his interview, Korotkov discussed the method by which Americans had been screened in North Korea and then transferred north for further interrogation in the USSR. In a subsequent interview, however, the colonel became more cautious. Korotkov explained that he had received phone calls and a late-night visitor whose behaviour left him with the impression that he was from the 'special services'. His subsequent testimony became more tentative, retracting key points Korotkov equivocated on the most politically sensitive details.[24]

During a subsequent Joint Commission meeting, Colonel Mazurov of the Russian security forces denied that any pressure had been brought to bear on Korotkov: 'I exerted no pressure – if I wanted to exert pressure, I wouldn't do it by telephone, but by other means.'[25]

In pursuit of such clues, the Joint Commission continued its work in Russia. Led by ageing witnesses, they searched for the missing American servicemen and found only the fragments of their lives. In 1999, their patience was, in a sense, rewarded when the American investigator Norman Kass unearthed the unpublished memoir of a Russian survivor of the camps, the response to another radio advertisement. The survivor was interviewed and his testimony judged to be the credible witness statement of a former prisoner in his late seventies, who had spent many years in the Gulag. Perhaps mindful of the forces brought to bear on previous witnesses, initially a decision was made to keep his identity secret. Only later was it revealed that Kass had discovered the memoir of Benjamin Dodin.

Key details of Dodin's recollections were checked against what was known of the historical record. The director of Memorial, the Russian organisation dedicated to the victims of Stalinism, confirmed the existence of Rybak, 'a top-secret uranium mine located on the Leningradskaya River' where Dodin reported he had encountered the 'citizen of the United States of America, Allied Officer

Dale'. No known archival records existed from Rybak, but geologists who had spent time there had passed on their knowledge to Memorial. When the Americans examined military records for the existence of the officer whose gaunt face Dodin remembered so clearly, they discovered two 'Dales' listed as missing from World War Two: Lieutenant Harvey Dale and Lieutenant William Dale.[26]

There were other American prisoners documented by name in the Dodin memoir. From the US Air Force archives, it was already established that an RB-29 aircraft stationed at Yokota Air Force Base, Japan, had been shot down on 13 June 1952 while on a reconnaissance mission over the Sea of Japan. During the American search-and-rescue efforts one, possibly two, empty life rafts were spotted in the water, but no survivors or bodies were picked up and a presumptive finding of death was issued to the entire aircrew on 14 November 1955. Benjamin Dodin had given the names of two of the men recovered by the Soviet authorities as 'Bush and Moore'. In the US Air Force records, the crew list of the lost RB-29 included a 'Major Samuel Busch' and a 'Master Sergeant David Moore'.

For decades sceptics had doubted the credibility of the witness testimony of Gulag survivors. In key details, Dodin's memoir validated the essential truthfulness of such men and women. It was also apparent that both Major Samuel Busch and Master Sergeant David Moore had been declared dead, when they were still alive and imprisoned in the USSR. After the shoot-down, the United States government had issued a formal diplomatic note asking for an investigation into the missing aircrew of the RB-29, among several other lost planes of the Cold War. But such diplomatic requests were routinely ignored or denied by the Soviet Foreign Ministry, and when released to the American media, had warranted only a scarce few lines in the *New York Times* of 17 July 1956. Nothing more was said or done, and just three years later Nikita Khrushchev received his rapturous welcome on a state visit to the United States.[27]

For Major Samuel Busch's surviving sister, Charlotte Busch Mitnik, the latest evidence was little comfort for the years spent agonising over her brother's fate. Her reaction was guarded: 'Time after time we asked the government to help us with our search for the truth. All we had received in the past were lies, half-truths and misinformation. How do you mourn a POW/MIA? You can't. You don't. We must insist that our government make North Korea, China, and Russia accountable as to what happened. These men paid the ultimate price, their lives. The cost was not too great for those men or their families to pay.' For certain families, the price paid was disproportionately high. The Busch family had already lost one son, Morris T. Busch, killed in action, during the liberation of France in the Second World War.[28]

What happened to Major Samuel Busch after the shoot-down of his plane remained unknown. However one document relating to his fate was discovered in the Russian state archives. A military report dated 13 June 1952 was sent to Joseph Stalin. The report, marked 'Top Secret', recorded the American search-and-rescue efforts for their missing aircraft and stated that the shoot-down had been recorded on film. But neither the photography nor the fate of the missing crew could be discovered.[29]

At their meetings, the Russian side of the investigation could seldom explain the American evidence. Usually an effort was made to call into question the authenticity of the American sources, which were usually eyewitness accounts with little or no documentation. And throughout the period of the investigation, the Russians stead-fastly refused to open the KGB archives or Stalin's personal archives for examination. It was evident, if always diplomatically expressed, that passive resistance took precedence over active quest. Any other outcome smacked too much of Cold War defeat for the Russians, or triumph on the part of the Americans. Colonel Mazurov, formerly of the KGB, first expressed this view in a meeting in 1993: 'We studied your report, sixty percent of the information was obtained from ex-prisoners . . . these people have their own axes to grind.' A decade later, a Colonel Vinogradov of the FSB reported 'to the incredulity of the US side' that 'a check of camp statistics revealed that there had been no American citizens detained anywhere in the camp system of the former USSR'.[30]

When the same Colonel Vinogradov was presented with the memoirs of Benjamin Dodin, he commented that such evidence was 'not realistic'. It was a 'waste of time for Russians and Americans to follow up on such bad information', which he claimed was like a 'fairy tale'. It was the same metaphor once used by the prisoners of Kolyma – 'just like a fairy tale', the years and their lives had disappeared.[31]

In August 2001, some fifty-seven years after Henry Wallace's ill-fated visit, Major-General Roland Lajoie boarded a plane for Far East

Russia. As the leader of the American commission, Lajoie was in charge of overseeing the examination of the crash site of a US Navy bomber missing since March 1944. Forensic scientists from the US Army's Central Identification Laboratory had recovered human bone fragments from the isolated site in Kamchatka scattered across the steep slope of a volcano, amid scrub brush and wild flowers. Despite months of painstaking investigation, the scientists had failed to locate the remains of the whole crew. Their bodies may have been taken away by wild animals; they may also have been removed by the authorities at the time. It was not known.

Standing next to the wreckage of the American plane, broken into silver pieces over the desolate landscape, Major-General Lajoie spoke cautiously to American and Russian television news: 'People are reluctant to talk about MIAs in the past tense for fear they might be alive, regardless of how many years go by.' If Lajoie understood that the history of the missing American servicemen cast a long shadow beyond this brief flare of media interest, then he was doubtless also aware that Russia's vast empty spaces had a habit of throwing up the most unlikely of survival stories.[32] Just the year before, in April 2000, a Hungarian soldier had been discovered in a psychiatric institute in the depths of rural Russia, missing since World War II, unclaimed and forgotten for over half a century. Judging from his physical condition, his doctors assumed that he was around seventy-five years old. His medical files stated that he had been in a 'pitiful state' when he had first arrived, 'emaciated in the extreme and suffering from extreme psychosis', a not uncommon condition for a Gulag survivor. Eventually with care and attention, the traumatised patient was able to tell his carers his real name was Andras Toma and that he came from a village in Eastern Hungary. Six weeks later, he was reunited with the brother and sister he had last seen as a nineteen-year-old conscript.[33]

Nor was Toma's case unique. Two years earlier, in 1998, Kenji Maruko, a Japanese prisoner of war was found living in Siberia and returned to a rapturous welcome in his home country – fifty years after being imprisoned in the Gulag at the end of the Second World War. Maruko told the press he had forgotten how to speak Japanese. In 1990, Ivan Bushilo, a Belorussian peasant, reappeared in his village after forty-two years as a hermit hiding in the dense forest. In 1947 he had been called an 'enemy of the people' by a local militia-man and Bushilo had fled to live alone for four decades in fear.[34]

A Polish prisoner, 'Mr. Strajinski', was reported to have died in a psychiatric prison hospital in Raizan, aged eighty-two, having survived fifty-one years of incarceration. Victor Hamilton, a defector from the National Security Agency, was discovered in 1992 at Special Hospital Number Five, near Moscow, where he had been held since 1962 and known only by the letter 'K'. The Memorial psychiatrists had long experience of treating such 'unknown people with unknown identities'. It would, of course, take a miracle to discover an aged American serviceman still alive in some remote Russian backwater.[35]

In September 1992, a letter was sent to investigators describing an American encountered in a Russian psychiatric hospital in 1979 who was seen again in 1986. The man went by the name of 'Vladimir', spoke fluent English and claimed to be an American pilot. Stripped of its wider context, the details of this single thread seemed far-fetched. And yet history is full of such improbabilities: the lost human casualties of a great ideological conflict. They were the men who were left behind. According to the American investigation, there were 'hundreds' like him.[36]

The work of the Russian–American Joint Commission has reached stasis in its second decade, as the search for witnesses and evidence struggles against time and the priorities of international relations. The last best hope lies within the archives of the former KGB, which may yet provide definitive knowledge for the families of the disappeared, for the men themselves, and for history. According to the American investigators, three-quarters of the available archival evidence has yet to be examined, despite the fact that Presidents George W. Bush and Vladimir Putin have described each other as friends and allies.[37]

While the KGB archives and Stalin's personal archives remain closed, there is little cause for optimism. In all likelihood the demands of realpolitik have already prevailed. From the Russian side, a view is likely to have been taken that the release of such information would be too damaging to the reputation of the former Soviet Union and, by extension, the contemporary Russian state. Vladimir Putin remains, after all, a former lieutenant-colonel of the KGB. In the past decade, sage eyes have long recognised the ongoing shifts in the political landscape of Russia – the signals that began with the reinstatement of the former Soviet national anthem, and the choice to commemorate the anniversary of Stalin's secret service with a set of postage stamps bearing the portraits of six NKVD agents.

The warnings which continued with the use of Stalin's portrait in campaign material for the ruling 'United Russia' party, and the murder of the FSB defector Alexander Litvinenko in London by the use of the poison Polonium-210, allowing his killers sufficient time to return to Moscow, leaving a trail of radioactivity in their wake. The chief suspect for the murder, a former FSB operative, Andrei Lugovoi, was then 'elected' to Russia's national parliament.

After two terms of Vladimir Putin's presidency, democracy in Russia exists only as a simulacrum – in the form required to maintain the pretence of its existence. Freedom of the press has long been silenced amid the ebb of murders of those Russian editors and journalists who were slow to grasp the rules of the new order. In such a political climate, the Russian government can no longer distance itself morally from the consequences of the 1917 Revolution. Nor could there ever be the national equivalent of a 'truth and reconciliation commission' – since the relapse into state authoritarianism has already taken place.

When the most famous critic of the abuses of the Putin government, Anna Politkovskaya was casually murdered in the elevator of her apartment building on 7 October 2006, the Russian judiciary blamed the killing on a plot organised from abroad. While such absurd explanations have a historical familiarity, the murder could only be regarded as another repressive signal to silence the voices of dissent. In her book published two years earlier in the West, Politkovskaya had detailed the promotion of six thousand former KGB servicemen into 'every conceivable nook and cranny in the power structure' of Russia: 'We dragged ourselves out of the USSR and into "The New Russia" still infested with our Soviet bedbugs . . . Everyone is convinced that the Soviet Union has returned, and that it no longer matters what we think.' She had then expressed her personal disregard for Vladimir Putin: 'In Russia we have had leaders with this outlook before. It led to tragedy, to bloodshed on a huge scale, to civil wars. I want no more of that. That is why I so dislike this typical Soviet Chekist as he struts down the red carpet in the Kremlin on his way to the throne of Russia.'[38]

None of which character evidence suggests that a Putin-controlled Russian government will ever voluntarily allow one of the Soviet Union's more cynical exploits to see the light of day. Rather it appears that the cause of the forsaken American servicemen will once again be sacrificed, now just as it was before, on the altar of the

American–Russian relationship. While the families of the disappeared will be denied resolution, the fate of the missing American servicemen will be forgotten, and the current American President will remain as silent as his predecessors – unless, of course, sufficient numbers of ordinary people seek justice for the missing.

27

'THE TWO RUSSIAS'

Russia is a Sphinx. Grieving, jubilant,
And covering herself with blood
She looks, she looks, she looks at you – her slant
Eyes lit with hatred and with love.

Alexander Blok, *The Scythians*[1]

In Vladivostok in Far East Russia – at the turn of the century – one of the last of the Liberty ships, the *Odessa*, sits rusting in harbour. Within weeks of her launch in 1942 from a slipway in Richmond, California, the 139-metre vessel was being used by the NKVD to ferry three thousand female prisoners across the Sea of Okhotsk to Magadan. Sixty years later, the gift of American democracy to the Gulag fleet lies waiting to be sold to scrap metal dealers from South Korea – and then the final substantiation of the cruelty inflicted upon the men and women packed below her decks will be lost.[2]

Across the wilderness of Kolyma, the remaining evidence of the camps is gradually disappearing. Within the realm now long abandoned, the wooden watchtowers have slowly fallen to pieces. Only a few still remain, as though awaiting the return of a familiar guard to climb the steps and, with the crack of a rifle shot, a cry to come echoing back across the zone. The camps that once swallowed men and women's lives are slowly returning into the desolate wilderness upon which they were built, their presence in the landscape marked by little more than the abandoned buildings and the rusted barbed wire which stubbornly refuses to yield. The perimeters of the zone that once carried a life-and-death distinction, have been rendered meaningless again, returned to the arbitrary by the death of an idea.

In the brief Kolyma summers the pathways and roads leading to the camps emerge from the ice and snow. From the wasteland the entrances to the mines reveal themselves clearly as the evidence of man's work. Black, perfectly rectangular holes appear in the sides of the mountains as though to warn of the horror which once lay within the darkness of the galleries. Beyond the broken-down fences, the aftermath of misery is strewn across the landscape: a heavy prison door swung free, a rusted padlock burst open, a pyramid of worn-out leather boots beside the human bones that emerge from the earth which cannot hold them. The human eye is constantly drawn to this debris: to an empty rusted iron bed on which only a guard had slept, or a collapsed barrack where the prisoners endured another night of cold and hunger. In an abandoned guards' building in Butugychag, a map of the world dated 19 July 1952 is pinned to the wall. Next to the map is a photograph of Comrade Stalin. The prison bars of the isolator cell are still strong, although the doors and roof have collapsed. There are watchtowers still standing, with their crude ladders leading upwards towards the sky. This is the abandoned archaeology of a forgotten genocide.[3]

The name Butugychag means 'Death Valley' in the local Yakut language. From the population of 50,000 at this particular camp, teenage prisoners from West Ukraine were selected to work four-hour shifts. The young men chosen for their 'special' task had viewed it with pleasure compared to the ordeal of the regular fourteen-hour shifts in the mines. A survivor from Butugychag remembered how they had lasted just twenty days before they were sent to the treatment zone. At first the Ukrainian boys lost their hair in chunks and then they started bleeding from their ears and nostrils, the first signs of radiation sickness. They were unaware that they were drying, stirring and baking the uraninite from the mine without any safeguards – their youth considered the property of the state.[4]

Only from the air does the taint of Dalstroi's intelligence fully reveal itself. The landscape bears the evidence of the work that sent the men and women to their deaths. During the short weeks of summer the breadth of this terminal point of the Gulag is revealed, and we are left to imagine the numbers required to tear the scars across the land, to build the roads, to build their own camps, to puncture the black holes into the sides of mountains in the endless forced pursuit of gold, or silver, or lead, or uranium. The same is true of every other terminal point of the Gulag across the wide space of the former Soviet Union. Within the archives there is a black-and-white photograph of an abandoned railway line built in the Far North, its sleepers buckled like a rollercoaster and covered in Arctic moss. The iron rails have long since rusted, useful only as evidence of the human labour which was consumed to lay them. On this forgotten line a train-engine stands slowly rusting, another decoration to the futility and anguish and unattenuated cruelty of Stalinism.[5]

Many of the current residents of Kolyma are the children and grand-children of those who survived the camps. In Magadan, the youngest of the former prisoners live on into old age. Occasionally they meet and help their former guards who have fallen into destitution. There coexists the uneasy consequence of Anna Akhmatova's 'two Russias' – the prisoners and their guards – whose fortunes have often been reversed by time. Very soon they will all be gone.

In the 1980s, the Soviet government began reworking the old mines of Kolyma in response to the rise in the world gold prices. According to Wladyslaw Cieslewicz, a Polish mining expert who sur-vived his sentence, the 'bodies of the victims, usually preserved in the permafrost, are being caught daily on dragline buckets and bulldozer blades'.[6] More than three hundred mass graves have been found thus far in Kolyma, and no one knows how many more remain. Many of the camps were so isolated, and their conditions so severe, that no one survived to remember where the prisoners were buried. But the bodies remain, perfectly preserved by the ice, and the principal evi-dence of this unpunished genocide lies waiting in the permafrost.[7]

It was a crime which lasted decades and required constant con-cealment by the state. Throughout the former USSR, the bodies of Stalin's victims had a tendency to reveal themselves with stubborn regularity. In 1979 at Kolpashevo, the twisting river Ob over-whelmed the site of a former NKVD prison in the Tomsk region, four thousand kilometres east of Moscow. From the shifting river bank thousands of corpses were released in a torrent into the water.[8] Eight years earlier, in 1971, two Russian journalists on a journey to Dudinka, the Siberian town on the Yenisei river, which led to the Gulag centre of Norilsk, recalled meeting an unexpectedly talkative riverboat captain: 'I made dozens of journeys, on the way out the holds were full and on the way back they were empty. I've seen people, and I've seen what you'd call non-people.' The island of Dikson lies five hundred kilometres further north.[9]

Near Minsk in Byelorussia, workers laying a gas pipeline through a pine forest discovered a mass grave dating from 1937 to 1941. The bodies were still clutching reading glasses, purses, children's toys, medicines and the host of random, day-to-day possessions which people take with them when they are seized.[10] The mass graves at Kuropaty Forest were estimated by Memorial to contain 150,000 victims. At Bykovna, outside Kiev, another mass grave was found in which an estimated 200,000 victims of the Terror lay buried.[11] In the Donetsk province, mass graves were discovered in Rutchenko fields containing 40,000 victims. On Golden Mountain near Chelyabinsk, Memorial discovered a mass grave containing an estimated 300,000 victims. And so it continues, until we are rendered senseless by the numbers.[12]

Here, too, in the catalogue of mass graves is a connection with the American emigration. In 1997, Memorial located the site of a mass grave near Sandarmokh in Karelia, one of four in the region. At this particular location nine thousand bodies were buried in trenches. The prisoners had been stripped to their underwear and shot on the edge of the pit with their hands and feet tied. The NKVD records revealed that in this particular mass grave was buried Oscar Corgan, and at least 140 other Americans, born in Minnesota, Michigan, Washington and San Francisco, who had arrived in the Karelia to work as loggers, truck drivers and mechanics. Among the victims was a young woman in her early twenties listed as Helen Hill, born in Minnesota. According to the NKVD file, Helen Hill had been executed for the crime of having 'maintained contacts with relatives in the US. Collected information in favor of Finland's intelligence service. Praised life in capitalist countries. Spoke of her intentions to cross the border creating a spirit of emigration in the workers.'[13]

Most of the mass graves were concealed beneath newly planted forests or newly built factories or apartment buildings. Often access to the land of these 'special zones' is still controlled by the Russian security services, and thus denied investigation by civic groups such as Memorial. In Moscow – where the crematoria were working overtime – the victims' ashes were often scattered in the bottomless 'Grave Number One' of the Donskoi cemetery. In 1991, a monument was added to this site with the words: 'HERE LIE BURIED THE REMAINS OF THE INNOCENT TORTURED AND EXECUTED VICTIMS OF THE POLITICAL REPRESSIONS. MAY THEY NEVER BE FORGOTTEN.'[14]

*

Through it all, long after the rise and fall of the statues of Stalin, and Russia's fitful emergence into the post-Soviet era, the embalmed corpse of Vladimir Ilyich Lenin remains in its red marble mausoleum in Red Square. The Russian state archives confirmed Lenin as the initiator of the use of terror by the Soviet state. On 11 August 1918, Lenin wrote to the party leaders in Penza giving instruction on how to deal with the peasants:

> Comrades! The revolt by the five kulak volosts must be
> suppressed without mercy . . . You need to hang (hang
> without fail, so that the public sees) at least 100 notorious
> kulaks, the rich and the bloodsuckers . . . Execute the
> hostages – in accordance with yesterday's telegram. This needs
> to be accomplished in such a way that people for hundreds of
> miles around will see, tremble, know and scream out: let's
> choke and strangle those blood-sucking kulaks. Telegraph us
> acknowledging receipt and execution of this. Yours Lenin.
> PS Use your toughest people for this.'[15]

Here also was Lenin's order for the 'execution by firing squad' of the priests of Shuia, his instruction to Nikolai Krestinsky: 'It is necessary secretly – and urgently – to prepare the terror', and his admission in 1920: 'We do not hesitate to shoot thousands of people.' Was it surprising, therefore, that Lenin, who began the process, gave way to Stalin, who accelerated the disappearance of millions? Stalin methodically and ruthlessly applied the same methods on a larger scale, but the rhetorical statement 'When we are reproached with cruelty, we wonder how people can forget the most elementary Marxism' was Lenin's own. The consequences of Stalinism were therefore neither accident nor a 'socialist aberration', as Khrushchev sought to portray. The Terror was a historical continuity within a political system which glorified 'Bolshevik ruthlessness' and denigrated the value of human life. In such a society, genocide was never a contingent aspect of this process. It was simply the casuistry of violence, the grim logic of an extermination process judged necessary to maintain absolute power.[16]

There have been bitter quarrels between the historians of Stalinism over the count of the dead. Scholars who rely on the official records from the Russian state archives arrive at counts in the single-figure millions. Those whose investigative evidence grants more credence to the insight of the survivors move substantially past ten million, towards twenty million victims. The truth is that no one can be sure. History was always propaganda for the Bolshevik state, and to place too much faith in the purely statistical evidence of the archives creates a modern danger of falling victim to a Potemkin village built from paper. It is to read the cause of death of 'alimentary dystrophy', without recourse to an accompanying vision of a human being worked and starved into a skeletal form – every bone in his body protruding, his teeth gone, his knees forming the thickest part of his leg, collapsing in the snow to die. It is to fall victim to the most insidious form of denial: that such a death is not murder.[17]

Estimates for the total population of the Gulag run as high as thirty million over its lifespan. The Soviet nuclear scientist turned dissident Andrei Sakharov estimated that between fifteen and twenty million people perished as victims of the Stalin era. Anastas Mikoyan, the Politburo survivor, wrote of a figure given to Khrushchev by the KGB that between 1 January 1935 and 22 June 1941 there were approximately twenty million arrests and eight million deaths.[18] Olga Shatunovskaya, a member of a 1960 commission to investigate the death of Kirov and herself a former camp prisoner, stated that as part of that commission she had seen a KGB report giving the figure of 19,840,000 people 'repressed' between 1935 and 1941, of whom seven million were shot. The percentage of the 'repressed' who subsequently died in the camps can only be guessed at.[19]

Shuffling around the pathways of his dacha settlement in Zhukovka, Moscow, his slab face lined by old age, Vyacheslav Molotov lived on undisturbed into the Gorbachev era. Stalin's functionary-in-chief, who signed the death lists and arranged Soviet foreign policy with Hitler and then Roosevelt, now tapped his walking stick on the path to market to buy cabbages, checking first that he had not left the lights burning in his dacha.[20] In retirement, the elderly Molotov was visited and interviewed by the Marxist historian Felix Chuev. In one of these discussions, Vycheslav Molotov revealed to Chuev that during the May Day celebration of 1953, Beria had whispered to him 'I did him!' as they stood next to each other on Lenin's mausoleum, 'I saved all of you!' Molotov took these words to mean that Beria was responsible for Stalin's death.[21] The former premier did not believe that Stalin died a natural death: 'He wasn't seriously ill. He was working steadily ... And he remained very spry.'[22] Later

Molotov confessed that even as a very old man, Joseph Stalin regularly visited him in his dreams. He would find himself lost in a destroyed city unable to find his way out, and then Stalin would appear before him to lead the way.[23]

Vyacheslav Molotov lived until the age of ninety-six, eventually dying on 8 November 1986. He was survived by his colleague in the administration of the Terror, Lazar Kaganovich, who lived until the age of ninety-seven, dying on 25 July 1991. It was just long enough for Kaganovich to watch the collapse of the Soviet Union unfold on his colour television. 'It's a catastrophe', were the last words his maid heard him say.[24]

If they survived the Terror, most of those who signed the lists lived on into retirement untouched. Some of the former NKVD executioners suffered psychological breakdowns, perhaps a self-inflicted form of retribution. In 1982, the writer Yuri Druzhinikov interviewed Spiridon Kartashov, a seventy-nine-year-old former member of the Special Department of the Tavda district of the Ural OGPU. The aged Kartashov was living in conditions which 'resembled a flophouse' but was nevertheless willing to talk openly about the methods he had once employed:

> I figure, that thirty-seven people were shot dead by me personally, and I sent even more to the camps. I can kill people so that the shot won't be heard . . . The secret's this: I make them open their mouth and I shoot down their throat. I'd only be splashed by warm blood, like eau-de-cologne, and it doesn't make a sound. That I can do – kill. If I didn't have seizures, I wouldn't have taken my pension so soon. I had seizures even before the war, but I didn't pay them any mind. And then during the war I went into the hospital.

In his medical records, Druzhnikov discovered that Kartashov had suffered from 'epilepsy aggravated by nervous exhaustion'. He was treated in a psychiatric hospital where the doctors listened to his confessions about how he 'ran the children through with a bayonet and trampled them on a horse'.[25]

During the early period of the Stalinist Terror, Bolshevik intellectuals spoke darkly of the violence of the French Revolution, not yet realising their own Thermidor would be far worse. In the mid nineteenth century the Russian writer Alexander Hertzen wrote of his fear of 'Gengis Khan with a telegraph', never suspecting that Stalin would belittle his premonition. In 1923, Vladimir Zazubrin wrote a novella called *The Chip* in which he described how:

> Future 'enlightened' human societies will rid themselves of their superfluous or criminal members by means of gas chambers, various acids, electricity or deadly bacteria. Then there will be no cellars and no 'bloodthirsty' Chekists. Learned scholars with learned expressions on their faces will quite calmly put live people into huge retorts and test tubes, and with all kinds of chemical compounds and reactions and distillations imaginable will turn them into shoe polish, vaseline, and lubricating oil.

For such dystopic speculations, Zazubrin was himself executed in the Terror of 1938.[26]

Now we may wait in turn for 'Stalin with a retinal eye scanner' and peer darkly down avenues of our own destruction. Perhaps our historical awareness will protect us from the creation of future tragedies of an electronic age to rival those of our recent past, and fend off our capacity to believe in a delusion. In Moscow during the 1990s, a historical exhibition was presented by the Russian state archives. An old man peered over an original copy of the Ribbentrop–Molotov Pact very intently before announcing: 'I heard about this, but I never believed it.' He then fainted over the cabinet and shattered the glass.[27]

The defining feature of the history of the Soviet Union, beyond which all else pales into insignificance, was the murder of millions of innocent citizens by the state. The Revolution began a process of imprisonment and killing that continued in virtually every country in which it was attempted. For while culturally distinct, the social experiment always reached a similar conclusion over the fate of those the regime had judged to be its 'enemies'. The 'Killing Fields' of Cambodia were not a 'socialist aberration' on the part of Pol Pot so much as the Stalinist principle applied to one third of the population. The Cambodia of the 1970s was therefore not an anomaly. It was repetition. Even in 2008, the 'corrective labour camps' still exist in North Korea and China. Yet the world shuts its eyes and looks the other way.

We know that mankind has always been capable of demonising

our fellow man. But where this cruelty comes from, this ability to kill en masse, defies explanation. The true nature of our humanity is a recurring argument, and one which occupied the minds of the greatest thinkers of the Enlightenment. In 1793, the philosopher Immanuel Kant reflected: 'It will be noted that the propensity to evil is here established (as regards actions) in the human being, even the best; and so it also must be if it is to be proved that the propensity to evil among human beings is universal, or, which amounts here to the same thing, that it is woven into human nature.' Beneath the veneer of our civilisation lies the warning of Immanuel Kant.[28]

28

THOMAS SGOVIO REDUX

My days have raced past like the sloping
run of deer. The time of happiness was briefer
than the flicker of an eyelash. Out of one final effort
I squeezed only a handful of the ashes of delight.

Osip Mandelstam, My Days Have Raced Past[1]

After his return to America, Thomas Sgovio lived for a while in Buffalo, the city in which he was born and raised. There he worked as a draughtsman, lived a happily married life and raised a family. In Buffalo, he visited the Volat family to deliver the news that Marvin Volat had died in a concentration camp in Kolyma. At the time, the family had refused to believe him and clung to their hope that Marvin might still be alive in Russia.[2]

During the day Thomas worked to support his family, but at night he laboured on his memoir, *Dear America*, which was published in a very small print run and soon fell out of print. Undeterred he gave lectures on his experience at the University of Buffalo, and used his artistic talent to draw illustrations of the scenes he had witnessed in Kolyma, which he donated to the Hoover Institution in Stanford, California. And in this way, he kept the promise he had made to the prisoners in the camps. He let the world know of the suffering that had been inflicted upon them.[3]

Eventually Thomas Sgovio retired, settling to live quietly in a suburb of Phoenix, Arizona. There he grew old under the desert sun, as far from the climate he had escaped as it was possible to find. In Phoenix he lived a normal life, one of the last survivors of a forgotten emigration, his grey hair and worn body hiding the glinting miracle of his life – the most extraordinary human history walking anonymously down a Phoenix sidewalk. His return defied every expectation.

In his retirement, Thomas was interviewed every once in a while by a local journalist or a documentary filmmaker who had learned of his existence through the Hoover Institution. Then the old man would come alive with a passionate advocacy that belied his years. As he spoke in a frantic rasp, his eyes would fill with tears and his lips stumble over his words in a struggle to articulate his experience, and a continued effort to justify the sacrifices of others who had kept him alive.[4] Most dearly of all, Thomas Sgovio wanted a younger generation to understand the terrible events that had taken place in Kolyma and across the Soviet Union. Although each explanation reawakened his trauma and caused him such obvious anguish, he willingly accepted his role as a historical witness of the Terror until the moment of his death. In fulfilling his perceived duty, this quiet American again showed evidence of the courage that had kept him alive.

In 1996, Thomas celebrated his eightieth birthday, an old age he had never expected to reach. His face was wrinkled, but his brown eyes still shone with the passion of a twenty-year-old baseball player. In 1995, he asked Chuck Hawley, a local journalist, 'Is that why God spared me? To come back fifty years later and tell the story? I don't know . . . We always said, if any of us survived, we would tell the world about Kolyma . . . I have kept my promise.' Having kept his promise, he was at peace.[5]

Fate, however, had one final hand to play. That year, Thomas Sgovio was shown a copy of his NKVD file, recently released by the Yeltsin government. On page eighty, he learned the details of how Lucy Flaxman had informed on him. The file revealed that she had reported his comment that 'Soviet power does not rest on the love of its subjects. It rests on fear'. Lucy had also passed on the information that Thomas was waiting for a war between the USSR and USA because if America won, he might be free. In 1948, she added that she had seen a copy of the *Saturday Evening Post*, an 'anti-Soviet' magazine, in his apartment.[6] Sitting back in his armchair with the file, Thomas remarked to the journalist Alan Cullinson who was interviewing him over the telephone: 'She was not a very courageous person. It was a frightening time for everyone.'[7]

At least there were happier times to remember. Sitting in the living room of his home in Phoenix, Thomas Sgovio could recall the

American baseball teams of Gorky Park. And, if only for a moment in a daydream, his old legs returned to their youthful state, running around the bases on a summer afternoon.

The following year, on 3 July 1997, Thomas Sgovio died.

NOTES

1 THE JOADS OF RUSSIA

1 Photo from the collection of Thomas Sgovio, courtesy of Joanne Sgovio, published in article by Alan Cullinson, 'A Secret Revealed: Stalin's Police Killed Americans', Associated Press, 23 November 1997.

2 *New York Times*, 17 November 1931, quoted in 'American Jobless Begin National March to Washington', *Moscow News*, 8 December 1931.

3 *United News*, Vol. 2, R.86; Vol.7, R.332; Vol 8 R.480, National Archives II, College Park, Maryland; Frank Tannenbaum, 'The Prospect of Violent Revolution in the United States', *Scribner's Magazine*, New York, May 1931.

4 Irving Howe and Lewis Coser, *The American Communist Party – A Critical History 1919–1957*, (Boston: Beacon Press, 1957), p.192.

5 Inaugural Addresses of the Presidents of the United States (Washington DC: US Government Print Office, 1952).

6 Peter G. Filene, *Americans and the Soviet Experiment, 1917–1933* (Cambridge, MA: Harvard University Press, 1967), p.255.

7 Mikhail Ilin, trans. George S. Counts and Nucia P. Lodge, *New Russia's Primer: The Story of the Five-Year Plan* (Boston: Houghton Mifflin, 1931), pp.148–160.

8 Andrew Smith, *I Was a Soviet Worker* (London: Robert Hale, 1937), p.24.

9 '6,000 Artisans Going to Russia Glad to Take Wages in Roubles' in *Business Week*, 2 September 1931, pp. 36–37.

10 'A Soviet Call for Yankee Skill', *Literary Digest*, 19 September 1931; *Business Week*, 7 October 1931.

11 'Russia Will Curb Job-Seekers' Entry', *New York Times*, 18 March 1932; 'Too Many Americans are Going to Russia', *New York Times*, 17 April 1932; 'American Immigrants in Russia', Ruth Kennell and Milly Bennett, *American Mercury*, April 1932, pp.463–472.

12 361.11 Employees/315, RG 59, National Archives II, College Park, Maryland.

13 861.5511/9, RG 59, National Archives II, College Park, Maryland.

14 Walter Duranty, 'Moscow Expects Immigration Soon', *New York Times*, 4 February 1931.

15 Albert Parry, 'A Gold Rush To Moscow', *Outlook*, 15 July 1931, p.331.

16 Albert Parry, 'A Gold Rush To Moscow', *Outlook*, 15 July 1931, p.338.

17 Boris Pilnyak, 'Moscow the Magnet', *Sovietland*, Issue 2, 1935, Moscow.
18 Elbridge Durbrow, 6 October 1934, Enc. No.1 to Despatch No. 156, RG 59, National Archives II, College Park, Maryland.
19 Radio broadcast, 11 October 1931, quoted from 'A Little Talk on America' by George Bernard Shaw (London: Friends of the Soviet Union, 1932).

2 BASEBALL IN GORKY PARK

1 Wedding is a suburb of Berlin, from *Za Industrializatsu*, Enclosure 3, to Despatch 8389, Riga, Latvia, 13 January 1932, National Archives II, College Park, Maryland.
2 'Reds Draft Many from US Trades', *Washington Post*, 1 November 1931.
3 Ruth Kennell and Milly Bennett, 'American Immigrants in Russia', *American Mercury*, April 1932, pp.463–472.
4 Letter from Anna Louise Strong to Eleanor Roosevelt, 29 January 1935, Eleanor Roosevelt Papers, 1933–1945, Library of Congress manuscripts, Washington DC.
5 'From a Professor's Diary', *Moscow News*, 12 October 1931; 'It Feels Good to Arrive in USSR Says American Workers', *Moscow News*, 17 October 1931.
6 'Admit Us to USSR', *Moscow News*, 12 January 1932.
7 Walter Duranty, 'Immigration Now an Issue in Soviet', *New York Times*, 14 March 1932, p.8.
8 Eugene Lyons, *Assignment in Utopia: On the Experiences of an American Journalist in the USSR* (London: Harrap, 1938), p.88.
9 'Hundreds at "Moscow News" birthday party', *Moscow News*, 26 October 1931.
10 'A Visit to Schools', *Moscow Pioneer*, No. 3, March 1932, p.4; Despatch No. 286, Riga, 22 April 1932, RG59, National Archives II, College Park, Maryland; 'Epic of Working Class Strength', *Moscow News*, 11 November 1931.
11 'How We Marched', *Moscow News*, 6 May 1932.
12 'Russian Athletes Want Baseball', *Moscow Daily News*, 14 May 1932; 'Baseball for USSR', *Moscow Daily News*, 1932; 'Russian Team Keen for Baseball – Put up Good Game', *Moscow Daily News*, 3 July 1932.
13 'Americans Bring Baseball to the Soviet Union', *Moscow News*, 20 May 1932; 'Baseball is Spreading', *Moscow Daily News*, 5 June 1932; Robert Edelman, *Serious Fun: A History of Spectator Sports in the USSR* (New York: Oxford University Press, 1993), p.73; 'Stalin Auto Plant Workers Take to Baseball', *Moscow Daily News*, 24 June 1934.
14 'Anglo-American School Challenges Leningrad Pupils', *Moscow Daily News*, 20 November 1932; 'English School Moves', *Moscow News*, 22 November 1931; 'Public Schools Here, Abroad', *Moscow News*, 27 February 1932.
15 James E. Abbe, *I Photograph Russia* (London: Harrap, 1935), p.272; MID 2070, 23 October 1929, RG 165, National Archives II, College Park, Maryland.

16 Elizabeth Hampel, *Yankee Bride in Moscow* (New York: Liveright, 1941) p.301.

17 'What do English Speaking Children Here Read?', *Moscow Daily News*, 8 July 1934.

18 861.01/A19, RG59, National Archives II, College Park, Maryland; Vladimir Zazubrin, 'The Chip: A Story about a Chip and about Her', 24 April 1923, trans. Graham Roberts from Oleg Chukhontsev (ed.), *Dissonant Voices* (London: Harvill, 1991) p.7.

19 'Anglo-American School Pupils Hold Own Court', *Moscow Daily News*, 29 January 1933.

20 'It's Such a Contrast to Boston', *Moscow Daily News*, 6 November 1934.

21 'Moscow Baseball Team Beats Visiting Gorki Nine by 16 to 5', *Moscow Daily News*, 8 June 1934; 'Shortcomings of Moscow–Gorki Baseball Game', *Moscow Daily News*, 10 June 1934; 'Baseball Asks for a Helping Hand', *Moscow Daily News*, 1934; 'Moscow, Gorki Players, Physical Culture Head Discuss Baseball', *Moscow Daily News*, 9 June 1934.

22 'Karelia Foreign Youth Club Wants to Get Into Inter-City Baseball', *Moscow Daily News*, 12 May 1934; 'Baseball Grows in Karelia', *Moscow Daily News*, c. 24 June 1934; 'Suggests Baseball Spartakiade for Players Here', *Moscow Daily News*, 14 August 1934.

23 'Moscow Baseball Team Leaves for Intercity Series in Karelia', *Moscow Daily News*, 16 July 1934; Mayme Sevander, Red Exodus: Finnish–American Emigration to Russia (Duluth, MN: Oscat, 1993), p.168; 'Moscow Team Drops Second Game in North', *Moscow Daily News*, 21 July 1934; 'Moscow Baseball Team's Faults, Misfortunes', *Moscow Daily News*, 4 August 1934; 'Missing Ball Players Found Gathering the Harvest', *Moscow Daily News*, August 1934.

24 'Baseball Comes to the USSR to Stay', *Moscow Daily News*, September 1934; 'Moscow Baseball Team Thanks Supporters as Season Ends', *Moscow Daily News*, 1934; 'The Hot Dog Makes its Bow', *Moscow Daily News*, December 1934.

25 'Baseball and Soccer at Dynamo', *Moscow Daily News*, 24 July 1932.

26 Jerzy Gliksman, *Tell The West* (New York: National Committee for a Free Europe, 1948), p.9.

27 'Foreign Workers to Stage Baseball Game at OGPU Labor Commune', *Moscow Daily News*, 17 June 1934; 'Teams Line Up for Baseball Tournament', *Moscow Daily News*, 21 February 1935.

3 'LIFE HAS BECOME MORE JOYFUL!'

1 'Record Attendance at Foreign Baseball Practice', *Moscow Daily News*, 26 1935.

2 Paul Robeson 'I Breathe Freely', Interview in Moscow by Julia Dorn, *New Theatre*, July 1935, p.5; Paul Robeson, Philip S. Foner (ed.), *Paul Robeson Speaks* (London: Quartet, 1978), p.102.

3 Paul Robeson Jr., *The Undiscovered Paul Robeson: An Artist's Journey, 1898–1939* (New York: John Wiley), p.280.

4 'Warm Welcome for Robeson at Foreign Workers' Club', *Moscow Daily News*, 2 January 1935.

5 'I am Home', interview by Vern Smith, *Daily Worker*, 15 January 1935 from Robeson, *Paul Robeson Speaks*, p.95.

6 Thomas Sgovio, *Dear America* (Kenmore, NY: Partners' Press, 1979), p.106.

7 Ibid., p.103.

8 Enc. No. 3 to Despatch no. 1133 of the Legation at Riga, Latvia, 8 February 1933, RG 59, National Archives II, College Park, Maryland.

9 Irena Wiley, *Around the Globe in Twenty Years* (New York: McKay, 1962), p.6.

10 Archibald Forman, *From Baltic to Black Sea* (London: Sampson Low,1933), p.86.

11 Thomas Sgovio interview with George Kovacs, tapes courtesy of David Elkind, LiveWire Media, San Francisco.

12 361.11, Employees/179, RG 59, National Archives II, College Park, Maryland.

13 *Moscow Daily News*, 2 August 1934.

14 Eugene Lyons, *Assignment in Utopia* (London: Harrap, 1938), p.421.

15 'Anglo-American Chorus to Give Concert, Jan. 6', *Moscow Daily News*, 28 December 1935.

16 'English Chorus Invited to Sing April 14', *Moscow Daily News*, 5 April 1935.

17 Thomas Sgovio, *Dear America*, p.112.

18 Ibid., p.29; Alan Cullinson, 'A Secret Revealed: Stalin's Police Killed Americans', Associated Press, 23 November 1997.

19 Walter Duranty, 'Million are Held in Russian Camps, 200,000 in Forests', *New York Times*, 3 February 1931.

20 Diane P. Koenker and Ronald D. Bachman (eds), *Revelations from the Russian Archives, Documents in English Translation* (Washington DC: Library of Congress, 1997), p.156.

21 Eugene Lyons, *Assignment in Utopia*, p.58.

22 Thomas Sgovio, *Dear America*, pp.7–8.

23 Boris Agapov, 'Abundance', *Sovietland*, April 1936, Moscow.

24 Thomas Sgovio, *Dear America*, pp.7–8.

25 Margaret Wettlin, *Fifty Russian Winters: An American Woman's Life in the Soviet Union* (New York: Pharos, 1992), p.102.

26 Sheila Fitzpatrick, *Everyday Stalinism – Ordinary Life In Extraordinary Times: Soviet Russia in the 1930s* (New York: OUP, 1999), p.90.

27 Thomas Sgovio, *Dear America*, p.119.

4 'FORDIZATSIA'

1 Alexander Blok, Retribution foreword, quoted from *Selected Poems*, trans. Alex Miller (Moscow: Progress, 1991).

2 Despatch No. 286, Riga, 22 April 1932, RG59, National Archives II, College Park, Maryland.

3 'Baseball Progresses Slowly but Surely at Kharkov Plant', *Moscow Daily News*, 3 July 1934.

4 Charles E. Sorensen, *My Forty Years with Ford* (New York: Norton, 1956), p.182; Peter G. Filene, *Americans and the Soviet Experiment, 1917–1933* (Cambridge, MA: Harvard University Press, 1967), p.117.

5 'Henry Ford Conquers Russia', *Outlook*, 29 June 1927.

6 Peter G. Filene, *Americans and the Soviet Experiment, 1917–1933*, p.124.

7 Carol Gelderman, *Henry Ford: Wayward Capitalist* (New York: Dial Press, 1981), pp.270–1.

8 Harry Bennett, *We Never Called Him Henry* (New York: Fawcett, 1951), p.32.

9 Charles E. Sorensen, *My Forty Years With Ford* p.145; Carol Gelderman, *Henry Ford: Wayward Capitalist*, p.53.

10 B. H. Berghoff, Report of the Ford Delegation to Russia and the USSR, April–August 1926; Acc 49, Box 1A, Benson Ford Research Center, Dearborn, MI.

11 Russian State Archive of Socio-Political History, Moscow – RGASPI, fond 17, opis 166, delo 296, list 5.

12 Charles E. Sorensen, *My Forty Years With Ford*, p.183.

13 Walter Duranty, 'Talk of Ford Favor Thrills Moscow', *New York Times*, 17 February 1928.

14 Contract 31 May 1929, Acc. 19, Box 1, Benson Ford Research Center, Dearborn, MI.

15 Robert Scoon, 'Those Communist Model A's', *The Restorer*, Vol. 14, Issue 6, March–April 1970; Benson Ford Research Center, Dearborn, MI.

16 Charles E. Sorensen, *My Forty Years With Ford*, pp.185–7.

17 Charles Sorensen, *Oral History*, Amtorg 1953, Acc. 65, Box 66; Benson Ford Research Center, Dearborn, MI.

18 Victor Herman, *Coming out of the Ice: An Unexpected Life* (New York: Harcourt Brace Jovanovich, 1979) pp.10–17.

19 Acc. 818, Box 1, Folder 1 of 4; Benson Ford Research Center, Dearborn, MI.

20 Victor Herman, *Coming Out of the Ice: An Unexpected Life*, p.27.

21 Eugene Lyons, Assignment in Utopia, p.351.

22 Kurt Schultz, 'Building The Soviet Detroit: the Construction of the Nizhni-Novgorod Automobile Factory, 1927-1932', Slavic Review, Spring 1990

23 Robert Scoon, 'More About Those Communist Model A's', *The Restorer*, Vol. 15, Issue 6, March/April 1971; Benson Ford Archives, Dearborn, MI.

24 Ellery Walter, *Russia's Decisive Year* (London: Hutchinson, 1932), p.143; 'Collective Feeding is Death Blow to Kitchen Drudgery', *Moscow Daily News*, 9 May, 1932.

25 Susan Buck-Morss, *Dreamworld and Catastrophe: The Passing of Mass Utopia in East and West* (Cambridge, MA: MIT Press, 2000), p.166.

26 '*Ekonomicheskaya Zhizn*', 1 November 1931, RGAE, f.7620, op.1, D.75, l.8906. From list compiled by Professor Boris Shpotov, Institute of World History, Russian Academy of Sciences, Moscow.

27 Ruth Kennell and Milly Bennett, 'American Immigrants in Russia', *American Mercury*, April 1932; 'In the Fatherland of the Proletarians of All Countries', *Za Industrializatsiu*, 7 November 1931, enc. 3 to despatch 8389, Riga, Latvia, 13 January 1932, RG59, National Archives II, College Park, Maryland.

28 Victor Herman, *Coming out of the Ice*, p.38.

5 'THE LINDBERGH OF RUSSIA'

1 Interviewed by Emil Ludwig, published in the *Moscow Daily News*, 5 June 1932.

2 Grant Hildebrand, *Designing for Industry: the Architecture of Albert Kahn* (Cambridge, MA: MIT Press, 1974), p.128; Mira Wilkins and Frank Ernest Hill, *American Business Abroad: Ford on Six Continents* (Detroit, MI: Wayne State University Press, 1964), p.217.

3 Robert Robinson, *Black on Red: Forty-Four Years Inside the Soviet Union* (Washington DC: Acropolis, 1988), p.29.

4 Maxim Gorky, *Those Who Built Stalingrad: As Told by Themselves*, (London: Martin Lawrence,1934), p.226.

5 'Crisis Turns Ford Plant into "Madhouse"', *Moscow Daily News*, 18 October 1932.

6 'Soviet Union Will Ask Fired Ford Men to Work Here', *Moscow Daily News*, 20 October 1932.

7 Robert Robinson, *Black on Red: Forty-Four Years Inside the Soviet Union*, p.66.

8 Walter Duranty, 'Americans Essay Color Bar in Soviet', *New York Times*, 10 August 1930, p.9.

9 William Henry Chamberlin, *Russia's Iron Age* (London: Duckworth, 1935), p.363.

10 'The Fascist Lewis is Sent Away From the USSR', *Trud*, 31 August 1930, 361.11/4045, RG59, National Archives II, College Park, Maryland.

11 '450 Americans Reported Held Captive by Reds', *Chicago Sunday Tribune*, 21 September, 1930.

12 Robert Robinson, *Black on Red: Forty-Four Years Inside the Soviet Union*, 1988) p.82.

13 'Black Blank', *Time*, 24 December 1934.

14 Robert Robinson, *Black on Red: Forty-Four Years Inside the Soviet Union*, pp.95–107.

15 Robert Scoon, 'Those Communist Model A's', *The Restorer*, Vol.14, Issue 6, March–April 1970, Benson Ford Research Center, Dearborn, MI.

16 8 July 1932, 861.911/1335, RG 59, National Archives II, College Park, Maryland.

17 Andrew Smith, *I Was a Soviet Worker* (London: Robert Hale, 1937), p.181.

18 'Memo on Autostroy', 861.797/31, 7 December 1932, RG 59; Enc. No. 1, to despatch 65, from Legation at Riga, Latvia, interview with John Karsky, 8 February 1932, RG59, National Archives II, College Park, Maryland.

19 Victor Reuther, *Commitment and Betrayal: Foreign Workers at the Gorky Auto Works*, ed. Paul T. Christensen (Unpublished: 2004), p.63.

20 '"Safety First" Psychology Needed at Nizhni', *Moscow News*, 30 May 1932, p.7.

21 'The Reminiscences of Mr Frank Bennett, Ford Motor Company Archives', Oral History Section, November 1954, Benson Ford Research Center, Dearborn, MI.

22 Susan Buck-Morss, *Dreamworld and Catastrophe: The Passing of Mass Utopia in East and West*, p.83.

23 Gene Tunney, 'So This Is Russia!', *Collier's*, 3 October 1931.

24 'Scare Stories of "Nizhny Defeat" Unwarranted, Says U.S. Engineers', *Moscow News*, 23 April 1932, p.3; '"Swellest Union Convention Ever Witnessed" say USA Delegates', *Moscow News*, 28 April 1932, p.3.

25 'The Man Who Abandoned Detroit', *Pravda*, 26 April 1932.

26 'At work and play – Americans at Gorki Help Build New Life', *Moscow News*, 12 May 1934, p.3.

27 Victor Herman, *Coming out of the Ice: An Unexpected Life*, pp.50–2.

28 Ibid., pp.54–6.

29 Ibid., pp.58–60

30 Victor Herman, *Coming out of the Ice: An Unexpected Life*, pp.75–6; 'Detroit Boy Wins Fame as "Lindy of Russia"', *Detroit Evening Times*, 18 February 1935.

31 Victor Herman, *Coming out of the Ice: An Unexpected Life*, pp.76–81

6 'THE CAPTURED AMERICANS'

1 Eugene Lyons, *Assignment in Utopia* (London: Harrap, 1938), p.240.

2 Eugene Lyons, *Assignment in Utopia*, pp.519–523.

3 Angus Ward, letter to Secretary of State, No. 484, 3 April 1935, 130–Traczewski, Walter. RG 59, National Archives II, College Park, Maryland.

4 Report No. 11, 580, 7 August 1931, Berlin, RG 165, National Archives II, College Park, Maryland.

5 Malcolm Muggeridge, *Winter in Moscow* (London: Eyre & Spottiswoode, 1934), p.ix.

6 Walter Duranty, 'Russians Hungry But Not Starving', *New York Times*, 31 March 1933, p.13.

7 James E. Abbe, *I Photograph Russia* (London: Harrap, 1935), p.280.

8 Eugene Lyons, *Assignment in Utopia*, p.237; State Archive of the Russian Federation, Moscow, GARF, fond 5515, opis 33, delo 26, listy 061, 062.

9 Willis B. Clemmit, 18 May 1935, Russian Subject Collection, Box 4, File 4, Hoover Institute, Stanford, CA; Eugene Lyons, *Assignment in Utopia*, p. 576.

10 Walter Duranty, 'Abundance Found in North Caucasus', *New York Times*, 14 September 1933, p.14.

11 S. J. Taylor, *Stalin's Apologist: Walter Duranty, The* New York Times' *Man in Moscow* (New York: Oxford University Press, 1990), p.221.

12 James E. Abbe, *I Photograph Russia*, p.32.

13 Edmund Wilson, *Red, Black, Blond, and Olive: Studies in Four Civilizations* (New York: Oxford University Press, 1956), p.381.

14 James E. Abbe, *I Photograph Russia*, p.181.

15 Victor Kravchenko, *I Chose Freedom: The Personal and Political Life of a Soviet Official* (New York: Scribner's, 1946), p.83.

16 James E. Abbe, *I Photograph Russia*, p.22.

17 Charles Ciliberti, *Backstairs Mission in Moscow* (New York: Booktab Press, 1946), pp.21–2.

18 Charles Thayer diary, 17 October 1933, Box 6, Charles Thayer papers, Harry S. Truman Library, Independence, MO.

19 James E. Abbe, *I Photograph Russia*, p.181–2.

20 Charles Thayer diary, 10 October 1933, Box 6, Charles Thayer papers, Harry S. Truman Library, Independence, MO.

21 Zara Witkin, *An American Engineer in Stalin's Russia: The Memoirs of Zara Witkin, 1932–1934*, ed. Michael Gelb (Berkeley: University of California Press, 1991), pp.127–134.

22 John N. Hazard, *Recollections of a Pioneering Sovietologist* (New York: Oceana, 1987), p.44.

23 Eve Garrette Grady, *Seeing Red: Behind the Scenes in Russia Today* (New York: Brewer, Warren and Putnam, 1931), pp.61–62.

24 'Roosevelt Confers on Russian Policy – Consults Walter Duranty in Regard to Suggestions That Our Attitude Should Change', *New York Times*, 26 July 1932, p.9; Loy Henderson, *A Question of Trust – The Origins of US–Soviet Diplomatic Relations: The Memoirs of Loy W. Henderson*, ed. George W. Baer (Stanford, CA: Hoover Institution Press, 1986), p.217; Walter Duranty, 'The Soviet and Us', *New York Times*, 31 July 1932, p.E1; 'Roosevelt Confers on Russian Policy', *New York Times*, 26 July 1932, p.1.

25 Walter Duranty, 'America Delights Envoy of Soviet', *New York Times*, 8 November 1933, p.25.

26 Dennis J. Dunn, *Caught Between Roosevelt and Stalin: America's Ambassadors to Moscow* (Lexington, KY: University Press of Kentucky, c.1998), p.37.

27 President Franklin Roosevelt's office files, 1933–1945, 2 May 1934; Part Two: Diplomatic Correspondence 'Russia', FDR Library, Hyde Park, New York.

28 Keith David Eagles, *Ambassador Joseph E. Davies and American–Soviet Relations, 1937–1941* (New York : Garland, 1987), p.27.

29 Peter G. Filene, *Americans and the Soviet Experiment 1917–1933*, pp.237–240.

30 Fred E. Beale, *Proletarian Journey: New England, Gastonia, Moscow* (New York: Hillman-Curl,1937), pp.295–307.

31 Loy Henderson, *A Question of Trust – The Origins of US–Soviet Diplomatic Relations: The Memoirs of Loy W. Henderson*, p.248.

32 711.61/343 2/8, RG 59, National Archives II, College Park, Maryland.

33 George Kennan, *Memoirs: 1925–1950* (London: Hutchinson, 1967), pp.50–53.

34 Robert Conquest, 'How Liberals Funked It', *Hoover Digest*, No.3, 1999.

35 Walter Duranty, 'President Reveals Pact', *New York Times*, 18 November 1933, p.1.

36 Eugene Lyons, *Assignment in Utopia*, p.346.

37 Yuri Druzhnikov, *Informer 001: The Myth of Pavlik Morozov* (New Brunswick, NJ: Transaction, 1997), p.96.

38 Eugene Lyons, *Assignment in Utopia*, pp.241–2.

39 Ibid., p.433.

40 Linton Wells, *Blood on the Moon: The Autobiography of Linton Wells* (London: Hamish Hamilton, 1937), pp.347–8.

7 'THE ARRIVAL OF SPRING'

1 Handwritten letter, John Match, 6 May 1935. Vol. 348, Moscow Post files, RG 84, National Archives II, College Park, Maryland.

2 Loy Henderson Papers, File 'Memoirs Vol. 9', 1938–42, Box 20, Library of Congress manuscripts, Washington DC.

3 Loy Henderson, *A Question of Trust – The Origins of US–Soviet Diplomatic Relations: The Memoirs of Loy W. Henderson*, pp.369–70.

4 Elbridge Durbrow collection, Box 68, interview with John Mason, 5 May 1981, Hoover Institution, Stanford, CA.

5 'The Stealthful Soviet Century', 9 July 1996, p.34, Elbridge Durbrow collection, Box 41, Hoover Institution, Stanford, CA.

6 American Consulate 1934, Vol. 94, RG 84, National Archives II, College Park, Maryland.

7 Enc. No. 1 to Despatch 65, from Legation at Riga, Latvia, interview with John Karsky, 8 February 1932, RG59, National Archives II, College Park, Maryland.

8 Ibid.

9 361.1115/43, RG 59, National Archive, Washington DC.

10 861.5017LC/678, 10 June 1933, RG 59, National Archives II, College Park, Maryland.

11 124.61/101, Decimal file 1930–1939, Box 0793, RG 59, National Archives II, College Park, Maryland.

12 Irena Wiley, *Around the Globe in Twenty Years*, p.11.

13 Ibid., p.13.

14 Lindsay Parrott, 'Bullitt Home in Moscow to Have 45 Rooms', Universal Service Special, 25 February 1934.

15 William C. Bullitt, letter to Eugene Lyons, 2 November 1937, Box 22, File 15, Bullitt papers, Yale University, New Haven, CT.

16 1 January 1934, William Bullitt in letter to the President, Franklin Roosevelt's office files, 1933–1945; Part Two: Diplomatic correspondence 'Russia', FDR Library, Hyde Park, New York.

17 22 May 1934, Charles Thayer diary, Charles Thayer papers, Harry S. Truman Library, Independence, MO.

18 'Retreat from Moscow', *Time*, 7 September 1936, p.12.

19 Charles Thayer diary, 14 April–20 May 1934, p.53, Charles Thayer papers, Harry S. Truman Library, Independence, MO.

20 William C. Bullitt, *For the President Personal and Secret – Correspondence Between Franklin D. Roosevelt and William C. Bullitt*, ed. Orville H. Bullitt (Boston: Houghton Mifflin, 1972), p.62; 'Envoy Bullitt in Plane Crash', Universal Service Special Cable, June 1934.

21 Ed Falkowski, 'Moscow Children Find Their Wonderland', *Moscow Daily News*, September 1934.

22 Franklin D. Roosevelt letter to Bullitt, 7 January 1934 in *For the President Personal and Secret – Correspondence Between Franklin D. Roosevelt and William C. Bullitt*, p.74.

23 21 April 1934, 840.6, Moscow Post files, RG 84, National Archives II, College Park, Maryland.

24 Charles Thayer diary, 14 April–20 May 1934, p.53a, Charles Thayer papers, Harry S. Truman Library, Independence, MO.

25 Harold Denny, 'Americans Mark the Fourth in Russia', *New York Times*, 5 July 1934.

26 Reels 16–19, Julian Bryan Collection, Library of Congress, Washington DC.

27 Franklin D. Roosevelt letter to Bullitt, 29 August 1934, Bullitt, *For the President Personal and Secret – Correspondence Between Franklin D. Roosevelt and William C. Bullitt*, p.95.

28 Vol.335, Moscow Post Files, RG 84, National Archives II, College Park, Maryland.

29 'Baseball Comes to the USSR to Stay – 1934 Summarized', *Moscow Daily News*, June 1934.

30 J. A. E. Curtis, *Manuscripts Don't Burn: Mikhail Bulgakov, A Life in Letters and Diaries* (London: Bloomsbury, 1991), pp.198–9; Irena Wiley, *Around the Globe in Twenty Years*, pp.31–5; Elbridge Durbrow, 'The Stealthful Soviet Century', 9 July 1996, p.41, Elbridge Durbrow Collection, Box 41, Hoover Institution, Stanford, CA.

31 Mikhail Bulgakov, *The Master and Margarita*, trans. Richard Pevear and Larissa Volkhonsky (London: Penguin, 1997), pp.261–273; Charles Thayer, *Bears in the Caviar* (London: Michael Joseph, 1952) pp.144–154.

32 William C. Bullitt Papers, Yale University, New Haven, CT.

33 William C. Bullitt, letter to Judge Moore, 30 March 1936, Bullitt, *For the President Personal and Secret*, p.150.

34 Anna Larina, *This I Cannot Forget: The Memoirs of Nikolai Bukharin's Widow* (London: Hutchinson, 1993), p.233.

35 William C. Bullitt to Secretary of State, 20 April 1936; 861.01/2120, RG 59, National Archives II, College Park, Maryland.

36 Letter from Loy Henderson to William C. Bullitt at State Department dated Moscow 26 June 1936, William C. Bullitt Papers, Yale University, New Haven, CT.

37 'Found the Russians Unfed and Unhappy', *New York Times*, 28 September 1931, p.11.

38 Reminiscences of Bredo Berghoff, Ford Motor Company Archives, Oral History Section, November 1957, Benson Ford Research Centre, Dearborn, MI.

39 William Henry Chamberlin, *Confessions of an Individualist* (London: Duckworth, 1940), p.170.

40 Elizabeth Hampel, *Yankee Bride in Moscow*, p.183.

41 'First Baseball Practice Game of Season', *Moscow Daily News*, c. 2 August 1936.

42 'Trial of Trotskyite–Zinovyevite Terrorist Center', *Moscow Daily News*, 23 August 1936.

43 'It is Because Everyone is Very Afraid', Edmund Wilson, *Red, Black, Blond, and Olive* (New York: Oxford University Press, 1956), pp.218–9.

44 861.74/73, 6 February 1934, RG 59, National Archives II, College Park, Maryland.

45 Despatch No. 1620, 27 May 1936, American Embassy, Moscow, RG 59, National Archive, Washington DC.

46 Whitman Bassow, *The Moscow Correspondents* (New York: William Morrow, 1988), p.84.

47 'American Embassy Announcement', *Moscow Daily News*, 28 February 1935, p.4.

48 Loy Henderson, 'Memoirs Vol. 7' Ch 10–13, 1934–38, Box 20, Loy Henderson Papers, Library of Congress Manuscripts, Washington DC.

49 'Russia, Pure Terror', *Time*, 17 December 1934.

50 'Retreat from Moscow', *Time*, 7 September 1936.

51 17 February 1933, 861.911/1403, RG 59, National Archives II, College Park, Maryland.

8 THE TERROR, THE TERROR

1 Rene Fueloep-Miller, *The Mind and Face of Bolshevism* (London: Putnams, 1927), p.270.

2 RTSKhiDNI, fond 629, op.1, d.150 ll.10–11, 17, 19 from Diane P. Koenker and Ronald D. Bachman (eds), *Revelations from the Russian Archives, Documents in English Translation* (Washington DC: Library of Congress, 1997), p.84.

3 Robert Conquest, *The Great Terror: A Reassessment* (London: Hutchinson, 1990), pp.38–40.

4 Irena Wiley, *Around the Globe in Twenty Years*, p.30.

5 Loy Henderson Papers, File 'Memoirs Vol 7', Ch10–13 1934–38, Box 20, Library of Congress manuscripts, Washington DC.

6 Irena Wiley, *Around the Globe In Twenty Years*, p.31.

7 *Moscow Daily News*, 31 December 1936.

8 Vadim J. Birstein, *The Perversion of Knowledge: The True Story of Soviet Science* (Boulder, CO: Westview, 2001), p.16.

9 Ivan Bunin, *Cursed Days: A Diary of Revolution*, trans. Thomas Gaiton Marullo (London: Phoenix Press, 2000), p.57.

10 Ibid., pp.138–139, 217.

11 361.00/11, RG 59, National Archives II, College Park, Maryland.

12 The NKVD HQ and local staff in 1939 numbered 365,839 people. From G. M. Ivanov, *GULAG v sisteme totalitarnogo gosudarstva* (GULAG in

the System of a Totalitarian State), (Moscow: 1997), p.161; Vladimir Petrov, *It Happens in Russia: Seven Years' Forced Labour in the Siberian Goldfields* (London: Eyre & Spottiswoode, 1951), p.17; Roy Medvedev, *Let History Judge: The Origins and Consequences of Stalinism*, trans. Colleen Taylor (London: Spokesman, 1976), p.341; Alexander Solzhenitysn, *The Gulag Archipelago, 1918–1956: An Experiment in Literary Investigation*, trans. Thomas P. Whitney; Vol.1 (London: Fontana, 1976), p.528.

13 Roy Medvedev, *Let History Judge: The Origins and Consequences of Stalinism*, pp.343, 351; Arnold Beichman, 'Sorting Pieces of the Russian Past', *Hoover Digest*, 2003, No.1; Hoover Institution, Stanford, CA.

14 Roy Medvedev, *Let History Judge: The Origins and Consequences of Stalinism*, p.344; Edvard Radzinsky, *Stalin: The First Biography Based on Explosive New Documents from Russia's Secret Archives*, trans. H. T. Willets (London: Hodder & Stoughton, 1996), p.390; Yuri Druzhnikov, *Informer 001: The Myth of Pavlik Morozov* (New Brunswick, New Jersey: Transaction, 1997), p.11.

15 Yuri Druzhnikov, *Informer 001: The Myth of Pavlik Morozov*, p.130; Kolya Voinov, *Outlaw: The Autobiography of a Soviet Waif* (London: Harvill, 1955) p.108.

16 Elena Bonner, *Mothers and Daughters* (London: Hutchinson, 1992), p.317; from Sheila Fitzpatrick, *Everyday Stalinism – Ordinary Life in Extraordinary Times: Soviet Russia in the 1930s* (New York: Oxford University Press, 1999), p.211.

17 Joseph Berger, *Shipwreck of a Generation: The Memoirs of Joseph Berger* (London: Harvill, 1971), p.14; Brian Moynahan, *The Russian Century: A Photographic History of Russia's 100 Years* (New York: Random House,1994), p.174; Nikita Khrushchev, Special Report to the 20th Congress of the CPSU, 24–25 February 1956; Dmitri Volkogonov, *Stalin: Triumph and Tragedy*; ed. and trans. Harold Shukman (London: Weidenfeld & Nicolson, 1991), p.200.

18 Marc Jansen and Nikita Petrov, *Stalin's Loyal Executioner: People's Commissar Nikolai Ezhov, 1895–1940* (Stanford, CA: Hoover Institution Press, 2002), p.100; Robert Robinson, *Black on Red: My Forty-Four Years Inside the Soviet Union*, p.116; Roy Medvedev, *Let History Judge: The Origins and Consequences of Stalinism*, p.284.

19 Aleksandr Orlov, *The Secret History of Stalin's Crimes* (New York: Random House, 1953), pp.226–8; Edvard Radzinsky, *Stalin*, p.337.

20 Dmitri Shepilov, from Marc Jansen and Nikita Petrov, *Stalin's Loyal Executioner: People's Commissar Nikolai Ezhov, 1895–1940*, p.195.

21 Marc Jansen and Nikita Petrov, *Stalin's Loyal Executioner: People's Commissar Nikolai Ezhov, 1895–1940*, p.207.

22 Nikita Khrushchev, *The 'Secret' Speech: Delivered to the Closed Session of the Twentieth Congress of the Communist Party of the Soviet Union* (Nottingham: Spokesman, 1976), p.44.

23 Roy Medvedev, *Let History Judge : The Origins and Consequences of Stalinism*, p.296. NB On the semantics of 'genocide'. For all their simi-

larities, the great historical crimes are also unique. There appears to have been a policy of eradication of segments of ethnic groups within the USSR who were seen as providing a source of opposition to the regime – the Ukrainians, Poles, Byelorussians, Latvians, Lithuanians, Germans, etc. – which was one part of the crime of 'Stalinism' that one could say was genocidal. Since the Americans were a tiny element of this anti-foreigner assault, were the individual actions directed against them part of this over-all genocide? I would argue that yes, this was the case. The Gulag camps certainly had a utilitarian motive for their existence, but an essential part of their utility was also the eradication and execution of the various oppo-nents of the regime. There was little expectation of survival in many of the worst camp centres. Their extinction was therefore also an end in itself. And if that is the case, then what took place within the camps was geno-cidal, if we perceive the intent as the eradication of life. Although one must be careful with language and use the word 'genocide' with care. When the count of the victims enters the millions then it appears justified and necessary.

24 Robert Conquest, *The Great Terror: A Reassessment*, p.287.

25 Hans Schaferenk and Natalia Musienko, 'The Fictitious "Hitler-Jugend" Conspiracy of the Moscow NKVD', from Barry McLoughlin and Kevin McDermott (eds) *Stalin's Terror: High Politics and Mass Repression in the Soviet Union* (Basingstoke: Palgrave Macmillan, 2003), p.213.

26 Marc Jansen and Nikita Petrov, *Stalin's Loyal Executioner: People's Commissar Nikolai Ezhov, 1895–1940*, p.92.

27 Barry McLoughlin, 'Mass Operations of the NKVD, 1937–8: A Survey', from Barry McLoughlin and Kevin McDermott (eds), *Stalin's Terror: High Politics and Mass Repression in the Soviet Union*, pp.129–130; Marc Jansen and Nikita Petrov, *Stalin's Loyal Executioner: People's Commissar Nikolai Ezhov, 1895–1940*, pp.84–5.

28 Iu. M. Zolotov (ed.), *Kniga pamiati zhertv politcheskikh repressi* (Ul'ianovsk, 1996), pp.797–8, quoted in Barry McLoughlin – 'Mass Operations of the NKVD, 1937–8: A Survey', from Barry McLoughlin and Kevin McDermott (eds), *Stalin's Terror: High Politics and Mass Repression in the Soviet Union*, p.129.

29 Marc Jansen and Nikita Petrov, *Stalin's Loyal Executioner: People's Commissar Nikolai Ezhov, 1895–1940*, p.86.

30 Barry McLoughlin, 'Mass Operations of the NKVD, 1937–8: A Survey', from Barry McLoughlin and Kevin McDermott (eds), *Stalin's Terror: High Politics and Mass Repression in the Soviet Union*, p.134.

31 Robert Conquest, *The Great Terror: A Reassessment*, p.287.

32 *The Challenge*, Bulletin of the Association of Former Political Prisoners of Soviet Labor Camps, Vol. 1, No. 3, January 1951.

33 Robert Conquest, *The Great Terror: A Reassessment*, p.287.

34 Hedrick Smith, *The New Russians* (London: Hutchinson, 1990), p.130.

35 Margarete Buber, *Under Two Dictators*, trans. E. Fitzgerald (London: Gollancz, 1949), p.10.

36 Laszlo Bekesi, *KGB and Soviet Security Uniforms and Militaria*,

1917–1991 (Marlborough: Crowood Press, 2002), p.16; Edmund Stevens, *This is Russia Uncensored* (New York: Didier,1950), p.98.

37 Louis Fischer, *Men and Politics: An Autobiography* (London: Cape, 1941) p.409.

38 Véronique Garros, Natalia Korenevskaya and Thomas Lahusen (eds), trans. Carol A. Flath, *Intimacy and Terror: Soviet Diaries of the 1930s* (New York: New Press, 1995), p.352.

39 Louis Fischer, *Men and Politics: An Autobiography* (London: Cape, 1941), p.411.

40 Nanci Adler, *Victims of Soviet Terror: The Story of the Memorial Movement* (Westport, CT: Praeger, 1993), p.21; John McCannon, *Red Arctic: Polar Exploration and the Myth of the North in the Soviet Union, 1932–1939* (New York: Oxford University Press, 1998), p.112; Robert Conquest, *The Great Terror: A Reassessment*, p.297; Freda Utley, *Lost Illusion: The Story of the Author's Life in Russia* (London: George Allen, 1949), p.163.

41 David Remnick, 'The Triumphant Merriment of Isaac Babel', *Moscow Times*, 26 April 1997; Véronique Garros, Natalia Korenevskaya and Thomas Lahusen (eds), *Intimacy and Terror: Soviet Diaries of the 1930s* (New York: New Press, 1995), p.358; Robert A. D. Ford, *Our Man in Moscow: A Diplomat's Reflections on the Soviet Union* (Toronto: University of Toronto Press, 1989), p.12; Slavoj Žižek – 'When the Party commits suicide', Human Rights Project, 1999; Elizabeth Wilson, *Shostakovich: A Life Remembered* (London: Faber, 1994), pp.124–5.

42 Vladimir Zazubrin, 'The Chip: A Story about a Chip and about Her', 24 April 1923, trans. Graham Roberts from Oleg Chukhontsev (ed.), *Dissonant Voices: The New Russian Fiction* (London: Harvill, 1991), p.55; Aleksandr Orlov, *The Secret History of Stalin's Crimes*, pp.215–6.

43 A. Ia. Razumov (ed.), *Leningradskii martirolog. tom 4, 1937 god* (St Petersburg: 1999) pp.675–81; quoted in Barry McLoughlin, 'Mass Operations of the NKVD, 1937–8: A Survey' from Barry McLoughlin and Kevin McDermott (eds), *Stalin's Terror: High Politics and Mass Repression in the Soviet Union*, p.136; Robert Conquest, *The Great Terror: A Reassessment* (London: Hutchinson, 1990), pp.241–271; Edvard Radzinsky, *Stalin*, p.379

44 J. Stalin, 'Defects in party work and measures for liquidating Trotskyite and other double-dealers', Report and speech in reply to debate at the plenum of the Central Committee of the CPSU, 3–5 March 1937, 361.00/11, RG 59, National Archives II, College Park, Maryland.

45 Marc Jansen and Nikita Petrov, *Stalin's Loyal Executioner: People's Commissar Nikolai Ezhov, 1895–1940*, p.93.

46 Ibid., pp.98–99.

47 Louis Fischer, *Men and Politics: An Autobiography*, pp.418–471; Harry and Rebecca Timbres, *We Didn't Ask Utopia: A Quaker Family in Soviet Russia* (New York: Prentice-Hall, 1939), p.220.

9 'SPETZRABOTA'

1 Anna Akhmatova, *The Complete Poems*, Vol. 2, trans. Judith Hemschemeyer (Somerville, MA: Zephyr Press, 1990), pp.106–7.

2 Walter Duranty, 'Lindberghs View Russian Air Fete', *New York Times*, 19 August 1938, p.17.

3 Marc Jansen and Nikita Petrov, *Stalin's Loyal Executioner: People's Commissar Nikolai Ezhov, 1895–1940*, pp.x, 108-110.

4 Stalin quoted in diary of Georgii Dmitrov from Fridrikh I. Firsov, Dmitrov, the Comintern and Stalinist Repression; Barry McLoughlin and Kevin McDermott (eds), *Stalin's Terror: High Politics and Mass Repression in the Soviet Union*, p.67.

5 Ronald Grigor Suny, 'Beyond Psychohistory: The Young Stalin in Georgia' *Slavic Review*, Vol. 50, No.1, Spring 1991.

6 Vadim Z. Rogovin, *1937: Stalin's Year of Terror*, trans. Frederick S. Choate (Oak Park, MI: Mehring, 1998), p.xv.

7 Czeslaw Milosz, *The Captive Mind*, trans. Jane Zielonko (London: Secker & Warburg, 1953), p.214, quoted in Stephen Kotkin, *The Magnetic Mountain: Stalinism as a Civilization* (Berkeley, C: University of California Press, 1995), p.556.

8 Arthur Talent's NKVD interrogation from the Adam Hochschild Collection, Hoover Institution, Stanford, CA; Alan Cullinson, 'A Secret Revealed', Associated Press, 23 November 1997.

9 Paul Robeson interviewed by Ben Davis Jr., 'Sunday Worker', 10 May 1936 from Paul Robeson, (ed.), *Paul Robeson Speaks*, ed. Philip S. Foner (London: Quartet, 1978), p.107.

10 Paul Robeson Jr., *The Undiscovered Paul Robeson: An Artist's Journey, 1898–1939* (New York: John Wiley, 2001), pp.281–306

11 Paul Robeson, 'To You Beloved Comrade', *New World Review*, April 1953, pp.11–13, from Robeson, *Paul Robeson Speaks*, p.347.

12 Peggy Dennis, *The Autobiography of an American Communist: A Personal View of a Political Life 1925–1975* (Berkeley, CA: Creative Arts, 1977), pp.119–20.

13 Paul Robeson Jr., *The Undiscovered Paul Robeson: An Artist's Journey, 1898–1939*, pp.289–90.

14 Yelena Khanga with Susan Jacoby, *Soul to Soul: A Black Russian-American Family, 1865–1992* (New York: Norton, 1992), p.90.

15 Paul Robeson Jr., *The Undiscovered Paul Robeson: An Artist's Journey, 1898–1939*, pp.294, 305–6.

16 Yelena Khanga with Susan Jacoby, *Soul to Soul: A Black Russian-American Family, 1865–1992*, pp.90–1.

17 Robert Robinson, *Black on Red : My Forty-Four Years Inside the Soviet Union*, p.361.

18 Harvey Klehr, John Earl Haynes and Kyrill M. Anderson, *The Soviet World of American Communism* (New Haven, CT: Yale University Press, 1998), pp.224–226; Alan Cullinson, 'The Lost Victims', Associated Press, 9 November 1997.

19 361.1163/7, Box 1594, RG 59, National Archives II, College Park, Maryland.

20 Interview with Marcella Hecker by Lyuba Vinagradova, Moscow, 25 June 2005.

21 Alan Cullinson, 'The Lost Victims', Associated Press, 9 November 1997.

22 Aleksandr Vatlin and Natalia Musienko, *Stalinist Terror in the Moscow District of Kuntsevo, 1937–8*; from Barry McLoughlin and Kevin McDermott (eds), *Stalin's Terror: High Politics and Mass Repression in the Soviet Union*, p.203.

23 Victor Herman, *Coming out of the Ice*, pp.94–5.

24 Ibid., p.99.

25 6 May 1935, 320, Grondon, Joseph, RG 59, National Archives II, College Park, Maryland.

26 861.60/305, RG 59, National Archives II, College Park, Maryland.

27 Interview with Sergei Dyakanov from *Yanks for Stalin* documentary film, Abamedia, Moscow.

28 Victor Herman, *Coming out of the Ice*, p.109.

29 James E. Abbe, *I Photograph Russia*, p.302.

30 Alan Cullinson, 'A Secret Revealed: Stalin's Police Killed Americans', Associated Press, 23 November 1997.

31 Victor Tyskewicz-Voskov, NKVD file from Adam Hochschild collection, Hoover Institution Archives, Stanford University, CA.

32 Barry McLoughlin, 'Documenting the Death Toll: Research into the Mass Murder of Foreigners in Moscow, 1937–8', *Perspectives* (American Historical Association Newsletter), Vol.37, (1999), pp.29–33.

33 Full title: The Rehabilitation Group of the Moscow Administration of the Ministry of Security (MB). Barry McLoughlin, 'Documenting the Death Toll: Research into the Mass Murder of Foreigners in Moscow, 1937–8, *Perspectives* (American Historical Association Newsletter), Vol.37 (1999), pp.29–33.

34 Brian Moynahan, *The Russian Century: A Photographic History of Russia's 100 Years*, p.182; Barry McLoughlin, 'Documenting the Death Toll: Research into the Mass Murder of Foreigners in Moscow, 1937–8, *Perspectives* (American Historical Association Newsletter), Vol.37, (1999), pp.29–33.

35 Vladimir Zazubrin, 'The Chip: A Story about a Chip and about Her', 24 April 1923, trans. Graham Roberts from Oleg Chukhontsev (ed.), *Dissonant Voices: The New Russian Fiction* (London: Harvill, 1991), p.11.

36 Lev Razgon, *True Stories*, trans. John Crowfoot (London: Souvenir Press, 1998) p.30.

37 Vitaly Shentalinsky, *The KGB's Literary Archive: The Discovery and Ultimate Fate of Russia's Suppressed Writers*, trans. John Crowfoot (London: Harvill Press, 1993) p.220; Barry McLoughlin, 'Documenting the Death Toll: Research into the Mass Murder of Foreigners in Moscow, 1937–8', *Perspectives* (American Historical Association Newsletter), Vol.37, (1999), pp.29–33.

38 Thomas Sgovio, *Dear America*, p.124; Paula Garb, *They Came to Stay: North Americans in the USSR* (Moscow: Progress, 1987), pp.72–3; Memo 7 January 1938; 800, RG59, National Archives II, College Park, Maryland; Davia Merkushen, 'Even Stalin Couldn't Scare Off This Expat', Moscow Times, 27 August 2001.

39 Alan Cullinson, 'A Secret Revealed: Stalin's Police Killed Americans', Associated Press, 23 November 1997.

40 Ibid.

41 Thomas Sgovio NKVD file, Adam Hochschild Collection, Hoover Institution, Stanford, CA; Thomas Sgovio interview with George Kovacs, tapes courtesy of David Elkind, LiveWire Media, San Francisco.

42 Memo regarding Henry Maiwin, 1 April 1937, American Embassy, Moscow, RG 59, National Archives II, College Park, Maryland.

43 16 February 1935, 361.1121, Maiwin, Henry, RG 59, National Archives II, College Park, Maryland.

44 George Kennan letter from Berlin to Consul General, 16 February 1931, RG 59, National Archives II, College Park, Maryland.

45 Alan Cullinson, 'A Secret Revealed: Stalin's Police Killed Americans', Associated Press, 23 November 1997.

10 'A DISPASSIONATE OBSERVER'

1 Annensky, quoted from Anna Akhmatova, *The Complete Poems of Anna Akhmatova*, vol. 1, trans. Judith Hemschemeyer (Sommerville, MA: Zephyr Press, 1990).

2 Elizabeth Kimball MacLean, *Joseph E. Davies: Envoy to the Soviets* (Westport, CT: Praeger, 1992), p.21.

3 Robert C. Williams, *Russian Art and American Money, 1900–1940* (Cambridge, MA: Harvard University Press, 1980), p.231.

4 The *Sea Cloud* was originally launched as the *Hussar V* but was renamed after Marjorie's divorce; Robert C. Williams, *Russian Art and American Money, 1900–1940*, p.249.

5 Elizabeth Kimball MacLean, *Joseph E. Davies: Envoy to the Soviets*, pp.21–22.

6 Ibid., p.21–2.

7 Ibid., p.26.

8 Charles Ciliberti, *Backstairs Mission in Moscow*, p.14.

9 Loy Henderson Papers, File 'Memoirs Vol. 9', 1938–42, Box 20, Library of Congress Manuscripts, Washington DC.

10 Marjorie Merriweather Post Collection, Hillwood Museum Archives, Washington DC.

11 Harpo Marx with Roland Barber, *Harpo Speaks* (London: Gollancz, 1961), p.307.

12 Elizabeth Hampel, *Yankee Bride in Moscow*, p.143.

13 Ibid., p.252.

14 Charles Thayer, *Bears in the Caviar*, p.88; Elizabeth Hampel, *Yankee Bride in Moscow*, p.228.

15 Charles Ciliberti, *Backstairs Mission in Moscow*, p.18.

16 Joseph Davies, *Mission to Moscow* (London: Gollancz, 1942), pp.33–4.

17 Véronique Garros, Natalia Korenevskaya and Thomas Lahusen (eds) trans. Carol A. Flath, *Intimacy and Terror: Soviet Diaries of the 1930s*, p.12.

18 Hans Von Herwarth, *Against Two Evils: Memoirs of a Diplomat Soldier During the Third Reich* (London: Collins,1981), p.110.

19 Elizabeth Kimball MacLean, *Joseph E. Davies: Envoy to the Soviets*, p.31.

20 Kolya Voinov, *Outlaw: The Autobiography of a Soviet Waif* (London: Harvill, 1955), p.119.

21 Eugene Lyons, *Assignment in Utopia*, p.127.

22 Roy Medvedev, *Let History Judge: The Origins and Consequences of Stalinism*, p.115; Aleksandr Orlov, *The Secret History of Stalin's Crimes*, 1953) p.260.

23 Anna Larina, *This I Cannot Forget: The Memoirs of Nikolai Bukharin's Widow*, p.312.

24 Robert Conquest, *The Great Terror: A Reassessment*, p.141; Vadim Z. Rogovin, *1937: Stalin's Year of Terror*, trans. Frederick S. Choate (Oak Park, MI: Mehring, 1998) p.69.

25 S. J. Taylor, *Stalin's Apologist: Walter Duranty, The New York Times' Man in Moscow*, pp.225–6.

26 *Neue Freie Presse*, 30 January 1937.

27 Joseph Davies to Secretary Hull, 17 Febuary 1937, from Joseph Davies, *Mission to Moscow*, pp.38–9.

28 'Speech of N. S. Khruschev', 1 February 1937, *Moscow Daily News*, p.1; Robert Conquest, *The Great Terror: A Reassessment*, p.149.

29 Robert Conquest, *The Great Terror: A Reassessment*, p.165.

30 George Kennan quoted in Keith David Eagles, *Ambassador Joseph E. Davies and American–Soviet Relations, 1937–1941*, p.127.

31 George Kennan, *Memoirs: 1925–1950* (London: Hutchinson, 1967), p.82.

32 Loy Henderson, *A Question of Trust – The Origins of US–Soviet Diplomatic Relations: The Memoirs of Loy W. Henderson*, p.423.

33 Elizabeth Hampel, *Yankee Bride in Moscow*, p.218; Elbridge Durbrow Collection, Box 68, interview with John Mason, 5 May 1981, Hoover Institution, Stanford, CA.

34 Joseph Davies, *Mission to Moscow*, p.62.

35 Joseph Davies diary, Moscow, 23 March 1937, from Joseph Davies, *Mission to Moscow*, pp.95–6.

36 Joseph Davies to Sumner Welles, 28 June 1937, from Joseph Davies, *Mission to Moscow*, p.111; Joseph Davies to Secretary of State, 28 July 1937, from Joseph Davies, *Mission to Moscow*, pp.129–138.

37 Aleksandr Orlov, *The Secret History of Stalin's Crimes*, p.241; John Reed quoted in 'Dybenko Persuades Cossacks to Surrender', *Moscow News*, 28 February 1935; Edvard Radzinsky, *Stalin*, p.387; Robert Conquest, *The Great Terror: A Reassessment*, p.212; Roy Medvedev, *Let History Judge: The Origins and Consequences of Stalinism*, p.341.

38 Joseph Davies letter to Mrs Millard Tydings, Moscow, 22 March 1937, from Joseph Davies, *Mission to Moscow*, p.94; Joseph Davies, *Mission to Moscow*, p.78; Robert C. Williams, *Russian Art and American Money 1900–1940*, p.249.

39 Irena Wiley, *Around the Globe in Twenty Years*, p.37.

40 Post Family Papers, Series II: Marjorie Merriweather Post Re: Joseph E. Davies, Scrapbooks, Russia, 1937, Marjorie Merriweather Post Collection, Hillwood Museum Archives, Washington DC.

41 Charles Ciliberti, *Backstairs Mission in Moscow*, p.38.

42 Hans von Herwarth, *Against Two Evils* (London: Collins, 1981), p.62; Journal, 5 July 1937, Joseph Davies Papers, Library of Congress Manuscripts, Washington DC.

43 Joseph Davies letter to Stephen Early, 9 March 1937, from Joseph Davies, *Mission to Moscow*, p.82; *Time*, 15 March 1937.

44 Moscow Post files, Vol. 394, 15 April 1937, RG 84, National Archives II, College Park, Maryland.

45 Charles Thayer, *Bears in the Caviar*, p.157.

46 Marjorie Merriweather Post interview with Nettie Major, 31 August 1964, PM4(50), Hillwood Museum Archives, Washington DC.

47 Keith David Eagles, *Ambassador Joseph E. Davies and American–Soviet Relations, 1937–1941*, p.211; Joseph Davies, *Mission to Moscow*, p.102.

11 'SEND VIEWS OF NEW YORK'

1 Nikolay Gumilyov, 'Heaven' from *The Pillar of Fire*, trans. Richard McKane (London: Anvil Press, 1999), p.106.

2 Joseph Davies journal, 18 June 1937, Joseph Davies Papers, Library of Congress Manuscripts, Washington DC.

3 Joseph Davies, *Mission to Moscow*, p.105.

4 Charles Ciliberti, *Backstairs Mission in Moscow*, p.14.

5 Despatch 10 August 1937, Decimal File 1930–39, Box 0793, RG 59, National Archives II, College Park, Maryland.

6 Elizabeth Kimball MacLean, *Joseph E. Davies: Envoy to the Soviets*, p.40.

7 Marjorie Merriweather Post interview with Nettie Major, 31 August 1964 and 1 September 1964, Hillwood Museum Archives, Washington DC.

8 Charles Ciliberti, *Backstairs Mission in Moscow*, p.26.

9 Ibid., p.16.

10 Ibid., pp.63–64.

11 Ibid., p.64.

12 Ibid., p.29.

13 Ibid., pp.19, 29, 44, 47.

14 Joseph Davies journal, 18 October 1937, Joseph Davies Papers, Library of Congress Manuscripts, Washington DC.

15 Charles Ciliberti, *Backstairs Mission in Moscow*, p.41.

16 Joseph Davies journal, 5 July 1937, Joseph Davies Papers, Library of Congress Manuscripts, Washington DC.

17 Joseph Davies journal, 27 July 1937, Joseph Davies Papers, Library of Congress Manuscripts, Washington DC.

18 Charles Ciliberti, *Backstairs Mission in Moscow*, p.85.

19 Ibid., pp.77, 84–85.

20 Loy Henderson, *A Question of Trust – The Origins of US–Soviet Diplomatic Relations: the Memoirs of Loy W. Henderson*, p.368.

21 361.1121, Belakoff, Timothy, RG 59, National Archives II, College Park, Maryland.

22 10 January 1939, 361.1115/84; 10 July 1939, 361.1115, Burton, Paul; 361.1115, Cooper, John; RG 59, National Archives II, College Park, Maryland.

23 Letter Mrs Hilma Oja, 1999 Madison Avenue, New York, New York. 24 October 1938, RG 59, National Archives II, College Park, Maryland.

24 361.1115 Jaffe, Harry, RG59, National Archives II, College Park, Maryland.

25 361.1115 Volat, Marvin, RG59, National Archives II, College Park, Maryland.

26 361.1115 Dubin, Ivan, RG 59 National Archives II, College Park, Maryland.

27 Robert C. Williams, *Russian Art And American Money, 1900–1940*, p.251.

28 'Soviet Silent to All Queries on Robinsons', *New York Daily News*, 14 December 1937.

29 361.1115, Robinson, Donald, RG59, National Archives II, College Park, Maryland.

30 Krivitsky FBI file, FBI Reading Room, Washington DC; Given that all bureaucracies, including that of the Soviet, were liable to error, the mechanics of this deception were occasionally revealed. On 20 March 1937, for example, the Soviet Foreign Office forwarded to the American Embassy the passport of one William Hill – a 24-year-old native-born American citizen – with a request that the passport be made valid so Hill 'might be deported to the United States'. In response, the American Embassy advised the Soviet Foreign Office that 'Hill would be required to appear at the Embassy to execute the necessary application for the renewal of his passport' and then nothing more was heard. Ten months later, on 10 January 1938, the American Embassy officials were advised by the Soviet authorities that 'Hill had died in Karelia during the summer of 1937'. The following year, the Soviet Foreign Office sent the Americans a copy of William Hill's death certificate, which gave the date of death as 11 July 1936, and the cause of death 'haemorrhage in cerebrum (murder)'. The circumstances of William Hill's death and the Soviet request for the renewal of his passport eight months later, raised the 'grave suspicions' of the American diplomats: 'the possibility that Hill was killed by a GPU agent either in resisting arrest or later while under detention is not to be dismissed.' 'The Murder of William Hill, American citizen', 28 July 1939, 361.113, Hill, William, RG 59, National Archives II, College Park, Maryland.

31 861.00/11847, RG59, National Archives II, College Park, Maryland; Edward Gazur, *Secret Assignment: The FBI's KGB General* (London: St Ermin's, 2001), p.166; Krivitsky FBI file, FBI Reading Room, Washington DC.

32 Loy Henderson, 'Memoirs Vol. 9, 1938--1942', Box 20, Loy Henderson Papers, Library of Congress Manuscripts, Washington DC.

33 361.1121, Sviridoff, George/22, RG 59, National Archives II, College Park, Maryland. Two years before George Sviridoff's arrest, the Swedish-American engineer Axel Markuson, upon his return from an Amtorg contract in Russia, had written a warning on behalf of such American teenagers 'who had come from the United States to Russia and cannot return as they would like, although they were born in the United States.' Axel Markuson's son had informed him of two boys both seventeen years old – 'one from Boston and the other from Cleveland – who had tried to escape by boat over the Black Sea but were caught by the GPU.' Their American passports had been taken from them when they first entered Russia, and they had nothing to prove their nationality: 'One of them had a sister, nineteen years old, who was thinking of marrying an American engineer in order to get out of Russia in that way ... The unfortunate plight of these poor American-born children is brought to the Department's special attention.' Interview with Axel Markuson, 18 January 1932, 861.5017, Living Conditions/423, RG 59, National Archives II, College Park, Maryland.

34 1 June 1938, Kennan note from 361.1121 Sviridoff, George/21, RG 59, National Archives II, College Park, Maryland.

12 'SUBMISSION TO MOSCOW'

1 Joseph Davies to Secretary of State, 28 July 1937, from Joseph Davies, *Mission to Moscow*, p.138; Joseph Davies to Secretary of State, 15 November 1937, from Joseph Davies, *Mission to Moscow*, p.159.

2 Joseph Davies to Cordell Hull, strictly confidential, 1 April 1938, Joseph Davies Papers, Library of Congress Manuscripts, Washington DC.

3 Charles Ciliberti, *Backstairs Mission in Moscow*, p.113.

4 Journal 2 March 1938, Joseph Davies Papers, Library of Congress Manuscripts, Washington DC.

5 Robert Conquest, *The Great Terror: A Reassessment*, p.241.

6 Walter Duranty, *The Kremlin and the People* (London: Hamish Hamilton, 1942), p.68.

7 Roy Medvedev, *Let History Judge: The Origins and Consequences of Stalinism*, p.175.

8 TSGAOR, Fond 7523 sch, op.66, d.58, ll.1–5 quoted from Diane P. Koenker and Ronald D. Bachman (eds), *Revelations from the Russian Archives, Documents in English Translation*, p.109.

9 William C. Bullitt to Franklin D. Roosevelt, 1 January 1934, Bullitt,

President FDR's office files, 1933–1945, Part 2: Diplomatic Correspondence 'Russia', Library of Congress Manuscripts, Washington DC.

10 Vitaly Shentalinsky, *The KGB's Literary Archive*, pp.277–8; Aleksandr Orlov, *The Secret History of Stalin's Crimes*, p.260.

11 'Krestinsky at his trial', *Moscow News*, 12 March 1938, p.9; Aleksandr Orlov, *The Secret History of Stalin's Crimes*, pp.289–90.

12 Roy Medvedev, Let History Judge: *The Origins and Consequences of Stalinism*, pp.186–7.

13 *Trud*, 26 May 1988 from Robert Conquest, *The Great Terror: A Reassessment*, p.237.

14 Aleksandr Orlov, *The Secret History of Stalin's Crimes*, p.284.

15 Louis Fischer, *Men and Politics: An Autobiography* (London: Cape, 1941), p.483.

16 Charles E. Bohler, *Witness to History, 1929–1969* (New York: Norton, 1973), p.51; Edvard Radzinsky, *Stalin*, transl. H. T. Willets (London: Hodder & Stoughton, 1996) p.334; Aleksandr Orlov, *The Secret History of Stalin's Crimes* (New York: Random House, 1953) p.207

17 Boris Souvarine, *Stalin: A Critical Survey of Bolshevism* (London: Secker&Warburg, 1939), p.476.

18 'Trotsky Sees "Witch Trial"', *New York Times*, 21 January 1937.

19 Joseph Davies to Secretary of State Hull, 17 March 1938, from Joseph Davies, *Mission to Moscow*, pp.178–9.

20 Charles Thayer diary, 2 March 1938; Charles Thayer Papers, Harry S. Truman Library, Independence, MO.

21 'US Painters Exhibit Here Lacks Life, Reality', *Moscow Daily News*, 16 October 1936.

22 Joseph Davies, *Mission to Moscow*, p.193.

23 361.1115 Aisenstein, Michael, RG 59, National Archives II, College Park, Maryland.

24 Loy Henderson, *A Question of Trust – The Origins of US–Soviet Diplomatic Relations: The Memoirs of Loy W. Henderson*, p.416.

25 RF FPA. S. 0129. SF. 20. F. 133a. C. 389(1). S. 1–2. Copy, [October] 1937, #355, Secret memo from the diary of M. M. Litvinov. Twentieth-Century Documents: Soviet–American Relationship in 1934–1939, compiled by B. I. Zhilyaev, scientific editor: G.N. Sevost'yanov, (Moscow, 2003).

26 Robert Conquest, *The Great Terror: A Reassessment*, p.424.

27 Fitzroy MacLean, *Eastern Approaches* (London: Cape, 1949), p.23.

28 Keith David Eagles, *Ambassador Joseph E. Davies and American–Soviet Relations, 1937–1941*, p.194; Joseph Davies to Secretary of State, 9 June 1938 from Joseph Davies, *Mission to Moscow*, pp.219–226.

29 Loy Henderson, *A Question of Trust – The Origins of US–Soviet Diplomatic Relations: The Memoirs of Loy W. Henderson*, p.417.

30 Joseph Davies letter to Emlen Knight Davies, 9 June 1938, from Joseph Davies, *Mission to Moscow*, p.230.

31 Elizabeth Kimball MacLean, *Joseph E. Davies: Envoy to the Soviets*, p.57; 'Farewell', *Time*, 20 June 1938.

32 APRF, fond 45, op.1, d.375, ll. 14–18, from Diane P. Koenker and Ronald D. Bachman (eds), *Revelations from the Russian Archives*, p.646.

33 861.00/11787, RG 59, National Archives II, College Park, Maryland; Loy Henderson papers, File 'Memoirs Vol.7', Ch.10-13, 1934–38, Box 20, Library of Congress Manuscripts, Washington DC.

34 Loy Henderson papers, File 'Memoirs Vol.7', Ch.10–13, 1934–38, Box 20, Library of Congress Manuscripts, Washington DC; Margarete Buber, *Under Two Dictators*, trans. E. Fitzgerald (London: Gollancz, 1949) p.13.

35 Loy Henderson papers, File 'Memoirs Vol.9', 1938–42, Box 20, Library of Congress Manuscripts, Washington DC.

36 Amb J. K. Huddle's Inspection Report, Moscow, April 17 1937, RG59, National Archives II, College Park, Maryland.

37 Ibid.

38 361.1121 Nausiainen, Elmer, RG 59, National Archives II, College Park, Maryland.

39 Mayme Sevander, *Of Soviet Bondage* (Duluth, MN: Oscat, 1996), pp.111–112.

40 Edwin McKee, 'The Purge at Petrozavodsk', 19 July 1938; 361.1121 Nausiainen, Elmer J., RG59, National Archives II, College Park, Maryland.

41 Loy Henderson to Moffat, Division of European Affairs, 30 November 1938; 361.1121 Nausiainen, Elmer J./6, RG 59, National Archives II, College Park, Maryland.

42 21 December 1938, RG 84, National Archives II, College Park, Maryland.

43 27 June 1938, Memo of conversation between K. A. Umanskii and J. Davies, Doc. 384, RF FPA. S. 05. SF. 18. F. 147. C. 132. S. 32–33. Twentieth Century Documents; Soviet–American Relationship in 1934–1939, compiled B. I. Zhilyaev, scientific editor: G.N. Sevost'yanov (Moscow, 2003).

13 'KOLYMA ZNACZIT SMERT'

1 Jean Améry, *At the Mind's Limits*, trans. Sidney Rosenfeld and Stella P. Rosenfeld (London: Granta, 1999), p.34.

2 Thomas Sgovio interview with George Kovacs, tapes courtesy of David Elkind, LiveWire Media, San Francisco; Thomas Sgovio NKVD file, Hoover Institution, Stanford, CA.

3 Louis Fischer (ed.), *Thirteen Who Fled: 13 Essays by Refugees from Soviet Russia* (New York: Harper, 1949), p.136; Thomas Sgovio, *Dear America*, p.20.

4 Thomas Sgovio, *Dear America*, pp.9–11.

5 *The Challenge*, Bulletin of the Association of Former Political Prisoners of Soviet Labor Camps, October 1950, Vol. 1, No. 2, p.14.

6 Edvard Radzinsky, *Stalin: The First Biography Based on Explosive New Documents from Russia's Secret Archives*, trans. H. T. Willets, p.398.

7 Arthur Koestler, *The Yogi and the Commissar* (New York: Macmillan, 1946), p.176.

8 Thomas Sgovio, *Dear America*, p.53.

9 Robert Conquest, *The Great Terror: A Reassessment*, p.288

10 Victor Reuther, *Commitment and Betrayal: Foreign Workers at the Gorky Auto Works*, edited by Paul T. Christensen (unpublished: 2004) p.93.

11 Victor Herman, *Coming out of the Ice: An Unexpected Life*, pp.154–8.

12 Robert Conquest, *Inside Stalin's Secret Police* (Basingstoke: Macmillan, 1985), p.87.

13 Diane P. Koenker and Ronald D. Bachman (eds), *Revelations from the Russian Archives: Documents in English Translation*, p.27.

14 Victor Herman, *Coming out of the Ice: An Unexpected Life*, pp.160–4.

15 Ibid., pp.172–5.

16 Ibid., pp.178–182.

17 Robert Conquest, *The Great Terror: A Reassessment*, p.125.

18 Alex Weissberg, *Conspiracy of Silence: An Account of Three Years Imprisonment by the GPU*, trans. Edward Fitzgerald (London: Hamish Hamilton, 1952), p.305.

19 Victor Herman, *Coming out of the Ice: An Unexpected Life*, pp.185–189.

20 Ibid., pp.190–2.

21 Ibid., p.200.

22 Feliks Lachman, *I Was a Gulag Prisoner, 1939–42* (London: Caldra, 1991), p.29; Thomas Sgovio, *Dear America*, pp.54, 132.

23 Roy Medvedev, *Let History Judge: The Origins and Consequences of Stalinism*, p.277.

24 Thomas Sgovio interview with George Kovacs, tapes courtesy of David Elkind, LiveWire Media, San Francisco.

25 Vitaly Shentalinsky, *The KGB's Literary Archive*, p.192.

26 Michael Solomon quoted in Robert Conquest, *Kolyma: The Arctic Death Camps* (London: Macmillan, 1978), p.23.

27 Thomas Sgovio, *Dear America*, pp.134–137.

28 Robert Conquest, *Kolyma: the Arctic Death Camps*, pp.25–7.

29 Michael Solomon, *Magadan* (Princeton NJ: Auerbach, 1971), p.85.

30 Thomas Sgovio interview with George Kovacs, tapes courtesy of David Elkind, LiveWire Media, San Francisco; Thomas Sgovio, *Dear America*, pp.138–9.

31 Aleksandr Gorbatov, *Years off My Life: The Memoirs of a General of the Soviet Army* (London: Constable, 1964), p.124.

32 Janusz Bardach and Kathleen Gleeson, *Man is Wolf to Man: Surviving Stalin's Gulag* (London, Simon & Schuster, 1998), pp.191–4.

33 Robert Conquest, *Kolyma: The Arctic Death Camps*, p.35.

34 Martin J. Bollinger, *Stalin's Slave Ships: Kolyma, the Gulag Fleet, and the Role of the West* (Westport, CT: Praeger, 2003), pp.1–5.

35 Thomas Sgovio interview with George Kovacs, tapes courtesy of David Elkind, LiveWire Media, San Francisco.

36 Robert Conquest, *Kolyma: The Arctic Death Camps*, pp.36–7.

37 Mikhail Mikhaeev (dir.), *Kolyma*, documentary film, Hoover Institution, Stanford, CA; Varlam Shalamov, *Kolyma Tales*, trans. John Glad (New York: Norton, 1980), p.46.

38 Robert Conquest, Kolyma: *The Arctic Death Camps*, pp.17–19.

39 Thomas Sgovio interview with George Kovacs, tapes courtesy of David Elkind, LiveWire Media, San Francisco.

40 Janusz Bardach and Kathleen Gleeson, *Man is Wolf to Man: Surviving Stalin's Gulag*, p.196.

41 Thomas Sgovio, *Dear America*, pp.141–3.

42 Janusz Bardach and Kathleen Gleeson, *Man is Wolf to Man: Surviving Stalin's Gulag*, p.195.

43 Stanislaw J. Kowalski, *Kolyma: The Land of Gold and Death* (online edition).

44 Walter Duranty, *The Kremlin and the People* (London: Hamish Hamilton, 1942), p.101.

45 10 October 1937, MID 2070–2316, RG 165, National Archives II, College Park, Maryland.

46 Boris Souvarine, *Stalin: A Critical Survey of Bolshevism* (London: Secker & Warburg, 1939), p.669.

47 Source Sergo Mikoyan, son of Anastas Mikoyan; *Literaturnya gazeta*, 9 August 1989 quoted in Robert Conquest, *The Great Terror: A Reassessment*, p.487; Adam Hochschild, *The Unquiet Ghost: Russians Remember Stalin* (New York: Viking, 1994) p.xi.

14 THE SOVIET GOLD RUSH

1 Lenin quoted in *Time*, 15 May 1964.

2 John Morton Blum, *From the Morgenthau Diaries: Years of Crisis, 1928–1938* (Boston: Houghton Mifflin, 1959), pp.69–70.

3 *Fortune*, 24 March 1934; from *The Presidential Diaries of Henry Morgenthau, Jr., 1933–1939*, FDR Library, Hyde Park, New York.

4 John Morton Blum, *From the Morgenthau Diaries: Years of Crisis, 1928–1938*, pp. 467–473.

5 Joseph Davies letter to Henry Morgenthau Jr., 15 March 1937, Moscow, from Joseph Davies, *Mission to Moscow*, p. 85.

6 Joseph Davies letter to Henry Morgenthau Jr., 12 Aug.12 1937, from Joseph Davies, *Mission to Moscow*, pp.143–4.

7 Harpo Marx with Rowland Barber, *Harpo Speaks*, p.322.

8 Eugene Lyons, *Assignment in Utopia*, p.249.

9 Walter Krivitsky, *I Was Stalin's Agent* (London: Hamish Hamilton, 1939), p.135.

10 Robert C. Williams, *Russian Art and American Money, 1900–1940*, p.40.

11 Ibid., pp.181–4.

12 Ibid., p.189.

13 Eugene Lyons, *Assignment in Utopia*, p.449.

14 John Littlepage with Demaree Bess, *In Search of Soviet Gold* (New York: Harcourt, Brace, 1938) pp.26–28.

15 Alexander P. Serebrovsky, *Soviet Gold* (Moscow: Co-operative

Publishing Society of Foreign Workers in the USSR, 1936), p.2.

16 John Littlepage with Demaree Bess, *In Search of Soviet Gold*, pp.4, 8.

17 John Littlepage, 'Hunting gold for Stalin', *Saturday Evening Post*, 18 December 1937; John Littlepage with Demaree Bess, *In Search of Soviet Gold*, p.7.

18 A. P. Serebrovsky, *Soviet Gold*, p.2, pp. 17–24.

19 16 December 1935, article written by Serebrovsky, 861.6341/71, RG59, National Archives II, College Park, Maryland; John Littlepage with Demaree Bess, *In Search of Soviet Gold*, pp.60, 181.

20 John Littlepage with Demaree Bess, *In Search of Soviet Gold*, p.14.

21 Ibid., pp.119–120, 124–125.

22 Ibid., p.81.

23 David J. Nordlander, 'Origins of a Gulag Capital: Magadan and Stalinist Control in the Early 1930s', *Slavic Review* 57, no.4, Winter 1998, p.793.

24 Thomas Sgovio, *Dear America*, p.159.

25 David J. Nordlander, 'Origins of a Gulag Capital: Magadan and Stalinist Control in the Early 1930s', *Slavic Review* 57, no.4, Winter 1998, p.799.

26 Russian State Archive of Socio-Political History, Moscow, RGASPI, fond 17, opis 166, delo 451, list 28.

27 David J. Nordlander, 'Origins of a Gulag Capital: Magadan and Stalinist Control in the Early 1930s', *Slavic Review* 57, No.4, Winter 1998, p.808.

28 David J. Nordlander, 'Origins of a Gulag Capital: Magadan and Stalinist Control in the Early 1930s', *Slavic Review*, No.4, Winter 1998, p.808; Silvester Mora, *Kolyma: Gold and Forced Labor in the USSR* (Washington DC: Foundation for Foreign Affairs, 1949), p.11.

29 Robert Conquest, *Kolyma: The Arctic Death Camps*, p.54.

30 *The Challenge*, Bulletin of the Association of Former Political Prisoners of Soviet Labor Camps, Vol.1, No.3 January 1951; Elinor Lipper, *Eleven Years in Soviet Prison Camps* (London: Hollis & Carter, 1951), pp.106–7.

31 Robert Conquest, *Kolyma: The Arctic Death Camps*, p.57.

32 Nikishov was born in 1894, the son of a peasant. He joined the Communist Party in 1919 then followed this with a career in the NKVD, becoming NKVD chief of Azerbaijan during 1937 and 1938. He rose to the rank of Dalstroi chief in July 1943. He was retired from 1948 onwards. Memorial Society, Russian State Archive of Sociopolitical History, State Archive of the Russian Federation; N. V. Petrov and K. V. Skorkin, *Who Headed the NKVD in 1934–1941*, ed. N. G. Okhotin and A. B. Roginskii (Moscow: 1999).

33 Mikhail Mikhaeev (dir.), *Kolyma*, documentary film, Hoover Institution, Stanford, CA; Robert Conquest, *Kolyma: The Arctic Death Camps*, pp.68–69; Elinor Lipper, *Eleven Years in Soviet Prison Camps*, pp.110–111.

34 Alexander Solzhenitysn, *The Gulag Archipelago, 1918–1956: An Experiment in Literary Investigation*, trans. Thomas P. Whitney, Vol.2 (London: Fontana, 1976), p.480; Elinor Lipper, *Eleven Years in Soviet Prison Camps*, p.111.

35 David J. Nordlander, 'Magadan and the Economic History of Dalstroi in the 1930s' from Paul R. Gregory and Valery Lazerev (eds), *The*

Economics of Forced Labor: The Soviet Gulag (Stanford, CA: Hoover Institution Press, 2003), p.119.

36 Anton Antonov-Ovseyenko, *The Time of Stalin: Portrait of a Tyranny*, trans. George Saunders (New York: Harper & Row, 1981), pp.172–5.

37 John Littlepage with Demaree Bess, *In Search of Soviet Gold*, p.132.

38 861.6341/90, RG 59, National Archives II, College Park, Maryland.

39 John Littlepage with Demaree Bess, *In Search of Soviet Gold*, p.306.

40 John Littlepage, 'Hunting Gold for Stalin', *Saturday Evening Post*, 18 December 1937.

41 MID 2070-2347, RG 165, National Archives II, College Park, Maryland.

42 Anatol Krakowiecki quoted in Stanislaw J. Kowalski, *Kolyma: The Land of Gold and Death* (online edition).

43 861.6341/56, RG 59, National Archives II, College Park, Maryland.

44 861.51, Soviet American Securities Corp. RG 59, National Archives II, College Park, Maryland; *New York Times*, 17 March 1935.

45 John Morton Blum, *From the Morgenthau Diaries: Years of Crisis, 1928–1938*, p.473.

46 11 April 1937, *The Presidential Diaries of Henry Morgenthau, Jr., 1933–1939*, FDR Library, Hyde Park, New York; Trade General Review, Memo 'Foreign trade of the USSR in 1937' January 1939, 661.00/216, RG59, National Archives II, College Park, Maryland.

47 John Littlepage with Demaree Bess, *In Search of Soviet Gold*, p.269.

15 'OUR SELFLESS LABOUR WILL RESTORE US TO THE FAMILY OF WORKERS'

1 Esenin quoted from Varlam Shalamov, *Kolyma Tales*, trans. John Glad (New York: Norton, 1980), p.109.

2 Varlam Shalamov, *Kolyma Tales*, quoted from Robert Conquest, *Kolyma: The Arctic Death Camps* (London: Macmillan, 1978) pp.52–4.

3 Michael Solomon, *Magadan* (Princeton, N.J.: Auerbach, 1971), p.119.

4 Michael Solomon, *Magadan*, quoted from Robert Conquest, *Kolyma: The Arctic Death Camps*, p.64.

5 David J. Nordlander, Origins of a Gulag Capital: Magadan and Stalinist Control in the Early 1930s, *Slavic Review* 57, No.4 (Winter 1998), p.804.

6 Joseph Berger, *Shipwreck of a Generation: The Memoirs of Joseph Berger* (London: Harvill, 1971), p.122.

7 Thomas Sgovio, *Dear America*, pp.141–3.

8 Thomas Sgovio interview with George Kovacs, tapes courtesy of David Elkind, LiveWire Media, San Francisco.

9 Thomas Sgovio, *Dear America*, p.154.

10 Thomas Sgovio interview with George Kovacs, tapes courtesy of David Elkind, LiveWire Media, San Francisco.

11 *New York Times*, 28 January 1939; Records of the Consular Section, Moscow Embassy, 1940, Box 1, RG84, National Archives II, College Park, Maryland.

12 Thomas Sgovio interview with George Kovacs, tapes courtesy of David Elkind, LiveWire Media, San Francisco.

13 Meyer Galler and Harlan E. Marquess, *Soviet Prison Camp Speech: A Survivor's Glossary* (Madison, Wisconsin: University of Wisconsin Press, 1972), p.39.

14 *The Challenge*, Bulletin of the Association of Former Political Prisoners of Soviet Labor Camps, January 1951, Vol.1, No.3.

15 Thomas Sgovio interview with George Kovacs, tapes courtesy of David Elkind, LiveWire Media, San Francisco; Thomas Sgovio drawings, Hoover Institute, Stanford, CA.

16 Thomas Sgovio interview with George Kovacs, tapes courtesy of David Elkind, LiveWire Media, San Francisco.

17 Thomas Sgovio, *Dear America*, p.151.

18 Thomas Sgovio interview with George Kovacs, tapes courtesy of David Elkind, LiveWire Media, San Francisco.

19 Ibid.

20 Ibid.

21 Silvester Mora, *Kolyma: Gold and Forced Labor in the USSR*, pp.18–19.

22 Varlam Shalamov, *Kolyma Tales*, pp.29–30.

23 Elinor Lipper, *Eleven Years in Soviet Prison Camps*, trans. Richard and Clara Winston, p.238.

24 Antoni Ekart, *Vanished Without a Trace: The Story of Seven Years in Soviet Russia* (London: Parrish, 1954), p.47.

25 Vladimir Petrov, *It Happens in Russia: Seven Years' Forced Labour in the Siberian Goldfields* (London: Eyre & Spottiswoode, 1951), p.181.

26 Janusz Bardach and Kathleen Gleeson, *Man is Wolf to Man: Surviving Stalin's Gulag*, p.266.

27 Bernhard Roeder, *Katorga: An Aspect of Modern Slavery*, trans. Lionel Kochan (London: Heinemann, 1958). pp.6–7.

28 Thomas Sgovio interview with George Kovacs, tapes courtesy of David Elkind, LiveWire Media, San Francisco.

29 Janusz Bardach and Kathleen Gleeson, *Man is Wolf to Man: Surviving Stalin's Gulag*, p.207.

30 Thomas Sgovio interview with George Kovacs, tapes courtesy of David Elkind, LiveWire Media, San Francisco; Thomas Sgovio, *Dear America*, p.161.

31 Mikhail Mikhaeev (dir.), *Kolyma*, documentary film, Hoover Institution, Stanford, CA.

32 Varlam Shalamov, *Kolyma Tales*, pp.121–2; Robert Conquest, *Kolyma: The Arctic Death Camps*, pp.79–80.

33 Thomas Sgovio, *Dear America*, pp.165–8.

34 Thomas Sgovio interview with George Kovacs, tapes courtesy of David Elkind, LiveWire Media, San Francisco.

35 'Gulag tattoos decoded', BBC, 22 May 2001.

36 Thomas Sgovio interview with George Kovacs, tapes courtesy of David

Elkind, LiveWire Media, San Francisco; Thomas Sgovio, *Dear America*, p.171.

37 Antoni Ekart, *Vanished Without a Trace: The Story of Seven Years in Soviet Russia*, p.53; Thomas Sgovio, *Dear America*, p.162.

38 Meyer Galler and Harlan E. Marquess, *Soviet Prison Camp Speech: A Survivor's Glossary*, p.27.

39 Roy Medvedev, *Let History Judge: The Origins and Consequences of Stalinism*, p.280.

40 Thomas Sgovio, *Dear America*, pp.194–5.

41 c.861.6362/48, RG 59, National Archives II, College Park, Maryland.

42 Elinor Lipper, *Eleven Years in Soviet Prison Camps*, pp.231–239.

43 Eugenia Ginzburg, *Within the Whirlwind*, trans. Ian Boland (London: Collins Harvill, 1981), pp.7–8.

44 Mikhail Mikhaeev (dir.), *Kolyma*, documentary film, Hoover Institution, Stanford, CA; Elinor Lipper, *Eleven Years in Soviet Prison Camps*, pp.120–122.

45 Eugenia Ginzburg, *Within the Whirlwind*, p.217.

46 Robert Conquest, *The Great Terror: A Reassessment*, p.249.

47 Elinor Lipper, *Eleven Years in Soviet Prison Camps*, pp.176–178.

48 Galina Ivanova, *Labor Camp Socialism: The Gulag in the Soviet Totalitarian System*, trans. Carol Flath (Armonk, NY: M. E. Sharpe, 2000), p.55.

49 Janusch Bardach and Kathleen Gleeson, *Man is a Wolf to Man: Surviving the Gulag*, p.133; Victor Herman, *Coming out of the Ice: An Unexpected Life*, pp.206–9; Ibid., pp.218–9; Janusch Bardach and Kathleen Gleeson, *Man is a Wolf to Man: Surviving the Gulag*, p.213.

50 Victor Herman, *Coming out of the Ice: An Unexpected Life*, pp.219–212.

51 Ibid., pp.222–3.

52 Victor Herman, *Coming out of the Ice: An Unexpected Life*, pp.229–30.

53 Ibid., pp.224–231.

54 Mayme Sevander, *Red Exodus: Finnish-American Emigration to Russia* (Duluth, MN: Oscat, 1993), pp.168–170; Victor Herman, *Coming out of the Ice: An Unexpected Life*, pp.240–1.

55 Mayme Sevander, *Red Exodus: Finnish-American Emigration to Russia*, pp.168–170; Victor Herman, *Coming out of the Ice: An Unexpected Life*, pp.246–9.

56 17 May 1939, press release from New York World's Fair, Russia subject collection, Box 24, Files, 1 and 2, Hoover Institution, Stanford CA.

57 Russia subject collection, Box 24, Files, 1 and 2, Hoover Institution, Stanford, CA.

58 'The Five Pointed Ruby Star', Russia subject collection, Box 24, Files 1 and 2, Hoover Institution, Stanford, CA.

16 22 JUNE, 1941

1 Quoted from Gordon E. Michalson Jr., *Fallen Freedom: Kant on Radical Evil and Moral Regeneration* (Cambridge: Cambridge University Press, 1990), p.287.

2 Edvard Radzinsky, *Stalin*, p.417.

3 Marc Jansen and Nikita Petrov, *Stalin's Loyal Executioner: People's Commissar Nikolai Ezhov, 1895–1940*, p.187.

4 Charles E. Bohlen, *Witness to History, 1929–1969* (New York: Norton, 1973), p.82; Hans von Herwarth, *Against Two Evils: Memoirs of a Diplomat-Soldier During the Third Reich* (London: Collins, 1981), p.150.

5 Winston Churchill, *The Second World War: The Gathering Storm, Vol.1* (London: Penguin, 2005), p.352.

6 Hans von Herwarth, *Against Two Evils: Memoirs of a Diplomat-Soldier During the Third Reich*, p.150.

7 Anton Antonov-Ovseyenko, *The Time of Stalin: Portrait of a Tyranny* (New York: Harper & Row, 1981), p.257.

8 Joseph Berger, *Shipwreck of a Generation: The Memoirs of Joseph Berger*, p.177; Loy Henderson Papers, Box 1, File 'Laurence A. Steinhardt', Loy Henderson Papers, Library of Congress Manuscripts, Washington DC.

9 Victor Kravchenko, *I Chose Freedom: The Personal and Political Life of a Soviet Official* (New York: Scribner's, 1946), p.333; Eugenia Ginzburg, *Within the Whirlwind*, trans. Ian Boland, p.26.

10 'Foreign Statesmen Greet Stalin on 60th Birthday', *Moscow News*, 1 January 1940.

11 Antoni Ekart, *Vanished Without a Trace: The Story of Seven Years in Soviet Russia* (London: Parrish, 1954), p.94.

12 Homer Smith, *Black Man in Red Russia: A Memoir* (Chicago: Johnson, 1964), p.107; Winston Churchill, *The Second World War: Their Finest Hour, Vol.2* (London: Penguin, 2005), p.118.

13 Louis Fischer, *Men and Politics: An Autobiography*, p.602.

14 Berthold Unfried, 'Foreign Communists and the Mechanisms of Soviet Cadre Formation in the USSR', from Barry McLoughlin and Kevin McDermott (eds), *Stalin's Terror: High Politics and Mass Repression in the Soviet Union*, p.189.

15 Alex Weissberg, *Conspiracy of Silence: An Account of Three Years' Imprisonment by the GPU*, trans. E. Fitzgerald (London: Hamish Hamilton 1952), p.487.

16 Olaf Groehler, *Selbstmörderische Allianz: Deutsch-Russische Militärbeziehugne, 1920–1941* (Berlin: Vision Verlag, 1992), pp.122–3, 139.

17 Margarete Buber, *Under Two Dictators*, p.195.

18 Louis Fischer (ed.), *Thirteen Who Fled: 13 Essays by Refugees from Soviet Russia*, p.36.

19 Kolya Voinov, *Outlaw: The Autobiography of a Soviet Waif*, p.174.

20 Obituary Jagna Wright, *Guardian*, 29 August 2007, the Polish film-maker quotes 1.7 million; Jozef Gebski (dir.) *From Archipelago Gulag to*

America: Part 3, Valley of Tears, documentary film, Hoover Institute, Stanford, CA. Quotes 1.5 million Poles sent into the Gulag during this period.

21 William L. White, *Report on the Russians* (London: Eyre & Spottiswoode, 1945), p.113.

22 Jerzy Gliksman, *Tell the West* (New York: National Committee for a Free Europe, 1948), pp.22–23.

23 Brian Moynahan, *The Russian Century: A Photographic History of Russia's 100 Years,* p.184.

24 Henry Morgenthau, Jr., The Presidential Diaries of Henry Morgenthau, Jr. (1938–1945), FDR Library, Hyde Park, New York.

25 711.61.7431/4, RG59, National Archives II, College Park, Maryland.

26 'Radio address by Comrade V. M. Molotov', *Moscow News,* 27 June 1941.

27 Anton Antonov-Ovseyenko, *The Time of Stalin: Portrait of a Tyranny,* p.183.

28 Felix Chuev (ed.), *Molotov Remembers: Inside Kremlin Politics – Conversations with Felix Chuev* (Chicago: Ivan Dee, 1993), pp.295–296.

29 Erskine Caldwell, *All-Out on the Road to Smolensk* (New York: Duell, Sloan & Pearce, 1942), pp.20–2.

30 Roy Medvedev, *Let History Judge: The Origins and Consequences of Stalinism,* p. 458.

31 Stepan Anastasovich Mikoyan, *Stepan Anastasovich Mikoyan: An Autobiography* (Shrewsbury: Airlife, 1999), p.107.

32 Alice-Leone Moats, *Blind Date with Mars* (Garden City, NY: Doubleday, Doran 1943), p.234; Richard Lourie, *Russia Speaks: An Oral History from the Revolution to the Present* (New York: E. Burlingame, 1991), p.218.

33 Brian Moynahan, *The Russian Century: A Photographic History of Russia's 100 Years,* p.212.

34 *Nightmare in Red,* NBC television film, 1955, National Archives II, College Park, Maryland; Hans von Herwarth, *Against Two Evils: Memoirs of a Diplomat-Soldier During the Third Reich,* p.198.

35 Robert Robinson, *Black on Red: My Forty-Four Years Inside the Soviet Union,* pp.161–162.

36 Alice-Leone Moats, *Blind Date With Mars,* pp.340–1.

37 Erskine Caldwell, *Moscow Under Fire: A Wartime Diary* (London: Hutchinson, 1942), p.40.

38 Benjamin B. Fischer, Review of V. S. Khristoforov et al, 'Lubyanka in the Days of the Battle for Moscow: Materials from the Organs of State Security SSR from the Central Archive FSB Russia', published in *Studies in Intelligence,* Vol.48, No.2, 2004; Victor Kravchenko, *I Chose Freedom: The Personal and Political Life of a Soviet Official,* p.374.

39 Dennis J. Dunn, *Caught between Roosevelt and Stalin: America's Ambassadors to Moscow* (Lexington, KY: University of Kentucky Press, 1998), p.151; Charles Thayer diary, 15 October 1941, Charles Thayer Papers, Harry S. Truman Library, Independence, MO.

40 Letter from Elbridge Durbow September 1946 to Frederick Lyon, Director of Office Controls, Department of State, Top Secret Records of the Office of the Ambassador, 1943–1950, Box 2 RG84, National Archives II, College Park, Maryland.

41 Charles Thayer diary, 25 November 1941; Charles Thayer papers, Harry S. Truman Library, Independence, MO.

42 Records of Consular Section, Moscow Embassy 1941, Box 22, 1941, RG 84, National Archives II, College Park, Maryland.

43 361.1121/2–1245 and 361.1121/1–548, RG59, National Archives II, College Park, Maryland.

44 Task Force Russia 36–108, RG 330, National Archives II, College Park, Maryland.

45 Vadim J. Birstein, *The Perversion of Knowledge: The True Story of Soviet Science*, p.136; 361.113 Oggins, Isaiah, RG59, National Archives II, College Park, Maryland; Task Force Russia 36–105, RG330 National Archives II, College Park, Maryland.

46 361.113 Speirer, Edward Henry (sic), RG59, National Archives II, College Park, Maryland.

47 330, Speier, Edward H, Moscow Embassy, Records of the Consular Section 1943: 310–621, Box 29, RG 84, National Archives II, College Park, Maryland.

48 Alice-Leone Moats, *Blind Date with Mars*, pp.433–4; Jozef Gebski (dir.), *From Archipelago Gulag to America: Part 3 – Valley of Tears*, documentary film, Hoover Institution, Stanford, CA.

49 383.6 USSR, Army Intelligence Project decimal file 1941–45, Box 1047, RG319, National Archives II, College Park, Maryland.

50 Antoni Ekart, *Vanished Without a Trace: The Story of Seven Years in Soviet Russia*, p.61.

51 Zygmunt Bauman, *Modernity and the Holocaust* (Cambridge: Polity Press, 1989), p.193.

17 THE AMERICAN BRANDS OF A SOVIET GENOCIDE

1 Published under the pseudonym Abram Tertz, *On Socialist Realism*, trans. George Dennis (Berkeley, CA: University of California Press, 1962), p.162.

2 General Hugh Johnson, quoted in George N. Crocker, *Roosevelt's Road to Russia* (Chicago: Henry Regnery, 1959), p.32.

3 Hubert P. van Tuyll, *Feeding the Bear: American Aid to the Soviet Union, 1941–1945* (New York: Greenwood, 1989), p.3; Henry Morgenthau, Jr., 4 August 1941. The Presidential Diaries of Henry Morgenthau, Jr. (1938–1945), FDR Library, Hyde Park, New York.

4 Box 21, Moscow Post 1943, RG 84; and Standley despatch 12 August 1943. Moscow Post, 1945, Box 21, RG84, National Archives II, College Park, Maryland.

5 Harry Hopkins, 'My Meeting with Stalin', *The American*, December 1941.

6 Memo of conversation between Hopkins and Stalin, 30 July 1941, Top Secret General Records 1941–8, Box 1, RG 84, National Archives II, College Park, Maryland.

7 FDR quoted from Cordell Hull to American Embassy, Moscow, 2 October 1941, 861.404/451 RG 59, National Archives II, College Park, Maryland.

8 Margaret Bourke-White and Erskine Caldwell, *Russia at War* (London: Hutchinson, 1942), pp.8–14.

9 Margaret Bourke-White, *Shooting the Russian War* (New York: Simon & Schuster, 1943), pp.208–215.

10 Telegram Bullitt to Moore, 14 November 1936, 361.6121/16, RG 59, National Archives II, College Park, Maryland.

11 840.4, Moscow 3 December 1937, RG 59, National Archives II, College Park, Maryland.

12 Received 11 August 1941, State Department, Box 1239, Decimal File 1940–1944, 361.1163, RG 59, National Archives II, College Park, Maryland.

13 Letter from M. A. Matthew of the First Presbyterian Church, Seattle, WA, to Cordell Hull, 19 September 1938, 361.1121 Voroneff, John, RG59, National Archives II, College Park, Maryland.

14 Leopold L. S. Braun, *Religion in Russia: From Lenin to Khrushchev, An Uncensored Account* (Paterson, NJ: St Anthony Guild Press, 1959), p.46.

15 Arnold Beichman, 'Sorting Pieces of the Russian Past', *Hoover Digest*, No.1, 2003; Hoover Institution, Stanford, CA.

16 Henry Morgenthau, Jr., 28 October 1941, The Presidential Diaries of Henry Morgenthau, Jr. (1938–1945), FDR Library, Hyde Park, New York.

17 John R. Deane, *The Strange Alliance: The Story of Our Efforts at Wartime Cooperation with Russia* (New York: Viking Press, 1947), p.93.

18 091.4 USSR 6 January 1944, Army Intelligence Project decimal file 1941–45, Box 1038, RG319, National Archives II, College Park, Maryland.

19 Martin J. Bollinger, *Stalin's Slave Ships: Kolyma, the Gulag Fleet, and the Role of the West*, pp.60–61, 89.

20 Varlam Shalamov, *Kolyma Tales*, pp.173–4.

21 Thomas Sgovio, *Dear America*, p.212.

22 Elinor Lipper, *Eleven Years in Soviet Prison Camps*, p.129.

23 Varlam Shalamov, *Kolyma Tales*, pp.175–6.

24 Ibid., pp.178-180

25 Goebbels' diary quoted from Roy Medvedev, *Let History Judge: The Origins and Consequences of Stalinism*, p.395.

26 Thomas Sgovio, *Dear America*, pp.201–3.

27 Ibid., pp.204–9.

28 Thomas Sgovio interview with George Kovacs, tapes courtesy of David Elkind, LiveWire Media, San Francisco; Thomas Sgovio, *Dear America*, p.214.

29 Thomas Sgovio interview with George Kovacs, tapes courtesy of David Elkind, LiveWire Media, San Francisco.

30 Chuck Hawley, 'Man Recalls Ordeal of Slave Labor Treatment', *Arizona Republic*, 28 June 1995.

31 Thomas Sgovio interview with George Kovacs, tapes courtesy of David Elkind, LiveWire Media, San Francisco.

32 Ibid.

33 Meyer Galler, *Soviet Prison Camp Speech* (Hayward, CA: Soviet Studies, 1977); Thomas Sgovio, *Dear America*, p.213; Victor Herman, *Coming out of the Ice: An Unexpected Life*, pp.249–56.

34 Ibid., pp.259–263.

35 Varlam Shalamov, *Kolyma Tales*, p.68; Victor Herman, *Coming out of the Ice: An Unexpected Life*, p.268.

36 Mayme Sevander, *Red Exodus: Finnish-American Emigration to Russia*, pp.168–170; Victor Herman, *Coming out of the Ice: An Unexpected Life*, pp.276–77.

37 Victor Herman, *Coming out of the Ice: An Unexpected Life*, pp.284–5.

38 Elinor Lipper, *Eleven Years in Soviet Prison Camps*, p.266; Suzanne Massie, 'Why Are We Always Wrong About Russia?', World Affairs Council of Washington DC, 16 May 2001; Eugenia Ginzburg, *Within the Whirlwind*, p.31; Elinor Lipper, *Eleven Years in Soviet Prison Camps*, p.267; Robert Conquest, *Kolyma: The Arctic Death Camps*, p.206.

18 AN AMERICAN VICE-PRESIDENT IN THE HEART OF DARKNESS

1 Quoted in Arthur Koestler, *Darkness at Noon* (New York: Macmillan, 1941), p.241.

2 Henry Morgenthau, Jr., October 1933, The Presidential Diaries of Henry Morgenthau, Jr., 1933–1939, FDR Library, Hyde Park, New York.

3 Mark O. Hatfield, with the Senate Historical Office, *Vice-Presidents of the United States, 1789–1993* (Washington DC: US Government Printing Office, 1997), pp.399–406.

4 Elliot Roosevelt and James Brough, *A Rendezvous with Destiny: The Roosevelts of the White House* (London: W. H. Allen, 1975), p.137.

5 Henry Wallace, Columbia University Oral History Collection, interview with Dean Albertson, November 1950–May 1951, p.1301, Columbia University, New York.

6 Norman D. Markowitz, *The Rise and Fall of the People's Century: Henry A. Wallace and American Liberalism, 1941–1948* (New York: Free Press, 1973), pp.46–49.

7 Lee Hays and Pete Seeger, 'Plough Under', 1941.

8 Norman D. Markowitz, *The Rise and Fall of the People's Century: Henry A. Wallace and American Liberalism, 1941–1948*, p.169.

9 Charles Lindbergh, *The Wartime Journals of Charles A. Lindbergh* (New York: Harcourt Brace Jovanovich, 1970), pp.538, 546–7. Most politicians

kept such opinions to themselves. The wartime administrator Leo Crowley explained privately in conversation with Henry Morgenthau that Franklin Roosevelt had 'for no apparent reason' launched into a lecture: 'Leo, you know this is a Protestant country, and the Catholics and the Jews are here on sufferance ... It is up to both of you to go along with anything that I want at this time.' The President then asked Crowley whether American Catholics would be opposed to having him send US troops to Russia, to which Crowley replied: 'The Catholics will not feel any differently about this than any other citizen.' – Henry Morgenthau, Jr. 27 January 1942, The Presidential Diaries of Henry Morganthau, Jr. (1938-1945), FDR Library, Hyde Park, New York.

10 Norman D. Markowitz, *The Rise and Fall of the People's Century: Henry A. Wallace and American Liberalism, 1941–1948*, p.165.

11 Eleanor Roosevelt, *This I Remember* (New York: Harper & Row, 1949), p.199.

12 George R. Jordan, *From Major Jordan's Diaries* (New York: Harcourt, Brace 1952), p.30.

13 Robert E. Sherwood, *Roosevelt and Hopkins: An Intimate History* (New York: Harper, 1948), p.566.

14 Henry A. Wallace, with Andrew Steiger, *Soviet Asia Mission* (New York: Reynal & Hitchcock, 1946), p.30.

15 Henry Wallace diary, Library of Congress Manuscripts, Washington DC; Henry A. Wallace, with Andrew Steiger, *Soviet Asia Mission*, p.20.

16 13 March 1944, Henry Wallace diary, Library of Congress Manuscripts, Washington DC.

17 Owen Lattimore, *Pacific Affairs*, September 1938; quoted from Robert Conquest, *The Great Terror: A Reassessment*, p.468.

18 3 June 1942, Henry Wallace diary, Henry Wallace Papers, Library of Congress Manuscripts, Washington DC.

19 'Memorial' Society, Russian State Archive of Sociopolitical History, State Archive of the Russian Federation, N. V. Petrov and K. V. Skorkin, 'Who Headed the NKVD in 1934–1941', ed. N. G. Okhotin and A. B. Roginskii.

20 Henry Wallace diary, Henry Wallace Papers, Library of Congress Manuscripts, Washington DC.

21 Folder 5, transcript of Journal 12, Box 57, Owen Lattimore Papers, Library of Congress Manuscripts, Washington DC.

22 Henry A. Wallace, with Andrew Steiger, *Soviet Asia Mission*, p.33.

23 Owen Lattimore, 'The New Road to Asia' – National Geographic Magazine, Dec. 1944.

24 Ibid.

25 Folder 5, Transcript of Journal 12, Box 57, Owen Lattimore Papers, Library of Congress Manuscripts, Washington DC.

26 Henry A. Wallace, with Andrew Steiger – *Soviet Asia Mission*, pp.120–121.

27 Ibid pp.35–6; Henry Wallace diary, Library of Congress Manuscripts, Washington DC.

28 Folder 5, Transcript of Journal 12, Box 57, Owen Lattimore Papers, Library of Congress Manuscripts, Washington DC; John N. Hazard, *Recollections of a Pioneering Sovietologist* (New York: Oceana, 1987), p.89.

29 25 May 1944, Henry Wallace diary, Henry Wallace Papers, Library of Congress Manuscripts, Washington DC.

30 Methodology from Raul Hilberg, *Perpetrators, Victims, Bystanders* (New York: Aaron Asher, 1992).

31 Elinor Lipper, *Eleven Years in Soviet Prison Camps*, p.268.

32 Henry A. Wallace, *Soviet Asia Mission*, p.120.

33 John N. Hazard, *Recollections of a Pioneering Sovietologist*, p.89.

34 Owen Lattimore, 'The New Road to Asia', *National Geographic*, December 1944.

35 Elinor Lipper, *Eleven Years in Soviet Prison Camps*, pp.267–8.

36 Thomas Sgovio, *Dear America*, pp.250–1.

37 Henry A. Wallace, with Andrew Steiger, *Soviet Asia Mission*, p.34.

38 Box 8, Entry 68A5159, RG84, National Archives II, College Park, Maryland.

39 Box 8, Entry 68A5159, RG84, National Archives II, College Park, Maryland; Elinor Lipper, *Eleven Years in Soviet Prison Camps*, p.113; Henry A. Wallace, with Andrew Steiger, *Soviet Asia Mission*, pp.127–8.

40 Owen Lattimore, The New Road to Asia', *National Geographic*, December 1944.

41 Owen Lattimore, 'Soviet Siberia and Central Asia, America's New Gateway to Asia, Scenes from Vice-President Wallace's Journey to China, Soviet Asia, 1944', Nail–111–LC–46072, National Archives II, College Park, Maryland.

42 'Summary of Political Maneuvering', Henry Wallace Diary, Henry Wallace Papers, Library of Congress Manuscripts, Washington DC.

43 *Paramount News*, 26 July 1944, 200–PN–3.95, National Archives II, College Park, Maryland; Norman D. Markowitz, *The Rise and Fall of the People's Century: Henry A. Wallace and American Liberalism, 1941–1948*, p.111.

44 Henry Wallace diary, Henry Wallace Papers, Library of Congress Manuscripts, Washington DC.

45 Norman D. Markowitz, *The Rise and Fall of the People's Century: Henry A. Wallace and American Liberalism, 1941–1948*, p.91.

19 'TO SEE CRUELTY AND BURN NOT'

1 Memo of a conversation between Roosevelt and Henry Morgenthau, 15 May 1942, The Presidential Diaries of Henry Morgenthau, Jr., 1938–1945, p.1093, FDR Library, Hyde Park, New York, quoted from Warren F. Kimball, *The Juggler: Franklin Roosevelt As Wartime Statesman* (Princeton, NJ: Princeton University Press, 1991), p.7.

2 Thomas Sgovio, *Dear America*, p.245.

3 Ibid., pp.249–50.

4 Ibid., p.245.

5 Roy Medvedev, *Let History Judge: The Origins and Consequences of Stalinism*, p.524.

6 Thomas Sgovio, *Dear America*, pp.239–40.

7 Thomas Sgovio interview with George Kovacs, tapes courtesy of David Elkind, LiveWire Media, San Francisco.

8 Silvester Mora, *Kolyma: Gold and Forced Labor in the USSR*, p.10.

9 Thomas Sgovio, *Dear America*, pp.240–1.

10 Alyce Alex, 261.0022/9-656, RG 59, National Archives II, College Park, Maryland.

11 Eddy Gilmore, *Me and My Russian Wife* (London: Foulsham, 1956), pp.215–216.

12 William. H. White, *Report on the Russians*, p.89.

13 Wallace Carroll, *We're in This with Russia* (Boston: Houghton Mifflin, 1942). p.79.

14 Eddy Gilmore, *Me and My Russian Wife*, p.159.

15 Howard Koch, *As Time Goes By: Memoirs of a Writer*, (New York: Harcourt, Brace, Jovanovich, 1979), pp.101–2.

16 AVPRF, Fond 6, op5, p.9, d.337, ll. 57, 60, 61, from Diane P. Koenker and Ronald D. Bachman (eds), *Revelations from the Russian Archives, Documents in English Translation*, p.649.

17 Elizabeth Kimball MacLean, *Joseph E. Davies: Envoy to the Soviets*, p.106.

18 20 May 1944, Joseph Davies diary, Joseph Davies Papers, Library of Congress Manuscripts, Washington DC.

19 Telegrams maintained by Ambassador W. Averell Harriman, 1944–45, Box 2, RG 84, National Archives II, College Park, Maryland.

20 361.1121/17A, RG 59, National Archives II, College Park, Maryland.

21 Ambassador Harriman telegram, secret despatch to Secretary of State, 24 March 1944, 124.613/1458, RG 59, National Archives II, College Park, Maryland.

22 124.613/1487 RG 59, National Archives II, College Park, Maryland.

23 John F. Melby Oral history interview, 7 November 1986, Harry S. Truman Library, Independence, MO.

24 Moscow post 1944, Box 47, RG 84, National Archives II, College Park, Maryland; Robert Pickens Meiklejohn World War II diary, Box 211, W. Averell Harriman Papers, Library of Congress Manuscripts, Washington DC.

25 John R. Deane, *The Strange Alliance: The Story of Our Efforts at Wartime Cooperation with Russia*, pp.58–59.

26 Kathleen Harriman letter, 9 June 1944, W. Averell Harrmian papers, Library of Congress manuscripts, Washington DC.

27 Box 19, Moscow post 1943, RG 84, National Archives II, College Park, Maryland.

28 Homer Smith, *Black Man in Red Russia*, pp.161–163.

29 Averell Harriman to Roosevelt, January 1944, W. A. Harriman Papers, Library of Congress Manuscripts, Washington DC.

30 President Secretary's File (PSF) Safe Files: GB diplomatic files, Box 37,

Churchill, Winston: 1943 Index, Churchill–FDR, 13 August 1943; FDR Library, Hyde Park, New York. Another document marked 'Top Secret' was delivered by the KGB Chief Alexander Shelepin to Nikita Khrushchev in March 1959, which confirmed that '21,857 person were shot, out of them 4,421 in the Katyn Forest (District of Smolensk), 3820 persons in the camp of Starobelsk close to Kharkov, 6311 persons in the camp of Ostashkovo (District of Kalinin), and 7305 persons were shot in other camps and prisons of the Western Ukraine and Western Byelorussia.', Wojciech Materski (ed.), 'Katyn, Documents of Genocide: Documents and Material from the Soviet Archives Turned Over to Poland on October 14, 1992' (Warsaw: Institute of Political Studies, Polish Academy of Sciences, 1993), p.27.

31 Wojciech Materski (ed.), Katyn, Documents of Genocide: Documents and Material from the Soviet Archives Turned Over to Poland on October 14, 1992', pp.18–23.

32 William Bullitt, 'How We Won the War and Lost the Peace' Life, 30 August 1948, p.94.

33 12 February 1946, conversation between William Bullitt and Henry Wallace from Henry Wallace diary, Library of Congress Manuscripts, Washington DC.

34 Robert Pickens Meiklejohn diary, Box 211, W. Averell Harriman Papers, Library of Congress Manuscripts, Washington DC.

35 Memorandum of Conference, 3p.m., 28 November 1943, Teheran, Harriman file 'Conferences Teheran Official Record', Box 187, Harriman Papers, Library of Congress Manuscripts, Washington DC.

36 Valentin Berezhkov interview 23 June 1997, Hoover Institution, Stanford, CA.

37 Ibid.

38 Gary Kern, 'How "Uncle Joe" Bugged FDR', Studies in Intelligence, Vol.47, No.1, 2003.

39 Memo, dinner 29 November 1943, 8.30 p.m., Harriman file 'Conferences Teheran Official Record', Box 187, W. Averell Harriman Papers, Library of Congress Manuscripts, Washington DC; Winston Churchill quoted from Winston Churchill, The Second World War: Closing the Ring, Vol.5 (London: Penguin, 2005), p.330.

40 New York Times, 25 December 1943, quoted from Gary Kern, 'How "Uncle Joe" bugged FDR', Studies in Intelligence, Vol.47, No.1, 2003.

41 Eleanor Roosevelt, This I Remember, p.247.

42 John R. Deane, The Strange Alliance: The Story of Our Efforts at Wartime Cooperation with Russia, p.160; Yalta Conference Newsreel, Department of Defense, 342–USAF–24228, National Archives II, College Park, Maryland.

43 Winston Churchill, The Second World War: Triumph and Tragedy, Vol.6 (London: Penguin, 2005), p.316.

44 Ibid., p.308.

45 Ibid., pp.333–6.

46 Winston Churchill, *The Second World War: The Hinge of Fate, Vol.4* (London: Cassell, 1951), pp.447–8.

47 Gary Kern, 'How "Uncle Joe" bugged FDR', *Studies in Intelligence*, Vol.47, No.1, 2003; Edmund Stevens, *This is Russia Uncensored* (New York: Didier,1950) p.97; Eva Troyer letter dated 10 February 1938, Enc. No.1 to Despatch No. 1128 of February 1938, from the American Legation, Riga, Latvia, RG59, National Archives II, College Park, Maryland.

48 Martin Gilbert, *Churchill: A Life*, (London: Heinemann, 1991), p.819.

49 Alexander Kirk quoted from Orville H. Bullitt (ed.), *For the President Personal and Secret: Correspondence between Franklin D. Roosevelt and William C. Bullitt*, p.611.

50 Henry Morgenthau, Jr., 11 April 1945, Diaries of Henry Morgenthau, Jr. (1938–1945), FDR Library, Hyde Park, New York.

51 Irwin F. Gellman, *Secret Affairs: Franklin Roosevelt, Cordell Hull and Sumner Welles* (Baltimore: John Hopkins University Press, 1995), p.375.

52 James Forrestal, *The Forrestal Diaries: The Inner History of the Cold War*, ed. Walter Millis (London: Cassell, 1952), pp.58–9.

53 Walter Bedell Smith, *Moscow Mission, 1946–49* (London: Heinemann, 1950), p.38.

54 'Gift from Stalin: Horses, 1945–9', Box 205, W. Averell Harriman Papers, Library of Congress Manuscripts, Washington DC.

20 'RELEASE BY THE GREEN PROCURATOR'

1 Varlam Shalamov, *Graphite*, p.131.

2 George Kennan, *Memoirs: 1925–1950*, p.242.

3 800–USSR, 15 November 1945, Box 81, Moscow Post 1945, RG84, National Archives II, College Park, Maryland.

4 Eugenia Ginzburg, *Within the Whirlwind*, p.139.

5 Kolya Voinov, *Outlaw: The Autobiography of a Soviet Waif*, p.238; Louis Fischer (ed.), *Thirteen Who Fled: 13 Essays by Refugees from Soviet Russia*, p.14.

6 Kolya Voinov, *Outlaw: The Autobiography of a Soviet Waif*, p.240.

7 I. Shcherbakova, 'How Buchenwald Became the NKVD's Torture Chamber', *Moscow News*, 4 June 1993, from Edwin Bacon, *The Gulag at War: Stalin's Forced Labour System in the Light of the Archives* (Basingstoke: Macmillan and Centre for the Russian and East European Studies, University of Birmingham, 1994), p.14.

8 John Noble, *I Was a Slave in Russia* (London: Brown Watson, 1963), p.32.

9 Ibid., pp.58–59; 7000 deaths quoted in CNN Cold War series, Episode 1 'Comrades' broadcast on 27 September 1998; 12,500 deaths quoted in Stephen Kinzer, 'Germans Find Mass Graves at an Ex-Soviet Camp', *New York Times*, 24 September 1992.

10 John Noble, *I Was a Slave in Russia*, pp.76–94.

11 361.1121 Rusinek, Mieczyslaw/2–1147, RG 59, National Archives II, College Park, Maryland.

12 Moscow Embassy Confidential File 1948, RG 84, National Archives II, College Park, Maryland.

13 Nikolai Tolstoy, 'Forced Repatriation to the Soviet Union: The Secret Betrayal', *Imprimis*, December 1988.

14 Letter from Norman Dacey, former psychological warfare operations at SHAEF, 3 October 1952 to State Department. 611.6124/10–352, RG59, National Archives II, College Park, Maryland.

15 Earl F. Ziemke, *The US Army in the Occupation of Germany, 1944–1946* (Washington DC: Center of Military History, United States Army, 1975), p.415.

16 335.11 USSR, Army Intelligence Project Decimal File 1941–45, Box 1041, RG319, National Archives II, College Park, Maryland.

17 Alexander Solzhenitsyn, *The Gulag Archipelago, 1919–1956, An Experiment in Literary Investigation, Vol.1*, p.259.

18 Nikolai Tolstoy, 'Forced Repatriation to the Soviet Union: The Secret Betrayal'; *Impri*, December 1988.

19 Roy Medvedev, *Let History Judge: The Origins and Consequences of Stalinism*, p.468.

20 Varlam Shalamov, *Kolyma Tales*, pp.89–103; Robert Conquest, *Kolyma: The Arctic Death Camps*, pp.154–8.

21 Thomas Sgovio, *Dear America*, p.247.

22 Varlam Shalamov, *Graphite*, p.250.

23 Thomas Sgovio, *Dear America*, pp.176–177.

24 Homer Smith, *Black Man in Red Russia*, pp.173–179.

25 Telegram of Elbridge Durbrow to Secretary of State, top secret, 26–29 October 1946, Moscow, 361.1115/10–2646, RG 59, National Archives II, College Park, Maryland.

26 George Kennan memo: 'Transmitting report on Soviet treatment of American citizens', Moscow, 14 November 1945, Harriman file 'Nov. 8–14, 1945', Box 184, W. Averell Harriman Papers, Library of Congress Manuscripts, Washington DC

27 879.6 Top Secret general records 1941–8, Box 1, RG 84, National Archives II, College Park, Maryland.

28 James Forrestal, *The Forrestal Diaries: The Inner History of the Cold War*, ed. Walter Millis (London: Cassell, 1952), pp.142–6.

21 THE SECOND GENERATION

1 Eugenia Ginzburg, *Within the Whirlwind*, trans. Ian Boland, p.161.

2 Thomas Sgovio, *Dear America*, pp.253–4.

3 Ibid.

4 Eugenia Ginzburg, *Within the Whirlwind*, pp.206–7.

5 Thomas Sgovio, *Dear America*, pp.260–1.

6 Ibid., pp.263–4.

7 Ibid., pp.265–7.

8 Ibid., pp.268–70.

9 Ibid., p.269.

10 Ibid., p.274.

11 Ibid., p.275.

12 Alexander Solzhenitysn, *The Gulag Archipelago, 1919–1956, an Experiment in Literary Investigation, Vol.1*, p.91.

13 Eugenia Ginzburg, *Within the Whirlwind*, trans. Ian Boland, p.279.

14 124.612 and 124.613/12–1845, State Department Decimal File 1945–9, Box 1160, RG59, National Archives II, College Park, Maryland.

15 Telegram from Byrnes, Secretary of State to American Embassy, 23 May 1946, 361.11/11-1445. RG 59, National Archives II, College Park, Maryland.

16 261.1111/3–1556, RG 59, National Archives II, College Park, Maryland.

17 Alexander Dolgun with Patrick Watson, *Alexander Dolgun's Story: An American in the Gulag* (London: Collins/Harvill, 1975), p.12.

18 124.613/8-249 and 124.613/1–1849, State Department Decimal File 1945–9, RG59, National Archives II, College Park, Maryland.

19 Alexander Dolgun with Patrick Watson, *Alexander Dolgun's Story*, p.30.

20 Ibid., pp.30–129.

21 Ibid., pp.163–177.

22 Letter from Professor Yakov Etinger, published in Moscow *Nezavisimaya Gazeta*, 14 May 1992, p.8, from Theodore Karasik collection, Hoover Institution, Stanford, CA.

23 'Treatment of American citizens in USSR', 361.1115/1–1249, RG 59, National Archives II, College Park, Maryland.

24 Letter from Walter Bedell Smith to James W. Riddleberger, Office of the US Political Adviser, Berlin, 20 February 1948, Moscow Embassy Confidential File, 1948: 1201.1–811.11, Box 128, RG 84, National Archives II, College Park, Maryland.

25 Thomas Sgovio, *Dear America*, pp.270–271.

26 18 May 1943, 124.613/1377 – RG 59, National Archives II, College Park, Maryland; Moscow Post 1941–2, Box 13, RG 84, National Archives II, College Park, Maryland; Thomas Sgovio, *Dear America*, p.270.

27 Thomas Sgovio, *Dear America*, p.275.

28 Ibid., p.277.

29 Margaret Wettlin, *Fifty Russian Winters: An American Woman's Life in the Soviet Union* (New York: Pharos, 1992), p.143.

30 Ibid., p.283.

31 Thomas Sgovio, *Dear America*, pp.280–1.

32 *New York Daily Worker*, 30 June 1943 and 8 July 1943.

33 David Horowitz, *Radical Son: A Generational Odyssey* (New York: Free Press, 1997), pp.73–74; Herbert Marshall, 'Paul Robeson's obituary – the aftermath', *Bulletin of the Center for Soviet & East European Studies*, Southern Illinois University at Carbondale, IL, Fall 1976.

34 Interview with Paul Robeson Jr., Cold War history project, Episode 6, 'Reds', 1 November 1998, National Security archive, George Washington University, Washington DC.

35 Barry Finger, 'Paul Robeson: A Flawed Martyr', *New Politics*, Vol.7, No. 1, Summer 1998.

36 Zhdanov quoted in René Fuelop-Miller, *The Mind and Face of Bolshevism* (New York: Harper & Row, 1965), p.300.

37 Joshua Rubinstein and Vladimir P. Naumov (eds), *Stalin's Secret Pogrom: The Postwar Inquisition of the Jewish Anti-Fascist Committee* (New Haven, CT: Yale University Press, 2001), pp.2–3.

38 Robert Robinson, *Black on Red: My Forty-Four Years Inside the Soviet Union*, p.314.

39 Ibid., p.317.

40 John Steinbeck, *A Russian Journal* (New York: Viking, 1948), pp.50–1.

41 John Steinbeck, *The Grapes of Wrath* (London: Penguin, 1992), p.206.

42 Ibid., p.407.

43 John Steinbeck, letter to Bo Beskow, quoted from Elaine Steinbeck and Robert Wallsten (eds), *Steinbeck: A Life in Letters* (London: Heinemann, 1975), p.403.

44 William. L. White, *Report on the Russians*, p.53.

45 Thomas Sgovio, *Dear America*, p.282.

46 Victor Herman, *Coming out of the Ice: An Unexpected Life*, p.286.

47 Ibid., pp.291–329.

48 Ibid., pp.5–6.

22 AWAKENING

1 Hannah Arendt, *The Origins of Totalitarianism* (New York: Harcourt Brace Jovanovich, 1951), p.388.

2 J. Edgar Hoover official and confidential Files, FBI Confidential Files, Library of Congress Manuscripts, Washington DC.

3 Dennis J. Dunn, *Caught Between Roosevelt and Stalin: America's Ambassadors to Moscow*, p.236.

4 Elizabeth Kimball MacLean, *Joseph E. Davies: Envoy to the Soviets*, p.125.

5 Victor Kravchenko, *I Chose Freedom: The Personal and Political Life of a Soviet Official*, p.198.

6 Ibid., pp.198, 289.

7 Joseph Berger, *Shipwreck of a Generation: The Memoirs of Joseph Berger*, p.244.

8 Victor Kravchenko, *I Chose Justice: An Account of the Action for Libel Brought by the Author Against 'Les Lettres Françaises'* (London: Robert Hale, 1951). pp.18–19.

9 *Paramount News*, 2 February 1949, 200–PN–8.46, National Archives II, College Park, Maryland.

10 Victor Kravchenko, *I Chose Justice*, pp.327–330.

11 Pierre Rigoulet, Stéphane Courtois and Martin Malia, *The Black Book of Communism: Crimes, Terror and Repression* (Cambridge, MA: Harvard University Press, 1999), pp.550, 750, xv, xvii.

12 Robert Conquest, *The Great Terror: A Reassessment*, pp.472–5.

13 Maurice Thorez quoted from 'Intelligence Reports on the USSR',

1942–1960, Box 10, Entry 5514, RG 59, National Archives II, College Park, Maryland.

14 Martin Malia, *The Black Book of Communism: Crimes, Terror and Repression*, p.xv.

15 André Gide, *Back from the USSR*, trans. Dorothy Bussy (London: Secker and Warburg, 1937), pp.62–63. Original published as *Retour de l'U.R.S.S.* (Paris: Gallimard, November 1936).

16 André Gide, *Afterthoughts: A Sequel to Back from the USSR*, trans. Dorothy Bussy (London: Secker and Warburg, 1937), pp.7–68.

17 Seth Mydans, 'First Meeting for Two Sons of a Defector', *New York Times*, 4 January 1992.

18 Vladimir Petrov, *It Happens in Russia: Seven Years Forced Labour in the Siberian Goldfields*, p.243.

19 The attitude of American academia to the Soviet Union can be partially explained by a letter from the office of the President of the University of Chicago, dated 17 May 1945, asking for Ambassador Harriman's help with the publication of a 'message to the American people' from Marshal Joseph Stalin: 'Some twenty to thirty thousand words or longer . . . in which he expressed quite frankly the contribution Russia has made toward world unity . . . The publication of Mr Stalin's writings by a great American University can only redound to the good of the world.' (800.1 Stalin Moscow Post 1945, Box 82, RG 84, National Archives II, College Park, Maryland). Or a similar example in the intervention of Charles B. Rugg in October 1945, an attorney acting for Harvard University in a letter to the Legal Division of the State Department asking them to support Harvard's refusal to return the manuscript of Trotsky's *Life of Stalin*: 'In view of the possible effect on Soviet-American relations, Harvard does not wish to release the documents.'(711.61/10–2545, Box 3332, RG 59, National Archives II, College Park, Maryland).

20 Norman D. Markowitz, *The Rise and Fall of the People's Century: Henry A. Wallace and American Liberalism, 1941–1948*, pp.188–9.

21 Henry Wallace interview with Dean Albertson, November 1950, May 1951, p.5123; Columbia University Oral History Collection, Columbia University, New York.

22 Adam Hochschild, *The Unquiet Ghost: Russians Remember Stalin*, p.270.

23 Norman D. Markowitz, *The Rise and Fall of the People's Century: Henry A. Wallace and American Liberalism*, 1941–1948, p.309; Henry Wallace FBI file, pp.309–317, FBI Reading Room, Washington DC.

24 Henry Wallace diary, 30 January 1950; Henry Wallace Papers, Library of Congress Manuscripts, Washington DC; Norman D. Markowitz, *The Rise and Fall of the People's Century: Henry A. Wallace and American Liberalism, 1941-1948*, p.309.

25 Leona Toker, *Return from the Archipelago: Narratives of Gulag Survivors* (Bloomington, IN: Indiana University Press, 2000), p.79; Elinor Lipper, trans. Richard and Clara Winston, *Eleven Years in Soviet Prison Camps* (London: Hollis & Carter, 1951) pp.287–8.

26 Graham White and John Maze, *Henry A. Wallace: His Search for a New World Order* (Chapel Hill, NC: University of North Carolina Press, 1995), 295–6.

27 Henry Wallace diary, Henry Wallace Papers, Library of Congress Manuscripts, Washington DC.

28 John C. Culver and John Hyde, *American Dreamer: The Life and Times of Henry A. Wallace* (New York: Norton, 2001), p.469.

29 Owen Lattimore Papers, Box 33, Folder 9, Library of Congress Manuscripts, Washington DC.

30 Robert Conquest, *Kolyma: The Arctic Death Camps*, p.211.

31 John Earl Haynes and Harvey Klehr, *Venona: Decoding Soviet Espionage in America* (New Haven, CT: Yale University Press, 1999), p.12.

32 Whittaker Chambers, *Witness: An Autobiography* (New York: Random House, 1952), p.466.

33 George N. Crocker, *Roosevelt's Road to Russia* (Chicago: Henry Regnery, 1959), p.250; John Earl Haynes and Harvey Klehr, *Venona: Decoding Soviet Espionage in America*, p.331.

34 George N. Crocker, *Roosevelt's Road to Russia* (Chicago: Henry Regnery, 1959), pp.238–9.

35 John Earl Haynes and Harvey Klehr, *Venona: Decoding Soviet Espionage in America*, pp.202–203.

36 Christopher D. O'Sullivan, *Sumner Welles, Postwar Planning and the Quest for a New World Order, 1937–1943* (Chichester, NY: Columbia University Press, 2003 and Gutenberg edition online); J. Edgar Hoover official and confidential files, FBI confidential files, Library of Congress Manuscripts, Washington DC.

37 Krivitsky FBI file, FBI Reading Room, Washington DC; Christopher D. O'Sullivan, *Sumner Welles, Postwar Planning and the Quest for a New World Order, 1937–1943*; Irwin F. Gellman, *Secret Affairs: Franklin Roosevelt, Cordell Hull and Sumner Welles* (Baltimore: John Hopkins University Press, 1995), pp.391–2.

38 George Racey Jordan, *From Major Jordan's Diaries* (New York: Harcourt, Brace and Company, 1952), pp.66–81.

39 Ibid., pp.92–94.

40 Hopkins quoted in George Racey Jordan, *From Major Jordan's Diaries*, p.31; Henry Wallace interview with Dean Albertson, November 1950–May 1951, p.3713; Columbia University Oral History Collection, Columbia University, New York.

41 George Racey Jordan, *From Major Jordan's Diaries*, p.122.

42 Christopher Andrew and Oleg Gordievsky, *KGB: The Inside Story of its Foreign Operations from Lenin to Gorbachev* (London: Hodder & Stoughton, 1990), p.233. In his book Oleg Gordievsky qualified Akhmerov's statement describing Hopkins as 'an unconscious rather than a conscious agent'.

43 James F. Byrnes, *Speaking Frankly* (London: Heinemann, 1947), p.263; Winston Churchill, *The Second World War: Triumph and Tragedy, Vol.6* (London: Penguin, 2005) pp.579–80.

23 'CITIZEN OF THE UNITED STATES OF AMERICA, ALLIED OFFICER DALE'

1 Michael Solomon, *Magadan* (Princeton N.J.: Auerbach, 1971), p.119.

2 Wringer Report: 71288-E–51–7623A, Box 998, RG 341, National Archives II, College Park, Maryland.

3 'The Memoirs', Defense POW/Missing Personnel Office, Joint Commission Support Directorate, Arlington, VA.

4 The Gulag Study, Joint Commission Support Directorate, Gulag Research Group, Defense POW/Missing Personnel Office, Arlington, VA, fourth edition, 22 June, 2002, p.30.

5 'The Memoirs', Defense POW/Missing Personnel Office, Joint Commission Support Directorate, Arlington, VA.

6 Ibid.

7 17 March 1945, FDR to Stalin, Map Room papers, September 1939–July 1942, FDR Library, Hyde Park, New York.

8 7 April 1945, Stalin to Roosevelt, Map Room papers, September 1939–July 1942, FDR Library, Hyde Park, New York.

9 Bill Paul, 'POWs: Four Decades of US Abandonment', *Wall Street Journal*, 13 August 1987.

10 Elbridge Durbrow letter dated 22 June 1963, Elbridge Durbrow collection, Hoover Institution, Stanford, CA.

11 *USIS News Bulletin*, 321.4 German PWs, Moscow Embassy Confidential File. 1950: 321.4–350 France, Box 146, RG84, National Archives II, College Park, Maryland.

12 Brian Moynahan, *The Russian Century: A Photographic History of Russia's 100 Years*, p.204.

13 25 January 1956, 661.6224/1–2556, RG 59, National Archives II, College Park, Maryland.

14 2 June 1954, 661.0024/8–1054, RG 59, National Archives II, College Park, Maryland.

15 'The five million slaves', *New York Times*, 18 July 1948.

16 Wringer Report No. 52A–E–5522A, Box 998, RG 341, National Archives II, College Park, Maryland.

17 Wringer Report No. 181385–59–B–1745–A, RG 341, National Archives II, College Park, Maryland.

18 Wringer Report No. E–53–12631–B, RG 341, National Archives II, College Park, Maryland.

19 014.5 Detention USSR, 16 November 1948, Army Intelligence Project decimal file, 1946–1948, Box No 279, RG319, National Archives II, College Park, Maryland.

20 611.61251/2–1854, Decimal file 1950–54, Box 2826, RG 59, National Archives II, College Park, Maryland.

21 611.61251/4–2554, RG59, National Archives II, College Park, Maryland

22 19 June 1952, 611.61241/6–1952, RG 59, National Archives II, College Park, Maryland.

23 611.61251/4–2554, 611.61251/6–2884, Decimal file 1950–54, Box 2826, RG 59, National Archives II, College Park, Maryland.

24 Gavril Korotkov quoted in Douglas Stanglin and Peter Cary, 'Generalissimo's last war', US News and World Report, 9 August 1993.

25 The figure of at least 2.5 million is from 'Korean War' entry, Encyclopaedia Britannica Online, 10 December 2007; the figures of 36,576 American servicemen and women killed during the conflict, 103,274 listed as wounded, 8126 missing in action or unaccounted for come from Washington HQ Services, Directorate for Information Operations and Reports, Department of Defense, Washington DC, published 15 June 2004.

26 Annex B13 to JCSB Triweekly Report, 21 August–10 September 1993, Task Force Russia, Report, June 1993, Box 3, RG330, National Archives II, College Park, Maryland.

27 Zygmunt Nagorski Jr., 'Unreported GIs in Siberia', Esquire, May 1953.

28 Letter 11 June 1958, to Jack D. Neal State Department from J. Edgar Hoover, FBI, Army Intelligence Project decimal file, 1946–48, Box 280, RG319; Report Lt. Col. E. Nichols, 25 October 1948, Army Intelligence Project decimal file, 1946–48, Box 280, RG319; Army Intelligence Project decimal file, 1949–1950, Box 192, RG319, National Archives II, College Park, Maryland; Vyacheslav Molotov interview from Felix Chuev (ed.), Molotov Remembers: Inside Kremlin Politics – Conversations with Felix Chuev (Chicago: Ivan Dee, 1993), p.71.

29 Moscow Embassy confidential file, Box 164, RG 84, National Archives II, College Park, Maryland.

30 Top Secret Dispatch, 24 September 1948, Kohler to Secretary of State, Top Secret Records from the Office of the Ambassador, 1948–1949, Box 3, RG84, National Archives II, College Park, Maryland.

31 23 March 1954, Moscow Embassy confidential file 1954, Box 191, RG84, National Archives II, College Park, Maryland.

32 Dwight D. Eisenhower Library memo, Abilene, Kansas, quoted in 'Korean War POWS in Siberia', Associated Press, 4 May 1996.

33 Interview with Lt. Col. (Retired) Philip Corso, Annex B to Task Force Russia Biweekly Report, 13 Novovember 1992, RG 330, National Archives II, College Park, Maryland. According to Task Force Russia operatives, the archives of the Eisenhower Library in Abilene, Kansas 'fully supported LTC Corso's statements as to what the US Government knew or had to reason to believe about prisoner transfers during the Eisenhower adminstration' – Task Force Russia (POW/MIA) Report 20 February 1993–5 March 1993, RG330, National Archives II, College Park, Maryland.

34 13th Plenum, USRJC, 24–25 September 1996, Box 1, DPMO, RG 330, National Archives II, College Park, Maryland.

35 611.61241/8–2156, 21 August 1956, RG 59, National Archives II, College Park, Maryland.

36 261.0022/9–656, RG 59, National Archives II, College Park, Maryland.

37 261.0011/2–554, RG 59, National Archives II, College Park, Maryland.

38 261.1111/7–1856, RG 59, National Archives II, College Park, Maryland.

39 321.4 USSR Moscow Embassy, classified records 1960–63, Box 4, RG84, National Archives II, College Park, Maryland.

40 William R. Tyler, 27 July 1960, American Embassy, Bonn, 321.4, classified general records, Box 4, RG84, National Archives II, College Park, Maryland.

41 261.1111/12–1256, RG 59, National Archives II, College Park, Maryland.

42 611.61241/11-453, RG 59, National Archives II, College Park, Maryland.

43 261.1111/7–1155, RG 59, National Archives II, College Park, Maryland.

44 George Kennan, Secret telegram to Secretary of State, Washington, 25 September 1956; filed 2 October 1945, State Department confidential file, RG59, National Archives II, College Park, Maryland; K. Belyaninov, 'May I not see the Statue of Liberty for as long as I live', *Komsomolskaya Pravda*, 11 June 1992, p.2, from concatenated JPRS reports, 1992, Final report DPMO, Redacted copies from Box 2, Box 2A, RG 330, National Archives II, College Park, Maryland.

45 Pavel Sudoplatov, *Special Tasks: The Memoirs of an Unwanted Witness – a Soviet Spymaster* (London: Little Brown, 1994), pp.270–271.

46 Galina Ivanova, *Labour Camp Socialism: The Gulag in the Soviet Totalitarian System*, trans. Carol Flath (Armonk, NY: M. E. Sharpe, 2000), p.190.

47 TFR 37–11 to 37–19, Minutes of the meeting between Comrade Stalin and Chou En-Lai, 19 September 1952. Box 3, RG330, National Archives II, College Park, Maryland.

24 'SMERT STALINA SPASET ROSSIIU'

1 Sergei Eisenstein, *Ivan The Terrible*, Part One, 1944.

2 Roy Medvedev, Let History Judge: *The Origins and Consequences of Stalinism*, p.151.

3 Nikita Khrushchev, *The 'Secret' Speech: Delivered to the Closed Session of the Twentieth Congress of the Communist Party of the Soviet Union* (Nottingham: Spokesman, 1976), p.70.

4 Edvard Radzinsky, *Stalin*, pp.3–4.

5 Milovan Djilas, *Conversations with Stalin*, trans. Michael Petrovich (London: Hart-Davis, 1962), pp.136, 145–146.

6 Ibid., p.97; Lev Razgon, *True Stories*, trans. John Crowfoot (London: Souvenir Press, 1998), p.18.

7 Valentin Berezhkov interview 6 May 1997, Hoover Institution, Stanford, CA; Edvard Radzinsky, *Stalin*, p.518.

8 Nikita Khrushchev, *Khrushchev Remembers*, trans. Strobe Talbott (London: André Deutsch, 1971), p.307.

9 Valentin M. Berezhkov, *At Stalin's Side: His Interpreter's Memoirs from the October Revolution to the Fall of the Dictator's Empire*, trans. Sergei V. Mikheyev (New York: Birch Lane Press, 1994), p.318.

10 Richard Hottelet, 'Soviet Union Can't Be Trusted or Appeased, Diplomat Litvinov Warned Western World', *Washington Post*, January 1952.

11 Pavel Sudoplatov, *Special Tasks: The Memoirs of an Unwanted Witness – a Soviet Spymaster*, p.306.

12 Nikita Khrushchev, *The 'Secret' Speech: Delivered to the Closed Session of the Twentieth Congress of the Communist Party of the Soviet Union*, p.63.

13 Valentin Berezhkov interview 6 May 1997, Hoover Institution, Stanford, CA.

14 Edmund Stevens, *This is Russia Uncensored* (New York: Didier, 1950), p.167.

15 Vadim J. Birstein, *The Perversion of Knowledge: The True Story of Soviet Science*, p.64.

16 'The Death of Stalin', NBC documentary film, 27 January 1963, National Archives II, College Park, Maryland; Valentin Berezhkov interview 6 May 1997, Hoover Institution, Stanford, CA.

17 Anton Antonov-Ovseyenko, *The Time of Stalin: Portrait of a Tyranny*, trans. George Saunders, p.294.

18 Pavel Sudoplatov, *Special Tasks: The Memoirs of an Unwanted Witness – a Soviet Spymaster*, p.327.

19 Edvard Radzinsky, *Stalin*, p.533; Vadim J. Birstein, *The Perversion of Knowledge: The True Story of Soviet Science*, p.61.

20 Svetlana Alliluyeva, *Twenty Letters to A Friend*, trans. Priscilla Johnson (London: Penguin, 1968), p.28.

21 Ibid., p.171; Svetlana Alliluyeva, *Only One Year*, trans. Paul Chavchavadze (London: Hutchinson, 1969), p.156.

22 Thomas Sgovio, *Dear America*, p.282.

23 Sheila Fitzpatrick, *Everyday Stalinism – Ordinary Life In Extraordinary Times – Soviet Russia in the 1930s* p.184.

24 John Noble, *I Was a Slave in Russia*, p.125.

25 Thomas Sgovio, *Dear America*, p.283.

26 Svetlana Alliluyeva, *Twenty Letters to A Friend*, p.17.

27 Robert A. Ford, *Our Man in Moscow: A Diplomat's Reflections on the Soviet Union* (Toronto: University of Toronto Press, 1989) p.23.

28 Robert Robinson, *Black on Red: My Forty-Four Years Inside the Soviet Union*, p.266.

29 Ibid., p.267.

30 Ibid., p.269.

31 Telegram sent by Beam 9 March 1953 and Letter from Beam to Malik, 6 March 1953, Moscow Embassy, confidential file 1953, Box 178, RG 84, National Archives II, College Park, Maryland.

32 *The Times of India*, 8 March 1953; Paul Robeson, 'To You Beloved Comrade', *New World Review*, April 1953, pp.11–13, from Robeson, *Paul Robeson Speaks*, ed. Philip S. Foner, pp. 348–9.

33 Zhores Medvedev and Roy Medvedev, introduction to Nikita Khrushchev, *The 'Secret' Speech: Delivered to the Closed Session of the Twentieth Congress of the Communist Party of the Soviet Union*, p.12.

34 Roy Medvedev and Zhores Medvedev, *Khrushchev: The Years in Power*, trans. Andre R. Durkin (London: Oxford University Press, 1977), pp.10–11; Nikita Khrushchev, *Khrushchev Remembers*, p.338; Roy Medvedev, *Let History Judge: The Origins and Consequences of Stalinism*, p.368; Robert Robinson, *Black on Red: My Forty-Four Years Inside the Soviet Union*, p.274; Don Richardson, *Moscow* (London: Rough Guides, 1995), p.154.

35 Edward Radzinsky, *Stalin*, trans. H. T. Willets (London: Hodder and Stoughton, 1996), p.561; Roy Medvedev, *Khrushchev*, trans. Brian Pearce (Oxford: Blackwell, 1982), p.67; TFR 376–1a, Alekandr Syrtsov, RG330, National Archives II, College Park, Maryland.

36 Zhores Medvedev and Roy Medvedev, introduction to Nikita Khrushchev, *The 'Secret' Speech: Delivered to the Closed Session of the Twentieth Congress of the Communist Party of the Soviet Union*, p.12; Moscow Embassy confidential file, 1954, Box 191, RG84, National Archives II, College Park, Maryland; Pavel Sudoplatov, *Special Tasks: The Memoirs of an Unwanted Witness – a Soviet Spymaster*, p.366; Memorial Society, Russian State Archive of Sociopolitical History, State Archive of the Russian Federation, N. V. Petrov and K. V. Skorkin, 'Who Headed the NKVD in 1934–1941', N. G. Okhotin and A. B. Roginskii (eds) (Moscow: 1999).

37 John Noble, *I Was a Slave in Russia*, p.128.

38 Ibid., p.139.

39 Ibid., p.142.

40 Alexander Dolgun with Patrick Watson, *Alexander Dolgun's Story: An American in the Gulag* (London: Collins/Harvill, 1975), pp.287–289.

41 Alexander Solzhenitsyn, *The Gulag Archipelago, 1918-1956: An Experiment in Literary Investigation*, pp.320–331; Geoffrey Hosking, *A History of the Soviet Union* (London: Fontana, 1985), p.33.

42 Mikhail Mikhaeev (dir.), *Kolyma* documentary film, Hoover Institution, Stanford, CA.

43 Bruno Bettelheim, *Surviving and Other Essays* (London: Thames & Hudson, 1979), p.95; the idea of the 'two tragedies of the twentieth century' is from Milan Kundera.

44 Lev Razgon, *True Stories*, trans. John Crowfoot (London: Souvenir Press, 1998), p.338.

45 Victor Herman, *Coming out of the Ice: An Unexpected Life*, pp.317–333.

46 Thomas Sgovio NKVD file, Hoover Institution, Stanford, CA.

47 Thomas Sgovio NKVD file, Hoover Institution, Stanford, CA.

48 Interview with Evgeny Bernadovich Chen by Lyuba Vinogradova, Moscow, 31 March 2006.

49 Boris Pasternak, *Doctor Zhivago*, trans. Max Hayward and Manya Harari (London: Collins Harvill, 1988), p.449.

50 Thomas Sgovio, *Dear America*, p.121.

25 FREEDOM AND DECEIT

1 Varlam Shalamov, *Graphite*, p.281; Nanci Adler, *The Gulag Survivor: Beyond The Soviet System* (New Brunswick, NJ: Transaction, 2002), p.64.

2 Thomas Sgovio, *Dear America*, p.284; Andrei Sinyavsky, *Soviet Civilization: A Cultural History*, trans. Joanne Turnbull and Nikolai Formozov (New York: Arcade, 1990), p.24; Geoffrey Hosking, *A History of the Soviet Union* (London: Fontana, 1985), p.342.

3 Joseph Berger, *Shipwreck of a Generation: The Memoirs of Joseph Berger*, p.243.

4 Richard Lourie, *Russia Speaks: An Oral History from the Revolution to the Present* (New York: E. Burlingame, 1991), p.188.

5 Pavel Sudoplatov, *Special Tasks: The Memoirs of an Unwanted Witness – A Soviet Spymaster*, p.419.

6 Nanci Adler, *The Gulag Survivor: Beyond the Soviet System*, p.172.

7 Varlam Shalamov, *Kolyma Tales*, pp.72–73.

8 Leona Toker, *Return from the Archipelago: Narratives of Gulag Survivors* (Bloomington, IN: Indiana University Press, 2000), p.150.

9 Vitaly Shentalinsky, *The KGB's Literary Archive*, pp.136–8.

10 Vadim J. Birstein, *The Perversion of Knowledge: The True Story of Soviet Science*, p.241; Bruno Bettelheim, *Surviving and Other Essays*, p.71.

11 David J. Dallin and Boris I. Nicolaevsky, *Forced Labor in Soviet Russia* (London: Hollis & Carter, 1948), p.144.

12 Geoffrey Hosking, *The History of the Soviet Union* (London: Fontana, 1985) pp.342–343.

13 Russian State Archive of Socio-Political History, Moscow, RGASPI, fond 17, opis 127, delo 1129, listy 35, 38, 39, 40, 41, 59.

14 Vadim J. Birstein, *The Perversion of Knowledge: The True Story of Soviet Science*, p.184.

15 Alexander Dolgun with Patrick Watson, *Alexander Dolgun's Story: An American in the Gulag*, pp.327–341.

16 Ibid., p.337.

17 25 September 1956 from the American Embassy, Vienna, Despatch 265, 261.1111/9–2566, RG 59, National Archives II, College Park, Maryland.

18 Alyce Alex had been released only to be rearrested in August 1949 – 261.0022/9-656, RG 59, National Archives II, College Park, Maryland; Dora Gershonowitz too survived her sentence and was reported to have arrived in Moscow at her mother's house on 3 November 1959. Her relatives in America were still attempting to obtain for her an exit visa to the United States (251.1111 Geroshonowitz, Dora. RG59, National Archives II, College Park, Maryland). The State Department, meanwhile, had published another memo in July 1954, entitled 'US Citizens in the USSR and its Eastern European Satellites', which reported the number of Americans held behind the Iron Curtain at 4766. The *New York Times* editorial 'The Other Prisoners' quoted the same source to comment that 'several times that number' were also regarded as 'possible claimants' to United States

citizenship.(611.61251/7–2354, RG 59, National Archives II, College Park, Maryland; 'The Other Prisoners', *New York Times*, 5 January 1954).

19 261.1111/8–1056, RG 59, National Archives II, College Park, Maryland.

20 30 September 1943; quoted in 310, Koppelman, RG 59, National Archives II, College Park, Maryland.

21 Zhores Medvedev and Roy Medvedev, introduction to Nikita Khrushchev, *The 'Secret' Speech: Delivered to the Closed Session of the Twentieth Congress of the Communist Party of the Soviet Union*, pp.9–10.

22 Nikita Khrushchev, *The 'Secret' Speech: Delivered to the Closed Session of the Twentieth Congress of the Communist Party of the Soviet Union*, p.46.

23 Irving Howe and Lewis Coser, *The American Communist Party – A Critical History,1919–1957* (Boston: Beacon Press, 1957), p.491.

24 Roy Medvedev, *Khrushchev*, trans. Brian Pearce (Oxford: Blackwell, 1982), p.99; Nanci Adler, *The Gulag Survivor: Beyond the Soviet System*, pp.23–24, 177.

25 Nikita Khrushchev quoted in Nanci Adler, *The Gulag Survivor: Beyond the Soviet System*, p.89.

26 Boris Pasternak, *Doctor Zhivago*, trans. Max Hayward and Manya Harari (London, Fontana, 1985), p.555.

27 Mayme Sevander with Laurie Hertzel, *They Took My Father: A Story of Idealism and Betrayal* (Duluth, MN: Pfeifer-Hamilton, 1992), pp.175–184.

28 Thomas Sgovio, *Dear America*, pp.284–6.

29 18 September 1959, Foreign Relations of the United States, 1958–1960, Vol X, Part 1:11, Soviet Union.

30 Victor Reuther, 'Commitment and betrayal: foreign workers at the Gorky auto works', ed. Paul T. Christensen (unpublished, 2004) p.191, p.66; Victor Reuther, *The Brothers Reuther and the Story of the UAW: A Memoir by Victor G. Reuther* (Boston: Houghton Mifflin, 1976), pp.396–8.

31 Nikita Khrushchev, 'Nations should live as good neighbours!', Khrushchev's address on United States television, Washington, 27 September 1959 (London: Soviet Booklets, 1959), pp.1–19.

32 Nikita Khrushchev, *Khrushchev Remembers*, p.417.

33 'Investigation of the Unauthorized Use of United States Passports – Part 3,' Hearings before the Committee on Un-American Activities, House of Representatives, Eighty-Fourth Congress, Second Session, 12 June 1956, Washington DC, 1956, pp.4492–4510; quoted from Paul Robeson, *Paul Robeson Speaks*, Philip S. Foner (ed.), pp.413–433.

34 Paul Robeson FBI file, FBI Reading Room, Washington DC; New York World Telegram 23 December 1963; Sterling Stuckey, *New York Times Book Review*, quoted in Rob Nagel, biography, Paul Robeson *Contemporary Musicians, Vol.8*, September 1992.

35 'Davies Reply to Gossip is "I Am a Capitalist"', *Milwaukee Journal*, 29 May 1952.

36 Elizabeth Kimball MacLean, *Joseph E. Davies: Envoy to the Soviets*, p.181.

37 'Walter Duranty, newsman, 73, dies', *New York Times*, 4 October 1957; Carl Blumay and Henry Edwards, *The Dark Side of Power: The Real Armand Hammer* (New York : Simon & Schuster, 1992), p.48.

38 Norman D. Markowitz, *The Rise and Fall of the People's Century: Henry A. Wallace and American Liberalism, 1941–1948*, pp.309–323; Graham White and John Maze, *Henry Wallace: His Search for a New World Order* (Chapel Hill, NC: University of North Carolina Press, 1995), p.296.

39 Henry Wallace interview with Dean Albertson, November 1950–May 1951, p.11, p.3657, Columbia University Oral History Collection, Columbia University, New York.

40 'The International Jew – The World's Foremost Problem – being a reprint of a series of articles appearing in the *Dearborn Independent* from May 22 to Oct 2, 1920', published by The Dearborn Publishing Co., Dearborn, Michigan distributed by the Ford Motor Company. Henry Ford's FBI file cited evidence produced in a German court in 1923 that Henry Ford had also contributed funds to Adolf Hitler's fledging Nazi Party. Winifred Wagner – the daughter-in-law of the Nazi's favourite composer and confidante of Hitler – recalled a conversation she had with Henry Ford on a visit to Dearborn in 31 January 1932: 'Ford told me that he had helped finance Hitler with money from the sales of automobiles and trucks that he had sent to Germany.' It helped to explain why Adolf Hitler – when interviewed by a journalist from the New York Times at his Munich head-quarters in 1922 – had a portrait of Henry Ford hanging behind his desk. Henry Ford was decorated by Hitler and praised by name in *Mein Kampf*. See Carol Gelderman, *Henry Ford: Wayward Capitalist*, p.223; Henry Ford FBI File, FBI Reading Room, Washington DC. Niven Busch, Jr., *Twenty-One Americans: Being Profiles of Some People Famous in Our Time* (Garden City, NJ: Doubleday, 1930), p.4.

41 Carol Gelderman, *Henry Ford: Wayward Capitalist* (New York: Dial Press, 1981), p.398; 'Recorded conversation between Comrade I. V. Stalin and Chairman of the Trade Chamber of the USA E. Johnston,' 26 June 1944, from Russian State Archive of Socio-Political History, Moscow, RGASPI, fond 558, opis 11, delo 374, listy 68–75.

42 Charles Sorensen, *My Forty Years with Ford*, p.18.

43 Victor Herman, *Coming out of the Ice: An Unexpected Life*, p.347; *New York Times*, 30 May 1977.

44 Molly Ivins, 'A former American exile awaits daughter's arrival from Russia', *New York Times*, 30 May 1977; Victor Herman, *Coming out of the Ice: An Unexpected Life*, p.49; *New York Times*, 14 June 1978; Frank J. Prial, 'Ex Soviet worker is rebuffed', *New York Times*, 14 June 1985; 'Victor Herman, exile in Soviet', *New York Times*, 29 March 1985; Jack Norworth, 'Take Me Out to the Ballgame', p908.

45 Craig Whitney, 'From idealism to misery', *New York Times*, 10 December 1977; Dan Fisher, 'Soviet utopia of 1931 now a prison for embittered American', *Washington Post*, 1 September 1977; John Gilardi, 'American Jew returns for visit after 58 years in Soviet Union', *New York Times*, 5 July 1989; *New York Times*, 25 December 1986.

46 Interview with Evgeny Bernadovich Chen by Lyuba Vinogradova, Moscow, 31 March 2006.

47 Geoffrey Hosking, *A History of the Soviet Union*, p.343.

48 Transcript of the interrogation of Andrey Sinyavsky, Andrei Sinyavsky, *On Trial: The Case of Sinyavsky (Tertz) and Daniel (Arzhak)*. Documents ed. and trans. Leopold Labedz and Max Hayward (London: Collins & Harvill Press, 1967), p.205.

49 Hannah Arendt, *The Origins of Totalitarianism*, p.465.

50 Nikita Khrushchev, *Khrushchev Remembers*, p.3.

51 Mikhail Gorbachev, *Mikhail Gorbachev: Memoirs*, trans. Georges Peronansky and Tatjana Varsovsky (London: Doubleday, 1996), p.13

26 THE TRUTH AT LAST

1 Joseph Brodsky, *Collected Poems in English*, tran. Anthony Hecht (Manchester: Carcanet, 2001), p.64.

2 'Remarks by President Bush and Russian President Boris Yeltsin Concerning the U.S.–Russia Agreement on Nuclear Weapons', 16 June 1992, transcript by News Transcripts Inc., Box 1, Theodore Karasik collection, Hoover Institution, Stanford, CA.

3 *Dateline* NBC, 16 June 1992, News Transcripts Inc., Box 1, Theodore Karasik collection, Hoover Institution, Stanford, CA.

4 'President Bush and Russian President Boris Yeltsin News Conference, White House East Room', 17 June 1992, transcript by News Transcripts Inc., Box 1, Theodore Karasik collection, Hoover Institution, Stanford, CA.

5 Task Force Russia report, November 1992, Box 2, RG 330, National Archives II, College Park, Maryland.

6 Donna Downes Knox, 'The Continuing Search for Answers in Russia', Coalition of Families, PO Box 7152, Roanoke, VA.

7 Task Force Russia (POW/MIA), Analytical Report No.2, Box 2, RG 330, National Archives II, College Park, Maryland.

8 Interview of Soviet General Fiodor Shinkarenko (retired) with Jane Reynolds Howard, Riga, Latvia, 2 September 1992, Box 2A, Defense POW MIA Office (DPMO), RG 330, National Archives II, College Park, Maryland.

9 Final Report DPMO, Redacted copies from Box 2, Box 2A, RG 330, National Archives II, College Park, Maryland; *Krasnaya Zvezda*, 13 Febuary 1993, 'Angels from the Pentagon and the CIA, Why are they cherished in Russia?', Annex A to TFR, 6–19 February 1993, RG 330, National Archives II, College Park, Maryland.

10 Task Force report, 25 September 1992, RG 330, National Archives II, College Park, Maryland.

11 '1992–1996 findings of the WWII Working Group', p.141, RG 330, National Archives II, College Park, Maryland.

12 Figure of 2,836 Americans from State Archive of Russian Federation, Moscow, GARF, f.9414, o.1393, d.14, quoted in Thirteenth Plenary Session US–Russia Joint Commission on POW/MIAs, 24 September 1996, RG 330, National Archives II, College Park, Maryland.

13 361.1121/12–1045, 10 December 1946, National Archives II, College Park, Maryland.

14 Dr Peterson, 11th Plenary Session, US–Russian Joint Commission on POWs/MIAs, 7 December 1994, Task Force Russia Box 4, RG 330, National Archives II, College Park, Maryland.

15 Task Force Russia (POW/MIA), report to the US Delegation, US–Russian Joint Commission on POW/MIAs, 12 March 1993, RG 330, National Archives II, College Park, Maryland.

16 'President Too Busy to Discuss Joint Commission with General Lajoie', August 2001, and 'Background of Korean War – POW issue', Statements issued by Coalition of Families, PO Box 7152, Roanoken, VA.

17 MSGs AMEMBASSY TALLINN, 201020Z April 1993 and AMEM-BASSY TALLINN 231223Z April 1993, Annex A to Task Force Russia Biweekly Report, 17–30 April 1993. Reports from US Russian Joint Commission, 1993, Box 3, RG330, National Archives II, College Park, Maryland.

18 '1992–1996 Findings of the WWII Working Group', pp.145–6, RG 330, National Archives II, College Park, Maryland.

19 Task Force Russia document No.382–3, RG 330, National Archives II, College Park, Maryland.

20 Comprehensive Report, USRJC, 17 June 1996, pp.146–153, 13th Plenum US–Russia Joint Commission on POW/MIA Affairs, 24-24 Sept.1996, Moscow; 196 JCSD–AMEMBASSY Moscow, 011207Z June 1995, RG 330, National Archives II, College Park, Maryland; James Brooke, 'Americans in Soviet Jails', *New York Times*, 19 July 1996.

21 Task Force Russia report, June 1993, Box 3, RG330, National Archives II, College Park, Maryland.

22 Transcript from interview in newspaper article *Komsomolskaia Pravda*, quoted in Comprehensive Report, USRJC, 17 June 1996, p.159, DPMO, Box 1, RG 330, National Archives II, College Park, Maryland.

23 R241259A August 1992 Fm Amembassy Moscow, Subject : POW/MIA Team interview with Colonel Korotkov, Annex C to Task Force Russia Biweekly Report, 17 March–16 March 1993, RG 330, National Archives II, College Park, Maryland.

24 Task Force Russia (POW/MIA) Report to the US Delegation, US–Russian Joint Commission on POW/MIAs, 25 September 1992, RG 330; Comprehensive Report, USRJC, 17 June 1996, pp.163–7, DPMO, Box 1, RG 330, National Archives II, College Park, Maryland.

25 Annex B To TFR Report for 29 January 1993, RG330, National Archives II, College Park, Maryland.

26 The Gulag Study, Joint Commission Support Directorate, Gulag Research Group, Defense POW/Missing Personnel Office, Arlington, VA, fourth edition, 22 June 2002, p.33.

27 Comprehensive Report, USRJC, 17 June 1996, DPMO, Box 1, RG 330, National Archives II, College Park, Maryland; 'US Says Soviet Holds Americans of 2 Lost Planes', *New York Times*, 17 July 1956; Draft Note to the US Embassy from the Ministry of Foreign Affairs, 9 August 1956, from Diane P. Koenker and Ronald D. Bachman (eds), *Revelations from the Russian Archives*, p.680.

28 Charlotte Busch Mitnik, 'A Family Member's Feelings', Coalition of Families, PO Box 7125, Roanoke, VA.

29 TFR 185–121, Comprehensive Report, USRJC, 17 June 1996, DPMO, Box 1, RG 330, National Archives II, College Park, Maryland.

30 Source Annex A to JCSB Triweekly report of the Period 21 August–10 September 1993, Task Force Russia, report, June 1993, Box 3; Meeting of Co-Chairmen, US–Russia Joint Commission on POW/MIAs, 28 May 2002, Moscow. DPMO, RG 330, National Archives II, College Park, Maryland.

31 16th Plenum, 1999, Cold War working group, DPMO, Joint Commission Support Directorate Report 9–13 September 2003, DPMO, RG 330, National Archives II, College Park, Maryland.

32 '56 Years Later, WWII Navy Bomber Found in Remote Russia', Associated Press, Honolulu-Star Bulletin, 14 August 200; Trip Report for TDY to Kamchatten Russia, 30 June–18 September 2001, US–Russian Joint Commission on POW/MIA, Department of Defense, Washington DC.

33 Amelia Gentleman, 'Europe's Last POW, the Man Locked Away for 56 Years', Guardian, 3 August 2000; Nick Thorpe, 'POW Gets Life Back After 55 Years', Guardian, 19 September 2000.

34 Vitaly Vitaliev, 'Echoes can still be heard of the tyranny of fear', Moscow Times, 6 March 2003.

35 'Thaw Brings Japan's POWs Back', Moscow Times, April 16 1998; Tom Lantos, Speech to House of Representatives, 5 October 1992; Adam Hochschild, The Unquiet Ghost: Russians Remember Stalin, p.275.

36 Report to the US Delegation, US–Russian Joint Commission on POWs/MIAs, 11 September 1992, RG 330, National Archives II, College Park, Maryland; In February 2005, the American investigator Norman Kass briefed the international press: 'I personally would be comfortable saying that the number [of Americans held in the gulags during the Cold War and Korean War] is in the hundreds', quoted in article, 'Official says hundreds of US Citizens likely died in gulags' – CNN, 11 February 2005.

37 Danz Blasser interview from Secrets of the Lost Fighter Pilots, documentary film broadcast Channel 5, 5 December 2006.

38 Anna Politkovskaya, Putin's Russia, trans. Arch Tait (London: Harvill Press, 2004) pp.vii, 96–271, 283.

27 'THE TWO RUSSIAS'

1 Alexander Blok, Selected Poems, trans. Jon Stallworthy and Peter France (Manchester: Carcanet Press, 2000), p.111.

2 Russell Working, 'Odessa Last Breath of Soviet Liberty', Moscow Times, 9 September 2000; Martin J. Bollinger, Stalin's Slave Ships: Kolyma, the Gulag Fleet, and the Role of the West, p.43.

3 Descriptions of Kolyma based upon footage from George Kovach (dir.), The Camps of Magadan, documentary film, 1990, Hoover Institute, Stanford, CA, and rushes courtesy of David Elkind, LiveWire Media, San Francisco.

4 Mikhail Mikhaeev (dir.), *Kolyma*, documentary film, Hoover Institution, Stanford, CA.

5 Photographs from Nanci Adler, *Victims of Soviet Terror: The Story of the Memorial Movement*.

6 'Gold and Human Rights', *Wall Street Journal*, 28 August 1985.

7 Adam Hochschild, *The Unquiet Ghost: Russians Remember Stalin*, p.255.

8 Nanci Adler, *Victims of Soviet Terror: The Story of the Memorial Movement*, p.93; Adam Hochschild, *The Unquiet Ghost: Russians Remember Stalin*, pp.198–199.

9 Ales Adamovich, 'Look About You!', from Vitaly Korotich and Cathy Porter (eds), *The Best of Ogonyok: The New Journalism of Glasnost* (London: Heinemann, 1990), p.7.

10 Adam Hochschild, *The Unquiet Ghost: Russians Remember Stalin* (New York: Viking, 1994), p.xxvi.

11 Edwin Bacon, *The Gulag At War: Stalin's Forced Labour System in the Light of the Archives* (Basingstoke: Macmillan Press, with the Centre for Russian and East European Studies, University of Birmingham, 1994), p.30.

12 Nanci Adler, *Victims of Soviet Terror: The Story of the Memorial Movement*, p.94.

13 John Earl Haynes and Harvey Klehr, *In Denial: Historians, Communism And Espionage* (San Francisco: Encounter, 2003), pp.117–118. Elmer John Nouisianen was *not* listed among the names of the dead buried in Sandormokh. The young man who had conveyed the news of the mass arrests of the Americans emigrants in Karelia – and was himself arrested outside the American Embassy in Moscow in 1938 – was sentenced to eight years in the Gulag. Remarkably, Elmer John Nousiainen survived his sentence in part through his ability to play the saxophone in a Gulag camp orchestra: See Mayme Sevander, *Of Soviet Bondage*, pp.111–112.

14 Source – Memo.Ru; Adam Hochschild, *The Unquiet Ghost: Russians Remember Stalin*, p.128; Edvard Radzinsky, *Stalin*, p.345; Vitaly Shentalinsky, *The KGB's Literary Archive*, p.70.

15 Diane P. Koenker and Ronald D. Bachman (eds), *Revelations from the Russian Archives: Documents in English Translation*, p.12

16 Richard Pipes (ed.), *The Unknown Lenin: From the Secret Archives*, trans. Catherine A. Fitzpatrick (New Haven, CT: Yale University Press, 1996) pp.56, 183; R. J. Rummel, *Lethal Politics: Soviet Genocide and Mass Murder since 1917* (New Brunswick, NJ: Transaction,1990), p.1.

17 Leona Toker, *Return from the Archipelago: Narratives of Gulag Survivors* (Bloomington, IN: Indiana University Press, 2000), p.3.

18 *Literaturnaya gazeta*, 9 August 1989 from Robert Conquest, *The Great Terror: A Reassessment*, p.487.

19 Edwin Bacon, *The Gulag at War: Stalin's Forced Labour System in the Light of the Archives*, p.36.

20 Felix Chuev (ed.), *Molotov Remembers: Inside Kremlin Politics – Conversations with Felix Chuev*, p.307.

21 Ibid., pp.161, 237.

22 Ibid., p.326.

23 Ibid., p.198.

24 Edvard Radzinsky, *Stalin*, p.563.

25 Yuri Druzhnikov, *Informer 001: The Myth of Pavlik Morozov*, pp.87–89, 95.

26 Vladimir Zazubrin, 'The Chip: A Story about a Chip and about Her', 24 April 1923, from Oleg Chukhontsev(ed), *Dissonant Voices*, p.54; Erika Gottlieb, *Dystopian Fiction East And West: Universe of Terror and Trial* (Montreal: McGill–Queens University Press, 2001), p.141.

27 Trudy Huskamp Peterson, 'Access matters: four documents', Cold War History Conference, 25 September 1998.

28 Immanuel Kant, *Religion Within the Boundaries of Mere Reason and Other Writings*, trans. and ed. Allen Wood and George Di Giovanni (Cambridge: Cambridge University Press, 1998), p.54.

28 THOMAS SGOVIO REDUX

1 Osip Mandelstam, *The Moscow and Voronezh Notebooks: Poems, 1930–1937*; trans. Richard and Elizabeth McKane (Tarset: Bloodaxe, 2003, p.79.

2 Tom Bukham, *Buffalo News*, 9 November 1997.

3 Ibid.

4 George Kovach (dir.) *The Camps of Magadan*, documentary film from Hoover Institute, Stanford, CA; Thomas Sgovio interview with George Kovacs, tapes courtesy of David Elkind, LiveWire Media, San Francisco.

5 Chuck Hawley, 'Stalin's Horrors Recalled' – *Arizona Republic*, 23 June 1995.

6 Thomas Sgovio NKVD file, Hoover Institution, Stanford, CA.

7 Alan Cullinson, 'A Secret Revealed', Associated Press, 9 November 1997.

BIBLIOGRAPHY

Abbe, James E, *I Photograph Russia*. London: Harrap, 1935.

Abolin, A, *The October Revolution and the Trade Unions*. Moscow: Co-operative Publishing Society of Foreign Workers in the USSR, 1933.

Adler, Nanci, *Victims of Soviet Terror: The Story of the Memorial Movement*. Westport, CT: Praeger, 1993.

—— *The Gulag Survivor: Beyond the Soviet System*. New Brunswick, NJ: Transaction, 2002.

Anna Akhmatova, *The Complete Poems of Anna Akhmatova*, trans. Judith Hemschemeyer. Somerville, MA: Zephyr Press, 1990.

Aleksander, Irina, *This is Russia*. Philadelphia: D. McKay, 1947.

Aleksandrov, Valentin, *The Wonderland Called Siberia*. Moscow: Novosti, 1977.

Alliluyeva, Svetlana, *Twenty Letters to a Friend*, trans. Priscilla Johnson. London: Penguin, 1968.

—— *Only One Year*, trans. Paul Chavchavadze. London: Hutchinson, 1969.

Alsberg, Henry A. (ed.), *America Fights the Depression: A Photographic Record of the Civil Works Administration*. New York: Coward-McCann, 1934.

Amalrik, André, *Involuntary Journey to Siberia*, trans. Manya Harari and Max Hayward. New York : Harcourt Brace Jovanovich, 1970.

—— *Will the Soviet Union Survive until 1984?* London: Penguin, 1970.

American Trade Union Delegation to Europe, 1951, 'American Workers Look at the Soviet Union. Impressions of the American Trade Union Delegation That Visited the Soviet Union in June and July 1951'. Moscow: Foreign Languages Publishing House, 1952.

Améry, Jean, *At the Mind's Limits*, trans. Sidney Rosenfeld and Stella P. Rosenfeld. London: Granta, 1999.

Amster, Gerald and Asbell, Bernard, *Transit Point Moscow*. London: André Deutsch, 1985.

Andrew, Christopher and Gordievsky, Oleg, *KGB: The Inside Story of its Foreign Operations from Lenin to Gorbachev*. London: Hodder and Stoughton, 1990.

—— *Comrade Kryuchkov's Instructions: Top Secret Files on KGB Foreign Operations, 1975–1985*. Stanford, CA: Stanford University Press, 1993.

Andrew, Christopher and Mitrokhin, Vasili, *The Mitrokhin Archive: The KGB in Europe and the World*. London: Allen Lane, 1999.

Annensky, Innokenty, *The Cypress Chest*, trans. R.H. Morrison. Ann Arbor, MI: Ardis, 1982.

Anonymous, *Dark Side of the Moon: On the Relations Between Poland and the USSR, 1939–1945*. London: Faber, 1946.

Anschel, Eugene (ed.), *American Appraisals of Soviet Russia, 1917–1977*. London: Scarecrow Press, 1978.

Antonov-Ovseyenko, Anton, *The Time of Stalin: Portrait of a Tyranny*, trans. George Saunders. New York: Harper and Row, 1981.

Applebaum, Anne, *Gulag: A History of the Soviet Camps*. London: Allen Lane, 2003.

Arendt, Hannah, *The Origins of Totalitarianism*. New York: Harcourt Brace Jovanovitch, 1951.

—— *Eichmann in Jerusalem: A Report on the Banality of Evil*. London: Faber, 1963.

Arrow, Jan, *Dorothea Lange*. London: Macdonald, 1985.

Asher, Oksana Dray-Khmara, *Letters from the Gulag: The Life, Letters, and Poetry of Michael Dray-Khmara*. New York: Robert Speller, 1983.

Baciu, Nicholas, *Sell Out to Stalin, The Tragic Errors of Roosevelt and Churchill: The Untold Story*. New York: Vantage, 1984.

Bacon, Edwin, *The Gulag at War: Stalin's Forced Labour System in the Light of the Archives*. Basingstoke: Macmillan Press, with the Centre for Russian and East European Studies, University of Birmingham, 1994.

Bailes, Kendall, *Technology and Society under Lenin and Stalin: Origins of the Soviet Technical Intelligentsia, 1917–1941*. Princeton, NJ: Princeton University Press, 1978.

Baitalsky, Mikhail, *Notebooks for the Grandchildren: Recollections of a Trotskyist who Survived the Stalin Terror*, trans. Marilyn Vogt-Downey. Atlantic Highlands, NJ: Humanities Press, 1995.

Bak, Richard, *Detroit, 1900–1930*. Chicago: Arcadia, 1999.

Baker, Vincent, 'American workers in the Soviet Union between the two world wars: From dream to disillusionment.' Thesis: West Virginia University, 1998.

Baltermants, Dmitri (photographs) and Von Laue, Theodore H. and Von Laue, Angela, *Faces of a Nation: The Rise and Fall of the Soviet Union, 1917–1991*. Golden, Colo.: Fulcrum, 1996.

Barbusse, Henri, *Stalin: A New World Seen Through One Man*, trans.Vyvyan Holland. London: John Lane, 1935.

Bardach, Janusz and Gleeson, Kathleen, *Man is Wolf to Man: Surviving Stalin's Gulag*. London: Simon & Schuster, 1998.

Barmine, Alexander, *Memoirs of a Soviet Diplomat: Twenty Years in the Service of the USSR*, trans. Gerard Hopkins. London: Dickson, 1938.

—— *One Who Survived: The Life Story of a Russian under the Soviets*. New York: Putnam's, 1945.

Bassow, Whitman, *The Moscow Correspondents: Reporting on Russia from the Revolution to Glasnost*. New York: William Morrow, 1988.

Bauer, Josef Martin, *As Far as My Feet Will Carry Me*, trans. Lawrence Wilson. London: André Deutsch, 1957.

Bauman, Zygmunt, *Modernity and the Holocaust*. Cambridge: Polity, 1989.

Beale, Fred E., *Proletarian Journey: New England, Gastonia, Moscow*. New York: Hillman-Curl, 1937.

de Beausobre, Julia, *The Woman Who Could Not Die: Reminiscences of Imprisonment in Russia*. London: Chatto & Windus, 1938.

Beckett, Francis, *Stalin's British Victims*. Stroud: Sutton, 2004.

Beevor, Anthony, *Stalingrad*. London: Viking, 1998.

Bekesi, Laszlo, *KGB and Soviet Security Uniforms and Militaria, 1917–1991*. Marlborough: Crowood Press, 2002.

Bely, Andrey, *Selected Essays of Andrey Bely*, trans. Steven Cassedy. Berkeley, CA: University of California Press, 1985.

—— *The First Encounter*, trans. Gerald Janecek. Princeton, NJ: Princeton University Press, 1979.

—— *The Silver Dove*, trans. John Elsworth. London: Angel, 2000.

Benjamin, Walter, *Moscow Diary*, trans. Richard Sieburth. Cambridge, MA: Harvard University Press, 1986.

Bennett, Harry, *We Never Called Him Henry*. New York: Fawcett, 1951.

Benson, Jackson J., *Looking for Steinbeck's Ghost*. Reno, NV: University of Nevada Press, 2002.

—— *The True Adventures of John Steinbeck, Writer: A Biography*. London: Heinemann, 1984.

Berezhkov, Valentin M., *At Stalin's Side: his Interpreter's Memoirs from the October Revolution to the Fall of the Dictator's Empire*, trans. Sergei V. Mikheyev. New York: Birch Lane Press, 1994.

Berger, Joseph, *Shipwreck of a Generation: The Memoirs of Joseph Berger*. London: Harvill, 1971.

Berle, Adolf A., *Navigating the Rapids, 1918–1971*. New York: Harcourt Brace Jovanovitch, 1973.

Bernikow, Louise, *Abel*. London: Hodder and Stoughton, 1970.

Best, Harry, *The Soviet Experiment*. New York: R.R.Smith, 1941.

Bethell, Nicholas, *The Last Secret: Forcible Repatriation to Russia, 1944–1947*. London: André Deutsch, 1974.

Bettelheim, Bruno, *Surviving, and Other Essays*. London: Thames and Hudson, 1979.

Bezborodov, S., *The Bolsheviks Discover Siberia*. Moscow: Co-operative Publishing Society of Foreign Workers in the USSR, 1933.

Biagi, Enzo, *Svetlana: The Inside Story*, trans. Timothy Wilson. London: Hodder and Stoughton, 1967.

Birstein, Vadim J., *The Perversion of Knowledge: The True Story of Soviet Science*. Boulder, CO: Westview, 2001.

Bishop, Donald Gordon, *The Roosevelt–Litvinov Agreements: The American View*. Syracuse, NY: Syracuse University Press, 1965.

Black, Edwin, *IBM and the Holocaust: The Strategic Alliance between Nazi Germany and America's Most Powerful Corporation*. London: Little, Brown, 2001.

Bloch, Sidney and Reddaway, Peter, *Russia's Political Hospitals: The Abuse of Psychiatry in the Soviet Union*. London: Gollancz, 1977.

—— *Diagnosis: Political Dissent, an abridged version of Russia's Political Hospitals, The Abuse of Psychiatry in the Soviet Union*. London: Overseas Publications Exchange, 1981.

—— *Soviet Psychiatric Abuse: The Shadow over World Psychiatry*. London: Gollancz, 1984.

Blok, Aleksandr, *The Twelve and Other Poems*, trans. Jon Stallworthy and Peter France. London: Eyre & Spottiswoode, 1970.

—— *Selected Poems*, trans. Alex Miller. Moscow: Progress, 1981.

—— *Selected Poems*, trans. Jon Stallworthy and Peter France. Manchester: Carcanet Press, 2000.

Blum, John M., *From the Morgenthau Diaries, Vol.1, Years of Crisis, 1928–1938*. Boston: Houghton Mifflin, 1959.

—— *From the Morgenthau Diaries, Vol.2, Years of Urgency, 1938–1941*. Boston: Houghton Mifflin, 1965.

—— *From the Morgenthau Diaries, Vol.3, Years of War, 1941–1945*. Boston: Houghton Mifflin, 1967.

Blumay, Carl and Edwards, Henry, *The Dark Side of Power: The Real Armand Hammer*. New York: Simon & Schuster, 1992.

Bohlen, Charles E., *Witness to History, 1929–1969*. New York: Norton, 1973.

Bolkhovitinov, Nikolai N., *Russia and the United States: An Analytical Survey of Archival Documents and Historical Studies*, trans. and ed. J. Dane Hartgrove. Armonk, New York: M.E. Sharpe, c.1986.

Bollinger, Martin J., *Stalin's Slave Ships: Kolyma, the Gulag fleet, and the Role of the West*. Westport, CT: Praeger, 2003.

Bonner, Elena, *Mothers and Daughters*, trans. Antonia W. Bouis. London: Hutchinson, 1992.

Borodin, Leonid, *The Year of Miracle and Grief*. London: Quartet, 1984.

Bourke-White, Margaret, *Eyes on Russia*. New York: Simon & Schuster, 1931.

—— *Shooting the Russian War*. New York: Simon & Schuster, 1943.

Bourke-White, Margaret and Caldwell, Erskine, *Russia at War*. London: Hutchinson, 1942.

Brackman, Roman, *The Secret File of Joseph Stalin: A Hidden Life*. London: Frank Cass, 2001.

Braun, Leopold L.S., *Religion in Russia: From Lenin to Khrushchev, an Uncensored Account*. Paterson, NJ: St Anthony Guild Press, 1959.

Brodsky, Joseph, *Collected Poems in English*, trans. Anthony Hecht. Manchester: Carcanet, 2001.

Bron, Saul, *Soviet Economic Development and American Business: Results of the First Year under the Five Year Plan and Further Perspectives*. New York: Horace Liveright, 1930.

Brown, Anthony Cave (ed.), *Operation World War III: The Secret American Plan 'Dropshot' for War with the Soviet Union, 1957*. London: Arms & Armour, 1979.

Brown, Archie (ed.), *The Soviet Union: A Biographical Dictionary*. London: Weidenfeld & Nicolson, 1990.

Brownell, Will, *So Close to Greatness: A Biography of William C. Bullitt*. New York: Macmillan, 1987.

Bryant, Louise, *Six Red Months in Russia: An Observer's Account of Russia before and during the Proletarian Dictatorship*. London: Heinemann, 1919.

Buber, Margarete, *Under Two Dictators*, trans. E. Fitzgerald. London: Gollancz, 1949.

Bucar, Annabelle, *The Truth about American Diplomats*. Moscow: *Literaturnaya Gazeta*, 1949.

Buck, Pearl, *Talk about Russia with Masha Scott*. New York: John Day, 1945.

Buck-Morss, Susan, *Dreamworld and Catastrophe: The Passing of Mass Utopia in East and West*. Cambridge, MA: MIT Press, 2000.

Bulgakov, Mikhail, *The Early Plays of Mikhail Bulgakov*, trans. Carl Proffer and Elleander Proffer. Bloomington, IN: Indiana University Press, 1972.

—— *The Heart of a Dog*, trans. Michael Glenny. London: Collins, Harvill, 1989.

—— *Manuscripts Don't Burn: Mikhail Bulgakov, a Life in Letters and Diaries*, trans. J.A.E. Curtis. London: Harvill, 1992.

—— *The Master and Margarita*, trans. Richard Pevear and Larissa Volkhonsky. London: Penguin, 1997.

Bullitt, Orville H., (ed.), *For the President, Personal and Secret: Correspondence Between Franklin D. Roosevelt and William C. Bullitt*. Boston: Houghton Mifflin, 1972.

Bullitt, William C., *The Bullitt Mission to Russia: Testimony before the Committee on Foreign Relations, United States Senate, of William C. Bullitt*. New York: Huebsch, 1919.

—— *Report to the American People*. Boston: Houghton Mifflin, 1940.

Bunin, Ivan, *Memories and Portraits*, trans. Vera Traill and Robin Chancellor. London: Lehmann, 1951.

—— *Cursed Days: A Diary of Revolution*, trans. Thomas Gaiton Marullo. London: Phoenix Press, 2000.

Buranov, Yuri, *Lenin's Will: Falsified and Forbidden*. Amherst, NY: Prometheus, 1994.

Burrell, George, *An American Engineer Looks at Russia*. Boston: Stratford, 1932.

Busch, Niven Jr., *Twenty-one Americans: Being Profiles of Some People Famous in Our Time*. Garden City, NY: Doubleday, Doran, 1930.

Byrnes, James F., *Speaking Frankly*. London: Heinemann, 1947.

Caldwell, Erskine, *All-out on the Road to Smolensk*. New York: Duell Sloan and Pearce, 1942.

—— *Moscow under Fire: A Wartime Diary*. London: Hutchinson, 1942.

Caldwell, Erskine and Bourke-White, Margaret, *Say, Is This the USA?* New York: Duell, Sloan & Pearce, 1941.

Carroll, Wallace, *We're in This with Russia*. Boston: Houghton Mifflin, 1942.

Cartier-Bresson, Henri, *About Russia: Photographs*. London: Thames and Hudson, 1974.

Cassidy, Henry, *Moscow Dateline, 1941–1943*. London: Cassell, 1943.

Chamberlin, William Henry, *Soviet Russia*. London: Duckworth, 1930.

—— *Russia's Iron Age*. London: Duckworth, 1935.

—— *The Russian Revolution*. London: Macmillan, 1935.

—— *Confessions of an Individualist*. London: Duckworth, 1940.

—— *America's Second Crusade*. Chicago: Regnery, 1950.

Chambers, Whittaker, *Witness: An Autobiography*. New York: Random House, 1952.

Chase, William J., *Enemies within the Gate: The Comintern and the Stalinist Repression*. New Haven, CT: Yale University Press, 2001.

Chen, Jack, *Soviet Art and Artists*. London: Pilot, 1944.

Cherkasov, Nikolai K., *Notes of a Soviet Actor*, trans. G. Ivanov-Mumjiev and S. Rosenberg. Moscow: Foreign Languages Publishing House, 1957.

Chudakov, Grigory, (ed.), *Twenty Soviet Photographers, 1917–1940*. Amsterdam: Fiolet and Draaijer, 1990.

Chuev, Felix (ed.), *Molotov Remembers: Inside Kremlin Politics, Conversations with Felix Chuev*. Chicago: Ivan Dee, 1993.

Chukhontsev, Oleg (ed.), *Dissonant Voices: The New Russian Fiction*. London: Harvill, 1991.

Churchill, Winston, *The Second World War: Vols. 1–6*. London: Penguin, 2005.

Ciliberti, Charles, *Backstairs Mission in Moscow*. New York: Booktab Press, 1946.

Ciszek, Walter J. with Flaherty, Daniel L., *With God in Russia*. London: Davies, 1965.

Cohen, Allen and Fillippelli, Ronald L., *Times of Sorrow and Hope: Documenting Everyday Life in Pennsylvania during the Depression and World War II, a Photographic Record*. University Park, PA: Pennsylvania University Press, 2003.

Communist Party of Great Britain, *History of the Communist Party of the Soviet Union*, (*Bolsheviks*), Moscow: Foreign Languages Publishing House, 1939.

Communist Party of the Soviet Union (Bolsheviks), Central Committee, *History of the Communist Party of the Soviet Union*. Moscow: Foreign Languages Publishing House, 1949.

Conquest, Robert, *The Courage of Genius, the Pasternak Affair: A Documentary Report on its Literary and Political Significance*. London: Collins and Harvill, 1961.

—— *The Great Terror: Stalin's Purge of the Thirties*. London: Macmillan, 1968.

—— *Kolyma: The Arctic Death Camps*. London: Macmillan, 1978.

—— *Inside Stalin's Secret Police: NKVD Politics, 1936–1939*. London: Macmillan, 1985.

—— *The Harvest of Sorrow: Soviet Collectivisation and the Terror-famine*. London: Hutchinson, 1986.

—— *The Great Terror: A Reassessment*. London: Hutchinson, 1990.

Contat, Michel and Rybalka, Michel, *The Writings of Jean-Paul Sartre*. Evanston, ILL: Northwestern University Press, 1974.

Cooke, Brett, *Human Nature in Utopia – Zamyatin's We*. Evanston, Illinois: Northwestern University Press, 2002.

Costello, John and Tsarev, Oleg, *Deadly Illusions*. London: Century, 1993.

Couloudre, Robert, *De Staline à Hitler: souvenirs de deux ambassades, 1936–1939*. Paris: Hachette, 1950.

Counts, George Sylvester, *A Ford Crosses Soviet Russia*. Boston: Stratford, 1930.

—— *The Soviet Challenge to America*. New York: John Day, 1931.

Craig, R. Bruce, *Treasonable Doubt: The Harry Dexter White Spy Case*. Lawrence, KS: University Press of Kansas, 2004.

Crocker, George N., *Roosevelt's Road to Russia*. Chicago: Henry Regnery, 1959.

Crowl, James William, *Angels in Stalin's Paradise: Western Reporters in Soviet Russia, 1917 to 1937, a Case Study of Louis Fischer and Walter Duranty*. Washington DC: University Press of America, 1982.

Culver, John C. and Hyde, John, *American Dreamer: A Life of Henry A. Wallace*. New York: W. W. Norton, 2001.

Curtis, J. A. E., *Manuscripts Don't Burn: Mikhail Bulgakov, a Life in Letters and Diaries*. London: Bloomsbury, 1991.

Dahlinger, John Cote, as told to Leighton, Francis Spatz, *The Secret life of Henry Ford*, Indianapolis: Bobbs-Merrill, 1978.

Dallin, David J. and Nicolaevsky, Boris I., *Forced Labor in Soviet Russia*. London: Hollis and Carter, 1948.

Daniel, Yuli, *Prison Poems*, trans. David Burg and Arthur Boyars. London: Calder and Boyars, 1971.

Davies, Joseph E., *Mission to Moscow*. London: Gollancz, 1942.

—— *Our Debt to Our Soviet Ally: How Can We Repay That Debt?* London: Russia Today Society, 1942.

—— *My Second Mission to Moscow*. London: Russia Today Society, 1943.

Deane, John R., *The Strange Alliance: The Story of Our Efforts at Wartime Cooperation with Russia*. New York: Viking Press, 1947.

Delafield, E. M., *I Visit the Soviets*. New York: Harper, 1937.

DeMott, Robert J., *Steinbeck's Reading: A Catalogue of Books Owned and Borrowed*. New York: Garland, 1984.

Dennis, Peggy, *The Autobiography of an American Communist: A Personal View of a Political Life 1925–1975*. Berkeley, CA: Creative Arts, 1977.

Denny, Harold, *Behind Both Lines: An Account of the Author's Experiences as a War Correspondent*. London: Michael Joseph, 1943.

De Santis, Hugh, *The Diplomacy of Silence: The American Foreign Service, the Soviet Union, and the Cold War, 1933–1947*. Chicago: University of Chicago Press, 1980.

Dimitrov, Georgi, *The Diary of Georgi Dimitrov, 1933–1949*, trans. Jane Hedges, Timothy Sergay and Irina Faïon. New Haven, CT: Yale University Press, 2003.

Djilas, Milovan, *Conversations with Stalin*, trans. Michael Petrovich. London: Hart-Davis, 1962.

Doenecke, Justus D. (ed.), *In Danger Undaunted: The Anti-interventionist*

Movement of 1940–1941 as revealed in the papers of the America First Committee. Stanford, CA: Hoover Institution Press, 1990.

Dolgun, Alexander with Patrick Watson, *Alexander Dolgun's Story: An American in the Gulag.* London: Collins/Harvill, 1975.

Dostoevsky, Fyodor, *The Brothers Karamazov*, trans. C. Garnett. London: Heinemann, 1920.

Drake, David, *Intellectuals and Politics in Post-war France.* Basingstoke: Palgrave, 2001.

Druzhnikov, Yuri, *Informer 001: The Myth of Pavlik Morozov.* New Brunswick, NJ: Transaction, 1997.

Dennis, J. Dunn, *The Catholic Church and the Soviet Government, 1939–1949.* Boulder Co: Eastern European Quarterly, 1977.

—— *Caught Between Roosevelt and Stalin: America's Ambassadors to Moscow.* Lexington, KY: University of Kentucky Press, 1998.

Duranty, Walter, *Duranty Reports Russia.* New York: Viking, 1934.

—— *I Write as I Please.* London: Hamish Hamilton, 1937.

—— *One Life, One Kopeck.* London: Hamish Hamilton, 1937.

—— *The Kremlin and the People.* London: Hamish Hamilton, 1942.

—— *USSR: The Story of Soviet Russia.* London: Hamish Hamilton, 1945.

—— *Stalin and Co: The Politburo, the Men Who Run Russia.* London: Secker and Warburg, 1949.

Eagles, Keith David, *Ambassador Joseph E. Davies and American–Soviet Relations, 1937–1941.* New York: Garland, 1985.

Eastman, Max Forrester, *Love and Revolution: My Journey Through an Epoch*, New York: Random House, 1964.

Eaton, Katherine Bliss (ed.), *Enemies of the People: The Destruction of Soviet Literary, Theatre, and Film Arts in the 1930s.* Evanston, ILL: Northwestern University Press, 2002.

Edelman, Robert, *Serious Fun: A History of Spectator Sports in the USSR.* New York: Oxford University Press, 1993.

Ehrenburg, Ilya, *The Thaw*, trans. Manya Harari. London: MacGibbon and Kee, 1961.

—— *Men, Years, Life, Vols. 1–6*, trans. Tatiana Shebunina and Yvonne Kapp. London: MacGibbon and Kee, 1961–1966.

—— *The Life of the Automobile*, trans. Joachim Neugroschel. London: Serpent's Tail, 1999.

Ehrenburg, Ilya and Grossman, Vasily (eds), *The Black Book: The Ruthless Murder of Jews by German-Fascist Invaders Throughout the Temporarily-Occupied Regions of the Soviet Union and in the Death Camps of Poland During the War of 1941–1945*, trans. John Glad and James S. Levine. New York: Holocaust library, 1981.

Eisenstein, Sergei, *Selected Works, Vols. 1–4*, trans. Richard Taylor. Bloomington, IN: Indiana University Press, 1988–1996.

Ekart, Antoni, *Vanished Without a Trace: The Story of Seven Years in Soviet Russia.* London: Parrish, 1954.

Elliot, Mark R., *Pawns of Yalta: Soviet Refugees and America's Role in their Repatriation*, Urbana, IL: University of Illinois Press, 1982.

Elvin, Harold, *A Cockney in Moscow*, London: Cresset Press, 1958.

Epstein, Edward J., *Dossier: The Secret History of Armand Hammer*. New York: Random House, 1996.

Ericson, Edward E. III, *The Apocalyptic Vision of Mikhail Bulgakov's The Master and Margarita*. Lewiston, NY: Mellen Press, 1991.

Ericson, Edward E., *Feeding the German Eagle: Soviet Economic Aid to Nazi Germany, 1933–1941*. Westport, CT: Praeger, 1999.

Ervin, Spencer, *Henry Ford vs. Truman H. Newberry: The Famous Senate Election Contest. A Study in American Politics, Legislation and Justice*. New York: R.R. Smith, 1935.

Esenin, Sergei, *Poems by Esenin*, trans. Charles Brasch and Peter Soskice. Wellington: Wai-Te-Ata, 1970.

—— *Confessions of a Hooligan: Fifty Poems by Sergei Esenin*, trans. Geoffrey Hurley. Cheadle Hulme: Carcanet, 1973.

Fainsod, Merle, *How Russia is Ruled*. Cambridge, MA: Harvard University Press, 1954.

—— *Smolensk under Soviet Rule*. New York: Random House, 1968.

Farnsworth, Beatrice, *William C. Bullitt and the Soviet Union*, Bloomington, IN: Indiana University Press, 1967.

Fehling, Helmut M., *One Great Prison: The Story Behind Russia's Unreleased POWs*, trans. Charles R. Joy. Boston: Beacon, 1951.

Fichelle, Alfred, *Russia in Pictures; from Moscow to Samarkand*. London: Duckworth, 1956.

Field, Harmann and Kate, *Trapped in the Cold War: The Ordeal of an American Family*. Stanford, CA: Stanford University Press, 1999.

Figes, Orlando, *Natasha's Dance: A Cultural History of Russia*. London: Allen Lane, 2002.

Filene, Peter Gabriel, *Americans and the Soviet Experiment, 1917–1933*. Cambridge, MA: Harvard University Press, 1967.

Fischer, Louis, *Machines and Men in Russia*. New York: H.Smith, 1932.

—— *Stalin and Hitler: The Reason for and the Results of the Nazi-Bolshevik Pact*. Harmondsworth: Penguin, 1940.

—— *Men and Politics: An Autobiography*. London: Cape, 1941.

Fischer, Louis (ed.), *Thirteen Who Fled: Thirteen Essays by Refugees from Soviet Russia*. New York: Harper, 1949.

Fitzpatrick, Sheila, *Everyday Stalinism: Ordinary Life in Extraordinary Times: Soviet Russia in the 1930s*. New York: Oxford University Press, 1999.

—— *The Russian Revolution*. New York: Oxford University Press, 1994.

Foglesong, David S., *America's Secret War Against Bolshevism: US Intervention in the Russian Civil War, 1917–1920*, Chapel Hill, NC: North Carolina Press, c.1995.

Ford, Henry, *My Life and Work*. London: Heinemann, 1923.

—— *My Philosophy of Industry*. London: Harrap, 1929.

Ford, Henry (publisher), *The International Jew: The World's Foremost Problem, being a reprint of a series of articles appearing in The Dearborn Independent from May 22 to October 2, 1920*. Dearborn, MI: Dearborn Publishing, 1920.

Ford, Henry, *Der internationale Jude*. Leipzig: Hammer-Verlag, 1940.

Ford, Robert A., *Our Man in Moscow: A Diplomat's Reflections on the Soviet Union from Stalin to Brezhnev*. Toronto: University of Toronto Press, 1989.

Forman, Archibald, *From Baltic to Black Sea*. London: Sampson Low, 1933.

Forrestal, James, *The Forrestal Diaries: The Inner History of the Cold War*, ed. Walter Millis. London: Cassell, 1952.

Foss, Kendall, *Black Bread and Samovars: An Account of an Unconventional Journey through Soviet Russia*. London: Arrowsmith, 1930.

Franck, Harry A., *A Vagabond in Sovietland: America's Perennial Rambler Goes Tourist*. New York: Stokes, 1935.

Frank, Waldo, *Dawn in Russia: The Record of a Journey*. New York: Scribner's, 1932.

French, Warren, *John Steinbeck's Non-fiction Revisited*. New York: Twayne, 1996.

Fueloep-Miller, René, *The Mind and Face of Bolshevism*. New York: Harper & Row, 1965.

Galler, Meyer and Marquess, Harlan E., *Soviet Prison Camp Speech: A Survivor's Glossary*. Madison, WI: University of Wisconsin Press, 1972.

Galler, Meyer, *Soviet Prison Camp Speech: A Survivor's Glossary Supplement*. Hayward, CA: Soviet Studies, 1977.

Garb, Paula, *They Came to Stay: North Americans in the USSR*. Moscow: Progress, 1987.

Garros, Véronique, Korenevskaya, Natalia and Lahusen, Thomas (eds), trans. Carol A. Flath, *Intimacy and Terror: Soviet Diaries of the 1930s*. New York: New Press, 1995.

Gates, John, *The Story of an American Communist*. New York: Nelson, 1958.

Gazur, Edward, *Secret Assignment: The FBI's KGB General*. London: St. Ermin's, 2001.

Gelderman, Carol, *Henry Ford: Wayward Capitalist*. New York: Dial Press, 1981.

Gelernter, David, *1939: The Lost World of the Fair*. New York: Avon, 1995.

Gellman, Irwin F., *Secret Affairs: Franklin Roosevelt, Cordell Hull and Sumner Welles*. Baltimore, MD: John Hopkins University Press, 1995.

Getty, J. Arch, *Origins of the Great Purges: The Soviet Communist Party Reconsidered*. Cambridge: Cambridge University Press, 1987.

Getty, J. Arch and Naumov, Oleg *The Road to Terror: Stalin and the Self-destruction of the Bolsheviks, 1932–1939*. New Haven, CT: Yale University Press, 2002.

Gide, André, *Travels in the Congo*, trans. Dorothy Bussy. New York: Knopf, 1930.

—— *Back from the USSR*, trans. Dorothy Bussy. London: Secker and Warburg, 1937.

—— *Afterthoughts: A Sequel to Back from the USSR*, trans. Dorothy Bussy. London: Secker and Warburg, 1937.

Gilbert, Martin, *Churchill: A Life*. London: Heinemann, 1991.

Gilmore, Eddy, *Me and My Russian Wife*. London: Foulsham, 1956.

—— *Troika*. London: Hamilton, 1963.

—— *The Cossacks Burned Down the YMCA: Russia Revisited*. London: Bodley Head, 1964.

Ginzburg, Eugenia, *Into the Whirlwind*, trans. Paul Stevenson and Manya Harari. London: Collins/Harvill, 1967.

—— *Within the Whirlwind*, trans. Ian Boland. London: Collins and Harvill, 1981.

Gliksman, Jerzy G., *Tell the West*. New York: National Committee for a Free Europe, 1948.

—— *Coercion of the Worker in the Soviet Union, Prepared by the International Commission Against Concentrationist Regimes*, trans. Charles R. Joy. Boston: Beacon, 1953.

Glinsky, Albert, *Theremin: Ether Music and Espionage*. Urbana: University of Illinois Press, c.2000.

Golden, Lily, *My Long Journey Home*. Chicago: Third World Press, 2002.

Goldman, Emma, *My Disillusionment in Russia*. London: Daniel, 1925.

Gonzalez, Valentin (El Campesino), *Listen Comrades: Life and Death in Soviet Russia*. London: Heinemann, 1952.

Goodwin, Doris Kearns, *No Ordinary Time: Franklin and Eleanor Roosevelt: The Home Front in World War II*. New York: Simon & Schuster, 1994.

Gorbachev, Mikhail, *Mikhail Gorbachev: Memoirs*, trans. Georges Peronansky and Tatjana Varsavsky. London: Doubleday, 1996.

Gorbatov, Aleksandr, *Years off my Life: The Memoirs of a General of the Soviet Army*. London: Constable, 1964.

Gorky, Maxim, *Those Who Built Stalingrad: As Told by Themselves*. London: Martin Lawrence, 1934.

Gottlieb, Erika, *Dystopian Fiction East and West: Universe of Terror and Trial*. Montreal: McGill–Queens University Press, 2001.

Gould, Jean and Hickok, Lorena, *Walter Reuther: Labor's Rugged Individualist*. New York: Dodd, Mead, 1972.

Gould, Margaret, *I Visit the Soviets*. Toronto: Francis White, 1937.

Graaff, Frances de, *Sergej Esenin: A Biographical Sketch*. The Hague: Mouton, 1966.

Grabbe, Alexander, *The Private World of the Last Tsar: In the Photographs and Notes of General Count Alexander Grabbe*, (eds) Paul and Beatrice Grabbe. London: Collins, 1985.

Grady, Eve Garrette, *Seeing Red: Behind the Scenes in Russia Today*. New York: Brewer, Warren and Putnam, 1931.

Graham, Loren R., *The Ghost of the Executed Engineer: Technology and the Fall of the Soviet Union*. Cambridge, MA: Harvard University Press, 1996.

Graves, William S., *America's Siberian Adventure*. New York: J.Cape and H.Smith, 1931.

Graziosi, Andrea, *The Great Soviet Peasant War: Bolsheviks and Peasants, 1917–1933*. Cambridge, MA: Harvard University Press, 1997.

Graziosi, Andrea, *A New Peculiar State: Explorations in Soviet History, 1917–1937*. Westport, CT: Praeger, 2000.

Gregory, Paul R. (ed.), *Behind the Façade of Stalin's Command Economy: Evidence from the Soviet State and Party Archives*. Stanford, CA: Hoover Institution Press, 2001.

Gregory, Paul R. and Lazerev, Valery (eds), *The Economics of Forced Labor: The Soviet Gulag*. Stanford, CA: Hoover Institution Press, 2003.

Grimsted, Patricia Kennedy, *The Odyssey of the Smolensk Archive: Plundered Communist Records for the Service of Anti-communism*. Pittsburgh, PA: The Center of Russian and Eastern European Studies, University of Pittsburgh, 1995.

—— *Archives of Russia Five Years After: 'Purveyors of Sensations' or 'Shadows Cast to the Past'?*, Amsterdam: International Institute of Social History, 1997.

Groehler, Olaf, *Selbstmörderische Allianz: Deutsch-russische Militärbeziehugne, 1920–1941*. Berlin: Vision Verlag, 1992.

Grossman, Vassily, *Forever Flowing*, trans. Robert Whitney. New York: Harper& Row, 1972.

—— *Life and Fate*, trans. Robert Chandler. London: Harvill, 1995.

Groves, Leslie R., *Now It Can Be Told: The Story of the Manhattan Project*. New York: Harper, 1962.

Gumilyov, Nikolai, *The Pillar of Fire: Selected Poems*, trans. Richard McKane. London: Anvil Press, 1999.

Hackel, Sergei, *The Poet and the Revolution: Aleksandr Blok's The Twelve*. Oxford: Clarendon Press, 1975.

Hagen, Charles (intro.), *American Photographers of the Depression: FSA photographs, 1935–1942*. London: Thames and Hudson, 1991.

Halasz, Mary, *From America with Love: Memoirs of an American Immigrant in the Soviet Union*. New York: Columbia University Press, 2000.

Hammer, Armand, *The Quest of the Romanoff Treasure*. New York: Payson, 1932.

Hammer, Armand with Neil Lyndon, *Hammer: Witness to History*. New York: Simon & Schuster, 1987.

Hampel, Elizabeth, *Yankee Bride in Moscow*. New York: Liveright, 1941.

Harp, Theodore, *Siberian Gold*. London: Hutchinson, 1937.

Harriman, W. Averell, *Peace with Russia?* New York: Simon & Schuster, 1959.

—— *America and Russia in a Changing World: A Half-century of Personal Observation*. Garden City, NJ: Doubleday, 1971.

Harriman, W. Averell and Abel, Elie, *Special Envoy to Churchill and Stalin, 1941–1946*. New York: Random House, 1975.

Hatfield, Mark O. with the Senate Historical Office, *Vice Presidents of the United States, 1789–1993*. Washington DC: US Government Printing Office, 1997.

Haynes, John Earl and Klehr, Harvey, *Venona: Decoding Soviet Espionage in America*. New Haven, CT: Yale University Press, 1999.

—— *In Denial: Historians, Communism and Espionage*. San Francisco: Encounter, 2003.

Hays Jr., Otis, *Home from Siberia: The Secret Odysseys of Interned American Airmen in World War II*. College Station, TX: Texas A & M University Press, 1990.

—— *The Alaska-Siberia Connection: The World War II Air Route*. College Station, TX: Texas A & M University Press, c.1996.

Haywood, Harry, *Black Bolshevik: Autobiography of an Afro-American Communist*. Chicago: Liberator Press, 1978.

Hazard, John N., *Recollections of a Pioneering Sovietologist*. New York: Oceana, 1987.

Hecker, Julius, *Moscow Dialogues: Discussions on Red Philosophy*. London: Chapman & Hall, 1933.

—— *Russian Sociology*. London: Chapman & Hall, 1934.

—— *The Communist Answer to the World's Needs: Discussions in Economic and Social Philosophy*. London: Chapman & Hall, 1935.

—— *Religion and Communism: A Study of Religion and Atheism in Soviet Russia*. London: Chapman & Hall, 1933.

Henderson, Loy, *A Question of Trust: The Origins of US–Soviet Diplomatic Relations/The Memoirs of Loy W. Henderson*, ed. George W. Baer. Stanford, CA: Hoover Institution Press, 1986.

Herman, Victor, *Coming out of the Ice: An Unexpected Life*. New York: Harcourt Brace Jovanovich, 1979.

Herwarth, Hans von, *Against Two Evils: Memoirs of a Diplomat-soldier during the Third Reich*. London: Collins, 1981.

Hilberg, Raul, *Perpetrators, Victims, Bystanders: The Jewish Catastrophe, 1933–1945*. New York: Aaron Asher, 1992.

—— *Sources of Holocaust Research: An Analysis*. Chicago: Ivan Dee, 2001.

—— *The Politics of Memory: The Journey of a Holocaust Historian*. Chicago: Ivan R. Dee, 1996.

—— *The Destruction of the European Jews, Vols.1–3*. New Haven, CT: Yale University Press, 2003.

Hilberg, Raul (ed.), *Documents of Destruction: Germany and Jewry, 1933–1945*. Chicago: Quadrangle, 1971.

Hildebrand, Grant, *Designing for Industry: The Architecture of Albert Kahn*, Cambridge, MA: MIT Press, 1974.

Hilton, Harold Boaz, *Cordell Hull: A Biography*. New York: Doubleday, Doran, 1942.

Hindus, Maurice, *Under Moscow Skies*. London: Gollancz, 1936.

—— *Hitler Cannot Conquer Russia*. Garden City, NJ: Doubleday, Doran, 1942.

—— *Russia Fights On*. London: Collins, 1942.

Hitler, Adolf, *Mein Kampf*, trans. Ralph Manheim. London: Hutchinson, 1969.

Hochschild, Adam, *The Unquiet Ghost: Russians Remember Stalin*. New York: Viking, 1994.

Holloway, David, *Stalin and the Bomb: The Soviet Union and Atomic Energy, 1939–1956*. New Haven, CT: Yale University Press, 1994.

Hokkanen, Lawrence and Sylvia, with Middleton, Anita, *Karelia: A Finnish-American Couple in Stalin's Russia*. St. Cloud, MN: North Star Press, 1991.

Hoover, J. Edgar, *Masters of Deceit: The Story of Communism in America and How to Fight It*. New York: Henry Holt, 1958.

Horowitz, David, *Radical Son: A Generational Odyssey*. New York: Free Press, 1997.

Hosking, Geoffrey, *A History of the Soviet Union*. London: Fontana, 1985.

Howe, Irving and Coser, Lewis, *The American Communist Party: A Critical History, 1919–1957*. Boston: Beacon Press, 1957.

Hughes, James Langston, *The Big Sea: An Autobiography*. New York: Knopf, 1940.

—— *I Wonder as I Wander: An Autobiographical Journey*. New York: Hill and Wang, 1964.

—— *The Collected Works of Langston Hughes*, (ed.) Arnold Rampersad, Columbia: University of Missouri Press, 2001.

Hull, Cordell, America Against Aggressors: A Verbatim Report of an Address Entitled 'The Spirit of International Law', Delivered by Mr Cordell Hull to the Tennesssee Bar Association on Friday, 3 June 1938. London: Peace, 1938.

—— *The Memoirs of Cordell Hull*. London: Hodder and Stoughton, 1948.

Ickes, Harold L., *The Autobiography of a Curmudgeon*. New York: Reynal and Hitchcock, 1943.

—— *The Secret Diary of Harold L. Ickes*. London: Wiedenfeld & Nicolson, 1955.

Ilf, Ilya and Petrov, Eugene, *Little Golden America: Two Famous Soviet Humourists Survey the United States*, trans. Charles Malamuth. London: Routledge, 1944.

Ilin, Mikhail, *New Russia's Primer: The Story of the Five-Year Plan*, trans. George S.Counts and Nucia P.Lodge. Boston: Houghton Mifflin, 1931.

Ivanov-Razumnik, R. V. *The Memoirs of Ivanov-Razumnik,* trans. P. S. Squire. London: Oxford University Press, 1965.

Ivanova, Galina, *Labor Camp Socialism: The Gulag in the Soviet Totalitarian System*, trans. Carol Flath. Armonk, NY: M. E. Sharpe, 2000.

Jaffe, Philip, *New Frontiers in Asia: A Challenge to the West*. New York: Knopf, 1945.

—— *The Rise and Fall of American Communism*. New York: Horizon, 1975.

—— *The Amerasia Case from 1945 to Present*. New York: Jaffe, 1979.

Jansen, Marc and Petrov, Nikita, *Stalin's Loyal Executioner: People's Commissar Nikolai Ezhov, 1895–1940*. Stanford, CA: Hoover Institution Press, 2002.

Johnpoll, Bernard K. and Klehr, Harvey, (eds), *Biographical Dictionary of the American Left*. New York: Greenwood, 1986.

Jordan, George R., *From Major Jordan's Diaries*. New York: Harcourt Brace, 1952.

Kahan, Stuart, *The Wolf of the Kremlin*. London: Robert Hale, 1989.

Kant, Immanuel, *Religion Within the Boundaries of Mere Reason and Other Writings*, trans. Allen Wood and George Di Giovanni. Cambridge: Cambridge University Press, 1998.

—— *Critique of Pure Reason*, trans. N. K. Smith. Basingstoke: Palgrave Macmillan, 2003.

Kapuscinski, Ryszard, *Imperium*, trans. Klara Glowczewska. London: Granta, 1994.

Keller, Judith, *Dorothea Lange: Photographs from the J. Paul Getty Museum*. Los Angeles: J. Paul Getty Museum, 2002.

Kennan, George, *Siberia and the Exile System*. Chicago: University of Chicago Press, 1958.

Kennan, George F., *Russia and the West Under Lenin and Stalin*. London: Hutchinson, 1961.

—— *Memoirs: 1925–1950*. London: Hutchinson, 1967.

—— *American Diplomacy, 1900–1950*. Chicago: University of Chicago Press, 1970.

—— *Memoirs, 1950–1973*. London: Hutchinson, 1973.

Kern, G. (ed.), *Zamyatin's We: A Collection of Critical Essays*. Ann Arbor, MI: Ardis, 1988.

Khanga, Yelena with Jacoby, Susan, *Soul to Soul: A Black Russian–American Family, 1865–1992*. New York: W.W. Norton, 1992.

Khlebnikov, Velimir, *Collected Works of Velimir Khlebnikov*, trans. Paul Schmidt. Cambridge, MA: Harvard University Press, 1997.

Khrushchev, Nikita, *Khrushchev Remembers*, trans. Strobe Talbot. London: André Deutsch, 1974.

—— *Nations Should Live As Good Neighbours!*, Khrushchev's address on United States television, Washington, 27 September 1959. London: Soviet Booklets, 1959.

—— *The 'Secret' Speech: delivered to the closed session of the Twentieth Congress of the Communist party of the Soviet Union*, with an introduction by Zhores A. Medvedev and Roy A. Medvedev. Nottingham: Spokesman, 1976.

Kimball, Warren F., *The Juggler: Franklin Roosevelt as Wartime Statesman*. Princeton, NJ: Princeton University Press, 1991.

King, David A., *The Commissar Vanishes: The Falsification of Photographs and Art in Stalin's Russia*. New York: Henry Holt, 1999.

—— *Ordinary Citizens: The Victims of Stalin*. London: Francis Boutle, 2003.

Kitchin, George, *Prisoner of the OGPU*. London: Longmans, Green, 1935.

Klehr, Harvey, *Communist Cadre: The Social Background of the American Communist Party*. Stanford, CA: Hoover Institution Press, 1978.

—— *The Heyday of American Communism: The Depression Decade*. New York: Basic, 1984.

Klehr, Harvey and Haynes, John Earl, *The American Communist Movement: Storming Heaven Itself*. New York: Twayne, 1992.

Klehr, Harvey, Haynes, John Earl and I. Firsov, Fridrikh, *The Secret World of American Communism*. New Haven, CT: Yale University Press, 1995.

Klehr, Harvey, Haynes, John Earl and Anderson, Kyrill M., *The Soviet World of American Communism*. New Haven, CT: Yale University Press, 1998.

Kleinman, Mark L., *A World of Hope, a World of Fear: Henry A. Wallace, Reinhold Niebuhr, and American Liberalism*. Columbus, OH: Ohio State University Press, c.2000.

Klinghoffer, Arthur Jay, *The Political Economy of Soviet Gold: Some Implications for American Foreign Policy*. Jerusalem: Hebrew University of Jerusalem, Soviet and Eastern European Research Centre, 1983.

Koch, Howard, *As Time Goes By: Memoirs of a Writer*. New York: Harcourt Brace Jovanovich, 1979.

Koenker, Diane P. and Bachman, Ronald D. (eds), *Revelations from the Russian Archives: Documents in English Translation*. Washington DC: Library of Congress, 1997.

Koestler, Arthur *Darkness at Noon*. New York: Macmillan, 1941.

—— *The Yogi and the Commissar and Other Essays*. New York: Macmillan, 1996.

—— *The God that Failed*. London: Hutchinson, 1949.

—— *The Invisible Writing: An Autobiography*. London: Collins, 1954.

Kollontai, Alexandra, *The Selected Writings of Alexandra Kollontai*, trans. Alix Holt. London: Allison & Busby, 1977.

Korotich, Vitaly and Porter, Cathy (eds), *The Best of Ogonyok: The New Journalism of Glasnost*. London: Heinemann, 1990.

Kotkin, Stephen, *Steeltown, USSR*. Berkeley, CA: University of California Press, 1991.

—— *Magnetic Mountain: Stalinism as a Civilization*. Berkeley, CA: University of California Press, 1995.

Kowalski, Stanislaw J., *Kolyma: The Land of Gold and Death*, online edition.

Kravchenko, Victor, *I Chose Freedom: The Personal and Political Life of a Soviet Official*. New York: Scribner's, 1946.

—— *I Chose Justice: An Account of the Action for Libel Brought by the Author Against 'Les Lettres Francaises'*. London: Robert Hale, 1951.

Krepp, Endel, *Mass Deportations of Population from the Soviet-Occupied Baltic States*. Stockholm, Estonian Information Centre, 1981.

Krivitsky, Walter, *I was Stalin's Agent*. London: Hamish Hamilton, 1939.

—— *In Stalin's Secret Service*. New York: Enigma, 2000.

Kugel, Barbara M., 'The export of American technology to the Soviet Union 1918–1933, including the Ford Motor Company–Soviet government relationship, 1918–1933'. Thesis: Benson Ford Archives, 1956.

Lachman, Feliks, *I was a Gulag Prisoner, 1939–42*. London: Caldra, 1991.

Lange, Dorothea, *Dorothea Lange: Photographs of a Lifetime*. Millerton, NY: Aperture, 1982.

—— *The Photographs of Dorothea Lange*. Kansas City, MO: Hallmark, 1995.

Lange, Dorothea and Taylor, Paul Schuster, *An American Exodus: A Record of Human Erosion in the 1930s*. New Haven, CT: Yale University Press, 1969.

Larina, Anna, *This I Cannot Forget: The Memoirs of Nikolai Bukharin's Widow*. London: Hutchinson, 1993.

Leahy, William D., *I Was There: The Personal Story of the Chief of Staff to Presidents Roosevelt and Truman*. London: Gollancz, 1950.

Lee, Albert, *Henry Ford and the Jews*. New York: Stein and Day, 1980.

Lengyel, Emil, *Secret Siberia*. London: Robert. Hale, 1947.

Lévi-Strauss, Claude, *The Savage Mind*. Oxford: Oxford University Press, 1996.

Levytsky, Borys, *The Stalinist Terror in the Thirties: Documentation from the Soviet Press*. Stanford, CA: Hoover Institution Press, 1974.

Lewis, John and Bishop, Reginald, *The Philosophy of Betrayal: An Analysis of the Anti-Soviet Propaganda of Arthur Koestler and Others*. London: Metcalfe & Cooper for Russia Today, 1945.

Leyda, Jay, *Kino: A History of Russian and Soviet Film*. London: Allen & Unwin, 1960.

Lih, Lars T., Naumov, Oleg V. and Khlevniuk, Oleg V. (eds), *Stalin's Letters to Molotov, 1925–1936*, trans. Catherine A. Fitzpatrick. New Haven, CT: Yale University Press, 1995.

Lindbergh, Charles A., *The Wartime Journals of Charles A. Lindbergh*. New York: Harcourt Brace Jovanovich, 1970.

Lipper, Elinor, *Eleven Years in Soviet Prison Camps*, trans. Richard and Clara Winston. London: Hollis and Carter, 1951.

Littlepage, John D. and Bess, Demaree, *In Search of Soviet Gold*. New York: Harcourt, Brace, 1938.

Lochner, Louis Paul, *America's Don Quixote: Henry Ford's Attempt to Save Europe*. London: Kegan Paul, 1924.

Long, Breckinridge, *The War Diary of Breckinridge Long, 1939–1944*, ed. Fred L. Israel. Lincoln, NE: University of Nebraska Press, 1966.

Louis, Victor and Jennifer, *Sport in the Soviet Union*. Oxford: Pergamon, 1964.

Loukomski, George, *The Face of Russia*. London: Hutchinson, 1944.

Lourie, Richard, *Russia Speaks: An Oral History from the Revolution to the Present*. New York: E. Burlingame, 1991.

Luciuk, Lubomyr (ed.), *Not Worthy: Walter Duranty's Pulitzer Prize and the New York Times*. Kingston, Ont.: Kashtan Press, 2004.

Lyons, Eugene, *Modern Moscow*. London: Hurst and Blackett, 1935.

—— *Assignment in Utopia: On the Experiences of an American Journalist in the USSR*. London: Harrap, 1938.

—— *Terror in Russia: Two Views*. New York: R.S.Smith, 1938.

—— *The Red Decade: The Stalinist Penetration of America*. Indianapolis, IN: Bobbs-Merrill, 1941.

McCannon, John, *Red Arctic: Polar Exploration and the Myth of the North in the Soviet Union, 1932–1939*. New York: Oxford University Press, 1998.

McCauley, Martin, *Who's Who in Russia Since 1900*. London: Routledge, 1997.

MacDonald, Dwight, *Henry Wallace: the Man and the Myth*. New York: Vanguard, 1948.

McIlroy, John, Morgan, Kevin and Campbell, Alan, *Party People: Communist Lives*. London: Lawrence and Wishart, 2001.

MacLean, Elizabeth Kimball, *Joseph E. Davies: Envoy to the Soviets*, Westport, CT: Praeger, 1992.

Maclean, Fitzroy, *Eastern Approaches*. London: Cape, 1949.

McLoughlin, Barry and McDermott, Kevin (eds.), *Stalin's Terror: High Politics and Mass Repression in the Soviet Union*. Basingstoke: Palgrave Macmillan, 2003.

McNeal, Robert H., *Stalin's Works: An Annotated Bibliography*. Stanford, CA: Hoover Institution, 1967.

Maisky, Ivan, *Memoirs of a Soviet Ambassador: The War, 1939–1943*. London: Hutchinson, 1967.

Mandelstam, Nadezhda, *Hope Against Hope: A Memoir*, trans. Max Hayward. London: Collins/Harvill, 1971.

—— *Hope Abandoned: A Memoir*, trans. Max Hayward. London: Collins/Harvill, 1974.

Mandelstam, Osip, *50 poems*, trans. Bernard Meares. New York: Persea, 1977.

—— *Poems*, trans. James Greene. London: Elek, 1980.

—— *The Moscow and Voronezh Notebooks: Poems, 1930–1937*, trans. Richard and Elizabeth McKane. Tarset: Bloodaxe, 2003.

Margulies, Sylvia, *The Pilgrimage to Russia: The Soviet Union and the Treatment of Foreigners 1924–1937*. Madison, WI: University of Wisconsin Press, 1968.

Mariengof, Anatoly, *A Novel Without Lies*, trans. Jose Alaniz. Moscow: Glas, 2000.

Markowitz, Norman D., *The Rise and Fall of the People's Century: Henry A. Wallace and American Liberalism, 1941–1948*. New York: Free Press, 1973.

Marx, Harpo with Barber, Rowland, *Harpo Speaks!* London: Gollancz, 1961.

Materski, Wojciech (ed.), Katyn, documents of genocide: documents and material from the Soviet archives turned over to Poland on October 14, 1992, Warsaw: Institute of Political Studies, Polish Academy of Sciences, 1993.

Mathewes, Charles T., *Evil and the Augustinian Tradition*. Cambridge: Cambridge University Press, 2001.

Matthiessen, Peter, *Baikal: Sacred Sea of Siberia*. London: Thames and Hudson, 1992.

Mayakovsky, Vladimir, *Poems*, trans. Dorian Rottenberg. Moscow: Progress, 1976.

—— *Selected Works Vol. 1*, trans. Dorian Rottenburg. Moscow: Raduga Publishers, 1985.

—— *Love is the Heart of Everything: Correspondence Between Vladimir Mayakovsky and Lili Brik, 1915–1930*, (ed.) Bengt Jangfeldt, trans. Julian Graffy. Edinburgh: Polygon, c.1986.

Medvedev, Roy A., *Let History Judge: The Origins and Consequences of Stalinism*, trans. Colleen Taylor. London: Spokesman, 1976.

—— *On Stalin and Stalinism*, trans. Ellen de Kadt. Oxford: Oxford University Press, 1979.

—— *Khrushchev*, trans. Brian Pearce. Oxford: Blackwell, 1982.

—— *All Stalin's Men*, trans. Harold Shukman. Oxford: Blackwell, 1983.

—— *The October Revolution*, trans. George Saunders. New York: Columbia University Press, 1985.

Medvedev, Roy A. and Medvedev, Zhores A., *Khrushchev: The Years in Power*, trans. Andrew R. Durkin. London: Oxford University Press, 1977.

Melgounov, Sergey P., *The Red Terror in Russia*. London: J.M.Dent, 1925.

Merleau-Ponty, Maurice, *Signs*, trans. Richard C. McCleary. Evanston, IL: Northwestern University Press, 1964.

—— *Humanism and Terror: An Essay on the Communist Problem*, trans. John O'Neill. Boston: Beacon, 1969.

Mezhlauk, Valery, *The Second Five-Year-Plan for the Development of the National Economy of the USSR, 1933–1937*. Moscow: Co-operative Publishing Society of Foreign Workers' in the USSR, 1936.

Michalson, Gordon E., Jr., *Fallen Freedom: Kant on Radical Evil and Moral Regeneration*. Cambridge: Cambridge University Press, 1990.

Mikoyan, Stepan A., *Stepan Anastasovich Mikoyan: An Autobiography*. Shrewsbury: Airlife, 1999.

Milosz, Czeslaw, *The Captive Mind*, trans. Jane Zielonko. London: Secker and Warburg, 1953.

Mitrokhin, L. V., *Friends of the Soviet Union: India's Solidarity with the USSR During the Second World War in 1941–1945*. Bombay: Allied, 1977.

Mitrokhin, Vasily, (ed.), *KGB Lexicon: The Soviet Intelligence Officer's Handbook*. London: Frank Cass, 2002.

Moats, Alice-Leone, *Blind Date with Mars*. Garden City, NY: Doubleday, Doran 1943.

Molchulsky, Konstantin, *Andrei Bely: His Life and Works*, trans. Nora Szalavitz. Ann Arbor: Ardis, 1977.

Monkhouse, Allan, *Moscow, 1911–1933: Being the Memoirs of A. Monkhouse*. London: Gollancz, 1933.

Mora, Silvester, *Kolyma: Gold and Forced Labor in the USSR*. Washington DC: Foundation for Foreign Affairs, 1949.

Moynahan, Brian, *The Russian Century: A Photographic History of Russia's 100 Years*. New York: Random House, 1994.

Moynihan, Daniel P., *Secrecy: The American Experience*, New Haven, CT: Yale University Press, 1998.

Muggeridge, Malcom, *Winter in Moscow*. London: Eyre and Spottiswoode, 1934.

Nabokov, Vladimir V., *Poems and Problems*. London: Weidenfeld & Nicolson, 1970.

—— *Lectures on Russian Literature*. London: Picador, 1983.

—— *Speak, Memory: An Autobiography Revisited*. London: Penguin, 2000.

Nekrasov, Nikolai A., *Poems*, trans. Juliet M.Soskice. London: Oxford University Press, 1929.

Neumaier, Diane, (ed.), *Beyond Memory: Soviet Nonconformist Photography and Photo-related Works of Art*. New Brunswick, NJ: Rutgers University Press, 2004.

Nevins, Allan and Hill, Frank E., *Ford, Vols. 1–3*. New York: Scribner, 1954–1963.

Newton, James D., *Uncommon Friends: Life with Thomas Edison, Henry Ford, Harvey Firestone, Alexis Carrel and Charles Lindbergh*. San Diego, CA: Harcourt Brace Jovanovich, 1987.

Nisbet, Robert, *Roosevelt and Stalin: The Failed Courtship*. London: Simon & Schuster, 1989.

Noble, John, *I Was a Slave in Russia: An American Tells His Story*. London: Brown Watson, 1963.

O'Malley, Owen, *The Phantom Caravan*. London: John Murray, 1954 .

—— *Katyn: Despatches of Sir Owen O'Malley to the British Government*. London: Polish Cultural Foundation, 1972.

O'Neill, William, *A Better World: The Great Schism, Stalinism and the American Intellectuals*. New York: Simon & Schuster, 1982.

Ohrn, Karin Becker, *Dorothea Lange and the Documentary Tradition*. Baton Rouge, Louisiana: Louisiana State University Press, 1980.

Oppenheimer, Francis, *Stranger Within: Autobiographical Pages*. London: Faber, 1960.

Orlov, Aleksandr, *The Secret History of Stalin's Crimes*. New York: Random House, 1953.

Orr, Charles A., *Stalin's Slave Camps: An Indictment of Modern Slavery*. Brussels: International Confederation of Free Trade Unions, 1951.

Orr, J. Edwin, *Prove Me Now: 10,000 Miles of Miracle to Moscow*. London: Marshall, Morgan and Scott, 1935.

Osokina, Elena, *Our Daily Bread: Socialist Distribution and the Art of Survival in Stalin's Russia, 1927–1941*, trans. Kate Transchel and Greta Bucher. Armonk, NY: M.E. Sharpe, 2001.

Orwell, George, *Nineteen Eighty-Four*. London: Secker and Warburg, 1949.

—— *The Collected Essays, Journalism and Letters of George Orwell*, (eds) Sonia Orwell and Ian Angus. London: Secker & Warburg, 1968.

O'Sullivan, Christopher D., *Sumner Welles, Postwar Planning and the Quest for a New World Order, 1937–1943*. New York: Columbia University Press, 2003 and Gutenberg edition online.

Partridge, Elizabeth (ed.), *Dorothea Lange: A Visual Life*. Washington DC: Smithsonian Institute Press, 1994.

Pasternak, Boris *An Essay in Autobiography*, trans. Manya Harari. London: Collins/Harvill, 1959.

—— *Poems*, trans. Eugene M. Kayden. Yellow Springs, OH: Antioch, 1964.

—— *Selected Poems*, trans. Jon Stallworthy and Peter France. New York: W.W.Norton, 1983.

—— *The Last Summer*, trans. George Reavey. Harmondsworth: Penguin, 1976.

—— *Doctor Zhivago*, trans. Max Hayward and Manya Harari. London: Collins/Harvill, 1988.

—— Tsevetayeva, Marina, Rilke, Rainer Maria, *Letters, Summer 1926,* (eds) Yevgeny Pasternak, Yelena Pasternak, and Konstantin M.Azadovsky, trans. Margaret Wettlin & Walter Arndt. London: Cape, 1986.

—— *Selected Writing and Letters*. Moscow: Progress, 1990.

Pells, Richard H., *Radical Visions and American Dreams: Culture and Social Thought in the Depression Years*. New York: Harper & Row, 1973.

Penkovsky, Oleg, *The Penkovsky Papers*. London: Collins, 1965.

Peris, Daniel, *Storming the Heavens: the Soviet League of the Militant Godless*. Ithaca, NY: Cornell University Press, 1998.

Perlmutter, Amos, *FDR & Stalin: A Not So Grand Alliance, 1943–1945*. Columbia: University of Missouri Press, 1993.

Persico, Joseph, *Roosevelt's Secret War: FDR and World War II espionage*. New York: Random House, 2001.

Petrov, Vladimir, *Escape From the Future: The Incredible Adventures of a Young Russian*. Bloomington, IN: Indiana University Press, 1973.

Petrov, Vladimir and Evdokia, *Empire of Fear*. London: André Deutsch, 1956.

Petrov, Vladimir, *It Happens in Russia: Seven Years' Forced Labour in the Siberian Goldfields*. London: Eyre and Spottiswoode, 1951.

Pipes, Richard, *Russia under the Bolshevik Regime*. New York: Knopf, 1993.

—— *A Concise History of the Russian Revolution*. London: Harvill, 1995.

—— *Communism: A Brief History*. London: Wiedenfeld & Nicolson, 2001.

Pipes, Richard (ed.), *The Unknown Lenin: From the Secret Archive*, trans. Catherine A.Fitzpatrick. New Haven, CT: Yale University Press, 1996.

Platonov, Andrei, *Collected Works*, trans. Thomas P.Whitney. Ann Arbor, MI: Ardis, 1978.

—— *Happy Moscow*, trans. Robert and Elizabeth Chandler. London: Harvill, 2001.

—— *The Fierce and Beautiful World*, trans. Joseph Barnes. New York: New York Review Books, 2000.

Plotinus, *The Enneads*, trans. Stephen MacKenna. London: Penguin, 1991.

Politkovskaya, Anna, *A Dirty War: A Russian Reporter in Chechnya*, trans. and ed. John Crowfoot. London: Harvill, 2001.

—— *A Small Corner of Hell: Despatches from Chechnya*, trans. Alexander Burry and Tatiana Tulchinsky. Chicago: University of Chicago Press, 2003.

—— *Putin's Russia*, trans. Arch Tait. London: Harvill Press, 2004.

Pollitt, Harry, *Salute to the Soviet Union*. London: Communist Party of Great Britain, 1937.

—— *Those Russians*. London: Communist Party, 1949.

—— *In Memory of Joseph Stalin and Klement Gottwald*. London: Communist Party, 1953.

Post, Marjorie Merriweather, *The Collection of Marjorie Merriweather Post. Hillwood, Washington DC*, Norman: University of Oklahoma Press, 1965.

Power, Samantha, *A Problem from Hell: America in the Age of Genocide*. New York: Basic, 2002.

Pushkin, Aleksandr S., *Three Russians Poets: Selections From Pushkin, Lermontov, and Tyuchev*, trans. V. Nabokov. Norfolk, CT: New Directions, 1944.

Pushkin, Aleksandr, *Collected Narrative and Lyrical Poetry*, trans. Walter Arndt. Ann Arbor, MI: Ardis, 1984.

Radzinsky, Edvard, *Stalin: The First Biography Based on Explosive New Documents from Russia's Secret Archives*, trans. H. T. Willets. London: Hodder and Stoughton, 1996.

Raiguel, George Earle and Huff, William Kisler, *This is Russia*. Philadelphia: Penn, 1932.

Rancour-Laferriere, Daniel, *The Mind of Stalin: A Psychoanalytic Study*. Ann Arbor, Michigan: Ardis, 1988.

Rawicz, Slavomir with Downing, Ronald, *The Long Walk*. London: Constable, 1956.

Razgon, Lev, *True Stories*, trans. John Crowfoot. London: Souvenir Press, 1998.

Read, Anthony and Fisher, David, *The Deadly Embrace: Hitler, Stalin and the Nazi-Soviet Pact*. New York: Norton, 1988.

Reed, John, *Ten Days That Shook the World*. New York: Random House, 1960.

—— *The Collected Works of John Reed*. New York: Modern Library, 1995.

Reuther, Victor, *The Brothers Reuther and the Story of the UAW: A Memoir*. Boston: Houghton Mifflin, 1976.

—— 'Commitment and betrayal: foreign workers at the Gorky auto works,' ed. Paul T. Christensen (unpublished, 2004).

Reuther, Walter Philip, *Selected Papers*, (ed.) Henry M.Christman. New York: Macmillan, 1961.

Reynolds, Quentin, *The Curtain Rises*. New York: Random House, 1944.

Rhodes, Richard, *The Making of the Atomic Bomb*. New York: Simon & Schuster, 1986.

Riehl, Nikolaus, *Stalin's Captive: Nikolaus Riehl and the Soviet Race for the Bomb*. Washington DC: American Chemical Society, 1996.

Riess, Steven A., *Touching Base: Professional Baseball and American Culture in the Progressive Era*. Westport, CT.: Greenwood, 1980.

Rigoulet, Pierre, Courtois, Stéphane and Malia, Martin, *The Black Book of Communism: Crimes, Terror and Repression*. Cambridge, MA: Harvard University Press, 1999.

Rivera, Diego with March, Gladys, *My Art, My Life: An Autobiography*. New York: Citadel Press, 1960.

Roberts, Graham, *Forward Soviet!: History and Non-fiction Film in the USSR*. London: Tauris, 1999.

Robeson, Paul, *Here I Stand*. Boston: Beacon, 1971.

—— *Paul Robeson Speaks: Writings, Speeches, Interviews, 1918–1974*, ed. Philip S. Foner. London: Quartet, 1978.

Robeson, Paul Jr., *The Undiscovered Paul Robeson: An Artist's Journey, 1898–1939*. New York: John Wiley, 2001.

Robinson, Robert, *Black on Red: My Forty-Four Years Inside the Soviet Union*. Washington DC: Acropolis, 1988.

Roeder, Bernhard, *Katorga: An Aspect of Modern Slavery*, trans. Lionel Kochan. London: Heinemann, 1958.

Rogers, William P., *There's Not a Bathing Suit in Russia, & Other Bare Facts*. London: Brentano's, 1927.

Rogovin, Vadim Z., *1937: Stalin's Year of Terror*, trans. Frederick S. Choate. Oak Park, MI: Mehring, 1998.

Roosevelt, Anna Eleanor, *This I Remember*. New York: Harper & Row, 1949.

Roosevelt, Elliot, *As He Saw It*. New York: Duell, Sloan and Pearce, 1946.

Roosevelt, Elliot and Brough, James, *An Untold Story: The Roosevelts of Hyde Park*. New York: Putnam, 1973.

—— *A Rendezvous with Destiny: The Roosevelts of the White House*. London: W. H. Allen, 1975.

Roosevelt, Franklin D., *FDR: His Personal Letters, 1928–1945*, ed. Elliot Roosevelt. New York: Duel, Sloan and Pearce, 1950.

—— *FDR's Fireside Chats*, (eds) Russell D. Buhite and David W. Levy. Norman: University of Oklahoma Press, 1992.

Roosevelt, Franklin, Churchill, Winston, Stalin, Joseph, *The Secret History of World War II, the Ultra-Secret Wartime Letters and Cables of Roosevelt, Churchill, and Stalin*. London: W.H. Allen, 1987.

Rossi, Jacques, *The Gulag Handbook: An Encyclopaedia Dictionary of Soviet Penitentiary Institutions and Terms Related to the Forced Labor Camps*, trans. William A. Burhans. New York: Paragon, 1988.

Rougle, Charles, *Three Russians Consider America: America in the Works of Maksim Gor'kij, Aleksandr Blok and Vladimir Majakovskij*. Stockholm: Almqvist & Wiksell, 1976.

Rubinstein, Joshua and Naumov, Vladimir P. (eds.), *Stalin's Secret Pogrom: The Postwar Inquisition of the Jewish Anti-Fascist Committee*. New Haven, CT: Yale University Press, 2001.

Rukeyser, Walter Arnold, *Working for the Soviets: An American Engineer in Russia*. New York: Covici-Friede, 1932.

Ruksenas, Algis, *Day of Shame*. New York: McKay, 1973.

Rummel, R. J., *Lethal Politics: Soviet Genocide and Mass Murder Since 1917*. New Brunswick, NJ: Transaction, 1990.

Rybin, A. T., *Next to Stalin: Notes of a Bodyguard*. Toronto: Northstar Compass Journal, 1986.

Salisbury, Harrison E., *American in Russia*. New York: Harper & Bros, 1955.

Sanders, James D., Sauter, Mark R., Kirkwood, Cort, *Soldiers of Misfortune: Washington's Secret Betrayal of America's POWs in the Soviet Union*. Washington DC: National Press, 1992.

Sartre, Jean-Paul, *Nekrassov*, trans. Sylvia and George Leeson. London: Hamish Hamilton, 1956.

—— *The Writings of Jean-Paul Sartre*, compiled by Michel Contat & Michel Rybalka, trans. Richard C.McCleary. Evanston: Northwestern University Press, 1974.

Satter, David, *Darkness at Dawn: The Rise of the Russian Criminal State*. New Haven, CT: Yale University Press, 2003.

Savelev, Boris, *Secret City: Photographs from the USSR*. London: Thames and Hudson, 1988.

Schaafsma, Petruschka, *Reconsidering Evil: Confronting Reflections with Confessions*. Leuven: Peeters, 2006.

Schecter, Leona and Jerrold, *An American Family in Moscow*. Boston: Little, Brown, 1975.

Schmidt, Karl M., *Henry A. Wallace: Quixotic Crusade, 1948*. Syracuse, New York: Syracuse University Press, 1960.

Schuetz, A.D. Hans, *Davai, davai!: Memoir of German Prisoner of World War II in the Soviet Union*. London: McFarland, 1997.

Scott, John, *Behind the Urals: An American Worker in Russia's City of Steel*. Cambridge, MA: Houghton Mifflin, 1942.

Serebrovsky, Alexander P., *Soviet Gold*. Moscow: Co-operative Publishing Society of Foreign Workers in the USSR, 1936.

Serge, Victor, *From Lenin to Stalin*, trans. Ralph Manheim. London: Secker and Warburg, 1937.

Sevander, Mayme, *Of Soviet Bondage*. Duluth, MN: Oscat, 1996.

—— *Red Exodus: Finnish-American Emigration to Russia*. Duluth, MN: Oscat, 1993.

Sevander, Mayme with Hertzel, Laurie, *They Took My Father: A Story of Idealism and Betrayal*. Duluth, MN: Pfeifer-Hamilton, 1992.

Sgovio, Thomas, *Dear America*. Kenmore, NY: Partners' Press, 1979.

Shalamov, Varlam, *Kolyma Tales*, trans. John Glad. New York: W. W. Norton, 1980.

—— *Graphite*, trans. John Glad. New York: W.W. Norton,1981.

Shane, Sylvan Myron Elliot, *As I Saw It in the Soviet Union, in Israel, in Auschwitz*. Baltimore, MD: Lowry and Volz, 1968.

Shaw, George Bernard, *A Little Talk on America*. London: Friends of the Soviet Union, 1932.

Shentalinsky, Vitaly, *The KGB's Literary Archive: The Discovery and Ultimate Fate of Russia's Suppressed Writers*, trans. John Crowfoot. London: Harvill Press, 1995.

Sherwood, Robert E., *Roosevelt and Hopkins: An Intimate History*. New York: Harper, 1948.

Shklovsky, Victor, *Third Factory*, trans. Richard Sheldon. Chicago: Dalkey, 2002.

Shoumatoff, Elizabeth, *FDR's Unfinished Portrait: A Memoir by Elizabeth Shoumatoff*. Pittsburgh, PA: University of Pittsburgh Press, 1990.

Shudakov, Grigory, Suslova, Olga and Ukhtomskaya, Lilya, *Pioneers of Soviet Photography*. London: Thames and Hudson, 1983.

Sics, Astrid, (ed.), *We Sang Through Tears: Stories of Survival in Siberia*. Riga: Janis Roze, 1999.

Simonov, Konstantin, *Always a Journalist*. Moscow: Progress, 1989.

Sinyavsky, Andrei, *On Trial: The Case of Sinyavsky, Tertz. and Daniel, Arzhak.*, trans. Leopold Labedz and Max Hayward. London: Collins/Harvill, 1967.

—— *Soviet Civilization: A Cultural History*, trans. Joanne Turnbull and Nikolai Formozov. New York: Arcade, 1990.

—— *The Russian Intelligentsia*, trans. Lynn Visson. New York: Columbia University Press, 1997.

Sinyavsky, Andrei, under the pseudonym Abram Tertz., *On Socialist Realism*, trans. George Dennis. Berkeley, CA: University of California Press, 1962.

Sinyavsky, Andrei, under the pseudonym Abram Tertz, *A Voice From the Chorus*, trans. Kyril Fitzlyon and Max Hayward. London: Collins, Harvill, 1976.

—— *The Trial Begins*, trans. Max Hayward. London: Fontana, 1977.

Smith, Andrew, *I Was a Soviet Worker*. London: Robert Hale, 1937.

Smith, Charles Andrew (ed.), *Escape From Paradise: By Seven Who Escaped and One who Did Not*. Boston: Beacon, 1954.

Smith, Hedrick, *The New Russians*. London: Hutchinson, 1990.

Smith, Homer, *Black Man in Red Russia: A Memoir*. Chicago: Johnson, 1964.

Smith, Robert Miller, *Baseball: A Historical Narrative of the Game, the Men who have Played it, and its Place in American Life*. New York: Simon & Schuster, 1947.

Smith, Walter Bedell, *Moscow Mission, 1946–49*. London: Heinemann, 1950.

Smyth, Henry DeWolf, *Atomic Energy for Military Purposes: The Official Report on the Development of the Atomic Bomb under the Auspices of the United States Government, 1940–1945*. Princeton, NJ: Princeton University Press, 1945.

Sobolev, P., Borodina, L., Korobkov, G., *Sport in the USSR*, trans. Dennis Ogden. Moscow: Foreign Languages Publishing House, 1958.

Solomon, Michael, *Magadan*. Princeton, NJ: Auerbach, 1971.

Solzhenitsyn, Alexander, *Cancer Ward*, trans. Nicholas Bethell and David Burg. London: Bodley Head, 1970.

—— *A Day in the Life of Ivan Denisovich*, trans. Gillon Aitken. London: Bodley Head, 1971 .

——*The Gulag Archipelago, 1918–1956: An Experiment in Literary Investigation*, trans. Thomas P Witney, Vols. 1-3, London: Collins/Fontana, 1976.

—— *The First Circle*, trans. Michael Guybon. London: Collins/Harvill, 1979.

—— *The Oak and the Calf: A Memoir*, trans. Harry Willetts. London: Collins/Harvill, 1980.

Sontag, Raymond and Beddie, James (eds.), *Nazi-Soviet Relations, 1939–1941: Documents from the Archives of the German Foreign Office*. New York: Didier, 1948.

Sorensen, Charles, *My Forty Years with Ford*. New York: Collier, 1956.

Souvarine, Boris, *Stalin: A Critical Survey of Bolshevism*. London: Secker and Warburg, 1939.

Spewack, Samuel, *Red Russia Revealed: The Truth about the Soviet Government and its Methods*. New York: World, 1923.

Stalin, Joseph, *The New Democracy: Stalin's Speech on the New Constitution*. London: Lawrence & Wishart for Friends of the Soviet Union, 1937.

—— *Defects in Party Work and Measures for Liquidating Trotskyite and Other Double-dealers*. Moscow: Co-operative Publishing Society of Foreign Workers in the USSR, 1937.

—— *Problems of Leninism*. Moscow: Foreign Languages Publishing house, 1953.

Standley, William H. and Ageton, Arthur A., *The Admiral Ambassador in Russia*. Chicago: Regnery, 1955.

Steinbeck. Elaine and Wallsten, Robert (eds.). *Steinbeck: a life in letters*. London: Heinemann, 1975.

Steinbeck, John, *A Russian Journal*. New York: Viking, 1948.

—— *The Grapes of Wrath*. London: Penguin, 1992.

Stettinius, Edward R., *Roosevelt and the Russians: The Yalta Conference*. London: Cape, 1950.

Stevens, Edmund, *This is Russia: Uncensored*. New York: Didier, 1950.

Stimson, Henry L. and Bundy, McGeorge. *On Active Service in Peace and War*. London: Hutchinson, 1949.

Strong, Anna Louise, *From Stalingrad to Kuzbas: Sketches of the Socialist Construction in the USSR*. London: Modern, 1932.

—— *I Change Worlds: On the Author's Experiences in America and Russia*. London: Routledge, 1935.

—— *This Soviet World*. New York: Holt, 1936.

—— *The New Soviet Constitution: A Study in Socialist Democracy*. New York: Holt, 1937.

—— *The Soviets Expected It*. New York: Dial Press, 1941.

—— *The Stalin Era*. New York: Mainstream, 1957.

Strong, Tracy B. and Keyssar, Helene, *Right in Her Soul: The Life of Anna Louise Strong*. New York: Random House, 1983.

Sudoplatov, Pavel, *Special Tasks: The Memoirs of an Unwanted Witness, a Soviet Spymaster*. London: Little Brown, 1994.

Sutton, Antony C., *Western Technology and Soviet Economic Development, 1917–1930*, Stanford, CA: Hoover Institution Press, 1968.

—— *National Suicide: Military Aid to the Soviet Union*. New Rochelle, NY: Arlington, 1973.

Sward, Keith Theodore, *The Legend of Henry Ford*. New York: Rinehart, 1948.

Swianiewicz, Stanislaw, *Forced Labour and Economic Development: An Enquiry into the Experience of Soviet Industrialization*. London: Oxford University Press, 1965.

Symons, Julian, *The Thirties: A Dream Revolved*. London: Cresset, 1960.

Tarkovskii, Arsenii, *Life, Life: Selected Poems*. Kidderminster: Crescent Moon, 2000.

Tarnopol, Daniel, 'Motivations for American-Soviet trade during the early Bolshevik era, 1919–1933.' Thesis: Rutgers, 2002.

Taubman, William, *Stalin's American Policy: From Entente to Détente to Cold War*. New York: Norton, 1982.

Taylor, Edmund, *The Strategy of Terror: Europe's Inner Front*. Boston: Houghton Mifflin, 1940.

Taylor, Richard, *Film Propaganda: Soviet Russia and Nazi Germany*. London: Tauris, 1998.

Taylor, Richard, (ed.), *The Film Factory: Russian and Soviet Cinema in Documents*. London: Routledge, 1994.

Taylor, S.J., *Stalin's Apologist: Walter Duranty, New York Times' man in Moscow*. New York: Oxford University Press, 1990.

Thayer, Charles, *Bears in the Caviar*. London: Michael Joseph, 1952.

—— *Diplomat*. London: Michael Joseph, 1960.

Thiel, Erich, *The Soviet Far East: A Survey of Its Physical and Economic Geography*, trans. Annielie and Ralph Rookwood. London: Methuen, 1957.

Thubron, Colin, *In Siberia*. London: Chatto & Windus, 1999.

Timbres, Harry and Rebecca, *We Didn't Ask Utopia: A Quaker Family in Soviet Russia*. New York: Prentice-Hall, 1939.

Toker, Leona, *Return from the Archipelago: Narratives of Gulag Survivors*. Bloomington, IN: Indiana University Press, 2000.

Tolstoy, Nikolai, *Victims of Yalta*. London: Hodder and Stoughton, 1977.

Tompkins, Stuart Ramsay, *A Canadian's Road to Russia: Letters from the Great War Decade*, (ed.) Doris H. Pieroth. Edmonton, Alberta: University of Alberta Press, 1989.

Trifonov, Yuri, *The House on the Embankment*, trans. Michael Glenny. London: Sphere, 1985.

Trotsky, Leon, *Stalin: An Appraisal of the Man and his Influence*, trans. and ed. Charles Malamuth. London: Panther, 1969.

Tsvetaeva, Marina, *After Russia*, trans. Michael M. Naydan with Slava Yastremski. Ann Arbor, MN: Ardis, 1992.

Tully, Grace, *FDR: My Boss*. New York: Scribner's, 1949.

Tumanova, Alla, *Where We Buried the Sun: One Woman's Gulag Story*, trans. Gust Olson. Edmonton, Alberta: Newest, 1999.

Tupitsyn, Margarita, *The Soviet Photograph: 1924–1937*. New Haven, CT: Yale University Press, 1996.

Tuyll, Hubert P. van, *Feeding the Bear: American Aid to the Soviet Union, 1941–1945*. New York: Greenwood, 1989.

Tyutchev, Fedor I., *Eighty Stars from Tyutchev's Galaxy*, trans. Alexander Podikov. Moscow: PoligrafAtelePlius, 2003.

Unknown author, *Guide to the City of Moscow: A Handbook for Tourists*. Moscow: Co-operative Publishing Society of Foreign Workers in the USSR, 1937.

Unknown author, *The World Hails Twentieth Anniversary of the Soviet Union*. Moscow: Co-operative Publishing Society of Foreign Workers in the USSR, 1938.

Unknown author, *Workaday Heroics: Life and Work in Socialist Fields*. Moscow: Co-operative Publishing Society of Foreign Workers in the USSR, 1932.

Unknown author, *USSR Builds the Socialism*. Moscow: Moskva, 1933.

Utley, Freda, *The Dream We Lost: Soviet Russia Then and Now*. New York: John Day, 1940.

—— *Lost Illusion: The Story of the Author's Life in Russia*. London: George Allen, 1949.

Valentinov, Nikolay, *Encounters with Lenin*, trans. Paul Rosta and Brian Pearce. London: Oxford University Press, 1968.

Various, 'We Have Learned the Truth about the Soviet Union', say British,

Americans, French, Italians, Canadians, Danes, Dutch, Swedes, Icelanders, Finns and Austrians, who Visited the USSR in May, 1951. London: Soviet News, 1951.

Vettenniemi, Erkki, *Surviving the Soviet Meat Grinder: The Politics of Finnish Gulag Memoirs*. Helsinki: Kikimora, 2001.

Vins, Georgi Petrovich, *Three Generations of Suffering*, trans. Jane Ellis. London: Hodder and Stoughton, 1976.

—— *Konshaubi: Free on the Inside: A True Story of the Persecuted Christians in the Soviet Union*. Eastbourne: Kingsway, 1989.

Viola, Lynne (ed.), *Contending with Stalinism: Soviet Power and Popular Resistance in the 1930s*. Ithaca, NY: Cornell University Press, 2002.

Vogelfanger, Isaac J., *Red Tempest: The Life of a Surgeon in the Gulag*. Montreal: McGill-Queen's University Press, 1996.

Voinov, Kolya, *Outlaw: The Autobiography of a Soviet Waif*. London: Harvill Press, 1955.

Volkogonov, Dmitri, *Stalin: Triumph and Tragedy*, trans. Harold Shukman. London: Wiedenfeld & Nicolson, 1991.

Vyshinsky, Andrei Y., *USSR at the Paris Peace Conference, July-October, 1946, Selected Speeches of A.Y.Vyshinsky.*, London: Soviet News, 1946.

Walker, Donald E. and Cooper, Lee B., *Baseball and American Culture: A Thematic Bibliography of Over 4,500 Works*. Jefferson, NC: McFarland, 1955.

Wallace, Henry A., *Democracy First: What We Fight For*. London: Oxford University Press, 1944.

—— *The Century of the Common Man*. London: Hutchinson, 1944.

—— with Steiger, Andrew, *Soviet Asia Mission*. New York: Reynal and Hitchcock, 1946.

—— *Toward World Peace*. New York: Reynal & Hitchcock, 1948.

Walter, Ellery, *Russia's Decisive Year*. London: Hutchinson, 1932.

Walton, Richard J., *Henry Wallace, Harry Truman, and the Cold War*. New York: Viking, 1976.

Ward, Yvette H., *American Women Behind the Iron Curtain*. Hudson, WI: Star-Observer Print, 1956.

Wat, Aleksander, *My Century: The Odyssey of a Polish Intellectual*, trans. Richard Lourie. New York: W.W. Norton, 1988.

Weinberg, Steve, *Armand Hammer: The Untold Story*. Boston: Little Brown, 1989.

Weissberg, Alex, *Conspiracy of Silence: An Account of Three Years' Imprisonment by the GPU*, trans. E. Fitzgerald. London: Hamish Hamilton 1952.

Welles, Sumner, *The Time for Decision*. London: Hamish Hamilton, 1944.

—— *Seven Major Decisions*. London: Hamish Hamilton, 1951.

Wells, Linton, *Blood on the Moon: The Autobiography of Linton Wells*. London: Hamish Hamilton,1937.

Welty, Eudora, *One Time, One Place: Mississippi in the Depression*. New York: Random House, 1971.

Wettlin, Margaret, *Fifty Russian Winters: An American Woman's Life in the Soviet Union*. New York: Pharos, 1992.

White, Graham and Maze, John, *Henry A. Wallace: His Search for a New World Order*. Chapel Hill, NC: University of North Carolina Press, 1995.

White, William Chapman, *These Russians*. New York: Scribner's, 1931.

White, William L., *Report on the Russians*. London: Eyre and Spottiswoode, 1945.

Wiley, Irena, *Around the Globe in Twenty Years*. New York: McKay, 1962.

Wilkins, Mira and Hill, Frank Ernest, *American Business Abroad: Ford on Six Continents*. Detroit: Wayne State University Press, 1964.

Williams, Robert C., *Russian Art and American Money, 1900–1940*. Cambridge, MA: Harvard University Press, 1980.

Wilson, Edmund, *Red, Black, Blond, and Olive: Studies in Four Civilizations*. New York: Oxford University Press, 1956.

—— *The Thirties: From Notebooks and Diaries of the Period*, ed. Leon Edel. New York : Farrar, Straus and Giroux, 1980.

Wilson, Elizabeth, *Shostakovich: A Life Remembered*. London: Faber, 1994.

Witkin, Zara, *An American Engineer in Stalin's Russia: The Memoirs of Zara Watkin, 1932–1934*, (ed.) Michael Gelb. Berkeley: University of California Press, 1991.

Wolin, Simon and Slusser, Robert M. (eds.), *The Soviet Secret Police*. London: Methuen, 1957.

Wright, A. Colin, *Mikhail Bulgakov: Life and Interpretations*. Toronto: University of Toronto Press, 1978.

Wynne, Greville, *The Man from Moscow: The Story of Wynne and Penkovsky*. London: Arrow, 1968.

Yakir, Petr I., *A Childhood in Prison*, (ed.) Robert Conquest. London: Macmillan, 1972.

Yesenin, Sergei, *The Collected Poems of Yesenin*, trans. Gregory Brengauz. Tallahassee, FL: Floridian, 2000.

Zamyatin, Yevgeny, *We*, trans. Bernard Guebey. London: Cape, 1970.

Zarod, Kazimierz, *Inside Stalin's Gulag: A True Story of Survival*. Lewes: Book Guild, 1990.

Zazubrin, Vladimir, 'The Chip: A Story About a Chip and About Her', from Chukhontsov, Oleg (ed.), *Dissonant Voices: The New Russian Fiction*. London: Harvill, 1991.

Ziemke, Earl F., *The US Army in the Occupation of Germany, 1944–1946*. Washington DC: Center of Military History, United States Army, 1975.

ARCHIVES

The Benson Ford Research Center, Dearborn, Michigan

GARF: State Archive of the Russian Federation, Moscow

Hillwood Museum and Archives, Washington DC

Hoover Institution on War, Revolution and Peace, Stanford, California

Library of Congress Manuscripts, Washington DC

National Archives I and II, Washington DC and College Park, Maryland

RGAKFD: The Russian State Archive of Documentary Films and Photographs, Krasnogorsk
RGASPI: Russian State Archive of Socio-Political History, Moscow
Yale University Manuscripts and Archives, New Haven, Connecticut

PERMISSIONS

ACKNOWLEDGEMENTS

All memoirs from the survivors of the camps are invaluable, but two books in particular I would like to acknowledge as primary sources for this one: Thomas Sgovio's *Dear America* and Victor Herman's *Coming out of the Ice: An Unexpected Life*. I would encourage all interested readers to search out and read these authors' first-hand accounts.

I would like to acknowledge the work of the journalist Alan Cullinson, who interviewed Thomas Sgovio and wrote a story on the American emigrants for his newspaper article, 'A Secret Revealed: Stalin's Police Killed Americans', published by the Associated Press in November 1997. I would also like to acknowledge the work of the writer Adam Hochschild who wrote a feature on the same subject for *Mother Jones* magazine, and in his book, *The Unquiet Ghost: Russians Remember Stalin*. I would like to recognise the work of the documentary filmmaker George Kovacs, who interviewed Thomas Sgovio after a visit to Kolyma, and his colleague on the trip, David Elkind, who were both very generous with their time in San Francisco and allowed me to view the rushes of their documentary film, *The Camps of Magadan*. Most importantly, I would like to thank Mrs Joanne Sgovio who welcomed me to Arizona with a generous heart, shared her memories of her husband's remarkable life, and kindly allowed me to view his personal archive.

I would like to acknowledge the importance of those authors and historians whose work was essential to my understanding of Soviet history – in particular but not only: Anne Applebaum, Robert Conquest, Vassily Grossman, John Haynes, Harvey Klehr, Elinor Lipper, Barry McLoughlin, Roy Medvedev, Zhores Medvedev, Richard Pipes, Edvard Radzinsky, Varlam Shalamov, Vitaly Shentalinsky, Alexander Solzhenitsyn and Dmitri Volkogonov.

I would like to thank the following individuals who helped me in so many ways, both large and small, for which I remain very grateful: Mario Argueta, Ed Barnes, Gennadij Bourdiougov, Richard Boylan, Stephanie Brown, Evgeny Chen, Paul Christensen, Allie Clarke, Rowan Cope, Rodrigo Corral, Jane Day, Rob Dinsdale, Jenna Dolan, Suzanne Fowler, Francesca Frigerio, Mihaly Fulop, Claudia Fumo, Amy Garrett, Bruce Giffords, Ann Godoff, Ksenia Gonchar, Julian Granville, Emily Haines, Nick Harris, Marcella Hecker, Antonio Hernandez, Emma Hinton, Nicole Hughes, Iain Hunt, Samantha Jackson, Norman Kass, Jim Kates, Starling Lawrence, Katie Lewis, Rachel Lewis, Larry McDonald, Molly Malloy, William Massa, Caroline Metcalf, Nathalie Morse, Jorg Muth, Bobby Nayyar, Francesca and Mark Nelson-Smith, Timothy Nenninger, Tara O'Donoghue, Declan O'Reilly, Emma Parry, Gillian Peele, Tony Rose, Bobby Sgovio, Roman Shebalin, Linda Silverman, Linda Skolarus, Jake Smith-Bosanquet, Mia Sorgi, Zbigniew Stanczyk, Susan Strange, Stefan Turnbull, Lindsay Whalen, Andrea Wulf, Herbert Wulf, Sergei Zhurahlev.

My thanks to Adam Wishart for his crucial wisdom at the beginning, and to my literary agent Patrick Walsh who took on this project with an enduring faith and enthusiasm.

I would like to thank Dr Lyuba Vinogradova and Dr Dimitri Konyushkov for their invaluable work with the Russian interviews, research, and archival translations in Moscow. And to thank and credit the work of my American and British editors who showed such care, patience, and critical engagement with this book: Vanessa Mobley, Scott Moyers and Richard Beswick.

Finally my thanks in the simplest way to my family – to my mother and three sisters and especially to my father, Dr V. Tzouliadis, for teaching me the value of politics and history.

INDEX

28, 56, 65, 222; American industry, 108–9

Ford, Edsel, 32

Ford, Henry, 17, 31–6, 38, 101, 164, 331–2

Ford Motor Company, 30–7, 39, 41, 44, 326, 332–3

Fordlandia, 31

Fort Dix, New Jersey, 251

Fort-Whiteman, Lovett, 18, 40, 98–9

Fosfortinaya camp, 185

Fourth of July, 68–9

France, 249; fall of, 190, 192; D-Day invasion, 251; and Kravchenko case, 276–9; liberation of, 348

Franciscans, 3

Franklin, Benjamin, 10

Franklin, Jay, 285

Fredericksburg, Virginia, 292

Freedman, Sam, 266

French Communist Party, 277–9

French nationals, 104, 342; prisoners of war, 291–2

French Revolution, 81, 359

Frison, Monsignor, 207

FSB, 339, 348, 351

Garanin, Colonel, 169, 176

Garner, 'Cactus' Jack, 216–17

Gary, Indiana, 12, 38

Gedritis, William, 56

Gehrig, Lou, 75

Geismann, Doctor, 293

Gelver, Alexander, 105

General Electric, 222

General Foods, 108

Geneva, 300–1

Genghis Khan, 360

genocide, 85, 104, 202, 275, 324, 354–5, 357

George VI, King, 122

Georgetown University, 280

Georgia, 221, 306

German army, Soviet citizens in, 251

German Embassy (Moscow), 297

German nationals, 44, 91, 104, 290; communists, 26, 191; returned from Soviet Union, 190–1; prisoners of war, 287, 290–2, 300; in labour camps, 291, 297, 341

German Sixth Army, 291

Germantown, Pennsylvania, 130

Germany, 102, 138, 153; Nazi, 191, 203, 218, 249, 279; post-war, 242, 249; see also East Germany; West Germany

Gershonowitz, Abe, 266

Gershonowitz, Dora, 257, 263–4, 266

Gestapo, 189–90

Gide, André, 279

Gilmore, Eddy, 231–3, 254–5

Glan, Betty, 68, 73

Goebbels, Joseph, 211, 238

Goglidze, General Sergei, 220–2, 224–5, 313

Gogol, Nikolai, 19

gold, 31, 161–3, 224; prices, 161, 170, 355; production, 165–74, 211, 221, 227, 231, 321; survivors' hatred of, 320

gold stores, 165

Golden, Bertha, 97

Golden, Oliver, 97–8

Golden Mountain, 356

Goldwyn, Sam, 225

Goncharov (criminal leader), 181

Goode, John, 95–6

Gorbach (NKVD chief), 85

Gorbachev, Mikhail, 335–6, 338, 358

Gorbatov, Aleksandr, 156

Gordievsky, Oleg, 286

Gori, Georgia, 305

Gorky, 1, 20, 49, 63, 75; city renamed, 42; automobile plant, 45–6, 100–1, 152, 326; 'foreigners' bureau', 49; NKVD activity, 150; prison, 185; see also Nizhni-Novgorod

Gorky Auto Workers' Club, 1, 19–20, 35

Gorky Park, 21, 73, 75, 255; baseball in, 2, 11, 15, 23, 76, 273, 329, 364; diplomatic baseball game, 68–9

Gorky, Maxim, 15, 42, 138

Goya, Francisco, 156

GPU, 22, 26, 28, 53–4, 56, 58–60, 63, 125, 165

Grapes of Wrath, The, 271, 273

Great Depression, 2–6, 31, 39–41, 54, 56, 146, 161, 186, 232; and emigration, 2, 5–6, 9, 144, 167, 186, 232, 295; American recovery, 56, 161, 272, 325; and food industry, 108–9; and agriculture, 216; Steinbeck's depiction, 271–2

Great Falls, Montana, 285

Greek nationals, 104, 147, 291

Gridassova, Aleksandra, 170, 225–6, 321

Grisha (chauffeur), 52, 60

Gromyko, Andrei, 281

Grondon, Benjamin, 1, 100

Grondon, Joe, 44–5, 100

Groton School, 192